FIFTH EDITION

PARTNERSHIPS

Families and Communities in Early Childhood

Lynn Wilson
George Brown College

NELSON / EDUCATION

NELSON EDUCATION

Partnerships: Families and Communities in Early Childhood, Fifth Edition
by Lynn Wilson

Vice President, Editorial Higher Education:
Anne Williams

Executive Editor:
Lenore Taylor-Atkins

Marketing Manager:
Terry Fedorkiw

Managing Developmental Editor:
Sandy Matos

Developmental Editor:
Alisa Yampolsky

Photo Researcher:
Julie Pratt

Permissions Coordinator:
Jessie Coffey

Content Production Manager:
Hedy Sellers

Production Service:
Cenveo Publisher Services

Copy Editor:
Karen Rolfe

Proofreader:
Gomathy

Indexer:
BIM Indexing Services

Design Director:
Ken Phipps

Managing Designer:
Franca Amore

Interior Design:
Sharon Lucas

Cover Design:
Trinh Truong

Cover Image:
ArtisticCaptures/iStockphoto

Compositor:
Cenveo Publisher Services

Library and Archives Canada Cataloguing in Publication

Wilson, Lynn, 1946 August 31-, author

Partnerships : families and communities in early childhood/Lynn Wilson. — Fifth edition.

Includes bibliographical references and index.
ISBN 978-0-17-650957-6 (pbk.)

1. Early childhood education—Parent participation—Canada.
2. Parent-teacher relationships—Canada. I. Title.

LB1139.35.P37W56 2013
372.119'2 C2013-903425-0

ISBN-13: 978-0-17-650957-6
ISBN-10: 0-17-650957-7

I dedicate this book to my students in recognition of their enthusiasm, creativity, and dedication to families. They will make a difference!

CONTENTS

EXHIBITS LIST

Partnerships was developed as a resource to encourage the development of meaningful and respectful relationships with families. Over the past few years, a significant shift has taken place in the relationship between families and teachers in both early learning and school environments. Many family members have demanded a more active role in their children's care and education and have challenged the notion of teacher as expert. Compelling research supports the benefits to children, educators, teachers, and families when a strong alliance between all parties is formed, and it is from this perspective that the text has been written.

The fifth edition of *Partnerships* differs in several ways from the previous versions. Because more children throughout the country enter full-day kindergarten programs, the text has been expanded to be more inclusive of primary school environments. There are more Inside Looks from educators and teachers, and other professionals in the field, as well as many more from ECE students themselves. Students have played a greater role in this text by providing their insights into their experiences while in their field placement experiences. Many experts from around the country have also shared their ideas, as well as examples of programs that have been successful in their own communities. There is no question that the impact of the Reggio Emilia approach has influenced educators around the world, and this edition continues to reflect its respect for families. New photos improve the text and provide useful examples; statistics have been updated based on the 2010 census where possible. Where appropriate, books have been suggested for children and adults on relevant topics, and URLs have been included throughout.

The companion website (**http://www.nelson .com/site/partnerships5e**) includes various forms, checklists, and other useful tools from the text that can be downloaded for student and instructor use. Throughout the text, a www icon will appear to signify to the reader that these items are available on the website. Students and instructors can easily access the companion website and be instantly connected to the websites that are highlighted throughout the book.

Chapter 1 discusses the very nature of families and how our own family experience impacts on our interactions with the families we meet in the field. We examine the various roles that family members play. We consider the many issues facing Canadian families and discuss the most recent research. New to the chapter is information on fertility and how science is impacting the family unit. The increasing diversity of Canadian society is explored in greater depth, as well as the impact of the country's increasing religious diversity. We also explore the impact of an aging Canadian population on the family unit. The section on the roles of men and women has been expanded, with an update on work and family conflict. The impact of feminism and gender inequality, poverty and its implications, and factors necessary for children's healthy development are also explored.

There are significant changes to Chapter 2, with an update on why child care is a good choice for many Canadian families. We explore how Canada compares to OECD (Organisation for Economic Co-operation and Development) countries in terms of child-care services. The research of Fraser Mustard, Margaret Norrie McCain, and their colleagues informs this chapter and explains the importance of support for young families and access to quality early learning environments. The descriptions of many innovative national programs designed to support children and their families have been expanded and updated.

Chapter 3 begins by outlining why we need partnerships with families. The rights of parents and rights of the child are discussed. We consider Epstein's Six Types of Parent Engagement, which provides insight into the role of families in early learning environments. We explore strategies for ensuring effective relationships, the benefits to all concerned, and the potential challenges. This chapter also includes input from students about their perceptions and the challenges they face in their work with families in their field placements. The section on men in early childhood education has been expanded, as has the section on the role of the supervisor and the teacher in providing leadership and support to families facing various challenges. The chapter also focuses on the need for a collaborative, inter-professional approach within our communities to ensure that families have the support they need to raise happy and healthy children.

Chapter 4 now includes more extensive information on orientations for new families, including family visits, and their importance in establishing positive relationships with families in early learning environments. The section on separation and transitions to new rooms has been expanded. Information on the transition from child care to school environments is also included as more four-year-olds enter full-day kindergarten. The challenges for latchkey children are also highlighted.

Chapter 5 highlights strategies for actively encouraging family involvement in both formal and informal gatherings. Opportunities for families to have significant influence in the early learning environment are discussed, as are strategies for creating more welcoming male-friendly environments.

Chapter 6 expands the content on verbal and nonverbal interactions between families, educators, and teachers. A section on gestures has been expanded, and the chapter provides practical ideas of what to say when challenging situations arise. Conflict resolution strategies are also outlined.

Chapter 7 explains the benefits of family–teacher conferences and strategies for successful interactions. It also discusses strategies for dealing with challenging situations that may arise in a conference.

Chapter 8 provides more guidelines for written communication. Many more practical examples have been added to the chapter, and the section on technology has been expanded.

In Chapter 9, the discussion of "family types" has been expanded and updated where possible, based on information that released from the 2010 census. Information on Aboriginal families has been greatly enlarged as has the section on multiracial families, older families, and grandparents raising their grandchildren. The chapter discusses the role of noncustodial grandparents in supporting young families. Information on foster and adoptive families reflects the opinions of experts in the field and the most recent statistics. The section on LGBTQ families has been expanded as has the information on teen families; separation and divorce; and blended, lone, widowed, and new-comer families. New to this chapter is a discussion

of military families and the challenges they may face. The role of the educator/teacher is expanded in all areas of this chapter.

Chapter 10 highlights the many challenges that may face the families with whom we may work. We analyze the impact of becoming a parent, the stages of parenthood, and the ways parenting styles influence children. We explore how siblings influence the family unit, and discuss children with special needs. Mental health issues, as well as chronic illness and its impact on the family, have been expanded upon. A section on children and hospitalization is included. The role of the teacher when a child or parent dies is examined, as is information on the grieving process. The substance abuse section is expanded, and homeless families are also included in the chapter. The family violence section is expanded with the most recent research. Stress is a mounting concern in the lives of young children, and this is also discussed. Information on natural disasters and how educators and teachers can help children deal with this type of crisis is included. The section on families with an incarcerated parent has been expanded to include a discussion of how the prison system is attempting to support parenting skills and to improve visitation opportunities for families.

Chapter 11 explores the family in a global context. Information includes the UN Convention on the Rights of the Child, UN Millennium Development Goals, and a global perspective on child survival. The underlying and structural causes of maternal and child mortality are explored. We discuss the impact of war and terrorism on families. A variety of Canadian aid organizations are highlighted. The final section of the text provides opportunities for ECE students to evaluate the competencies required for working in the international community and explores options for volunteering or working abroad.

THE INSTRUCTOR'S MANUAL

The accompanying Instructor's Manual outlines strategies for in-class exercises on a chapter-by-chapter basis. The manual contains learning outcomes, examples for classroom discussions, and assignments. It is available as a downloadable resource on the instructor companion website (**http://www.nelson.com/site/partnerships5e/instructor**).

A NOTE ON TERMINOLOGY

Those who work in early learning environments are referred to by many different titles. These titles differ from province to province. Throughout the text you will see the terms *educator* and *teacher* used interchangeably, given that the text is targeted to those who work in many different types of child-care environments as well as those who work in primary school settings. The terms *mother* and *father* are used in this text but may refer to any significant woman or man in a child's life.

ACKNOWLEDGMENTS

I would like to thank the children, educators, managers, students, and families of the Queen Street Child Care Centre, Esther Exton Child Care Centre, Scotia Plaza Child Care Centre, and Richmond Adelaide Child Care Centre for their participation in our photo shoots. Many of the photographs appear in the pages of the book, and I thank you. A special thank-you is extended to the children who contributed their exceptional drawings that are seen throughout the text.

I want to thank the many individuals who have contributed their time and expertise to this latest edition. Each contributor is credited in the body of the text, but I want to acknowledge all of them for their outstanding efforts. They have greatly influenced my work and I know students will benefit from their insightful passages.

To the staff at Nelson Education Ltd., I am deeply indebted to my Developmental Editors, Alisa Yampolsky and Sandy Matos; Executive Editor, Lenore Taylor-Atkins; Content Production Manager, Hedy Sellers; freelance copy editor Karen Rolfe; Proofreader, Gomathy; Permissions Editors, Jessie Coffey and Julie Pratt; Indexer, BIM Indexing Services; and Project Manager, Sangeetha Vijay. Their professional approach and many kindnesses extended to me made this edition a positive writing experience.

On a more personal note, I would like to thank my family: Charlie Dougall and my four children whose love, patience, and support have been a gift to my life. I have learned much from my children, Kelsey, Alexander, Kristen, and Katherine. They enrich my life in ways that words cannot express.

I would like to acknowledge the enormous support and generosity of my colleagues at George Brown College. It has been a privilege to work with such dedicated professionals, committed to the well-being of young children and their families! My heartfelt thanks for their encouragement and guidance. Throughout the years I have met many brave and inspired parents. Some remain my friends and many of their experiences are highlighted in the text. I would also like to thank the many students who have contributed ideas to this book and made me rethink others.

Finally, the following quotation from Barbara Coloroso perhaps best conveys the spirit of the text: "Power is like a candle with a huge flame. Our flame as teachers can light up every child/family we come into contact with and never be diminished itself. The beauty of empowering another human being is that we never lose our own power. Instead what we have is a greater light by which to see." Source: Winning At Teaching (Conference, 1989)

Lynn Wilson

ABOUT THE AUTHOR

Lynn Wilson taught in a variety of teaching environments since her graduation in 1966 from teachers' college. She spent a number of years in the public school system in primary classrooms, helped to establish a parent cooperative, and taught in a full-day kindergarten program in a child-care environment. Lynn supervised a George Brown College lab school and, in 1990, became a member of the faculty. She travelled to many child-care centres in Western Canada as the project director of a Child Care Initiatives Fund project of Health and Welfare Canada on extended-hour child care. In cooperation with Ryerson Polytechnic University's School of Early Childhood Education, she delivered training workshops with colleagues to front-line teachers in Bosnia during the summers of 1999 and 2000. She was the technical advisor on a five-year Partnership Project in Early Childhood Education in Jamaica with the Association of Canadian Community Colleges. In 2008, funding for a Scaling Up Project in Jamaica allowed her and her colleagues to continue their work in Jamaica. In 2006, Lynn won a National Teaching Excellence Award from the Association of Canadian Community Colleges. Currently retired from her faculty position at George Brown College, Lynn has used this time to write another book that reflects her passion for outdoor experiences for young children, *Outdoor Playscapes—Breaking New Ground.*

Chapter 1

THE CHANGING FACE OF CANADIAN FAMILIES

wong sze yuen/Shutterstock.com

"Here is where one has the first experience of love, and of hate, of giving, and of denying; and of deep sadness.… Here the first hopes are raised and met—or disappointed. Here is where one learns whom to trust and whom to fear. Above all, family is where people get their start in life."

—*Amy Swerdlow, Renate Bridenthal, Joan Kelly, and Phyllis Vine (cited in Samovar and Porter, 2007)*

LEARNING OUTCOMES

After studying this chapter, you will be able to

1. describe families in today's society

2. identify various factors affecting families in Canada today

3. explore the implications of brain research on the role of the teacher and the family in providing optimal learning opportunities for children

In this chapter we examine the complex nature of today's families and the many factors that influence them. Though every attempt has been made to provide the most recent information on Canadian families, the student is encouraged to conduct individual research in order to obtain the most meaningful statistics, which are those that best reflect his or her own community.

DEFINING A FAMILY

> "A family is people who love each other."
>
> —Kate, age 5

Poet Robert Frost once said that home is the place where, when you go there, they have to let you in. He could have defined *family* in much the same way, but the term has legal, political, sociological, and personal definitions. It is critical to a deeper and more meaningful understanding of the family in a global society that we, as teachers, extend our understanding of family beyond the North American perspective.

> In the face of dramatic social, economic and cultural change over the past 30 years, many of the accepted assumptions about what it means to be a family have given way to increasingly diverse forms and practices. Traditional roles, responsibilities and boundaries have been challenged, blurred and redrawn. (de Vries, 2010: 1)

It is clear that there is no one-size-fits-all approach to understanding the complex pluralistic nature of families in Canada today. Families are never static. They are fluid, always in motion, constantly changing and realigning themselves; events such as marriages, births, deaths, and divorce will shift and alter the relationships and living arrangements among family members, and a definition of family must respond to these changing variations. A family may include blended family members; grandparents parenting their grandchildren; siblings assuming responsibility for each other; families with children who are adopted; families headed by gay and lesbian parents; and those living with aunts, uncles, more distant relatives, recent immigrants, and friends. In attempting to categorize families, we discover the difficulty in finding one definition that fits all. Families are not homogeneous groups: each one will have different perspectives, attitudes, and values based on its cultural identity. Even within cultural groups, the family may be different from others who ascribe to similar cultural underpinnings. For example, children of second- or third-generation immigrants may have ideas about how they will construct their own families that are dissimilar to their parents' ideas. An individualistic approach versus a collectivist approach may alter family relationships and create harmony or conflict. Every individual's understanding of family is shaped by his or her past: family is what we remember it to be.

> "Everything about family in Canada today is shaped by our remembered past, our social memory."
>
> —Sager, 2010: xvi
>
> "We all grow up with the weight of history on us. Our ancestors dwell in the attics of our brains as they do in the spiraling chains of knowledge hidden in every cell of our bodies."
>
> —Shirley Abbott

The birth of a child has a tremendous impact on the family unit.

EXHIBIT 1.1   Canada: A Quiz

1. What percentage of fathers take parental leave in Quebec?

2. What percentage of fathers take parental leave in the rest of Canada?

3. What percentage of children who are 5 years old attend kindergarten?

4. What percentage of children enter school with vulnerabilities?

5. What percentage of lone-parent families are headed by women?

6. Which province or territory has the highest fertility rate according to the 2011 census?

7. How many babies are born each day in Canada?

8. How many minutes per day do experts recommend preschoolers should be read to?

9. What percentage of boys meet Canadian physical activity guidelines?

10. What percentage of girls meet Canadian physical activity guidelines?

11. How many Quebec mothers are working because of the low cost of child care?

12. How many provinces offer full-day kindergarten?

13. What percentage of First Nations children are receiving child care promoting traditional cultural values and customs?

14. What percentage of same-sex partners are married?

15. What percentage of children live in a stepfamily?

16. True or False: There are more childless couples in Canada than those with children.

"The family. We were a strange little band of characters trudging through life sharing diseases and toothpaste, coveting one another's desserts, hiding shampoo, borrowing money, locking each other out of our rooms, inflicting pain and kissing to heal it in the same instant, loving, laughing, defending, and trying to figure out the common thread that bound us all together."

—Erma Bombeck (cited at goodreads.com)

Family scholars Bubolz and Sontag (1993: 435) have developed the following definition, which attempts to reflect the changing face of Canadian families: "We define families in an inclusive sense to be composed not only of persons related by blood, marriage, or adoption, but also sets of interdependent but independent persons who share some common goals, resources, and a commitment to each other over time." But the most prevalent definition that is used in Canadian research and policymaking is Statistics Canada's *census family*. This unit includes a married couple with or without children living with them, or a single parent or

Inside LOOK

In our family, my two sisters and I often argue about who our parents will live with when they get old. We all want them to live with us! We are what the census data would call a multigenerational household. My grandmother has lived with us for as long as I can remember and my mother's sister and her child have also come from Pakistan to be with us. I see this as a model for family living. My mother has been able to work, volunteer, and engage in our community in ways that would not have been possible if we had not had this extended family with us—all eight of us! I love the energy and laughter in our house!

grandparent sharing a dwelling with only his or her children or grandchildren. These children may be any age and be brought into the household through birth, marriage, or adoption, but they cannot have their own offspring living with them. Cohabiting couples living together for longer than one year are considered to be married although separate statistics are kept for legally married and cohabiting couples. Now a married couple can be opposite or same sex.

In the past, the traditional *nuclear family*—husband, wife, and children in one household—was referred to as the modern family. The increasing family diversity that we see now has led some scholars to refer to today's family as the *postmodern family*.

Some societies organize their kinship relationships so that monogamy is the exception rather than the rule. Some of the world's cultures are polygamous, that is, one man legally has several wives. Families may be organized not only as an emotional unit but also as a unit of economic production, whether based in an agricultural or industrial community. Some languages have no word for *family*; rather, the social unit is identified as a "house" that may include many people. "Truly understanding what it means to be a family in Canada, however, requires looking beyond our own immediate experience to include the diverse spectrum of relationships and responsibilities that make up family life from coast to coast to coast" (Sager, 2010: 5).

HOW CANADIANS VIEW THE FAMILY: WHAT THE RESEARCH TELLS US

In *The Future Families Project* (2004), Bibby found about 6 in 10 Canadians see the traditional family as the ideal family arrangement, while most of the remaining 40 percent—led by younger adults—take the position that there is no one ideal form. Although many people find a variety of family forms that work for them, relatively few put forward any specific alternative as ideal beyond the traditional family. However, the results are nearly unanimous in emphasizing the importance of the family. As can be seen on the Vanier Institute of the Family website at **http://www.vifamily.ca,**

- **97 percent of respondents say that the family is essential to personal well-being.**

- **97 percent also agree that the family is essential to instilling values that are needed for interpersonal relationships.**

- **95 percent say the family is essential to healthy communities.**

- **95 percent think the family is essential to a healthy nation.**

- **90 percent say their mothers provided them with a good model for family life generally. Just over 80 percent say the same thing about their fathers.**

Inside LOOK

What Children Have to Say About Relationships

- "When my grandmother got arthritis, she couldn't bend over and paint her toenails anymore. So my grandfather does it for her all the time, even when his hands got arthritis too. That's love." Rebecca, age 8
- "When someone loves you, the way they say your name is different. You just know that your name is safe in their mouth." Billy, age 4
- "Love is when you go out to eat and give somebody most of your French Fries without making them give you any of theirs." Chrissy, age 6
- "If you want to learn to love better, you should start with a friend who you hate." Nikka, age 6
- "When you love somebody, your eyelashes go up and down and little stars come out of you." Karen, age 7

Source: Reprinted by permission of Art Schrage, boardofwisdom.com.

- 77 percent say their mother provided a good model for marriage. 72 percent say the same thing for their fathers. (This means that 1 in 4 Canadians *do not* think their parents provided good marriage role models.)[*]

In a 2007 Ipsos-Reid survey, a majority of Canadians agreed that there is no such thing as a typical family (cited in Sager, 2010: 8). Despite its challenges, it is clear that social scientists will continue to redefine the family as it continues to evolve throughout our history.

THE ROLE OF THE FAMILY

We all have strong feelings about our families. We may have positive feelings of love and caring for people in our family; however, for others, the family is a place of misery and neglect. The family does not exist in a vacuum, and children may adopt the culture, social class, status, and religious and moral teachings of their family. Nevertheless, personal choices are also shaped by our family circumstances and events in the wider society, such as changes in educational opportunities, employment trends, social policies, technological innovations, media representations, and new ideas about human rights or personal entitlements (Baker, 2007: 2).

Yet the evolution of the family has not diminished the importance of its role. In the words of Alvi (1994: 11):

The family constitutes the basic unit of society; it is appreciated for the important socio-economic functions that it performs. In spite of the many changes in society that have altered its role and functions, it continues to provide the natural framework for the emotional, financial and material support essential to the growth and development of its members, particularly infants and children, and for the care

[*]Bibby, R. 2004. "The Future Families Project: A Survey of Canadian Hopes and Dreams." Ottawa: Vanier Institute of the Family. Available at http://www.vifamily.ca. http://www.vanier institute.ca/include/get.php?nodeid=42. Reprinted by permission of The Vanier Institute of Family.

| TABLE 1.1 | Couple Families by Presence of Children in Private Households, 2011 Counts, Children (all ages), for Canada, Provinces, and Territories |

| | | CENSUS FAMILY STRUCTURE OF COUPLES[1] | | | |
| | | MARRIED COUPLES | | COMMON-LAW COUPLES | |
GEOGRAPHIC NAME	ALL COUPLES	WITH CHILDREN	WITHOUT CHILDREN	WITH CHILDREN	WITHOUT CHILDREN
Canada	7,861,855	3,402,735	2,891,215	706,555	861,350
Newfoundland and Labrador	134,965	55,180	59,155	9,290	11,335
Prince Edward Island	34,270	15,035	14,660	1,955	2,615
Nova Scotia	223,335	87,115	97,760	14,985	23,475
New Brunswick	188,405	70,380	82,075	15,790	20,160
Quebec	1,048,350	547,225	596,140	360,500	334,250
Ontario	3,007,560	1,522,150	1,090,740	158,660	236,010
Manitoba	271,685	126,245	106,390	17,295	21,765
Saskatchewan	238,550	100,030	102,740	16,195	19,585
Alberta	855,020	405,130	314,230	52,230	83,430
British Columbia	1,048,350	465,680	442,310	54,935	105,425
Yukon	7,420	2,675	2,400	980	1,360
Northwest Territories	8,600	3,505	1,960	1,770	1,365
Nunavut	5,585	2,385	655	1,965	580

Note:
1. Refers to the classification of census families into married couples (with or without children of either and/or both spouses), common-law couples (with or without children of either and/or both partners), and lone-parent families by sex of parent.

Source: Statistics Canada: http://www12.statcan.gc.ca/census-recensement/2011/dp-pd/hlt-fst/fam/Pages/highlight.cfm?TabID=1&Lang=E&As c=1&PRCode=01&OrderBy=999&View=1&tableID=301&queryID=1&Children=1

of other dependants, including the elderly, disabled and infirm. The family remains a vital means of preserving and transmitting cultural values. In the broader sense, it can, and often does, educate, train, motivate and support its individual members, thereby investing in their future growth and acting as vital resources for development.

The Western association of love and marriage is unique to our modern culture. Historically, marriages were often arranged as business deals. In traditional cultures many elements of the basic exchange (a man providing financial support in exchange for the woman's childbearing and child-rearing capabilities, domestic services, and sexual availability) remain. Few traditional societies allowed young people to choose partners without the approval of parents or other relatives. In contemporary arranged marriages, the child's preference is often considered but not always deferred to.

> Despite the apparent differences between arranged marriages and free-choice marriages, decisions are influenced by some of the same considerations. In Western marriages, couples expect to marry for "love" but at the same time people marry for a variety of reasons, including companionship, emotional stability, regular and safe sex, the desire for children, and additional financial support. (Baker, 2010: 72)*

* From Baker, Maureen, *Choices and Constraints in Family Life* 2/e © Oxford University Press Canada 2010. Reprinted by permission of the publisher.

Social scientists produce extensive research every year on the family and kinship systems. It is beyond the scope of this text to include them all in this chapter, so we will focus on the work of one researcher, psychologist Urie Bronfenbrenner.

Bronfenbrenner (1979) studied the family and described what he called the *human ecological system*. He stated that the individual is linked to the family and the community in a reciprocal, influential relationship and that "the family seems to be the most effective and economical system for fostering and sustaining the child's development. Without family involvement, intervention is likely to be unsuccessful, and what few effects are achieved are likely to disappear once the intervention is discontinued." Bronfenbrenner stated unequivocally that parents are more capable of providing for the physical and psychological needs of a child when they have a third party who admires and loves them for their caregiving; he described four systems that influence individuals (see Figure 1.1).

Enormous pressures are exerted on families today. As the building blocks of our society, families provide social benefits that extend beyond their own homes. They enrich all our lives in ways more complex than those that can simply be deduced from a census form. But in our rapidly changing society, families need constant care and support in order to succeed. Ideally, who is responsible for children and families? The answer is both simple and complex: we all are! Families, professionals,

FIGURE 1.1 Bronfenbrenner's System

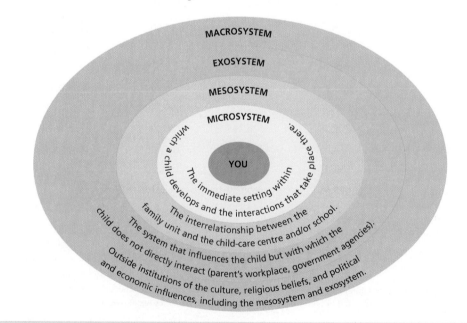

Source: Bronfenbrenner, 1990

Characteristics of Functional Families

- *Family Pride.* Families are unified and loyal; they view their family positively and cooperate with one another
- *Family Support:* Families spend time together and provide love and support to each member for a growth-producing environment
- *Cohesion:* In addition to cooperating with each other, members respect one another's individuality. Family members are interdependent without being too dependent or too independent
- *Adaptability:* In the face of change, families can adapt. Tasks may rotate or are completed by those who have time and skills
- *Communication:* Both sharing of self and careful listening to others is important
- *Social Support:* Family members accept responsibility for supporting community endeavours
- *Values:* Families who function well know their values and they work to practice and live by them
- *Joy:* Families know how to have fun together

Source: From COUCHENOUR/CHRISMAN. *Families, Schools and Communities, 4E.* © 2011 Wadsworth, a part of Cengage Learning, Inc. Reproduced by permission. www.cengage.com/permissions.

Courtesy of Scotia Plaza Child Care Centre

It is clear that this mother takes great pride and joy in her son.

residents of communities and neighbourhoods, and taxpayers are all responsible in different ways. "In a system of shared responsibility, government is responsible for providing incentives and vehicles with which to empower families in caring for themselves and their children" (Kagan and Neville, 1994: 8). While governments at all levels could be doing much more to support healthy family functioning, Marian Wright Edelman of the Children's Defence Fund states the need for collaboration:

> No single person, institution, or government agency can meet all of our children's and families' needs. But each of us, taking one or more of those needs, can together weave the seamless web of family and community and private sector support that

children need. We must work together and resist the political either/or-ism and organizational turf-ism that plague so much policy development, advocacy, service, and organizing today. Good parenting and good community, employer, and governmental supports for parents are inextricably intertwined. (cited in Gestwicki, 2010: 472)*

CANADA AT A GLANCE

The 2011 census estimated the population of Canada at 34.6 million people. Our population grew by 5.9 percent between 2006 and 2011, the highest growth among G8 countries. Only two other G8 countries have registered increases in their population growth in recent years: Britain and Russia. From Manitoba to the Pacific, the 2011 census showed impressive gains in population. Alberta topped the country in population growth, with British Columbia right behind. Saskatchewan reversed a decade of population decline with impressive gains, and Manitoba is growing twice as quickly as it was before. Ontario's growth dropped below the national average for the first time in 25 years. It lost 57,000 people to other provinces and accepted nearly 100,000 fewer immigrants than in the previous census period. Oil, gas, potash, and other resources drew newcomers west.

*From GESTWICKI, *Home, School, and Community Relations*, 7E. © 2010 Cengage Learning. Reproduced by permission. www.cengage.com/permissions.

For the first time, the population of the four Western provinces exceeded that of the four Atlantic provinces and Quebec. Immigration accounted for about two thirds of Canada's population gains, while the other third was due to natural increase (Friesen and Wingrove, 2012).

HOW FAMILIES ARE CHANGING

Since the 2008 economic downturn, Canadian families have been impacted in many ways: government spending has decreased and families are expected to cover more of their own expenses. Health care, education, housing, recreation, and cultural activities have been hard hit by government cutbacks.

With better medical care more readily available, infant mortality rates are decreasing, we are living longer, and our population is aging.

Technology has had an enormous impact not only in the workplace but also in our homes. More and more of us are achieving higher education credentials; however, stimulating early learning environments for our youngest children are still not a national standard. Religion in Canada now encompasses many groups, and the freedom of religious practice is an important part of Canadian culture. Increased immigration has enriched the lives of all Canadians as we celebrate our multicultural society. Many families move from place to place in search of employment and experience the isolation of being far from extended family. Other families rely heavily on their extended family members. The feminist movement has had an enormous impact on women's roles in both their work and their home environments. Many women in Canada today are financially independent, allowing them more control over their lives. Young adults are staying home longer, because of a variety of factors, but many are attending postsecondary institutions, the cost of which prohibits them from living independently. Many couples are postponing marriage as they establish their work lives, and so cohabitation is much more common.

Some common-law partnerships are a prelude to marriage, with just under one-half of people ever in a common-law union ending up marrying their common-law partner. Surprisingly, the probability of divorce is greater, on average, for couples who marry after having lived together than for couples who marry without first living together. (McDaniel and Tepperman, 2011: 107)

Smaller families are more the norm today; they allow for greater independence and financial stability, and many couples are also choosing to remain childless. This push for personal autonomy

Today's families are smaller than ever before.

may also be a factor in the rising divorce rate, and there are more lone-parent families than ever before. There is also increasing acceptance of same-sex partners in Canada. There is a changing perception of the child within the family unit: while it appears that our society embraces a child-centred approach, many children live in situations that put them at risk. All of these factors have tremendous influences on the fabric of Canadian lives.

FAIRNESS IN FAMILIES INDEX

The Fatherhood Institute was challenged to find out if men and women are sharing the care of their children more equitably. To create the *Fairness in Families Index*, research was done in 21 industrialized countries, examining how well they were promoting and sustaining greater equity in men and women's division of labour in the home and in the workplace. There are 10 indicators of gender equality in the index:

- **gender equality in parental leave**

- **gender pay gap**

- **percentage of men in the part-time workforce**

- **percentage of women sitting in Parliament**

- **percentage of women in management positions**

- **percentage of children in lone-parent families**

- **percentage of GDP spent on child care and education of children under 5**

- **ratio of men's to women's time spent caring for children**

- **ratio of men's to women's time spent on unpaid work**

- **maximum leave available for fathers**

RANK	COUNTRY	AVERAGE RANKING
1.	Sweden	4.00
2.	Finland	4.90
3.	Norway	5.00
4.	Denmark	6.78
5.	Portugal	7.44
6.	Belgium	7.67
7.	Greece	8.89
8.	France	8.90
9.	New Zealand	9.50
10.	Italy	10.11
11.	Netherlands	10.33
12.	USA	10.44
13.	Spain	10.50
14.	Germany	10.80
15.	**Canada**	**11.50**

TABLE 1.2 The Fairness in Families Index: Overall Ranking on 10 Indicators of Gender Equality

Source: "The Fairness in Families Index", *The Fatherhood Report, 2010-2011*. http://www.fatherhoodinstitute.org/wp-content/uploads/2010/12/FI-FiFI-Report-2010_FINAL.pdf. Reprinted by permission of The Fatherhood Institute.

SCIENCE AND THE FAMILY

In-vitro fertilization and genetic testing are increasingly used, and recent scientific breakthroughs have made it possible to scan every chromosome in a single embryonic cell to test for genes involved in hundreds of conditions. In the future, DNA microchips will be able to analyze more than a thousand traits at once. These genes will be linked not only to a child's health but also to appearance—such as height and hair, skin, and eye colour—and athletic ability. These tests were devised to help those dealing with infertility, but people able to have babies the old-fashioned way may now opt for IVF and embryo screening, paying a high price in return for the chance to have greater genetic control over their children.

"We now have the potential to banish the genes that kill us; that make us susceptible to cancer, heart disease, depression, addictions and obesity; and to select those that may make us healthier, stronger, and more intelligent. The question is, should we?" (Abraham, 2012). Preimplantation genetic diagnosis (PGD) extracts a cell from a newly created embryo and amplifies enough of its DNA to check for mutations.

Some couples in Canada may find themselves facing infertility challenges that are emotionally, financially, and physically exhausting. For example, women who have waited to have children later in life may have trouble conceiving. Those who are determined to have children, however, may seek out reproductive treatments, such as in-vitro fertilization and artificial insemination. The results are increasingly positive: the overall live birth rate among women who received fertility treatment at one of Canada's 28 IVF centres in 2009 was 30 percent per cycle started. Of these births, 71 percent were singletons, 28 percent were twins, and 1 percent were triplets or more (Vanier Institute of the Family, 2012a).

The development of sperm banks has allowed prospective parents to screen potential donors for qualities they want in their child. One extreme example was the Repository for Germinal Choice in California (now closed), which preserved sperm from outstanding scientists and professionals, including Nobel Prize winners. More than 230 children from these donors were born to women who had also been screened for intelligence (Goodwin, 2000 in Ward and Belanger, 2011: 132–133).

For some women, the new technology succeeds too well; they bear far more children than they had bargained for. A famous set of octuplets were born in 2009 through artificial reproduction to a California woman who already had six children! For many families, reproductive technology has succeeded, but for many others it is a disappointing and difficult experience. These families may continue to look for other options; as a consequence, surrogate motherhood is on the rise.

FERTILITY RATES IN CANADA

Below are 2009 fertility statistics:

- **1.67**—The fertility rate of Canadian women (total fertility rate is the average number of children per woman)

- **3.9**—The fertility rate of women in 1959 at the height of the baby boom

- **2.1**—The number of children Canadian women would need to have to replace the current population in the absence of migration

- **1.50**—The fertility rate of women in British Columbia and Nova Scotia—the lowest in the country

- 31.7 percent—The proportion of babies born to women aged 30 to 34 years—the highest among all age groups

- 51.3 and 48.3 percent—The proportion of male and female babies born, respectively

- 60.1 percent—The proportion of babies born to mothers who were married (27.2 percent to single/never married women, 0.9 percent to divorced women, 0.4 percent to separated women and 11.3 percent to women whose marital status was not stated) (Vanier Institute of the Family, 2012g) [*]

The most recent census data tell us that the number of young children in Canada is increasing.

The population of children aged 4 and under increased 11.0% between 2006 and 2011. This was the highest growth rate for this age group since the 1956 to 1961 period during the baby boom. This was the result of [a] slightly higher fertility level and an increase in the number of women aged between 20 and 34 during that period. (Statistics Canada, 2011b) [†]

AN AGING POPULATION

There is no question that the Canadian population is aging.

In 2011, the median age in Canada was 39.9 years, meaning that half of the population was older than that and half was younger. In 1971, the median age was 26.2 years. Seniors make up the fastest-growing age group. This trend is expected to continue for the next several decades due mainly to a decreased fertility rate (i.e. number of children per woman), an increase in life expectancy, and the effects of the baby boom. In 2011, an estimated 5.0 million Canadians were 65 years of age or older, a number that is expected to double in the next 25 years to reach 10.4 million seniors by 2036. (Human Resources and Skills Development Canada, 2012) [‡]

---

[*] Vanier Institute of the Family, 2009. "Just the Facts: Births And Babies in 2009." Ottawa: Vanier Institute of the Family. Available at http://www.vanierinstitute.ca/include/get.php?nodeid=1898& format=Download. Reprinted by permission of The Vanier Institute of the Family.

[†] Statistics Canada. 2011. *The Canadian Population in 2011: Age and Sex.* Available at http://www12.statcan.gc.ca/census-recensement/2011/as-sa/98-311-x/98-311-x2011001-eng.cfm

[‡] *Canadians in Context, Aging Population.* URL: http://www4.hrsdc.gc.ca/.3ndic.1t.4r@-eng.jsp?iid=33. Human Resources and Skills Development Canada, 2012. Reproduced with the permission of the Minister of Public Works and Government Services, 2013.

THE INCREASING DIVERSITY OF CANADIAN SOCIETY

The majority of Canadians were born in Canada. However, over the past 200 years, many newcomers helped to build a better Canada. In that span, the largest groups were the English, French, Scottish, Irish, German, Italian, Chinese, Aboriginal, Ukrainian, Dutch, South Asian, and Scandinavian. Since the 1970s, most immigrants have come from Asian countries (Discover Canada, n.d.).

Languages other than French and English are often spoken in Canadian homes. Chinese languages are the second most spoken at home, after English, in two of Canada's biggest cities: In Vancouver, 13 percent of the population speak Chinese languages at home; in Toronto, the number is 7 percent (Citizenship and Immigration Canada, 2012).

The following numbers give us a glimpse into newcomers to our country:

RANK	COUNTRY	NUMBER
1	Philippines	36,578
2	India	30,252
3	People's Republic of China	30,197
4	United Kingdom	9,499
5	United States of America	9,243
6	France	6,934
7	Iran	6,815
8	United Arab Emirates	6,796
9	Morocco	5,946
10	Republic of Korea	5,539
Total Top 10		147,799
All Other Source Countries		132,882
TOTAL		280,681

Source: Citizenship and Immigration Canada, Facts and Figures 2010. Annual Report to Parliament on Immigration, 2011. Retrieved February 7, 2013, from http://www.cic.gc.ca/english/resources/publications/annual-report-2011/section2.asp

Canadians consistently express the most positive attitudes toward immigration compared with people in other countries (Pew Research Centre, 2003; Adams 2007, 2010).

National polls in Canada portray a country where, according to Canadian pollster Michael Adams, people "consistently express positive attitudes … towards immigration" and that a large majority, 75%, of "Canadians, believe that overall, immigrants have a positive influence on the country." These findings from

2006 were repeated in 2010 as a new poll found that over 80% of Canadians supported wholly or somewhat the thesis that immigration is "a key positive feature of Canada as a country." (SWR International, 2012)

The Pew Research Centre conducted an international survey of 38,000 people in 44 countries, and found Canada to be the only nation where the majority (77 percent) of respondents said immigrants have a good influence on their country. "Canadians appear to believe that in Canadian culture, intolerance of immigrants is not socially acceptable"* (Adler et al., 2012: 26). Importantly for the immigrants and their families "who have experienced oppression in their country of origin because of their 'race' or ethnicity, immigration to Canada may provide an opportunity to celebrate a status that was previously devalued by others"† (Riedmann, Lamanna, and Nelson, 2003: 18).

Quebec is unique in its composition of immigrants. Blacks, mostly from Haiti, are the largest group at 188,000, followed by Arabs, mostly from the French-speaking Maghreb, at 109,000 (Siddiqui, cited in Cohen, 2008).

Experts predict that the number of foreign-born Canadians will continue to grow:

Like population aging, this trend will have wide ranging ramifications. Sustained levels of immigration from increasingly diverse source countries is transforming communities, neighbourhoods, schools, workplaces, and public institutions, especially in Canada's largest cities. Increasing diversity challenges us to rethink how we understand families—how they operate and how we collectively support them. (Sager, 2010: 6)

For many, life in Canada is not what they expected:

The better life immigrants come to Canada in search of remains elusive to many visible minorities who face language barriers, discrimination, culture shock, and the rejection of foreign credentials. And that's despite the fact that visible minorities are more likely than non-visible minorities in Canada to have a post-secondary education. (Siddiqui, 2008)

RELIGIOUS DIVERSITY

Canadians are religiously diverse with more now reporting being followers of religions such as Islam, Hinduism, Sikhism, and Buddhism.

*From Adler, Ronald, et al., *Interplay: The Process of Interpersonal Communication* 3/Ce © Oxford University Press Canada 2012. Reprinted by permission of the publisher.

†From LAMANNA/RIEDMAN/NELSON. *Marriages and Families, 1E.* © 2003 Nelson Education Ltd. Reproduced by permission. www.cengage.com/permissions.

Before 1971, less than 1 percent of Canadians ticked the "no religion" box on national surveys. Two generations later, nearly a quarter of the population, or 23 percent, say they aren't religious ... In 2002, 34 percent of 15–29 year olds said religion was highly important to them while data from Statistics Canada's 2009 General Social Survey show that number tumbling to 22 percent ... Only the persistence of religious traditions among immigrants, whose religiosity has increased slightly over the past 25 years, has slowed the march away from our places of worship. (Valpy and Friesen, 2010: A17)

With Canada's increasing cultural diversity, inter-religious conjugal unions are on the rise. A study based on census data by Clark (2006) found that

the likelihood of an interreligious union was associated with where you lived, how homogenous the religious mix of your community was, how religious you were, how traditional the doctrine of your religion was, and how long you had been in Canada. People in communities which were religiously homogenous and people who were highly religious were less likely to be in interreligious unions, as were immigrants and older individuals.

Spiritual practice is strongly interwoven through most cultures of the world. While not every person understands the sacred in exactly the same way, and significant numbers of people around the world remain agnostic, many parents speak of the important role spirituality and religion plays in their parenting practices. Teachers often may not know the religious background of a family, but it may be an important element in family dynamics. Some families will share information that impacts on practices in the child-care centre, such as religious celebrations. Variations in religious beliefs must be respected in the way that all other elements of acceptance of family practices are embraced. The world's great religious traditions also have some similar values that bind people together (see Figure 1.2):

- *Buddhism*: Hurt not others in ways that you yourself would find hurtful (Udana Virga, 5:8).

- *Christianity*: All things whatsoever ye would that men should do to you, do ye even so to them (Matthew, 7:12).

- *Confucianism*: Do not do unto others what you would not have them do unto you (Analect, 15:23).

- *Hinduism*: This is the sum of duty: do naught unto others which would cause you pain if done to you (Mahabharata, 5:1517).

FIGURE 1.2 The Golden Rule

Source: Courtesy of Paul McKenna.

- *Islam*: No one of you is a believer until he desires for his brother that which he desires for himself (Sunnah).

- *Jainism*: In happiness and suffering, in joy and grief, we should regard all creatures as we regard our own self (Lord Mahavira, 24th Tirthankara).

- *Judaism*: What is hateful to you; do not to your fellow man. That is the law: all the rest is commentary (Talmud, Shabbat, 31a).

In all of the important human characteristics, we are all very much alike. What is important to remember is the need to see the commonalities within a multicultural world (Samovar, Porter, and McDaniel, 2007: 359). Educators should be knowledgeable of the religious affiliations of the families with whom they are working and encourage people to share information about their faiths. By learning more about the community, educators are in a position to educate children and help them develop tolerance for others.

BOOKS FOR ADULTS

How to Be a Perfect Stranger: The Essential Religious Etiquette Handbook, 4th ed., by S.M. Matlins and A.J. Magida

Understanding Religion in a Global Society, by E.M. Rapple, J.C. Modschiedler, and R.D. Peterson

Religions in Global Society, by P. Beyer

CHANGES IN THE LABOUR FORCE

For many Canadians, temporary job have become the norm.

Today, as many as one in eight Canadians hold temporary jobs and unlike in past downturns where laid-off workers were eventually rehired by firms, there's no signs the trend is about to slow down. For workers, the changing employment landscape requires major, life-altering adjustments. Those who are entrepreneurial with a stomach for risk will find opportunities. But many others risk being dragged under by a new corporate reality where they can be hired and fired at a moment's notice … The rise of the contract worker may also be having a more wide-scale impact than previously realized. A growing gap between rich and poor in countries like Canada has been blamed, in part, on a growing number of poor quality jobs … The trend reflects on-going skittishness by employers about the health of the economy, particularly given the ongoing crisis in Europe and the sluggish recovery south of the border. (Sorensen, 2012)[*]

In its abstract of *The Current State of Canadian Family Finances* (2012b), the Vanier Institute of the Family finds

many Canadian families struggling to balance persistently high debt loads against modest savings and often precarious income flow. [Former] Bank of Canada Governor Mark Carney has described family debt as "the greatest risk to the domestic economy." For the one million Canadian

---

[*]Sorensen, C. 2012. "The end of the job," *Maclean's*, January 30, vol. 125, no. 3, pp. 32-34. Reprinted by permission.

Inside LOOK

- 3.9 million—The number of mothers (including biological, adoptive, and stepmothers) in Canada with children under 18 living with them.
- 69%—The proportion of lone working mothers with children under the age of 16 living at home.
- 39% and 73%—The employment rate for mothers with school-age children in 1976 and 2009, respectively.
- 4.6 hours—The amount of time spent daily by mothers on unpaid work.
- 6.6 hours—The amount of time spent daily by women on caring for children aged 0 to 4.
- 1/5—The proportion of employed females who work part time to accommodate child care or other family responsibilities.
- 26%—The proportion of working women who are the sole or primary earner in their household.

Source: Vanier Institute of the Family. 2012. "Mothers In Canada." Available at http://www.vanierinstitute.ca/modules/news/newsitem.php?ItemId=435. Reprinted by permission of The Vanier Institute of the Family.

families with a debt-service ratio of 40% or more, vulnerability to rising interest rates, consumer price increases or job loss is high.

Younger and older members of Canadian families, in particular, are struggling with the lingering effects of the recession. Youth are finding it hard to get into today's job market while workers aged 55 and older have garnered over half the net jobs created since the low point of the recession in 2009. And yet, despite their increased labour market participation, the Institute notes an increase in the number of seniors declaring bankruptcy, an incredible seventeen hundred percent rise over the last 20 years.[*]

Many families attempt to restructure their work and private lives to reach some balance. Parents whose work falls outside the standard workweek find it doubly difficult to coordinate child care and other family responsibilities. Spouses may work on different shifts—a strategy called "off-shifting"—to reduce child-care expenses, but these irregular hours may have a negative impact on relationships within the family. "Working non-standard hours has negative consequences for individual and family wellbeing. The proportion of Canadians aged 20–64 years who worked other than a regular time daytime schedule increased from 22.8% in 1992 to 25.2% in 2009" (Canadian Index of Wellbeing, 2010a).[†]

The safety net that so many of us have relied on in the past is now not always available to the most disadvantaged people in our society.

Certain key social programs for working age people now provide less income support to the disadvantaged than they did in the past. Employment insurance in 2008 was less generous, in terms of required qualification period, coverage, and duration of benefits, than in 1981. These developments have likely contributed to the increase in income inequality. On the other hand, the introduction of the Child Tax Credit and the National Child Benefits Supplement in the mid-1990s, the only major new social program established since the 1970s, has provided additional income to poor working families and lowered the poverty rate for this group somewhat. (Canadian Index of Wellbeing, 2009)[‡]

EMPLOYER ATTITUDES

Many factors affect employer attitudes to their workforce. "In recent decades, globalization, technological change, freer trade agreements and new government policies have altered labour markets and employment patterns for men and women"[§] (Baker, 2010: 144). This has increased pressure on employers and resulted in downsizing, contract work, and, for the employee, increased workloads and the need to acquire new skills in many areas. Employers are noticing the effect of work–family conflict on their companies, particularly in terms of productivity and the bottom line, and "are looking for ways to support their employees in order to remain competitive and responsive to their own ever-changing operating environments" (Johnson, Lero, and Rooney, 2001: 1). Governments have also been examining the effect of

---

[*]Vanier Institute of the Family. 2012. "The Current State of Canadian Family Finances." Available at http://www.vanierinstitute.ca/modules/news/newsitem.php?ItemId=421. Reprinted by permission of The Vanier Institute of the Family.

[†]Canadian Index of Wellbeing. 2010. *Community Vitality*. Available at http://www.ciew.ca/en/TheCanadianIndexOfWellbeing/Domains. Reprinted by permission.

[‡]Canadian Index of Wellbeing. 2010. *Community Vitality*. Available at http://www.ciew.ca/en/TheCanadianIndexOfWellbeing/Domains. Reprinted by permission.

[§]From Baker, Maureen, *Choices and Constraints in Family Life* 2/e © Oxford University Press Canada 2010. Reprinted by permission of the publisher.

The CIBC Children's Centre is designed to provide a back-up child-care service when full- or part-time staff members' regular child-care arrangements are not available. A comprehensive child-care service for infants through school-age children up to 13 years of age includes special play areas for infants, toddlers, preschoolers, and school-age children, with activities designed specifically for each age group. Lunch is to be provided by the employee, and the centre will provide two snacks per day. CIBC employees may use the centre up to 20 days a year, but may not use it for more than five consecutive days without special authorization. The centre is open from 8:00 a.m. to 6:00 p.m. Monday to Friday. Staff may call as far ahead as 30 days in advance or as late as the morning of the day that care is needed. Reservations are taken on a first-come, first-served basis. CIBC pays for the operation of the CIBC Children's Centre; there is no direct charge to employees. Employer-provided child care is a taxable benefit in Canada, and that after-tax cost to most employees is about $20.00 per day of use. There is a one-time cost of $20.00 to reflect a first-time administration fee. Trained early childhood teachers provide developmentally appropriate care and education.

Source: Canadian Imperial Bank of Commerce http://www.brighthorizons.com/back-up/sheets/fs

work–family conflict on individuals and families. However, corporations have been slow to respond many have not adopted progressive changes in the workplace, such as the following:

- more flexible work schedules
- jobs that support young families (hours from 9 to 5, with no shift work)
- flex time for child care and school involvement
- a shorter workweek at full pay or a compressed workweek
- salary deferrals
- sabbaticals
- opportunities to work at home
- compassionate care leave
- job-sharing schemes
- voluntary part-time work
- telecommuting, mobile offices, and satellite offices
- counselling services
- workplace child care or extended-hour child care
- child-care resource and referral services
- supplementary unemployment benefits plan
- phased return from maternity leave
- voluntary summers off without pay
- respite care and other emergency referral services
- job training and retraining
- parenting courses
- prenatal and postnatal care for families and their babies
- a voucher system in which families choose from a range of company benefits those that best meet their needs, including reimbursement for child-care expenses for work responsibilities outside regular hours

WORK–FAMILY CONFLICT

Balancing work and family life is challenging for many Canadians, who would appreciate and benefit from a more supportive work environments.

STRESS

The sources of stress are varied, and so too are the abilities of and resources for families to deal with these challenges. These disparities highlight the importance of informal and formal support networks and the need for community resources and family-friendly workplace programs. Across the country, people are experiencing increasing levels of stress. In a study by the Vanier Institute of the Family (2012c)

Employers like Ontario Power Generation recognize the competing demands employees face in trying to balance their work and family responsibilities. The connection between organizational culture and employee performance, recruitment, and retention is clear. High-performing organizations—and those listed as Canada's Top 100 Employers—all have a spectrum of strategies and programs to attract new talent and enable employees to participate fully and effectively in all aspects of their lives. Workplaces that acknowledge and support the multiplicity of needs, interests, and responsibilities of employees tend to have an environment and culture that fosters engagement, commitment, and creativity.

At OPG, valuing diversity isn't just about respecting differences between the genders or different ethnic groups. Diversity is about acknowledging the different and changing life circumstances and situations of individual employees. An effective and supportive work culture views the employee not just as a worker, but as a "whole person." Employees cannot easily park their personal lives at the office or plant doors. Responsibilities, problems, and worries are baggage employees bring with them wherever they go. But we also know that what employees do outside of work can contribute in very real ways to their capabilities, creativity, and commitment to the job. So, regardless of the nature of work–life needs or interests, the company is committed to helping ensure that the different dimensions of employees' lives harmonize and complement each other—rather than conflict and collide. By reducing the potential for work–life conflict and minimizing the effects of role overload, we can help ease stress and increase engagement—resulting in healthier, happier employees in healthier, happier workplaces.

While achieving total work–life balance may be an elusive goal, employees of all ages and stages consider the management of work–life responsibilities and priorities as an important quality of life issue. It seems the roles and responsibilities of individual employees are increasing in number and complexity, especially with the significant numbers of workers today who are members of the "sandwich generation"—people who are attending to the needs of aging or ailing parents or other family members, while at the same time raising their own children. For these workers, the "struggle to juggle" may be particularly intense, especially if their family members do not live in the same city or country. But other workers feel the crunch too, in different ways. For new parents, the issue of finding and keeping quality child care is often a challenge. And across North America, younger employees without children are indicating they would prefer to work for employers that enable them to achieve balance in their lives. They are not adopting a "work-centric" style, preferring instead to find satisfaction on a number of different levels, such as getting more education, volunteering, travelling, or spending time with family and friends.

Clearly a "one size fits at all" approach is not the most effective way of finding solutions to the work–life challenges that confront us. Generally, the first step towards identifying a solution involves dialogue. Through dialogue and joint problem-solving, issues and ideas are explored. Usually what's called for is reciprocal flexibility—or some movement on both sides to find a mutually satisfactory solution. But what's the starting point for these discussions? Policies and programs, plus collective agreements, all serve as a vital springboard for work–life dialogue between employees, their managers and supervisors, and employee representatives or bargaining agents. While employers are not responsible for creating balance in the lives of their employees, OPG is proud of its long history helping employees find ways to effectively manage their work–life responsibilities. By providing an array of policies, programs, resources, and supports, we seek to enable our employees as they navigate the "every-day-a-thon" of modern life—contributing to individual and organizational well-being, and to the health of families, communities, and society.

Source: Reprinted by permission of Kim Taylor, Manager, retired, Recruitment Solutions and Diversity, Corporate Human Resources, Ontario Power Generation.

FIGURE 1.3 Multitasking Is a Fact of Life for Many Parents

just under one-quarter of Canadians aged 15 and older (23.5%) report that most days are extremely stressful, according to the 2010 Canadian Community Health Survey: 24.9% of women and 22.0% of men. Across all age groups, women are more stressed than men. The biggest difference is among teenagers; 23.2% of young women aged 15 to 19 years report high levels of stress compared to only 13.7% of young men. The degree of stress peaks among persons aged 35 to 44, with about three in ten men and women (29.8%) experiencing "quite a lot" of stress each day. This is the age group that is most likely to be juggling multiple responsibilities.

A poll commissioned by *The Globe and Mail* (cited in Agrell, 2012) found that Canadians experience, on average, 14 stressful moments in a week. Recently the Canadian Index of Wellbeing revealed that one in five working people experience high levels of "crunch time" when they feel overwhelmed by full inboxes and busy weekly schedules (Agrell, 2010).

The work–family balance is a constant struggle:

> Juggling the demands of paid and unpaid work is one of the most common sources of family stress today. One-quarter of Canadian workers aged 15 and older report being unsatisfied with their work/family balance (Turcotte, 2011). And over one-third worry that they don't spend enough time with their family or friends. (Statistics Canada, 2011; Vanier Institute of the Family, 2012e)*

---

*Vanier Institute of the Family. 2012. "Stress: A Family Matter." Available at http://www.vanierinstitute.ca/modules/news/newsitem.php?ItemId=315. Reprinted by permission of The Vanier Institute of the Family.

The impact of stress is experienced not only by individuals but also by all family members. According to Lero (2003: 24),

> Role overload and work–family interference are significantly related to employees' job stress, job satisfaction, organizational commitment, and absenteeism, and also are correlated with family outcomes. The latter include a higher incidence of work demands negatively affecting time with their spouse, perceived poor quality of couple and family relationships, lower levels of family satisfaction, and a great tendency to miss family activities due to work.

According to Statistics Canada (2003c), managers and professionals were significantly more likely than workers in primary industries to report stress from too many demands or hours. Stressed employees may consider quitting their job; turn down promotions that require travel, relocation, overtime, or extra responsibilities; or leave their job to find new employment where family needs are more easily met.

New parents, half of whom are in their mid 30s, are connected to their parenting role in ways that could not have been imagined by their own parents. One trip to a bookstore's parenting section will show hundreds of experts who have written about every possible aspect of child rearing and parenting. Parents are sure to feel overwhelmed by the responsibility of their task when each expert has a different strategy for raising successful and caring children. Internet access through blogs, email alerts, and health care and parenting sites exacerbates the situation since it allows parents to retrieve more information than was ever thought possible. For many parents who are educated and environmentally conscious, this information supports their demanding role. For others, it may make them feel not just anxious but overwhelmed as the content may be too complicated, too basic, or in conflict with cultural practices.

Often emotional exhaustion goes hand-in-hand with physical exhaustion. Lero (2003: 24) states that

> many families report cutting back on sleep as a primary strategy for dealing with time conflicts. The stressed individual may also suffer psychologically. The reduced sense of accomplishment and self-esteem that accompanies burnout and the accompanying loss of zest for life are the central characteristics of depression.

Employees have voiced strong concern over the child-care difficulties they experience. Research shows consistently that compared to employees without child-care responsibilities, parents experience higher stress levels, lower productivity, and higher absenteeism, all of which have a negative effect on their workplace performance. Organized labour and other concerned groups have proposed that child care be universally accessible and publicly funded. In taking this position, they support the view that child care is not a women's issue or a parental responsibility but a societal issue that requires community involvement and support as well as family participation. It is interesting to note that today's 30-year-olds are the first generation of parents who may have been in child care themselves but they may be experiencing the frustration of not being able to find it for their own children.

Changing family structures, economic pressures, eroding community support systems, and government cutbacks at all levels contribute to stressors on the family that can lead to clinical burnout and that affect children's social, emotional, and intellectual development. According to Galinsky (1999), the amount of time that parents have to spend with their children matters a great deal:

When children spend more time with their parents on both workdays and nonworkdays, they see their parents as putting their family first. Nevertheless, many children mention that the time they spend with their parents feels rushed and hectic, and they comment on the lack of focus from many parents, indicating that families today need to find ways of getting out from under the stress to make changes that will benefit all. (Gestwicki, 2010: 59)[*]

One of the manifestations of the control that parents exercise over their children is found in the "hurried child syndrome" (Elkind, 1981). What happens to the family when child/parent schedules and needs collide?

At a time when wage-earning single parents and dual-earner families are the norm, there is an inevitable conflict between the pace of a child's life and the imposed pace of a parent's schedule. In this regard, time awareness in the family can be like a collective bargaining agreement whereby children gradually learn to ignore their own natural rhythms

---

[*]From GESTWICKI, *Home, School, and Community Relations*, 7E. © 2010 Cengage Learning. Reproduced by permission. www.cengage.com/permissions.

Inside LOOK

Balancing Work and Caregiving in Canada

A major Canadian study was conducted in 2012 by Linda Duxbury, Carleton University, and Christopher Higgins, Western University. This study, their third on work-life balance in two decades, found that work demands have risen, flexible work arrangements are rare, and career mobility is an issue. Their study looked at the work–life challenges of 25,000 Canadians working full time in all provinces and territories. Two thirds of the participants were parents.

"Stress levels have gone up and life satisfaction has gone down," said Duxbury. "Email use has gone up, as have work demands. There are more employees balancing work, elder care and childcare. But despite the talk, many companies have not made progress in the area of work-life balance and employee well-being."

Among the findings:
- Most Canadian employees still work a fixed nine-to-five schedule—about two-thirds.
- Overall, the typical employee spends 50.2 hours in work-related activities a week. Just over half of employees take work home to complete outside regular hours.
- The use of flexible work arrangements such as a compressed work week (15 per cent) and flexible schedules (14 per cent) is much less common.
- Fifty-seven per cent of those surveyed reported high levels of stress.
- Employees in the survey were twice as likely to let work interfere with family as the reverse.
- Work-life conflict was associated with higher absenteeism and lower productivity.

Source: Reprinted by permission of Dr. Linda Duxbury, Carleton University.

EXHIBIT 1.2   A Mother's Memories of Poverty

How does poverty affect Canadian families? We can gain some understanding of this issue by considering Linda Marchotte's memories of mothering in poverty:

- the kids always having stained, patched, or out-of-fashion clothes;
- sending them to school with plain, unexciting lunches every day;
- no hot-dog or doughnut treats at school fundraising days;
- no cable TV, actually no TV for five years;
- no movies;
- arriving places tired from carrying stuff and worn out from waiting in the cold or wet or hot;
- shame in inviting kids over: "Where's the couch?" "Where's your stereo?" "Where's your room?" were the kinds of questions from these young visitors;
- birthday parties, where kids asked, "Is this all there is?";
- worry and anxiety about money—"Will we make it to cheque day?"—and being scared anything will happen that costs anything, this fear taking energy away from living, having fun, and paying attention to the children;
- dragging the kids and two garbage bags full of dirty laundry on the bus every week to do laundry;
- always looking for money or returnable bottles on the ground;
- being constantly worried the kids weren't getting enough nutritious food to grow and be healthy;
- being homeless for four months and living with friends and at two different friends' houses while they were away, with our things stored on another friend's back porch;
- being aware of how outside of their peers' culture and experience my children were, and being powerless to do anything about it.

Source: Baxter, S. 1993. *A Child Is Not a Toy: Voices of Children in Poverty.* Vancouver: New Star Press. Reprinted by permission of the publisher.

... and absorb the messages and attitudes about time sent by their busy parents." (Erkel, 1995: 36)

When stress induces parents to put their own needs ahead of children's, then children are expected to adapt to adult schedules and timetables rather than adults adapting themselves to the pace of childhood.

POVERTY

What are the implications of poverty? According to a Senate Standing Committee,

To be born poor is to face a greater likelihood of ill health—in infancy, in childhood, and throughout one's adult life. To be born poor is to face a lesser likelihood that you finish high school; lesser still that you attend university. To be born poor is to face a greater likelihood that you are judged a delinquent in adolescence and, *if* you are, a greater likelihood that you are sent to a correctional institution. To be born poor is to have the deck stacked against you at birth and to find life an uphill struggle ever after. (1991: 74)

Regional variations and the different issues facing urban and rural populations make it difficult

to measure precisely the depth of poverty in this country. One of the striking facts about poverty in Canada is that many people who live in poverty have jobs! We also know that a significant number of children in Canada live in circumstances that place them at social, physical, and emotional disadvantage.

Campaign 2000's website has a comprehensive overview of child poverty in Canada (**http://www .campaign2000.ca**). This group has proposed a strategy of joint federal–provincial action to reduce child poverty by at least 25 percent by 2012 and by at least 50 percent by 2017. The four cornerstones of its strategy are outlined below:

1. *Make Work Pay:* **Any parent or adult working full-time, full-year, for 30 hours a week (1,500 hours a year) should not live below the poverty line.**

2. *Dignity for People with Disabilities:* **A basic income system for people with disabilities equivalent to social security benefits available for seniors should be implemented.**

3. *Safety Net for the Unemployed:* **For families with children in which the parents are**

unavailable for work because of temporary or extended difficulties , an income system is needed that does not leave them destitute (i.e., welfare rates for families to be equivalent to 80 percent of minimum income earned by families working full-time for a full year).

4. *Public Supports for Families and Children:* Employment Insurance coverage should be restored and basic drug and dental benefits should

be provided for all workers, as well as more afford-able housing and universal access to affordable child care (Monsebraaten and Whittington, 2007).

According to the Canadian Council on Social Development (2003), Canada now has the highest level of college and university graduates in the Organisation for Economic Co-operation and Development and average earnings reflect this. Income and level of education are well known to have

FIGURE 1.4 Incidence of Absolute Poverty among Children in the Early Years, Study 3

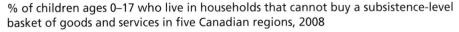

% of children ages 0–17 who live in households that cannot buy a subsistence-level basket of goods and services in five Canadian regions, 2008

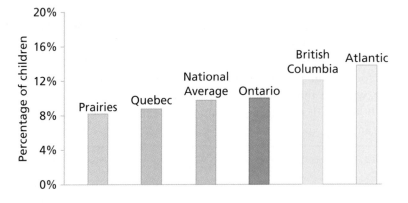

Source: Norrie McCain, M., Mustard, F.J., McCuaig, K. 2012. *Early Years Study 3. Making Decisions Taking Action.* Margaret & Wallace McCain Family Foundation. Reprinted by permission.

Inside LOOK

Money may not buy happiness, but it does afford a myriad of options, from sufficient and nutritious food to eat; to comfortable residences; to better health care; to education at prestigious universities; to vacations, household help, and family counselling. Consider that, among two-parent Canadian families with children aged 4 to 11:

- Nearly 30 percent of poor children had changed school three times before they were 11 years of age, in contrast to about 10 percent of children in upper-income families. Children experiencing frequent transitions tend to have lower math scores, more grade failures, and more behaviour problems than children who remain in the same school.
- One third of poor children 4 to 5 years of age display delayed vocabulary development, while less than 10 percent of children from high-income families are behind in vocabulary development.
- Organized and unorganized sports are less likely to be part of a poor child's activities than an advantaged child. About 25 percent of poor children participate in organized sports in contrast to 75 percent of children in high-income families.

Sources: From LAMANNA/RIEDMAN/NELSON. *Marriages and Families, 1E.* © 2003 Nelson Education Ltd. Reproduced by permission. www.cengage.com/permissions

Neserita Gascon sacrificed a teaching career and the joy of raising her two school-age children when she left the Philippines for Canada in 1985 to build a better future for her family. But after working for a family for nine years, she had to leave that job when she developed a severe skin allergy to harsh cleaning chemicals and rubber gloves. The timing couldn't have been worse as her two children, 17 and 19, had just arrived in Canada. It was the mid-1990s and jobs were scarce and welfare and social programs were slashed. Gascon learned about a free program to become an early childhood assistant. It was her ticket out of welfare, out of social housing, and eventually out of poverty. The six-month program led to two years of daycare supply teaching, a full-time job, and an opportunity to upgrade her credentials to a registered early childhood educator as well as a pay hike. Today Gascon, who recently turned 65, earns about $38,600 with benefits. The Learning Enrichment Foundation and the University of Toronto's Ontario Institute for Studies in Education (OISE) conducted a research project that looked at 60 long-time child-care workers at Learning Enrichment Foundation's 17 daycare centres in 2011 and measured how the workers' quality of life changed as they upgraded their skills and climbed the non-profit organization's pay scale. The results of this survey and continuing investigation will be published in 2013 in *Social Purpose Enterprises: Case Studies in Doing Business Differently* (Monsebraaten, 2012).

Source: Monsebraaten, L. 2012. "The Cost Of Really Living," *The Toronto Star*, February 11, A6. Reprinted by permission of Torstar Syndication Services.

an impact on parental beliefs, values, and practices. The Canadian Centre for Policy Alternatives (2007—the latest data available) reported that by 9:46 a.m. on January 2, 2007, the country's 100 highest paid business executives had earned, on average, an amount equal to what the average Canadian would earn in all of 2007—$38,010.

Often people of the same socioeconomic status from different countries have more in common than people of different socioeconomic status within the same country. "Contrary to the expectation of a better life, immigrants and refugees often find that their socioeconomic status lowers dramatically when they arrive and for a number of years afterwards" (Mawani, 2004: 1). Statistics Canada (2007) reports that second-generation women earn more than women with similar education whose parents were born in Canada, while second-generation men earn considerably less than their male peers. "It is suggested that delayed marriage and child rearing, as well as better access to high-paying jobs in urban areas may contribute to the comparative success of second-generation women" (Grewal, 2007).

So what are the real implications of gender inequality in the workforce? Ambert (2006) claims, "If women were paid equitably, the poverty rate in Canada could be cut in half. The economic disadvantages to women are exacerbated for single mothers" (in Shimoni and Baxter, 2007: 159).

The Canadian Teachers' Federation characterizes the negative consequences of poverty in general:

> Outside of the classroom, social inequity looms affecting educators' ability to maximize every child's potential. Inequity comes in many forms including discrimination and reduced socioeconomic opportunity. Of special concern to the Canadian Teachers' Federation is poverty. Poverty stunts the potential of the one in ten Canadian children affected by it. Empty stomachs and less money for extracurricular activities can translate into lower achievement levels. Poverty's symptoms include reduced motivation to learn, delayed cognitive development, lower achievement, less participation in extracurricular activities, interrupted school attendance, increased illiteracy and higher dropout rates. Not surprisingly, children who grow up in poverty have lower university attendance rates. (Tremblay, 2012)[*]

HOUSING

Peters (2011) points out that housing prices have risen much more quickly than income:

[*]Claire Tremblay, "Canada's A Grade Teachers." Reprinted by permission from *Ottawa Life Magazine*.

Second Harvest

Given the pressing nature of poverty, many organizations have sprung up to provide community support to those in need. Every month in Canada, 93,000 people access a food bank for the first time. In 1985, Ina Andre and Joan Clayton started Second Harvest by using their station wagon to pick up fresh food, which would have otherwise gone to waste, and delivering it to local shelters and drop-in centres. In 2011–2012, Second Harvest in Toronto distributed 7.2 million pounds of food donated by grocery stores, food manufacturers, processors and distributors, hotels, restaurants, and caterers. Using a value of $2.50 per pound of food (based on consultation with Food Banks Canada), this food was worth over 18 million dollars. This surplus food went to 215 community agencies and provided enough food for over 19,000 meals every day. Second Harvest relies on approximately 1,600 volunteers, in addition to financial donations and sponsorships. Many businesses support Second Harvest by donating products and services, and in 2011–2012 this support was valued at nearly $1,700,000 and included truck insurance, courier costs, cell phone service, creative design and print work, event involvement, promotion, and prizing. What started as a two-person operation has grown to address the pressing needs of the poorest in this community. You can read more about Second Harvest at **http://www.secondharvest.ca.**

Source: Contributed by Katherine Moffat, Interim Director of Communications, Second Harvest, 2013.

Average household income has flat lined since the mid-1970s while housing prices have increased 76 percent across Canada, leaving parents of young children facing a higher cost of living. In Ontario, housing prices jumped eight times faster than household incomes for young couples, even though women have increased their participation in the labour force by almost 40 percent since 1976.[*]

[*]Gordon, A. 2011. "Young Parents Squeezed For Time and Money Report Finds," *The Toronto Star*, November 1. Reprinted by permission of TorStar Syndication Services.

Today's young families are pressed for time at home, pressed for money because of the increasing cost of living, and pressed for child-care services that would support them in balancing work and family (Gordon, 2011). Far too many families in Canada are living in conditions that put children and their families at risk: 750,000 children in Canada under 15 years live in housing that is either unaffordable, substandard, overcrowded or all three (Co-operative Housing Federation of Canada, 2009).

Feminist theorizing has contributed to political action regarding families in the following ways, among others:

1. Changes in policies that economically weaken households headed by women (for example, efforts to end gender and race discrimination in wages).
2. Changes in laws that reinforce the privileges of men and heterosexual nuclear families compared to other family types (for example, divorce laws that disadvantage women economically or laws that exclude non-traditional families from economic and legal supports offered to married people).
3. Efforts to stop sexual harassment and sexual and physical violence against women and children.
4. Advances in securing women's reproductive freedom (for example, through abortion rights).

5. New recognition and support for women's unpaid work, by involving men more fully in house-work and child care and by efforts to fund good-quality daycare and paid parental leaves.

6. Transformations in family therapy so that counsellors recognize the reality of gender inequality in family life and treat women's concerns with respect.

Source: Goldner, V. 1993. "Feminist Theories." In P.G. Boss and J. William, eds., *Sourcebook of Family Theories and Methods: A Contextual Approach*. New York: Plenum Press, pp. 623-625, with kind permission from Springer Science+Business Media B.V.

Inside LOOK

In her ground-breaking book of the early 1960s, *The Feminine Mystique,* Betty Friedan chronicled women's struggle to break out of the confines of their domestic straitjacket. But Friedan also argued that the new role of women didn't mean they had to hate men or give up fulfilling romantic and sex-ual relationships with men. Much of the backlash against feminism in the past 30 years has centred on feminists as man-haters. Some believe being a feminist means women have to hate men or give up on marriage. Others say simply that the idea of romantic love is so entwined with traditional gender roles that it dies when those roles change and overlap. Still others say men react to the feminist challenge with a powerful backlash that includes violence. Friedan herself believed that feminism was not in-compatible with romantic love and that the liberation of women would lead to the liberation of men.

Source: Angelini, 2007: 220.

FEMINIST MOVEMENTS

The first wave of the women's movement was successful in gaining voting rights for women. The second wave, during the 1960s, included radical, liberal, and socialist feminist movements, and also achieved many important victories.

With the increase of mothers in the workforce, child care continues to be a critical issue. Rosenberg (2001: 312) states,

attempts to socialize child care outside the house-hold—a project crucial to the redesign of moth-erwork and parenting—continue to meet with enormous resistance. In North America there is still much popular and official hostility to "insti-tutionalized" daycare.

Their roles have changed over time, but living in our society remains a different experience for men and women. Spousal roles continue to be blurred, and there are conflicting ideas about these roles in all sectors of society. The role of mothers varies from family to family, from culture to culture, and from province to province.

According to Lero (2003: 13–14), a number of factors have influenced women's employment and family roles. They include the following:

- A rapid rise in divorce rates, a lower mar-riage rate, and the tendency toward later marriages. Larger numbers of working-age women are spending longer periods unmar-ried, a condition that requires that they be self-supporting. When married or involved in a common-law relationship, women are less likely to relinquish their economic indepen-dence or risk the loss of their job or future career prospects.[*]

- Low fertility rates, along with the tendency to delay marriage and childbearing. On average,

[*]Lero, D.S. 2003. "Dual-Earner Families." In M. Lynn, ed., *Voices: Essays on Canadian Families*, 2nd ed. Toronto: Thomson Nelson Learning. P. 24. Reprinted by permission of Donna Lero.

women are deferring having children until their late 20s or 30s (with some having children in their 40s). As well, women are having fewer children, in part because of work demands and income security (Belanger and Ouellet, 2002). An extended period of time before childbearing allows women to establish themselves in the paid workforce, which promotes their ongoing involvement. In addition, the period of time when older mothers have young children at home is compressed, since they are likely to have only one or two children.

- Greater access to postsecondary education. Access to education and advanced professional training has enabled women to prepare themselves for a wider variety of occupations, including higher-paying professional and managerial positions. Today's women are the most highly educated of any generation; now more women than men have university degrees. Both young men and women increasingly want work that enables them to use their education, skills, and talent to contribute in a meaningful way. "Nexus generation [the generation that represents a link between the Industrial Age and the Information Age]" and younger

cohorts (both men and women) expect to have families and satisfying work.

- Changes in social attitudes toward women working outside the home, the influence of second-wave feminism, growing workplace diversity, and the demand for talent. General attitude change and government commitments to gender equality have led to increased acceptance, at least in principle, of women's rights to economic and social equality. To the extent that this leads to increased opportunities for women and the removal of systemic barriers, it promotes men and women being involved as equal partners, both at home and in the paid workforce. Faced with an increasingly diverse workforce, a shrinking labour pool, and the need for new talent, employers are more likely to hire and promote women, providing additional opportunities and economic rewards for their participation.

- Additional opportunities in professions and in senior service-sector positions.

A Conference Board of Canada study last August found that women [had] made virtually no progress in the past two decades in reaching senior management levels. Even in middle management—a key

Inside LOOK

The First, Second and Third Wave of Feminism

The first wave [of the feminist movement] began in the mid-1800s, with efforts devoted to the fight for women's suffrage as well as advocating for expanded educational and employment opportunities. The second wave in the 1960s and 70s was fuelled by books by Betty Friedan [including] *The Feminine Mystique*, Simone de Beauvoir's *The Second Sex* and Kate Millett's *Sexual Politics*. Issues were social and economic reforms, the perpetuation of male dominance and [how] educational and occupational opportunities were structured to maintain gender inequities. National organizations were founded to coordinate political lobbying efforts and to represent the diverse voices of Canadian women but federal funding has [now] been largely eliminated. The third wave is often rumoured to be obsolete. In contrast to the collectivist drive of the first two waves, the third wave of feminism is sometimes characterized as more individualistic in approach, and as lacking cohesion. But those active in the movement contend that their movement has broadened to allow for expanded areas of social concern, and to accommodate multiple voices and viewpoints. Their global perspective includes challenging universal definitions of femininity, fighting against racism and homophobia, and embracing diverse identities. Perhaps the greatest shift is in the use of the term *feminist*. Both men and women may prefer to express their views on complex issues such as abortion, sexual harassment, pornography and welfare individually rather than under the banner of feminism. (Witt and Hermiston, 2010: 273–274)

pipeline for future executives—the portion of women has grown only by 4 per cent since 1987. At that rate, it would take 151 years before gender equality is reached at the management level. (Grant, 2012)[*]

WOMEN AND THEIR INCOME

Eichler (1997: 36) states,

In spite of the great influx into the labour force, wives continue to be economically disadvantaged compared to husbands. This is the result of being female and married and/or a mother. Women as a group continue to have lower incomes than men.

Statistics Canada (2010) reports that

Average annual earnings for both women and men rose with their level of education. However, the education premium was greater among women. In 2008, women with less than a Grade 9 education earned $20,800 on average, compared with earnings of $62,800 for women with a university degree. In contrast, men who had less than Grade 9 education earned $40,400, compared with $91,800 for those with a university degree. While the earnings gap narrowed for those with higher levels of education, women working full year full time with a university degree earned about 30% less than men with a university degree.[†]

More than two million women, or 14 percent of the total female population, are members of a visible minority; most are located in Toronto and Vancouver. Twenty-one percent of visible minority women aged 15 or older have a university degree, compared with 14 percent of other women. But while visible minority women are better educated on average than other Canadian women, they are somewhat less likely to be employed and earn less at their jobs than do other women (Statistics Canada, 2006).

In 2011, there were 2.67 million self-employed workers, representing around 15.4 percent of all employed workers in the Canadian economy. Slightly more than one third of self-employed workers were female—the share of female self-employment rose steadily from 1976 to 1998, from 26 percent to 36 percent, and has remained at around 35 percent since 1999. (Statistics Canada, 2012c)

Self-employment allows some women greater flexibility in their work–home balance.

For women who work part-time, Perry (2003), states that they are less likely than their full-time counterparts to win promotions or supervise other workers, despite high levels of education and long job tenure. Women in these positions often take unpaid leave from paid employment in order to raise children, either by choice or necessity (affordable child care might be unavailable, for example). The implications of unpaid leave can be far-reaching and may include lost ground in their careers as technological advances outpace them, reduced contributions to pension plans, or the necessity of taking part-time employment that offers fewer benefits.

Despite this, research has shown that within the last 35 years the ratio of wives who earn more than their husbands has grown significantly. In 1976, 11 percent of women earned more than their spouses; by the 1980s this had grown to 19 percent, and in 2009 the figure was 31 percent.

Women also obtain a higher number of undergraduate and postgraduate degrees as they are

increasingly better suited to occupy the post-industrial economy; they're making gains in lucrative fields such as medicine, law, upper management and

[*]Grant, T. 2012. "EU Eyes Quotas For Women On Corporate Boards," *The Globe and Mail*, March 6. © The Globe and Mail Inc. All Rights Reserved.

[†]Statistics Canada. 2011. "Women In Canada: Paid Work," July 5. Available at http://www.statcan.gc.ca/daily-quotidien/101209/ dq101209a-eng.htm

I feel as if I have already put in a full day's work by the time I get to the child-care centre. It takes incredible organization to have everything go smoothly so that I can get to work on time. All it takes is one broken shoelace or a stubborn daughter dawdling over her cereal to wreak havoc. At work I'm doing the work of two people as our organization has downsized—there is no relief at work. At the other end of the day my life is programmed around Girl Guides and swimming lessons, not to mention Saturdays at the hockey arena. After I finally get everyone into bed and do laundry, make lunches for the next day, I fall into bed completely exhausted.

high finance. Job losses during the last recession were mostly incurred by men, who dominate the hardest hit sectors such as construction and manufacturing. For all the challenges facing female breadwinner families, most experts agree that more and more couples are succeeding at this non-traditional model by freeing themselves from traditional gender roles and realizing that, in many cases, the tables could turn again, depending on how the economy and their personal vocations change over time. (Gulli, 2012: 48)

THE ROLE OF WOMEN

Many women have two jobs—their work job and their home job! Witt and Hermiston (2010) have found that mothers spend approximately 13 hours a week caring for their children and 19 hours on work in the home. Fathers, on the other hand, spend 7 hours caring for their children and only 10 hours working in the home.

Unless we value the work that women have traditionally done, few men will want to do it:

> Unpaid work is perhaps the biggest contribution that women make to the economy. In Canada unpaid work is estimated to be worth up to $319 billion in the money economy or 41% of the Gross National Product; globally the numbers skyrocket to $11 trillion US. (Women and the Economy, 2011)*

Women continue to be held disproportionately responsible for the well-being of all members of the family. Indeed, many women with children in child care and those who are working in the field of early childhood are also faced with caring for aging parents. The "superwoman" concept continues to drive women in all areas of their lives, as illustrated by Helen Schulman's (2003) anecdote:

---

*Reprinted by permission of UNPAC.

I was guiding my father back to his wheelchair when I looked up and saw my son hanging precipitously off a climbing apparatus. Where was King Solomon when I needed him? If I let go of my father, who wavered like a feather in the air, he would have no choice but to fall. If I didn't run to my son, he would surely topple and hit the playground's cement hardtop. What would you have done?

Helen held onto her father, and watched her toddler drop to the ground. The child escaped with nothing worse than scraped palms. But that doesn't make the choice any less excruciating, the dilemma any less stark. Schulman's vignette, from her essay in *The Bitch in the House* (2003), illustrates a tug-of-war being lived out by a rising number of women everywhere, every day; mothers simultaneously tending growing children and aging parents—tiptoeing through a minefield of teenage rebellion at one end and seniors grasping their independence at the other, balancing the needs of kids on bicycles and elders on walkers. Statistics show that more than one in four Canadians is a caregiver and 70 percent of baby boomers expect to care for an older family member in the near future. Overwhelmingly, the caregivers are women. Most are working full-time.

Smaller family size has spread available family resources among fewer people. This is particularly relevant in the context of caregiving and population aging. Caring responsibilities are now carried by fewer family members, a situation complicated by the fact that extended families often live at a great distance from each other. In 2007, one-fifth of the population aged 45 and over who provided care to a parent lived more than an hour away from the parent in need. More than 2.3 million Canadian employees currently have caregiving responsibilities (Sager, 2010: 8).

With more and more young adults staying at home longer, the family dynamic is further complicated.

As the workforce ages, as we extend our working lives and as our longevity continues to increase, caring for an adult (adult child, sibling, spouse, parent, grandparent, senior and/or elder with a disability, recovering from illness or injury, or coping with a chronic or episodic health condition) is one of the fastest growing work–life challenges.

Caregiving is, and always has been, at the heart of family life. It is estimated that family/friend caregivers provide 70–80% of care to individuals with a chronic health condition or disability. Sixty-one percent of all adult/elder caregivers are in the paid workforce: 37% of employed women and 28% of employed men age 45+ provide care to another adult. Most work full-time. The majority provide care to parents, while 1 in 5 cares for a friend. As we marry later in life and start families later in life, employed caregivers are increasingly providing care for two or more generations at the same time. Caregivers with dual (or multiple) responsibilities are most vulnerable to the negative impacts of stress and work overload. Working long hours to make up for lost time—typically borne from either arriving late or leaving early or from sheer exhaustion and inattention—can tip an already precarious balance. While, in general, women provide more personal daily care and emotional support, men are engaged in less time-sensitive tasks, such as financial management, household management, maintenance and running errands. The lack of control over when care might be needed can make combining work and caregiving particularly difficult. Missing work, reducing hours and turning down assignments or career opportunities to meet caregiving responsibilities is common practice among employed caregivers. Providing care can mean forfeiting pay, job security or work advancement. The impact of juggling paid work with caregiving, however, goes well beyond lost wages and missed promotions—the physical, social and emotional costs can be high, too. For many caregivers, offering support to family or friends means spending less time on social activities or with spouses/partners and children. Opportunities for rest, relaxation and self-care often become few and far between. Dr. Janet Fast, Director of Research on Aging Policies and Practice at the University of Alberta, estimates that the costs to the economy of lost work time due to caregiving is the equivalent of 157,000 full time employees annually. In this context, the development of workplace policies and programs that acknowledge and support working caregivers makes sense from both an employee and employer perspective. (Spinks and Lero, 2011: 1–3).

Source: Spinks, N., and Lero, D. 2011. "Combining Caregiving and Work in Canada: Achievable or Not?" *Transition*, Winter, pp. 1-3. Reprinted by permission of The Vanier Institute of the Family.

Another factor to consider in the changing role of women is the number of women from immigrant and refugee families who have settled in Canada. Far from their families and support systems, many of these mothers parent in isolation in a country where their language and customs are not well understood. Their traditional values and ways of parenting may be very different from those they see around them.

THE CHANGING ROLES OF MEN

According to the Vanier Institute of the Family (2012e), there are over 8 million fathers in Canada (including biological, adoptive, and stepfathers).

Just under half (3.7 million) have children under 18 at home. Fathers today, on average, tend to be older than in the past. The role of fathers has changed, and bookstores abound with titles that support fathers in their role in the birthing process, their parenting skills, and their role in the family. Fathers' interaction within the structure of the family is based on many variables—the attitude of partners toward traditional roles, the number of people living in the home, work responsibilities, income, number and ages of the children, health of family members, and so on. Historically, fathers have been the major providers for their family. In many cultures, fathers are the decision makers in the family and in the community, and they are often

Ottawa mother Maithreyi Ramanathan grew up in south India, where she says that, typically, a mother goes to her own mother's house when she is eight months pregnant and doesn't return home until the baby is three or four months old. When Ramanathan was pregnant in Canada with her son Sanjay, her grandmothers were genuinely worried. "How could you do this on your own? Who is going to help you? they asked. I told them my husband would," she says. "But what good is a man's help?" they asked. Her grandmothers couldn't have appreciate that in today's North America, parenting takes place in more isolated nuclear families, often far removed from extended family members and without the support of once every-present neighbours—who now head off to work each day. In that context, a father's effective early involvement is arguably a necessity.

Source: Hoffman, 2005.

supported in this role by religious beliefs. Because status in the family and community may depend on a father's ability to provide financially for his family, the shifting reality of our economic times is altering this position for fathers. And so the challenge for fathers today is that, for many, they cannot look back to their own fathers as role models. Their fathers may in fact be less than supportive of those who become stay-at-home dads or fathers who see themselves as more than just the breadwinner.

According to Intini (2010: 71), "Between 1976 and 2009, the number of stay-at-home dads in Canada jumped from 20,000 or one percent of all stay-at-home parents, to nearly 60,000 or 12 percent."

The biggest roadblocks to active participation in child care by fathers are still sociocultural, with regard to how fathers see themselves. Practices related to pregnancy and childbirth have changed over time and now involve fathers more, contributing significantly to changing fathers' perceptions of their own role in the family. Bigner (2005) says, "Several studies conclude that the father's participation at birth helps the mother assume her role; the birth itself may be a strong stimulus for nurturing behaviours from both fathers and mothers, as well as a time for attitude formation" (in Gestwicki, 2010: 81).[*]

All research shows that it is women who take up the slack when social services are slashed, although many wish that men played a more active role. Yet, "some research projects also show that men who attempt to take on more family responsibilities get increased negative feedback from grandparents and even from wives. The legacy of the model of male as breadwinner and female as caregiver may create stress for men trying to find new roles" (Geswicki, 2010: 47).[†] Many women define their status within the family and community by their ability to care for and nurture their children. These women may be resistant to allowing fathers greater involvement with the children, since it may undermine their position. Also, if extended-family members live in the home, such as grandparents who aid in the caregiving of children, the father may play a more limited role.

The past two decades have seen a shift in fathers' involvement in their children's lives and in child-care settings, and some fathers struggle to balance the sometimes conflicting roles of successful breadwinner and nurturing parent.

The quality of the marital relationship is significantly associated with the nature of both the father–child and mother–child interaction. The more positive the marital relationship, the more involved the father is likely to be in child care and vice versa. Fathers who have, at times, exclusive responsibility for the child develop caregiving skills and gain confidence. It is also important to note that fathers may play different roles at different stages of their children's development.

There are many ways in which the concept of "good fathers" is interpreted, particularly across

[*]From GESTWICKI, *Home, School, and Community Relations*, 7E. © 2010 Cengage Learning. Reproduced by permission. www.cengage.com/permissions.

[†]From GESTWICKI, *Home, School, and Community Relations*, 7E. © 2010 Cengage Learning. Reproduced by permission. www.cengage.com/permissions.

When Sanjay was born, Ramanathan's husband was excited about playing an integral role in the raising of their son. But for Ramanathan, although she knew she wanted his help, she could not completely relinquish Sanjay's care. She would often hover, correcting and instructing to the point that her husband began to withdraw, feeling incompetent and unappreciated. Researchers have labelled this *gatekeeping*. In the end, both the mother and the father feel resentful. The lesson here is that together, both mothers and fathers need to redefine their roles.

Source: Hoffman, 2005.

cultures, although comparisons reveal more similarities than differences. Fagan and Palm (2004) point out that a study by Wilcox (1999) indicated that fathers who consider themselves religious are more likely than fathers who are nonreligious to be connected to their children in one-on-one interactions and group experiences; to be physically affectionate; and to be less likely to raise their voices in anger.

Concerns about absent fathers through divorce, separation, or incarceration continue to rise. With the high incidence of divorce, many fathers are estranged from their children. Some can't or won't pay support and, as children age, they may be less likely to want to spend time away from their friends. If a new family is started, the father may spend less time with his original family. Some fathers may also resent having to support two families. On the other hand, some fathers may see more of their children and take on more child-related responsibilities than they did when they were living with their partner. There is no question that interactions between fathers and their children are now much more complex:

> On one hand there is growing pressure on fathers residing with their children to be actively involved in the care and rearing of offspring. On the other hand, fathers are increasingly less likely to live with their biological children, and they are more likely to live with other children (i.e., children of their current partner). (Fagan and Palm, 2004: 5–6)

Clearly, more analysis needs to be done on paternal involvement, cross-cultural differences, the impact of religious beliefs, and the impact of paternal involvement in the lives of their children.

After the federal government's extension of parental benefits, fathers' participation in the program rose from 38 percent in 2001 to 55 percent in 2008 (Statistics Canada, 2008). This claim rate for fathers moves Canada ahead of many other countries, but still leaves us considerably behind those that offer fathers nontransferable leave. In Norway, for example, almost 80 percent of fathers take parental leave (Statistics Canada, 2003).

> Women who return to work after maternity leave undergo far more stress than men who take similar time off. In fact, 62 percent of mothers reported that the transition between leave and work was stressful and 20 percent described it as very stressful. Sixty-five percent of fathers rated the transition as not too stressful or not stressful at all. The data shows that nearly half of the parents cited balancing job and family responsibilities as the main source of stress associated with their return to work. (Statistics Canada, 2008)[*]

Many fathers play an active role in their children's lives.

[*]Statistics Canada. 2008. "Labour Productivity, Hourly Compensation and Unit Labour Cost." *The Daily*. June 13. Available at http:// www.statcan.ca/Daily/English/080613/d080613b.htm.

IMMIGRANT FATHERS

Immigrant fathers are

dealing with multiple and often interrelated stressors such as unemployment and underemployment, social isolation, barriers to accessing services, role reversal (when their partners are the first to find employment), and trauma induced by war or enforced refugee status. In addition, these men may have strong beliefs, values, and traditions about the nature of the family and father–child relationships that may or may not be supported in Canada. When cultural expectations of fathers' roles change as a result of immigration, there is a risk of significant pressure to either adapt or adopt new roles. Many immigrant and refugee fathers are at risk for stress factors, requiring for increased social support. Some of the pertinent stressors include the following.

- *Underemployment or Unemployment:* These factors can be devastating to the self-esteem of fathers. The loss of the traditional role as breadwinner has been linked to the use of punitive measures with children, increased alcoholism, and domestic abuse.

- *Social Isolation:* Many immigrant and refugee new Canadians are of diverse religious and cultural backgrounds. Feelings of isolation and discrimination intensify the social, psychological, and economic pressures they face. In addition, many immigrants and refugees come from countries that were at war with one another and, as a result, those hostilities further prevents community integration in Canada.

Fathers who are new immigrants and/or refugees to Canada face multiple stressors. These stressors are often interrelated and may include underemployment or unemployment. These men may also be impacted by trauma induced by war and forced into refugee status that may lead to feelings of loss, grief, and depression.

- *Barriers to Accessing Services:* There is a growing awareness of the barriers that prevent new Canadians from fully utilizing community social and health services that offer support to individuals and families. Fathers who seek support for this role face an additional barrier: women provide most of the child-focused services, and some men do not feel comfortable accessing these services. Also, women workers may be uncomfortable in their role with fathers.

- *Role Reversal:* Among immigrant and refugee families where the father is unemployed, many fathers are, through a lack of choice, fulfilling the primary caregiving and child rearing roles.

With appropriate support and training, fathers can help their children make the transition to their new country and provide for the children's healthy development. Role reversal occurs when mothers obtain work outside the home, resulting in fathers facing social isolation and loss of self-esteem.

- *Trauma Induced by War or Enforced Refugee Status:* It is well accepted that families who have been affected by traumatic events or who are forced into refugee status require special intervention and attention. Adults appear to need to move through several stages as they seek to restore mental health after being uprooted and displaced. (Este, 2006; Father Involvement Community Research Forum Spring 2006)[*]

BRAIN RESEARCH AND THE EARLY YEARS STUDY: IMPLICATIONS FOR FAMILIES

The 1999 *Early Years Study* co-written by the Honourable Margaret Norrie McCain and J. Fraser Mustard, and the subsequent publications, *Early Years Study 2* (2007) and *Early Years Study 3* (2011), provided the Ontario government with options and recommendations with respect to the best ways to prepare young children—including those at risk or with special needs—for scholastic, career, and social success. Research on brain development has helped families and teachers in their effort to understand its implications on their day-to-day lives with children. Fraser Mustard stated that "it is now understood not only that the environment affects how the brain cells are wired, but that these effects are long-lasting and that stress on early brain development has a measurable negative impact" (McCain and Mustard, 1999: 17). The *Early Years Study 2—Putting Science into Action* was an audit of what happened in early child development science and practice in the eight years after the publication of the first volume. The findings continue to acknowledge that Canada is a long way from the universally accessible high-quality programs necessary. The *Early Years Study 3—Making Decisions, Taking Action* expands on previous documents and discusses

the social, economic and scientific rationale for increased investments in early childhood education. It also introduces the Early Childhood Education Index to monitor the funding, policy, access and quality of early education

---

[*]Reprinted by permission of David Este.

programming. Together, the three Early Years Studies argue that if we truly wish to provide our children with an equal opportunity to maximize their potential, it is vital that we do everything we can to enhance their early development. Our survival as a species will depend on our children acquiring the skills they will need to cope with the social and environmental revolutions of the 21st century. Canada's tomorrow depends on our ability to leverage what we know into policies and practices that support families and benefit children today. Now, as never before, knowledge needs to be harnessed to serve not just every individual in our society, but every society around the globe. (Norrie McCain, Mustard, and McCuaig, 2012)*

Marie Goulet, a retired faculty member at the School of Early Childhood at George Brown College, contributes the following information about the importance of brain development and the role of parents and educators:

The brain is the master control of our health and well-being, competencies and coping skills. It directs all aspects of bodily functions through established biological pathways. We have long accepted the involvement of the brain in intellectual pursuits. We now know that there is a clear physiological basis that links stressful circumstances and increased vulnerability to disease (Bertrand: 2001). Brains are central to health, learning, and coping, and families are central to the environments that support brain growth. Parents' genes make a major contribution to who we become. Most researchers estimate that genetic inheritance accounts for about 50 percent of that outcome, leaving 50 percent to be influenced by life's experience. The brain integrates genetic and environmental influences. We now know that genes are not blueprints that create destiny. Genes have chemical switches that control how, when, and if that gene is expressed. A variety of environmental factors influence these switches. Parents play a significant role in passing on genes and in the expression of genes, beginning in the womb. The womb can be a child's most powerful environment. The mother's health, nutrition, exposure to toxins, and emotional well-being are important to brain development. The womb is naturally stimulating, providing the fetus with the sensory stimulation it requires. The fetus's brain is protected when maternal stress is low. This keeps cortisol, the stress hormone, at safe levels that will

not interfere with brain development in utero. The unborn child's brain development is also protected when the mother's environment is free of contaminates like lead. "Between about four months in utero and two years after birth, babies' brains are exquisitely sensitive to the quantity and quality of nutrients consumed" (Eliot, 1999: 445). "The World Health Organization and the Canadian Pediatric Society recommend breastfeeding into the second year of life" (Canadian Child Care Federation, 2001). A diet made for brain development during those years consists of breast milk, protein, dairy products, grains, and fresh vegetables and fruits.

Touching also plays an essential role in brain growth. Physical affection produces oxytocin, which is an antidote to cortisol. In infancy, touching and physical affection not only protect the child from stress, they are the means by which infants orient to and learn from visual and auditory stimulation. Parental warmth and affection continue to contribute to intellectual and emotional well-being throughout the early years and into adolescence. Responsiveness is also important from birth. Responsiveness means responding to the child's physical needs, and his or her needs for stimulation and for social interaction. Responsiveness requires parents to recognize that each child is unique. This means that they determine their child's individual needs. Uniqueness includes a child's preference for stimulation. Individuals have preferences for the type and amount of stimulation they experience. Young children require adults who help manage stimulation so that children do not become overwhelmed. Responsive parents protect their children from over-stimulation and they aid in recovery when children are overwhelmed. This protection and responsiveness strengthen brain structures involved in self-regulation and coping. When parents are sensitive to their child's signals and respond predictably, they support the child's competence and security. Security produces the brain's chemical balance that supports learning and coping. Secure children are free to explore and their repeated explorations strengthen brain connections.†

When parents and children are involved in one-on-one play where the parent and child focus attention on the same activity and have fun, the conditions are right for learning, concentrating, and coping. Joint attention and fun experienced in the child's most important relationship ensure

---

*Norrie McCain, M., Mustard, F.J., McCuaig, K. 2012. *Early Years Study 3*. Making Decisions, Taking Action. Margaret & Wallace McCain Family Foundation. Reprinted by permission.

†Reprinted by permission of Marie Goulet.

THE CHANGING FACE OF CANADIAN FAMILIES

Children deserve the best start in life.

that learning will persist and that the brain chemicals required to turn short-term memories into long-term learning are present. In the warmth of the relationship, parents provide appropriate challenges that a brain requires for learning. Parents do not provide the answers; they help the child figure out what to do to meet the challenge. This ensures that the child's brain is active. The more the child thinks, the better he or she becomes at thinking.

Parents' genetic gifts, the provision of a healthy environment (from conception), and parents' responsive relationships with their children play important roles in their children's brain development. These positive family factors produce brains that are ready for life—brains that are central to good health, learning, emotional well-being, competence, and coping.

CRITICAL FACTORS NECESSARY FOR CHILDREN'S HEALTHY DEVELOPMENT

Couchenour and Chrisman (2011) help us to understand what children need for healthy development:

Four External Assets

- *Support:* Children need care and love from families, neighbours, and community groups.

- *Empowerment:* Children are empowered when communities value them and keep them safe and secure.

- *Boundaries and Expectations:* Children need to know what is expected of them. Limits should be clear, realistic, and responsive.

- *Constructive Use of Time:* Children need to have opportunities to play safely. Choices should be provided with many varied activities. Both developmental level and individual differences should be considered.

Four Internal Assets

- *Commitment to Learning:* Families and communities encourage children to be lifelong learners.

- *Positive Values:* Children are exposed to examples of caring, fairness, social justice, integrity, honesty, responsibility, and healthy life choices.

- *Social Competencies:* Children have opportunities to learn how to get along with others, to celebrate similarities and differences, and to peacefully resolve conflicts.

- *Positive Identity:* Children have positive role models and responsive nurturing so that they can develop a sense of self-worth and caring for others.[*]

WHAT DO WE NEED?

The premise that all children have a right to sensitive nurturance and that no citizen has a right to ignore children's needs is a common thread throughout much of the work examining children's irreducible needs. Couchenour and Chrisman (2011) rely on T. Berry Brazelton and Stanley Greenspan in their work as pediatric professionals when they discuss the stress of young families in today's society. Couchenour and Chrisman speak to the need for community support and believe that we are in grave danger of failing children and their families. They believe that society will pay the price of ignoring the needs of young families when children do not receive what they need for optimal development. The cost many well reflect a culture where street gangs flourish, drug and alcohol dependence increases, and many children end up behind bars. They remind us that we are all responsible for the children in our communities and we need to be champions for their right to a healthy and caring society.

Paul Steinhauer was a professor of Psychiatry at the University of Toronto's Division of Child Psychiatry and the Hospital for Sick Children who best summed up this chapter when he stated,

We have to get to the point where governments do not just talk about doing what is right for

[*]From COUCHENOUR/CHRISMAN. *Families, Schools and Communities*, 4E. © 2011 Wadsworth, a part of Cengage Learning, Inc. Reproduced by permission. www.cengage.com/permissions.

children, but will give it the highest priority. We must get informed and stand up in community meetings at all levels and make contact with elected politicians on a regular basis—to let them know that there is a community of people out there who care just as much about what is happening to the nation's children as what is happening to the nation's economy … our children should be our nation's most important interest.

ANSWERS TO EXHIBIT 1.1 FAMILIES IN CANADA: A QUIZ

1. 82%
2. 12%
3. 99.2%
4. 25%
5. 80%
6. Saskatchewan
7. 1060
8. 20
9. 9%
10. 4%
11. 70,000
12. 6
13. 24%
14. 32.5%
15. 10%
16. True

REFERENCES

Abraham, C. 2012. "Unnatural Selection." The Globe and Mail. January 7. F1, F5–F7.

Adams, M. 2007. *Unlikely Utopia: The Surprising Triumph of Canadian Pluralism*. Toronto: Viking Canada.

Adams, M. 2010. *Stayin' Alive. How Canadian Baby Boomers Will Work, Play and Find Meaning in the Second Half of Their Lives*. Toronto: Viking Canada.

Adler, R.B., L.B. Rosenfeld, R.F. Proctor II, and C. Winder. 2012. *Interplay. The Process of Interpersonal Communication*. Oxford University Press.

Agrell, S. 2010. "Part 1: Stress: Public Health Enemy No. 1." *The Globe and Mail*. October 30. A14. Retrieved February 20, 2013, from http://www.theglobeandmail.com/news/national/time-to-lead/part-1-stress-public-health-enemy-no-1/article1318732/?page=3

———. 2010. "Totally Freaked Out." *Toronto Life*. March.

———. 2012. "Part 1: Stress: Public-Health Enemy No. 1? June 21. Retrieved February 14, 2013, from http://m.theglobeandmail.com/news/national/time-to-lead/part-1-stress-public-health-enemy-no-1/article1318732/?service=mobile

Alvi, S. 1994. *The Work and Family Challenge: Issues and Options*. Ottawa: Canada Committee for the International Year of the Family, the Conference Board of Canada.

Anderssen, E., and A. McIlroy. 2004. "Study Names Canadians World's Best Dads." *The Globe and Mail*. April 2. Retrieved February 19, 2013, from http://www.theglobeandmail.com/life/study-names-canadians-worlds-best-dads/article1135373

Angelini, P.U. 2007. *Our Society. Human Diversity in Canada*, 3rd ed. Toronto: Thomson Nelson.

Baker, M. 2007. *Choices and Constraints in Family Life*. Oxford University Press.

———. 2010. *Choices and Constraints in Family Life,* 2nd ed. Oxford University Press.

Baxter, S. 1993. *A Child Is Not a Toy: Voices of Children in Poverty*. Vancouver: New Star Press.

Belanger, A., and G. Ouellet. 2002. "A Comparative Study of Recent Trends in Canadian and American Fertility, 1980–1999." In A. Belanger, ed., *Report on the Demographic Situation in Canada 2001: Current Demographic Analysis*. Catalogue no. 91-209-XPE. Ottawa: Ministry of Industry, Statistics Canada.

Bertrand, J. 2001. *Children's Developmental Health: Nourish, Nurture and Neurodevelopment*. Ottawa: Canadian Child Care Federation.

Bibby, R. 2004. "The Future Families Project: A Survey of Canadian Hopes and Dreams." Ottawa: Vanier Institute of the Family. Retrieved from http://www.vifamily.ca

Bigner, J.J. 2005. *Parent–Child Relations: An Introduction to Parenting*, 7th ed. New York: Prentice Hall.

Brazelton, T. B., and S.I. Greenspan, 2000. The Irreducible Needs of Children: What Every Child Must Have to Grow, Learn and Flourish. Cambridge, MA: Perseus.

Bronfenbrenner, U. 1979. *The Ecology of Human Development*. Cambridge, MA: Harvard University Press.

———. 1990. The *Ecology of Human Development: Experiments by Nature and Design*. Cambridge, MA: Harvard University Press.

Bubolz, M.M., and S. Sontag. 1993. "Human Ecology Theory." In P.G. Boss, W.J. Doherty, R. LaRossa, W.R. Schumm, and S.K. Steinmetz, eds., *Sourcebook of Family Theories and Methods: A Contextual Approach*. New York: Plenum Press.

Canadian Centre for Policy Alternatives. 2007. "No New Year's Hangover for Top CEO's." January 2. Retrieved February 14, 2013, from http://www.policyalternatives.ca/newsroom/updates/new-years-party-still-going-top-ceos

Canadian Index of Wellbeing. 2009. "Living Standards." Retrieved from http://uwaterloo.ca/canadian-index-wellbeing/our-products/domains/living-standards

Canadian Index of Wellbeing. 2010a. "Time Use." Retrieved from https://uwaterloo.ca/canadian-index-wellbeing/how-are-canadians-really-doing/domains-wellbeing/time-use

Canadian Index of Wellbeing. 2010b. "Community Vitality." Retrieved from https://uwaterloo.ca/canadian-index-wellbeing/how-are-canadians-really-doing/domains-wellbeing/community-vitality

Citizenship and Immigration Canada. 2012. "Who Are We?" Retrieved from http://www.cic.gc.ca/english/resources/publications/discover/section-05.asp

Clark, W. 2006. "Interreligious Unions in Canada." *Canadian Social Trends*. Catalogue no. 82 (11-008-XWE). Retrieved from http://www.statcan.ca/english/freepub/11-008-XIE/2006003/main_interreligious.htm#study.

Cohen, T. 2008. The Latest Canadian Portrait. *Toronto Star*. April 2. Retrieved from http://www.thestar.com/news/canada/census/article/409103--visible-minorities-hit-5-million

Co-operative Housing Federation of Canada. 2009. *The Dunning Report: Dimensions of Core Housing Need in Canada*. CHF Canada. Retrieved from http://www.chfcanada.coop

Couchenour, D., and K. Chrisman. 2011. *Families, Schools and Communities. Together for Young Children*, 4th ed. Wadsworth, Cengage Learning.

de Vries, B. 2010. "Friendship and Family: The Company We Keep." The Vanier Institute of the Family. *Transition*. Winter.

Discover Canada. n.d. "The Rights and Responsibilities of Citizenship." Study Guide. Citizenship and Immigration Canada. Retrieved February 14, 2013, from www.cic.gc.ca/english/pdf/pub/discover.pdf

Eichler, M. 1997. *Family Shifts: Families, Policies, and Gender Equality*. Toronto: Oxford University Press.

Elkind, D. 1981. *The Hurried Child: Growing Up Too Fast Too Soon*. Reading, MA: Addison-Wesley Publishing Company.

Erkel, R.T. 1995. "Time Shifting." *Family Therapy Networker* 19: 33–39.

Este, D. 2006. *Immigrant Fathers*. Retrieved February 2, 2012, from http://fira.ca/cms/documents/45/Immigrant_Fathers.pdf

Fagan, J., and G. Palm. 2004. *Fathers and Early Childhood Programs*. New York: Thomson Delmar Learning.

Father Involvement Research Alliance. 2006. "Immigrant Fathers Cluster Executive Summary." Retrieved February 23, 2013, from fira.ca/cms/documents/45/Immigrant_Fathers.pdf

Friesen, J. and J. Wingrove. 2012. "Ontario Cedes Centre Stage to Thriving Western Provinces." *The Globe and Mail*. February 9, A12.

Galinsky, E. 1999. *Ask the Children: What America's Children Really Think About Working Parents*. New York: Morrow.

Gestwicki, C. 2010. *Home, School and Community*, 7th ed. Wadsworth Cengage Learning.

Goldner, V. 1993. "Feminist Theories." In P.G. Boss and J. William, eds., *Sourcebook of Family Theories and Methods: A Contextual Approach*. New York: Plenum Press.

Goodwin, C. 2000. "Nobel Sperm Bank Babies and How They Grew." *Toronto Star*. Retrieved from http://www.thestar.ca/thestar/editorial/life/20000116BOD016_BS-BRAINS.html

Gordon, A. 2011. "Young Parents Squeezed for Time and Money Report Finds." thestar.com. November 1. Retrieved from http://mobile.thestar.com/mobile/NEWS/article/1071806

Grant, T. 2012. "EU Eyes Quotas for Women on Corporate Boards." *The Globe and Mail*. March 6. Retrieved February 20, 2013, from http://www.theglobeandmail.com/report-on-business/international-business/european-business/eu-eyes-forced-quotas-for-women-on-corporate-boards/article551278

Grewal, S. 2007. "The Stronger Sex." *Toronto Star*. November 3. Retrieved January 19, 2012, from http://www.thestar.com/article/273126--why-immigrant-women-may-be-the-stronger-sex

Gulli, C. 2012. "The Richer Sex." *Maclean's*. March 12.

Hoffman, J. 2005. "When Dads and Babies Build a Strong Relationship, Everybody Wins." *Today's Parent*. April.

Human Resources and Skills Development Canada. 2012. "Indicators of Well-Being in Canada." Aging. Retrieved February 14, 2013, from http://www4.hrsdc.gc.ca/.3ndic.1t.4r@-eng.jsp?iid=33

Intini, J. 2010. "Why Our Boys Are Growing Up to Be Underachieving Men." *Macleans*. October 25.

Johnson, K.L., D.S. Lero, and J.A. Rooney. 2001. *Work–Life Compendium 2001*. Centre for Families, Work and Well-Being. Guelph, ON: University of Guelph, Human Resources Development Canada.

Kagan, S.L., and P.R. Neville. 1994. "Parent Choice in Early Care and Education: Myth or Reality?" *Research and Clinical Issues, Zero to Three* 14 (4). February–March.

Lero, D.S. 2003. "Dual-Earner Families." In M. Lynn, ed., *Voices: Essays on Canadian Families*, 2nd ed. Toronto: Thomson Nelson Learning.

Luxton, M. 2001. "Family Coping Strategies: Balancing Paid Employment and Domestic Labour." In B. Fox, ed., *Family Patterns: Gender Relations*, 2nd ed. New York: Oxford Press.

Mallick, H. 2012. "Working Women with Kids Need a Workplace Revolution … Or Else." *Toronto Star*. June 22. Retrieved from http://www.thestar.com/news/world/article/1216067--seo-head-working-women-with-kids-need-a-workplace-revolution-or-else

Mann, B. 1996. "New Times, New Fathers." Retrieved January 20, 2013, from http://www.ottawamenscentre.com/news/19960807_new_fathers.htm

Mawani, F.N. 2004. "Attachment Across Cultures." National Advisory Panel. Retrieved February 24, 2013, from http://www.phac-aspc.gc.ca/hp-ps/dca-dea/publications/attach-cultures/attach-cultures-eng.php

McDaniel, S.A. and L. Tepperman. 2011. *Close Relations. An Introduction to the Sociology of Families,* 4th ed. Pearson Canada.

Monsebraaten, L. 2012. "The Cost of Really Living." *Toronto Star*. February 11. A6.

Monsebraaten, L., and L. Whittington. 2007. "Politicians Challenged to Combat Child Poverty." *Toronto Star*. September 12. A1.

Norrie McCain, M., Mustard, F.J., and McCuaig, K. 2012. *Early Years Study 3. Making Decisions, Taking Action*. Margaret & Wallace McCain Family Foundation.

Norrie McCain, M.N., and J. F. Mustard. 1999. *Early Years Study: Final Report*. April. Toronto: Children's Secretariat. Retrieved from http://www.childsec.gov.on.ca

Olson, D.H., H.I. McCubbin, H.L. Barnes, M.J. Muxen, A.S. Larsen, and M.A. Wilson. 1989. *Families: What Makes Them Work*. Newbury Park, CA: Sage.

Perry, A. 2003. "Long-term Effects of Part-Time Hours: Study Finds Women Bear Costs in Job Quality—Fewer Promotion, Supervisory Roles and Lower Wages." *Toronto Star*. 5 July.

Peters, T. 2011. "The Next Generation of Parenting. Young Parents Squeezed for Time and Money Report Finds." October 19. Retrieved February 14, 2013, from http://tonivpeters.wordpress.com/2011/10/page/4

Pew Research Centre for the People and the Press. 2003. *Global Attitudes Project.* Washington, DC: Pew Research Centre.

Riedman, A., M.A. Lamanna, and A. Nelson. 2003. *Marriages and Families.* Toronto: Thomson Nelson.

Rosenberg, H. 2001. "Motherwork, Stress, and Depression: The Costs of Privatized Social Reproduction." In B. Fox, ed., *Family Patterns: Gender Relations*, 2nd ed. New York: Oxford Press.

Sager, E. 2010. "Family and Social Memory: Why History Matters." *Transition* 40(2). Summer. The Vanier Institute of the Family.

Samovar, L.A., R.E. Porter, and E.R. McDaniel. 2007. *Communication Between Cultures*, 6th ed. New York: Thomson Wadsworth.

Schulman, H. 2003. "My Mother's Ring: Caught Between Two Familes." In C. Hanauer, ed., *The Bitch in the House: 26 Women Tell the Truth about Sex, Solitude, Work, Motherhood, and Marriage.* New York: HarperCollins.

Search Institute. n.d. "What Kids Need to Succeed." Retrieved February 14, 2013, from http://www.search-institute.org

Senate Standing Committee. 1991. Official Report of Debates of the Legislative Assembly. Retrieved January 21, 2013, from http://www.leg.bc.ca/Hansard/34th2nd/34p_02s_880412p.htm

Shimoni, R. and J. Baxter. 2007. *Working with Families*, 4th ed. Pearson, Addison Wesley. 172.

Spinks, N. and Lero, D. 2011. "Combining Caregiving and Work in Canada: Achievable or Not?" *Transition.* Winter. The Vanier Institute of the Family.

Statistics Canada. 2001. "Census Families in Private Households by Family Structure, Presence of Children and Labour Force Activity of Husband/Male Common-law Partner, Showing Labour Force Activity of Wife/Female Common-law Partner or Lone Parent, for Canada, Provinces and Territories, 1996 Census." Retrieved from http://www.statcan.ca/english/census96/june9/econ2.htm

———. 2003. "Benefiting From Extended Parental Leave." *The Daily.* Retrieved from http://www.statcan.gc.ca/daily-quotidien/030321/dq030321b-eng.htm

———. 2006. "Visible Minority Women. A Well Educated Population. Retrieved from http://www.statcan.gc.ca/pub/89-503-x/2010001/article/11527-eng.htm#a11

———. 2008. "Labour Productivity, Hourly Compensation and Unit Labour Cost." *The Daily.* June 13. Retrieved from http://www.statcan.gc.ca/daily-quotidien/080613/dq080613b-eng.htm

———. 2010. "Women in Canada: Economic Well Being." *The Daily.* December 16. Retrieved February 2013, from from http://www.statcan.gc.ca/daily-quotidien/101216/dq101216c-eng.htm

———. 2011a. "Women in Canada: Paid Work." July 5. Retrieved January 21, 2013, from http://www.statcan.gc.ca/daily-quotidien/101209/dq101209a-eng.htm

———. 2011b. "The Canadian Population in 2011: Age and Sex." Retrieved January 21, 2013, from http://www12 .statcan.gc.ca/census-recensement/2011/as-sa/98-311-x/98-311-x2011001-eng.cfm

———. 2012a. "Canada's Population Clock." Retrieved from http://www.statcan.gc.ca/ig-gi/pop-ca-eng.htm

———. 2012b. "Couple Families by Presence of Children in Private Households, 2011 Counts, Children (All Ages), for Canada, Provinces and Territories." Retrieved January 21, 2013, from http://www12.statcan.gc.ca/census -recensement/2011/dp-pd/hlt-fst/fam/Pages/highlight .cfm?TabID=1&Lang=E&Asc=1&PRCode=01&OrderBy =999&View=1&tableID=301&queryID=1&Children=1

———. 2012c. "SME Research and Statistics. "Key Small Business Statistics." July. Retrieved February 14, 2013, from http://www.ic.gc.ca/eic/site/061.nsf/eng/02724.html

Steinhauer, P. 1998. "How a Child's Early Experiences Affect Development." Paper presented at Linking Research to Practice: A Canadian Forum, Banff, Alberta. 25–27 October.

Swerdlow, A., R. Bridenthal, J. Kelly, and P. Vine. 1989. *Families in Flux.* New York: Feminist Press.

SWR International. 2012. "Canada: A Welcoming Model of Immigration?" Retrieved from http://www .swr.de/international/en/-/id=233338/nid=233338/did=10518238/5pwv2/index.html

Tremblay, C. 2012. "Canada's A Grade Teachers." Canadian Teachers Federation. Retrieved February 8, 2013, from http://www.ctf-fce.ca/Priorities/default.aspx? ArtID=1942 &year=2012&index_id=65551&lang=EN

Valpy, M. and Friesen, J. 2010. "A Twist of Faith." *The Globe and Mail.* December 11.

Vanier Institute of the Family. 2012a. Trying to Conceive: Infertility in Canada. Retrieved January 21, 2013, from http://www.vanierinstitute.ca/modules/news/newsitem .php?ItemId=425

———. 2012b. "The Current State of Canadian Family Finances." Abstract retrieved January 18, 2013, from http://www.vanierinstitute.ca/modules/news/newsitem .php?ItemId=421

———. 2012c. "Mothers in Canada." Retrieved January 21, 2013, from http://www.vanierinstitute .ca/modules/news/newsitem.php?ItemId=435

———. 2012d. "Fathers in Canada." Retrieved from http://www.vanierinstitute.ca/modules/news/newsitem .php?ItemId=441

———. 2012e. "Stress: A Family Matter," January 16, 2012 Issue #43.

———. 2012f. "Births and Babies in 2009." Retrieved January 21, 2013, from www.vanierinstitute .ca/modules/news/newsitem.php?ItemId=431

Ward, M. and M. Belanger. 2011. *The Family Dynamic: A Canadian Perspective,* 5th ed. Nelson.

Wilcox, W.B. 1999. "Emerging Attitudes About Gender Roles and Fatherhood." In D. Eberly, ed., *The Faith Factor in American Fatherhood: What America's Faith Communities Can Do to Restore Fatherhood.* Lanham, MD: Lexington Books.

Witt, J. and A. Hermiston. 2010. *SOC: A Matter of Perspective.* McGraw-Hill Ryerson.

Women and the Economy. 2011. "Women and Unpaid Work." Retrieved January 21, 2013, from http://www .unpac.ca/economy/unpaidwork.html

Chapter 2

SUPPORTS TO CHILDREN AND FAMILIES

"I implore you to see with a child's eyes, to hear with a child's ears, and to feel with a child's heart."

—*Antonio Novello*

LEARNING OUTCOMES

After studying this chapter, you will be able to

1. analyze the effects of the changing family on the early learning community

2. evaluate the benefits of universal quality early learning environments for children and their families

3. discuss ways in which employers and governments can support families

4. evaluate the range of services from which families can choose and the ways in which children, family members, and teachers can benefit from them

5. discuss the role of teachers in a wide range of services to families

It is not possible in the context of this book to capture all the inventive, responsive, and resourceful programs that communities have put in place to support children and their families. The following information provides an overview of early learning environments in Canada and highlights a variety of different programs and initiatives. In this text, early childhood education is defined as any program that cares for children from birth to age 8 in both formal and informal settings.

THE FIELD OF EARLY CHILDHOOD EDUCATION IN CANADA

Without a national child-care policy in place, services for families in Canada are a patchwork of programs that do little to respond to the ever-growing demand for care. "Fewer than 20 percent of Canadian children under age 6 have access to government-regulated care. Meanwhile, more than 70 percent of mothers of young children are in the paid labour force—one of the highest workforce participation rates for mothers in the developed world" (Monsebraaten, 2011a: A1).

Provincial and territorial governments have jurisdictional authority for child care; they are responsible for setting licensing standards and operational regulations for group-care facilities for children and for controlling the supply of and funding to these programs, but there is no central organization at any level of government. Most child-care centres in our country are nonprofit. Commercial centres or for-profit centres are privately owned businesses. About 25 percent of Canada's child-care centres operate as commercial businesses, ranging from small, owner-operated programs to large chains. In Newfoundland and Labrador, Alberta, Prince Edward Island, and New Brunswick, most child-care centres are commercial operations, whereas other provinces or territories, such as Manitoba, have no commercial child-care centres. Public child-care centres, which are directly operated by a government, are less common in Canada (Bertrand and Gestwicki, 2012: 11).

Throughout the country, child-care spaces have been provided by community organizations and many early childhood graduates have started their own small business to provide this much-needed care. Of growing concern is the advancement of commercial child-care chains that are more profit oriented and often less likely to provide quality, affordable

Inside LOOK

The NLSCY (*National Longitudinal Survey of Children and Youth*), a joint project of Human Resources Development Canada and Statistics Canada) data tells us most kids are doing okay. That's good news, but we could make it much easier for families. During the Early Years Study we were confronted by the array of services—child care, drop-in play groups, nursery schools, kindergarten, Head Start, family resource and parenting centres, among others. It may sound as if the field is covered but, in fact, we were witnessing the fallout of inadequate public policy—a scattering of disconnected, poorly resourced programs. Few parents know what services exist or what they do. The quality of parenting is paramount for children but parents are under a great deal of pressure. We add to their stress and guilt by loading them with information and then abandoning them to the hunt for quality child care. What parent of a young child doesn't need help? It is difficult for an individual parent to replicate the stimulation provided by a good-quality child-development program. For example, how many would consider that mucking around in goop is a great sensory experience for a toddler? Or who is prepared to cover their floor in paper every day so a child doesn't have to focus on "being careful" as she develops her fine motor skills with paint and markers? Mothers are in the work force—over 60 percent will return to work by the time their child is three—and there are plenty of economic, social, and political reasons to support their participation. There is also ample brain research indicating we should be very concerned about the non-parental care their children receive. Now we have to wait for governments to catch up.

Source: From BERTRAND. *Understanding, Managing, and Leading, 1E.* © 2008 Nelson Education Ltd. Reproduced by permission. www.cengage.com/permissions.

services. Unfortunately, most children in Canada are cared for in unregulated arrangements where there are no program standards or early childhood training required.

For some families, hiring a nanny is a better fit for their lifestyle. Many nannies come from developing countries where jobs are scarce, having left their own children behind—a painful and difficult life decision. Canada offers a *Live-in Caregiver Program* with permits that allow nannies to move from their sponsoring family without losing their ability to stay in Canada while they await their permanent resident permit. This program is a result of the serious concerns raised about the working conditions under which many nannies are employed.

IS CHILD CARE A GOOD CHOICE FOR CHILDREN, FAMILIES, AND CANADA?

After years of supportive research, there is no question that quality and accessible child care is good not only for families but also for Canada. It makes Canada more competitive as it allows women to receive further education and training, providing not only economic but also social returns. Women and men are better able to work while having a family. As more women are able to enter the workforce, families benefit financially—keeping many out of poverty—and women attain greater financial independence. With an aging society and diminishing labour force, we need to provide child care

to support a new generation of workers (Childcare Resource and Research Unit, 2008). While those of us in the field understand the need for quality early learning environments, our advocacy work is supported when others speak up on behalf of families.

The research evidence is clear: the foundations for good adult physical health, social competence, communication skills, adaptability, literacy, and numeracy are laid down before entry into kindergarten (Norrie McCain, Mustard, and Shanker, 2007). But we need a child-care system that is inclusive of all children.

High-quality early learning and care is particularly important for children living in poverty, children with special needs, new Canadians, and children in minority communities: it gives them opportunities to develop the foundational knowledge and skills, resilience, and emotional maturity they need to succeed in school and society. High-quality care is equally important for children from stable, advantaged families who experience negative effects if the programs do not provide responsive, stimulating environments. The quality of early learning and care services depends on four key factors:

- Effective policies, funding, and infrastructure;
- Knowledgeable, committed practitioners with post-secondary education in early childhood development who are appropriately compensated for their work;
- Well-designed programs with the capacity to meet the needs of all children; and
- Strong partnerships with parents. (Report of the Expert Panel on Quality and Human Resources, 2007)

Inside LOOK

In a 2008 comparison of child-care services in 25 developed countries, Canada met only one international benchmark—staff training—a measure most other countries also met. Canada's poor showing represents a lost opportunity for economic growth at a time of economic uncertainty, said the report by UNICEF's Innocenti Research Centre in Florence, Italy. UNICEF Canada's response to the report states that investing in early child care and education is a key strategy to respond to current economic challenges and to promote economic stimulus and recovery. Below is the criteria and the results of the report:

The 10 Criteria

1. Parental leave of 1 year at 50 percent of salary
2. A national plan with priority for the disadvantaged
3. Subsidized and regulated child-care services for 25 percent of children under 3
4. Subsidized and accredited early education services for 80 percent of 4-year-olds
5. 80 percent of all child-care staff trained

continued

6. 50 percent of staff with relevant postsecondary education (Canada)
7. Minimum staff to child ratio of 1:15 in preschool education
8. 1 percent of GDP spent on early childhood services
9. Child poverty rate less than 10 percent
10. Near universal outreach of essential child health services

The Country Results

1.	Sweden	10
2.	Iceland	9
3.	Denmark	8
4.	Finland	8
5.	France	8
6.	Norway	8
7.	Belgium	6
8.	Hungary	6
9.	New Zealand	6
10.	Slovenia	6
23.	Canada	1

Canada and Ireland were tied for last place in this list.

Source: UNICEF, 2008.

Inside LOOK

Prince Edward Island

Prince Edward Island demonstrates what is possible when government assumes responsibility for providing for all children. In 2008, PEI Premier Ghiz recognized the role of quality early childhood education as part of a strategic plan for PEI created to embrace new social and economic realities. Actions emanating from the strategic plan included publicly funded full-day kindergarten in elementary schools across the island, the movement of responsibility for early years programming to the newly formed Department of Education and Early Childhood, and the development of a network of publicly managed Early Years Centres (EYCs) providing quality early learning and care for children under 4 years.* This full-day kindergarten program is publicly managed but community delivered—a unique model that shares some similarities with Quebec's and Manitoba's. The initiative also includes new infant spaces to start to make up for the shortage of infant care in the province. All EYCs must have at least three infant spaces and will also create infant homes for parents who prefer a smaller setting. Upgrading of training is a major component of this plan, along with increases in wages.**

Sources: *University of New Brunswick, 2012; **Child Care Human Resources Sector Council, 2011.

Children benefit from a quality child-care setting with responsive and caring teachers.

THE EARLY YEARS STUDIES

In the first of three important documents, *The Early Years Study* (1999), conducted in Ontario by Fraser Mustard and Margaret Norrie McCain, the authors found that child care and other early child development opportunities are important in the development of a child's brain. They made two key recommendations: (1) that learning in the early years be based on high-quality and developmentally attuned interactions with primary caregivers, and (2) that children be given opportunities for play-based problem solving with other children. The authors also recommend that parents be a key part of early child development programs.

Norrie McCain, Mustard, and Shanker's *Early Years Study 2: Putting Science Into Action* (2007: 80–81), outlines the Early Development Instrument (EDI) developed by Magdalena Janus and Dan Offord, which was released in 2000. This tool assesses community outcomes in child development in respect to health, learning, and behaviour. It is completed by kindergarten teachers after several months of observations and provides a population-level measure. Results then can be interpreted for groups of children and used to identify the weak and the strong sectors of a community and, therefore, to mobilize for improved child outcomes. The EDI assesses five child development domains: physical health and well-being, social competence, emotional maturity, language and cognitive development, and communication skills and general knowledge. Since its inception, the EDI has been used in all Canadian provinces.

Mustard et al. proposed a

system of community hubs—ideally located in schools—that would offer play-based preschool activities, help for parents, social service referrals, and

child care. In Ontario alone, Mustard estimates the cost of behavioural and mental health problems triggered by problems in early childhood to be $30 billion. With the right programs in place that number could decrease to less than $15 billion a year, and probably even lower than that. If Ottawa spent at least one percent of its GDP, that would more than cover the cost of child/parenting centres. (cited in Rushowy, 2007)[*]

In *Early Years Study 3,* the authors state that by broadening education's mandate to include younger children, we can bridge the gap between parental leave and formal schooling. Promoting public investment similar to that made for children from 6 to 18, a system may emerge that will support families with young children.

By including the option of extended-day activities for families who request it, Canada can have its long-demanded early learning and care program. The fight for high-quality, universal early education is part of a larger battle to broaden the scope of government responsibility to ensure the success of young children and their families. The corollary of failing to act is deleterious for the individual and for society. The developmental gap that emerges so soon after birth for so many children not only robs individual potential, it also creates an unsustainable burden for our education, health and mental health systems. It deprives the economy of productive capacity and society of engaged, contributing participants. Reversing this trend requires smart decisions about program and system design. (Norrie McCain, Mustard, and McCuaig, 2012: 3)[†]

There is no question that much needs to be done to provide quality, universally accessible early learning environments for all families in Canada who need this care.

FINDING HIGH-QUALITY CHILD CARE

The challenge of locating high-quality care is an issue for families across the country, regardless of income level. Many families seek a community support system to strengthen their family unit. Child-care choices are made based on factors such as whether the family needs full-time or part-time care; even more problematic is care for families who work extended hours.

---

[*] Rushowy, K. 2007. "Canada 'Dead Last' In Spending," *The Toronto Star*, 26 March, A1. Reprinted by permission of Torstar Syndication Services.

[†] Norrie McCain, M., Mustard, F.J., McCuaig, K. 2012. *Early Years Study 3. Making Decisions, Taking Action*. Margaret & Wallace McCain Family Foundation. Reprinted by permission.

Other factors include the age of the child (it is especially difficult to find infant group care and school-age care), the distance from the child-care centre to home and work, the centre's hours of operation, the cost of the service compared to family income, and parental understanding of the available options. Most parents rely on an informal network of friends and relatives for information about child care—information that may or may not be comprehensive or accurate. The more knowledgeable the family is, the more likely it is that it will find the type of care that works for the family. Families are encouraged to become good consumers by accessing information within their community, visiting programs, and talking with the professionals in each location.

Child care is difficult to find but

> the search for child care is especially problematic for disadvantaged groups. Already burdened by subtle, overt biases against parents as a whole, subgroups of disadvantaged and minority parents may experience additional disenfranchisement and choice limitation. Victimized by stereotypes regarding both their effectiveness as parents and their abilities as citizens in comparison with mainstream groups, low-income parents are in double jeopardy; they lack real options and are often encumbered by the unfounded opinions and low expectations of others. (Kagan and Neville, 1994: 14)

Quality is key. The benefits from high-quality early education and care have been firmly established, but poor-quality programs can be worse than nothing, retarding children's development, wasting taxpayers' money, and inflicting long-term harm on efforts to expand preschool when they fail to deliver promised results (Norrie McCain, Mustard, and McCuaig, 2012: 3).

Each jurisdiction across the country has established health and safety regulations that operators must meet as a condition of licensing. However, like public health inspections of restaurants, child-care regulations are intended to protect children's safety but tell us little about the quality of the experience. Some jurisdictions apply additional criteria beyond basic licensing. The *Toronto Operating Criteria* is one example of an assessment tool that reflects the quality of the entire learning environment; Alberta has a voluntary accreditation system for child-care programs that ties the maintenance of quality benchmarks to funding. Several jurisdictions use the *Early Childhood Environment Rating Scale* to monitor quality. It looks at both the physical space children occupy and the quality of interactions between adults and children, allowing centres to be reflective about their practices. Parents seeking programs for their children can use quality ratings as information in making their program choices (Norrie McCain, Mustard, and McCuaig, 2012).

QUEBEC LEADS THE WAY

There is no question that Quebec is a classic example of what is possible!

> Child-care centres in Quebec are known as *Centres de la petite enfance*, or CPEs; there are 1,000 CPEs in the province. In 1997, after the Social and Economic Summit of 1996, the Quebec government announced a family policy to create a Quebec child-care system where parents could pay $5-a-day per child; this figure was raised to $7 in 2004. Children of parents on social assistance are entitled to free enrolment for 22.5 hours a week (Bertrand, 2008: 49).*
>
> After 12 years, the Quebec scheme more than pays for itself through mothers' annual income and consumption taxes, says Pierre Fortin, an economics professor at the University of Quebec at Montreal. For every dollar Quebec invests, it recoups $1.05 while Ottawa receives a 44 percent windfall. By 2008, about 70,000 more women with young children had entered the workforce who would not otherwise have been working, a 3.8 percent increase. The ripple effect of their employment pumped an additional $5.2 billion into the Quebec economy. The increased economic activity, which includes mothers' income and consumption taxes, more than covered the province's $1.6 billion annual child-care costs that year. The province subsidizes each spot by about $10,000 annually. And it poured more than $700 million in additional revenue into federal coffers. This is why the federal government should make a contribution to Ontario and other provinces. (Monsebraaten, 2011b)†

In recognition of the direct link between specialized training and quality child care, the Quebec government has imposed stricter regulations regarding training in early childhood care and education. The government provides financial support to child-care providers who are already actively working in the sector and enrol in college-level courses, making it easier for them to access professional development. This may be a response to a study done in Quebec in 2003 that looked at home-based and centre-based

---

* From BERTRAND. *Understanding, Managing, and Leading, 1E.* © 2008 Nelson Education Ltd. Reproduced by permission. www.cengage.com/permissions.

†Monsebraaten, L. 2011. "Quebec's Child Care Scheme Pays For Itself, Economist," *The Toronto Star*, June 27. Reprinted by permission of Torstar Syndication Services.

FIGURE 2.1 ECEC Programs and Private Nonparental Care Arrangements for Newborns to 12-Year-Olds in Canada

ECEC PROGRAM	CHILDREN 0–12 ATTENDING
Centre-based program*	750,000
Kindergarten/prekindergarten	500,000
Regulated family child care	150,000
Aboriginal Head Start	12,000
Early intervention programs	50,000
Private Nonparental Care Arrangements	
Unregulated family child care**	750,000
In-home care	400,000
Self/sibling care	345,000

* Includes regular full-time or part-time participation in nursery schools, child care centres, preschool centres, and after-school programs.
** Includes both relative and nonrelative home-based nonparental care arrangements.
Sources: From BERTRAND/GESTWICKI. *Essentials of Early Childhood Education*, 4E. © 2012 Nelson Education Ltd. Reproduced by permission. www.cengage.com/permissions

care and reported that, overall, 26 percent were good quality, 61 percent were mediocre, and 13 percent were poor quality (Japel et al., 2005).

WHERE ARE THE CHILDREN?

Because there are so many different types of early learning programs and no organized system for early childhood, it is difficult to determine exactly how many children and families are participating in specific programs. The following programs are examples of only a few of the many early learning and care environments offered throughout the country for children and their families.

REGULATED FAMILY CHILD CARE

Family child care is a term used to describe the care of young children in the home of a caregiver. Unlike informal, unlicensed home care, under regulated family child care, an agency is licensed to contract with own-home caregivers and operates according to existing regulations, which vary from province to province and address issues such as the number of children who may be in care, qualifications of the caregivers, registration, and so on. Caregivers who work for a licensed agency work with a team of professionals to ensure the best possible care for the children and families they serve. Although agencies across the country differ from one another, many consider it their mandate to provide trained staff to

- support the caregiver and the family of the children in care

- train caregivers in child development and appropriate programming, nutrition, and first aid

- monitor the child-care home for safety, cleanliness, and the number and ages of children in care in each home

- ensure that prospective caregivers and their families are in good health and have completed a criminal reference check

For some families, regulated family care is the best possible fit. Some children may be more comfortable in a smaller, more intimate group of children in a home setting. With a smaller group, the caregiver is able to get to know the child intimately and has more flexibility throughout the day than he or she would in many child-care centres. Families who find licensed care near their home may significantly reduce travel time. The caregiver may also be able to support the family's varying work schedule. Other families may like the idea of their child being cared for in a multi-age setting. Through the agency, families will be able to visit a number of homes that may be available to them.

NANNIES AND OTHER IN-HOME CARE ARRANGEMENTS

Many families prefer the flexibility of having their children cared for in their own home, where the child will be secure in his or her own environment

Razzle Dazzle Kids Konnection Family Day Home Agencies operates in central Alberta in both urban and rural settings. Services offered to day homes and providers registered with the agencies include

- screening of all providers in accordance with Alberta government standards
- monthly/bimonthly monitoring of all day homes to ensure compliance with standards, agency requirements, policies and procedures
- referral of families to potential family day homes for child-care

Central to all services to the child-care operation is a strong mandate to enrich the lives of children through quality and developmentally appropriate practices. In order to facilitate understanding and implementation of this mandate a variety of unique practices are employed. These may include

- workshops on specific topics identified
- yearly retreat to demonstrate appreciation and to foster partnerships
- yearly thank-you banquet
- resource room with up-to-date resources
- purchase of innovative child resources to present to family day home providers
- financial support to family day home providers to attend a yearly conference
- use of consultants and experts to provide training on site or during workshops
- timely provision of resources to aid daily operations within day homes
- open-door policy to assist day home providers and families
- development of provincial and local resources
- partnerships with community organizations and agencies to build strong childhood programs

Source: Reprinted by permission of Dr. Ingrid Crowther, Executive Director, ICC Lifelong Learn Inc.

with a consistent caregiver. This arrangement may also provide parents with more flexibility with regard to their work and travel schedules and may meet their need for evening, weekend, or extended-hour care. These caregivers—often referred to as nannies—may live in the home with the family or live elsewhere. Many families may specifically seek out early childhood educators to provide this in-home care. Other nannies immigrate to Canada through the Live-in Caregiver Program (LCP), as noted earlier. This federal immigration program allows future employers to sponsor immigrants who wish to enter Canada to provide in-home child care.

The LCP helps to protect people who come to Canada as nannies by allowing them to leave their sponsoring family, if necessary, but stay in the country until they are granted a permanent resident permit. The program took this step because, in some cases, employers took advantage of their

Nannies may allow parents greater flexibility in their child-care arrangements.

Healthy Images/Public Health Agency of Canada

EXHIBIT 2.1   How Do I Find a Good Home Child-Care Arrangement?

Start by making some lists:

- A list of your child-care requirements including hours of care, days of care, ideal locations (e.g., near home, school, or work), and special needs of your children (e.g., food requirements, allergies)
- A list of the child-care arrangements your friends, neighbours, or co-workers have made or researched
- A list of the child-care agencies working in your neighbourhood
- A list of the phone numbers of the agencies you want to call
- A list of the questions you want to ask about the offered child care, including questions about
  - the length of time in operation
  - experience of caregivers
  - training and support offered to caregivers
  - insurance coverage
  - vacation and sick policies
  - fee schedule and availability of fee assistance
  - average length of stay of children in homes
  - availability of care that meets your particular needs
  - support given to the family by the agency
- Learn about the caregiver by asking:
  - What formal or informal training and education has she completed?
  - What other jobs has she done?
  - Why has she chosen home child care as her work?
  - How many children are in the home? Are her own children in care?
  - What are her thoughts on child development and parenting?
  - How does she handle discipline when it is required?
  - What is her policy on television and videos? Is it similar to your own?
  - Will the caregiver be driving the children? Is the car safe and equipped with seatbelts and car seats?
  - What equipment will you need to supply to the caregiver?
  - What meals and snacks are available to your child? Will a variety of foods be available?
  - What are the daily routines for activities and outdoor play?
  - What are the learning and reading opportunities?
  - Are there quiet-time activities?
  - What about sleep schedules and meal times?

Source: Reprinted by permission of Family Day Care Services.

---

employees. The nannies endured unfair employment conditions, with no option but to stay until the permit was issued. Their long work hours and low wages were at odds with their dream of moving to Canada and providing a better life for the family they left behind.

WORKPLACE CHILD CARE

Although they still account for a minority of centre-based spaces, the number of child-care facilities sponsored by an employer, union, or employee group has grown. Workplace child care may take many forms. It may be an on-site centre run by an independent operator, or it may be managed by the employer. It may be a centre organized off-site, perhaps for reasons of safety or lack of space. A consortium may be an option for some employers, joining with other companies to provide child care for all employees and to share the cost of operation. Employers may offer other options such as a subsidy to a worker who has found a child-care space in the community. Referral services offered by the employer might provide information and guidance for employees searching for child care, or they may connect employees with family child care providers or private-home child-care agencies.

Many benefits accrue to companies that offer child care. They may be better able to market their company, thus attracting more suitable candidates and raising their employee-retention rate; they may reduce absenteeism and tardiness; and they are more likely to benefit from increased morale and productivity. The employer is also seen in a more positive light in the community. Employees are less stressed and conflict is reduced when they're able to stay close to their children. This is especially apparent when children become ill while in the child-care centre. The family enjoys cost savings, and the child-care centre may provide flexible hours to accommodate the parents' work schedules.

Inside LOOK

The Copper House, a workplace child-care centre at Husky Injection Moulding Systems Ltd., in Bolton, Ontario, serves 98 children with a staff of 15 and reflects an outstanding commitment to the families. The centre's approach is rooted firmly in the commitment to continually ask if the expectations for a child's well-being and development are ever high enough. The magic of the Copper House does not lie in the aesthetics of the building but rather in the sustained commitment of its team. At the root of our approach lies a passion for nurturing the child and family. If we can provide the opportunity for child and family to spend quality time together with minimal outside interference, then we are meeting our primary objective. Ours is a passionate vision, and we strive to do what has not been done before. By sharing the following we will perhaps motivate others to meet child and family needs beyond the too-established and structured manner of child care today. A more effective partnership between families and community must be encouraged. We need to support our working parents more effectively, by taking an active role in decreasing the stress that they and their children experience daily. If we achieve this, we give the parent and child a gift that lasts a lifetime—saved time and energy to nurture one another. What an excellent contribution to give to young children.

The Copper House's initiatives are many. The following are done with minimal cost, if any, to the parent, team, or centre:

- Team members attend school activities—parent–teacher interviews; classroom visits; holiday concerts; field trips; communions, and so on—in an effort to unite child, school, home, and child care and provide opportunity for parental support.
- Team members may work privately for parents on evenings or weekends in another effort to encourage parents to plan for quality time together.
- We pick up or drop off a child to help out when the parent is away on business.
- Light suppers are served to children who are busy with extracurricular activities so that parents won't have to scramble to fit this in before the lesson.
- Child-care pyjama parties are provided for the children to encourage parents to have quality time together—uninterrupted time together that allows them to nurture their own relationship.
- Piano or music lessons are provided at the Copper House, and practice time is supported at any time during the child's day.
- Team members will drive a child to hockey, swimming, or gymnastic lessons when possible to help decrease parent stress.
- Haircuts are given during Copper House time to remove one item from the parents' weekend errands list.
- The centre provides the opportunity for parents to purchase supplies, equipment, and food items through the centre itself.

Source: Reprinted by permission of Valerie Nease, former Director, The Copper House.

Courtesy of Scotia Plaza Child Care Centre

In this workplace early learning environment, this father is able to visit his child during his breaks and on his lunch hour.

CHILD-CARE CO-OPERATIVES

> "As parent co-operatives spread, develop, and extend their influences further, they will develop world kinship at the very roots of being in the growth of children, their families and their teachers."
>
> —K. Whiteside Taylor

Community members, including parents, have been operating co-operative child-care services in Canada for over 65 years. The country's oldest co-op nursery, Manor Road Co-operative, celebrated its 70th anniversary in Toronto in 2007. There are over 400 child care co-operatives (over 500 if we include parent-run child-care centres, which are not legally co-operatives but operate like them in BC, Alberta, and Ontario). Ontario, Saskatchewan, and Manitoba have the largest concentration of formal child-care co-operatives, with British Columbia having a considerable number of co-op-like organizations. An estimated 9 percent of Canadian child care spaces are in centres operated by co-operatives (Anderson et al., 2007). Many of these co-operatives arose through a period of rapid development in the 1970s and 1980s.

Co-ops are democratic organizations owned and controlled by their members. All child-care co-ops are nonprofit and use any surplus funds to increase or improve their services. Most co-ops are incorporated provincially under a provincial co-operative statute. Child-care co-ops are developed by parents, early childhood educators, and community members. Parents are active on the board of directors, work on committees, and assist with various other tasks.

Inside LOOK

Co-operative child care has a long and successful record in Canada and is often described as the nation's best-kept secret. Community members, including parents, have been operating co-operative child care services in Canada for over 75 years. It is where parents, teachers, and children learn together. Across the co-op child-care sector, many options are available, including playschools, nursery schools, kindergarten enrichment, full-time day care, part-day programs, before- and after-school activities for school-age children, and flexible hours and after-hours care. The trend for a majority of nonprofit centres, whether they are preschools or child care, is building on parent partnerships, which is one of the cornerstones of the PCPC [Parent Co-operative Preschool Council] philosophy. The Early Years Study reiterated what all educators know; that the earlier a parent is involved in his or her child's education and social well-being and the continuation thereof, the better the child will do in the public school system. With a limited number of spaces in traditional daycares and a growing group of parents determined to be actively involved in raising and educating their children, the co-operative approach is an effective model for many families. They are a powerful and democratic way to put decision making into the hands of those who need and use the services.

When families with diverse backgrounds share their expertise and talents with teachers, other families, and the children, a rich and stimulating environment for learning is created. Family involvement has a direct impact on the quality of care the child receives and allows the parent to ensure continuity of care. Because of family involvement, staff costs and overhead are reduced through the provision of services on a voluntary basis. Since these costs amount to 80 percent of operational expenditures, budgets are smaller than in non-co-operative centres.

continued

Co-operatives are run by a board of directors and provide a wonderful opportunity for parents to gain administrative skills as well as political savvy. Staff do not sit on the board but they are invited to be part of the organizational structure that works together to run the centre. Boards have insurance that protects them while they are making decisions as volunteers at the centre. In general, parents who belong to a co-op are expected to work on scheduled duty days, attend or organize parent meetings that deal with school administration or family life education, serve on parent committees, and assist with fundraising projects. Working parents who are unable to commit to regular participation during the day may contribute by serving on committees, on the board of directors, or in other tasks outlined by the co-op. In some instances, additional monetary payments are required. In some co-operatives, other family members or nannies may fill in for parents on their duty days—that is, days on which they serve as members of the playschool teaching team. With growing demands on families, co-operatives have adapted and changed based on the needs of the community they serve. In some centres, more staff have been hired in place of family volunteers; in others, hours have been extended to include after-school programs.

Source: Reprinted by permission of Nancy Bradley, Executive Director, PCPC.

Inside LOOK

The playschool was my first opportunity to see a large number of children the same age as my son Ryan. I had always felt that Ryan was a very demanding and challenging child, and when I saw other children interacting in such a positive way with their parents, I realized that something was not working in our relationship. Over the two years that we were in the playschool, the teacher worked closely with us to help us set reasonable limits for Ryan and then, most importantly, to follow through with them. I realized that Ryan was desperate for us to put some boundaries on his behaviour. I'll be forever grateful to that teacher and to the families who supported us.

Inside LOOK

When I first heard about the co-op, I was very excited about the prospect of having a group experience for my daughter Susan. But I was also terrified. I'm a very shy person and the prospect of having to deal with so many children and their families seemed overwhelming. Two years later, I can honestly say that the playschool has changed my life. With the support of a terrific teacher and a wonderful group of families, I have become a more confident and capable person. I look forward to my days at playschool with enthusiasm and energy. I have discovered talents I never knew I had, and I am now attending night classes at a local community college where I hope to obtain a diploma in Early Childhood Education. My goal is to continue working with the playschool when my daughter goes into the public school system.

Co-ops get their revenues from fees charged to parents, minimal direct operating grants from municipal or provincial governments, and fundraising. Co-operatives recognize the importance of people and communities defining their own needs and working together to meet those needs. They are a powerful and democratic way to put decision making into the hands of those who need and use the services.

Co-ops provide a friendly, natural source of support and advice to parents. Included in the mandate of most co-ops is a commitment to parent education, which may come in the form of workshops, meetings, and the active support of the playroom teacher. Families are encouraged to share their knowledge, expertise, and ideas with others. Through direct involvement with the program, parents can have their concerns answered and feel more confident in their child-raising ability. The centre provides an opportunity for children and adults to learn together and is active in the inclusion of children with special needs.

Relationships developed in a co-op may become a springboard for lifelong friendships. Some parents are so inspired by their experiences in the playschool that they go on to train for employment in co-operative and teaching environments. For those teaching in a co-operative setting, it is both a rewarding and challenging experience—one that requires excellent communication and interpersonal skills, confidence in one's teaching abilities, the flexibility to support and encourage families from a wide range of backgrounds, and unfailing enthusiasm.

PARENT CO-OPERATIVE PRESCHOOLS INTERNATIONAL (PCPI)

PCPI is a non-profit international council dedicated to the family and the community. PCPI represents more than 50,000 families and teachers, providing ongoing support to families, educators, and social agencies who recognize the value of parents as teachers of their children and the necessity of educating parents to meet the developmental needs of their children. Membership is open to schools, councils, libraries, and individuals who uphold its purposes. The organization was founded in 1960 on the initiative of Katharine Whiteside Taylor who was inducted into the Co-operative Hall of Fame in 1996 in recognition of her work on behalf of co-operative child care. (Parent Co-operative Preschool International, 2010)*

---

*Reprinted by permission of Parent Co-operative Preschools International.

THE COMMUNITY ACTION PROGRAM FOR CHILDREN (CAPC)

At the 1990 United Nations World Summit for Children, the leaders of 71 countries made a commitment to invest in the well-being of vulnerable children. The Government of Canada responded with the Child Development Initiative (CDI). The Community Action Program for Children (CAPC) is the largest program of this initiative under the auspices of the Public Health Agency of Canada (2010a).

CAPC provides long-term funding to community coalitions to deliver programs that address the health and development of children (0–6 years) who are living in conditions of risk, recognizing that communities have the ability to identify and respond to the needs of children. CAPC places a strong emphasis on partnerships and community capacity building.

CAPC targets children living in low-income families; children living in teenage-parent families; children experiencing developmental delays or social, emotional, or behavioural problems; and abused and neglected children. Special consideration is given to Métis, Inuit, and off-reserve First Nations children, and to the children of recent immigrants and refugees, children in lone-parent families, and children who live in remote and isolated communities.

There are 441 CAPC projects in 3,000 communities across Canada, serving 65,000 children, parents, and caregivers in a typical month. The federal government provides $52.4 million directly to CAPC communities to fund their projects. Guiding principles for all CAPC projects are

- children first
- equity and accessibility
- a community base
- strengthening and support for families
- flexibility
- partnerships

KIDS R FIRST, SUMMERSIDE, PEI

Kids R First, which operates in Summerside, PEI, offers a wide range of family and child-oriented programs and supports for parents and children. The CAPC in Prince Edward Island was formed to work collaboratively to develop projects that could serve a diverse range of needs and populations and address the seven provincial priority areas for CAPC:

- child abuse and neglect

- lack of economic resources

- mental and physical disabilities

- poor health and nutrition

- substance abuse and its negative impact on the child

- unplanned pregnancies

- youth and inexperienced parents

All members of the coalition agreed that a Family Resource Centre model was the solution. This is a unique model on the island and capable of providing a wide range of services and activities to people around Summerside. Activities such as play groups, clothing exchanges, community kitchens, and toy-lending libraries are available at the main Kids R First location and at its three outreach sites in Kensington, Borden, and Wellington (a francophone site). All services at Kids R First are free in order to make them accessible to low-income families. Transportation to and from the centre is also included. The sites also offer prenatal support and emergency respite for postnatal mothers whose babies are over six months old but who still need help (Parents' Time Out); breastfeeding moms groups; home visiting; and a very popular cooking program, Maggie's Kitchen. Various parenting programs such as Nobody's Perfect and Magic 1-2-3 (an effective discipline for children 2 to 12 years old developed by Thomas W. Phelan) are run by the centre to support young or inexperienced parents. Cyber Camp and Adult Computer Training are also available.

THE CANADIAN PRENATAL NUTRITION PROGRAM (CPNP)

Similar to CAPC, the Canadian Prenatal Nutrition Program (CPNP) provides funding to community groups that aid vulnerable pregnant women. There are currently 325 CPNP sites serving close to 50,000 women in over 2,000 communities across Canada each year. In addition, a separate stream of the program administered through Health Canada serves Inuit and First Nation women living on-reserve. This exceptional program targets women in need.

> CPNP is not a universal program; instead it is targeted specifically at women facing challenging life circumstances such as poverty, teenage pregnancy, alcohol or substance use, family violence, social and geographical isolation, and recent arrival in Canada. CPNP projects also increase the availability of culturally sensitive prenatal support for Aboriginal women living off-reserve. (Public Health Agency of Canada, 2010b)

These projects reach pregnant adolescents; youth at risk of becoming pregnant; pregnant women who abuse alcohol or other substances; pregnant women living in violent situations; pregnant women living in isolation or without access to services; refugee and immigrant women; and Métis, Inuit, and First Nations women. CPNP provides support to services that offer nutrition, health, and lifestyle education and counselling with the goal of improving the health of mothers and babies. Additional services include one-on-one and group prenatal nutrition counselling; food supplements; collective kitchens; peer counselling; access to mothers who are mentors; breastfeeding education and support, and postpartum support; and information about infant attachment and child development. Projects are delivered in partnership with community organizations such as Rotary clubs, food banks, high schools, school boards, liquor control boards, physicians, public health units, religious groups, and professional organizations such as the Canadian Dietetic Association (Public Health Agency of Canada, 2010b).

FAMILY RESOURCE PROGRAMS

The Canadian Association of Toy Libraries (CATL) was established in 1975. Thirteen years later, CATL merged with a network of parent–child resource centres to form the Canadian Association of Toy Libraries and Parent Resource Centres (TLRC Canada). In 1994 the name of this organization was changed to the Canadian Association of Family Resource Programs. The association is also known as FRP Canada. Its mission is to promote the well-being of families by providing national leadership, consultation, and resources to those who care for children and support families. Parent or caregiver education and support stand out as one of the most important and common types of services offered by family resource programs (FRPs). The association is dedicated to strengthening families through community-based prevention-oriented programs and services. The association also has links with other national and international groups that support families and children. In 2012, FRP Canada had over 500 member organizations: family resource programs providing services to 2000 communities and reaching over 500,000 families across Canada. FRP Canada holds a biennial national conference

The diversity in programs reflects the needs of individual communities. Some programs are mobile services; others have their own facilities. Still others share facilities with community centres, churches, schools, libraries, hospitals, or military bases.

Resources available through FRPs may include

- parent–child drop-in centres

- play groups or nursery schools

- toy-lending libraries

- child-care registries

- mobile resource units for parents and caregivers

- parent discussion groups or support groups

- warm line (telephone service offering noncrisis support and information for parents)

- food banks or community kitchens

- breakfast clubs or nutrition programs

- programs for teen mothers

- counselling (peer, professional, etc.)

- programs for families with children who have special needs (crisis intervention, infant stimulation programs, toy libraries with adapted toys, etc.)

- respite care

- emergency care for sick children

- summer camps

- training courses or workshops (e.g., volunteer and board training)

- conferences or symposiums

- information services (prenatal or childbirth education)

- referral services

- consultation with child-care and other community groups

- student placements

- hub model

- outreach (home visits, play groups in parents' or caregivers' homes)

- literacy, ESL, and life-skills programs

- health care and information

- participation in or sponsorship of community planning

- advocacy on behalf of resource programs, parents, and children

No individual program offers all of the above services; each community attempts to target the resources that are most relevant and meaningful to the families it serves.

The following statistics illustrate the wide reach of these programs:

- 40 percent of FRPs serve children with special needs, the majority integrate these children into existing programs.

- 65 percent serve single parents.

- 64 percent serve fathers as well as mothers.

- 35 percent serve teenage mothers.

- 18 percent serve teenage fathers.

- 29 percent serve the unemployed and students.

- 27 percent of FRPs in large urban areas have ethno-cultural minorities as a major user group.

- 21 percent of Aboriginal peoples located off-reserve are major users of FRPs.

To encourage working parents to participate, many FRPs extend their hours of operation by scheduling events on weekends or on Friday evenings from 6 p.m. to 8 p.m. and by offering parent–child programs from 4:30 p.m. to 7 p.m., with supper served. These programs connect with the workplace too, by holding brown-bag lunch sessions and workshops (Canadian Association of Family Resource Programs, 2012).

FRPs are a great support to military families. According to Norrie McCain, Mustard, and McCuaig (2012), the Department of National Defence/Canadian Forces supports 43 Military Family Resource Centres in Canada and abroad, one of which is found on each major military base.

They are part of a network of centres sponsored and managed by the Canadian Forces Personnel Support Agency and each one is independent of, but enjoys the support of, the military chain of command. The MFRC provides a range of programmes and support for families from arranging for babysitters, to daycare, to counselling sessions. The MFRC acts as a drop-in centre or it can be a refuge in times of stress. They run Reunification Workshops to help families adjust to the return of a parent from overseas. Deployment workshops are conducted for the children of service personnel, to help them understand and cope with the departure, or return, of a parent. The average MFRC agenda is a model of service. MFRCs are guided by a Board of Directors, usually composed of wives or husbands of military members and representatives of the military chain of command. The MFRC functions under the day-to-day management of an Executive Director and a small staff. The majority of the work is done by a corps of volunteers from the military community. (Casson, 2007)*

Though evidence shows that these preventive, less costly services are critically important, their real and potential contributions are often ignored. For the most part, FRPs in Canada have developed in the absence of a clear legislative and funding framework. Because many of them cut across categorical approaches to service delivery by combining health, recreation, educational, and social services (including social support, child welfare, and child care), they do not easily fit into traditionally structured government departments and funding categories and thus often fail to obtain recognition and funding. Visit **http://www.frp.ca**.

KINDERGARTENS

According to Norrie McCain, Mustard, and McCuaig (2012), approximately 350,000 children attend public education kindergarten or senior kindergarten programs and 150,000 children attend junior kindergarten or pre-kindergarten programs in Canada. Provincial ministries of education have responsibility for kindergarten.

> Full-day kindergarten has become the norm for five-year-old Canadian children. In September 2010, British Columbia, Prince Edward Island and Ontario joined New Brunswick, Quebec, and Nova Scotia in offering full-day kindergarten. In other jurisdictions most kindergarten is offered on a part-time basis, either half-days (morning or afternoon) or two to three full days per week. (Bertrand and Gestwicki, 2012: 18)†

SCHOOLS WITH SPECIAL PROGRAMS

Private schools may offer care for children of all ages and may offer special training in music, computers,

---

*Casson, R. 2007. *Canadian Forces In Afghanistan. Report of the Standing Committee on National Defence.* 39th Parliament, 1st Session. Reprinted by permission of the House of Commons.

†From BERTRAND/GESTWICKI. *Essentials of Early Childhood Education, 4E.* © 2012 Nelson Education Ltd. Reproduced by permission. www.cengage.com/permissions.

religion, art, and so on; the costs for these programs vary from community to community. Each setting will have its own specific philosophy, reflecting a unique program. Three examples of these philosophies and programs are introduced below.

MONTESSORI SCHOOLS

Dr. Maria Montessori (1870–1952) trained in engineering and medicine, and was the first Italian woman to earn a medical degree. During her medical training she worked with children who were at the time classified as mentally retarded; as a result, she went on to further her studies in education. She began her work in a housing project in Rome and developed a radically different approach to education that became the *Montessori Method*. Dr. Montessori designed equipment specifically for young children and developed materials to teach specific concepts. Her system of teaching was developed over her lifetime, and her goal to find a better way to educate children became grander with each passing year. She said her ultimate aim was to help humanity be its best self: "Our principal concern must be to educate humanity—the human beings of all nations—in order to guide it toward seeking common goals. We must turn back and make the child our principal concern. The efforts of science must be concentrated on the child, because he is the source of and the key to the riddles of humanity.... He needs much broader opportunities than he has been offered thus far. Might not this goal be reached by changing the entire structure of education?" (in Lillard, 2007: 31).

Specifically,

> [t]he Montessori philosophy includes introducing children to varieties of practical life skills, such as washing dishes, sweeping floors, and watering plants. The curriculum also includes sensorial components, which involve providing materials to help children broaden and refine their sensory perceptions, and conceptual components, which means using concrete academic materials to introduce children to reading, writing, mathematics, and social studies.... One abiding distinction of the Montessori philosophy is the respect for children and their abilities and accomplishments. (Gestwicki and Bertrand, 1999: 44–45)

During the later years of her life, Montessori devoted her time and energy to developing schools throughout Europe and North America, and she trained thousands of teachers in the Montessori

Method. Note that the name Montessori is in the public domain, so anyone can use it. The Canadian Council of Montessori Administrators (CCMA) urges parents to learn what constitutes a legitimate Montessori education and which Montessori schools are accredited.

WALDORF EDUCATION

First developed by Rudolf Steiner in 1919 in Germany, the Waldorf philosophy emphasizes a child's learning experiences and the development of the whole child. There are over 900 Waldorf schools worldwide, and many mainstream schools now use Waldorf techniques (Boyd, 2012). The Waldorf philosophy is an international movement that develops a long-term relationship between teacher and child. The teacher moves with the class from Grades One to Eight and his or her role is that of a mentor. The children are coached, rather than instructed, on understanding the how and why of learning—inquiry and emergent curriculum through experimentation and action. Waldorf classrooms use natural fabrics and natural lighting to instill a sense of tranquillity and peace. Children are given materials that allow them to engage in practical tasks such as bread making, table setting, dish washing, knitting, sewing, and cleaning up at the end of the day. The children are fully involved in the planning and organization of their play environment. Involving families is integral to the Waldorf philosophy, and families are encouraged to participate in celebrations at Waldorf schools.

> "Central to Waldorf education is the belief that the deepest and most universal human values can only arise when education brings into healthy balance the faculties of thinking, feeling and willing that live in each child. Learning at the Waldorf School is a vital and dynamic process, permeated with the power of imagination and working with the spiritual, emotional, and physical development of the individual within the social context. Reverence and awe for the wonders of nature, gratitude and respect for the efforts and accomplishments of others, and the responsibilities of dutiful self-discipline are guiding principles of Waldorf Education."
>
> —**Andre and Neave, 1992: 148**

HIGHSCOPE

This section was contributed by Moya Fewson, senior trainer, retired, Sheridan HighScope Teacher Education Centre, 2012.

HighScope is based on longitudinal research and is not only research based but also research validated. HighScope uses key developmental indicators as the basis of its curriculum. Key developmental indicators (KDIs) are learning objectives that cover all domains of child development. KDIs include objectives under Approaches to Learning, Social and Emotional Development, Physical Development, Language, Literacy and Communication, Creative Arts, Mathematics, Science and Technology, and Social Studies. The cornerstone of the HighScope curriculum is *active learning*. Research has shown that children learn best when they are actively involved with people and things. By providing materials that children can manipulate, by embedding choice in what children do, by promoting language, and by giving ongoing adult support and scaffolding, teachers help children develop initiative, autonomy, and self-confidence. Children learn to manage their day through the *plan–do–review process:* they make plans, carry them out, and reflect on their actions. Plan–do–review increases cognitive ability and allows children to feel in control of their actions. The daily routine in a HighScope classroom includes child-initiated times such as work time and adult-initiated times such as group time. The routine is consistent so that children can feel secure. The learning environment in a HighScope program is carefully planned to allow children to make choices and to use interesting and stimulating materials.[*]

Adult–child interactions are very important in a HighScope program. Adults and children share control: children are in control of "child-sized" decisions while adults take care of adult responsibilities. Adults develop genuine, respectful relationships with children. Furthermore, HighScope programs use a problem-solving approach to social conflict. Children are taught how to negotiate, communicate, and compromise. Adults use encouragement techniques with children, including making specific comments about the children's efforts, and putting children in control of judging their own work.

HighScope has a strong focus on developing and supporting early literacy. Adult-initiated times are

---

[*]Reprinted by permission of The HighScope Foundation and Moya Fewson.

SUPPORTS TO CHILDREN AND FAMILIES

based on early speaking, listening, reading, and writing experiences. Math and science are also a focus of adult-initiated times. Parents are an important part of HighScope and their input is highly valued. Classrooms reflect the positive aspects of children's families and communities. Parents and educators see themselves as partners in learning. Parents are given feedback on their child's interests and progress on a regular basis both through the sharing of anecdotal notes taken on an ongoing basis by teachers and through parent/teacher interviews held to discuss findings on the Child Observation Record (COR). HighScope teachers and programs are accredited using the Program Quality Assessment tool. This validated instrument assesses the learning environment, the daily schedule, how adults interact with children, and curriculum and assessment. It is used by both HighScope programs and non-HighScope programs as a self-assessment and training tool. HighScope is widely used in infant, toddler, preschool and school aged programs throughout the world.

Other programs have been developed, too, such as the Froebel Schools, which are based on the philosophy of Freidrich Froebel, the German educator who coined the term *kindergarten*, or *garden of children*. Throughout the country many communities have organized programs and initiatives that support families. They are as varied as the communities that they serve.

HOME INSTRUCTION PROGRAM FOR PRESCHOOL YOUNGSTERS (HIPPY)

This section was contributed by Susanne Nahm from HIPPY Canada.

Developed in 1969 at the Hebrew University of Jerusalem in Israel, the HA'ETGAR (HIPPY in English) Program is now used in 13 countries and serves over 22,000 families who want to provide stimulating experiences for their children in their home. HIPPY programs currently operate in Australia, Canada, El Salvador, Germany, New Zealand, South Africa, and the United States, to name a few. Discussions are underway regarding new programs in China, Portugal, Singapore, and Zimbabwe (Hepworth Berger, 2004: 332).

HIPPY Canada is a nonprofit organization that receives its revenue from the federal government, donations, and fundraising. In 2010–2011, 673 low-income families were served for an expenditure of $1,318,443 through six sites in British Columbia, one in Calgary, one in Red Deer, one in Montreal, four in Toronto, one in Oakville, one in Ottawa, and one in Halifax. Five of the HIPPY sites in British Columbia serve Aboriginal families. The skill areas included are tactile, visual, auditory, and conceptual discrimination, in addition to language development, verbal expression, eye–hand coordination, pre-math concepts, logical thinking, self-concept, and creativity.

A professional coordinates the program, but paraprofessionals are selected from parents whose children have already been in the program. The HIPPY program builds on the basic bond between parents and children. Supported by easy-to-use activity packets, home visits, and group meetings, HIPPY parents learn how to prepare their children for success in school and beyond. Children enter the program at the age of 3; families are required to commit to two years participation in the program for 30 weeks during the school year. The family is visited at home every second week to review materials with the parent through role-playing; parents are then expected to spend a minimum of 15 minutes daily doing the activities with their child. The HIPPY program is very structured and is implemented across sites in the same way using a standard curriculum and standard materials. Parents receive a progressive series of 60 weekly packets of daily activities. All of the parent instructional materials are prepared at a Grade Three level and are available in a number of languages; in 2008 HIPPY Canada incorporated Canadian content into the program by replacing 18 of the 27 books with books by Canadian authors and illustrators (including Aboriginal and multicultural content) and updating the curriculum to support the new reading material. Every other week parents attend group meetings with other parents and HIPPY staff.*

More information is available at **http://www.hippycanada.ca**

NOBODY'S PERFECT PROGRAM

Nobody's Perfect is a community-based parenting education and support program that was developed in the early 1980s by the Public Health Agency of Canada (then Health and Welfare Canada) and the

---

*Reprinted by permission of Susanne Nahm.

four Atlantic provincial departments of health. It was developed specifically for young, single, socially, culturally, or geographically isolated parents of children from birth through age five who have limited formal education and low income. In 1987 it was introduced nationally and was eagerly adopted across the country. The program has been offered in every Canadian province and territory and has been one of the most popular parenting programs in the country. Across Canada, over 5,000 community workers, parents, and public health nurses have been trained as Nobody's Perfect facilitators. Networks in every province and territory provide ongoing support for facilitators and trainers. Several major evaluation and impact studies have found Nobody's Perfect to be successful at reducing isolation and increasing parenting skills and confidence.

The overall goal of the program is to improve parents' capabilities to maintain and promote the health of their young children, and the specific objectives of the program are

1. to increase participants' knowledge and understanding of their children's health, safety and behaviour;

2. to effect positive change in the behaviour of participants in relation to their children's health, safety and behaviour;

3. to improve participants' confidence and self-image as parents;

4. to improve participants' coping skills as parents; and,

5. to increase self-help and mutual support among parents.

(Health Promotion Directorate, Atlantic Region, 1987: 12–13)

Nobody's Perfect is offered by a trained facilitator, or co-facilitators, to small groups of parents in weekly sessions over a six- to eight-week period. When developed in the early 1980s, Nobody's Perfect was before its time in terms of philosophy and approach. It is based on an adult learning model and uses a learner-centred and strengths-based empowerment model. Parents' own experiences are recognized and valued and the program builds on parents' existing knowledge and capacities through group discussion and problem-solving learning activities. Facilitators create opportunities for change by building trusting relationships with parents and creating groups characterized by mutual support. These program features are now

well accepted as best practices in parenting education and family support (Campbell and Palm, 2004; Mann, 2008; and Skrypnek and Charchum, 2009).

SUCCESS BY 6

Success By 6 was founded by the United Way in the Minneapolis area in 1988 and is one of the largest networks of early childhood coalitions, with more than 350 initiatives across the United States and Canada. Operating under local United Way organizations, Success By 6 is a community partnership dedicated to increasing awareness of and investment in early child development. Success By 6 coalitions galvanize businesses and governments around early learning by raising awareness of the importance of early childhood development, increasing access to services, advocating for public policies and improving systems—budgets, laws, and supports—to improve young children's lives.

The goal of Success By 6 is to offer all children a good start in life so that by the time they begin Grade One, they are physically, socially, and emotionally healthy and ready to learn. The focus is on supporting parents, promoting healthy births, promoting early learning programs, protecting children from abuse and neglect, and supporting neighbourhoods. From 2007 to 2012, more than 500,000 children benefited from Success By 6's early learning, child-care, parent education, health, literacy, and family resource centre programs.

THE PARENT–CHILD MOTHER GOOSE PROGRAM

This section was contributed by Catherine Melville, director, Toronto Parent–Child Mother Goose Program, 2012.

The Mother Goose Program (Programme la Mere l'Oie pour parents et enfants) (P-CMGP) is a non-profit organization that has been operating in eight provinces and Yukon for more than 20 years. It receives funding through donations; provincial and municipal government grants; and agency-paid fees for staff training, the use of the program materials, and daily operations. The program provides a one-hour group experience for parents/

caregivers and their children for 30 consecutive weeks. Participants receive education, and watch demonstrations, on how to use interactive rhymes, stories, and songs with their children to enhance the child's language and communication skills. Printed versions of the rhymes and songs are supplied to participants for use at home, but there is no requirement that parents work with their child between sessions. Connecting through the rhythm, sound, and meaning of language helps parents and caregivers experience joy with their babies and creates positive family patterns. Parents gain confidence as learners and parents and develop a network of friendship and support. Children show a marked improvement in language, preliteracy, and cognitive skills, and gain self-esteem and develop social skills. Nationally, the agencies delivering the program have reported serving a total of 1,649 adults.

Recent initiatives include the development of a new multicultural workshop called "Your Grandma, My Grandma: Connecting Cultures through the Parent-Child Mother Goose Program" and a partnership with the Hospital for Sick Children to produce *It Was Midnight on the Ocean,* a book of rhymes and stories for parents [with children] in the neonatal intensive care unit. The P-CMGP also provided several teacher training workshops along with manuals and other training materials to the Ontario Cultural Society for the Deaf (OSCD) to help that organization develop an ASL [American Sign Language] program for parents and infants modelled on the Parent-Child Mother Goose Program and continued to collaborate with the OCSD as it developed the American Sign Language workshops and materials it now offers.*

A study by the British Columbia arm of the Mother Goose organization surveyed parents, teachers and other community members on their 10th anniversary in 2007. The following are some of the results:

- 91.6% of parents agreed that participating had enhanced their relationship with their child
- 95% of parents said the program had lasting effects on them as parents
- 83% said the program had lasting effects on their family
- 95% of parents reported that they used the songs, rhymes and stories learned at home with their children

- 96% of parents continued to sing and rhyme with their children after the program finished
- 78.3% of parents keep in touch with other families met through Parent-Child Mother Goose (Hutchinson, 2008: 11)†

PARENTING AND FAMILY LITERACY CENTRES

Parenting and Family Literacy Centres (PFLCs) were first established in 1981 in five Toronto inner-city schools where students were at risk for academic failure. Parents and their preschool children in these neighbourhoods were invited to take part in this local school program aiming to engage parents positively in the school system, offer support in parenting, and lay the foundation for successful transition for young children into kindergarten. These ground-breaking programs were the first and largest programs of their kind in Canada. Currently, the Toronto District School Board (TDSB) has 76 PFLCs located in high-density, culturally diverse neighbourhoods throughout the city. In 2007, the Ontario Ministry of Education adopted this model and, since then, more than 156 PFLCs have been established in 16 school boards across the province. Every PFLC is free and accessible, and does not require preregistration.

PFLCs help prepare children for starting school and encourage families to be a part of their children's learning by

- supporting children's early learning through a play-based program that promotes the optimal development of the child
- helping children build essential literacy and numeracy skills through stories, music, reading, and playing
- encouraging families to engage in their children's learning
- familiarizing children and families with school routines
- giving children and families the chance to spend time with other families

---

†B. Hutchinson, 2008. "Singing and Rhyming, Bonding and Learning. The Results of the Parent-Child Mother Goose Program Province- Wide Survey, 2007-2008," *IMPRINT: The Newsletter of Infant Mental Health Promotion* 52 (Winter): 11. The Hospital for Sick Children, Infant Mental Health Promotion, Toronto. Reprinted by permission.

---

*Reprinted by permission of Catherine Melville.

- linking families with appropriate community resources for special needs, health, and other related services

- offering a book lending library in different languages so parents can read to their children in their first language

PFLCs give parents a positive introduction to the school environment and deliver a range of play-based, problem-solving activities to parents and children ranging in age from newborn to age 6. Each PFLCs is unique, as it reflects its immediate neighbourhood, so programs are delivered in a culturally sensitive environment. Respect for the values of the parents is paramount; staff work with parents to establish the needs that the parents themselves identify. Parenting staff (parent workers) are trained in the identification of early disabling conditions and routinely refer children to appropriate medical services.

In addition to being highly multicultural, PFLCs tend to be multigenerational. At one centre, three Chinese grandfathers socialize as they care for their grandchildren, while at the opposite end of the city, teenage mothers meet with their infants and often bring along their own mothers or sisters. Most centres have three generations represented at every session.

This section was contributed by Joanne Davis and Ruth Sischy of Parenting and Family Literacy Centres, Toronto District School Board.

The centres tend to be located in our most inner-city schools and reflect the typical issues facing the community. Therefore, staff (parent workers) need to familiarize themselves with local resources in the community so that they can make referrals around issues such as housing, legal advice, food banks, ESL classes, and family shelters.*

> The parent is seen as the first and most important teacher and is supported in this role. In keeping with the special focus of literacy and numeracy learning, parents and their children are read to many times a day. Each centre has a range of inexpensive "in-house" learning materials which offer parents opportunities to teach their young children literacy and numeracy concepts in a non-threatening play environment. Parents are exposed to age-appropriate activities and develop realistic expectations for their children.
>
> We are constantly explaining child development to the parents so they can recognize the milestones and enjoy them. The common denominator

here is fun. If a child feels loved and connected to one parent, their classroom learning will improve.

These centres provide many opportunities to engage children and their families through a play-based environment that also includes a multilingual lending library for children and adults. There are also CDs and DVDs to support both literacy and numeracy, fundamental elements of this program. The environment reflects what you might find in any early learning environment: sand, water, dramatic play, art materials, blocks, puzzles, physical activity equipment, and places for gathering for circle time.

The notion that ESL parents who read to their children in their first language are inhibiting the development of English-language skills is strongly rejected by parenting centres. Programs are premised on the belief that the intimacy of the parent–child relationship drives literacy learning and that if the first language is subtracted from this relationship, the learning is diluted. In the words of one parent worker:

> Working from the Parenting Centres with families in a respectful, inclusive way raises the parents' self-esteem and empowers them to be advocates for their children's education. The informal visits from teachers and principals to the parenting centres go a long way to [evening] the power imbalance that many low-literacy parents feel in our schools. We find that [when we demystify] the school system [for] parents, they are far more likely to become involved with their children's education. Parents will show up for interviews and help in the classroom when they understand jargon such as "literature-based reading programs" or "invented spelling" and when they feel welcomed by teachers.

Mary Gordon, founder of the PFLCs, believes that society has lost the fabric of the community and that parenting centres knit community members together once again. The most important thing the parents are told is that they are their child's first teacher. When parents realize they have this power, they can help their children learn (*Toronto Star,* 1998). The centres' work is supported by the National Longitudinal Study, which found that children whose mothers read to them more than once a day scored about 6 percent higher in reading skills than children whose mothers seldom read to them. Regularly reading to a preschool child not only improves vocabulary skills but also has a stronger effect on behaviour than any other factor.

---

*Reprinted by permission of Ruth Sischy.

Parent Attending a Parenting and Family Literacy Centre

The Parenting Centre gave my son and I the ability learn about the education system and to network with the school and other parents, and made it easier for us to make the transition from one country to another and be a part of the community. For me, the parenting centre was more than a place to take my son to learn through play; it made the challenges he was facing moving to a new culture less difficult for him. He learned to socialize with other children, by engaging in activities such as singing, story time, gym, and other social events within the school community. I was able to network and bond with other parents as we encouraged one another and shared our experiences, parenting ideas, trials and triumphs.

Principal

Our Parent and Family Literacy Centre has provided our families with an opportunity to build a positive relationship with our staff and administration, as well as allowed us to teach the necessary skills that our young learners need to effectively make the transition to kindergarten. Our Parent and Family Literacy Centre has created the feeling that our school is truly the "hub of the community."

Principal

For our families, the Parenting and Family Literacy Centre represents a welcoming introduction to the world of school, allowing an opportunity for parents, grandparents, extended family, and caregivers to share important learning together. We firmly believe the Parenting and Family Literacy Centre will have a tremendous impact on our future kindergarten students. Watching the children attending the centre participate in play-based activities while parents learn how to further develop their parenting skills will have a huge impact on the children's readiness for our all-day kindergarten program in September.

WHAT THE RESEARCH SAYS

Since 1999, the TDSB has conducted three phases of formal research to assess the immediate and long term impact of the program—with each successive phase involving larger samples of students and numbers of Centres.

The latest analysis of data in 2008–09 validated earlier findings about the immediate positive impact of the program in preparing children for school entry. The most recent research results demonstrate that the initial gains PFLC students had made could be extended to their later school years.

For children who had attended PFLCs with their parents/caregivers, their odds of receiving low Early Development Instrument (EDI) readiness scores in the five developmental areas (physical well being, social competence, emotional maturity, language and cognitive development, and communication skills and general knowledge) was significantly smaller than their school peers who had no exposure to the program.

This was especially true for those who attended the program regularly; their likelihood of being

assessed low on at least four of the five EDI domains was also less than that of the general population. These recent results demonstrate the measurable difference that PFLCs can make on students in high risk neighbourhoods. The results are immediate as they facilitate a smooth transition for pre school children into formal schooling, as well as provide long term benefits by developing social, learning and academic skills children need to succeed in school. These benefits are a direct result of the active participation of the parents/caregivers in the PFLCs offered in their local schools. (Research Today, 2010)[*]

A PROGRAM LIKE NO OTHER: ROOTS OF EMPATHY

The early years are critical in the development of social and moral knowledge. It is during this time

---

[*]Research Today. 2010. *PFLC: Making a Difference Beyond Early School.* Vol. 5, Issue 2, Winter. http://www.tdsb.on.ca/wwwdocuments/parents/parenting_and_family_literacy/docs/Research%20Today%20brochure%20winter%202010.pdf. Reprinted by permission of Maria Yau, Research Coordinator, Toronto District School Board.

that children's ideas and beliefs about equality or inequality, and differences in gender, race, and disability manifest themselves. Paley (1992: 3) notes

> by kindergarten ... a structure begins to be revealed and will soon be carved in stone. Certain children will have the right to limit the social experiences of their classmates. Henceforth, a ruling class will notify others of their acceptability and the outsiders learn to anticipate the sting of rejection. Long after hitting and name-calling have been outlawed by the teachers, a more damaging phenomenon is allowed to take root, spreading like a weed from grade to grade.

Fortunately, an innovative and powerful program, Roots of Empathy (ROE), was developed by Mary Gordon, a kindergarten teacher by training and creator and former administrator of the Parenting and Family Literacy centres at the Toronto District School Board. Gordon brings tremendous passion and energy to her work, which has been celebrated through numerous awards and honours. When she speaks, she recounts one success story after another, and those who have heard her will not be surprised to learn that the Clinton administration, the Manitoba government, the United Nations, the Nelson Mandela Children's Fund, and the Organisation for Economic Co-operation and Development have studied her techniques.

Roots of Empathy's mission is to build caring, civil, and peaceful societies through the development of empathy in children and adults. The long-term focus of ROE is to build the parenting capacity of the next generation of parents. More immediately, ROE focuses on raising levels of empathy, which results in more respectful and caring relationships and the reduction of bullying and aggression. The innovative classroom program is offered to hundreds of thousands of students, from kindergarten to Grade Eight in every province of Canada in English and French, and in countries of three continents. The Roots of Empathy program uses the loving relationship between a parent and an infant as a concrete, hands-on, interactive approach to demonstrate empathy. Throughout the school year, a volunteer family with a newborn baby and a trained instructor visit a classroom. The instructor coaches the students to observe how the baby forms an attachment to the parents and makes his or her needs known. The infant's development is chronicled and children learn to recognize the baby's cues and unique temperament while celebrating developmental milestones. Knowledge of infant development and safety issues (shaken baby syndrome, fetal alcohol spectrum disorder, SIDS) prevents future child abuse and builds parenting skills for the next generation. Inclusion, respect, and good citizenship are core values in Roots of Empathy instruction. The instructor conducts additional sessions before and after each family visit, for a total of 27 sessions over the course of a year. Roots of Empathy has been evaluated in both comparative and randomized controlled studies designed to measure changes in the behaviour of participating students. Independent research has been conducted in Australia, the Isle of Man, and New Zealand, as well as through five university-based Canadian studies. Key research findings show that children perceived a more positive classroom environment by the end of the program. Children also exhibit a decrease in aggression, an increase in prosocial behavior, an increase in social and emotional understanding, and an increase in knowledge of parenting. A follow-up study of the program also indicates that improvements in prosocial behaviour and reduced aggression are maintained and enhanced for years afterward. Looking ahead, new national and international brain-based studies will expand our understanding of the impact of Roots of Empathy beyond behavioural observation. Measuring brain activity will yield important information in relation to the development of social and emotional learning and self-regulation. Studies are currently in progress in Canada, the United States, Northern Ireland, and Scotland.
http://www.rootsofempathy.org

SEEDS OF EMPATHY

In 2005, Mary Gordon created Seeds of Empathy as a program to bring the messages of Roots of Empathy to preschoolers. Seeds of Empathy is designed for early childhood settings to foster social and emotional competence and early literacy skills and attitudes in children 3 to 5 years of age, while providing professional development for their educators.[*]
Source: **http://www.seedsofempathy.org**

BOOKS FOR ADULTS

Roots of Empathy: Changing the World Child by Child, by M. Gordon

[*]Reprinted by permission of Roots of Empathy.

INNOVATIVE INITIATIVES ACROSS THE COUNTRY
EARLY LEARNING AND CHILD CARE/EARLY CHILDHOOD DEVELOPMENT IN SASKATCHEWAN

Saskatchewan parents have the primary responsibility for the care and learning opportunities for their own children, but everyone in Saskatchewan shares an interest in their physical, intellectual, social, and emotional development. Children's well-being is a measure of the community's development. Early childhood educators play a key role in supporting parents to fulfill that important responsibility by providing quality care and education opportunities that serve the dual roles of nurturing children to reach their fullest potential, and supporting parents to work or go to school. In Saskatchewan, early childhood educators work with families in a range of settings and programs. The largest number of educators work with preschoolers, infants, toddlers, and school-age children in licensed child-care centres. Children who are identified as having special needs, either at birth or soon after, may be eligible for the Early Childhood Intervention Program (ECIP). Early childhood educators employed through this home visiting program work with children and their families, both at home and at child care if applicable, to ensure that the children benefit from stimulating activities to enhance their development prior to entering school. The relationships between early childhood educators and families are the key component of the ECIP program. Early childhood educators are also employed as family support workers in other family services organizations that provide children's programs as part of their supports to families. These include women's shelters and parenting centres, as well as programs sponsored by the Government of Canada such as Community Action Program for Children (CAPC) and Aboriginal Headstart (AHS). In many Saskatchewan schools, particularly in areas with large numbers of families living in circumstances of risk, pre-kindergarten programs are offered to 3- and 4-year-old children. Some pre-kindergartens offer the children's program four half-days per week, with the remaining half-day reserved for family activities. Early childhood educators are hired as assistants in pre-kindergarten, kindergarten, and elementary classrooms.

FORT MCMURRAY, ALBERTA, REGIONAL MUNICIPALITY OF WOOD BUFFALO

This section was contributed by Hope Moffatt, Instructor, Keyano College, Fort McMurray, Alberta, 2012.

Three preschool programs in Fort McMurray recognized the importance of family involvement and designed their programs to include parental components. The Children's Centre, which was founded in 1993, directs its attention to families in the high-risk category and offers preschool, parent–toddler drop-in, prenatal, and new mother programs, as well as focusing on children on the fetal alcohol syndrome spectrum. Educare Early Intervention program was launched in 1997 by the determined work of one woman, Kim Farrell, who wanted to address the language, academic, and social needs of the children who came into her kindergarten classes. It now includes early childhood development (preschool) with speech-language and family literacy components, a Rock-A-Tots music program, and a sensory integration program. The HUB Family Resource Centre opened in 2003 and won the Fort McMurray Chamber of Commerce Not for Profit Flame of Excellence Award for 2007. In its first year, the HUB Family Resource Centre partnered with approximately 26 agencies, business, and organizations to provide programs and services to the public. Partnerships with Keyano College Childhood Studies Programs, Fort McMurray Housing, FCSS Family and Community Support Services, Alberta Alcohol and Drug Abuse Commission (AADAC), Educare Preschool Program, and the RCMP allowed the HUB to deliver multilevel services free of charge. Attendance Centre exceeded 10,100 visits in the first year alone, with individuals accessing services, programs, or information on a wide variety of community programs and resources. In response to the community growth and needs, and in recognition of the HUB's success, Alberta Children's Services named the HUB as an Alberta Parent Link Centre. This initiative brought new opportunities with the creation of the HUB on Wheels program, which allowed the HUB to take its programs to various areas within the city and to the outlying communities of Anzac, Janvier, and Conklin. The HUB on Wheels program addresses a major barrier for families who do not always have access to transportation to attend programs in another part of the city or region. As a result of this innovative program, attendance at HUB programs jumped to over 15,000 visits in 2004. In 2008, the HUB opened a second site to accommodate the huge influx of new families. By 2011, 1700 families were registered with the HUB, and those families visited the various HUB programs an astonishing 42,850 times. The demographics at the HUB, and in Fort McMurray, continue to change and evolve: there are more than 15 first languages spoken by HUB families and staff. The HUB fulfills the important function of helping them find each other and form those important friendships necessary when extended families are thousands of miles away. It also informs families about community events and resources.

In the spring of 2008, Children First: Community Child Care Network Society was born and, with it, a vision of how a community can put "circles of support" around its families to help care for and educate their children. Children First's mandate was to create additional affordable, accessible child-care services for the families of Fort McMurray. Forming the society was just the beginning: the new Children First society applied for Creating Spaces funding from Alberta Children and Youth Services, and started the Children First: Community Day Home Agency, which immediately applied to become an accredited Agency. Operated as a nonprofit, the board of directors comprises both volunteers who are newcomers as well as long-time residents of the community. Because Children First had been formed from the Community Child Care Coalition—a loosely formed group of representatives from early childhood programs as well as community and oil sands industry stakeholders—it became aware that the Oil Sands Secretariat had been working with the local Child and Family Services Authority staff and administrators, and applied for a $2 million grant to build a new child-care centre. Beginning with the shells of two houses, community partners at Stratford Contracting worked alongside Children First as they designed and adapted the space so that it was purpose-built for child care. From March 2009 until the doors opened in May 2010, the board was consumed with the acquisition, design, creation, and building of Children First: Eagle Ridge Nest Child Care Centre, which is licensed for 58 children aged 5 months to 6 years. Parents have formed a parent advisory committee, helped with fundraisers, participated in community events, shared multicultural feasts, and formed new friendships. In February 2012 both Children First: Community Day Home Agency and Children First: Eagle Ridge Nest Child Care Centre received accreditation from Alberta's Accreditation of Early Learning and Care Services—a huge accomplishment in a short period of time. The organization moved from a vision in 2008 to become centres of excellence and models of best practice in terms of emergent curriculum, antibias education, and family involvement in less than two years.[*]

QUEBEC'S SERVICES INTEGERS EN PERINATALITE ET POUR LA PETITE ENFANCE A L'INTENTION DES FAMILLES VIVANT EN CONTEXTE DE VULNERABILITE (SIPPE)

SIPPE, a program that targets women who are pregnant, under age 20, or living in extreme poverty, and recent immigrants, is provided across Quebec. The mother and father may continue to participate in the program until the child is 5 years of age. Participants are referred by hospitals, or by other health and social services. In 2006–2007, SIPPE served 5,240 women—an estimated 56 percent of the eligible population—and had an annual budget of $48 million. Participants are provided with a variety of support including home visits lasting 60 to 90 minutes every second week beginning in the 12th week of pregnancy, information about good nutrition and health practices, food coupons, and prenatal vitamins. After the birth, there are weekly home visits until the child is 6 weeks old, every second week until he or she is 12 months old, and then monthly until the age of 5. The home visitors' activities are tailored to meet the needs of families, which may include child development information, effective parenting strategies, educational activities to do with the child, budgeting and other life skill counselling, assistance in accessing other services such as child care and job training, and accompanying a parent to an appointment. Generally, the home visitor is a nurse who has access to many other specialists such as speech and language therapists, medical doctors, nutritionists, social workers, etc. Home visits are supplemented by group activities for parents and their children, and parents are encouraged to enroll their preschool-aged child in regulated child care as a means of providing a group educational experience (Doherty, 2008).

[*]Reprinted by permission of Hope Moffatt.

BETTER BEGINNINGS, BETTER FUTURES PROGRAM

Better Beginnings, Better Futures, led by Ray Peters at Queen's University, is one of the most ambitious research projects on the long-term impact of early childhood development programming ever initiated in Canada. The Better Beginnings, Better Futures model is designed to prevent young children in low-income, high-risk neighbourhoods from experiencing poor developmental outcomes, which then require expensive health, education, and social services. It has been implemented in eight socioeconomically disadvantaged communities in Ontario since 1991. The model consists of programs that deliver at three levels: child-focused programs that enrich children's social and academic environments; parent- and family-focused programs that provide parent support and parenting education; and community-focused programs that work to improve conditions such as neighbourhood safety and cohesion.

This project is the first early childhood intervention project of its kind in Canada. The communities themselves define the services they need to promote their children's development and to alleviate the impact of economic disadvantage. Each project is unique, but most now offer early childhood intervention services, such as home visits, family support programs, and school and child-care centre enrichment, which are coordinated with other early childhood development services in each community.

One of the most ambitious research projects on the long-term impacts of early childhood prevention programming for disadvantaged children in Canada, this project has received wide national and international attention, interest, and support. Better Beginnings is a unique opportunity to apply knowledge about Canadian community-driven solutions that are countering the negative effects for at risk children living in poverty through early childhood intervention. The diversity of the participating communities (Francophone, Aboriginal, recent immigrants, and multicultural) increases the likelihood that findings will be applicable to children across Canada. Findings will provide specific direction to the development of prevention and intervention programs and will enable more informed decision-making about social policy. (Better Beginnings, 2012)[*]

ONTARIO'S EARLY LEARNING FOR EVERY CHILD TODAY (ELECT)

Early Learning for Every Child Today: A Framework for Ontario's Early Childhood Settings (ELECT) is a province of Ontario Best Start initiative that describes how young children learn and develop. It is a framework that can accommodate and enhance a range of curriculum and pedagogical approaches that are now used in Ontario's early childhood programs. For example, the Ontario Kindergarten Program, HighScope, and Creative Curriculum recognize developmental consideration that can be elaborated with the Continuum of Development that is a central component of the framework. The Continuum supports the abilities of educators to observe and document children's activities and interactions in order to assess their progress, plan curriculum and talk with families and other caregivers. ELECT provides a curriculum guide for early childhood settings with a statement of six principles. One of the six principles in ELECT states that "partnerships with families and communities strengthen the ability of early childhood settings to meet the needs of young children."

The explanation of this principle begins as follows:

The web of family and community is the child's anchor for early development. Families are the first and most powerful influence on children's early learning and development. Families live in, and belong to, multiple communities that may support or thwart their ability to support young children's optimal development. Relationships between early childhood settings and families and their communities benefit children when those relationships are respectful of family structure, culture, values, language and knowledge. (Weiss, Caspe, and Lopez, 2006)

The Better Beginnings bus provides transportation to and from the centre.

---

[*]Reprinted by permission of Better Beginnings, Better Futures Research Coordination Unit.

This important principle invites early childhood educators to expand their practice to include parents in decision making and planning curriculum; to expand their knowledge and presence in centre and family communities; to connect families with each other; to provide families with information and links to resources that support them meeting the diverse needs of their children; and to exchange observations and information on each child's learning, development, and daily experiences. Family and community involvement is a focus for educational change and improvement that promotes children's learning and development, health, and well-being.

Early Learning for Every Child Today: A Framework for Ontario's Early Childhood Settings (ELECT) is available at **http://www.children.gov .on.ca/htdocs/English/topics/earlychildhood/early _learning_for_every_child_today.aspx**.

ONTARIO EARLY YEARS CENTRES

Ontario Early Years Centres are family resource programs delivered in local communities that provide central locations for children up to the age of 6 and their parents and caregivers to take part in programs and activities together and get information about the programs and services that are available for their children. Funding for Ontario's Early Years initiatives is part of the National Children's Agenda, through which the federal government transfers funds to provinces to enhance Early Years programs and services. The centres give caregivers the chance to speak to Early Years professionals and other families in their community. Programs focus on the important role a parent has as primary teacher to his or her child, and all centres provide literacy and interactive learning activities involving parents and children, as well as parenting programs covering all aspects of early child development, prenatal and post-natal resources, training, referrals to link families with external services, and outreach to encourage parent participation across the province. A total of 106 centres operated in Ontario in 2012 (Ontario Ministry of Children and Youth Services, 2010).

FIRST CALL BRITISH COLUMBIA

This section was contributed by Gyda Chud of Vancouver Community College.

As a child-care advocate, my involvement with First Call has been a deepening and broadening experience in a multitude of ways. First Call is a coalition of over 90 organizations in British Columbia that advocate on behalf of children, youth, and families. While each organization has its own particular focus and mandate, First Call brings us together in a powerful collective voice regarding issues and activities of shared concern.

To this table I have brought information and advocacy initiatives to advance high-quality, affordable, accessible child care. At this table I have found important new allies to help take the child-care message forward. Through this table I have learned from others and have become informed and engaged in a myriad of other concerns—child poverty, child labour, the plight of sexually exploited youth, the desperate need for preventative services to families, and the lack of coherent social policies and programs to meet community needs.

Within First Call I have developed personal and working relationships with many knowledgeable, passionate activists, who are tireless in their effort to promote social justice, equity of outcomes, meaningful community development, and citizen empowerment. From them I have learned how interconnected our issues really are, and how child care is indeed a cornerstone in the building of healthy families. Thanks to First Call I have sharpened my own skills in effective advocacy strategies and have in turn been able to share those skills with students, colleagues, and the many child-care organizations in which I volunteer. Having taken part in brief writing, postcard campaigns, media connections, public rallies, and networking in the family services community, I say hats off to First Call for the energy, mutual support, organizational strength, and collaborative approach they model.

CHILD CARE IN RURAL AND FARMING COMMUNITIES

Having a greater understanding of the rural population in Canada helps us to understand the unique needs of farming families. The proportion of Canada's total population classified as farm population is 2.2 percent. In 2006, there were 229,000 farms in Canada, and 27.7 percent of farm operators in Canada are female. The average size of a census farm family is 3.1 people (Vanier Institute of the Family, 2012).

According to Adler et al. (2012: 260),

There has long been the popular idea that people living in rural areas and small towns enjoy greater intimacy with their friends and neighbours when compared to people living in large urban centres like Toronto, Montreal, Vancouver, and Ottawa.[*]

Statistics Canada (2005) explored some of these ideas in the 2003 General Social Survey on Social Engagement and here is what they discovered:

- Rural people are more likely than city dwellers to know most or all of their neighbours and more likely to trust them.

- Between 52 and 61 percent of rural Canadians said they knew all their neighbours. That's three times higher than people from the four largest urban centres mentioned above where only 16 percent said they knew all their neighbours....

- 32 percent of rural residents expressed a strong sense of belonging to the local community compared to only 19 percent of those living in cities with a population over 1 million.

It can be hard to find and access services in rural Canada, whether for children, families, youth, adults, or seniors. Even if social services are available, they are often not available in all communities, during the hours families need them or in a way that responds to individual needs. Governments and social service agencies across Canada struggle to successfully respond to the specific challenges of rural, remote, and northern communities. These challenges include large geographic distances, low population base, cultural diversity, seasonal employment patterns, and rural demographics. The Integrated Hub Model (IHM) examines ways to make a wide range of support

[*]From Adler, Ronald, et al., *Interplay: The Process of Interpersonal Communication* 3/Ce © Oxford University Press Canada 2012. Reprinted by permission of the publisher.

Inside LOOK

As a farm child growing up in the farm workplace, my safety was often compromised due to lack of child-care options. I can remember having heat stroke from long hours in the hayfield sitting on my mom's knee on the tractor mowing or raking. Almost every farmyard has a dugout [pond]. I remember my brother and I playing a game of Russian Roulette with ours—using an old car hood as a raft to see if we could make across before it would sink. Neither one of us could swim. As children, we had no fear; after all, we were invincible then.

Now as a parent of farm children, I have a lot of fear. I fear for my children's safety, that they might not be as lucky as my brother and I were to escape unhurt. When my husband and I were first married, we both inherited a basic assumption from our farm parents—that it was possible to be both farmers and parents at the same time. If we survived being farm children, so would our children. The children would be safe with us while we worked. There was no daycare in our town for our two boys to attend. My parents were running their own farm and my husband's parents were willing but not able to care for two active children. Regular babysitters were not available and the ones that were sometimes were not reliable. We were clever at devising ways to keep our children safe while we worked. During calving time, the boys rode in a wooden box attached to the rear of our three-wheeler Honda, much like a miniature set of stock racks. We could drive from calf to calf, tagging, castrating, doctoring, while they played inside this box. We also had a child's car seat mounted inside our cab tractor for seeding and haying time.

Of course, there were problems with these ideas. The Manitoba climate is not always kind to young children, being very cold in the winter and hot in the summer. Mosquitoes were bad and conditions were dusty and noisy. It seemed like we were working twice as hard and getting half as much done, trying to keep the boys safe and happy. Our third child was three weeks old when we finally admitted to ourselves that the situation was not good. We were loading cattle. Our two older boys were inside the truck and our baby was sleeping in the baby carriage. I had parked the carriage in front of the truck for shelter, not realizing my husband could not see it over the hood of the truck. Just minutes before my husband drove over the carriage, my baby cried and I picked him up to comfort him. If he had not awakened, he would have been in the carriage when it was crushed by our farm truck.

This incident shook both myself and my husband and opened our eyes to the dangers our children were facing in the farm workplace. Dangerous equipment, chemical use, noise levels, extremes in weather—we may do our best to protect them from these. But under stress, we can all make mistakes. Stress from heavy workloads is the unseen danger that threatens every child attending the farm workplace with their parents. Without alternative child-care options, I decided to stay home with the children. We would not place our children's lives at risk again.

My husband worked longer hours, seven day a week, to get all the work done on his own. This was very difficult on our family life. Then an option never before considered possible in a small town like ours became a reality; or should I say a miracle. Lakeview Children's Centre opened its doors. It began as a pilot project with federal grants to see if rural day care was needed and if it was viable. That year I enrolled our three boys and started helping my husband farm full-time. We got our work done faster, more efficiently, and with less stress. We discovered more leisure time to spend with our children, as my husband could now take weekends off work.

The child-care centre provided for our children all the things that family, baby-sitter, and the car seat in our tractor could not:

- flexible hours, open from 6:00 a.m. to 10:30 p.m. if needed
- affordable, through subsidy programs, for low-income families
- quality, with experienced, educated caregivers
- structure, in the lives of our children; they knew what to expect on a day-to-day basis
- and, as a bonus, it was guilt-free—our children loved it

We could see them growing and blossoming in the positive atmosphere of our rural child-care centre. Our children and our family life benefited from daily interaction at Lakeview Children's Centre. Day-care funding cuts have forced us to face an important question: "Could we go back now, to the way things were before?" NO. We have discovered a child-care system that is truly viable—that cares for the lives of our children and keeps them safe and happy while we are at work. My greatest wish is that all farm kids will someday have equal access to the same care that my kids have right now.

As farm parents who want the best for our children, we must unite on this issue and fight for a universal child-care policy that includes the needs of the farm child. We must do this for the sake of our children's safety, physical and mental well-being, and for the overall health of the farm community. I am not talking about a temporary measure, but in fact a permanent, structured, quality system where we can entrust our most precious resource, our children to grow, flourish, and remain safe while we are at work.

Source: JoAnn Egilson, "Viable Child Care Options," *Child Care Focus*, Fall 1993, Manitoba Child Care Association. Reprinted by permission.

services more available and accessible to families living in these rural, remote, and northern communities.

A VISION FOR RURAL CHILD CARE

Statistics Canada defines a rural area as one that has a population concentration of fewer than 1,000 people and has a population density of fewer than 400 people per square kilometre. Doherty (1994) states that rural characteristics and their implications for child care include

- seasonal variation as a predominant work pattern
- fluctuations in the need for child care from year to year
- a scattered population with relatively few users for any one type of service
- long travel distances and lack of public transportation
- the presence of commuters who live in rural areas but work in a town or city and drive long distances to work each day

- the presence of stay-at-home parents who may be without a car all day.

She points out that in many rural locations, there are few licensed child-care options, and centre-based care is expensive to provide; many centres cannot afford to hire the number of staff required to operate age-segregated groups (1994: 19). The needs of rural families are varied and include seasonal care, extended hours, emergency care, and full-time or part-time care. Finding teachers who are willing to engage in seasonal care is a particular challenge for centres in such regions.

The Northern Community Partnership Initiative is a multi-government horizontal coordination and collaborative approach that allows governments to work together at streamlining programs and service delivery for northern communities. This approach is being tested with federal and territorial government partners in Nunavut in one community—Pangnirtung—in its development and implementation of the Nunavut Partnership Pilot Project. The pilot project is focused on crime prevention through social development of children, youth, and their families. The project will evaluate the effectiveness of participatory approaches in building community capacity and fostering change through the management and delivery of the model.

Inside LOOK

I had an opportunity to work with diverse rural families and in different environments. An Ontario Early Years Centre provided drop-in centres, programs, and farm care for families in need. I worked on an "on call," basis which meant that I would be scheduled and booked for a different farm family daily. My shifts would range from 7:30 a.m.–3:30 p.m., 8:00 a.m.–4:00 p.m., 9:00 a.m.–5:00 p.m., 10:00 a.m.–6:00 p.m.; flexibility was the order of the day. My responsibilities included preparing meals for the children as well as supervising and implementing activities. I also communicated with families to find out the types of experiences or activities they would like their children to engage in. Working in the family's homes made the interactions more personal and this strong relationship made it easier to provide quality care since, in most cases, I watched the children grow.

Source: Reprinted by permission of Stefani Chiapponi, RECE.

Inside LOOK

The biggest benefit I have experienced working with children and families in a small northern community is the coming together for the good and the bad. When a crisis hits a family the entire community is there to help and to support them through it. No matter how small the contribution is, everyone has a part to play in a crisis. Families can be there to support each other, and help carry the load.

Source: Reprinted by permission of Patty Wiseman, Manager, Teslin Tlingit Council Daycare.

The Sister Celeste Child Development Centre, Tulita, Northwest Territories

Tulita is an isolated Native community of approximately 500 people in the Northwest Territories. It is situated where the Great Bear River meets the Deh Cho (Mackenzie) River. The symbolic Bear Rock overlooks the community. The Sister Celeste Child Development Centre was established in 1981. It has half-day programs for 3- and 4-year-olds that promote the continuity of learning between the highly valued family and the Child Development Centre. Community involvement is one of the primary strengths of the program. The centre is staffed by Native women and men from Tulita, coordinated by Sister Celeste, and is governed by a committee of community members. Another strength of the program is its continuously developing blend of Native culture and early childhood practices. Play is the form of curriculum that includes cultural values and customs as well as opportunities for exploration and the practice of developing skills. The centre includes a Slavey language program. Local stories from elders and others in the community have been translated into preschool books written in both Slavey and English for use in the centre and in homes. In response to the concerns of elders, the children receive instruction from a local Native drummer on how to dance, how to listen to the drum, and how to play hand games. Community members bring local stories to life with handmade dolls and props that illustrate values and tell how the Slavey people live in the far North. The program includes opportunities for children to snowshoe in the long winter months and snare rabbits in the nearby bush. The rabbit is then prepared and shared first with elders at the feast.

Source: Reprinted by permission of Marie Goulet retired faculty, George Brown College.

REFERENCES

Adler, R.B., L.B. Rosenfeld, R.F. Proctor II, and C. Winder. 2012. *Interplay. The Process of Interpersonal Communication*. Oxford University Press.

Ambert, A. 2012. *Changing Families. Relationships in Context*. 2nd ed. Pearson Canada.

Anderson, J., L. Markell, C. Brown, and M. Stuart. 2007. *Child Care Cooperatives in Canada 2007: A Research Report*. March 1. Prepared for the Cooperative Secretariat and Human Resources and Social Development Canada. Retrieved January 28, 2013, from http://childcarecanada .org/documents/research-policy-practice/07/09/child-care-co-operatives-canada-2007-research-report

Anderson, L., and S. Harney. 2012. "Briefing Update of *A Tale of Two Canadas: Implementing Rights in Early Childhood*." Pre Sessional Working Group of the U.N. Committee on the Rights of the Child. Coalition of Child Care Advocates of B.C. and Child Care Advocacy Association of Canada. February 6. Retrieved January 28, 2013, from http://cccabc .bc.ca/res/rights/files/CCRight_briefing_update.pdf?utm _source=Copy+of++Advocacy+Update+February+6 &utm_campaign=child+care+canada&utm_medium=email

Andre, T., and C. Neave. 1992. *The Complete Canadian Day Care Guide*. Toronto: McGraw-Hill Ryerson.

Beach, J., M. Friendly, C. Ferns, N.Prabhu, N., and B. Forer. 2009. *Early Childhood Education and Care in Canada, 2008*, 8th ed. Toronto: Childcare Resource and Research Unit.

Bertrand, J. 2008. *Understanding, Managing and Leading Early Childhood Programs in Canada*. Toronto: Nelson.

Bertrand, J. and C. Geswicki. 2012. *Essentials of Early Childhood Education*. Nelson Education.

Better Beginnings, 2012. Queens University. Retrieved from http://bbbf.queensu.ca/research.html

Boyd, H. 2012. "Waldorf Schools: What You Need to Know." Retrieved January 28, 2013, from http://www.education .com/magazine/article/Ed_Waldorf_Schools_What

Campbell, D., and G.F. Palm. *Group Parent Education: Promoting Parent Learning and Support*. Thousand Oaks, CA: Sage.

Canadian Association of Family Resource Programs. 2012. "What Is FRP Canada?" Retrieved January 28, 2013, from http://www.frp.ca

Child Care Human Resources Sector Council. 2011. *Province Introduces ECEC System, Invest in Training and Wages*. Spring. Retrieved January 21, 2013, from http://www.ccsc-cssge.ca/sites/default/files/uploads/CCHRSCspring11.pdf

Childcare Resource and Research Unit. 2001. *What Does Research Tell Us about Quality in Child Care?* Toronto: University of Toronto.

Childcare Resource and Research Unit. 2008. *Why Canada Can't Work Without Good Child Care: How Early Childhood Education and Care Supports the Economy*. Briefing Notes. Retrieved January 21, 2013, from http://www.childcarecanada.org/publications/briefing-notes/08/09/why-canada-can%E2%80%99t-work-without-good-child-care-how-early-childhood

Doherty, G. 1994. "Rural Child Care in Ontario." *Occasional Paper No. 4*. Childcare Resource and Research Unit and the Centre for Urban and Community Studies, University of Toronto.

———. 2008. *Ensuring the Best Start in Life*. Institute for Research on Public Policy.

Gestwicki, C., and J. Bertrand. 1999. *The Essentials of Early Education*. Toronto: Thomson Nelson Learning.

Gordon, M. 1992. "Family Literacy: Centres Involve Parents Early." *Literacy Works* 3 (3): 2–3.

Health Promotion Directorate, Atlantic Region. 1987. *Program Plan for Nobody's Perfect*. pp. 12–13, January.

Hepworth Berger, E. 2004. *Parents as Partners in Education: Families and Schools Working Together*, 6th ed. Columbus: Pearson Merrill Prentice Hall.

Hutchinson, B. 2008. "Singing and Rhyming, Bonding and Learning. The Results of the Parent-Child Mother Goose Program Province-Wide Survey, 2007–2008." *IMP: The Newsletter of Infant Mental Health Promotion*. Winter.

Japel, C., R. Tremblay, and S. Côté. 2005. "Quality Counts! Assessing the Quality of Daycare Services Based on the Quebec Longitudinal Study of Child Development." *Institute for Research on Public Policy* 11(5).

Kagan, S.L., and P.R. Neville. 1994. "Parent Choice in Early Care and Education: Myth or Reality?" *Research and Clinical Issues, Zero to Three* 14 (4). February–March.

Leighton, D. 2005. "The Waldorf Experience: A Parents' Perspective." *Canadian Children: Journal of the Canadian Association for Young Children* 30 (1). 40.

Lilliard, A.S. 2007. *Montessori: The Science behind the Genius*. New York: Oxford University Press.

Mann, B. 2008. *What Works for Whom? Promising Practices in Parenting Education*. Ottawa: Canada.

———. 2011a. "Five Years On, Children Still Wait for Quality Care." *Toronto Star*. February 4. Retrieved January 28, 2013, from http://www.thestar.com/parentcentral/education/childcare/article/933823--five-years-on-children-still-wait-for-quality-care

Monsebraaten, L. 2011b. "Quebec's Child Care Scheme Pays for Itself, Economist." *Toronto Star*. June 27. Retrieved January 28, 2013, from http://www.thestar.com/NEWS/article/1012855

Norrie McCain, M., and F.J. Mustard. 1999. *Early Years Study: Final Report*. April. Toronto: Children's Secretariat. Retrieved from http://www.childsec.gov.on.ca.

Norrie McCain, M., F.J. Mustard, and K. McCuaig. 2012. *Early Years Study 3. Making Decisions Taking Action*. Toronto: Margaret & Wallace McCain Family Foundation.

Norrie McCain, M.N., F.J. Mustard, and S. Shanker. 2007. *The Early Years Study 2: Putting Science into Action*. Toronto: Council for Early Child Development.

OECD (Organisation for Economic Cooperation and Development). 2011. "Investing in High Quality Early Childhood Education and Care." December 1. Retrieved January 28, 2013, from http://childcarecanada.org/documents/research-policy-practice/12/02/investing-high-quality-early-childhood-education-and-care-e

Ontario Ministry of Children and Youth Services. 2010. "Ontario Early Years Centre. A Place for Parents and Their Children." Retrieved January 28, 2013, from http://www.children.gov.on.ca/htdocs/English/topics/earlychildhood/oeyc/index.aspx

Paley, V.G. 1992. *You Can't Say You Can't Play*. Cambridge, MA: Harvard University Press.

Parent Cooperative Preschool International. 2010. "History." Retrieved January 28, 2013, from http://www.preschools.coop/v/history

Public Health Agency of Canada. 2010a. "Summative Evaluation of the Community Action Program for Children 2004–2009." Retrieved January 28, 2013, from http://www.phac-aspc.gc.ca/about_apropos/evaluation/reports-rapports/2009-2010/capc-pace/overview-survol-eng.php

———. 2010b. "Summative Evaluation of the Canada Prenatal Nutrition Program 2004–2009." Retrieved January 28, 2013, from http://www.phac-aspc.gc.ca/about_apropos/evaluation/reports-rapports/2009-2010/cpnp-pcnp/summary-resume-eng.php

Report of the Expert Panel on Quality and Human Resources. 2007. *Investing in Quality: Policies, Practitioners, Programs and Parents*. March. Retrieved from http://www.children.gov.on.ca/htdocs/English/topics/earlychildhood/investing_in_quality.aspx

Research Today. 2010. *PFLC: Making a Difference Beyond Early School* 5(2). Winter. Retrieved January 28, 2013, from http://www.tdsb.on.ca/wwwdocuments/parents/parenting_and_family_literacy/docs/Research%20Today%20brochure%20winter%202010.pdf

Rushowy, K. 2007. "Canada 'Dead Last' in Spending." *Toronto Star*. March 26. A1.

Skrypnek, B.J. and J. Charchun. 2009. *An Evaluation of the Nobody's Perfect Parenting Program*. Canadian Association of Family Resource Programs.

Statistics Canada. 2005. 2003 General Social Survey on Social Engagement. Cycle 17. An Overview of Findings. Retrieved January 28, 2013, from http://www5.statcan.gc.ca/access_acces/archive.action?loc=/pub/89-598-x/89-598-x2003001-eng.pdf

Toronto Star. 1998. "Praised Parenting Centres Feel Future Slipping Away." April 22. B1.

UNICEF. 2008. "The Child Care Transition: Innocenti Report Card 8." Retrieved January 21, 2013, from http://www.unicef-irc.org/publications/pdf/rc8_eng.pdf

University of New Brunswick. 2012. *Year Two Research Report, New Brunswick Early Childhood Centres*. January. 3.

Vanier Institute of the Family. 2012. "Family Farms In Canada." Ottawa. Retrieved from http://www.vanierinstitute.ca/modules/news/newsitem.php?ItemId=427

Weiss, H., M. Caspe, and M. Lopez. 2006. "Family Involvement in Early Childhood Education." *Family Involvement Makes a Difference*. Harvard Research Project Series, No. 1. Cambridge, MA: Harvard University.

MADELINE   CONNOR   DAD

Created by Madeline

Chapter 3

BUILDING EFFECTIVE PARTNERSHIPS

*"Transformative education is defined as two people or groups coming together and interacting in such a way that both parties learn something and are changed for the better by the interaction"**

—*Janet Gonzalez-Mena (2007)*

LEARNING OUTCOMES

After studying this chapter, you will be able to

1. identify the key features of successful family-centred practice

2. discuss the particular benefits of partnerships for family members, children, and teachers

3. describe the barriers to effective partnerships

4. identify the policies and procedures that supervisors and teachers can use to build effective partnerships with families

---

"When you heal a child you heal a family. When you heal a family you heal a community. When you heal a community you heal a nation. The same can be said for the love and care of a child: When you provide love, support and care to a child, you provide care and support to a family. When you provide care and support to a family, you provide care and support to a community. When you provide care and support to a community, you provide care and support to a country."

—Ovide Mercredi, 1992

WHY WE NEED PARTNERSHIPS WITH FAMILIES

Developing partnerships with families is an integral part of the role of an early childhood educator. To work effectively with children, educators must work effectively with their families. But how do we define this partnership? Since different early learning environments have varying perspectives and serve different communities, it is not surprising that family–teacher partnerships may take many forms. The child and family centre is a microsystem—it operates within a community, never in isolation, influenced by a larger macrosystem of political, economic, and social issues. All the elements of the microsystem and macrosystem influence relationships between families and teachers (see Figure 3.1).

Across the country, there is growing consensus that bolder approaches and break-through strategies are necessary to improve early childhood education. Declining achievement scores, rising educational costs, and a growing distrust of bureaucratic institutions have focused attention on parents' rights and responsibilities with respect to their child's education.

FAMILY–CENTRE COLLABORATION VERSUS PARENTAL INVOLVEMENT

The National Network for Collaboration states that

Collaboration is a process of participation through which people, groups, and organizations work together to achieve desired results. Collaborations accomplish shared vision, achieve positive outcomes for the audiences they serve, and build an interdependent system to address issues and opportunities. Collaborations also involve the sharing of resources and responsibilities to jointly plan, implement and evaluate programs to achieve common goals. Members of the collaboration must be willing to share vision, mission, power, resources and goals. (Learning Circle Five, n.d.)

At first glance, the term *family–centre collaboration* may be easily confused with the term *parental involvement.* Yet these terms represent significantly different paradigms about the nature of the family–centre relationship. Whereas parental involvement depicts a one-way flow of information between schools and parents, family–centre collaboration involves a two-way exchange of information (Christenson and Sheridan, 2001). Collaboration is key! "In addition, while parent involvement focuses on parents becoming involved in their children's education, family-school collaboration focuses on the joint involvement of parents/caregivers and school staff in children's education"* (Amatea, 2009: 27). Families must feel that they have significant influence.

Pusher (2007: 8) believes that

the shared role between staff and families is critical to a family-centric program. Living a story of parent engagement means living out a new story of school. A world which is co-constructed and shared with parents and community members is a world with a side-by-side structure rather than a hierarchical one.

WHAT THE EXPERTS SAY

Research tells us that family involvement is critical to children's development and achievement and in preventing or remedying educational and developmental problems. The benefits of family collaboration include higher achievement rates, higher

---

*AMATEA, ELLEN S., BUILDING CULTURALLY RESPONSIVE FAMILY-SCHOOL RELATIONSHIPS, 1st Edition, © 2009. Reprinted and Electronically reproduced by permission of Pearson Education, Inc., Upper Saddle River, NJ.

attendance rates, lower delinquency and dropout rates, and higher high school completion and college or university admission rates. Importantly, most of this research is based on families whose children are at high risk for school failure. Most researchers also agree that parental attitudes have a major effect on children's learning and acceptance of school.

Parental self-esteem is critical: "The most important predictor of children's school success is related to positive parental self-esteem. Studies indicate that there is a definite impact on the development of feelings of competence and self-esteem in parents involved in their children's schools" (Epstein, 2000: Fig. 5-8).

The attitudes of school personnel also affect how children learn. Many leading early childhood organizations and experts support the critical need for collaborative partnerships with families from a strength-based perspective. Several examples of this support are listed below.

In his report *With Our Best Future in Mind,* Dr. Charles Pascal (2009) states that "joint responsibility between parents and educators is an important difference maker, when it comes to the developmental progress of children. Outreach to parents can be informal, but some parents will need to be brought into the process through flexible program models that support a two way relationship" (29).* So perhaps we need to use new language—instead of *child-care centres,* use *child and family centres.* Pascal's vision for these centres would provide families with

- flexible, part-time/full-day/full-year early learning/care options for children up to age 4;

- prenatal and postnatal information and supports;

- parenting and family support programming, including home visiting, family literacy, and playgroups;

- nutrition and nutrition counselling;

- early identification and intervention resources;

- links to special needs treatment and community resources, including libraries, recreation and community centres, health care, family counselling, housing, language services, and employment/training services.

"… [E]very neighbourhood shall have access to a Child and Family Centre that offers one-stop services and supports for children and families" (Hiscott, 2010: 8–9).

*Pascal, C. 2009. *With Our Best Future In Mind,* http://www.ontario.ca/en/initiatives/early_learning/ONT06_018876. © Queen's Printer for Ontario, 2009. Reproduced with permission.

FIGURE 3.1   Links

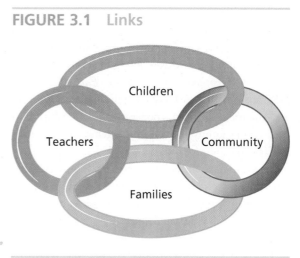

Children

Teachers

Community

Families

The *Canadian Child Care Federation's Code of Ethics* (2011: 28) underscores the importance of parent partnerships:

Quality child care maintains an open, friendly and informative relationship with each child's family and encourages their involvement. The interaction among all persons in a child care setting reflects mutual respect, trust and co-operation. The family and the child care providers become partners who communicate openly for the mutual benefit of the children and themselves.

The *National Statement on Quality Early Learning and Child Care* (2007: 20) describes a collaborative partnership as one that "honours the family's role

Teachers play a powerful role in the lives of children.

Courtesy of Ingrid Crowther

as the child's primary caregivers, respects its child-rearing beliefs and values, and provides meaningful opportunities for families to determine their children's early learning and care experiences." This is supported by the *Occupational Standards for Early Childhood Educators* (2010), which state that the ability to establish and maintain an open, cooperative relationship with each child's family is a key competency of educators. In 2006 the same standards stated that "administrators need to have the ability to create a family-friendly environment, and those administrators play an important role in providing a positive experience for the family and the child, and they also support families with their child-rearing responsibilities" (52).

UNICEF's priority is that family and community capacities are strengthened to promote caring, supportive, and protective environments in which children can reach their fullest potential.

It is clear that we have a great deal of direction from prestigious organizations and individuals and many principles upon which to build. The real test is how this theory is translated into practice!

PARTNERS IN QUALITY STUDY

Gillian Doherty (1997) shared the results of the Canadian Child Care Federation (CCCF) study *Partners in Quality,* a mail-out survey conducted in the fall of 1997, in which 42 percent of respondents (carers and parents) identified parental involvement as one of the most important elements of quality care. Although a more recent study of this magnitude has not been completed, there are many lessons to be learned from this research:

- Among people who worked directly with children (family- and centre-based care providers and centre directors), 54 percent identified the need for two-way communication between parent and care provider.

- Among the people identifying this as an important mechanism, 84 percent felt that such communication should be daily.

The CCCF survey also asked people how, apart from face-to-face communication, their settings communicate with parents.

- 33 percent identified written notes or journals.
- 32 percent reported that their setting has an open-door policy.
- 19 percent reported encouraging parents to be involved in program activities.

The most frequently cited desirable way of reaching out to parents was through a program or social event (43 percent of people working directly with children). When asked how child and family settings can support parents, respondents suggested the following:

- supporting frequent two-way communication (59 percent)
- providing resources such as information on child development or information on other community services (56 percent)
- providing a caring and nurturing environment for the child (52.3 percent)
- offering parent workshops or other forms of parent education (16 percent)

When differences of opinions were cited,

- 71 percent of the field respondents identified parents as the main barrier to family involvement in the child-care setting.
- Only 21 percent of respondents identified staff as a barrier.

Look carefully at these percentages! This survey provides valuable insight into the attitudes of staff toward the concept of a collaborative partnership with families. It demonstrates that teachers and parents are *not* equal partners in the child-care setting. Instead, the power rests with the teachers, who remain the perceived experts in the child-care context and in many cases indifferent to family engagement. While there has been an increased emphasis on working effectively with families in student training and in professional development for seasoned educators, clearly, much work remains to be done to establish a true partnership among equals.

According to the National Parent Teacher Association (PTA), roadblocks to parent collaboration are

- lack of time
- not feeling valued
- feeling unwelcome
- not knowing how to contribute
- not understanding the school system
- parents in need
- lack of child care
- language barriers
- special needs
- lack of transportation (National PTA, 2000)

This chapter will outline how we can address many of these family concerns.

As we become more whole as parents, as we are given dignity, listened to, and have a safe and joyous place to learn and express ourselves, we offer this to our children. We do this not only by way of example, but also by empathizing and connecting to our children's developing sense of becoming their full selves—listened to, respected, questioning, discovering, and ultimately empowered.

Source: Hartzell and Zlotoff, 2004: 113.

THE RIGHTS OF PARENTS

Loris Malaguzzi (n.d.) outlines the Reggio Emilia approach's *Charter of Rights for Parents* below:

It is the right of parents to participate actively and with voluntary adherence to the basic principles in the growth, care, and development of their children who are entrusted to the public institution. This means no delegating and no alienation. Instead, it confirms the importance of the presence and the role of parents, who have always been highly valued in our institutional tradition. Parent participation enables a communication network that leads to fuller and more reciprocal knowledge, as well as to a more effective shared search for the best educational methods, content, and values. Then we have parents who are mainly young, of different trades and professionals, different backgrounds and experiences, and often of different ethnic origins. But all these parents have to struggle against the lack of available time, the cost of living, the difficulty of their responsibilities as parents, and the desire to identify, discuss, and reflect on their problems, especially those concerning the growth and education of their children. When school and parents are able to converge toward a cooperative experience, an interactive experience that is the rational and advantageous choice of everyone concerned, then it is easy to see how hostile and mistaken is the pedagogy of self-sufficiency and prescription, and how friendly and fertile is the strategy of participation and shared research.

New families may be confused by the hundreds of "experts" who offer conflicting opinions on raising children. Parenting is a demanding role that requires ongoing support systems within the extended family as well as within the community. Some parents feel that they are ill prepared since in their own lives they had few role models to provide the skills they feel are necessary. Yet when parents are encouraged and believe that they have an important role to play, they act in ways that support their child's development and at the same time grow in their skills as a parent. When families and teachers work together and set goals and objectives, the chances for the child's success increase significantly. Involved parents are more likely to communicate the value of the program to their children and to reinforce the program's goals within both the child-care setting and the home. Treating parents respectfully, asking for their opinions, and making use of the information they provide are crucial steps to building alliances—to developing "we-ness." When parents and teachers successfully become a "we,"

November 20 is National Child Day, a special day set aside each year to honour and respect children. In 1993, the Canadian Government chose this date to commemorate the adoption by the United Nations of two human rights documents, each adopted on November 20: the *Declaration of the Rights of the Child* in 1959 and the *Convention on the Rights of the Child* in 1989.

they can truly work as partners (Rudney, 2005). According to Bronfenbrenner (1974), parents' self-esteem increases as they become more effective parents; once they see they can do something about their child's education, they see also that they can do something about housing, their community, and their jobs. Establishing teacher training that emphasizes the family's primary caregiving role and is responsive to different parenting practices is critical to the work of early childhood educators.

THE RIGHTS OF THE CHILD

All children have the right to families that support and protect them. The United Nations *Convention on the Rights of the Child* emphasizes the importance of families to a child's socialization. Governments are expected to make every effort to keep families intact and to provide support and assistance to parents so they can fulfill their responsibilities. Even young children are entitled to know about their human rights; families can engage in activities that help children learn about their rights and help put their rights and responsibilities into practice as they prepare to become responsible citizens. (For a more detailed discussion about the rights of the child, see Chapter 11.)

REACHING OUT TO FAMILIES

> "You can't stay in your corner of the forest waiting for others to come to you. You have to go to them sometimes."
>
> —**A.A. Milne, author of *Winnie the Pooh***
> **(Goodreads, n.d.)**

We need to rethink our approach to families. Too often professional boundaries get in the way of meaningful relationships in support of young children and their families.

> What we need to do today is to focus not on whether family involvement is important but to get to how we can do this! For families to expect teachers to care for their children without the needed supports and alliances is irresponsible. Likewise, for teachers to see their teaching role as limited to the children in their classroom is foolish. Only as teachers and families develop a vision of themselves as highly important and positive partners in children's lives can these strategies carry meaning. (Swick, 1991: 34)

Gestwicki (2010: 151) agrees:

we need to rethink the idea of a welcoming environment. If a partnership is to exist, the impetus must come from the program staff. It is our responsibility to extend a welcoming hand to all of the families in our program. We must ensure that all families regardless of family structure; socioeconomic status, racial, religious and cultural backgrounds; gender; abilities; or preferred language are included in all aspects of the program including volunteer opportunities. These opportunities should consider families' interests and skills and the needs of the program staff.[*]

So how do we begin to develop meaningful relationships? It begins with trust. According to Swick (2003), four communication behaviours are most likely to build trust:

1. Approachability—making others feel comfortable and secure
2. Sensitivity—understanding others in supportive ways
3. Flexibility—adapting to needs or concerns of others
4. Dependability—counting on one another to provide continuity (in Couchenour and Chrisman, 2011: 220)[†]

How we see families, and our perceptions and ideas about family collaboration, will have an impact on how successfully we are able to build authentic partnerships. Gonzalez-Mena and Widmeyer (1989: 23) help us to understand the progression that many teachers make in their work with families:

first, they may see themselves as saviours, rescuing the children from their parents. *Second*, they move toward a perception of parents as clients, whom they work toward reeducating, and *third* they come to see parents as partners, whose needs are listened to and integrated with the teacher's professional expertise to provide what is best for the children without a sense of imposing ideas.

SHARING EXPERTISE

We can maximize a child's learning opportunities when we work closely with families, sharing our insights and collaborating together.

---

[*]From GESTWICKI, *Home, School, and Community Relations, 7E.* © 2010 Cengage Learning. Reproduced by permission. www.cengage.com/permissions.

[†]From COUCHENOUR/CHRISMAN. *Families, Schools and Communities, 4E.* © 2011 Wadsworth, a part of Cengage Learning, Inc. Reproduced by permission. www.cengage.com/permissions.

When working together, teachers and families should remember that many of their goals are similar, but their areas of expertise are not. Their spheres of knowledge and influence are complementary, and together they hold an amazing amount of information about children. The teachers are knowledgeable about subject matters, pedagogy, and the general characteristics of the age group they teach. They are experts at working with children in group. Parents have a different sphere of knowledge, one that is equally important to the children and very useful to the teacher. Parents know their children's history, strengths and weaknesses, favourite foods, and whether they get scared at night or not. They have seen the children at their best and their worst, and they love them anyway. They also have information about how the children learn that can help the teacher. (Rudney, 2005)*

It is also important to note that parents will have difficulty moving away from a subjective approach to their children. Teachers can provide that objectivity that makes goal setting developmentally appropriate.

*Reprinted with permission of Corwin Press, from G. Rudney, 2005. *Every Teachers Guide To Working With Parents*; permission conveyed through Copyright Clearance Center, Inc.

EXHIBIT 3.1　What Makes Relationships Work?

SIX BASIC QUALITIES

1. **A relationship needs to balance reason and emotion.** Many aspects of a relationship are not rational. We often react emotionally, not logically, in pursuit of some purpose. Emotions such as fear, anger, and frustration may disrupt otherwise thoughtful actions. Emotions are normal, necessary, and often essential to problem-solving. They can convey important information, help us marshal our resources, and inspire us to action. Wisdom is seldom found without them. Nonetheless, the ability of two people to deal well with their differences will be greater to the extent that reason and emotion are in some kind of balance.

2. **Understanding helps.** If we are going to achieve an outcome that will satisfy the interests of both and leave each of us feeling fairly treated, we will need to understand each other's interests, perceptions, and notions of fairness. Whether we agree or not, the better we understand each other, the better our chance of creating a solution we can both accept.

3. **Good communication helps.** The more effectively we communicate about our differences, the better we understand each other's concerns and the better our chances for reaching a mutually acceptable agreement. The more openly we communicate, the less basis there is for suspicion.

4. **Being reliable helps.** Well-founded trust, based on honest and reliable conduct over a period of time, greatly enhances our ability to cope with conflict. The more honest and reliable we are with respect to each other, the better our chance of producing good outcomes.

5. **Persuasion is more helpful than coercion.** Each of us will try to affect the other's decisions, and the way in which we do so will have a profound effect on the quality of the relationship. At one extreme, I can try to inspire your voluntary cooperation through education, logical argument, moral persuasion, and my own example. At the other extreme, I can try to coerce you by worsening your alternatives and by warnings, threats, extortion, and physical force. The more coercive the means of influence, the less likely it is that the outcome will reflect both our concerns, and the less legitimate it is likely to be in the eyes of at least one of us. The less coercive the modes of influence, the better our ability to work with each other.

6. **Mutual acceptance helps.** If we are to deal well with our differences, we need to accept each other as someone worth dealing with. Feeling accepted, worthy, and valued is a basic human psychological need. Unless you listen to my views, accept my right to have views that differ from yours, and take my interests into account, I am unlikely to want to deal with you. And if we do not deal with each other, we will not even begin to resolve our differences.

Based on these six concepts, here is a checklist that will help teachers assess their relationships with families:

1. **Goal:** Am I trying to win the relationship or improve it? How well do we resolve differences? How often do I think about improving the process for working together over the long term?

continued

2. **General Strategy:** Do serious issues disrupt our ability to work together? Do I tend to retaliate by doing things that weaken our ability to deal with each other in the future? Do I ignore problems or sweep them under the rug rather than deal with them?

3. **Balance of Emotion and Rationality:** *Awareness*: What emotions, mine and yours, are affecting our interactions? *Effect*: How are emotions helping and hurting our decision-making?

4. **Degree of Understanding:** How well do I empathetically understand your perceptions, interests, values, and motivation? How well can I state them to your satisfaction? How well do you understand mine? Can you state them to my satisfaction?

5. **Effectiveness of Our Two-Way Communication:** How regularly do I consult you before making decisions? What important subjects don't we discuss? Why? How extensively and frequently do we communicate? Do I listen?

6. **Reliability, or Your Degree of Confidence in My Future Conduct:** Might I be more reliable? How? How could I be more worthy of trust? Do your perceptions suggest some changes I might make? What risks do I see in relying on you? Are those risks well-founded?

7. **Persuasion or Coercion:** Do I try to persuade you on the merits? Could I be more open to persuasion? How? How well do I avoid threats, warnings, and commitment tactics?

8. **Degree of Mutual Acceptance:** Do I fully accept you as someone with whom to deal? Do you matter in my scheme of things? Am I giving serious attention to your interests and views? Do I recognize the potential long-term quality of this relationship?

Source: Adapted from GETTING TOGETHER by Roger Fisher and Scott Brown. Copyright © 1988 by Roger Fisher and Scott Brown. Reprinted by permission of Houghton Mifflin Harcourt Publishing Company. All rights reserved.

FIGURE 3.2 Cultural Identity Circle

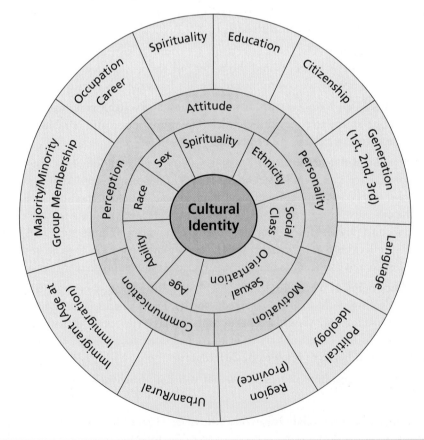

Source: James, Carl E. 1999. *Seeing Ourselves: Exploring Race, Ethnicity and Culture*, 2nd Edition. Toronto: Thompson Education Publishing. Reprinted by permission.

FAMILIES, TEACHERS, AND CULTURAL INFLUENCES

> "Culture of the mind must be subservient to the heart."
>
> —Mahatma Gandhi

Gonzalez-Mena (1998: 224) believes that

Culture is invisible. It has been said that one moves in one's culture the way a fish moves through water. The water is so much a part of the fish's experience that the only time it becomes aware of the water is when it suddenly finds itself surrounded by air. We are immersed in our culture the way the fish is immersed in water. We may be unaware of how much our culture influences our actions, our thoughts, our very perceptions.

When we speak about cultural differences we often refer to ethnic, racial, and linguistic diversity, but other important elements are also factors that should be considered—where we live, our socioeconomic status, and our religion. Religion plays an important role in many families in Canada.

The term *religiosity* refers to the degree of emphasis families place on religion in their lives. This may not be immediately evident to early childhood professionals, both because of the variety of religious practices and because of the tremendous differences in degree of practice from family to family. Some families may discuss their religion with teachers in the context of specific classroom practices such as holiday celebrations. Others may have unexpressed concerns, and still others may have no need to be open with their child's teacher about their religious views. Variations in religious beliefs and practices must be respected by early childhood teachers, just as teachers respect differences in culture, ethnicity, gender and abilities. (Couchenour and Chrismas, 2011: 49)*

Where we live will also have an impact. One director working with families from a rural area says that families in her rural setting have a very independent culture and are reticent to ask for help. They're suspicious of outside interference in their family structure, and teachers have to gain their trust. If you're not from that little geographical area, you're an outsider; they don't think you understand how they do things.

Therefore, strategies for effective partnerships will vary from community to community and from family to family. Families are not a homogeneous group, and each will have different perspectives, attitudes, and values that need to be reflected on and openly discussed. As illustrated in Figure 3.2, each family develops its own cultural identity based on (starting from the inner circle) individual factors, personal factors, and psychological and social factors.

THE ROLE OF THE EDUCATOR

Vygotsky's contextual theory supports the fundamental ideology that knowledge comes from culture and helps us to understand our role as educators more clearly:

Appreciating/honouring family cultural diversity means:

(a) reaching out to people with cultural identities different from your own by learning about the assumptions, belief systems, role perceptions, and prejudices that may affect how families rear their children and interact with the school and larger community;

(b) developing opportunities to incorporate the unique skills of families from different cultural contexts into their children's learning;

(c) creating comfortable, respectful relationships with them; and

(d) tailoring family-school activities to the constraints and capacities of individual families." (Amatea, 2009: 74–75)[†]

Children thrive when their identity, culture, and home language are recognized and supported.

[†]AMATEA, ELLEN S., BUILDING CULTURALLY RESPONSIVE FAMILY-SCHOOL RELATIONSHIPS, 1st Edition, © 2009. Reprinted and Electronically reproduced by permission of Pearson Education, Inc., Upper Saddle River, NJ.

---

*From COUCHENOUR/CHRISMAN. *Families, Schools and Communities, 4E.* © 2011 Wadsworth, a part of Cengage Learning, Inc. Reproduced by permission. www.cengage.com/permissions.

Merely being aware of cultural and linguistic differences is not enough to work effectively with families. Awareness implies knowledge but no action. Most of us are confident when asked if we provide culturally inclusive care, but it is when we encounter someone from other culture who challenges our own ways of thinking and acting that we are forced to overcome cultural assumptions and stereotypes. We are often not aware of how our actions and interactions are shaped by our own cultural upbringing. However, when we discuss families and their cultural identity, we must always remember the great diversity within cultures and avoid stereotyping because it ignores the great individuality among group members. As educators in the ever-changing diverse landscape of Canada, we have an incredible opportunity to learn from each other.

> Learning to embrace diversity is not intended to threaten anyone's way of living and being; nor is it about cultures being right or wrong. It is about understanding and accepting difference and extending equal human rights to all. Each of us is entitled to the way of living and being that is best for us. However, as early childhood educators, when we enter the workplace, we are in a public arena, one that must be accepting of all children and their families. If we are not, we devalue children and families in our care. (Dever and Falconer, 2008: 277)

Teachers must remember that difference does not mean deficit and that we have a responsibility to bring compassion and understanding to our relationships in the spirit of openness and acceptance.

Families will bring different beliefs and expectations to their child-care experience. Some will come from cultures where involvement in the child-care centre is not encouraged and others may openly challenge policies and procedures in the centre. Some parents may be reluctant to engage because they are uncomfortable with their language skills. Early childhood programs must adapt and respond to the needs of families and their communities. *Enculturation* is the process by which families and society enable children to take their place in a global society. Early childhood educators play an enormous role in supporting *acculturation*, as children encounter groups outside their ethnic roots. Acculturation is the transfer of culture from one ethnic group to another. It is an exciting yet challenging process, and one that is completely congruent with the principles and practices of honouring diversity. It is exciting, too, in that it opens

doors to reconceptualizing work with families, and challenging in that it places the onus on early childhood programs and staff to elicit, respect, and respond to families' needs, wants, and desires.

Chud and Fahlman (1995) state that underlying the concept of family-centred, culturally sensitive child care are the following core beliefs (146–47):

- The family is central to the child's life.

- Each family has its own particular strengths, competencies, resources, and ways of coping.

- Each family must be accepted and respected on its own terms, with no judgments or preconceptions.

- The racial, cultural, ethnic, religious, and socioeconomic diversity of families must be honoured.

- Services and programs for families are effective only insofar as they support the family in meeting its own identified needs and concerns.

- Policies or practices that limit access or exclude families from service because of their diversity must be eliminated.

Our capacity to respond thoughtfully and sensitively to family diversity depends on the following:

- our respect for the role and importance of family in the lives of children;

- our understanding of the challenges which are common to all parents and those that may be shared particularly by parents in minority positions;

- our commitment to the concept of family-centred, culturally sensitive child care; and

- our personal willingness to open our hearts and minds to family viewpoints and perspectives that might be different from our own.

We know that, to live in a just and civil society, children need the knowledge and skills to live peacefully with others, and to be aware of injustice and prejudice and prepared to act on behalf of others when this occurs. Children must recognize how important it is for children from minority groups that their culture, language, and way of life are respected and valued. Derman-Sparks and Olsen Edwards (2010) point out that children notice gender and racial differences as early as the second year of life and by age 3 may already have been exposed to biases that the authors call "preprejudice." "For children to have equitable education, it is important for educators and administrators to create anti-bias classrooms that focus on the reality of children's lives, taking into consideration the many cultural aspects of all of the children in the class" (Hepworth Berger and Riojas-Cortez, 2012: 50).

EPSTEIN'S SIX TYPES OF PARENT ENGAGEMENT

> "When parents, teachers, students, and others view one another as partners in education, a caring community forms around students and begins its work."
>
> **—Dr. Joyce Epstein**

Epstein (1995: 9) identified six types of parent engagement and suggested strategies that teachers could employ to develop a working partnership with parents.

1. *Parenting:* Help all families establish home environments to support children as students through parent education and family support programs assisting families with health, nutrition information and engaging in home visits.

2. *Communication:* Design effective forms of school-to-home and home-to-school communications about school programs and children's progress through a variety of media and family-teacher conferences.

3. *Volunteering:* Recruit and organize parent help and support.

4. *Learning at Home:* Provide information and ideas to families about how to help students at home with homework and other curriculum-related activities, decisions, and planning.

5. *Decision Making:* Include parents in school decisions, developing parent leaders and representatives through active engagement in PTA, advisory councils, networking with families and advocacy in the community.

6. *Collaborating with Community:* Identify and integrate resources and services from the community to strengthen school programs, family practices and student learning and development.[*]

STUDENT PERCEPTIONS

Considerable research has been conducted on preservice elementary schools teachers' beliefs about family involvement (Aldemir, 2008; Graue and Brown, 2003) but less is known about what preservice early childhood educators think about collaborating with parents. Beliefs about family involvement are based on past experiences, as well as professional training, and they influence how educators interact and engage with families when those educators enter the workforce. Connie Winder (2009) surveyed ECE students during the third semester of their two-year ECE program at a community college in a large urban area in Ontario. She found that, like students in teacher preparation programs, ECE students recalled high levels of family involvement in their own early education and they rated ECE knowledge of child development and curriculum as higher than parent knowledge of child development and curriculum. It is understandable that ECE students would rate ECEs as more knowledgeable than parents about curriculum, but it was somewhat surprising that they perceived parents as knowing less about their own child's social-emotional development than ECEs did. Winder argues that this may be due to the fact that the students were surveyed before they had completed a course about working with families, and they had not yet developed a greater appreciation for the scope of parents' knowledge about their children.

Gestwicki (2000) also notes that ECE students are aware that they may have an ideal image of the family and an understanding of how societal influences helped produce it. Nevertheless, "they may be unaware of how insidiously this subliminal image can influence their encounters with real families. If an ideal, lurking unknowingly in the teacher's value system, is considered the 'good,' a negative evaluation can be made of any family that does not measure up to this standard."[†]

For many ECE students, their first field placement and the knowledge that they are expected to work with not only the children but also their families raises many concerns. Being able to identify these potential "triggers" allows us to discuss these concerns in a frank and open manner in class and during field seminars. Some of the most worrisome issues for ECEs are

---

[*]Epstein, J. L. 1995. "School / family / community partnerships: Caring for the children we share," *Phi Delta Kappan*, 76, 701-712. Reprinted by permission of Phi Delta Kappan.

[†]From GESTWICKI, *Home, School, and Community Relations, 7E.* © 2010 Cengage Learning. Reproduced by permission. www.cengage.com/permissions.

A Map for Early Childhood Educators

According to Swick (2000), there are five starting points for early childhood professionals to use to craft their "map" for being truly high-quality family helpers:

1. The human development and learning process is the result of everyone's effort, that is, it is an interactive and renewing process that is influenced by all parts of the human community.
2. An empowering approach to working with the diverse and ever-changing needs and contexts of children and families must replace a deficit-oriented way of relating to children and families.
3. The power of parents and families to nurture healthy and proactive ways of living in children can occur within various forms and structures—the key is for families to have strong and nurturing relationships with each other and their supportive helpers.
4. Early childhood educators must create diverse and adaptive ways to support families in a world of constant change and stress.
5. Early childhood educators must lead the way for "community transformation" to create family-embracing ways of functioning.

Source: From COUCHENOUR/CHRISMAN. *Families, Schools and Communities, 4E.* © 2011 Wadsworth, a part of Cengage Learning, Inc. Reproduced by permission. www.cengage.com/permissions.

- What if I disappoint them?

- What if I don't know as much as they think I should or perform as well as they would like?

- How can I effectively communicate with families whose home language is not English?

- What if I am culturally insensitive without being aware of it?

- How can I hope to know everything I should about so many diverse families?

- How will I address controversial issues such as spanking when we have conflicting ideas about what is best for the child?

- What happens when families do not respect or agree with my teaching methods?

- I know that I lack confidence. I'm worried because I am shy and stepping up into the role of the teacher will be hard for me.

- I'm worried how older parents will respond to me. Will they think I am mature enough to work with their children?

- How will I deal with criticism and conflict?

- What if we just don't connect?

FAMILY TYPES

At the beginning of each semester, I surveyed my students (in an urban community college) to determine the "family types" with which they are most familiar and comfortable. Based on their responses, I modify my course to ensure we broaden their perspective by addressing the family types with which they are least familiar and comfortable. Over the last several years, we have discussed the following family types. Figure 3.3 ranks the family types from "least comfort/exposure/experience" to "most comfort/exposure/experience" based on feedback from my students:

A key feature of the family–centre collaboration is that it is a constantly evolving relationship. As Braun (1992: 186) observes,

> Working with parents ... provides workers with sources of help, of friendship and of support—but also of challenge and a constant need to review and rethink approaches. It ensures that no one and no place becomes static and complacent, but that things change to meet changing people, circumstances, and needs. (in Pugh, 2006)

Different types of families are discussed in greater detail in Chapter 9.

FIGURE 3.3 Comfort/Exposure/Experience with Family Types

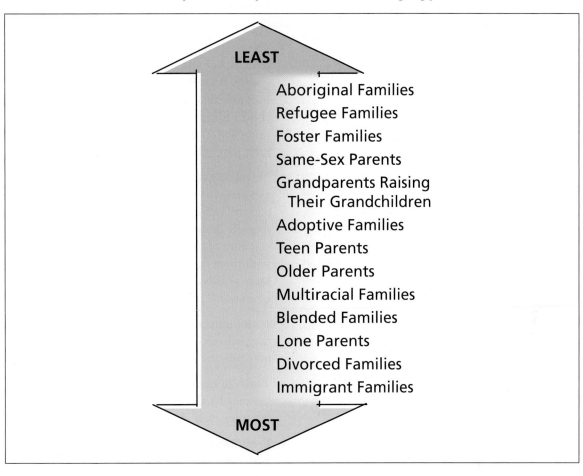

LEAST

Aboriginal Families
Refugee Families
Foster Families
Same-Sex Parents
Grandparents Raising
   Their Grandchildren
Adoptive Families
Teen Parents
Older Parents
Multiracial Families
Blended Families
Lone Parents
Divorced Families
Immigrant Families

MOST

EXHIBIT 3.2   Parents' Common Bond

No matter where parents come from or their socio-economic status there are many characteristics that are common to all parents:

1. **Parents love their children.** The vast majority of parents experience the bond with their children as a love relationship. Children's innocence, dependence, freshness, and beauty evoke feelings of protectiveness, nurturing, caring, and connectedness.

2. **Parents want the best for their children.** At the heart of the parent–child relationship is the parents' desire for the child to experience a good and happy life and to reach full potential—in ways the parents themselves may have failed. Whether "the best" means meeting basic needs for food, shelter, or clothing or, for parents of greater means, providing opportunities for education and other life-enhancing experiences, most parents want for their children the things they value in their own lives and in their own dreams. Wanting the best for their children often motivates parents to make sacrifices on their children's behalf.

3. **Parents learn to parent from their own parents.** The primary and most powerful teachers of parenting attitudes and skills are our own parents.… Whether our experiences in being parented were characterized by warmth or coldness, nurturance or neglect, permissiveness or authoritarianism, the likelihood that we will later display those characteristics ourselves, as parents, is great.

4. **Parents can learn new ways of parenting.** Despite the power of the past, parents can and do make the choice to unlearn old ways of behaving and learn new ways of relating to children. A belief in the capacity of parents to discard unsuccessful child-rearing practices in favour of new practices is at the core of all parent-education endeavours.

Source: Chud, G., and R. Fahlman. 1995. *Honouring Diversity within Child Care and Early Education: An Instructor's Guide*, vol. 11. Vancouver: British Columbia Ministry of Skills, Training and Labour and the Centre for Curriculum and Professional Development.

THE BENEFICIARIES OF EFFECTIVE PARTNERSHIPS

Families are the first and most important teachers in the child's life. Much can be accomplished when families and teachers work effectively in an atmosphere of mutual trust and respect that honours diversity while exchanging ideas and exploring goals for the child. Partnerships mean equity and shared power. Family-centred care and education in a partnership that includes the community is the focus of this text. There are so many opportunities for programs to complement existing services, to build networks and linkages, and to advocate for policies, services, and systems that support families' abilities to raise healthy children. With an asset-based approach that is respectful of families and their choices, we can build better communities that encourage mutual assistance and peer support.

BENEFITS FOR FAMILIES

- With trained teachers working in partnership, families have access to information and resources that may assist them in building on their knowledge of their child in all areas of development.

- Educators can help them locate needed human services in the community such as directories of local services, adult education programs, library services, clinics, English language classes, health care professionals, food banks, etc.

- Teachers who welcome all family members, from older siblings and grandparents to aunts and uncles, create an extended family experience where everyone focuses on enriching the child's life and everyone benefits.

- With an open-door policy at the centre, families will always feel welcome.

- Getting to know everyone at the centre—all the teachers, the cook, the bus driver, and the janitor—helps to create a welcoming and inclusive environment for everyone.

- In a caring environment, families may add to their own repertoire of parenting strategies, such as expanding effective prosocial techniques.

- When teachers invite families to engage with their children's education, families are more

likely to act. This positive action contributes to pathways for lifelong learning, behaviour, and health.

- "Not only do parents become more effective as parents, but also they become more effective as people. It's a matter of higher self-esteem. Once they saw they could do something about their child's education, they saw they could do something about housing, their community, and their jobs" (Bronfenbrenner, 1974).

- "Involving families in meaningful learning experiences with their children can increase parents' self-esteem. Parents who have a positive self-image tend to have a deeper understanding of their children, to spend more time with them in learning activities, and to have a more positive attitude toward teachers and the educational process" (Swick, 1991: 34).

- A strong relationship with the child-care team may help to lessen the isolation some parents may feel.

- Through examples seen in the playroom, families may be able to create activities and experiences for their child in the home environment.

- Families who observe their child's interaction with other children and adults, and observe their child's development and progress, set realistic goals.

- Parenting can be a daunting task but when families and teachers develop a reciprocal relationship, it allows the partners to problem solve and openly and safely share their frustrations and concerns.

- Effective partnerships provide an opportunity for parents to share exciting moments with other adults who know and care about their child.

- In situations where strong bonds exist between families and teachers, it can be theorized that teachers play a significant role in the "extended family."

- Some families may develop a supportive network with other families as well as with the educators in the early childhood environment.

- As children develop social networks within their own peer group, play dates can be arranged and families often find ways of supporting each other as their bond strengthens; in some cases, lifelong friendships develop.

- As volunteers in the program, parents may acquire new skills or expand on existing skills that can augment their résumés.

- The more involved parents are in the program, the more they may come to appreciate and value the efforts and dedication of the teachers, further enhancing the relationship.

- Family members may also be able to make meaningful suggestions for improvement in all areas of the program, including curriculum development.

- Families develop a better understanding of the goals of the centre.

BENEFITS FOR CHILDREN

- The climate of mutual respect engendered by an effective partnership enables teachers and families to create a consistent, nurturing, and emotionally stable environment for the child through trust, security, and attachment.

- A strong connection between home and the early learning environment makes the transitions between these two settings less stressful.

- As the parenting skills of the family members improve through direct observations, sharing of resources, and so on, the child is guided by confident parents who display increased self-esteem.

- Extensive research suggests that children achieve more when families are actively involved in their child-care and school experiences. Larsen and Haupt (1997) state that family participation has been linked to greater awareness and responsiveness in children, more complex language skills, greater problem-solving abilities in children, increased academic performance, and significant gains in cognitive and physical skill development.

- When families, as the primary caregivers, share information about their child, the teacher is better able to support the child in all areas of his or her development. Conversely, when teachers share information about the child, families are better able to establish for their child realistic goals that will maximize his or her growth and therefore improve the family–child bond.

- When children see their families validated by teachers they trust and respect, their own self-esteem is enhanced.

- Resources available at the centre can be shared with children and their families. Items such as travelling suitcases with storybooks, art supplies, science experiments, etc., can enrich the home environment.

- As family members become more involved, benefits accrue also to younger siblings, who will reap the rewards of strong ties to the centre.

- Children are constantly absorbing cues about how to behave from those people in their lives who are important to them. An effective teacher has the opportunity to model moral and ethical behaviours in everyday interactions with the children, other teachers, and the community at large.

- Through watching interactions between their parents and teacher, children can learn about communication skills and how issues can be resolved in a respectful and caring manner.

BENEFITS FOR TEACHERS

- Having their work valued and respected by families is important to teachers' self-confidence and professionalism.

- When the partnership goes well, teachers have the gratification of knowing that they have made an important contribution to the lives of the families with whom they work.

- When challenges arise and are successfully resolved, teachers and families strengthen their partnership and become more confident in their interactions.

- The more experience teachers have with families, the more they develop effective interpersonal strategies for dealing with all types of situations. The teacher experiences ongoing learning as each new family joins the centre.

- Learning about the child from the family enables the teacher to use that information to plan successful and relevant learning experiences.

- Many teachers feel positively toward families whose members actively participate in the program, since participation underscores the value that families place on the teachers.

- When families share their expertise, experiences, and resources, they enrich the program and the lives of everyone who works in the centre.

- When families volunteer in the playroom, teachers are able to engage in more one-on-one time with the children.

- Some families may involve themselves in decision making at the centre or volunteer on committees and thus share the workload and common goals with supervisors and educators.

- When strong relationships exist between families and teachers, a positive work environment is established, teachers' morale improves, and they experience less stress and anxiety.

- Educators are more likely to stay in centres where there are high levels of trust with families and where educators feel that parents support their work and respect them.

- Detached from the intensity of family relationships, the teacher is often in a good position to observe the interaction between family members and their children and is thus able

to contribute valuable information to the partnership.

- Evaluations of the program completed by families provide opportunities for improved teacher performance and provide insight into the families' perceptions of the early learning environment.

- Informally, many families who have had strong relationships with teachers who value their relationship benefit as the "parent grapevine" spreads the word among other families.

- In some situations, family members and teachers may become lifelong friends, an unexpected but positive connection.

Courtesy of Lynn Wilson

Children in diverse settings have much to learn from one another.

"When I chose to work with young children, I did it because children inspired me" says Amanda Hestbak, a recent graduate who works at the Wetaskiwin Head Start Society in Wetaskiwin, Alberta. "I've quickly discovered that children come with families and that being with children involves being with parents, too." Penny Pelton has watched many students come to this realization in her years of teaching in the Early Childhood Care and Education Program at Heritage College in Gatineau, Quebec. Penny compares the relationship between a family and their child-care practitioner to paddling a canoe together on the river. "When we pay attention to our partner and coordinate our strokes, the canoe moves smoothly through the water. We glide along and everyone can relax and enjoy the ride. Then if we do happen to hit rough water, we know we can get through it because we have practiced working together. There is trust that we can cooperate and keep the canoe upright and moving forward."

Source: Mann, B. 2008. "Welcoming Families As Partners In Child Care." *Interaction*. Spring. Reprinted by permission.

BENEFITS FOR EVERYONE: COMMUNITY INVOLVEMENT

> "What the best and wisest parent wants for his own child, that must the community want for all its children. Any other ideal for our schools is narrow and unlovely; acted upon, it destroys our democracy."
>
> —John Dewey (John Dewey Source Page, 2007)

The Canadian Index of Wellbeing (2010: 4) claims that

> Vital communities are characterized by strong, active and inclusive relationships between residents, private sector, public sector and civil society organizations that work to foster individual and collective wellbeing. Vital communities are those that are able to cultivate and marshal these relationships in order to create, adapt and thrive in the changing world and thus improve well-being of citizens.[*]

How can the community support young families raising their children?

> One key characteristic of vital communities is healthy families and children—not just physically healthy, but socially, emotionally and intellectually as well. And we know from research that healthy children begin with parents who have the knowledge, skills, confidence and support they need to do their most important job—raising a child. A vital community is one in which parents of young children feel supported in their role as parents, where every member of the community feels valued and our youngest children arrive at school with the developmental abilities to be ready to learn and make the most of their abilities. (Birnbaum, Crill Russell, and Clyne, n.d.: 1)[†]

---

[*]Canadian Index of Wellbeing. 2010. Community Vitality. Canadian Council On Social Development, p. 4. Available at http://www.ciew.ca/en/TheCanadianIndexOfWellbeing/Domains. Reprinted by permission.

[†]N. Birnbaum, et al., *Vital Communities, Vital Support: How well do Canada's communities support parents of young children. Phase 1.* (Toronto:

Our communities' greatest assets are people. Educators are becoming more and more aware of the interconnectedness of families and their communities. Besides the physical dimensions of a community, communities are also opportunities for social networking. When families feel comfortable, Ramsey (2004) believes that

> positive interactions between community and family give a sense of security and well-being to all. These communities help families provide the kind of nurturing that children need. Regrettably, not all communities provide healthy conditions for children. Community tolerance for gangs, illicit activities or establishments with erotic content will have unhealthy and negative influences on children's growth and the experiences they have. Violence in the streets limits everyone's sense of security. Yet, even in neighbourhoods besieged by poverty, extended family, churches, social and service organization and neighbourhood groups can make a positive different in children's lives and support and extend the work of families and schools. (in Heath, 2009: 14–16)

Families cannot function in a vacuum. The support or lack of support within the community will have a dramatic impact on the family unit. Educators should expand their understanding of the dynamics of their community by looking at demographic data that will give the centre a greater insight into the families that it may serve. Being aware of and connecting with the community's urban, suburban, rural, and cultural resources are critical to understanding the interconnectedness of communities. Strong communities can lessen the stressors facing families and, when they work, provide support services for children, parents, and families. As we have moved from an agricultural to a more industrialized culture, the feeling of community connectedness has

---

Invest in Kids; Pembroke, Phoenix Centre), page 1. Reprinted by permission of the Phoenix Centre for Children and Families.

Inside LOOK

The *Occupational Standards for Early Childhood Educators* (2010) affirm that ECEs establish relationships with and use the resources of the children's communities to support the achievement of program objectives, including the establishment of reciprocal relationships with agencies that support goals for curriculum, health promotion, children's transitions, inclusion, and diversity. ECEs must possess a familiarity with the resources available within their community and network with these resources to form partnerships and develop awareness programs.

not always been maintained. Big-box stores have replaced neighbourhood businesses and, in urban settings, vertical housing creates an environment where many people are isolated and do not know their neighbours. The kinds of protective services available and the attitudes and values modelled by citizens and leaders send children clear messages about community values and concerns. Lessons emerge as children sense their community at work and at play, when celebrating, and when struggling economically and politically or with natural disasters.

Every neighbourhood has a stake in early childhood education. Every individual—including teachers—has a responsibility for making the community a safe and productive place for all families. As teachers, we have specialized education that can help and support families but, most importantly, we must provide leadership in our communities. Family members may be surprised to find educators of their children in community meetings, strengthening these relationships. The opportunity to connect families and professionals from diverse backgrounds such as health, social work, and education also allows for a family-centred interprofessional association. This collaboration allows partners to work together in support of healthy families. Educators should make available information on all resources in the community that support families in the raising of their children: counselling services, job training, social services, housing referrals, addiction services, respite care, food banks, and so on.

- Promoting community involvement requires establishment of networks and connections evidenced by policies, procedures, and actions which extend and support all adults' and children's engagement with the wider community.

- Parents rarely have a say in program design, development, delivery or evaluation. Very little research focuses on what parents want and need in order to be and feel supported in their role as parents—we need to ask them!

- As a society we need to normalize the concept of support for all parents of young children, removing the stigma around "not knowing how to parent." We need to create and foster a community culture that supports parents and their young children, and that sees parenting as a shared responsibility between parents and their community. (Birnbaum, Crill Russell, and Clyne, n.d.: 3)[*]

"It is interesting, as soon as we made clear the importance of the first five years of a child's life, the agenda was overtaken by professionals and caregivers—not parents—despite the clarity in the literature about how central the role of parents and parenting actually is. Parents seem to be the forgotten piece of the puzzle."[†]

—**David Young, Executive Director, FRP in Birnbaum et al., n.d.: 9**

- Child-care centres and schools are well placed in most communities to foster the community connections that create some of the knowledge, confidence, relationships, and sense of connectedness that families need for effective child rearing.

- Professionals in the community may be more than willing to come and speak to teachers and families on a variety of issues facing families.

- Visiting members of the community, local business owners, etc. on field trips strengthens the children's comfort and sense of security. In times of trouble they are familiar with safe places in their community. This is very important for children who are no longer in child care or after-school programs and are on their own.

- Child-care centres must have a professional, collegial relationship with other services and with local schools to ensure smooth transitions and to benefit from shared best practices.

- Family members who establish strong, supportive working relationships with teachers in child-care centres tend to anticipate continuing their active participation when their child enters the elementary-school system.

- Family involvement provides children with a positive role model of active participation in the community.

- Highly involved families are more likely to support program policies, offer financial assistance, participate in fundraising efforts, and rally community efforts in support of the centre.

- Community businesses may be more than ready to support projects initiated at the early learning centre (for example, construction, fundraising, donating materials). These connections may provide great financial relief to the centre!

---

[*]N. Birnbaum, et al., *Vital Communities, Vital Support: How well do Canada's communities support parents of young children. Phase 1.* (Toronto: Invest in Kids; Pembroke, Phoenix Centre), page 3. Reprinted by permission of the Phoenix Centre for Children and Families.

[†]N. Birnbaum, et al., *Vital Communities, Vital Support: How well do Canada's communities support parents of young children. Phase 1.* (Toronto: Invest in Kids; Pembroke, Phoenix Centre), page 9. Reprinted by permission of the Phoenix Centre for Children and Families.

- Consider all of the resources in the community; artists, actors, and musicians and others involved in the arts may provide support and assistance. Perhaps their artistic endeavours could be highlighted at the centre or school.

- Family members who are involved in child care may well become effective long-term advocates for families, children, and teachers. We have an opportunity in our child-care centres to create the foundation for life-long advocacy for children and their families.

- Advocacy should extend beyond our local communities. We need to gain a commitment from all levels of government to implement a stable, high-quality, universally accessible child-care system in Canada. Teachers, families, and all concerned citizens should lobby and help to educate members of all political parties.

- Together we all have the responsibility when we see injustice, inappropriate practices taking place, or others being harmed to speak on behalf of the children.

In 2009, in his report *With Our Best Future in Mind*, Charles Pascal envisioned

the transformation of elementary schools into child and family centres, welcoming infants to adolescents and operating year-round. [The report] pleads with all concerned to break down their legislative, administrative and funding silos, and leave territorial and professional jealousies behind. The report argues that all the elements exist in the hodgepodge of child care, public health, education and family support services to create a consolidated program that can actually work for families. (in Norrie McCain, Mustard, and McCuaig, 2012: 16)[*]

The hub model is a blend of supports and services that respond to the particular community's needs and link early childhood environments with health services, local food banks, employment agencies, and social services that would greatly benefit families.

CHALLENGES TO EFFECTIVE PARTNERSHIPS

In this section we will examine the potential barriers to meaningful partnerships with families.

[*]Norrie McCain, M., Mustard, F.J., McCuaig, K. 2012. *Early Years Study 3. Making Decisions Taking Action*. Margaret & Wallace McCain Family Foundation. Reprinted by permission.

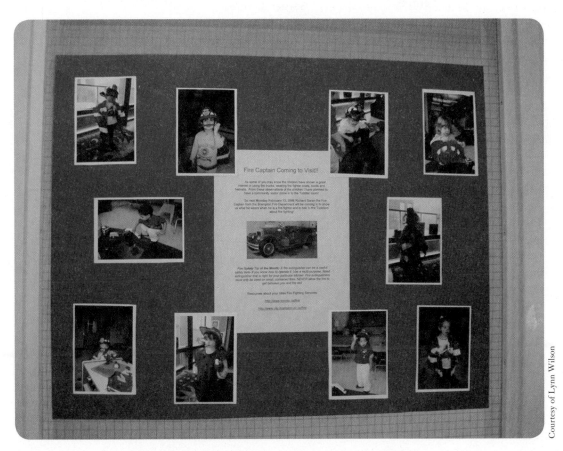

Courtesy of Lynn Wilson

Look to the community: a visit from the local fire captain was a highlight for these children.

FIGURE 3.4 Integrated Hub Model

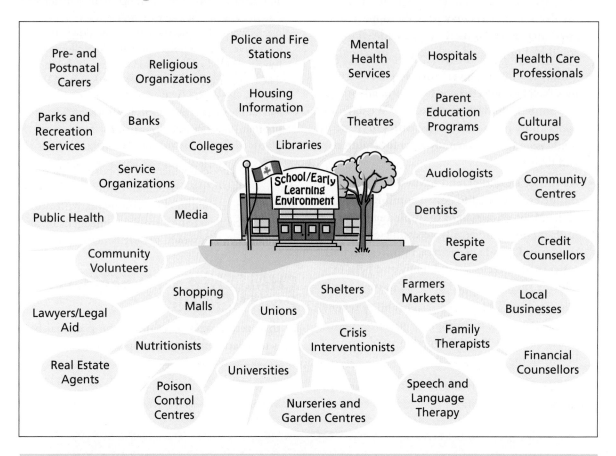

Leaders from the early childhood education and care sector, faith communities, housing providers, employers, labour unions, the education system, public health, social planning and development organizations, academic community, chambers of commerce, policy "think tanks," the justice system, and government are collaborating in the *About the Community Indicators Project*. The project is underway to raise public awareness about early childhood education and care in participating provinces and across Canada and to foster and strengthen the links between the early childhood education and care sector and the broader community. Four provinces—Newfoundland and Labrador, Ontario, Saskatchewan, and British Columbia—piloted this project. The project participants include a project advisory committee comprising representatives from the following national partners:

- Campaign 2000
- Canadian Association of Family Resource Programs
- Canadian Child Care Federation
- Child Care Advocacy Association of Canada
- Childcare Resource and Research Unit
- Citizens for Public Justice
- Family Services Association of Toronto

More information about this project is available at **http://www.campaign2000.ca**.

The Perceived Neighbourhood Scale (PNS) is a measure of neighbourhood perceptions for parents of young children. The PNS was designed to measure subjective perceptions of neighbourhood residents. The PNS consists of four subscales and 34 items. The four subscales represent four dimensions of neighbourhood context: (1) social embeddedness: formal and informal social interaction between neighbours; (2) sense of community: feelings of membership and belonging to the community, ties with neighbours; (3) satisfaction with neighbourhood: quality of the physical environment of the neighbourhood in relation to childrearing, use of local resources; and (4) fear of crime: perceived threat and occurrence of crime and violence in the neighbourhood.

Source: Martinez, Black, and Star (2002).

The scale is available at **http://somvweb.som.umaryland.edu/growth/docs/Martinez_JCP_2002.pdf**.

HAVING UNREALISTIC EXPECTATIONS

Rudney (2005) conducted a survey of parents and found that they have much to say in answer to the question of "What qualities in a teacher are most important to you?"

They value subject matter knowledge and the ability to communicate with them and with their children. The parents appreciate the teacher's qualities of enthusiasm, patience, honesty, creativity and firmness. Many liked to see a good sense of humour. These qualities establish a classroom environment that is both pleasant and focused on learning. The top two answers—listed by approximately 90% of the parents—are linked to the learning environment and beyond. The two things parents want first and foremost are that the teachers care about their children and know them as individuals. The desire for these qualities reveals how sensitive parents are to their children's emotional needs and how deep their concern is about their children's lives at school. (Rudney, 2005: 37)*

Galinsky (1988) reports that having realistic expectations is important:

> When we consider the diversity that exists among families—the myriad of beliefs, values, feelings, and concerns that each parent brings to the child-care centre—and the diversity of staff attitudes and behaviours, effective family engagement may seem an overwhelming task. The mix of older and younger families and staff, experienced and inexperienced families, and teachers presents many roadblocks to forming positive relationships. When families and teachers work together, it is only natural that there will be occasions, as in any relationship, when difficulties arise. Both parents and teachers experience job stress. For parents, the number of hours they work, the amount of job autonomy and job demands, and relationships with supervisors affect their other relationships. For teachers, the job stress also is affected by the number of hours worked, schedules, amount of autonomy, role ambiguity, physical demands of the job, and clarity of the program. (pp. 4–12)†

Teaching is physically and emotionally exhausting, and reaching out to families is sometimes viewed as one more burdensome task. So, in fact, both parties to the relationship are buffeted by strains and tensions in their worlds.

TEACHERS' CONFLICTING ATTITUDES ABOUT PARTNERSHIPS

While conflict in any relationship is inevitable, "teachers often enter the field expecting challenging relationships with parents. We expect conflict and judgment and so adopt a defensive attitude. Many teachers feel that they must educate children "in spite" of their parents, rather than in partnership with them" (Baum and McMurray-Schwarz, 2004: 58). Much of what happens in the family–teacher relationship is based on power and control. Too often teachers operate from a "teacher as expert" approach.

> The tendency to treat parents as inferior in some way, and in need of advice, has obscured the fact that most parents are well able to contribute to, as well as receive, services. Parents can be effective partners only if educators take notice of what they

say and treat their contributions as intrinsically important. (Kastings, 1992: 9)

When teachers focus on the family's problems or deficits rather than on their strengths, a collaborative relationship is unlikely. Anderson and Minke (2007: 311) found that "*specific invitations* from teachers to parents for *specific forms of participation* in their child's education had the largest effect on parental involvement at home and school." While the concept of families as partners in their child's early learning experience is gaining in popularity, it is not always supported in practice.

- Family roles and responsibilities may not be entrenched in the centre's philosophy. Even if they are so entrenched, they may be poorly communicated to families. A philosophy statement that sets forth strong ideals about family partnership is worthless if these ideals never translate into action.

- Teachers may be convinced that parents are unwilling or unable to participate, so they make no effort to involve them.

- Some centres fail to encourage participation; they never take the time to explain to families how they might become involved. It is not uncommon for families to be unsure of the rules and boundaries that are in place, and conflict and tension result.

- Some educators continue to believe that home and centre responsibilities should be separate, believing that family involvement in decision making or problem solving interferes with their professional autonomy. These teachers believe that communication with families is unnecessary unless there is a problem. This is confirmed by Kagan and Neville (1994), who note that many teachers see themselves as the experts in the parent–teacher relationship. Such partnerships tend to be based on the communication of knowledge from teacher to parent. Parents are left out of the decision-making process and are thereby rendered powerless. Worse still, they may come to internalize teachers' negative assessments of their abilities to make good decisions and choices.

- In many centres, when families are invited to participate, it is on the teachers' terms and they may limit that participation to tedious tasks.

- Some teachers who are less confident in their teaching abilities may try to keep families at arm's length because they fear criticism of their work.

---

*Reprinted with permission of Corwin Press, from G. Rudney, 2005. *Every Teachers Guide To Working With Parents*; permission conveyed through Copyright Clearance Center, Inc.

†Galinsky, E. 1988. "Parents and Teacher–Caregivers: Sources of Tension, Sources of Support," *Young Children* 43 (3): 4-12. © NAEYC. Reprinted with permission.

- Some teachers worry that involving families will place an additional burden on their limited time and energy, because some families may be too forward and, in their efforts to protect their children or change parts of the school program, they become abrasive and difficult.

- Other family members may need considerable direction and support.

- Teachers may worry about confidentiality as well, when parents witness incidents in the room that they might inappropriately share with other families.

- Other teachers worry that parents, lacking formal training, will deal with the children inappropriately.

- An unwillingness to respond to family suggestions—even when the ideas are appropriate and innovative—undermines the partnership. There is no point in stating that the centre has an open-door policy if the teachers have closed minds!

- Teachers may be resentful of families who do not actively participate in the centre or who fail to demonstrate qualities teachers feel are important to effective parenting. They focus on the family's faults rather than their strengths.

- A parent who tries to micromanage the teacher's interactions with his or her child may really be feeling like the "gatekeeper" of the child's well-being. Teachers need to understand that there may be many reasons for this behaviour; for example, they may be unaware of the guilt that some parents may feel about leaving their child in the care of others.

- Not understanding the complexities of a parent's life, some teachers become resentful when parents arrive late, don't keep diapers in their child's bin, or fail to comply with what the teacher perceives to be a "simple" request.

- Many teachers become discouraged when their attempts to build relationships with families are not appreciated and, in some cases, are rebuffed.

- When a parent is angry, it is hard for teachers to remember that it is important for families to be advocates for their own child; all children need an advocate who will be on their side.

- Teachers may also be resentful of parents who earn more money than they do and have higher-status jobs, although the work of caring for and nurturing children is critical.

- Some teachers comment that some families do not value or respect the importance of the work they do with children—that they don't see them as professionals and think that they just "play all day."

- This lack of societal acknowledgment is reflected in the low pay generally afforded educators who work in early childhood environments. Many teachers comment on how unappreciated they often feel.

- Some families simply do not understand the challenges of working with young children or the implications of working in group care.

- Many families never really acknowledge how talented, caring, resourceful, and committed most teachers are.

Some ECE students report that they are often shocked by the negative way in which children and families are discussed in staff rooms. Some co-operating teachers have attributed children's problems in school to the fact that their "parents just don't care." Research suggests, however, that parents do care and that "star teachers" see how much parents care, value this, and benefit from it. But negative images and assumptions result in parent–teacher relationships filled with mistrust and defensiveness (Rudney, 2005). This leads to a concern that impressionable students are being influenced by seasoned teachers and may adopt this negative approach to working with families. Other educators may also be influenced by their colleagues' comments and carry these biases into their interactions with their families.

Finding the right fit is critical. New teachers should consider the philosophy and practices of potential employers to determine whether these are compatible with their own deeply held personal convictions:

> Nothing more quickly destroys the joy of personal or professional life than working in a setting that calls for dissonance with self. To be able to maintain congruent feelings of personal and professional integrity, early childhood educators will need to identify those ideals and issues for which there is no room for compromise. (Bertrand and Gestwicki, 2012: 85)*

A full partnership between a family and the early learning environment means that a family will have significant influence over their child's experience in the centre, including curriculum issues, allocation of resources, and family policies.

*From BERTRAND/GESTWICKI. *Essentials of Early Childhood Education*, 4E. © 2012 Nelson Education Ltd. Reproduced by permission. www.cengage.com/permissions.

Inside LOOK

Dr. Alan Pence of the School of Child and Youth Care, University of Victoria, has worked extensively with Aboriginal communities in Canada and with a number of African nations to develop culturally and community-appropriate early childhood care and development programs. As child care professionals, he says

we have to remember that there is not just one way to competent adulthood. Indeed, seeking to learn from the parents we work with, to identify strengths in a family environment is an important starting point in a professional interaction. The European or Western culture is a very verbal culture; we talk all the time. But in some cultures, the ability to be silent, to tune into other elements in the environment, is highly valued. Yet children from such cultures also develop effective language abilities. So we need to allow for differences, to not say 'oh, they are doing it wrong.' They are just doing it differently. We can share what we know from our research and our perspective, but we also need to accept that parents' values and ways of being may not be familiar, but they can still be effective.

Source: Miller, R.J. 2008. Language, Literacy and Social Development. You Can't Have One Without The Other. *Interaction*. CCCF/Spring. Reprinted by permission.

Inside LOOK

If you feel concerned about parent empowerment, it is important to remember that people who feel powerless are more likely to be critical and demanding, needing to have everything go their way. They are less likely to see others' perspectives. On the other hand, parents and teachers who feel genuinely competent and resourceful are much better at "sharing the care," listening to others' ideas, and becoming mutual advocates for children.

Source: From *Parents to Partners: Building a Family-Centered Early Childhood Program* by Janis Keyser. Copyright © 2006 by Janis Keyser. Reprinted with permission of Redleaf Press, St. Paul, MN; www.redleafpress.org.

Inside LOOK

This early childhood educator left her first job after several months:

I didn't realize how strongly I felt about teamwork. I now know that being part of a supportive community of adults and children is necessary for my ability to grow and see myself as a real contributor in the small world of the child care centre. I will never again take a job that doesn't emphasize that feeling of community.

Source: From BERTRAND/GESTWICKI. *Essentials of Early Childhood Education, 4E.* © 2012 Nelson Education Ltd. Reproduced by permission. www.cengage.com/permissions.

The reality check is whether or not the parent feels that he or she has significant influence

FAMILIES' CONFLICTING ATTITUDES ABOUT PARTNERSHIPS

While family members and teachers share equal responsibility for making the relationship work, parents filter their perceptions of teachers through their own experiences, stereotypes, and ideas about educational settings.

- Family members who have had negative experiences with school settings in the past may bring feelings of discomfort and apprehension into the child-care environment—feelings so strong, in some cases, that a parent will refrain from any form of involvement in the centre. For some, even just coming into the school or early learning environment may bring back unpleasant memories.

- Some parents may be uncomfortable because they dropped out of school and did not complete their education.

- Other family members may see the teacher as another part of the "system," and not as someone they can count on.

- When families have not developed a trusting relationship with the teachers, they may feel that a teacher's questions and interest in their family is invasive.

- Some families may be reluctant to share personal information because they do not trust the teacher to respect confidentiality.

- Other families may defer to the teacher as the authority figure because they feel that the teacher is the one who knows best, and any criticism would be unthinkable.

- Some families don't know what to expect from the centre and lack an understanding of their rights and their ability to voice concerns.

- Others may have difficulty seeing themselves as the child's first teacher and feel intimidated or overwhelmed by the teacher's expectations.

- Many parents are unsure of their parental abilities and indicate that they lack the skills that the teachers demonstrate in the centre.

- Some families may not understand the importance of early intervention and the benefits for their child; they may feel that asking for support from the centre undermines their role.

- Some families say that teachers demonstrate little appreciation or understanding of their cultures or values.

- They feel that educators are always watching them and assessing their parenting skills; as a result, parents can end up feeling too intimidated to ask for help or to offer to volunteer.

- Many families feel that they have nothing to contribute and lack the self-esteem to participate.

- Other families may feel that by paying their fees they fulfill their responsibility to the centre.

- In some homes, a situation such as family violence or substance abuse may be occurring and this family "secret" may not be revealed, particularly when the parent does not have a trusting relationship with the teacher.

- Even families who are motivated to work with the centre may come to resent the fact that child-care decisions are made by teachers and administrators without parental input. Nothing is more demoralizing for families than to realize that the centre's idea of involvement is the rubber-stamping of decisions made by staff.

- Some families complain that centres are slow to respond to concerns and provide families with no opportunity for evaluation or feedback.

We often hold misconceptions about families based on their socioeconomic status:

> Disadvantaged parents generally value education as much as their wealthier counterparts do. But they often have low achievement expectations for their own children because several problems stand in their and their children's way that prevents the actualization of their values. These obstacles then lower their aspirations. Indeed, studies indicate that parental expectations are key predictors of school achievement. Families encounter several problems that prevent them from actualizing their high value for education. They may lack the skills to help their children when they have school problems and they often feel intimidated or stigmatized by teachers. Teachers make more frequent requests for involvement from disadvantaged parents but these requests are often negative and when parents want to help their children with school work, they often meet resistance because the youngsters lack confidence in their competence. (Ambert, 2012: 162–163)[*]

---

[*]From Ambert, *Changing Families: Relationships in Context* 2/e
© Pearson Canada 2010. Reprinted by permission of the publisher.

When I look back on that period what I regret the most is the way I treated my mother; just because we were poor I felt that she was not as good as other mothers and whenever she'd try to help me with homework, I'd turn to her and give her my most despising look. Not only did I hurt her a lot and made her feel useless as a mother but I made her feel worthless as a person because even then she was more educated than I am now.

Source: From Ambert, *Changing Families: Relationships in Context* 2/e © Pearson Canada 2010. Reprinted by permission of the publisher.

Teachers should be mindful of the strong ties that exist between families and their children.

Lillian Katz notes that families are particularistic—they favour their own children over others, have an emotional stake in their children's welfare, are biased in favour of their own children, and put the needs of their own children first, even at the expense of other children's needs. (Gonzalez-Mena, 2010: 28)*

Teachers should make every effort to create welcoming environments!

Courtesy of Ingrid Crowther

*GONZALEZ-MENA, JANET, 50 STRATEGIES FOR COMMUNICATING AND WORKING WITH DIVERSE FAMILIES, 2nd Edition, © 2010. Reprinted and Electronically reproduced by permission of Pearson Education, Inc., Upper Saddle River, NJ.

DEMANDS ON FAMILIES

"Feelings of worth can flourish only in an atmosphere where individual differences are appreciated, mistakes are tolerated, communication is open, and rules are flexible—the kind of atmosphere that is found in a nurturing family."

—**Virginia Satir (Thinkexist.com)**

Each family has its own set of values, challenges, and needs. The extent to which families choose to be involved in a child-care centre's activities is determined by many factors, including the demands of the parents' work, family responsibilities, relationships with the staff, language proficiency, and general interest in participating. Often it is not a lack of interest that keeps families from becoming involved in the centre. Many families, overwhelmed by the stresses and responsibilities of their day-to-day life (see Figure 3.5), are unable to do more than engage in minimal interactions with teachers during drop-off and pick-up

A.N. Maslow (1954) created a hierarchy of human needs. Basic needs must be met before higher-level needs are addressed. These needs are

- biological—food, rest, water, shelter, clothing
- safety—protection from physical danger, absence of abuse or neglect
- love and belongingness—friendship, affection, acceptance
- self-esteem—self-esteem, respect, independence
- intellectual—social and academic endeavours, internally motivated
- aesthetic—to produce art, philosophy, creativity
- self-actualization—realizing one's own potential

FIGURE 3.5   Parental Responsibilities

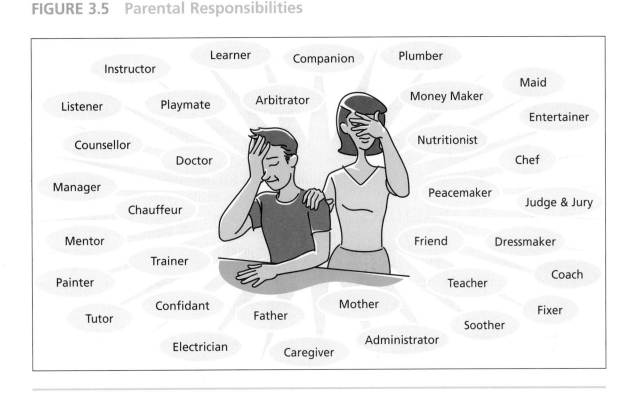

It is not hard to understand, after reviewing this model, that a family may not be interested in volunteering in the playroom because its members are concerned with where their next meal will come from or how to pay the gas bill. Their energies are taken up by providing basic needs for their family. Other families may be facing issues that make it difficult for them to focus on the needs of their children—drug and alcohol abuse in the home, divorce, family violence, caring for elders in

Parents wanting to be involved with their children are not always able to participate in the child-care centre because of family and work pressures.

BUILDING EFFECTIVE PARTNERSHIPS

their family, etc. Placing additional demands on this family would be unacceptable.

Galinsky (1988: 5) suggests that parental involvement in large measure reflects the characteristics of a parent's work life. "[J]obs differ a great deal and … certain characteristics of jobs such as autonomy (whether one has control over the tasks and timing of the job) and job demands (whether the job is demanding and hectic) affect parents' stress, health, marriages, and feelings of satisfaction and effectiveness as parents."

DEMANDS ON TEACHERS

> "Teachers are expected to reach unattainable goals with inadequate tools. The miracle is that at times they accomplish this impossible task."
>
> — **Dr. Haim Ginott** (Thinkexist.com, n.d.)

STRESS IN THE WORKPLACE

The changing nature of today's families has had a tremendous impact on family–teacher relationships. As a result of shifts in roles and responsibilities, the diverse, mobile group of families teachers may now serve may be very different from the small community that teachers may have served in the past. The support, income, and resources made available to teachers have not kept pace with the increasing workload placed on them, creating, in some situations, very stressful working environments. The commitment to integrating children with special needs into child-care programs, for example, has not always resulted in the provision of training and ongoing support for teachers.

Canada's changing demographics have challenged teachers to learn more about different cultures and values. Others may be working with an age group that does not suit their preferences or abilities; still others may not share the philosophical approach of other staff members or have not participated in workshops or upgrading to enhance their skills or knowledge. Teachers may be apprehensive about their relationships with families when working with wealthy or prominent community members (Rockwell et al., 2010). Some teachers suffer from low self-esteem, but professional development can strengthen their skills and therefore their self concept.

Though early childhood education professionals have nothing to be ashamed of, many of those who work with children under 5 still have difficulty feeling good about themselves, especially when the pay of teachers isn't as high as that of other professionals and the average preschool teacher or child care provider['s pay], even [for] those with bachelor's and master's degrees, keeps them at the poverty level on the economic scale. (Gonzalez-Mena, 2010: 15)[*]

Government legislation and changes in government policy can place more demands on teachers, who—recognizing the importance of advocacy work in the field of early childhood education—often stretch themselves too thin as they lobby and meet with other advocates. Some teachers are often just overwhelmed with the problems that many families are facing, such as poverty, housing issues, and employment, and don't know where to begin to provide support. Finally, many teachers are parents themselves, with the same demands on their time and energy as the families with whom they are working. All these factors tend to raise a teacher's stress level.

MENTAL HEALTH ISSUES

Like many in the population, teachers may suffer mental health issues:

Teachers and school staff take all of the demands placed upon them with an exceptional sense of personal commitment and responsibility that can exacerbate any problems they may be having. When it comes to mental health, their dedication can work against their ability to cope. Common mental health problems arise from life events as well as the pressure of work—and this is as true for teachers as it is for anyone else. Bereavements, divorces, financial difficulties, family history and personal characteristics can trigger mental health problems. These problems are common. Some people put off looking for help because they think that they will inevitably lose their job if they have a problem. In fact most staff are easily treated and with temporary adjustments do return to work. Very few people are permanently affected or so badly affected that they have to leave teaching. The earlier help is sought the more likely it is that any difficulty will be overcome. (Dept. for Children, Schools and Families, 2008)

Helpful advice for supporting coworkers and for managers can be found at *Common Mental Health Problems: Supporting School Staff by Taking Positive Action*:

http://www.lge.gov.uk/lge/aio/428696

LACK OF COMMUNICATION

> "Seek first to understand, then to be understood."
>
> —Stephen Covey (Thinkexist.com, n.d.)

Lack of communication is a key barrier to an effective partnership. It is sometimes difficult for families and teachers to know where the boundaries lie in their interactions: families may wonder how much information they should share with teachers, while teachers may worry that families will regard their requests for information as intrusive. But when teachers don't know the "family story," they can't understand why a simple request is met with resistance. Teachers may also be unsure of the extent to which families should be involved in programming for the children. Parents may feel that they have nothing to contribute to the centre if teachers make no effort to communicate exactly how families can participate. Many parents do not understand how the centre is run and, as a result, just don't know how to be involved. But teachers have a role to play in this:

> Too often teachers are quick to blame parents when they do not "come when called" by the school for various events or conferences and are viewed as "not caring," "deficient" (i.e., lacking time, interest or competence), "hard to reach" and having little to offer to the education of their children. (Amatea, 2009: 9)*

When issues arise, teachers may not always respond appropriately. Avoiding parents who the teacher believes are challenging does nothing to resolve the underlying issues. Because our culture encourages avoiding conflict in the workplace, teachers are often reluctant to speak directly about their concerns with families over things such as sleep routines, feeding, toilet learning, guiding behaviour, developmental issues, educational philosophy, and roles and responsibilities. In other situations, teachers may offer advice that is unwanted or, in a misguided effort to console a family member, make statements such as "I know just how you feel."

When teachers and families fail to communicate clearly with one another, children are put in an unenviable position. As York (1991: 188) observes,

> A teacher may expect children to behave one way and the parents expect their child to behave in an opposite way. [Thus] a child is caught in the middle

---

when a teacher wants him to ask for the toy that he wants to play with and his Native culture teaches him that it is selfish to ask for what he wants.

TEACHER AS EXPERT

> "Good teachers are those who know how little they know. Bad teachers are those who think they know more than they don't know."
>
> —R. Verdi (Karen's Linguistic Issues, n.d.)

Feeling that families are flawed by problems or deficiencies and that they need the teacher's support to "fix" their family is a negative and destructive approach to partnerships. This reinforces the "teacher as expert" model of one-way communication. Some educators believe that their view of what children need to learn to succeed should be dominant—that they know best. Educators who embrace this approach perceive that their job is to tell parents what they need to do at home to support their children's learning. If educators invite parents into the school, a "come when called" approach, they are asking parents to support the teacher's plan and routine, not to contribute to it.

> Parents may be asked to perform a myriad of tasks at the school or for the school (e.g., helping in the library, preparing food for school parties, building playgrounds, raising money, or serving on advisory boards or in parent–teacher associations), but in each of these they are expected to play a subordinate role. Because this is grounded in a mind-set of perceived parental deficits, educators often describe parents or caregivers—especially members of immigrant, low-income or culturally diverse families—in terms of their deficiencies. (Amatea, 2009: 31–33)

OPPOSING VALUES AND ATTITUDES

> "I have just three things to teach: simplicity, patience, compassion. These three are your greatest treasures."
>
> —Lao Tzu (Brainyquote.com, n.d.)

Conflict is bound to arise when teachers and families—each with their own values and attitudes—interact. Teachers and families will have divergent styles, cultural backgrounds, approaches, and interpersonal skills. People often have different perspectives on the same issues. Preconceived ideas of the role of the parent and teacher will affect teacher–family attitudes.

Families may be emotional about anything to do with their child. The child is seen as a reflection of themselves and any criticism may be seen as a personal attack. Issues such as independence versus dependence and autonomy versus compliance may affect the family–teacher relationship, and so too may cultural influences such as individualistic versus collectivist approaches. As Lieberman (1998: 15) states,

in individualistic cultures, people who sacrifice important personal goals for the sake of others may be considered masochistic, immature or overly dependent. In a collective culture, a person who fails to sacrifice personal goals for the welfare of others is often rebuked as selfish, disloyal and untrustworthy. Issues such as the child as part of a group vs the child as an individual, interdependence and helpfulness vs independence, cooperation vs competition, patience vs assertiveness etc. are just some areas that educators must consider when dealing with a diverse population.*

Many teachers grew up in middle-class families where education was valued and where emotional and economic support was available. Not all family members have had the same experience; for some, their interactions with schools and authority figures have been negative experiences. Some may be embarrassed by their lack of education and their memories of schools may be of humiliation and the resulting anger.

Research by the Institute for Responsive Education on educators' attitudes toward low-income parents shows that many didn't expect low-income parents to be productive participants in their children's education and, in turn, those parents felt that their participation wouldn't have much effect, and therefore they often had negative attitudes toward the school. Children internalize these attitudes of mutual disrespect. Children's self-worth is diminished or enhanced as the children sense how school personnel view the lifestyle and culture of their families, and these attitudes can breed tolerance or intolerance for others. (Barbour, Barbour and Scully, 2008: 6)

Yet Lott (2001: 247–259) reported that low-income parents describe their involvement with the school as meaningful when they have opportunities for informal communication with school staff and feel "invited in"; when they have a meaningful role in school activities other than that of consent giver or signer of notes; when they can rely upon teachers

and administrators to bridge the gap between themselves and school staff; when they can sense that teachers and administrators value their role in their child's learning; and when they believe that their involvement makes a difference in their child's educational experience and can see the direct benefits of their involvement for their children.

Families who are affluent and well educated may present other challenges. David Elkind (1981) wrote about the "hurried child" and many parents are in a rush to provide all of the resources to produce a "super child." They believe that by providing every possible benefit, their child will have the edge—the ability to rise above others. These families may pressure the teacher to push their child ahead to the older group long before the teacher believes that the child is ready, or be critical of the curriculum offered to the children. Teachers must do their best to help families understand the need for a developmentally appropriate environment that focuses not only on academics but also on play.

While we should not use our own family experience as the measuring stick for all families, Gestwicki (2010: 206) believes that

it is difficult not to look through our own "lens" when interacting with families. Teachers need to realize how their unconscious reactions to parents are influenced by their relationships with their own parents. A teacher who has unresolved hostilities with her own parents may have trouble relating comfortably to others who bear the label "parent." A teacher's experiences that have shaped his values about family life may conflict with the reality of parents with whom he works. People alienated by unconscious emotional responses can never really hear or speak to each other clearly.†

With an ethnocentric point of view, we view our own group (or family structure) as normal and often as best, safest, and most trustworthy. This tendency has been studied in the workplace, where it was found that the further people moved from their own sphere of knowledge and experience, the less likely they were to trust in the ability, competence, and even goodwill of others. Even when we have much in common with others, we still have a natural, egocentric tendency to value highly our own decisions, performance, and experiences while underestimating the value of others (Rudney, 2005).

*A.F. Lieberman, 1998. "Culturally sensitive intervention with children and families," *IMPRINT: The Newsletter of Infant Mental Health Promotion* 22 (Fall): 17. The Hospital for Sick Children, Infant Mental Health Promotion, Toronto. Reprinted by permission.

† From GESTWICKI, *Home, School, and Community Relations, 7E.* © 2010 Cengage Learning. Reproduced by permission. www.cengage.com/permissions.

Another area of conflicting values and attitudes in the guiding of behaviour is the one in which an authoritarian outlook meets a more democratic approach. Issues related to the development of morality, spoiling, self-help skills, spanking, and gender may all be contentious areas. Each teacher will have issues to which he or she reacts with great passion. One teacher may be resentful of families who send their ill child to the centre while another teacher may have the preconceived idea that children raised in a lone-parent family are disadvantaged. Issues that arise may relate more to the fact that parents do not always demonstrate their caring for their child in a way that meets the teacher's expectations.

Families too will feel more strongly about some issues than others. They may be shocked to learn that their child, who is used to sleeping with them, is required to sleep in a dark room, away from other adults and children during naptime. Other parents may rely on nontraditional health interventions and use rituals or practices that are foreign to the teachers in the room, some of which they may misconstrue as child abuse!

How do we maintain a professional approach when parents challenge our role?

"One infant-toddler care teacher, when told she had to wear an apron, refused to do so, because she in no way wanted to suggest to the parents that she was like their maid" (Gonzalez-Mena, 2010: 15).*

---

*GONZALEZ-MENA, JANET, 50 STRATEGIES FOR COMMUNICATING AND WORKING WITH DIVERSE

Without understanding the pressure that families face, sometimes teachers may believe that parents don't care about their child since they are not involved in the child-care centre. However, Yao (1988: 223–225) says,

It is important to remember that involvement and specific roles and responsibilities mean different things in different cultures. Consider the perception of many Asian immigrant parents. Due to cultural differences, many of these parents view communication with teachers as "checking up on them" and as an expression of disrespect. (pp. 223–225)

As a result, what appears to be apathy is more likely, in these cases, to be a sign of respect. Other cultures hold similar views. Unless they receive sincere, personal invitations to become involved, many parents will continue to stay away; not out of disdain, but out of respect. (Whitaker and Fiore, 2001: 33)

DIFFERING EDUCATIONAL PHILOSOPHIES

> "Education is not filling a pail but the lighting of a fire."
>
> —**William Butler Yeats**
> **(The Quotations Page, n.d.)**

FAMILIES, 2nd Edition, © 2010. Reprinted and Electronically reproduced by permission of Pearson Education, Inc., Upper Saddle River, NJ.

Inside LOOK

How each of us treat a cold or a fever is most likely embedded in the rituals and traditions of our childhood. In China, Old Chinese "cash coins"—round copper or bronze coins with a square hole in the middle surrounded by four Chinese characters—served as the major form of currency in China for 2000 years. Chinese cash coins are believed to have curative powers and have historically played a role in traditional Chinese medicine. *Gua sha* is a Chinese medical technique historically used to reduce fever in patients suffering from cholera but also used in cases of sunstroke, asthma, bronchitis, headaches, digestive disorders, etc. Oil is first placed on the skin and then the edge of an old cash coin is used to scrape the skin along acupuncture meridians. It is believed that this medical procedure will help release the disease stagnant under the patient's skin. The technique leaves some skin bruises but these fade away in a few days. Practices from other cultures include taking oil of oregano to cure a cold or a mustard plaster on the chest. What remedies exist in your home culture?

BUILDING EFFECTIVE PARTNERSHIPS

Families may not fully understand the educational goals that teachers have established for the children with whom they are working. Conversely, teachers may give little time or thought to the goals the families would like their children to achieve.

> The desire to improve children's readiness for school learning may lead to an emphasis on early academics or direct instruction of reading and number skills during the early years. How much academic content and method is appropriate for children in their early years? Although many professional early childhood educators understand and support developmentally appropriate practices for young children, some are less grounded in developmental knowledge. They are more easily influenced by administrators, parents and policymakers who push for academic experiences for young children that look a good deal like those presented to older children. (Bertrand and Gestwicki, 2012: 61)[*]

Murphy Kilbride (1997: 72) states,

> [A]s early childhood educators, we are sometimes guilty of preaching pompously to parents. We tell them that they just don't understand the developmental needs of young children. We say that all children benefit most from an unstructured, open-ended, play-based program. This says two things to some parents: the highly structured, very strict programs they went through as children were all wrong; they have no idea what is best for their own

child. These messages are not only confusing and insulting, they are untrue.

Gonzalez-Mena (2008: 28) draws attention to another pressure faced by many families: "parents are targets for marketers who want to sell them goods and services. Virtually all parents want the best for their children. They want their children to be smart, competent, and successful and marketers prey on parents' hopes and dreams."[†] One only has to walk into the parenting section of any bookstore or go online to see the hundreds of selections by physicians or child development experts with advice for raising the "perfect" child. The pressure on parents to raise exceptional children is enormous. If you look even more carefully at the bookshelves you will see many titles designed to either assist parents in holding their children's schools accountable or inform them about problems in the school system: *Left Back: A Century of Battles Over School Reform, The School Leaders Our Children Deserve, Leadership for Change and School Reform, Bad Teachers: The Essential Guide for Concerned Parents, Waiting for a Miracle: Why Schools Can't Solve Our Problems—And How We Can, Angry Parents, Failing Schools*. When you consider these titles, it is clear that these authors believe that there is something wrong with our school system and that parents need to do something about it. Powerful DVDs such as *Waiting for Superman*— not to mention

---

[*]From BERTRAND/GESTWICKI. *Essentials of Early Childhood Education, 4E.* © 2012 Nelson Education Ltd. Reproduced by permission. www.cengage.com/permissions.

[†]GONZALEZ-MENA, JANET, 50 EARLY CHILDHOOD STRATEGIES FOR WORKING AND COMMUNICATING WITH DIVERSE FAMILIES, 1st Edition, © 2007. Reprinted and Electronically reproduced by permission of Pearson Education, Inc., Upper Saddle River, NJ.

Inside LOOK

Equinox Holistic Alternative School, founded in 2009, is located in Roden Public School in Toronto. This school supports children from junior kindergarten to Grade Eight. Roden also includes a child care centre for children 2 1/2 to 12 years of age, as well as a Parenting and Family Literacy Centre for parents, caregivers, and children up to 6 years of age. There is a strong relationship with staff in these programs to ensure that the children's individual needs are met. Equinox's open-concept school houses a large music room, art room, gym, library, and computer lab. The values of this school environment support a holistic approach to teaching with the total engagement of the children. Kindergarten children spend most of their day outside and older children engage in trips to local parks and ravines to interact with nature. Equinox is a recognized TDSB Eco-School with Gold Standing. A school council ensures that families are actively involved in decision making. Parents meet on a regular basis to plan events and to discuss current educational practices.

Source: Toronto District School Board (n.d.).

magazines, websites, and blogs—continue to add to parent worries. While many forms of media refer to the school system and not necessarily early childhood environments, as teachers, we face the difficult task of changing these prevalent misconceptions by providing high-quality learning and care.

Lowell Krough (1994: 327–328) provides an account of the conflicting educational philosophies that arose at a Montessori school that functioned as a parent co-operative:

> [O]ne year, a couple of the fathers decided that the teachers should be more accountable for the progress of their pupils. They put forth the idea that charts should be made showing how many children in each class had "mastered" each of the pieces of Montessori equipment. Teachers with the highest score would get the biggest raises. The teachers were horrified at this total misinterpretation of Montessori's views of individualized, self-paced learning. Banding together, they realized that they hadn't been doing a sufficient job of parent education. The result was a monthly newsletter containing articles about Montessori's philosophies, and guest-teacher visits at the parent meetings in which the teachers answered questions about what was happening in the classrooms. The fathers eventually agreed to retreat from their plan until they received more information on the Montessori philosophy. While they later tried to reintroduce the plan, other families had become sufficiently knowledgeable that it was voted down.

It is critical for teachers to understand how education is delivered around the world. Many families come to us from an educational system that is very formal and teacher directed, very different from the play-based, child-centred emergent curriculum approach that is utilized in early childhood environments today. It is our role as ECE teachers to help parents understand the benefits of this play-based, child-centred method. A family's approach to an individualistic or collectivist viewpoint will also influence their interactions with teachers. Parents with a strong individualistic approach will see the importance of children learning that they are unique and special individuals, and expect their child to receive much individual attention, failing to understand group needs. Those with a collectivist perspective are more likely to value cooperation with others and respect for authority, are more likely to support group needs over the individual, and want teachers to reflect a sense of social responsibility within the centre. They may be very reluctant to openly discuss their child.

Parents are often reluctant to discuss how to manage their child's behaviour. They may find it is embarrassing and assume that it implies some negligence on their part. They often hear advice from relatives, neighbours, and the Internet, much of which is inaccurate and perhaps not applicable to their child at all!

We need to help families understand that children who are pushed beyond their developmental capabilities may suffer a loss of self-esteem, feel additional stress, and lose the confidence to try new things. We need to assure families that an active play-based environment that focuses on all domains of the

Inside LOOK

Observation tools from the Early Learning for Every Child Today (ELECT) model will ease discussions between parents and teachers. A well-run emergent curriculum forms a solid base for meaningful communication with all parents. The teacher's written observations of each child's development and interests can be shared frequently with the families of each child. The parents have the opportunity to make and share their written or verbal observations of their own child. These observational exchanges offer several benefits:

- They can help parents understand both the curriculum and their child.
- They give parents objective and reliable information about child development (in itself a teaching tool).
- Parents realize that a teacher is paying individual attention to their child, not just to the group as a whole.
- They encourage meaningful dialogue between parents and teacher around expanding on the child's interests (more than buying more toys). Parents then feel valued and more motivated to take an interest in their child and the program.
- They provide an opportunity to mutually discuss appropriate behaviour guidance strategies.

child's growth is the best preparation possible for a positive start to more formal school learning.

Some families may be reassured when they can see that their child is developing "normally" and may benefit from the teacher's sharing of developmental benchmarks; for example, at the Hanen Centre website, guidelines for language and literacy development can be accessed. This may relieve some of the pressure that families may be feeling.

http://www.hanen.org/Home.aspx

BOOKS FOR ADULTS

Simple Signing with Young Children: A Guide for Infant, Toddler, and Preschool Teachers, by C. Garboden Murray

How Children Acquire Language: A New Answer, by Dr. Laura-Ann Petitto

Baby Signs, by Linda Acredolo and Susan Goodwyn

Inside LOOK

Using new languages with some families and their children may include more than just communication interactions. Delia Avarell is a deaf bilingual ECE graduate and currently an educational assistant; she is also an American Sign Language (ASL) and Early Literacy Consultant for the Ontario Cultural Society of the Deaf. She contributes the following:

While I was in my field placement, some children were curious and asked questions about why we had an interpreter and others asked why I use a language that they don't use. Some of the preschoolers picked up some basic ASL words quickly during lunch, snacks, play activities, and outdoors. One preschooler liked reading books with me because I believe she enjoyed seeing the new language. I found it very challenging since our use of languages (American Sign Language and English) were different. However, I felt they were lucky to have exposure to a deaf ASL-using student teacher. Since interpreter support was not always available during the day, using a new language with families can be a challenge. It emphasizes the importance of having a full-time interpreter available for the staff working at the child care centre when ECE deaf students are doing their placements in an English-speaking environment. Many parents were thrilled for me to use ASL with their children. Deaf ASL-using students can use text messaging and videophone (iChat, Skype, ooVoo, etc.). English-speaking parents can also write on paper if necessary. Hearing parents and deaf student-teachers need to be patient with each other and show respect for their cultures, languages and differences.

Dr. Laura-Ann Petitto's book *How Children Acquire Language: A New Answer* suggests that using American Sign Language with deaf babies from birth helps them acquire skills on the identical maturational time course as hearing babies acquire spoken language. As indicated by Acredolo and Goodwyn, signing babies understood more words, had larger vocabularies, and engaged in more sophisticated play than babies who did not learn to sign. In my field placement, I gained a lot of experience teaching bilingual (American Sign Language and English) children. I felt I had a positive relationship with the deaf bilingual students. I looked up to the deaf bilingual teacher as a role model and mentor and she taught me many things. It has been a real investment in my future career and it has enriched my life. I have strong interpersonal communication skills, and my positive approach enabled me to work effectively with a number of teachers and staff at the school. I have a passion about the cultural and linguistic needs and accessibility of child-care centres for the Deaf ASL-using community. American Sign Language and Deaf ASL culture are critical to effective communication and interaction and its effect on children's health, safety, cognition and well-being in both the Deaf and hearing communities. I am a Deaf advocate in early childhood education and I support the delivery of high-quality care and education for children and their families. My interest is to protect the rights of deaf bilingual children by working with their families for the best life possible by helping them become effective advocates who are knowledgeable about their child's rights and their rights as parents.

Source: Reprinted by permission of Delia Averall.

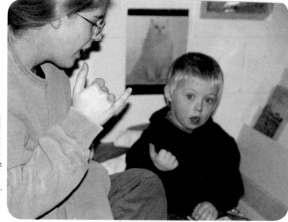

Even very young children can learn to sign.

EXCLUSIONARY OR OFFENSIVE TERMINOLOGY AND PRACTICE

It would be an interesting exercise for students to brainstorm about the many rules in place in child-care centres that present barriers to families' full participation. Flexibility is essential to stay focused on our goals. No matter how well planned our efforts, there are always details to work out, new information to absorb, and new ways to incorporate change that supports our families. Every family and every child is unique; there is no "one size fits all"!

Often the practices and language teachers' use offend or exclude families. Here are some examples:

- Centres where hours of morning entry are rigidly reinforced; for example, "All children must be in the centre by 9:30 a.m." does not respect the fact that many families may work nontraditional hours and the early morning hours may be the one time that the family can be with each other.

- Teachers use the terms *they* or *those parents* rather than referring to family members as individuals. The use of these terms creates a feeling of exclusion while creating an "us" versus "them" mind-set among the teachers.

Teachers who describe parents and other family members as noncompliant, uncooperative, or difficult convey the message that only teachers should dictate the conditions of the partnership. Similarly, labelling families as dysfunctional, in denial, overprotective, uninvolved, or uncaring may imply a judgment that fails to incorporate a full understanding of a family's circumstances. (Hughson, 1994–95: 56)

- The terms *atypical* and *at risk* should be avoided. They imply that there is something

wrong with the child or the family and that somehow they are to blame for their problems.

- To refer to children as coming from "broken homes" is to ignore the fact that many children live in lone-parent homes where they are well cared for, stimulated, nurtured, and loved.

- The term *one-parent family* is misleading, since many children continue to have contact with both parents as well as other relatives. To use the term *single-parent family* denotes marital status that may not reflect the family's situation.

- Terms such as *reconstituted*, *blended*, and *step* are used to describe some families. It is important for teachers to know which term each family prefers.

- Some families may object to siblings who are not related by blood being called *stepsister* or *stepbrother* or *half-sister* or *half-brother* and may prefer the term *sister* or *brother*.

- For gay and lesbian parents, forms that request information about *father* and *mother* instead of *parent* or *co-parent* set them apart.

- For parents who are illiterate, complicated written communications make understanding centre practices, policies, and events nearly impossible.

Centres that do not consider the importance of communicating in the parents' first language exclude those families. For example, avoid saying things like "I only speak a little bit of Swahili—I just can't do it." It is offensive to parents because this gives a signal that their native language is not valued. Instead say, "I really like learning other languages even though it is difficult for me," and show interest by asking how to say a phrase in the parents' native language. (Hepworth Berger and Riojas-Cortez, 2012: 5)[*]

- The celebration of Father's Day and Mother's Day may be stressful for children who have only one parent, who have gay or lesbian parents, who are adopted, or who are in foster care.

- Some teachers are unaware of how their use of language may offend adoptive parents—when, for example, a teacher refers to the birth parent

---

[*]BERGER, EUGENIA HEPWORTH; RIOJAS-CORTEZ, MARI R., PARENTS AS PARTNERS IN EDUCATION: FAMILIES AND SCHOOLS WORKING TOGETHER, 8th Edition, © 2012. Reprinted and Electronically reproduced by permission of Pearson Education, Inc., Upper Saddle River, NJ.

as the "real" parent or "natural" parent rather than the "biological" parent (see Chapter 9).

- Some educators, when using the term *primary caregiver*, seem to forget that families are the primary caregivers. Educators must not forget that families are the primary caregivers, and families have the long-term relationship with the child. Educators need to see themselves as supplements and supports to the family, and not assume parental responsibilities.

- What's in a name? Some parents may feel that their child is accepted into the child-care program more easily if the child has an English-sounding name. We must reassure parents that all children are welcomed with their given names and that teachers will pronounce these names correctly.

- Favouritism is another behaviour that leads to exclusion. Few things are more destructive to the family–teacher relationship than the thought that the teacher prefers some families and children over others.

- When teachers are not sincere in their praise of the children, families may not trust the teacher's opinion. Authentic praise is critical.

BIAS, PREJUDICE, RACISM

"Once social change begins, it cannot be reversed. You cannot under educate the person who has learned to read. You cannot humiliate the person who feels pride. You cannot oppress the people who are not afraid anymore."

—Cesar Chavez, American farm worker, labour leader, and civil rights activist (Goodreads, n.d.)

Our society continues to struggle to eradicate actions and words that are associated with racism, ethnocentrism, elitism, sexism, homophobia, and discrimination against people with disabilities. Bullying and other types of violence among children are often associated with prejudice. Families and educators have a responsibility to confront bias and prejudice when it occurs. In the process of doing this, teachers need to examine their own biases and expectations regarding their relationships with families.

In many early childhood environments, invisible (but not imaginary) lines exist based on race and class that prevent effective interaction. Indeed, there may be real differences in backgrounds between teachers and parents. Some teachers may unconsciously demonstrate an ethnocentric approach, the tendency to assume that one's culture and way of life represent the norm or are superior to all others.

Britzman (1998) suggests that we unconsciously desire learning only that which affirms what we already know and our own sense of self. In fact, it would be argued that we unconsciously desire to learn only that which affirms our sense that we are good people and that we resist learning anything that reveals our complicity with racism, homophobia, and other forms of oppression. Anti-oppressive education, then, needs to involve overcoming this resistance to change and learning, instead to desire change, to desire difference. (Kumashiro, 2010: 43)

Some teachers have acquired biases and prejudices towards others; for example, teachers' reactions to families who are more educated or economically advantaged may differ from their reactions to families with lower education and economic status, and these reactions affect the family–teacher relationship. The more similar parents are to us, the more credit we give them for good things that happen and the more forgiveness and understanding we give when bad things happen. It is a natural human response, but it is not the perspective that leads to the most success (Rudney, 2005).

The communication that low-income parents have with schools is typically negative and problem-focused. Most of these parents perceive themselves as being talked down to and blamed when required to interact with school staff. Despite wanting an equal, person-to-person relationship and not a "professional-client" relationship with school staff, many parents report that they are often dissatisfied with school personnel who are "too business-like" or "patronizing" or who "talk down" to them. Culturally disenfranchised groups are particularly vulnerable to feelings of judgment and blame. (Amatea, 2009: 9)[*]

Painful as it is to admit, when we reflect on why socioeconomic minority families come to school less than we think they should, we need to remind ourselves of realities such as those Carol Phillips has written about:

We must examine institutional racism and how it operates. Many of us have been taught to understand racism only as an individual attitude, and therefore

[*]AMATEA, ELLEN S., BUILDING CULTURALLY RESPONSIVE FAMILY-SCHOOL RELATIONSHIPS, 1st Edition, © 2009. Reprinted and Electronically reproduced by permission of Pearson Education, Inc., Upper Saddle River, NJ.

we believe that individual "bigots" are responsible for all the racist damage.... We must explore the stereotypes we have learned that are racist and ethnocentric and develop strategies for changing what we believe about ourselves and others. Too many of us still unconsciously treat light-skinned children better than dark-skinned ones, and the working mother better than the one on welfare. (in Greenberg, 1989: 70)

As one parent says,

As I see it, the "multiculturalists" fail to exhibit any sign of awareness of cultural diversity within a race (i.e., they don't distinguish between Northern Chinese, Cantonese, Fukienese, Shanghai people, etc., let alone Japanese, Vietnamese, Malays, Lao, etc.); they tend to lump us all into one group, implying "they're all the same, you can treat them all this way." And they have nothing to offer as solutions to conflicts within a race, e.g., the long-standing tension between Chinese and Japanese. They don't even acknowledge that such intra-racial conflicts exist. I say if they don't know about this, the cultural differences or conflicts, it's hard for me to believe they care. (in Lindsay, 1999)

It is my conviction that, although we are not born with racial and prejudicial concerns, through experience, observation, learning and interactions with society as a whole, we soon develop these characteristics and they become ingrained into our personalities whether we realize it or not.... Through an intelligent examination of our belief and value systems, we can perhaps begin to focus on where our biases have come from and help to change where they may be heading. (James, 1989: 68)

Janmohamed (2005) has suggested that in an effort to be inclusive and to encourage a pluralistic approach to education, we have lost the opportunity to challenge the dominant culture and seem unable to equip students for putting antiracism education principles into practice. Racism, sexism, and class bias are economically, politically, educationally, and institutionally produced. Faculty can help ECE students overcome these social barriers by engaging them in explorations of different ways to resist oppression. When ECE students are asked how they integrate antibias approaches in field placement, countless numbers have discussed the Spanish music they shared, or how they made fruit salad with "exotic" fruit.

Clearly a more strategic process needs to be developed within the discourse of antiracism, antibias education so that students with early childhood diplomas do not limit their experience to simulated or mock celebrations of Diwali and Hanukkah. Instead of focusing on festivals, we need a greater emphasis on diverse child-rearing practices beyond the dominant Western understanding. The shift from an antibias perspective to an antiracist education perspective is

Inside LOOK

A classroom teacher's experience highlights the influence of background and the challenges to re-creating a bridge. Participating in a teacher group discussion of intercultural communication, a teacher wrote (as if realizing it for the first time):

Culture means more than holidays and food; it includes all of the subtle patterns of communication, verbal and nonverbal, that people use every day. I noticed how easily I valued cultural diversity in the abstract or in the form of occasional holidays yet how readily I rejected cultural differences when they appeared in the form of parents' different approaches to child rearing.

She went on to write about the group's reflection:

We realized that unexamined values, beliefs, and patterns of interaction learned when we were children exert a powerful influence on our communication and care giving routines. Our sincere intentions didn't prevent us from rejecting parents' diverse values when they challenged our own cherished beliefs. We were often unable to set aside our own cultural values long enough to listen to parents.

Source: Sturm, C. 1997. "Creating Parent–Teacher Dialogue: Intercultural Communication in Child Care," *Young Children* 52 (5): 34–38. © NAEYC. Reprinted with permission.

a difficult one that questions the implications of how ECE training programs are delivered. However, if there is a desire to ensure that real change happens, changes do not happen without teachers, and teachers do not institute changes unless they understand them and believe in them (Gaine, 2000).

Unfortunately, as James and Muhammad (n.d.: 1) argue, "The culture of minorities tends to be seen as 'foreign' or 'add-on' rather than an integral part of our Canadian culture." We nurture racism in children until, by the time they are adults, they fit into the structures of racism that is our society. Society should intervene at the earliest possible time in a child's life with positive initiatives in the area of racial attitudes.

Howard Clifford, child-care advocate, has said, "A daycare program that results in a child's feeling ashamed of his family or shaken in his confidence and pride in his ethnic or cultural heritage is a failure." The need to create a better atmosphere has even been touched on and lobbied for by those outside the child-care education sector. Maya Angelou said,

> We must re-create an attractive and caring attitude in our homes and in our worlds. If our children are to approve of themselves, they must see that we

approve of ourselves. If we persist in self-disrespect and then ask our children to respect themselves, it is as if we break all their bones and then insist that they win Olympic gold medals for the hundred-yard dash. Outrageous.

It is necessary for us as teachers to examine our own attitudes, experiences, and impressions in regards to oppression, marginalization, and racism in order to create a community that is inclusive of all.

GUILT

> "Calvin: There's no problem so awful, that you can't add some guilt to it and make it even worse." *
>
> **Taken from a CALVIN AND HOBBES cartoon © 1986 Watterson. Dist. By UNIVERSAL UCLICK. Reprinted with permission. All rights reserved.**

It is astonishing how frequently today's parents refer to guilt. Many factors precipitate this feeling, including the ideal parent imaged in the various media; the changes in lifestyles and role behaviours,

---

Inside LOOK

Pro-Diversity Education

Anti-bias work or more appropriately pro-diversity work, is essentially optimistic work about the future for our children. Pro-diversity teachers are committed to the principle that every child deserves to develop to his or her fullest potential. Pro-diversity work provides teachers a way to examine and transform their understanding of children's lives and also do self-reflective work to more deeply understand their *own* lives. Even when we believe that we are not biased against others, at times our language may reflect otherwise. Phrases like "throws like a girl," "that movie was gay," "she's retarded" are all examples of words that can cause a great deal of pain. The heart of pro-diversity work is a vision of a world in which *all* children are able to blossom, and each child's particular abilities and gifts are able to flourish. Pro-diversity education has four core goals. Together, they provide a safe, supportive learning community for all children.

- **Goal 1:** Each child will demonstrate self-awareness, confidence, family pride, and positive social identities.
- **Goal 2:** Each child will express comfort and joy with human diversity; accurate language for human differences, and deep, caring human connections.
- **Goal 3:** Each child will increasingly recognize unfairness, have language to describe unfairness, and understand that unfairness hurts.
- **Goal 4:** Each child will demonstrate empowerment and the skills to act, with others or alone, against prejudice and/or discriminatory actions".

Source: Derman-Sparks, L., and Olsen Edwards, J. 2010. *Anti-Bias Education for Young Children and Ourselves*. Washington, DC: NAEYC. © NAEYC. Reprinted with permission.

which mean that many parents live quite differently than their parents did; the prevalent feeling that parents should produce children who will do better than they have done and the social attitude that "there are no bad children, only bad parents." The working mother may feel guilt because she is breaking a known pattern and is aware of the mixed reviews coming in from researchers and society. This is a strong message to fight against for most mothers. Probably a good portion of the Supermom phenomenon is fed by this guilt, pushing her to make sure her child misses no right or privilege. Much of today's materialism and marketing frenzies feed off this emotion of guilt. If the child has been deprived of time and interaction, at least he or she can have the latest item advertised. (Gestwicki, 2010: 112–113)[*]

In her study of mothers who had children in child-care arrangements, Uttal (2002) found that the responsibility for choosing care and education programs for their children was left up to mothers, even if fathers or other family members were involved. With responsibility comes the potential for error. The mothers wanted very much to believe that their children were getting high-quality care, but they were worried that perhaps they had made a bad choice and their children were not in the best situation. Gestwicki (2004: 200) reports that "50 percent of all parents and 59 percent of minority parents report that they are never sure how well their children will be treated when they leave them in a centre."

Worries about safety, programming, and staffing were high on the list of concerns for mothers in Uttal's (2002) study. Every article printed in the paper or broadcast on television about suspected child abuse only adds to a parent's worry. This is particularly evident in families where their children are in unregulated private home care in which other adults are not present to monitor each other's behaviour. Uttal's study confirmed that the mother's comfort level with the child-care professionals made a difference. Relationships matter!

RIVALRY

"Will the teacher replace me in the eyes of my child given that I spend all that time away from him when I am working?"

A parent comes into a centre one morning and enthusiastically says, "I have to tell you, Lily took her first step yesterday!" The teacher smiles and replies, "Oh, she walked here last week." The teacher's remark wasn't meant to hurt, but it made the parent feel unimportant—and, what's more, it created competitive feelings (Weissbourd, 1992). It is important that as teachers we never take these moments away from families. Firsts—whether they are a first step, a first tooth, or a first word—should be left for families to discover.

Some families may secretly resent the ease with which their child has made the transition from home care to child care, and their underlying fear is that the teacher will replace them in their child's affection. When rivalry exists between a parent and an educator, the child is placed in the untenable position of having to decide where his or her loyalty lies, which can be devastating for the child.

When the most personal aspects of a child's care are taken over by another, it is understandable that parents may feel uncertain. A mother may feel that she is losing her child to another which threatens her own identify as feelings of jealousy and competition arise. There are often ambivalent emotions here: a mother wants her child to be independent and happy away from her but resents the perception that a teacher is taking over in the child's regard. (Gestwicki, 2010: 207)[†]

Teachers may also become strongly attached to children in their care. At times they may cross the boundary between the appropriate practice of caring for and supporting the child to inappropriate thoughts of "rescuing" the child. This may be a reflection of the teacher's need to be wanted and loved, as well as the feeling that the teacher would be a better parent. This feeling is an occupational hazard for those who work with children; teachers need to monitor their emotional dependence.

Rivalry may also occur when teachers feel resentful of the income disparity between themselves and some of the parents in the centre or are envious of a particular family and their lifestyle or relationship.

FEELINGS OF VULNERABILITY AND FEAR

"There can be no vulnerability without risk; there can be no community without vulnerability; there can be no peace, and ultimately no life, without community."

—M. Scott Peck (Based on a True Story, n.d.)

[*] From GESTWICKI, *Home, School, and Community Relations, 7E.* © 2010 Cengage Learning. Reproduced by permission. www.cengage.com/permissions.

[†] From GESTWICKI, *Home, School, and Community Relations, 7E.* © 2010 Cengage Learning. Reproduced by permission. www.cengage.com/permissions.

Fear affects teachers as well as parents, and teachers may do little to encourage family engagement when they are uncertain or insecure about their teaching skills. When families have contact with teachers, they, like the teachers themselves, may feel vulnerable to criticism—criticize my child and you criticize me! After all, their child, who is an extension of themselves, is on view.

> First-time parents particularly can be quite frightened of the teacher's opinion, and all families yearn to know that the teacher likes their child and that the child is doing well. The relationship can be doubly sensitive when a parent, usually the mother, seeks validation of her own worth as a person by ascertaining that the teacher approves of her offspring. She is all too ready to believe the teacher (and to feel threatened and angry) if blame is implied. (Hendrick and Chandler, 1996: 162)

Fear of reprisal against their children silences many parents. They fear that if they speak up about a concern or an issue, the teacher may be upset and take out his or her anger out on the child. Teachers, too, may withhold information that parents should have because they fear reprisal from the parents.

Some parents would be surprised if they knew how vulnerable some teachers really are, especially inexperienced ones. Both families and teachers may feel anxious about one another. Both may be eager to please, hold the other in awe, feel respect or fear, feel hostile or submissive—a full range of emotions may be clearly evident. For Gestwicki (1992: 122–125), a barrier to effective parent–teacher relationships is fear: *fear of criticism* (both families and teachers can be concerned about being judged by the other); *fear hidden behind a professional mask* (an insecure teacher may use his or her status as a professional to intimidate families or keep them at arm's length); *fear of failure* (teachers need to understand that it takes work, time, and energy to build effective partnerships); and *fear of differences* (many teachers have difficulty relating to or accepting cultures, values, or customs that differ from their own).

However, when families and teachers share observations and information about the child, "this sense of sharing and cooperation [can serve to diminish] competitive and critical feelings" (Pawl, 1993: 223).

The inclusion of children with special needs began in the mid-1970s and today is much more common. However, some teachers may have negative feelings about working with children with special needs. These feelings may be grounded in their fear of not knowing how best to support the child and family in this situation, they may be afraid of doing something that harms the child, or they may be reluctant to learn about the equipment or medical intervention that the child requires.

It is important for teachers to recognize the limitations of their ECE training and engage with resource personnel in the community, such as counsellors, parent support groups, pediatricians, or psychologists. This interprofessional approach will provide a deeper understanding of how educators can support not only the child but also the family.

Inside LOOK

Shortly after the beginning of a program, I would suddenly note an increase in the number of [teachers'] complaints about parents: 'That father is dressing his child too warmly,' 'That mother is feeding her child junk food.' … I would greet this phenomenon with pleasure, because it indicated to me that the teacher was becoming attached to the children; yet I saw this time as an important crossroad. Without help and support, the staff complaints could turn into a real rivalry for the child's affection, including child rescue fantasies. With staff discussion, however, this caregiver–child attachment could be seen as positive and channelled away from rivalry into a caring that would not undermine the parents.

Source: Galinsky, E. 1988. "Parents and Teacher–Caregivers: Sources of Tension, Sources of Support," *Young Children* 43 (3): 4-12. © NAEYC. Reprinted with permission.

LACK OF TEACHER TRAINING AND PROFESSIONAL DEVELOPMENT

> "The illiterate of the 21st century will not be those who cannot read and write, but those who cannot learn, unlearn, and relearn."
>
> **—Alvin Toffler (Goodreads, n.d.)**

Many teachers enter the field of ECE because they want to work with children, but they underestimate the importance of family involvement and the amount of time that teachers spend interacting with other adults. The very qualities that enable teachers to work effectively with young children may make them uncomfortable in their dealings with adults. Galinsky (1988: 8) reports on a study that found that "professionals with the most positive perceptions of parents were more likely to have more education and to be more experienced."* Therefore, there clearly is a need for educators to pursue on an ongoing basis the knowledge, skills, and self-awareness needed to be professionally competent by participating in life-long professional development and continuous learning activities.

Not surprisingly, teachers who have been in the field for a number of years may be susceptible to burnout. Hepworth Berger (2004: 411) states that

[b]oth teachers and parents experience burnout. It is felt most when what you are trying to do seems unproductive, or you may think you have few alternatives that would change or improve the course of events. This frustration can lead to a feeling of being trapped. It can happen to any teacher and any parent.... Those who set high standards and aim for perfection are sometimes more likely to experience burnout, as are those who feel a need to be in control. Feelings of anger, guilt, depression, self-doubt, and irritability are symptoms of burnout.

Unfortunately, this condition is rarely addressed in the context of family–teacher interactions. Support for teachers who are tired and overworked should be an ongoing part of professional development. Too often, professional development is not supported by the administration of the centre. Many administrators lack a clear understanding of how their support would ensure a healthy and revitalized staff or have no resources to draw on. As for any professional, keeping up with new research should be an integral part of a teacher's and centre's responsibility. As

*Galinsky, E. 1988. "Parents and Teacher–Caregivers: Sources of Tension, Sources of Support," *Young Children* 43 (3): 4-12. © NAEYC. Reprinted with permission.

an example, centres must invest time in training educators to learn more about the variety of communication opportunities via technology and find money for technology upgrades in the centre. The question is not *if* we should use technology, but *how* and *why* we use technology to improve program quality, increase responsiveness to families, and expand opportunities for professional development.

It is reasonable to assume that technology will continue to dramatically change the way we live and work. Donohue (2010: 1) believes that "when used effectively, technology tools can support and enhance learning, teaching, documentation, program management, customer service, staff and parent communication, marketing, staff development, networking, and advocacy."

The Internet also provides a wide range of professional development opportunities for staff. For example, the Childcare Resource and Research Unit at **http://www.childcarecanada.org** allows teachers to build a library of reference materials on all sorts of topics related to working with families. Subscribing to magazines and journals such as *Interaction* (Canadian Child Care Federation) and *Young Children* (National Association for the Education of Young Children), and to provincial newsletters and bulletins, provides other sources of relevant information. Teachers may compile a list of agencies where parents can access information and DVDs in the community. Joining a child-care organization both locally and internationally will keep teachers abreast of the newest research. Sharing websites and establishing blogs with colleagues is also a positive step in growing and learning. Our world is becoming smaller through our ability to connect with each other through the Internet. In some countries—including Sweden, Iceland, Denmark, Finland, and France—innovative and comprehensive early childhood services are supporting young families and their children. Research on this may inform practice and provide opportunities for advocacy at the municipal, provincial, and federal level.

Community college and university training programs need to reflect the needs of families as partners in education. Students' field experiences seldom provide enough emphasis or time to develop meaningful relationships with families. Students have difficulty practising the skills they learn in their courses because most family members want to speak to the teacher rather than the student to discuss issues or concerns. Since surveys show that new teachers are unprepared to work with families, perhaps it is time to review the delivery of early childhood programs

I have been a faculty in the field of early childhood for many years, but my background was as a playroom teacher working over many years with infants, preschoolers, and kindergarten children. I am sometimes amazed at the stories from playroom teachers that my students relate to me after their field placement experiences. Many have said that their co-operating teachers say that "those people in the college who are teaching you these courses haven't got a clue. They don't know what it is like to work on the floor day after day. All of these fancy ideas just don't work." I am so disappointed to hear these comments and really see it as a way of just not being open to innovative or new ways of thinking and not valuing the ideas that students bring to their field experiences. More importantly I am concerned about how this affects my students, who are so eager and excited about their work with children and their families! I did work on the floor, and I do know that strong relationships with families are not only possible, they are necessary!

to place greater emphasis on the importance of family engagement. Colleges and university should also be strategically involved in providing opportunities for teachers currently in the field who would benefit from deepening their knowledge and skills about the need for family engagement through professional development opportunities.

NEGATIVE ATTITUDES ABOUT MEN IN ECE

"A teacher affects eternity; he can never tell where his influence stops."

—Henry Adams (Teacher Appreciation, n.d.)

The College of ECE in Ontario reports that its current membership comprises more than 36,000 members and 1.2 percent (or 432) of their membership is male registered early childhood educators (RECEs).

National statistics are difficult to ascertain but Beach, Bertrand, and Cleveland (1998) estimate that men make up 3 percent of all early childhood educators. A study by Robinson (1988: 55) revealed that men working in child care were motivated by "their love and enjoyment of working with children, appeal of the content of the child-care program and desire to contribute something of value to the young children for whom they cared."

Despite the publication date of Essa and Young's (1994: 445) research, their work is still relevant today:

men leave the field of early childhood education at an even greater rate than women do. Some male teachers who changed careers reported that they were subject to subtle prejudicial attitudes from parents, female co-workers, and administrators. They were considered not as good as women because "they had never been mothers."

Hinsliff (2003) points out that "just as women breaking into male-dominated professions may fall victim to an old boys' network, research found that some male child-care providers complained of being patronized by female colleagues.... One complained of being 'cut off' by a female colleague who would interrupt him when he talked to parents, while another two men reported that women colleagues 'would "jump in before a possible problem could occur" or would assume they couldn't do some things with the children properly.'"

In his study of men still working in the field, Robinson (1988) reports on attitudes to men in the field:

Sixty percent of the men were discontent about subtle unspoken assumptions from parents, the women they worked with or their administrators simply because they were men. Many said they were treated with mistrust and suspicion by parents and their co-workers. Several men said that their colleagues believed that they, as women, were better equipped by nature to work with young children. Others reported beliefs that because they had never been mothers, their co-workers felt they could not make accurate judgments concerning discipline, the health of the children and approaches to teaching and supervising children.

Becker (2005), a member of a men's networking/support group offered through the Manitoba Child Care Association, states, "the biggest factor for leaving reported was low pay. It was unrealistic to try and support a family on a child-care worker's salary, and so a few returned to higher paying vocations even though they expressed a wish to stay in the field."[*] Bertrand and Gestwicki (2012: 167) agree:

> The main reason men do not work in child care is not that they are not capable or suited for the work but because the rewards of salary and status do not meet their expectations. It is not difficult to understand how raising a family on the salary of an ECE teacher would be arduous. Early childhood educators and assistants still earn much less than other

workers and less than most women in other occupations. There is also considerable variation across the country. For example, in some regions educators are likely to receive not much more than provincial or territorial minimum wage, while in other regions annual salaries may start at $35,000 plus benefits."[†]

The large wage gap between early childhood educators and teachers is emerging as a major issue as early childhood programs become integrated into the education sector and schools (Beach and Flanagan, 2010a).

Becker (2005) writes that

> knowing the barriers to male participation in the ECE field is the first step towards changing the future. But real change starts with the individual. As

---

[*]Becker, S. 2005. "The Good, The Bad And The Few: Men In Child Care." Available at http://www.cccf-fcsge.ca/practice/policy/men_en .html. Reprinted by permission.

[†]From BERTRAND/GESTWICKI. *Essentials of Early Childhood Education, 4E.* © 2012 Nelson Education Ltd. Reproduced by permission. www.cengage.com/permissions.

Inside LOOK

"Who is that man in the classroom?" This was the first question indirectly asked about me by a mother on entering the preschool room to drop off her son. It was the first day of my first field placement. This question has since come to signify how I have often found myself positioned in the field of Early Childhood Education—that of the unexpected outsider who must defend and justify his presence and make clear his intentions before acceptance may be granted. When I reflect back on that first day, I often wonder if this question would have been asked had I been a new female adult seen interacting with the children that morning.

Prior to my becoming an early childhood educator I had the privilege of working with and supporting children and their families as an educator in a variety of settings on four different continents. The shift from elementary school teacher to early childhood educator was a natural one. It came as I became increasingly aware of how the early years presented a meaningful intersection where my knowledge of pedagogy, personal and professional experiences, commitment to social justice, and desire to educate, could be applied to the benefit of our most vulnerable members of society with far reaching effects. An educator colleague of mine informed me that he had discussed my move to ECE with the supervisor of his son's daycare. She told him that she would never hire a male, as 'that would never go over with the parents at her centre.' Prior to my making this career transition, being male had never presented as an issue. So, in a time when there is an identified need to more actively recruit men into the field, the question then becomes, how do we shift our present paradigm? How do we effectively problematize our current ways of thinking about men and their role in lives of young children? What steps then need to be taken in order to reduce the isolation and marginalization felt by many male early childhood practitioners? What say will men be given in the establishing of a framework toward an inclusive model that meets their needs, and weaves them more seamlessly into the fabric of early childhood education? While many do claim that they are all for having more men in the field, what taken-for-granted and heteronormative biases still remain naturalized and unchallenged—biases that lead to a question such as, 'Who is that man in the classroom?'"

Source: Bill Vizard BFA, Dip Ed Primary, RECE, M.I.T.R. Bill Vizard is a Field Faculty with George Brown College. Reprinted by permission.

Neugebauer wrote, "we all like to see ourselves as open minded and accepting. But if you, the director, or front-line worker believe that men aren't by nature nurturing, or that men are more likely to be abusers, your efforts to employ men or accept them as peers will be half-hearted. When staff recognize their own attitudes towards men as caregivers, they can work together to create a healthy and positive, gender-inclusive environment."[*]

Bertrand (2008: 173) points out that

In England and Scotland, targeted marketing to men includes television, newspaper, and poster campaigns featuring male workers, handing out brochures (including one with the provocative title "Are You Man Enough for Childcare?") at venues where men are likely to be found, and providing men-only orientation sessions at secondary schools and career fairs. Several Nordic countries also use targeted marketing.[†]

[*]Becker, S. 2005. "The Good, The Bad And The Few: Men In Child Care." Available at http://www.cccf-fcsge.ca/practice/policy/men_en .html. Reprinted by permission.

[†] From BERTRAND. *Understanding, Managing, and Leading, 1E.* © 2008 Nelson Education Ltd. Reproduced by permission. www.cengage.com/permissions.

Inside LOOK

Ten years ago I was invited to write a reflection on my commitment to the field of early childhood education for a yet-to-be-published edition of *Partnerships*. At that time I was a second-year student at George Brown College with limited front-line experience. Having just completed my final placement for the program, I spoke of initial fears that are common to males in this profession. In particular, I wrote of the stereotypes ascribed to men who voluntarily choose to work with young children and contemplated the following related questions: (1) Would my interest in working with this vulnerable population be misconstrued as pathological? (2) Would families, faculty, and colleagues judge my competence as a nurturing presence in the lives of children based solely on my skill as an early educator or simply on the basis of my sex/gender? and (3) Would my decision to enter a profession with so few males as front-line workers yield assumptions about my sexual orientation and promote further discrimination? These questions, initially the source of much hesitation and self-doubt, remained with me for some time following my formal entry into the field.

Since graduating with my ECE diploma in 2003 I've amassed a wealth of diverse experience—first as a front-line early childhood educator; then as a centre supervisor and, most recently, as a full-time faculty in Humber College's Department of Early Childhood Education. As I contemplate these years with a critical eye I can say that my male status, to my immediate knowledge, has rarely been an issue for the families with whom I've worked. In fact, in some cases, it's even served to nurture my professional development when, for example, I've been invited to various field-specific functions to speak to ECE students and colleagues about the experience of being a male in a female-dominated vocation. Moreover, I've had the privilege of being mentored by some of the most respected names in ECE, many of whom have made a concerted effort to support my personal and professional growth. It is for this reason that I routinely seek similar opportunities to reach out to male students enrolled in the ECE programs in which I've taught in recent years. So too has this experience served as the impetus for research I've proposed to conduct as part of the doctoral program in which I'm currently enrolled at OISE/U of T.

With the establishment of the College of Early Childhood Educators in Ontario and the implementation of full-day early learning/kindergarten, the continued evolution of the field is inevitable. Of the many potential changes to anticipate, I'm especially interested in the impact that these systemic measures (and future ones like them) will have on the recruitment and retention of males as front-line staff. If the move by other female-dominated disciplines to professionalize is any indication, it is likely that ECE will also benefit from a much-needed influx of male practitioners in the not-so-distant future.

Source: Reprinted by permission of Ryan Campbell, BA (ECE), MA (ECS), RECE, Faculty, Humber College.

Greater male involvement in the field of early childhood education is long overdue.

STRATEGIES FOR ACHIEVING EFFECTIVE PARTNERSHIPS

In this section we look at what supervisors and individual teachers can do to promote meaningful relationships with families.

WHAT CAN THE SUPERVISOR DO?

> "A leader is best when people barely know he exists, when his work is done, his aim fulfilled, they will say: we did it ourselves."
>
> —Lao Tzu

The leadership provided by a supervisor in an early childhood environment and a principal in a school setting are responsible for setting the stage for quality experiences for children and their families. According to Bertrand (2008: 215), "The early childhood program director/supervisor is the keystone to carrying the program's vision (purpose and philosophy) forward. He or she can bring clarity or confusion, calm or chaos, stability or fragility to the daily lives of children, their families and the staff team."* Strong leaders empower, encourage, and support others in a shared vision to achieve goals or create change.

*From BERTRAND. *Understanding, Managing, and Leading, 1E.* © 2008 Nelson Education Ltd. Reproduced by permission. www.cengage.com/permissions.

CREATE ADMINISTRATIVE POLICIES THAT STRENGTHEN PARTNERSHIPS

It is critical that the policies and procedures that are embedded in the mission or philosophy statement of the early learning environment clearly outline the partnership with families and their role in the day-to-day operation of the centre. The supervisor's leadership will be strongly influenced by the policies and procedures established by the administration of the centre, such as a board of directors. The board should ensure that the philosophy of the centre entrenches active family involvement and is reviewed on a regular basis.

GOAL SETTING

Families must be able to see how the philosophy or mission statement translates into action; this is effectively accomplished by stating the centre's goals. These goals summarize the ways in which the families and staff work together to provide the best possible environment for the children. These goals should be specific, measureable, and "top of the mind" for supervisors. The vision should be clear and understandable; all staff should be able to identify the centre's goals. A strong leader empowers others to achieve these goals.

MODEL THE WAY

The supervisor should model relationships that are authentic, empathetic, and trustworthy. The supervisor must actively demonstrate that he or she believes that all families are knowledgeable experts who influence their children's learning and invite them to be significant participants in the early learning environment. Teachers should be able to see that the supervisor "walks the talk," is aware, tuned in, and connected to families in the centre. Supervisors must demonstrate the ability to accept failure and criticism in an open manner that demonstrates that healthy learning moments come from experience. As the supervisor engages families and staff in a truly humble fashion, it will be easy to see that she is leading with hope and vision, working quietly without demanding recognition and praise but motivating those around her to lead the way. Strong relationships help to prevent the many conflicts that can arise in an early childhood environment; with an open-door policy, much can be accomplished!

BE AN EFFECTIVE COMMUNICATOR

The supervisor's role in a child-care centre is a multidimensional one, rooted in an understanding of the importance of effective interpersonal communication. Her positive and enthusiastic attitude toward families provides an example for teachers. The supervisor should be comfortable and confident in relating to people and have the ability to establish a positive, trusting rapport with families. As a communicator, she should be able to interact in a consistent manner, clearly and concisely. It should be clear that the supervisor cares about what she does and how she does it and feels a sense of responsibility to do it well. She is responsible for ensuring that orientation information and all other forms of written communication are relevant, up-to-date, and inclusive of all types of families. Having material translated into the first language of the families in the centre and, for example, providing interpreters for deaf parents are critical to effective communication. As the supervisor becomes more familiar with the families in the centre, she can catalogue their various skills, talents, and resources, and encourage them to share them with the centre. Overall, families should be able to see that the supervisor is committed to excellence and has high expectations to ensure best practices.

BE ACCESSIBLE

Accessibility is an important issue. Supervisors with busy schedules should set aside periods when they will be available to families, since in many small

An open-door policy should be in place; everyone should feel welcome.

It is important that the supervisor has a strong visible presence in the centre.

centres the supervisor is also a playroom teacher. The supervisor who is on the floor during drop-off and pick-up times can free up teachers so that they can discuss important issues with families. Floor time also provides supervisors with opportunities to speak with families themselves and to observe the family–teacher interactions.

HIRE OUTSTANDING STAFF

Supervisors are often in the position of hiring new staff, and this often involves members of the board of directors as well. One way to create a strong team is to hire outstanding teachers who reflect the community served and to make every effort to hire male teachers. All hires must be able to demonstrate a commitment to working with families, and a clear and concise job description should exist for each position in the centre.

We know that our ECE workforce is not stable—many teachers leave the profession because of poor working conditions, low pay, and lack of career opportunities. The supervisor needs to consider how multiple caregivers or frequent changes in staff may impact the ability of families and teachers to build strong relationships with each other. When staff turnover is high, it is detrimental to the children's ability to create attachments, and families may wonder if there is a serious problem in the centre that they may not be aware of. While many of these issues are out of the supervisor's control, it is the supervisor's responsibility to create a work climate that is rewarding and supportive while also knowing how to keep and nurture knowledgeable, committed teachers who understand the importance of partnerships with families. In order to maintain a climate of acceptance and trust, it is important that new hires understand this and that the message to families is consistent across all teachers. Successful hiring also applies to those who also work in the centre to support families, including cooks, caretakers, and others who may volunteer, who have enormous opportunities to contribute to a congenial workplace.

It is also important that whenever possible at the beginning and end of the day there are additional staff on site so that meaningful exchanges can take place between teachers and families. It is difficult to exchange information if the playroom teacher arrives after families have dropped off their children and only part-time staff are on site at the end of the day.

DEVELOP A TEAM APPROACH

Supervisors are responsible for establishing a sense of common purpose among a group of teachers who may come from diverse backgrounds and who may have different training and philosophical

Inside LOOK

One of the things that was most reassuring to me as a parent was that Pam was always there. She would be busy with one parent or another, helping out in a room or making coffee for parents who wanted to stay behind and talk. Pam was quick to assess situations where her helpful support would be welcome. She had the uncanny knack of being able to talk my 4-year-old into getting on his snow pants long after I had given up in exasperation. I appreciated the encouragement and support she gave to our family.

approaches to their work, as well as conflicting attitudes toward family involvement. Establishing a sense of group identity is an enormous undertaking but necessary for creating an effective team.

Jorde Bloom (1995) describes the culture of a centre as encompassing the basic assumptions and shared beliefs that unite the staff. These assumptions and beliefs include standards of appropriate everyday behaviour and a shared code of ethics guiding professional practice. The supervisor's role is to mesh the home cultures of the families in the centre with the early childhood culture. This "climate" or "culture" should be warm and welcoming to all who enter.

Staff meetings are also a good forum for providing psychological support and time for reflection. Journal writing, on a regular basis, may also provide insight and topics for discussion at these meetings. Rather than focus on curriculum, timetables, or other business items, reflective practice allows staff members to share their feelings, their successes, and their concerns about their work with families and with one another. In a trusting environment, these reflective practice meetings are real opportunities for change. When staff believe that the supervisor is truly concerned about them, they are more likely to share openly without fear of recourse. Relationships are enhanced and sustained by working together to achieve a common goal.

Educators learn to bridge differences in life experiences and interpretations, recognize the humanity of one another, share meaning, and find solutions that help them work more effectively with families.

SUPPORT FAMILIES AND TEACHERS

According to research, several characteristics appear to positively influence parent–teacher partnerships. The relationships are enhanced when teachers' personal attributes include warmth, openness, sensitivity, flexibility, reliability, and accessibility (Swick, 1992). The partnerships are positively influenced when parents' personal attributes include warmth, sensitivity, nurturance, the ability to listen, consistency, a positive self-image, personal confidence, and effective interpersonal skills (Ibid.). While neither teachers nor parents may have all these positive personal attributes, supporting both families and teachers requires tact and sensitivity on the part of supervisors. There will be times when the supervisor has the difficult task of supporting educators while at the same time giving due consideration to family concerns and complaints. Being an effective listener is crucial to the supervisor in her role as a mediator in family–teacher disputes, and as an objective observer, she may be able to suggest strategies for improving the relationship. Both parties need to know that

Inside LOOK

Commandments for an Enthusiastic Team

1. Help each other be right—not wrong.
2. Look for ways to make new ideas work—not for reasons they won't.
3. If in doubt—check it out! Don't make negative assumptions about each other.
4. Help each other win and take pride in each other's victories.
5. Speak positively about each other and about your organization at every opportunity.
6. Maintain a positive mental attitude no matter what the circumstances.
7. Act with initiative and courage as if it all depends on you.
8. Do everything with enthusiasm—it's contagious.
9. Whatever you want—give it away.
10. Don't lose faith—never give up.
11. Have fun!

Source: © Ian Percy Corporation. 2003. Used with permission. IanPercy.com.

the supervisor is trustworthy and will respond with honesty and integrity. It is important that all parties understand that she will deal with issues directly and be quick to find equitable solutions. Supervisors need to let educators know that they expect to be informed when conflicts with families arise; supervisors can then follow up as appropriate, perhaps with a phone call or a discussion at the end of the day to reassure the family.

The supervisor is also able to monitor the degree to which the families who are active in the centre reflect the centre's family population as a whole. It is not uncommon for a group of active and influential parents to form a clique and, intentionally or not, exclude other families who want to participate. The supervisor is in a position to advocate for all families to be involved in decision making by identifying groups not represented and targeting them for involvement.

The supervisor must also be able to appraise the skills of centre staff and determine where further support is needed. For example, she may note times when teachers show an unconscious preference for a child or a family; she can bring this favouritism to the attention of teachers and redirect them into fair and more consistent practice. The work of educators in early childhood environments is demanding, and it is incumbent on supervisors to help create support systems that encourage and motivate staff.

At the same time, supervisors need to be aware of when staff are struggling for personal or professional reasons and be ready to provide support and encouragement. It is at these times that teachers need appreciation the most. In addition to providing regular feedback to teachers about their role in the playroom, their interpersonal skills, and their ability to work effectively with colleagues and families, the supervisor can help those educators who require additional training to access the necessary resources or workshops. The supervisor will be aware that some staff are outgoing and personable and establish relationships with families in an authentic and meaningful way quite easily. Other staff may have a more introverted personality and may need more support in building their confidence and being less timid in their interactions with families. This may also be true for staff for whom English is not their first language; they may be reluctant to engage families verbally and in a written format. There may also be cultural barriers that the supervisor needs to be aware of in order

to support staff. Supervisors also should advocate at the board level for paid time for staff during family–teacher conferences, home visits, or staffing at the end of the day so teachers have real time to communicate with families.

SUPPORT FAMILIES EXPERIENCING POVERTY OR FINANCIAL DIFFICULTIES

In conjunction with the supervisor, the administration of the centre can provide assistance to families experiencing financial difficulty. Supervisors should know which support agencies, charities, and businesses are available in the community so that they can quickly help families access the resources they need. The addresses of local food banks should be prominently displayed on the bulletin board so that families are aware of them and do not have to ask. Centres should consider providing breakfast programs and hearty snacks for their school-age children. Centres that receive discounted rates for buying in bulk could allow families to purchase staple items at a reduced rate. Centres in which the cook prepares nutritionally sound "one-pot meals" could allow families to purchase these economical meals to take home. It may also be possible to purchase public transportation tickets so families can attend meetings and other events at the centre.

Centres may need to spread child-care payments over a longer period of time to help families experiencing financial difficulty. Centres should also be aware of the impact of asking families for extra funds to cover special events, field trips, etc. Children of unemployed parents will need extra attention and reassurance; these parents may be invited to the playroom to volunteer or to share a special skill, which might provide a needed boost to a worried or concerned child. Families could be encouraged to participate in exchanges (clothing, shoes, skates, and so on) as their children outgrow their belongings. Families with a garden and surplus produce can establish a help-yourself table at the centre. On this note, using food in art or sensory experiences should be discouraged. Families that have lived subsistence lives or that find it difficult to make ends meet may find such activities particularly offensive. Where space allows, centres could create a neighbourhood garden in order to further strengthen their ties with the community. This also provides a vehicle for compassion and empathy for those in our communities who need support—a valuable lesson for young children. Centres can approach local

Time Banks—Building a Community One Hour at a Time!

Exchanging Time and Talent with Your Community Members

A TimeBank is "a chance to exchange time and talent with your neighbours in your community. In TimeBanking members earn TimeCredits for helping each other—one hour of your time entitles you to one hour of another TimeBank member's time.

1. Become a member for free.
2. List time and talents you are willing to provide to other.
3. Review time and talent offers from other members.
4. When you see something that another member is offering that you would like to receive respond online to their offer.
5. Come to agreement about the offer.
6. Complete what was offered.
7. Log in to the exchange TimeBank and record the amount of time received.
8. When another member contacts you about your offer follow the same steps above except now you are giving them your time.
9. Both members can review the completed online exchange and any errors are corrected with the assistance of the TimeBank coordinator.
10. Every member can view and update their offers, requests and other info anytime online.

Unlike money, anyone and everyone can earn TimeCredits—no one is excluded (see Figure 3.6). What help would you like to receive and what would you enjoy doing for others in your community? Everyone has something to offer of value and we all enjoy the opportunity to share our time and talents with others who value them. The more members there are the greater selection of different types of exchanges of time and talent can take place!

For more information, view Lower Mainland, British Columbia's TimeBank at **http://lmtimebank.org/index.html**.

Source: Reprinted by permission of Bruno Vernier, LM timebank.org

companies that may be generous with goods if they know the cause is genuine and children are involved. Supervisors and educators should work closely with antipoverty groups in pressing governments at all levels for a comprehensive plan to eliminate poverty. For example, supervisors and teachers may look for innovative ways of supporting families in their communities by searching for and participating in antipoverty organizations.

ACKNOWLEDGE TEACHERS' STRENGTHS

Supervisors need to carry out performance evaluations on a regular basis. Acknowledging the efforts and strengths of teachers in the centre is an important part of a supervisor's job. Too often the contributions of teachers go unnoticed; too often others take credit for their ideas. When teachers feel that they have no ability to suggest or make changes in their work environment, they become discouraged. The best way for any supervisor to gain the loyalty and support of others is to acknowledge and appreciate the efforts of staff by celebrating their accomplishments so they feel an improved sense of self. Articles in local and community newspapers, television, radio interviews, and public meetings are some of the means by which the supervisor can share the important work that teachers and families are accomplishing in the centre. Celebrate every good piece of news! Displaying photos of the teachers and a biographical sketch in the centre for families to read also enhances the role of the teacher. With the teachers'

FIGURE 3.6 Ideas for TimeCredits

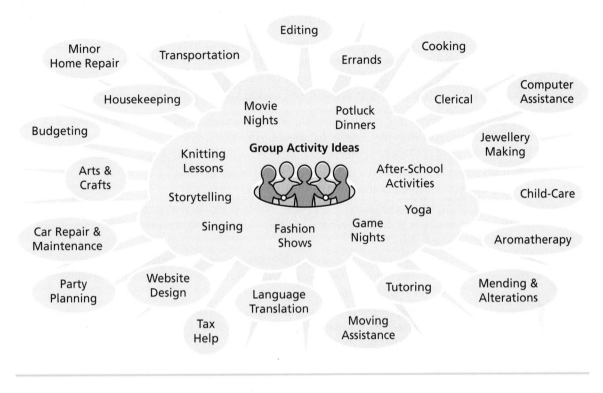

permission, the supervisor can profile teachers in newsletters, letting families know about professional and personal milestones reached.

> One supervisor adds a personal note to each week's pay stub. It has words of encouragement and details positive effort, strengths and appreciation. Another site has a fall breakfast called 'Our Teachers Are Stars Because ... ' Secret letters are distributed from the centre to parents requesting donations for staff gifts. Children fill out paper stars with reasons why their teachers are stars and they are displayed in the centre. (In some communities asking for a contribution may be a hardship and the stars in themselves may be enough of a reward). (Kiefer and Cohen, 2004: 29)

One centre had their holiday concert recorded for broadcasting on the local radio station. At another centre, the supervisor and board annually celebrate the teachers at a special dinner; all the families are invited. Teachers are "roasted" in good-natured fun and praised for the contributions they have made all year.

Supervisors can make teacher recommendations to local community colleges when they are in need of part-time or sessional ECE appointments, and she can encourage staff to supervise student field placements. Supervisors can also organize workshops in

the community for teachers to lead. One supervisor approached a local bookstore, and staff conducted Saturday story times for children in the community, a great addition to their résumés. Supervisors should also look for opportunities to nominate teachers for special community awards. Jorde Bloom (1995) recommends giving business cards to teachers and encouraging them to use them. They help teachers feel more professional, and they also publicize the centre.

Supervisors can encourage teachers to create a portfolio that reflects their academic achievements and is an ongoing record of events and milestones they deem memorable and worth celebrating. It is also important that the supervisor model continuing professional development. As she attends workshops and seminars or returns to school to upgrade her own academic credentials, she may well inspire staff to do the same. A good leader should be constantly learning and improving!

When times are difficult at the centre, a team-building exercise or a retreat may be a helpful strategy. A concentrated block of time to work on goals and expectations, and to plan new events will be much more productive than a short staff meeting. Social get-togethers may also be a welcome idea.

While families are often surveyed for their opinions, teachers are often overlooked. Conducting an in-house survey about new strategies for creating

Being aware of the newest research is part of a supervisor's responsibilities and an opportunity to demonstrate leadership in its implementation. As Director of Programs at the Chicago Commons Association, Karen Haigh (2004) has been working with staff to explore and experiment with various ideas and influences from Reggio Emilia. She lists the following ways that staff have worked together at Chicago Commons:

1. Learning to share, revisit, and reflect together at weekly meetings, in-services, out-of-town conferences, and seminars by allowing time for dialogue among staff.
2. Viewing videotapes of children together to see and discuss strengths and abilities of children, which has grown into searching for children's interests or areas to pursue.
3. Talking and thinking together about why photos are taken.
4. Reviewing and interpreting children's work (actual words, drawing, videotapes, slides, etc.).
5. Developing environment plans that consider the entire building, such as classrooms, bathrooms, hallways, and entrance ways.
6. Viewing slides together as a means of looking at the environment or the languages of children.
7. Allowing teams to have their own exploration. Each site developed research questions to explore as they were asked, "What do you wonder about children?"
8. Experiencing staff explorations of materials such as watercolours, wire, charcoal, clay, and paper.
9. Learning to think about how and why portfolios are used to collect children's work.
10. Talking and thinking together about how to ask questions.
11. Sharing and discussing documentation among sites.
12. Doing presentations for each other within the agency.
13. Viewing each other's environments.
14. Sharing, documenting, and revisiting our ideas, especially when we go to seminars and conferences.
15. Having an introduction to the Reggio Approach for new staff.
16. Focusing on specific research for each year.
17. Focusing on questions to think about and discuss together during the year.
18. Thinking about the purpose and meanings of journals.
19. Thinking and talking about "What is society's image of the child and what is the public schools' image of the child?"
20. Choosing, designing, executing, and evaluating documentation panels together.
21. Using quality circles to make decisions, policies, and procedures about specific aspects of our program (e.g., choosing agency-wide topics for research).
22. Planning, executing, and evaluating two-day Learning Tours together.

Haigh states, "I believe staff at the Commons have had the most dramatic change in terms of relationships, as they have had to reconstruct their relationships with children, with parents, with the community, and with each other." (pp. 83–84)

Source: HENDRICK, JOANNE, NEXT STEPS TOWARD TEACHING THE REGGIO WAY: ACCEPTING THE CHALLENGE TO CHANGE, 1st Edition, © 2004. Reprinted and Electronically reproduced by permission of Pearson Education, Inc., Upper Saddle River, NJ.

an effective team environment will give the supervisor important feedback for change.

ESTABLISH MENTORING

The importance of mentoring for both new and experienced educators cannot be overlooked, and supervisors will also benefit. In mentoring programs, experienced and effective early childhood educators are given specialized training to help beginning educators gain skills and become more effective practitioners. Educators may feel more comfortable in sharing their challenges with someone who is independent from the centre.

A report of the Expert Panel on Quality and Human Resources in 2007 identified a gap between education requirements and job expectations for directors and supervisors of child-care programs. Training is limited for the growing demand and responsibilities of the supervisory role. In response to this need, the Government of Ontario funded the Early Childhood Community Development Centre (ECCDC) to develop a province-wide mentoring program and related resources and services for licensed child-care supervisors.

The goal of the Mentoring Pairs for Child Care (MPCC) is to support and enhance child-care quality by matching less experienced child-care supervisors (mentees) with more experienced child-care supervisors (mentors) in their own communities. These mentoring pairs complete a year-long training program that incorporates group learning, one-on-one conferencing, networking, and guided communication to develop their management skills. The Child Care Human Resources Sector Council's *Occupational Standards for Child Care Administrators* provided the framework for the program. Since funding was available after the first year, new mentoring pairs were selected and the project continued for a second year of success.

Mentors and mentees participated in monthly group meetings facilitated by animators. During these meetings mentoring pairs focus on the tasks and subtasks specific to the group's interests in the *Occupational Standards for Child Care Administrators*. Self-assessment and planning tools were used to help members to reflect on their performance and identify what is needed to enrich the quality of their child-care practices. Group members are encouraged to recognize, trust, value, and respect each other's skills, knowledge, and abilities. They engaged in cooperative inquiry and dialogue that helped individuals to facilitate self-reflection. Safe dialogue and inquiry created a sense of understanding and comradeship that led to the formation of a mentoring culture. In addition, reflection journals helped mentoring pairs identify the wisdom they have accumulated through practice, charted individual progress, and reinforced reflection on action. It is a process that allows mentors and mentees to be more aware of what they do, how they do it, why they do it, identify useful problem solving strategies, and recognize and work with their own strengths and weaknesses.

For more information on mentoring, see McCormick and Ressler's 2011 article at Child Care Connections, NS: visit **http://www.cccns.org/pdf/14.3.pdf**.

Source: Reprinted by permission of Joyce Gee, Manager, Esther Exton Child Care Centre, George Brown College.

SUPERVISE THE DEVELOPMENT OF APPROPRIATE EMERGENT CURRICULUM

The supervisor has a role to play in helping staff develop an emergent curriculum that is relevant, inclusive, and reflective of all the families in the centre—and who better to provide this insight than the families themselves! Staff meetings and individual room meetings held at convenient times provide opportunities for the supervisor and teachers to evaluate the curriculum and develop strategies for remedying those aspects of the curriculum that serve as barriers to effective family–teacher partnerships. Creating a curriculum that reflects caring—for ourselves, others, and the environment—will help to create a positive and empowering culture within the centre. Input from families should be an integral part of this process. The first consideration in communicating the curriculum to families is the cultural context. Many families come from an educational system that is very formal and teacher directed, and relies somewhat on rote learning; many of these cultures are collectivist in nature. The play-based, child-centred emergent curriculum approach that is generally used in our individualistic culture will be difficult for many parents to appreciate at first. It is our role as ECE teachers to help all parents witness the benefits of this method.

Perhaps one of the best models of community involvement in early childhood is in the town of Reggio Emilia in Italy. After World War II, preschools opened in this northern Italian town and

Students, too, have much to contribute and bring many strengths to the program.

today the municipal government supports 35 Reggio Emilia schools. Adults and children work collaboratively with teachers in creating positive learning environments. Families are actively involved in critical decision making and the strong sense of community is evident in the connectedness among all participants. While Canadian supervisors cannot exactly replicate the Reggio model, both the connection to the community and the vision that the centre is part of a cohesive, healthy, and productive community are critical.

We must be in our communities! Amatea (2009) believes

> Supervisors and educators must know the values and attitudes of the community ... to truly engage the community. Beneficial in establishing trust in teacher-parent relationships is visibility in the community. Teachers can send a powerful message of interest and demonstrate cultural reciprocity by actively becoming visible in the community. Visibility can be in the form of attending a community event, festival or patronizing municipal services or businesses. (163–164)*

Families may see teachers at the grocery store or library, providing an informal opportunity to make connections in meaningful ways with parents. Educators recognize that a friendly open attitude and genuine interest in the children is critically important and many make time to attend special events that the children participate in outside the early childhood environment; for example, the season's final community championship soccer match. These moments are long remembered by the children and their families.

Supervisors should be aware of agencies and support services that would benefit families—local physicians, dentists, child-care subsidy offices, mental health professionals, parenting programs, assessment services, special needs consultants, linguistic services, parks and recreation, etc. Supervisors can contact local hospitals to find out what types of programs are available for families; do they have a library that is accessible to the public? Do local police and fire departments have programs for children, or will they come and visit the centre?

* AMATEA, ELLEN S., BUILDING CULTURALLY RESPONSIVE FAMILY-SCHOOL RELATIONSHIPS,

1st Edition, © 2009. Reprinted and Electronically reproduced by permission of Pearson Education, Inc., Upper Saddle River, NJ.

Child Care and Much More!

With a small, one-time grant from the York Board of Education in 1978, The Learning Enrichment Foundation (LEF) has grown to become a model of community economic development through the integration of services that meets local needs. LEF's 30 child-care programs lay a solid foundation for approximately 1,000 children every day. The magic of LEFs centres is in the wide breadth of support offered: sensitivity to families' cultural needs, integration of children with special needs, professional development, strong evaluations, nutritious meals and snacks, and parent workshops. LEF ensures that language and settlement needs of the newcomer community are addressed in a comprehensive and caring way. LEF offers language training to eligible adult newcomers who are assessed for language proficiency and enter one of the programs of English instruction. Participants are offered child care, transportation assistance, a computer lab, field trips, and volunteer opportunities. They also have the opportunity to use other LEF services for job search skills, employment, financial management, resource centre access, and additional skills training. Skills training may include forklift certification, and training in cooking, industrial skills, early childhood assistant skills, project management, bicycle assembly and maintenance, and caretaking. LEF also provides a variety of workshops to meet the needs of the participants. LEF has more than 200 partners in the community that assist in a variety of ways to help meet its goals of providing community-responsive programs and services that enable individuals to become valued contributors to their community's social and economic development.

Source: Reprinted by permission of The Learning Enrichment Foundation. http://www.lefca.org/about_us/index.shtml.

What resources are present in the community? What resources are needed? Many businesses have budgets for community efforts, and this is an opportunity for the supervisor and staff to put together a brief but compelling description of the support that the centre might need—perhaps for a large project to convert the playground from asphalt to a green space, or a smaller project that involves small centre repairs or donations to a barbeque. Posters or certificates should be given to thank businesses; and others should be posted in the centre thanking them for their community service and commitment to the early childhood.

The supervisor should be responsible for sharing with the community education, social, and family needs that exist and participate in problem-solving strategies. "The supervisor can develop multiple outreach mechanisms to inform families, businesses, and the community about family involvement policies and programs through newsletter, slide shows, videotapes and local newspapers" (Whitaker and Fiore, 2001: 161). Many local television stations have community information programs; it may be possible to post a short video about the centre for families looking for child care.

Classes and programs take place in libraries, museums, zoos, and other community facilities and supervisors can support teachers in their efforts to move beyond the playroom. Invite or visit members of the visual arts and performing communities who can share their interests and talents with the children. Public spaces that support young families are critical. Bertrand (2008: 252) states that

> raising the social capital of communities raises social cohesion—the level of trust and sharing, a recognition that we are all responsible in some sense for each other, and that we all share a responsibility for the next generation. Socially cohesive neighbourhoods are better places to live, characterized by less crime and isolation, more public and community spaces, and greater volunteerism and intergenerational reciprocity.[*]

---

[*] From BERTRAND. *Understanding, Managing, and Leading, 1E.* © 2008 Nelson Education Ltd. Reproduced by permission. www.cengage.com/permissions.

We know the importance of physical activity and the benefits for children and their families, so actively soliciting funds to create green spaces, playgrounds, and gathering places greatly benefits the community.

Supervisors can initiate relationships with community leaders from a wide range of cultures, seeking their advice and support and encouraging staff to engage in life-long learning. Supervisors can also use the child-care facility to serve community needs and to facilitate learning for the wider community. Because child-care centre supervisors are in a position to form networks, they can connect with agencies in the community that support families, businesses that may lend their assistance, media, and so on. Every community has programs that receive great praise for the quality of care, their outstanding outdoor environments, innovative programming, etc. Supervisors can arrange to meet with fellow supervisors to visit these sites and encourage their staff to visit these centres as well. We have much to learn from each other. According to Jorde Bloom, "Directors who have ... buil[t] strong community connections report a lower incidence of vandalism at their centres, fewer problems in recruiting volunteers and prospective staff, and longer waiting lists"* (1995: 49).

The *You Bet I Care!* study (2000) asked supervisors about their satisfaction with the availability of support from 11 different community sources. Their responses indicate that their greatest support comes from their health unit or nurses (56 percent), from other centre directors (54 percent), and from resource teachers (41 percent). This interdisciplinary approach has much to offer.

If they are not already based in a school setting, supervisors of child-care centres can also reach out to elementary schools in their community to help ease the transitions for families and their children, and they can encourage teachers in early childhood environments to hold meetings with families, children, and teachers in their new school environments to share goals for each child.

It is also important to stay connected to post-secondary institutions that offer early childhood education, where new research may be of benefit to teachers and families. Looking for opportunities to take students from ECE programs for field practicums provides an opportunity for mentoring and staying by hearing new ideas and techniques.

WHAT CAN TEACHERS DO?

"I have come to a frightening conclusion.
I am the decisive element in the classroom.
It is my personal approach that creates the climate.
It is my daily mood that makes the weather.
As a teacher I possess tremendous power to make a child's life miserable or joyous.
I can be a tool of torture or an instrument of inspiration.
I can humiliate or humor, hurt or heal.
In all situations, it is my response that decides whether a crisis will be escalated or de-escalated, and a child humanized or de-humanized."[†]

—**Dr. Haim Ginott (Thinkexist.com, n.d.)**

Courtesy of Lynn Wilson

This child-care centre, Studio 123, is housed in a building where many artists have their studios. One contributed this spectacular whimsical sculpture for the children's playground.

*Jorde Bloom, P. 1995. "Building a Sense of Community: A Broader View." *Child Care Information Exchange 101.* January–February, p. 47.

[†]Reprinted by permission of Alice Ginott Cohn.

COMMIT TO FAMILY INVOLVEMENT

Programs that fail tend to do so not because teachers lack the skills but because they lack sufficient commitment to family involvement. Before teachers work on building and refining the skills they need to create effective partnerships, they must first ask themselves if they truly want to involve families in the first place. Pelletier and Brent (2002: 45) identify the teacher as key to facilitating parental involvement in early childhood education programs. This implies that teachers possess certain skills, attitudes, and behaviours that translate into strategies to encourage parent participation. Swick and McKnight (1989) found that teachers who were educated with regard to the value of parent education and involvement, who were encouraged to remain active through professional organizations, and who were given the essential supports, such as small class size, administrative help, and appropriate working conditions, were the most supportive of parental involvement and education. There has been concern regarding an overemphasis on "large group" parental involvement; research suggests that a more successful approach entails increased individual contact among parents and teachers, conferences, small group discussions,

Inside LOOK

Expanding Horizons—Reaching Out to the Community

The bustling nature of early learning and care centres often draws the attention of supervisors inward. The many competing demands of parents, children, staff, and licensing requirements may make it difficult to find either the time or the energy to reach out to the broader community.

Early learning and care centres are just one, albeit a very important, component of a continuum of programs and services for young children and their families. In recognition of the benefits of a truly integrated service delivery system, centre directors and staff must seek every opportunity to develop a more comprehensive understanding of the range of supports available within their community.

Equally important is participation at local planning tables or children's services networks. Unfortunately, child-care centre directors may not be invited to these tables. In some communities, licensed child care is viewed as separate and apart from the range of agencies providing children's mental health, public health, and parent support programs. However, while participation at these tables does take time and energy, it is critical that the child-care community be well represented.

The benefits of active participation at planning tables are the following:

- increased capacity to provide "one-stop shopping" for parents seeking additional programs and services for their children
- the ability to provide parents with current and accurate information about a wide range of support services in response to specific requests or needs
- enhanced opportunities for shared, multisectoral professional development, which strengthen the capacity of all sectors to provide comprehensive, quality programs and services
- increased knowledge about the important role played by licensed child care in a continuum of supports and services that support healthy children and families
- increased ability to share resources (financial, physical, human) effectively, potentially increasing the overall capacity of the children's services sector

Parents who require additional supports and services for themselves or their children endure additional stresses over and above the day-to-day challenges faced by all working parents. The capacity to get informed information from one place reduces the number of times that a parent has to share what may be a difficult story and increases the likelihood that the services sought will best fit family needs.

Source: Reprinted by permission of Susan Elisabeth Hunter, Principal, Hunter Consultants.

and the use of parents' talents and skills. Teacher strategies that incorporate this approach encourage family involvement and overcome barriers to communication often perceived by teachers and parents in a culturally diverse context. When parents learn how to talk and interact with teachers, they feel capable of making changes themselves and realize their own possibilities for involvement; teachers, in turn, come to recognize these parents as effective participants in their children's education (Bernhard et al., 1998). Family-centred care must find the strengths in every family and include not just parents but all of the people that are significant in the child's life. Create a sense of belonging!

LAY THE FOUNDATION

When families first arrive at the child-care centre, the concept of family involvement is articulated, expectations are discussed, roles are established, and the partnership begins. Successful encounters early on in the family–teacher relationship are critical to its long-term success and have a ripple effect since many families spend several years connected to the centre as new siblings are born. Teachers should envision the child inside the circle of his or her own family and understand the intricate tapestry that each family weaves. Simple strategies such as knowing how each family member wants to be addressed—for some a formal approach is best and for others being on a first-name basis would be expected—help to get the relationship off on the right foot. The home visit is also an integral part of this connection because it is crucial that teachers become well acquainted with families. This visit allows families to discuss their hopes for their child and for the teacher to begin the partnership. Teachers should plan for and encourage the involvement of fathers as well as mothers and other significant family members, focusing on the whole family unit.

BOUNDARIES

Far too often there are too many rules in early learning environments that create unnecessary boundaries and barriers to meaningful relationships. Wright, Stegelin, and Hartle (2007) ask

> What is the appropriate role of the school in the lives of children and families? How involved should the school and the child-care or classroom teacher become in the personal lives of the children whom they teach and care for? How far into the home and the neighbourhood should the school's responsibility extend? What forms should partnerships take? These are all important questions for teachers to ask. Boundaries that separate home, school and neighbourhoods are blurring and thus provide a rich opportunity for teachers to connect with parents and families in new and creative ways. (20)

Families may also be interested in learning more about you and not just about your professional qualifications. Relationships are reciprocal and as families share with you, you may be willing to share with them.

SHARE THE POWER!

It is only when we share the power that meaningful relationships can be established.

> Teachers and parents who are able to relate to each other as real people with strengths and vulnerabilities can validate each other, share responsibilities, and focus on the common goal of providing the best growing ground for the child. In this way, teachers and parents develop authentic relationships as partners, collaborators, co-educators, and co-decision makers in the life of the child. (Coleman, 1997: 14)

Families have every right to expect to be involved in decisions that affect their children. The closer we move to establishing equal and trusting relationships with the families we work with, the more realistic our expectations will be. True collaboration occurs when cooperative planning and problem solving takes place when all of the partners trust each other and communicate openly about concerns and expectations. Act with humility. Families are seen as competent contributing members of the program with much to offer. Power is shared!

MAINTAIN CONFIDENTIALITY

Teachers often establish such trusting relationships with families that they are often privy to very personal information. Greenman and Stonehouse (1996: 263) state

> It is tempting to justify knowing the details of a family's private life because it may help us "understand" or "teach" a child. But we have no right to know the ins and outs of family life any more than parents have a right to know about *our*

Boundaries! I taught for a very long time in early childhood environments, and the word *boundaries* always troubled me. I cared deeply about the children and their families, and the word suggests that there must be some "box" I was supposed to put around my interactions and connections with them. I have stayed in touch with so many of the families that I have worked with; some of the children are now getting married and having children of their own. I have been privileged to share in important moments in their lives—graduations, marriages, baby showers, difficult times, and sometimes someone just dropping by my office for a chat and a word of encouragement. Over the years I have received awards and accolades for my teaching, but the real reward has been my connection with these families. Boundaries just didn't work for me.

private lives in order to monitor program quality or to better understand the centre … Respect for parents demands that unless the situation is one of abuse or neglect, the parents control what information they wish to share. If we come to know something about the family, as professionals we should ask the parent if they mind our sharing the information with colleagues or supervisors.

DEVELOP STRONG INTERPERSONAL SKILLS

By the time students graduate from their ECE programs, they have gained valuable insight into the strengths and challenges in their communication style. Field placement experiences, feedback from faculty and co-operating teachers, and opportunities to interact with families will help the student teacher formulate a personal action plan for building stronger interpersonal skills. Teachers who are successful at involving parents tend to possess the same skills that make good teachers: an ability to be caring, to individualize and personalize their interactions, and to be self-reflective and evaluate their interactions with families. They must also be able to integrate their theoretical knowledge of effective communication into their interpersonal style. Understanding the impact of body language and how it can enhance or undermine communication is critical, as is voice pitch and tone. Active listening is directly related to showing respect for families. Effective communicators have a strong sense of self, an awareness of their strengths and weaknesses, and a desire to improve their skills.

A new definition of professionalism includes humility—the ability to wait, be silent, and listen. Teachers with humility are able to step outside standard frames of reference and find creative, novel ways to work with families because they are not limited by believing only the traditional methods will work. This allows teachers to take a nondefensive "why not" approach to parent requests. In this approach parent requests are recognized as legitimate ideas to mull over, rather than eliciting knee-jerk responses that "we just can't do that" or "our policies state" or even an automatic yes. (Gestwicki, 2010: 224)[*]

COMMUNICATE ON A REGULAR BASIS

"All change, even very large and powerful change, begins when a few people start talking with one another about something they care about."

—**Margaret J. Wheatley**
(Wisdom Quotes, n.d.)

Despite the fact that much of the information we exchange with parents happens at drop-off and pick-up, when both teachers and families are tired or rushed, these daily interactions are critical to successful relationships. Teachers can get the relationship off on the right foot by communicating with families on a regular basis and by sharing with them

[*]From GESTWICKI, *Home, School, and Community Relations, 7E.* © 2010 Cengage Learning. Reproduced by permission. www.cengage.com/permissions

Sensitive, caring teachers understand the importance of strong partnerships with families.

information and positive stories about their child; for example, "Samir has been really supportive to the new child in our room. He spent most of the morning with her explaining the different activities and showed her how we help ourselves at lunch. He was a great help." Sharing such personal information indicates to families that the teacher really is connected to their child. Teachers must also listen attentively and act accordingly when families share pertinent information about their child—his health, mood, whether he has had breakfast or not, events happening in the family, etc. Teachers must also consider the multitude of ways in which they can connect with families. There are many verbal, written, and visual means of communicating, all of which should be implemented to strengthen the centre–family bond (see chapters 5, 7, and 8).

> Educators are often very good at mass communications via newsletters, calendars, letters, and handbooks, but mass communications are not effective in shaping or changing attitudes. In order to change attitudes, educators must become effective at interpersonal communication with a target audience. (Rogers and Wright, 2012: 36–37)

When teachers share something of themselves, families are more likely to see a human side to the teacher. We are all more than our "presentation self." It is important for teachers to be insightful observers because much of what we communicate is done nonverbally. When we see parents having difficulty separating from their children, we can encourage their participation in a variety of ways in order to help them deal with the stress and, for some, the guilt of leaving their child in care. Teachers can support these parents by making them feel that they are an integral part of the child-care community. When family members are involved, it provides an opportunity to exchange information about the child and a chance for the teacher to encourage parents in their critical role. This partnerships allows the teacher to plan in a more sensitive and responsive manner for the child.

BE RESPONSIVE AND ACCOMMODATING

Teachers should try to organize their time so that they are available to talk to families at both the beginning and the end of the day. The supervisor can play a supportive role here. Home visits, family–teacher conferences, and social and educational events should be organized with a view to accommodating family schedules; child care should be provided when needed. This flexibility is critical. It is important that teachers acknowledge parental

Supervisors need to organize time for teachers to discuss issues with family members.

concerns and then act on them immediately. An educator who promises information or specific support should always follow through. This allows a climate of trust to develop between teacher and family.

Many teachers encounter families who are in crisis or who have great difficulty meeting the most basic of their children's needs. Teachers need to be able to respond to these situations in an appropriate manner. Warren (1979) suggests that teachers recall difficult moments with their own children or the children they have worked with in order to find common ground with parents "whose good moments are rare and whose self-image as parents may be so tarnished and torn that they present an outward appearance of not caring, or self-righteousness, or abdication of parenthood" (1979: 9).

If teachers hope to develop a partnership with parents and families that encourages the holistic development of children, they must learn to recognize the strengths inherent in every family. When parents are discouraged, teachers can help families feel hopeful. In many situations, families are supported by the simplest of gestures. Offering to make coffee, finding a moment to talk, being a responsive listener—these can make all the difference.

Teachers may want to consider what professional behaviour is: Does it mean keeping families at arm's length or does it mean reaching out, crossing traditional boundaries? A teacher who stays past her shift to care for a sick child because she knows it will be hard for this parent to leave work early is demonstrating a very different approach from the teacher who works according to the theory that "this child is sick and must go home!"

Teachers must be aware of all families, especially the ones who appear to be withdrawn or uncomfortable in the centre. They need to take the time to find out about the family's interests and concerns and to look for opportunities to include them. For example, teachers should try to figure out why a parent drops his or her child off without a word or calls for the child to leave at the end of the day without entering the room. Rather than labelling the parent as "uninterested" or "difficult," teachers should avoid making judgments and be curious about why this is happening. They need to look to themselves first before laying blame on the parent. Remembering that the centre is the teacher's "home" environment, how can she create a more welcoming situation for this parent? When educators put time and effort into doing this, they are rarely disappointed in their efforts.

TELL THE TRUTH AND BE PATIENT

A teacher's credibility depends on his or her ability to be truthful. We need to be honest with the families we serve, and they will expect this of us. Truth telling is often most challenging for teachers when they know that sharing difficult information will be painful for parents. Despite this, educators have the professional responsibility to share information in a kind and respectful manner. The way in which the information is given is critical; it is most likely to be received in a positive manner when the parents and teachers have mutually respectful relationships. There may be times when parents do not believe what the teacher has to say because they are shocked, hurt, or embarrassed. It is important for teachers to be patient and to continue to provide support and encouragement to these parents. Change is difficult for many of us and so the ability to take time to be patient and tolerant as parents struggle with difficult issues is critical.

DEMONSTRATE EMPATHY

> "One looks back with appreciation to the brilliant teachers, but with gratitude to those who touched our human feelings. The curriculum is so much necessary raw material, but warmth is the vital element for the growing plant and for the soul of the child."
>
> —Carl Jung

Empathy is perhaps a teacher's greatest quality. Our interactions with families provide us with insight into many of the stressors that make parenting challenging. "Empathy has been recognized as important to both general communication competence and as a central characteristic of competent and effective intercultural communication. It is the bedrock of intercultural communication" (Samovar et al., 2007: 341).*

An empathic person takes the perspective of another person. The empathic person experiences the emotions of another, demonstrating understanding and concern through verbal and nonverbal cues. We must also be aware of how our own cultural orientation will impact our interactions with others. For some, "saving face" will sometimes result in a comment when the speaker really means something very different. Learning to suspend judgment about issues that reflect your own experiences and knowing that others will have a different frame of reference will help you to be more open to others' words and actions.

The ability to respond to a family in crisis may make all the difference, as the Inside Look below demonstrates.

In other situations empathy may be displayed by planning workshops in the centre that support family needs. At a parent's request, a lawyer in the community gave a free seminar on preparing wills. In another centre, teachers hold a sleepover pyjama party on Valentine's Day. The children look forward to the event, and it allows parents to have time alone with each other, strengthening their

*SAMOVAR/PORTER/MCDANIEL. *Communication Between Cultures*, 6E. © 2007 Wadsworth, a part of Cengage Learning, Inc. Reproduced by permission. www.cengage.com/permissions

Inside LOOK

When Barinder's mother, Sarah, became critically ill after the birth of her second child, we knew that the family was under considerable stress. At a staff meeting we discussed ways in which we might support the family through this trying time. We knew that Barinder's dad wanted to spend as much time at the hospital with Sarah as he could, so doing the drop-off and pick-up at daycare was very difficult for him. One staff member suggested that he could pick up Barinder on his way to work and drop him off at his grandmother's house on his way home. Two other staff members who lived close to the family offered to look after Barinder in the evening when his grandmother was unable to provide child care. Several other staff members dropped off food for the family. Fortunately, Sarah fully recovered and the family was very appreciative of our support. We were all invited to a wonderful home-cooked meal where we celebrated her return to good health. This simple gesture, which in the end was so easy for us to organize, made a significant difference to this family, and in the process we became part of their extended family.

relationship. This is especially helpful for families who cannot afford a babysitter. Parents have been very receptive and appreciative of staff efforts.

At times an observant teacher can smooth the way for more active participation in the centre. One teacher organized a car pool for a group of families when she realized that many were not attending meetings because they lacked transportation. She also helped parents who lived near one another organize a walking pool so that when they left meetings at night they had someone to walk home with.

Greenman and Stonehouse (1996: 286) suggest that

> nothing communicates caring and goodwill so much as unexpected acts of kindness and generosity, such as a card on the parent's birthday, an unexpected appreciative note, an offer of tea, coffee, or a breakfast roll, perhaps a photograph of their child, or marking the anniversary of the family's time in the center. Offer a needed ride to the repair shop or home on a rainy day. If the program seeks out ways to make families happy, the resulting parent–staff relationships should weather nearly any storm.

RESPECT DIVERSITY IN FAMILIES AND SUSPEND JUDGMENT

Successful teachers are those who truly value and respect children, and who accept that children have their own worldviews, life experiences, and likes and dislikes. Successful teachers are concerned with broadening and expanding children's experiences, not discounting or trivializing them. Successful teachers are able to enter a child's world rather than simply demanding that the child enter *their* world. Successful teachers do not give children mixed messages or resort to such phrases as "Do as I say, not as I do."

An integral part of respecting children is accepting and celebrating their diversities. In nurturing diversity, teachers need to assess their own values and attitudes when developing and implementing a bias-free approach to their work. This approach must include not only cultural sensitivity but also inclusive practice incorporating ability, age, appearance, beliefs, family composition, gender, race, socioeconomic status, and sexuality. Teachers need to be able to critically evaluate materials such as books, kits, teaching aids, and DVDs and to replace those that promote stereotypes with more sensitive materials. Gonzalez-Mena and Bernhard (1998: 15) state,

> Caregivers must become aware that there is nothing in a young child's day that comes separate

from its cultural context. Culture is not directly taught, but grows out of the interactions between caregivers and children. Babies are born with the need to attach to and become involved with other people and their surroundings; they naturally observe and attend. Sensitive adults respond by constantly adjusting their behaviours and structuring the environment in ways that provide support for development and learning. Culture is the medium in which all this occurs and in child care, whether that medium matches or is in conflict with the home culture is very important. Steps should be taken to create an optimum match for infants and toddlers, especially those at risk of losing or rejecting their home culture.[*]

The curriculum must be developed in a manner that combats sexism, ageism, and racism. The teacher must demonstrate inclusive strategies that develop respect and tolerance for each child and family. The teacher will demonstrate zero tolerance for racist or exclusionary behaviour. This approach has the additional advantage of modelling for the children how to stand up for themselves and for others when dealing with bias of any kind. There may be times when teachers are called on to correct misinformation or to challenge racist or ethnic jokes made by colleagues or parents.

Derman-Sparks and the ABC Task Force (1989) suggests that teachers deal with parental biases in the following manner:

> Invest time and energy with individual parents by engaging them in a series of conversations. Find out what underlies the parent's racist (or sexist or handicappist) stance. Remember that none of us is free from bias. Each of us needs other people to help us sort through our experiences and identify contradictory attitudes and areas we want to change. (107)

"Cultural differences and conflicts will be overlooked, transgressions forgiven, and children will thrive as long as teachers care and value their students. Children treated with respect, dealt with honestly, and lavished with kindness succeed"[†] (Cardinal, 1994: 23–24). When the same generosity is applied to relationships with parents and the child's extended family, the groundwork is established for effective partnerships.

---

[*] Gonzalez-Mena, J., and J.K. Bernhard. 1998. "Out-of-Home Care of Infants and Toddlers: A Call for Cultural Linguistic Continuity." *Interaction* 12 (2). Reprinted by permission.

[†]Cardinal, E. 1994. "Effective Programming: A Native Perspective." *Early Childhood Education* 27 (1): (Spring– Summer). Reprinted by permission of the Alberta Teachers' Association.

Inside LOOK

Essential Connections: Ten Keys to Culturally Sensitive Care

1. Provide cultural consistency in harmony with what goes on at home.
2. Work toward representative staffing.
3. Create small groups.
4. Use the home language verbally and in writing.
5. Make environments relevant, reflecting the culture of the families served.
6. Uncover your cultural beliefs.
7. Be open to the perspectives of others.
8. Seek out cultural and family information.
9. Clarify values.
10. Negotiate cultural conflicts.

Lieberman (1998: 17) states that our own strong personal feelings about families may put us in a position where

> we can fall prey to [our feelings] when working with people from another culture. It is easy to experience their values and beliefs as hurdles that we need to surmount if we are to help the child. We need instead to search for an understanding of how their values fit into the very fabric of who parents are and how they see their children, themselves, their families, their lives, us, and the world at large. This enhances our empathy for parents and cuts down to size our preconceptions of what we can accomplish in "improving" each family's life.[*]

[*]A.F. Lieberman, 1998. "Culturally sensitive intervention with children and families," *IMPRINT: The Newsletter of Infant Mental Health Promotion* 22 (Fall): 17. The Hospital for Sick Children, Infant Mental Health Promotion, Toronto. Reprinted by permission.

Practice in the child-care centre needs to reflect an understanding that there is more than one way to raise a child.

EXPECT CONFLICT AND BE OPEN-MINDED

Conflict is an inevitable aspect of any working relationship; it can even be a catalyst for positive change. Teachers should learn to expect conflict and to value it as an opportunity to improve their communication skills. It is also important for teachers to examine their own feelings and biases when a conflict arises. Both teachers and parents will filter their perceptions about a conflict through their own experiences in both their personal and professional lives. Teachers are faced with many types of families. Some may be reluctant to be

Inside LOOK

At the Little River Child Care Centre, the older children invited parents and planned their own celebration for the holidays, with staff playing a supporting role. Whereas festivities in the past had always emphasized Christmas, this year things are different. Small groups of children speak and sing in honour of Chanukah, the Hindu festival of Diwali, and the African-American celebration, Kwanza. One parent speaks with great passion about her hopes for a future in which celebrations such as these are commonplace in child-care centres across Canada.

involved in the centre, while others may be over-involved in a manner that is not supportive. Some will have blind trust in teachers; others will challenge them at every turn.

Teachers need to feel confident that they have the ability to resolve problems. Remaining professional in any conflict, staying calm when a parent's anger escalates, and working toward common ground is critical when tempers are high. Teachers should strive to avoid being defensive, arguing, or becoming aggressive with the parent. They need to be respectful and remember that for many family members it takes great courage to bring forth a concern. There is also a strong possibility that if one parent is concerned, others are too. When listening to criticism, teachers should keep an open mind and try to see things from the parent's perspective.

They should also solicit the parent for ideas about possible solutions. Rather than give up on parents or react angrily or defensively, teachers should concentrate on searching for common ground (see Chapter 6 for more strategies for resolving conflict).

Further, as Elkind (1998) points out, teachers need to be flexible enough to adapt to a wide variety of families. Educators should involve parents who see teachers as hired help differently from parents who see teachers as in a class above themselves. To involve parents who see teachers as employees means that we have to take away parents' feeling of superiority. We do this best by communicating that we are professionals. We convey this impression when we refer to our training as well as to theory and research in our discussions with these parents and by always being professional in our work and

Inside LOOK

I worked in a centre that believed kids should get dirty and be little scientists—it had a wonderful adventure playground. Parents … would say: "We don't want our kids going outside. We spend an hour and a half on their hair. Two minutes later they are covered with sand. We can't get that stuff out and we spend our whole evening cleaning it up. So we don't want our kids going outside." For a while our earnest and empathetic response was "Gee, that's too bad. But this really is good for the children." Of course, our knowing response implied, "You poor, ignorant person, valuing appearance over good child development." Conflict continued and we learned.

Now the response to this sort of issue is "Okay, let's figure this out. Obviously it's important to you how your child looks. And you know it's very good for children to have these sorts of experiences. Let's come up with a solution." The assumption is two legitimate points of view—let's work it out together. In this instance, the answer was shower caps for the kids (Greenman, 1989: 11).

Source: Greenman, J. 1989. "Living in the Real World: Diversity and Conflict." *Exchange* 69 (October), p. 11. Reprinted by permission.

Inside LOOK

The other day I was trying to put together a camping curriculum, and I just mentioned in passing to a parent that I was looking for small tents. She said she had a couple I could use, and then she got so excited about the curriculum that she offered to bring in some camping pictures and equipment we could use. She even called another parent to ask if they had some old flashlights to donate. I keep forgetting what incredible resources families are to our program. Somehow, I always think I have to do everything myself.

Source: From *Parents to Partners: Building a Family-Centered Early Childhood Program* by Janis Keyser. Copyright © 2006 by Janis Keyser. Reprinted with permission of Redleaf Press, St. Paul, MN; www.redleafpress.org.

communications. With parents who are intimidated by the school and by us, our task is the opposite. We need to take away their feeling of inferiority and give these parents a sense of being competent and involved in their child's education. We do this best by "giving away" early childhood education.

ASK FOR HELP

Too often, teachers feel that they have to shoulder the burden of so many tasks in the centre and often forget that many parents are anxious to help. In many situations, just asking is all that is necessary. This allows families to enjoy the feeling of accomplishment that comes with partnering with the teacher.

ENGAGE IN REFLECTIVE PRACTICE

Effective teachers often engage in reflective practice. Whether done individually or in a group setting, self-reflection provides an opportunity for growth, insight, and professional development. Perhaps some of the following questions will help to begin the process:

- How do I really feel about partnerships with families?

- Do I have an understanding of the family's hopes and dreams for their child?

- Do I really have an open-door policy?

- Do my families really feel welcome in my room?

- Am I making the same effort with every family? If not, why?

- Do I worry when families are in the room? If so, why?

- Am I as open and honest as I can be with families?

- Am I a good listener?

- Do I see families as a great resource?

- Have I really looked at my biases and how they might be impacting my relationships?

These questions are just the beginning. Some teachers have benefited from being videotaped in the room and have found this to be an insightful tool to improving their practice. In a staff meeting, teachers may brainstorm other questions that require some reflective thought and then hopefully some purposeful action will be the result. The more we are able to understand our own reactions and emotions in regards to family involvement, the more we are able to try out new ways of doing things. Part of being a reflective professional is to continually examine our profession, its practices, and standards and to question the status quo. Especially as a student, you need to ask yourself—and others—why our profession values this, believes that, or does the other. Being reflective means not accepting current assumptions and practices without question.

BE INVOLVED IN PROFESSIONAL DEVELOPMENT

Teaching is a demanding job. According to Jorde Bloom (1995: 47),

Most people who enter the child-care field are caring and compassionate people. But the treadmill of activity that consumes their time and

Inside LOOK

When I look back on my first few years of teaching, I realize how important my relationship with the more experienced staff and the supervisor in my centre was. I often worried about whether parents would accept me in my role as a teacher, and I worried about whether I handled situations appropriately. One teacher in particular was always willing to help me sort through the range of emotions I felt as I tried to improve on my skills and learn the ropes. I remember that she suggested that I attend a parent meeting at another centre, and I learned so much about how I could change the way we approached meetings at our centre. Now, years later, I try to provide the same kind of support to new teachers as they are hired on in our centre, as well as to the ECE students I am supervising. I still remember how vulnerable I felt.

Community Program, San Romanoway Revitalization Association

The Jane and Finch area continues to be known as one of Toronto's toughest neighbourhoods. Three apartment buildings —No. 5, No. 10, and No. 25 San Romanoway—are among the most populated buildings in the area. They buildings contain 892 units and are home to approximately 4,400 residents, of whom 2,800 are children and youth. The crime rate within the San Romanoway neighbourhood was a staggering 128 percent above the national average in 2002, according to the *Neighbourhood Quality of Life Survey*, which was conducted by Dr. George S. Rigakos, Professor of Law and Criminology at Carleton University in Ottawa, Ontario. Stephnie Payne, a nurse who emigrated from England almost 40 years ago has lived, she says, "in the shadow of these buildings." Seeing children, youth, and families in crisis, Stephnie identified an immediate need for safe and supportive programs for the residents. Her desire to increase community capacity for all people, and the promise of dedicated resources and support from all levels of government and public and private agencies, with local involvement of residents, formed the basis for the creation of the *San Romanoway Revitalization Association (SRA)*. The SRA is a charitable, nonprofit organization serving approximately 4,400 people living in the Jane and Finch community. To-day, the SRA works collaboratively with all stakeholders and oversees culturally sensitive programs for children, youth, seniors, and families. Along with the original programs started in 1999, in recent years the organization has been focusing its efforts on supporting its youth and seniors. Gang prevention is at the heart of many of the newer initiatives. An underutilized indoor pool was transformed into a space that now houses a cinema, a recording studio, a computer lab, an art gallery, a place for seniors to gather during the day, and a rental space for community events.

Youth 'N' Charge is a youth-led, youth-driven initiative that features a fully operational recording studio. Those aged 16–29 years are provided with engaging artistic, recreational, and leadership programs such as Music Entrepreneurship and Publishing Skills where youth work under the mentorship of experienced entrepreneurs, and music industry professionals can pursue their own business. Beat the Street is an artistic program that provides youth with instruction in the area of beat production. Strong Women provides young women with positive recreational and leadership opportunities in an outdoor setting, and Rhythm Defines Movement provides high school youth with a creative steel-pan, drumming, dance and storytelling program that highlights the diversity of the community.

The Youth Host program is a one-on-one befriending program that facilitates friendships with individuals, newcomers, and volunteers from the Jane-Finch community. The host is someone who lives in the area and can assist in educating participants on the customs, norms, and traditions of Canada while gaining an understanding of the experiences and lifestyles of the newcomers' countries.

The SRA's motto, "Making It Happen Together," continues to be based on an innovative, collaborative community-private sector approach to revitalization. "We have proven that our support for, and efforts on behalf of, the neighbourhood families, children, at-risk youth and seniors is creating a safer and healthier community," says Stephnie Payne, Executive Director of San Romanoway Revitalization Association.

For more information about this unique collaborative community initiative, visit the website at **http://ckc.tcf.ca/org/san-romanoway-revitalization-association**.

Source: Reprinted by permission of Lisa Teskey, Associate Dean, School of Health Sciences, Humber College.

energy on the job often keeps them from establishing close relationships with one another. The physical layout of space, time pressures, and conflicting schedules are just some of the barriers that prevent staff from exchanging information, sharing ideas, and lending and receiving support.[*]

Other barriers include the cost of conferences and professional development opportunities, the lack of wage-related recognition for any advanced training, the lack of paid professional development time, and the cost to the centre of providing replacement teachers. Teachers need time to meet with their peers and exchange concerns and ideas. Receiving positive, constructive feedback helps a teacher to build both self-confidence and the energy to deal with everyday situations that arise in the centre. An environment of empathy and support is especially important for new teachers, who may be enthusiastic about relationships with families but lack the expertise of their more seasoned colleagues. New graduates are most likely to succeed and stay in the field when they have been mentored by gifted teachers who are committed to the field. A mentoring approach is necessary to help create a stable and strong early childhood community.

No teacher should feel that the responsibility for strong family–centre relationships rests entirely on his or her shoulders alone. Each teacher brings his or her own strengths and by sharing these with other teachers in the centre, a more cohesive and effective approach can be forged. For example, one teacher may be a gifted writer, another a budding artist; each can utilize his or her individual strengths and apply them to projects and events at the centre. There is strength in individual talents and expertise that is combined for the greater good. It is also important for teachers to link with other teachers in a variety of different programs in their community. These collaborative ventures allow teachers to share new ideas.

Personal development and growth are also fundamental to teachers. According to Swick (1991: 40), "Teachers who are in a process of continuing personal growth are more receptive to parental involvement and actually take more initiative to pursue the partnership process." He goes on to say that teachers secure in their personal development are more likely to be responsive to both children and parents in terms of their cultural and individual needs. He believes that teachers trained in early childhood education programs (where parent–teacher involvement courses are often mandatory), instead of elementary or middle-school programs, more fully support parental involvement and education (Swick, 1991: 19–30). This information is further supported by the National Institute for Early Education at Rutgers University, which reports that young children's learning and development clearly depends on the educational qualifications of their teachers. In the United States, the most effective preschool teachers have at least a four-year college degree and specialized training in early childhood (Barnett, 2004).

REFERENCES

Aldemir, J. (2008). Pre-Service Teachers' Beliefs About Young Children, Their Parents and Teaching in Early Childhood Education. *Dissertation Abstracts International Section A. Humanities and Social Science*, 68, (10-A). 4189.

Amatea, E. 2009. *Building a Culturally Responsive Family-School Relationship*. Merrill.

Ambert, A. 2012. *Changing Families:Relationships in Context*. 2nd ed. Pearson Canada.

Anderson, K.J., and K.M. Minke. 2007. "Parental Involvement in Education: Toward an Understanding of Parents' Decision Making." *The Journal of Educational Research*, 100(13). 311.

Angelou, M. 1993. *Wouldn't Take Nothing for My Journey Now*. Random House.

Barbour, C., N.H. Barbour, and P.A. Scully 2008. *Families, Schools, and Communities. Building Partnerships for Educating Children*. Pearson Merrill Prentice Hall.

Barnett, S.W. 2004. "Better Teachers, Better Preschools: Student Achievement Linked to Teacher Qualifications. Preschool Policy Matters." National Institute For Early Education Research. Issue 2. Retrieved January 28, 2013, from http://www.nieer.org.

Based on a True Story. n.d. Retrieved January 23, 2013, from http://currierose.wordpress.com/2010/09/16/%E2%80%9Cthere-can-be-no-vulnerability-without-risk-there-can-be-no-community-without-vulnerability-there-can-be-no-peace-and-ultimately-no-life-without-community-%E2%80%9D-m-scott-peck/

Baum, A.C., and P. McMurray-Schwarz. 2004. "Preservice Teachers' Beliefs About Family Involvement: Implications for Teacher Education" *Early Childhood Education Journal,* 32(1).

Beach, J., and K. Flanagan. 2010. *Examining the Human Resource Implications of Emerging Issues in ECEC*. Ottawa. Child Care Human Resource Sector Council.

Beach, J., J. Bertrand, and G. Cleveland. 1998. *Our Child Care Workforce: From Recognition to Remuneration*. Ottawa: Child Care Human Resources Steering Committee.

Becker, S. 2005. "The Good, the Bad and the Few: Men in Child Care." Retrieved from http://www.cccf-fcsge.ca/practice/policy/men_en.html

Bernhard, J., M.L. Lefebvre, K.M. Kilbride, G. Chud, and R. Lange. 1998. "Troubled Relations in Early Childhood Education: Parent–Teacher Interactions in

[*]Jorde Bloom, P. 1995. "Building a Sense of Community: A Broader View." *Child Care Information Exchange 101*. January–February, p. 47. Reprinted by permission.

Ethnoculturally Diverse Child Care Settings." *Early Education and Development* 9 (1): 5–28.

Bertrand, J. 2008. *Understanding, Managing and Leading Early Childhood Programs in Canada*. Toronto: Thomson Nelson.

Bertrand, J., and C. Gestwicki. 2012. *Essentials of Early Childhood Education*. Nelson Education.

Birnbaum, N., C. Crill Russell, and G. Clyne. n.d. *Vital Communities, Vital Support. How Well Do Canada's Communities Support Parents of Young Children*. Phase 1. Invest In Kids.

Brainyquote.com. n.d. Lao Tzu. Retrieved January 23, 2013, from http://www.brainyquote.com/quotes/keywords/teach.html#EhGrQrS74QLV2d8Z.99

Britzman, D.P. 1998. *Lost Subjects, Contest Objects: Toward A Psychoanalytic Inquiry of Learning*. Albany: State University of New York Press.

Bronfenbrenner, U. 1974. *A Report on Longitudinal Evaluations of Preschool Programs: Is Early Intervention Effective?* Vol. 2. Washington, DC: DHEW Publishing.

Calvin and Hobbes Wonderland. n.d. Retrieved January 23, 2013, from http://www.lovine.com/hobbes/quotes.html

Canadian Child Care Federation. 2011. *Code of Ethics. Occupational Standards for Child Care Practitioners*. Retrieved February 15, 2013, from http://www.ccsc-cssge.ca/projects-publications/completed-projects/occupational-standards-for-early-childhood-educators

Cardinal, E. 1994. "Effective Programming: A Native Perspective." *Early Childhood Education* 27 (1): (Spring–Summer).

Christenson, S.L., and S.M. Sheridan. 2001. *Schools and Families: Creating Essential Connections for Learning*. New York: Guilford Press.

Chud, G., and R. Fahlman. 1995. *Honouring Diversity within Child Care and Early Education: An Instructor's Guide*. Vol. 11. Vancouver: British Columbia Ministry of Skills, Training and Labour and the Centre for Curriculum and Professional Development.

Coleman, M. 1997. "Families and Schools: In Search of Common Ground." *Young Children*, 52(5). 14–21.

Couchenour, D., and K. Chrisman. 2000. *Families, Schools, and Communities: Together for Young Children*. New York: Delmar Thomson Learning.

Couchenour, D., and K. Chrisman. 2011. *Families, School, and Communities: Together for Young Children*. Wadsworth Cengage Learning.

Department for Children, Schools and Families. 2008. *Common Mental Health Problems: Supporting School Staff by Taking Positive Action*. Sherwood Park, UK: DCSF Publications.

Derman-Sparks, L., and J. Olsen Edwards. 2010. *Anti-Bias Education for Young Children and Ourselves*. NAEYC.

Derman-Sparks, L., and the ABC Task Force. 1989. *Anti-Bias Curriculum: Tools for Empowering Young Children*. Washington, DC: National Association for the Education of Young Children.

Dever, M.T., and R.C. Falconer. 2008. *Foundations and Change in Early Childhood Education*. Toronto: John Wiley and Sons.

Doherty, G. "Partners in Quality." 1997. Canadian Child Care Federation. Retrieved from http://www.cccf-fcsge.ca/publications/piq_en.html

Donohue, C. 2010. *Technology in Early Childhood Education*. Child Care Exchange.com. Retrieved January 28, 2013, from http://www.ccie.com/resources/view_article.php?article_id=50154

Early Learning for Every Child Today (ELECT). 2007. "A Framework for Ontario Early Childhood Settings." Retrieved January 28, 2013, from http://www.children.gov.on.ca/htdocs/English/topics/earlychildhood/early_learning_for_every_child_today.aspx

Elkind, D. 1981. *The Hurried Child: Growing Up Too Fast Too Soon*. Boston: Da Capo Press.

———. 1998. "From Our President, David Elkind." *Young Children*. January.

Epstein, J. 2000. *School and Family Partnerships: Preparing Educators and Improving Schools*. Boulder, CO: Westview.

Epstein, J. and Associates. 2009. *School, Family and Community Partnerships. Your Handbook for Action*, 3rd ed. Corwin Press.

Epstein, J.L. 1995. "School/Family/Community Partnerships: Caring for the Children

Essa, E., and R. Young. 1994. *Introduction to Early Childhood Education*. Toronto: Nelson Canada.

Fisher, R., and S. Brown. 1988. *Getting Together: Building a Relationship That Gets to Yes*. Boston: Houghton Mifflin.

Gaine, C. 2000. "Anti-racist Education in 'White' Areas: The Limits and Possibilities of Change." *Race, Ethnicity and Education* 3 (1): 65–79.

Galinsky, E. 1988. "Parents and Teacher–Caregivers: Sources of Tension, Sources of Support." *Young Children*, 43(3),4–12.

Gestwicki, C. 1992. *Home, School and Community Relations: A Guide to Working with Parents*, 2nd ed. New York: Delmar.

———. 2004. *Home, School and Community Relations*, 5th ed. New York: Thomson Delmar Learning.

———. 2000. *Home, School and Community Relations: A Guide to Working with Parents*, 4th ed. New York: Delmar.

———. 2010. *Home, School and Community Relations*. 7th ed. Wadsworth Cengage Learning.

Gonzalez-Mena, J. 1998. *Foundations: Early Childhood Education in a Diverse Society*. Toronto: Mayfield Publishing.

———. 2007. "50 Early Childhood Strategies for Working and Communicating with Diverse Families." Pearson Merrill Prentice Hall.

———. 2010. *50 Early Childhood Strategies for Working and Communicating with Diverse Families*. Columbus, OH: Pearson, Merrill Prentice Hall.

Gonzalez-Mena, J., and E.D. Widmeyer. 1989. *Infants, Toddlers, and Caregivers*. Mountain View, CA: Mayfield.

Gonzalez-Mena, J., and J.K. Bernhard. 1998. "Out-of-Home Care of Infants and Toddlers: A Call for Cultural Linguistic Continuity." *Interaction* 12 (2).

Goodreads. n.d. "Alvin Toffler." Retrieved January 23, 2013, from http://www.goodreads.com/author/quotes/3030.Alvin_Toffler

———. n.d. "Cesar Chavez." Retrieved January 23, 2013, from http://www.goodreads.com/quotes/47934-once-social-change-begins-it-cannot-be-reversed-you-cannot

———. n.d. "Winnie-the-Pooh Quotes." http://www.goodreads.com/work/quotes/1225592-winnie-the-pooh

Graue, E., and C. Brown. 2003. "Pre-Service Teachers' Notions of Families and Schooling." *Teaching and Teacher Education*, 19, 719–735.

Greenberg, P. 1989. "Parents as Partners in Young Children's Development and Education: A New American Fad?" *Young Children.* May.

Greenman, J. 1989. "Living in the Real World: Diversity and Conflict." *Exchange* 69 (October).

Greenman, J., and A. Stonehouse. 1996. *Prime Time. A Handbook for Excellence in Infant and Toddler Programs.* St. Paul, MN: Redleaf Press.

Haigh, K. 2004. "Creating, Encouraging, and Supporting Relationships at Chicago Commons Child Development Program." In J. Hendrick, ed., *Next Steps toward Teaching the Reggio Way: Accepting the Challenge to Change.* Columbus, OH: Pearson Merrill Prentice Hall.

Hammer, K., and Bascaramurty, D. 2012. "School Clinics Making Big Strides in Public Health." *The Globe and Mail,* March 17. A4. Retrieved February 20, 2013, from http://www.theglobeandmail.com/news/national/school-clinics-making-big-strides-in-public-health/article4171836

Hartzell, M., and B. Zlotoff. 2004. "Parents as Partners." In J. Hendrick, ed., *Next Steps Toward Teaching the Reggio Way: Accepting the Challenge to Change.* Columbus, OH: Pearson Merrill Prentice Hall.

Heath, P. 2009. *Parent-Child Relations: Context, Research, and Application,* 2nd ed. Prentice Hall.

Hendrick, J., and K. Chandler. 1996. *The Whole Child: Developmental Education for the Early Years,* 6th ed. Toronto: Prentice Hall Canada.

Hepworth Berger, E. 2004. *Parents as Partners in Education. Families and Schools Working Together,* 6th ed. Columbus, OH: Pearson Merrill Prentice Hall.

Hepworth Berger, E., and M. Riojas-Cortez, M. 2012. *Parents as Partners in Education. Families and Schools Working Together,* 8th ed. Columbus, OH: Pearson.

Hinsliff, G. 2003. "Men Battle Prejudice in Childcare. *The Guardian.* June 7. Retrieved from

Hiscott, K. 2010. "Child and Family Centres—A Part of an Early Learning System for Ontario." *Interaction.* Fall. http://www.guardian.co.uk/uk/2003/jun/08/schools.children

Hughson, P. 1994–1995. "Learning Together: A Parent's Perspective. *Research and Clinical Issues, Zero to Three* 15 (3). December–January.

James, C.E. 1999. *Seeing Ourselves: Exploring Race, Ethnicity and Culture,* 2nd ed. Toronto, Thompson Education Publishing.

James, C.E., and H.H. Muhammad. n.d. *A Study of Children in Childcare Programs: Perceptions of Race and Race-Related Issues.* Toronto: Municipality of Metropolitan Toronto Children Services and Multicultural and Race Relationships Divisions.

Janmohamed, Z. 2005. "Rethinking Anti-bias Approaches in Early Childhood Education: A Shift Toward Anti-racism Education." In George Dei and Gurpreet Singh Johal, eds., *Critical Issues in Anti-racist Research Methodologies.* New York: Peter Lang.

John Dewey Source Page. (2007). Retrieved January 23, 2013, from http://www.brocku.ca/MeadProject/Dewey/Dewey_1907/Dewey_1907a.html

Jorde Bloom, P. 1995. "Building a Sense of Community: A Broader View." *Child Care Information Exchange* 101. January–February.

Kagan, S.L., and P.R. Neville. 1994. "Parent Choice in Early Care and Education: Myth or Reality?" *Research and Clinical Issues, Zero to Three.* February–March.

Karen's Linguistics Issues. "R. Verdi." Retrieved January 23, 2013, from http://www3.telus.net/linguisticsissues/quotes.HTM

Kastings, A. 1992. "Partnerships with Parents: What Centres Say." *The Early Childhood Educator: The Journal of Early Childhood Educators of British Columbia.* April.

Keyser, J. 2006. *From Parents to Partners: Building a Family-Centered Early Childhood Program.* St. Paul, MN: Redleaf Press.

Kiefer, H., and N. Cohen. 2004. *Handle with Care. Strategies for Promoting the Mental Health of Young Children in Community-Based Child Care.* Canadian Mental Health Association. The Hinks-Dellcrest Centre.

Kumashiro, K.K. 2010. *Toward a Theory of Anti-Oppressive Education.* American Educational Research Association. Retrieved January 28, 2013, from http://rer.sagepub.com/cgi/content/abstract/70/1/25

Larsen, J.M., and J.H. Haupt. 1997. "Integrating Home and School: Building a Partnership." In C.H. Hart, R. Charlesworth, and D.C. Burts, eds., *Integrated Curriculum and Developmentally Appropriate Practice Birth to Age Eight.* Albany, NY: SUNY.

Learning Circle Five. n.d. "Definition of Collaboration. Collaboration Framework—Addressing Community Capacity: the National Network for Collaboration." Retrieved from http://crs.uvm.edu/nnco/collab/framework.html

Lieberman, A.F. 1998. "Culturally Sensitive Intervention with Children and Families." *Newsletter of the Infant Mental Health Promotion Project* 22. Fall.

Lindsay, J. 1999. "Public Education: Views of a Concerned Parent." Retrieved January 28, 2013, from http://www.jefflindsay.com/Education.shtml

LMTimebank.org. n.d. Retrieved January 24, 2013, from http://lmtimebank.org/blog/how_tb_works

Lott, B. 2001. "Low-Income Parents and the Public Schools." *Journal of Social Issues,* 57.

Lowell Krough, S. 1994. *Educating Young Children: Infancy to Grade Three.* Toronto: McGraw-Hill.

Malaguzzi, L. n.d. "A Charter of Rights for Parents."

Mangione, P.L., J.R. Lally, and S. Signer. 1993. "Essential Connections: 10 Keys to Culturally Sensitive Child Care." Sacramento, CA: CDE Press.

Mann, B. 2008. "Welcoming Families as Partners in Child Care." *Interaction.* Spring.

Martinez, M.L., M. Black, and R.H. Starr. 2002. "Factorial Structure of the Perceived Neighborhood Scale (PNS): A Test of Longitudinal Invariance." *Journal of Community Psychology,* 30(1), 23–43. 38–40. Retrieved from http://ibs.colorado.edu/cspv/databases/record_details.php?record number=701&vio_name=vioeval&cur_page_limit=50

Maslow, A.H. 1954. *Motivation and Personality.* New York: Harper and Row Publishers.

Mercredi, O. 1992. "Our Traditions, Our Children, Our Future: Native/Aboriginal Early Childcare." Fredericton, New Brunswick. 6–7 November.

Miller, R.J. 2008. "Language, Literacy and Social Development. You Can't Have One Without the Other." *Interaction.* CCCF/Spring.

Murphy Kilbride, K. 1997. *Include Me Too! Human Diversity in Early Childhood*. Toronto: Harcourt Brace Canada.

National Network for Collaboration. 1995. Collaboration Framework—Addressing Community Capacity. Retrieved from http://crs.uvm.edu/nnco/collab/framework .html

National Parent Teacher Association. 2000. *Building Successful Partnerships: A Guide for Developing Parent and Family Involvement Programs*. Bloomington, IN: National Educational Service. Retrieved January 28, 2013, from http://www.njpirc.org/documents/resourcesEducators ParentInvolvement/Roadblocks%20and%20Detours.pdf

National Statement on Quality Early Learning and Child Care. 2007. Canadian Child Care Federation: Families Building Partnerships with Practitioners.

Neugebauer, R. 1994. "Recruiting and Retaining Men in Your Center." *Child Care Information Exchange*. May/June: 5–11.

Norrie McCain, M., F.J. Mustard, and K. McCuaig. 2012. *Early Years Study 3. Making Decisions Taking Action*. Margaret & Wallace McCain Family Foundation.

Occupational Standards for Child Care Administrators. 2006. Child Care Human Resources Sector Council. Retrieved January 28, 2013, from http://www.ccsc-cssge.ca/projects -publications/publications

Occupational Standards for Early Childhood Educators. 2010. Child Care Human Resources Sector Council. Retrieved January 28, 2013, from http://www.ccsc-cssge.ca/projects -publications/publications

Pascal, C. 2009. *With Our Best Future in Mind*. Retrieved January 28, 2013, from http://www.ontario.ca/en/ initiatives/early_learning/ONT06_018876

Pawl, J.H. 1993. "Impact of Day Care on Parents and Family." *Pediatrics* 91 (1). January.

Pelletier, J., and J.M. Brent. 2002. "Parent Participation in Children's School Readiness: The Effects of Parental Self-Efficacy, Cultural Diversity and Teacher Strategies." *International Journal of Early Childhood*, 34: 45–61.

Percy, I. 2003. *Commandments for an Enthusiastic Team: Collaboration with Purpose and Passion*. Inspired Production Press.

Pugh, G. ed. 2006. *Contemporary Issues in the Early Years: Working Collaboratively for Children*. London, UK: Paul Chapman Publishing in association with the National Children's Bureau.

Pusher, D. 2007. Parent Engagement: Creating a Shared World. Ontario Education Research Symposium. January 18–20.

Quotations Page. n.d. William Butler Yeats. Retrieved January 23, 2013, from: http://www.quotationspage.com/forum/ viewtopic.php?t=1886

Ramsey, P.G. 2004. *Teaching and Learning in a Diverse World: Multicultural Education for Young Children,* 3rd ed. New York: Teachers College Press.

Robinson, E.C. 1988. "Vanishing Breed: Men in Child Care Programs." *Young Children* 43 (6).

Rockwell, R.E., L.C. Andre, and M.K. Hawley. 2010. "Families and Educators as Partners." Belmont, CA: Wadsworth/ Cengage Learning.

Rogers, R.H., and V.H. Wright. 2012. *Assessing Technology's Role in Communication between Parents and Middle Schools*. Retrieved from http://www.ejite.isu.edu/Volume7/Rogers.pdf

Rudney, G. 2005. *Every Teacher's Guide to Working with Parents*. Corwin Press.

Samovar, L.A., R.E. Porter, and E.R. McDaniel. 2007. *Communication between Cultures*, 6th ed. Thomson Wadsworth.

Sturm, C. 1997. "Creating Parent–Teacher Dialogue: Intercultural Communication in Child Care." *Young Children* 52 (5): 34–38.

Swick, K. 1991. *Teacher–Parent Partnerships to Enhance School Success in Early Childhood Education*. NEA Early Childhood Education series. Washington, DC: National Education Association and Southern Association on Children under Six.

———.1992. "Teacher–Parent Partnerships." *ERIC Digest*. Champaign, IL: ERIC Clearinghouse on Elementary and Early Childhood Education.

———. 2003. "Communication Concepts for Strengthening Family-School-Community Partnerships." *Early Childhood Journal* 30. 275–80.

Swick, K., and S. McKnight. 1989. "Characteristics of Kindergarten Teachers Who Promote Parent Involvement." *Early Childhood Research Quarterly* 4: 19–29.

Switsun, D. 1994. "Do You Know Your Anti-Bias Curriculum?" *Child Care Focus* 29. Spring.

Teacher Appreciation. n.d. Retrieved January 23, 2013, from http://www.teacher-appreciation.info/Quotations_on_ teaching

Thinkexist.com. n.d. "Haim Ginott." Retrieved January 23, 2013, from http://thinkexist.com/quotation/i-ve-come-to -the-frightening-conclusioin-that-i/347295.html

———. n.d. "Haim Ginott." Retrieved January 23, 2013, from http://thinkexist.com/quotation/teachers_are _expected_to_reach_unattainable_goals/202932.html

———. n.d. "Stephen Covey." Retrieved January 23, 2013, from http://thinkexist.com/quotation/seek_first_to _understand-then_to_be/178484.html

———. n.d. "Virginia Satir." Retrieved January 23. 2013, from http://thinkexist.com/quotation/feelings_of_worth_can _flourish_only_in_an/184239.html

Toronto District School Board. (n.d.) Equinox Holistic Alternative School. Retrieved March 28, 2013, from http://www.tdsb.on.ca/schools/index.asp?schno=5903

Uttal, L. 2002. *Making Care Work: Employed Mothers in the New Childcare Market*. New Brunswick, NJ: Rutgers University Press.

Warren, R.M. 1979. *Accepting Parents*. Washington, DC: National Association for the Education of Young Children.

We Share." *Phi Delta Kappan*, 76, 701–712.

Weissbourd, B. 1992. "Building Parent Partnerships." *Scholastic Pre-K Today*. August–September.

Whitaker, T., and D.J. Fiore. 2001. *Dealing with Difficult Parents and with Parents in Difficult Situations*. Larchmont, NY: Eye on Education.

Winder, C. (2009). "Early Childhood Education Students' Perceptions of Family Involvement." Poster presented at the Sixth Annual Summer Institute on Early Childhood Development, OISE, Toronto.

Wisdom Quotes. n.d. "Margaret J. Wheatley." Retrieved January 24, 2013, from http://www.wisdomquotes.com/ topics/compassion

Wright, K., D.A. Stegelin, and L. Hartle. 2007. *Building Family, School, and Community Partnerships*, 3rd ed. Pearson Merrill Prentice Hall.

Yao, T. 1988. "Working Effectively with Asian Immigrant Parents." *Phi Delta Kappan*, 70(3).

York, S. 1991. *Roots and Wings*. St. Paul, MN: Redleaf Press.

You Bet I Care! Survey. 2000. Ottawa: Human Resources Development. Retrieved from action.web.ca/home/ cfwwb/attach/ybic_report_1.pdf

Created by Owen

Chapter 4

FIRST IMPRESSIONS

Courtesy of Atelier Child Care Centre, Vancouver, British Columbia

"It is well to give when asked, but it is better to give unasked, through understanding."

—*Kahlil Gibran*

LEARNING OUTCOMES

After studying this chapter, you will be able to

1. identify effective communication practices educators can use in their initial contact with families

2. describe the process of orienting a new family to an early learning environment

3. outline the elements of a successful family visit and identify some of the barriers to family visits

4. discuss the separation process and how teachers can facilitate childrens' transition to the child and family centre, to new playrooms, and to school environments

INITIAL CONTACT WITH A CHILD AND FAMILY CENTRE

We know that beginnings are critical. You never get a second chance to make a first impression! Initial contact is a process that should not be rushed and from the first contact, families should feel a connection. Many families who are searching for child care for the first time are unsure of how to make the right choice and their options may be limited. Different families require different types of care and there is no one-size-fits-all approach. Most families are introduced to a centre when they phone to ask about a space for their child. This call is usually followed by a visit to the centre and a meeting with the supervisor and teachers. If their first impressions are favourable and a position is available for their child, the family may make a commitment to enroll. Then, once the child is registered, the family begins what may be a long-term relationship with the centre.

The first few months in this new environment often set the stage for the type of interaction that will characterize the family–centre relationship—hence the importance of a systematic orientation process. The following information illustrates the process most families follow when they enter an early learning environment for the first time.

THE FIRST TELEPHONE CALL

The phone rings. A harried staff member, dealing with a sick child in her arms, picks up the phone and curtly names the centre. She informs the parent that she is too busy to deal with her questions and tells her to call back when the supervisor can speak to her. The parent, listening to the crying child in the background and the teacher's agitated voice, consults her list and decides to call another centre.

Working in an early learning environment sometimes can be frantic. Not only must teachers deal with sick children on a regular basis, but because most centres cannot afford the luxury of full-time secretarial support, most of the day-to-day administrative responsibilities fall to the supervisor and teachers. Given that the first impression of the centre is usually based on a phone call, the development of telephone skills is essential.

Information given over the telephone should be communicated in a positive, caring manner. Families are listening not only for details about the centre but also for a tone of warmth and genuine interest in their participation. Though supervisors and teachers may repeat this information many times over the course of a year, it is important to remember that families will be hearing it for the first time. Personalizing the call and asking questions about what the family is looking for will help the centre begin the process of building a positive relationship. A good strategy is to record all the information from the call on a standard form. If the family decides to visit the centre, this form can be used by the supervisor to prepare for the visit.

WRITTEN COMMUNICATION

Once families have expressed interest, the next step is to send them written information about the centre. Because families continue to evaluate the centre on the basis of this written material, it should be professional in appearance and error-free; it should also effectively convey the philosophy of the centre. (Detailed guidelines for written communication with families are provided in Chapter 8.) When necessary, this information should be translated into the family's first language. While email may be more expedient, it is important not to assume that all families will have access to a home computer.

VISITING THE CENTRE

The first visit will no doubt set the tone for the relationship between the families and the staff.

> We know that first impressions don't mean everything but we also know that they do matter. Therefore, we need to plan carefully for the *feeling tone* of the first meeting with parents. In addition to organizing information materials, we need to plan on demonstrating our openness, interest, concern and willingness to collaborate. (Rudney, 2005)[*]

For families whose children will be starting around the same time, a group orientation may be set up to facilitate introductions. Not all new families are able to visit during the day; staff may need to make arrangements to meet with these families at the end of their workday or on weekends. Visits that are set up outside business or school hours may allow other family members to come to this first, most important, visit. Visits are best timed when staff members are available to talk to families.

When setting up the first visit, it may be appropriate for families whose first language is not English to bring along another family member or trusted friend who speaks English to help them feel more comfortable. If this is not possible, a centre staff member who comes

---

[*]Reprinted with permission of Corwin Press, from G. Rudney, 2005. *Every Teachers Guide To Working With Parents*; permission conveyed through Copyright Clearance Center, Inc.

from the same cultural and language background may be able to assist in the orientation, or a professional interpreter may be hired. From the moment families enter the centre, they are gathering information about the culture of this environment. Creating a positive impression is based on many factors.

CREATING A WELCOMING ENVIRONMENT

It is important that families are able to see as soon as they walk through the door that they will be valued partners in this early learning environment. In practical terms, this could mean taking down the many signs that abound on a school landscape—staff parking only, no food or drinks, visitors please report to the office. These signs prohibit, admonish, or regulate, and send a message to parents and community members that they are, at best, inconvenient guests and, at worst, trespassers or interlopers. It could mean putting up new signs and displays with welcoming and culturally representative messages, in the language(s) of the community. "Hospitality and invitation remain empty gestures until they are made with the genuine intention to open up the school space and agenda, to co-create it with parents and other caregivers as well as with students" (Pushor, 2007: 7).

This poster represents many languages that may be spoken at the centre.

Environments send powerful messages.

The importance of a welcoming physical environment cannot be underestimated; it plays a crucial role in our ability to adapt and adjust. As Greenman (1988: 44) notes, "children reared in fortresses barricaded against the world outside, or in dingy basements, or in worlds of fluorescently-lit plastic and tile will have different aesthetic sensibilities than those raised in light, airy, open places with plants and easy access to the outside."

The physical design of a centre can affect the relationships among those who work there and those who visit. The family's impression of the centre begins before they meet anyone who works there: parking should be accessible, and there should be a safe drop-off and pick-up location for children who arrive by bus or in a car pool. The early learning environment should also be accessible for people with disabilities. Staff should routinely check for things such as peeling paint, unweeded flower beds, and cluttered walkways. The means of entry should be clearly explained at the entrance. (For example, a security code is required in many centres to ensure the safety of the children.) A welcoming foyer provides a gradual transition to the playrooms and a calming gathering place for families, especially when comfortable seating is in place. Too often, early learning centres are designed only with

children in mind. There should be designated spaces just for adults—places to hang up their coats, places to store strollers, safe places to store their bags and briefcases, and a comfortable location for reading family resource materials.

A home-like atmosphere will have more appeal to families than an institutional look. Function and comfort should go together. Cubby areas should be designed so that families can easily assist their children in their dressing routine. Families can personalize this space with family artefacts or pictures to make the connection from home to centre.

Maintaining a bulletin board near the main entrance helps keep families informed about relevant news and events. The bulletin board might include

- photographs of families involved in centre activities

- photographs of children's experiences

- names and brief biographies of permanent staff and regular supply teachers

- students who are doing field placements

- volunteers

- information about upcoming centre events

Emily's shadow box helps her identify her space as well as reminding her of home.

Biographies of the teachers, which include their educational qualifications, help reassure families that their children are being cared for by professionals.

Imagine a room where there are bright splashes of colour, often attached to moving bodies, and warm, muted hues on the carpet and walls. Sunshine catches the light of a prism in one corner and on the floor is a patch of sunlight so bright it makes you squint. There are soft, indirect lights, as well as shadows and cool, dark corners. There are hanging baskets of trailing green plants, flowers, pussy willows and cattails, angel hair, and dried grasses. The beauty of life is captured in artwork by Monet and Wyeth and assorted four-year-olds. There are the smells of fresh earth, lilacs and eucalyptus, garlic, and baking bread. One hears laughter and singing, animated conversation, soft classical music, and the backbeat of reggae from somewhere in the corridor. There is a ticking of clocks, a chirping of birds, and the squeaking and rustling of a guinea pig. There is a breeze from an open window as one walks around feeling heavy, dark wood and silky fabric; hard, cold metal and warm fur; complex textures and watery, slippery, gooey things.

Source: Greenman, 1988: 63.

- copies of recent newsletters

- copies of the latest minutes of the board of directors meeting

Playrooms should be labelled by age group, with the names and photos of the teachers prominently displayed. Students completing their field placements in the room should also be provided with an opportunity to post their photos and a brief biography. Labelling throughout the room should reflect the linguistic diversity of the community. Bulletin boards placed directly outside the playrooms can be used to keep families up to date about happenings specific to each playroom.

Families should see open spaces, cozy spaces, bright spaces, peaceful spaces, gathering places,

Courtesy of Scotia Plaza Child Care Centre

A simple gesture, such as having a comfortable place to sit and read, can make a difference to a weary parent.

working places, loft spaces, climbing spaces, resting spaces, and outdoor spaces. Variety is essential! The environment must be functional, too, in the sense that it accommodates the specific needs of the children and adults in the room. Is there easy access for the children to the outdoor environment—sliding glass doors to a green environment? Organizing bulletin boards, displaying artwork, and storing children's equipment should be done in a manner that avoids visual clutter. Lighting should be adequate, with the opportunity to raise and lower the levels of light. Are there lots of windows that let in natural light? Plants help to green the space and demonstrate the importance of nature to the children. Are animals cared for? Are there area rugs on the floor? Are there pictures and posters on the wall? Is music being softly played? Are there display tables showing off the children's work? Particular attention should be given to "soft" spaces to create an inviting and comforting feel. In other words, is the centre's "story" evident?

Inside LOOK

We were nervous when we arrived at the centre. Mario is our first child. We were undecided about whether to look for someone in our neighbourhood to look after him once I went back to work or to bring him to the Janeway Child and Family Centre. We had heard a lot of positive things about the centre, so we wanted to take a look. Theresa, the supervisor, was very friendly, and it wasn't long before we felt comfortable enough to ask the 1001 questions we had about group care. She was very patient with us. It was clear that she was very proud of the centre and the teachers who worked there. She took us on a tour of the centre, and when we got to the infant room we were very impressed with what we saw. The teachers were warm and caring, and despite the constant activity they handled everything in a calm manner. There was even a private space for me so that I could continue to breastfeed Mario when I could. All the information about the centre was reviewed with us, and we especially enjoyed the DVD of the infant room that showed us what a typical day for Mario might be like. This first visit really made a difference for us. Now we know that this centre is where we want him to be.

EXHIBIT 4.1   Two Different First Impressions

CENTRE VISIT A

Dalisay and Bayani Villanueva are looking for a daycare space for their 3-month-old daughter, Mayumi. Unaware that they needed to plan so far in advance, both parents are worried they will not find a suitable centre before Dalisay has to return to work in four weeks.

They arrive at the Janeway Child and Family Centre. The supervisor of the centre, Theresa Sanchez, had provided clear directions in an earlier—and very positive—telephone exchange. Some of the windows at the front of the centre are decorated with children's artwork. A large and colourful sign out front provides directions to the daycare. Instructions for entering the centre are located above the intercom system on the outside door. A pleasant-sounding voice responds to their request for entry, and they are buzzed in.

Inside, they are greeted by a large bulletin board that features photographs and short but informative biographies of the teachers and supervisor. Dalisay and Bayani are very impressed with the educational credentials of the staff; they are especially interested to see that one of the teachers was raised in the Philippines, their home country.

Samples of children's artwork line the hallway. At the end of it is a large sign with the word "welcome" written in a number of languages. Dalisay and Bayani are encouraged by the bright and warm feeling exuded by the centre.

As they reach the entrance to the playrooms, the supervisor approaches them, her hand extended in a gesture of welcome. She shows them an area designated for families where they can hang up their coats and leave their bags and briefcases. She then invites them into her office for a cup of coffee and freshly made fruit bread. The orientation process and the partnership between the centre and the family have begun.

Centre Visit B

Gabriella is a single parent who is new to this neighbourhood. As the mother of two children—a school-age child and a preschooler—she is pleased to discover that the local school has a daycare centre attached to it. She hopes to be able to place her two children in one location.

Gabriella calls the centre for information about the availability of spaces. She is told that the teacher is too busy to talk to her and she should call again later and speak to the supervisor. Gabriella calls back and leaves a message for the supervisor. Two days later she has still not heard from her. Knowing she has only a few days left before she must return to work, Gabriella decides that she will pay the centre a visit in the hopes of meeting with the supervisor.

At the school's front entrance there is no sign to indicate the location of the child care. Gabriella tries to get directions from the main office, but the secretary is busy with a student and the principal is in a meeting with a parent. Finally, Gabriella is given directions by one of the children sitting in the office.

Finding her way to the centre but feeling like an intruder, Gabriella is debating whether to leave when she finds that no one in the office when finally, the supervisor appears in the hallway. After Gabriella explains her situation, the supervisor tells her she is on her way to a meeting but will call her as soon as she can. As she talks, the supervisor escorts Gabriella outside the building. She seems reluctant to allow Gabriella to observe the centre without her being present. The supervisor does not apologize for failing to return her phone call. Gabriella leaves the centre with no information but with very strong reservations about placing her children in such an inhospitable environment.

The two very different experiences outlined in Exhibit 4.1 demonstrate the importance of the human connection. When we welcome families into the centre in the way that we would welcome friends into our home, we understand the impact of the role of the staff.

THE ROLE OF THE SUPERVISOR

Introducing new families to the centre is one of the supervisor's most important roles, and one that requires a great deal of thought and effort. When the supervisor's office is near the entrance to the centre, it is well situated as a place not only to welcome visitors but also as a place where families can touch base as they come and go. One centre supervisor has framed all the teachers' ECE diplomas, other educational diplomas, degrees, and professional development certificates on the wall above her desk, and several families have informed her that they were reassured to see these.

The supervisor should be waiting when the family arrives. An enthusiastic, friendly greeting gets the visit off to a good start. Using the parents' names is a sociable way to begin and since names are one of our most prized possessions, it is important to be respectful by using them correctly. Some families will encourage the use of their first names, while others will prefer a more formal approach. An assortment of toys, books, papers, and markers should be kept on hand for children who are accompanying their families on this visit. This is a big day for the child, so the visit should be as pleasant and stress-free as possible. Families are alert to how the supervisor interacts with their child; this interaction sets the tone for the visit.

An offer of refreshments as everyone gets acquainted is a good way to begin the orientation and demonstrates that the centre has planned for the visit. While refreshments are being organized, the supervisor might show families a photo album featuring family members, children, and educators

Seeing children actively engaged sends positive messages to new families.

in a variety of centre-related activities. Supervisors should be wary of sitting behind their desk and creating barriers between themselves and the parents. In the ensuing discussion, supervisors should provide families with a clear understanding of the licensing requirements (and how the centre meets them) and the philosophy of the centre. The supervisor should ask questions about what the family is looking for, what special interests they have, and so on. This is an opportunity to find out more about the family, not only as parents but also as persons in their own right. Families will want to know what makes this centre unique and if it will be a good match for them.

It is important for the supervisor to listen as much as she talks. Families will have an in-depth understanding of their child; for example, they will know if their child is very physical and active. In such a case the family may be looking for a centre with an emphasis on outdoor play—a "forest school" approach—that will support this area of their child's development. Families will also want to know how you will respond to their child's individual temperament despite a group care situation.

Some centres have developed a DVD that takes families through a typical day at the centre; families may also be provided with one to take home in which the information given during the visit is summarized. The take-home DVD is particularly helpful if some family members are not able to attend the orientation. There may be resistance to the concept of group care from family members who did not grow up with this option, and the DVD may help support the parents' choice. This information can also be conveyed in brochures or family handbooks. Previous issues of the centre's newsletters provide additional insight into the centre and highlight milestones and achievements. All of this information can be organized ahead of time and presented to families as they leave.

Supervisors can prepare themselves for parents' questions by keeping a record of commonly asked questions. It is important for supervisors to strike a balance between overwhelming families with material and conveying too little information. What they should emphasize is the importance of the family–educator relationship to the centre experience and the centre's professional approach.

TOURING THE CENTRE

A tour of the centre early in the visit helps consolidate the information provided during the opening discussion. During the tour the supervisor can point out ways in which the centre's philosophy translates into action. The supervisor should also point out contributions families have made in order to reinforce the active role families play in the centre. A parent of a child already attending the early learning environment may also be asked to join the orientation at this point, to contribute a family's perspective.

Teachers in each of the rooms should be prepared for the visit and greet the visitors with enthusiasm. If appropriate, family members should be encouraged to call the teachers and the supervisor by their first names. The supervisor should give the family some basic information about the teacher's education and work experience. It is reassuring for families to know about the people who will be working with their child. The supervisor should point out the important areas of the room and the materials that are available to the children. If learning outcomes are posted in each of the interest centres, families will see the possibilities for active child participation and growth (see Chapter 7). The daily schedule and the program plan can also be discussed.

Families often worry that group care will make it impossible for their child to receive the individual attention he or she needs. The supervisor should review with families the ratios in the room and the size of the group. Staff willingness to celebrate the uniqueness of each family should be evident in their interactions and be embedded in the environment. Family members should be invited to stay and observe in the playroom. Opportunities will arise to demonstrate the centre's philosophy with respect to guiding children's behaviour, exploration of materials, and problem solving. Talking about children in the group who may share interests with the visitors' child can help instill in new families a sense of belonging; for example, "You mentioned that your child is very interested in dinosaurs. Sarah, our resident dinosaur expert, is the same age as your daughter. She will look forward to having someone to share her dinosaurs with."

In their discussion of the role of the supervisor in talking to prospective parents, Kaiser and Rasminsky (1994: 30) offer this insight:

> Small events tell families a great deal about the atmosphere at your centre. If a child asks you to tie his shoe or an educator wants you to stay with her group while she takes someone to the bathroom, parents will notice that the children all know you and the staff is relaxed when you are around. Seeing this level of comfort is very reassuring.[*]

Families should also visit the kitchen and meet the cook, with whom menus and food issues can be discussed. Not unlike a home environment, the kitchen is the heart of the centre. Parents often come to seek advice and problem solve. The cook, like each member of the childcare team, plays an integral role and reflects

---

[*]Kaiser, B., and J.S. Rasminsky. 1994. "Encouraging Parent Participation." *Interaction*. CCCF/Summer. Reprinted by permission.

Inside LOOK

Having a simple activity for parent and child to participate can set a welcoming one:

> After brief introductions, Ms. Bender gave Avi and his mom a pencil and a "Treasure Map" to locate various places in the classroom. As they explored the room, checking off the locations of coat hooks, bathroom, and learning centres and locating Avi's name on a bulletin board and on his cubby, Ms. Bender chats with other arriving families. Avi and his mother leave talking excitedly about the start of the new school year.

Source: Barbour, Barbour, and Scully, 2008: 289.

As a parent and teacher, I understand the challenges of bringing your child to a group setting for the first time. Parents of infants often seem the most vulnerable. In some families, this is the first time that a child may be cared for by someone other than a family member, and this can increase the level of anxiety and sometimes conflict within the extended family itself. One of the ways in which I have tried to support families in their transition is to ask them to write a letter to me telling me everything that they want me to know about their child. Some letters were very extensive and others only a few sentences, but I always learned information from the families that filling out the orientation forms just didn't capture. These were heart-warming and passionate words, and it was a wonderful opportunity for me to discuss their letters. This clearly strengthened our bond with each other, and we all got off to a positive start!

The environment should reflect a wide range of cultures.

commitment and constant attention to the children and their families.

The tour can conclude with an examination of the outdoor environment. This is an opportunity to explain the benefits across all curriculum areas when children are actively engaged in the outdoors in all kinds of weather! With increased concerns regarding obesity in young children, families should be able to see that the outdoor environment is an integral part of the child's day. The outdoor environment must reflect places for active play, solitude, groups, art, blocks, dramatic play, woodworking, puzzles, reading, interactions with nature, gardens, sand, water, birds, etc. Here the supervisor can talk about the measures taken to ensure the safe use of equipment and, more generally, about the importance of an exciting outdoor play-based green environment.

New families should be able to see how the centre's outdoor play space provides meaningful learning opportunities for children.

ENSURING QUALITY: HELPING PARENTS KNOW WHAT TO LOOK FOR

In the initial written communication with the family, it may be helpful to include a checklist advising families on what to look for in any child and family centre. Families will become better, more discriminating consumers who are more informed about issues that are critical to the development of quality care when they are given this information. The Canadian Child Care Federation (CCCF), provincial ministries, or municipal agencies are good sources. For example, *Making a Quality Child Care Choice* is available from CCCF: **http://www.cccf-fcsge.ca/store/elc-resource-sheets**.

In 2011 research conducted in Toronto and Colorado, Michal Perlman, associate professor in the Department of Human Development and Applied Psychology at OISE/UT, and her colleagues found that parents rate their child's centre highly on just about any and all dimensions of quality. The research team used standardized measures of quality to conduct extensive assessments in a variety of child-care centres. These evaluations were then compared with ratings by parents whose children attended those centres. The gap was enormous! Research on parental choice and knowledge regarding early childhood environments reveals that parents select a program for pragmatic reasons—location, scheduling to fit their circumstances, costs, and availability of a scarce spot. Basically, due to scarcity, most parents take the first program they can find. The researchers also found that parents spend very little time in their child's program. In one study, they observed more than 1000 children being dropped off in the morning in over 100 classrooms in Toronto. Adults spent an average of 62 seconds dropping off their children. These findings suggest that parents have little opportunity to become knowledgeable about their child's program. At the heart of this challenge is the fact that many parents simply want to believe the centre is fine; parents who are dissatisfied with their child's program have very few options. Dealing with guilt when there's little you can do about it is a lot to handle. This highlights the important role of government and other agencies in helping to monitor quality and in providing parents with tools to make informed decisions for their children. We need to raise the level of parental literacy regarding the child care they need, not just the child care they can get (Perlman, 2011).

Some centres may create an observation sheet that draws the visiting family's attention to quality indicators in their program (see Exhibit 4.2).

When it is time for the family to leave, a thoughtful gesture may be to take a photo of the child in the room and print it for the child to take home. The child can share this picture with others in the family, and it may ease some of the tension related to the forthcoming, official first day. After the tour, the family may return to the supervisor's office for a discussion of any issues that arose from their observations. If the supervisor, parents, and educators have planned carefully for this visit, the family should begin to feel a sense of belonging and connection!

EXHIBIT 4.2   Sample Item from Observation Sheet

In our preschool room, you can observe the following ways in which we encourage self-help skills:

- At meal time, children serve themselves from small serving bowls and pour their own milk and juice.
- Snack is set up during the morning, and the children decide when they will come and eat, after washing their hands.
- After eating, children return their plates and utensils to labelled bins on the serving cart.
- The washroom is located in the room and has child-sized toilets and sinks for easy access. Children use it independently during the day.
- Children are encouraged to brush their teeth after lunch, following criteria for storage required by the Public Health Department.
- Recycled paper cups are stored in the washroom so that when the children are thirsty they can help themselves.
- Cubbies are set up for easy access to assist the child in retrieving clothes when dressing.
- The equipment in the room is scaled to children's height to allow for independent use.
- Equipment is stored in small bins that are easily lifted out and returned by the children.
- Playroom carts are labelled pictorially so that children can return their bins to the correct space.

Haigh (2004: 79) recounts an innovative strategy developed by the Chicago Commons Child Development Program for demonstrating the importance of children and their families:

We saw that photos of children or families displayed within a center can become documentation of the history and life of the center itself. We asked each child who attends the center to make a simple self-portrait with black marker on a beige tile ... In this way, we have created a way to respect the children and support the center's history as we portray work from all who have attended the program.

Source: HENDRICK, JOANNE, NEXT STEPS TOWARD TEACHING THE REGGIO WAY: ACCEPTING THE CHALLENGE TO CHANGE, 1st Edition, © 2004. Reprinted and Electronically reproduced by permission of Pearson Education, Inc., Upper Saddle River, NJ.

If a space is not currently available, the supervisor may outline the waiting-list procedures and advise families that they will be kept informed about their status. Supervisors can stay in touch with those families on the list by sending invitations to centre events and copies of newsletters. Some families may also request the names of families in the centre who may be willing to speak to them about their experience at the centre. While they are waiting, families should also be encouraged to visit as many programs in their community as possible in order to determine the best possible fit for them.

If a space is available and the family decides that they would like to come to the centre, the family should review the required forms and policies of the centre. A comprehensive family handbook (see Chapter 8) will provide families with an overview of important centre information. The issue of fees should be clearly addressed. Supervisors may assist English language learner families if forms are not available in their first language. Forms translated into the most common languages in the community will greatly assist non-English-speaking parents. The supervisor should outline who will have access to the child's file; families will be reassured to know that all information is confidential. Parents should be encouraged to provide relevant information about their child, including possible separation issues, experiences in previous child-care settings, and so on. Finally, the ways in which families can play an active role in the centre can be highlighted to reinforce the partnership approach!

FAMILY VISITS

"I want you to come to my house,
and yet I don't.
You're so important,
but our screen door has a hole in it,
and my mother has no fancy cake to serve.
I want you to come to my house, teacher,
and yet I don't.
My brother chews with his mouth wide open,
and sometimes my dad burps.
I wish I could trust you enough, teacher,
to invite you to my house." Cullum (1971: 50)

The family visit is one of the most effective ways of creating a sense of partnership with families. Kyle et al. (2002) promote the use of teacher-initiated visits but prefer to call these visits not home visits but, rather, family visits. The former term has a negative connotation for some because it has been used by different agencies when there are issues in the family that need to be addressed. According to Brooks (1994: 17), the family visit enables the teacher "to establish a personal and authentic relationship with individual children who are able to see the teacher as someone their parents invite into their homes. This parental approval is reassuring for children."

Family visits are positive options for families who, because of work schedules or other family issues, are unable to spend much time at the centre. Families may also feel more comfortable interacting with the teacher in their home. Family visits provide educators with insights into family–child interactions, the care strategies that work best for parents, and the values and priorities that families wish to instill in their child. "The information we gather in the home in just one hour would perhaps take us several months to collect in a more alien environment of the classroom with other children demanding our attention" (Brooks, 1994: 17). When teachers have an opportunity to see what families are trying to accomplish at home with their children, they can look for ways to support these efforts in the early learning environment.

Through the family visit, a teacher can learn about a child's

- relationship with family members and siblings

- position in the family (effects of being the youngest, oldest, etc.)

- living environment (blended family, lone-parent, joint-custody situation, two-parent, parent who is ill, elderly parents living with the family, etc.)

- developmental level of play

- parental attitude to play

- social skills

- communication skills

- exposure to books and materials for manipulation and exploration

- level of independence

- general knowledge and interests

- favourite playthings

- access to available neighbourhood resources (library, community centre, etc.)

Haigh (2004) states that in Head Start programs in the United States, home visits are now mandatory at the start of the year for all families. Staff have attempted to reframe their approach to these visits and, rather than overwhelming parents with information, they began to ask them about their ideas:

This was done by asking them their hopes and dreams for their children. Interestingly enough, parents did not say that they hoped their children would learn their ABCs and 1, 2, 3s. Some examples of their hopes are:

"I hope he grows up to be a professional person."

"I hope he has a sense of humour."

"I hope my child finishes school before having children."

"I hope my child will do for others."

We have now added other questions to encourage parents to share their ideas. Some of them are:

"What kind of adult would you wish your child to be?"

"What was your favourite family activity as a child and what is your family's favourite activity now?"

"What was your first day of school like and do you have a picture of yourself as a young child?"

Inside LOOK

A Parent/Teacher Home Visiting Program in Sacramento, California, allows teachers to build a relationship with families, learn more about their students' strengths and weaknesses, and pave the way for future home-school communication that will ultimately improve their teaching and outcomes for students. Evaluations show increased parental involvement and improved parent–teacher relationships and communication. These studies have also found positive student outcomes, including improved performance (e.g., attendance and grades), more academic credits, and higher graduation rates. In 1999, the Sacramento efforts became a model for a state-wide program providing millions of dollars for K–12 home visiting in California. That resource renewed again in 2006 facilitated hundreds of schools' ability to launch home visiting efforts, and the state has been invited by over a dozen other states to help train teachers on home visits.

Source: Lopez et al., 2010: 10.

The ideas that parents have shared are then displayed within the centre or the classroom, so in some way the voice of the parent is included and visible within the program. (p. 78)*

The family visit provides families with an opportunity to ask more questions about the centre and its philosophy, and to learn more about the person who will be working closely with their child. The educator might bring with her a few photographs

*HENDRICK, JOANNE, NEXT STEPS TOWARD TEACHING THE REGGIO WAY: ACCEPTING THE CHALLENGE TO CHANGE, 1st Edition, © 2004. Reprinted and Electronically reproduced by permission of Pearson Education, Inc., Upper Saddle River, NJ.

that reflect more personal information—a photo of her family, her enjoying a favourite sport, the family dog, etc. The main benefit of family visits for children is that they begin their relationship with the teacher on familiar territory and will not be encountering a stranger when they come to the centre for the first time. With this information the teacher can plan a more meaningful entry for the child by incorporating activities and experiences that are sure to be of interest.

Some centres continue to use family visits throughout a child's time at the centre. Additional family visits can be especially beneficial for those

Inside LOOK

When I arrived, the first place Jeremy took me was to his room. It was filled with models and books about dinosaurs. He even had dinosaur wallpaper! When I asked him to show me his favourite book, he brought me *Patrick's Dinosaur*. On Jeremy's first morning at the centre I set up the sand table with dinosaurs and rocks and created a tropical feel by adding plants from our garden. In the library area I brought out books about dinosaurs and on the table I stood *Patrick's Dinosaur*. When Jeremy entered the room, he was very hesitant and stuck close to his father. They slowly walked around the room and eventually they wandered over to the sand table. Jeremy noticed the dinosaurs right away. He turned to look at me and a huge smile spread across his face. He let go of his father's hand and from that moment on he was actively involved. The look of relief on the Jeremy's father's face was overwhelming!

Inside LOOK

Personally, our family visits changed our lives. We came away from our children's homes with respect and admiration for families doing the best they could, some under dire circumstances. We realized that all parents want a good education for their children … In the past it was easy to blame parents for a child's lack of school success by saying, "I wish someone at home cared about this child." We discovered instead that of course parents do care! When teachers make an effort to meet parents a little more than halfway, they find many ways to help children. After our family visits we found ourselves relating more often, verbally and emotionally, with the children. The children were delighted to tell their classmates that last night the teachers came to visit. After talking to parents in such a personal way, we began to view all of the children in our classes more compassionately and with greater understanding. Now we know that each child has a unique and special life. Our goal is to nourish the skills children do have and to appreciate parents and encourage them to be an integral part of their child's education.

Source: Gorter-Reu, M.S., and Anderson, J.M. 1998. "Home Kits, Family Visits, and More!" *Young Children* 53: 71–74. © NAEYC. Reprinted with permission.

children who have had difficulty adapting to life in the centre. Visits might also be scheduled when an important event has occurred in the home (the birth of a baby, for example). A child-centred family visit also affords older children an opportunity to show initiative. As host, the child can help organize the event. Family visits are also warranted when families are unable or reluctant to meet with the teacher at the centre.

ELEMENTS OF A SUCCESSFUL FAMILY VISIT

Family visits should be discussed with the family in the initial meetings with the supervisor as part of the orientation process. Families should understand the purpose of the visit—it's an opportunity to lay the foundation for a strong partnership between the home and the centre. They should also be reassured that any special planning or preparation for the visit is not necessary. A telephone, written, or email reminder to families just before the date of the visit is a good idea. Teachers should be thoughtful about how they dress for this occasion in order to create a comfortable but professional impression. Parents should know the expected length of the visit in advance. While family visits usually last from 30 minutes to an hour, teachers should be sensitive to indications that they are overstaying their welcome or, in some instances, teachers may stay even longer if the family is engaged and anxious to talk. It is important for the teacher to arrive on time.

The teacher may wish to bring a small gift or book for the child. Some resourceful teachers create a box of goodies that they take on all their family visits. These colourful inexpensive boxes might include age-appropriate puzzles, puppets, or books, and they serve as a nice icebreaker. If the teacher brings markers and paper, the child might create a picture that the teacher can take to the centre. When the child arrives at the centre, he or she will see the picture proudly displayed. The teacher might also consider bringing a small photo album with photographs of children playing in the room at the various interest centres. The teacher and child can talk about the fun things that will happen when the child arrives at the centre. Taking a photo of the child and his or her family and placing it on a bulletin board will provide both

a way to introduce the family to existing parents and a fun reminder of the family visit for the child. If the centre has a website, the teacher could post the photo with a short welcoming caption. The child might also email the teacher before the big day. If there are other children in the family, the educator should be prepared for this and should include them in the visit in order to avoid feelings of exclusion. For the families, teachers might bring a brochure about centre involvement or a booklet that provides information about all the community resources that they might want to access—upcoming special family events, libraries, community centres, swimming pools, clinics, special attractions, and so forth.

Perhaps the most essential element for a successful family visit is an ability to accept family behaviours and conditions that differ from those the teacher has experienced. An open and accepting attitude on the part of the teacher is essential to the success of a family visit. Respect for individual family styles and cultural preferences are a critical part of providing support to families and of building a trusting relationship. Professionals must seek to understand the uniqueness of each family. For teachers who are unsure of cultural expectations, they might, in advance, consult with colleagues or friends to understand appropriate cultural etiquette. An effective family visitor will be sensitive to the expressed and unexpressed needs of the child and other family members, will demonstrate versatility and flexibility during the visit, and will avoid alienating families by coming across as an expert. It's important to be informal and approachable, but not too casual.

The family visit is a good chance for the teacher to underscore the importance that he or she places on the parents' input and to learn more about the uniqueness of each family. Asking families to provide reading material that reflects their values and cultural beliefs may also be an important learning opportunity for an educator. Reinforcing the importance of the role of the family in the centre is critical to building lasting partnerships.

Teachers and families might address some, or all, of the following topics during the family visit; however, assure families that if there are questions that they are not comfortable answering, they may decline to respond.

- previous experiences in child care

- life in other cities or countries

- important events in the child's life

- strengths and positive qualities in the child

- activities the child likes to do at home

- outdoor activities the child enjoys

- things the family likes to do together

- favourite toys, snuggle blankets, and so on

- whether the child likes to read or to be read to

- responsibilities in the home

- schedules and routines

- things that upset the child

- comforting strategies

- the child's fears or concerns

- relationship with siblings

- other friendships

- food restrictions and nutrition generally

- eating habits (favourite and least favourite foods)

- child's attitude toward coming to the centre

- upcoming separation and how everyone in the family is feeling

- ways of incorporating religious or family customs into centre life

- family expectations for the child

- family interests and skills (create a skills bank for later use)

- nature and degree of possible family involvement in the centre

- community supports

- family members' memories of their early years in school

It is also possible to find out during a family visit how family members might be interested in participating in the centre. The teacher should be careful not to pressure families but suggest a variety of ways in which the centre might utilize their skills and talents; for example, teachers can ask how family members might be willing to participate: attending meetings on topics relevant to the families; collecting "trashables" for art experiences; helping with gardening activities; building equipment or doing repairs in the centre; driving or supporting field trips; working on a newsletter or participating on the board of directors; volunteering in the play room; arranging a visit to their workplace; contributing children's books or dramatic play items; carrying out an activity based on their interests or skills; or contributing to the planning of curriculum and community activism are just some examples. One teacher was admiring the necklace the child was wearing and the child mentioned that her mother had made it. The mother showed the teacher her work and the teacher was so impressed that she invited the mother to the centre to demonstrate her jewellery making to the children.

Teachers can also use the family visit to find out more about special family arrangements. In the case of divorced families, for example, teachers will want to know if visitation restrictions apply to the other parent and if that parent should receive centre mailings and invitations to family–teacher conferences. If foster families are involved, what role would they like to play? In a more relaxed environment, one that is familiar territory for the

Inside LOOK

As we drove up to the house we could see Jill watching out the window for our arrival. By the time we had walked up the path, she was already hopping up and down in the doorway. Mom, with Jill's baby brother on her hip, was just behind her. "'Do you like banana muffins?" [asked Jill], searching our faces anxiously and reaching for her mom's hand.... When we assured her that they were indeed our very favourite kind, her face broke into a wide grin of relief. "Good, we made some for you!"

Source: Brooks, 1994: 14.

parent, this opportunity for one-on-one interaction allows for more direct communication. Feedback is immediate and various family members may participate in the conversation.

It is not uncommon for families to offer refreshments. It is important for teachers to take part in the sharing of this food. Many families will have gone to a great deal of trouble. Teachers might also bring food that reflects their family favourites.

Finally, it is critical that the teacher maintain confidentiality, respecting the family and their lifestyle.

FOLLOW-UP TO THE FAMILY VISIT

Following the family visit, the teacher should send the family a note, which could be addressed to the child, expressing enthusiasm about the visit and thanking them for their hospitality. The teacher might also include a picture of the playroom so the child can show this to other family members. This could also be done by email. If a centre website has been created, an innovative approach might be to have a virtual tour of each of the playrooms for families to show to others or as a strategy for preparing the child for this transition. The teacher should also add to the child's file any information that might assist other teachers in supporting both the child and the family. In assessing the success of the family visit, teachers can use the self-review checklist included in this chapter to rate their own performance.

WHY FAMILY VISITS AREN'T DONE MORE OFTEN

There are a number of reasons family visits, despite their benefit to all concerned, are not a more regular part of a centre's interaction with families.

TIME

Many ECE educators say their work is too demanding and time consuming to allow for family visits. However, all centre staff must look for creative ways to accommodate these visits. For example, constructing a visiting schedule by grouping children by neighbourhoods will minimize travelling time. It may not be possible to begin by visiting all existing families, but the process can be used as each new family arrives. Teachers must weigh the demands on their own time against the benefits of these visits. Family visits may feel labour intensive upfront, but the benefits are enormous.

MONEY

Some teachers may insist on being paid for conducting visits on their own time. Many centres lack overtime budgets, and they can't afford to hire extra staff to replace teachers who are away on family visits during regular work hours. One solution is to have volunteers or the supervisor take over while teachers visit families. Centres should also consider paying staff for mileage.

RELUCTANT FAMILIES

For any of several reasons, families may be reluctant to have the teacher visit them in their home. Those who have not developed a trusting relationship with teachers may view the visit as an invasion of their privacy, as a form of harassment, or as an opportunity for the teacher to make judgments about their family life. Some families worry that

Inside LOOK

I find it interesting that here in Canada, teachers very seldom interact with the children and their families in their homes. In China, my home country, our teacher was much revered in our village. She was an honoured guest at our birthday gatherings and would often share a meal with us. We took great pride in her visits, which were often discussed long after they were over. We considered her a part of our extended family.

As a teen parent, I could tell that the teachers in the infant room felt that I was less than capable in my parenting role. This was never openly discussed but I could tell by the looks they exchanged with each other and their voice tone when they spoke to me. They played the role of "expert," as if I didn't really understand the importance of nutrition, responsive caregiving, and so on. So I decided to invite the teachers to my apartment for a family visit. We spent a long time talking. I shared my dreams for my daughter and talked about my role as a mother. There was a marked change in their attitude toward me. It was more respectful and they were more willing to work with me instead of against me. Several years later when we were leaving the centre, one of the teachers in the infant room confided to me that I had helped her become a better teacher. She explained that the family visit had not only changed her attitude about me as a teen parent but more importantly made her examine her own bias about teen parents.

the teacher wants to visit because their child is not doing well and the teacher plans to instruct them on how to be a better parent. Other families may be so overwhelmed by problems resulting from situations such as poverty or illness that they cannot deal with a visitor to their home. Teachers should respect the wishes of such families and perhaps arrange for meetings to take place in the centre. For some families a neutral place in the community may make them feel more comfortable.

RELUCTANT CENTRES

In some situations, teachers may see the real benefits of family visits but receive little or no support from their supervisor. When, for some reason, a family visit is not feasible, the teacher can invite families to the centre for a special lunch or even to his or her own home. Families who are unwilling to meet under any circumstances can be contacted by letter, email, or telephone.

RELUCTANT TEACHERS

Some teachers are discouraged by the time and effort required to plan and carry out a family visit. Others are unsure what to expect or how to conduct themselves outside the confines of the teaching environment. Some teachers feel that a family visit might be too intrusive, while others worry about offending families from other cultures because of

their own lack of understanding. However, there may be well-respected community members able to provide support and guidance on these issues.

In some rural communities great distances must be travelled to meet with families. In other situations, some teachers feel that they are putting themselves at risk by visiting families with histories of drug or alcohol abuse. "High-crime neighbourhoods or ... isolated rural areas can be dangerous. Visitors in problem areas often carry cellular phones in case of emergencies" (Rockwell, Andre, and Hawley, 1996: 185). In such cases, teachers may decide to visit in pairs or the teacher and supervisor may visit together. In some situations it may be more appropriate to arrange to meet in the centre or a local park or other community location.

Being concerned about your safety is a positive thing and some situations warrant it. At the same time, it will benefit you to really consider what is holding you back from wanting to visit a student's home—is it that the family is different from yours? Is it that they live in a neighbourhood different from the one you grew up in? Distinguishing between legitimate safety concerns and unwarranted assumptions is important. (Amatea, 2009: 229)*

*AMATEA, ELLEN S., BUILDING CULTURALLY RESPONSIVE FAMILY-SCHOOL RELATIONSHIPS, 1st Edition, © 2009. Reprinted and Electronically reproduced by permission of Pearson Education, Inc., Upper Saddle River, NJ.

Janeway Child and Family Centre

THE FAMILY VISIT: TEACHER SELF-REVIEW

Did I:

- ☐ contact families well in advance?
- ☐ let families know ahead of time the purpose of the visit?
- ☐ arrange the meeting at the parents' convenience?
- ☐ call, email, or send home a note confirming the date and time of the visit?
- ☐ arrive on time?
- ☐ bring something special to share with the child?
- ☐ interact with all family members?
- ☐ allow the child to lead the play, show me his or her room, favourite toys, pets, and so on?
- ☐ concentrate on paying attention to the family rather than scrutinizing their home?
- ☐ listen more than I talked?
- ☐ remember my role as a "support person" as opposed to an "expert"?
- ☐ act in a respectful and mannerly fashion?
- ☐ find out more about the family's philosophy of child-rearing?
- ☐ encourage family participation in the centre?
- ☐ help ease any anxieties that the child or family members may have had?
- ☐ send a thank-you note?

Do I:

- ☐ feel that the family visit made a positive difference in my partnership with this family? If not, why?
- ☐ feel the child and I have become closer as a result of the visit?
- ☐ feel more informed and more able to support this family?

Family Visits from Primary School Teachers and Staff

Nancy Steinhauer, principal of George Webster Elementary School—one of 80 schools of the most needy in the city—is visiting low-income homes, one way of closing the opportunity gap. She visited Mujib's family along with school personnel on a community walk organized to help staff better understand students and vice versa.

Mujib, who came to Canada from Bangladesh as a refugee five years ago, said schools need to know the challenges faced by poor families. "Being poor is already devastation. You are weak, you have less brain power and you feel you are less important to your society," said the car salesman who has a BA in accounting from his home country. "I understand being a poor dad. It is not only painful; it breaks your heart. Sometimes I did not have money to buy milk for my child. We had no luxuries, lived hand to mouth, and we did not understand the schools here were so welcoming to families until they invited us to visit."

George Webster is part of the Toronto District School Board's poverty busting *Model Schools for Inner Cities Program*, which distributes an extra $8 million among the poorest 128 schools for extra field trips, free medical clinics, parenting workshops and time off for community walks—all to help shrink the class

continued

divide. "A community walk can be culture shock for teachers," states Harpreet Ghuman of Shoreham Public School. "It can force them to confront their middle class bias. Some teachers assumed poor parents don't care about education because they don't show up for school events. But when they went to the homes, many parents explained that education is their No. 1 priority." Mujib says, "I felt proud to see all these busy people coming to our home. I gave them a speech about how Bengali families run." Nahida, his wife served homemade chicken biryani, four different curries and sweets to the visitors, all to be eaten by hand while sitting on a mattress on the floor. Jan Olson of Barrie states "it's an 'aha' moment' when you realize our middle-class school system has focused on different cultures, but it's the forgotten culture—lower socio-economic status—that's the final taboo in education."

Source: Brown, L. and Rushowy, K. 2011. "Teachers See Families' Lives First-Hand," *The Toronto Star*, September 3, GT4. Reprinted by permission of Torstar Syndication Services.

Inside LOOK

A Different Type of Family Visit—A Block Walk

If it is appropriate in your circumstances, try a block walk while the weather is warm and sunny. Map the location of all your students' homes and divide the area into blocks. Schedule a series of block walks, and escort the children living in each block area to their homes on a selected day. Let families know that you will be coming. On the appointed day, walk or ride the bus to the chosen block. Meet the parents outside if they are at home and chat with them about school. You may also accumulate some curriculum materials such as leaves, sidewalk rubbings, or bits of neighborhood history to be used later by the children in the classroom. This initial contact with parents will be positive and possibly make a second meeting even more productive.

Source: Hepworth Berger, 2008: 151.

GETTING STARTED

For centres that would like to begin this process, they might begin with all new incoming families; for other families, the supervisor might send home a letter to families, explaining the purpose of the family visit and asking them to respond if they are interested in participating.

THE SEPARATION PROCESS

A child's first entry into an early childhood environment is a major separation event and is a difficult transition for families. Much of the literature on separation focuses on the child, and very little of it considers the parents. It is critical for teachers to recognize that powerful emotions are at work. How well parents separate affects how well their children adjust to the centre and has an enormous impact on the teacher–family relationship. Some families may be so distressed by, and so filled with guilt at, their child's anguished response to separation that they find it difficult to leave the centre each day. Other parents may be so desperate for the new arrangement to succeed that they unconsciously place untenable pressures on the child or the educators. Helplessness, denial, guilt, sadness, anger, relief, jealousy, resentment—all are emotions that may be felt by parents at one time or another. No matter what the parent's response, it is critical for teachers who work with families to understand the seriousness and complexity of this transition. Discussing these responses ahead of time with families may help them acknowledge their own feelings in an atmosphere that is empathetic and understanding of the process of separation. Any family member or friend who will be picking up or dropping off the child should be included in the orientation. It is natural for babies to feel anxious when their mother or father leaves them. This anxiety usually first appears at six months, when infants gain an awareness of their parents, and themselves, as separate beings. Afraid of being abandoned, they become wary and anxious around strangers. Separation anxiety can continue to occur in children of all ages and may be aggravated by divorce, illness, hospitalization, or a parent's sudden return to work.

Separations are hard for everyone involved. "Family members are not the only people a child becomes attached to. Although a child is likely to become strongly attached to one or two particular persons and prefer them to all others, the child may also form deep attachments to other people, such as daycare providers" (Bowlby, cited in Barker, 1993: 4).* Therefore, it is also

---

*Barker, K. 1993. "Infancy: New Perspective for Caregiving." *Ideas: The Journal of Emotional Well-Being in Child Care* 1 (1). May. Reprinted by permission.

important to acknowledge that a child who has difficulty separating can also be difficult for teachers! But as teachers we also know that this is a rite of passage for the child:

> Despite the fact that we know that this is a natural and typically a manageable event in a child's developing a sense of autonomy and independence and while it can be stressful for all, it does demonstrate healthy attachment. This attachment theory explains why children who have formed positive attachments to an attachment figure instinctively respond with anxiety, sadness or anger to an unwanted separation, or even a threat of separation from that person. Illness, fatigue, hunger or strange situations intensify these reactions, especially for children, as does the child's individual temperament. (Jervis and Polland: 2007:9)

Preparing written information for families—magazine or journal articles on the subject of separation, for example—ahead of time may be useful. Teachers might ask families who are well established in the centre to describe their first few months in a centre and provide some guidance and support. In some family situations, siblings may now be separated for the first time, and that should also be taken into account.

This skillful teacher eases the transition for this parent and child by focusing on the child's interest in dinosaurs.

Jason was a wonderful participant in the three-year-old nursery. He painted with flourishing strokes at the easel and built bridges and roads in the block corner. His only difficulty seemed to be separating from his mother each morning. He happily appeared each morning at the door with mother in tow. The teacher encouraged him to hang up his coat and to say good-bye, which he did. The mother stood at the door with some last-minute reminders: "Mommy will be back in three hours, Jason!" "Don't be upset when Mommy leaves, Jason." "Mommy loves you, Jason." With each comment, Jason became a little less certain of his willingness to move into the room. The teachers who watched this display were somewhat annoyed at this over-protective mother. After a few weeks, a parent conference was scheduled. The teacher shared that she wanted to help Jason separate more easily each morning and so asked his mother for her perspective. During the conversation, Jason's mother shared that Jason was her only child and that she and her husband had waited years to adopt a baby. Their first attempt at adoption had resulted with the child being given back to the birthmother, who had changed her mind about the adoption. It was a heart-breaking story, but the teacher understood a great deal more about the separation dilemma. During the next few weeks, the mother and the teacher worked together to transition Jason into school and to alleviate the mother's fears.

Source: SPRINGATE, KAY WRIGHT; STEGELIN, DOLORES A., BUILDING SCHOOL AND COMMUNITY PARTNERSHIPS THROUGH PARENT INVOLVEMENT, 1st Edition, © 1999. Reprinted and Electronically reproduced by permission of Pearson Education, Inc., Upper Saddle River, NJ.

The length of time it takes a child to adjust to centre life varies. Most children take two to three weeks to settle in, but the range is great. Gregarious children may take off without a backward look, leaving their families feeling a bit downcast. Some children seem fine for a week or so—or even six months—and *then* fuss, as though testing to see whether you are serious about this new routine. The "novelty" affect may have also worn off and they start to miss the way things used to be. A few children can take as long as three months to settle in. Children who find it hard to adapt to new things may have the occasional tearful episode when they abruptly remember where they are—or, rather, where they are not. The separation may also become more acute as events in the child's family life take a turn.

Each child will have an individual approach to this separation. Bowlby claims that

> since the manner in which infants are nurtured varies within each subculture as well as across cultures, the well-being of the child is affected by the quality of care as well as the resiliency of the child. One child may thrive while another deteriorates, in environments that seem identical. The child, the caregiver, and the environment intertwine in the child-rearing process, making every child's experience unique. The essential bond between

child and caregiver emphasizes the significance of the parents' role. (cited in Barker, 1993: 1)[*]

ROLE OF THE TEACHER IN THE SEPARATION PROCESS

Teachers may have strong feelings associated with separations, and these events can remind them of painful or difficult experiences in their own lives. They need to be aware that this may affect their ability to respond appropriately to families and children. To instill a sense of empathy in the child, Weissbourd (1992) suggests that teachers draw on memories of their own experiences with separation, "whether it was losing a best friend when he or she moved, losing a pet, or even tougher situations such as being a child of divorce or losing a parent" (68).

Teachers need to be patient in the separation process. They need to realize that families respond to separation in different ways, and that having a tearful child is generally not a reflection on their skill as a teacher. The teacher needs to be in tune with each child's abilities and rhythms and respond in those

*Barker, K. 1993. "Infancy: New Perspective for Caregiving." *Ideas: The Journal of Emotional Well-Being in Child Care* 1 (1). May. Reprinted by permission.

terms. This means the teacher sets aside his or her rhythms to accommodate the child—challenging work when a child is distressed and there are several children's needs to meet. Stable staffing is also critical; children suffer another difficult transition when educators leave or move to another room.

Bell and Ainsworth (1972) identify promptness as the single most important factor in stopping crying: responding immediately to crying does not spoil the child. Bell and Ainsworth's research demonstrates that among infants 6 to 12 months old, those whose mothers respond immediately cry less. Conversely, ignoring a baby's cries may increase crying. Teachers should comfort a distressed child in a manner that is consistent with the child's preferences. For example, though some children like to be held, others prefer to be engaged by a stimulating toy or object.

More recently, Gunnar (n.d.) has shown that "by the end of the first year, children who have received consistent, warm, and responsive care produce less of the stress hormone cortisol, and when they do become upset, they turn off their stress reaction more quickly. This suggests that they are better equipped to respond to life's challenges."

Having one teacher who consistently cares for the new infant or toddler has a positive effect on the child's ability to separate successfully. It is also important to consider that the relationship between other parents and other children is a factor in separating. If an older child looks forward to seeing a playmate in the room in the morning, this enhances the morning routine. Families with similar experiences have opportunities to discuss the issues that are of concern to both parties.

While continuity is desirable, its complexities make it far from easy to achieve. Children in groups may be happy, resilient, and alert or depressed and lethargic; tall or short; self-actualized or dependent

A sympathetic and responsive adult can ease the child's transition.

on direction; secure and outgoing, or reticent and shy. Children encounter a wide variety of teachers—creative or structured; open or closed; authoritarian, laissez-faire, or authoritative; self-actualized or discouraged—and each of these may vary day by day. Families are just as varied—disorganized or stable, extended or nuclear, enriching or restrictive, verbal or nonverbal, nurturing or punishing—with many of the characteristics changing with conditions." (Hepworth Berger, 1991: 4)

Inside LOOK

It was like having my heart ripped out. I know that sounds melodramatic, but hearing Emma screaming for me as I left the centre on that first morning after our orientation week was absolutely overwhelming. I was in tears, and if the teacher hadn't sent me an email to say that Emma was happily playing with her new friends, I'm not sure I would have made it through the day. The photo that the teacher attached of Emma's smiling face now sits framed on my desk!

To help ease the transition, for example, the parents and the child might discuss what the day will be like for both of them, or they might participate in rituals such as packing a lunch. Educators can suggest to families that they engage in an activity with their child at the centre before saying good-bye. For example, a parent might say, "I will read one book and we'll paint one picture together and then I must go." It may also be useful for the child and family member to create a ritual that is practised every day, helping the child recognize the stages of saying good-bye. Cueing the child as to what is happening next is also a good strategy for some children. If the child is crying, parents should acknowledge that he or she is upset but remain calm themselves, reassuring the child (as they give their parting kisses and hugs) that they will return and letting the child know that they will miss the child too. Leaving the child with a positive thought about the end of the day is always helpful ("When I pick you up we will go to Grandma's house for supper").

A "cuddle couch" or a "cuddle chair"—a space by the exit where children and parents can say good-bye with words, hugs, and kisses—may help in the transition. A wind-up music box, a sand

Consistent goodbye routines are important to young children.

clock, or a kitchen timer can help set limits once the routine is established: "when the music stops … or the sand is finished … or the timer rings, it will be time to say goodbye" (Jervis and Polland, 2007: 32).

Gestwicki (2004: 261) provides a handout for parents that suggests things they can do in the classroom during the first few days of school.

You're welcome to stay! As you and your child get used to life in our classroom, feel free to stay if you can. Some things you could do:

- Help your child develop a morning routine of putting things in the cubby.

- Find the child's name tag and move it to our "We're Here" board.

- Wash hands in the bathroom.

- Look around at each interest centre to notice new materials.

- Go say good morning to our fish Henry.

- Choose a book and read to your child and any other child who wants to join you.

- Say good-bye and leave without lingering when you are ready—teachers will help you say good-bye.

- Feel free to call or stop back and see us later in the day.*

Teachers can facilitate the separation process in the following ways:

- **Be set up and ready to receive the children and their parents.**

- **Greet children warmly as they arrive (commenting on a new haircut or a big smile will go a long way to easing a child's anxieties). Observe the child's emotional and physical state.**

- **Plan activities that will instantly captivate children as they enter the room.**

- **Involve the children in each other's play.**

- **Give older children a job when they arrive (let them check themselves in on a giant attendance sheet, for example, or help with the setup).**

- **Ask children already in the program to be a "buddy" for the new child, helping them get started upon arrival.**

- **Have a fishbowl filled with folded slips of paper, each with the name of one of the various**

Courtesy of Ingrid Crowther

Her mother was dropping off 3-year-old Sarah one morning at child care. After she kissed her daughter good-bye for the day, the little girl rubbed her lips vigorously with her hand. The mother moaned, "Sarah, why do you always wipe off my kisses?" To which her daughter replied, "Oh Mommy, I'm not wiping them off. I'm rubbing them in."

Source: Jervis and Polland, 2007: 32.

Create a visual schedule so the child can see how long it will be before a parent arrives to pick them up.

centres in the room. Invite the children to pick one slip and start their day off there.

- Create lotto games or memory games by using photos of the children and their families.

- Invite family members to stay for tea or coffee, if they have the time.

- Have the child's mother leave a "lipstick kiss" on the child's hand.

- Spray the mother's perfume on a sleep blanket.

- Take a picture of the child at the centre and give it to the child to share with other family members.

- Take a picture of the child at the centre and give it to family members to keep in their workplace.

- If they are interested and would like more photos, have families leave a disposable camera with the teachers.

- Keep a collection of comfort toys in the room so that the children can help themselves.

Many children are reassured by a familiar photo.

- Play calming music. (In one centre the parent taped herself singing her child's favourite sleep song, and it was played during naptime.)

- Have a photo of the family scanned onto a pillowcase or blanket for nap time or on the wall at the child's eye level.

- Leave welcoming messages or photos in the children's cubbies.

Courtesy of Richmond Adelaide Child Care Centre

- Give families a small photo album and ask them to fill it with family photos and return it to the centre. These can be stored in the book centre or in the child's cubby and may come in handy during sleep time when families are often missed most.

- Give parents a disposable camera to take to their work. Have a co-worker take photos and create a bulletin board or placemat for the child, or put the photo under the Plexiglas at the lunch table.

- Tape positive "happenings" for families to view.

- Record families on their first day so they can watch at home with family members who could not be there.

- Ask parents to provide a video or audio recording of home and family. For children and teachers who do not share a common language, a recording in the child's language can provide comfort during the day. Parents can record directions for naptime and other routines in the family's home language so the child will know what to do (Jervis and Polland, 2007: 40–41).

- Ensure that there are sheltered spaces where children can retreat.

- Make use of the indoor and outdoor environments to engage children in dramatic play to sort out their feelings.

- Encourage children to create drawings for their parents, expressing, if appropriate, their feelings about the separation.

- Phone, email, or text families who were especially anxious about the separation to reassure them that their child is all right.

- Invite the parent to extend an invitation to a grandparent or an older sibling for the child to take on a tour of the room. If people they trust are in this space, then it must be a good place!

- Avoid high-energy activities at the end of the day, and help the children wind down in anticipation of the arrival of their parents.

- Set up a craft activity at the end of the day to engage both parents and children, in order to help them reunite with each other in a positive way, and to make the transition from centre to home smoother.

- Create a cross-over activity in which children and families complete a simple project at home to be brought to the centre.

Courtesy of Scotia Plaza Child Care Centre

When families can spend a few minutes helping their child settle into the program, it can be time well spent for everyone.

THE FIRST DAY AT THE CENTRE: STRATEGIES FOR A SUCCESSFUL TRANSITION

A child's first day at the centre is a major event for all family members. It is important for families to understand that they set the tone for what will happen. A positive, cheerful approach with the child is critical to a successful transition. Children are quick to notice any tension in the parent's touch, voice, and mannerisms. The age of the child is another factor; a school-aged child who has been in care for most of his or her life will probably make an easier transition than an 18-month-old toddler who is coming into care for the first time.

To make the transition as smooth as possible for the child, teachers should encourage families to

- ensure that the child gets a good night's sleep before the big day

- have positive conversations with the child about their previous visit to the centre

- make use of the centre-supplied "What to Bring on First Day" list

- invite the child to participate in labelling with his or her name the items that will be coming

to the child and family centre (blanket, pillow, comfort toy, and so forth)

- have the child select the family photo that will go into his or her cubby

- write down key words in the child's language if it is a language other than that spoken by the teachers

- complete all the necessary paperwork (medical documentation, for example) and bring it to the centre

- arrive after the morning rush, when things are not quite so hectic at the centre

For their part, teachers should

- ensure that interpreters are available for families who need them

- be on hand to greet the family as they arrive and have bright and colourful name tags ready for them

- ensure that the child's cubby and any other storage areas are labelled with their name and cleaned in advance

- introduce families to staff members and other parents who might be in the centre at the time of arrival

Children in a new environment are reassured by a familiar face.

Courtesy of Scotia Plaza Child Care Centre

- create a bulletin board message with a photo and a description of the family as a welcoming gesture

- have a parent, as part of a welcoming committee, meet with them in the playroom for a brief period to reassure the new family and discuss some of the strategies that helped his or her family over the first few weeks

- look for common interests or needs between parents—those who use the same bus line, live in the same area, or have jobs, hobbies, or languages in common

- ensure that all staff members (cooks, caretakers, security people, and so on) understand their important role in supporting and welcoming new families

- give parents specific instructions about how they might be involved during the orientation period, since many family members are unsure of what to do in the room

- refer to planning sheets to give family members an idea about emergent curriculum

- fill out any necessary paperwork, and assist the parents in understanding their role in completing them

- show family members where the centre keeps its medication sheets, permission forms, and other paperwork

- show the families the message area so they know where to pick up communiqués

- confirm with parents how staff should contact them if an emergency occurs

- share positive stories about the child when parents return at the end of the day

- be available to meet with parents to discuss how the transition is proceeding

Ideally, the transition should be a gradual one, occurring over the course of a week. However, teachers need to be flexible in supporting parents who may not be able to take long periods of time off work. Creative planning might involve having the mother available on the first day, the father on the second, and a grandparent the next. Older children might be paired with a preschool or school-aged child who is familiar with the centre and can help the newcomer through the routines for the first week or so. Parents might also appreciate a written overview of their child's adjustment to the centre. Teachers can record their observations of the child's progress in a journal for the first few weeks or so and then share it with parents. This might also be a good time to suggest a variety of children and adult books on separation. Even better, if these books are available in the family resource area, collect some and loan them to the families. Try to collect resources in the languages of your centre's families.

Exhibit 4.3 provides information about how a one-week orientation might unfold.

EXHIBIT 4.3   Sample Orientation Week for Younger Children in Care Situations

MONDAY

- Parent and child arrive after 9 a.m., when much of the hustle and bustle of early arrivals is winding down.
- Parent and child are greeted by supervisor and directed to the playroom.
- Teacher greets child and invites parent and child into the room.
- Parent and child are introduced to parents, children, and teachers.
- Teacher shows child the cubby in which his or her special items will be stored.
- Parent is given a detailed tour of the room.
- Parent and child stay for the morning program and the child is gently encouraged to participate.
- Parent discusses with staff the child's likes and dislikes, medications, schedules, sleep-time rituals, feelings about separation, and so forth.
- Parent and teacher ensure that paperwork (for example, completing charts, permission to give medications) is in order.
- Teachers encourage parents to participate as much as they feel comfortable.
- Supervisor is available throughout the day to answer parent's questions or to cover for teacher while she spends time with parent.
- Based on the child's response, a few hours may be enough for the first day.

TUESDAY

- Parent and child arrive at regular drop-off time.
- Child and parent are invited to participate.
- As child's comfort level increases, parent assumes a more passive role, observing and encouraging child to interact with other children and teachers.
- Toward the end of the morning, parent leaves the room for a cup of coffee or a chat with the supervisor.
- After lunch, parent and child observe beginning of nap-time procedure and leave shortly thereafter.

WEDNESDAY

- Parent continues to support the child through the program but spends increasingly longer periods away.
- Parent and child stay through the lunch program and nap time.
- Parent and child leave about 3 p.m., following a short play at wake-up.

THURSDAY

- Parent and child stay for a full day.
- Throughout the day, the parent's time away from child is lengthened.

FRIDAY

- Similar to the Thursday schedule but with longer periods of separation between parent and child.

Janeway Child and Family Centre

THE ORIENTATION PROCESS: FAMILY QUESTIONNAIRE

- How well did the orientation support your and your child's entry into the centre?
- What were your first impressions of the centre?
- Was there anything about your initial contact with the centre that you think we might have handled better?
- Do you have any questions that were not addressed during the orientation process?
- What aspects of the orientation process could the centre improve on?
- How helpful was the written information you were provided with in advance of the first day?
- Did the DVD help solidify the information you received on your first visit?
- Did you feel the staff members were warm and welcoming?

Leaving my grandson when I drop him off at child care is hard for me. I know my daughter depends on me to do this task. At first, I was disappointed with my daughter and son-in-law for not staying home and looking after my grandson as my wife had done. I know financially my daughter has to work in order for her to support her family, but at the same time it is hard to let old ideas go. The staff at the centre encouraged me to stay longer and longer and now I feel they really appreciate the time I spend with the children and my grandson certainly enjoys my "position" in the child-care centre. Surprisingly, I am enjoying my time at the centre, and my latest project is showing the school-age children how to build a bird house. I was a cabinet maker before I retired, and I'm having fun sharing my skills with the children. My wife kids me about the amount of time I'm spending at the centre.

END OF THE DAY

Greenman (1988) suggests awarding the family a congratulatory certificate from the teachers and the supervisor at the end of the first day that the family and child spend apart. The certificate reinforces the partnership while acknowledging that the first day is always the hardest. Children may also respond at the end of the day in ways parents don't always anticipate. The child who does not rush into his or her parents' arms may upset the parent; however, the child may be so engrossed in an activity that he or she doesn't want to leave. In other situations, the child may be resisting another transition, or the child may be so secure in his or her attachment that he or she sees no need to jump up and go home. Some children may act out to test the limits and some to let their parents know they weren't happy about being left behind in the morning! Others may refuse their parents' hugs and hold tightly to the teacher's hand. Some will be so attached to a particular toy that they can't bear to leave it behind. This is when a "travelling suitcase" in which the child places the favourite toy and is allowed to bring it home overnight may help in saying goodbye. Another strategy might be to take a picture of the child and toy and send that home. Each child will have his or her own individual response to leaving the centre and reconnecting. Acknowledging that these end-of-day experiences will change over time may help to ease the transition when they don't go well.

After the family has been in the centre a few months, it might be helpful and informative for the staff to carry out another family visit, organize a conference at a convenient time for all parties, or arrange for the family and supervisor to meet to review the orientation process. Parents who are unable to meet centre staff in person might be provided with a written questionnaire or agree to take part in a telephone discussion or respond by email.

TRANSITIONS TO NEW PLAYROOMS: SUPPORTING FAMILIES

A new transition will be required as the child moves to the next age group. As teachers, we tend to focus on the needs of the child during this time, forgetting how difficult the new transition can be for parents, especially those who have built strong relationships with the infant staff and have come to rely on them for support and advice. Such parents may be anxious and reluctant to begin a relationship with the toddler staff. Teachers can remind parents that it took time to build their relationship and this will no doubt happen again in the toddler room. Infant teachers need to encourage parents to build a partnership with the toddler staff while at the same time letting parents know they can stay in touch with them, and that they, too, will assist in the child's transition. Remember that all of the teachers are responsible for all of the children in the centre; it is not the case that infant teachers interact only with infants. Some families may be reassured to learn of this inclusive approach.

Continuity of care is a critical factor in the life of a young child. Some centres use a system that allows the same caregiver to remain with the child throughout the infant and toddler years. The teacher moves up with the child until the transition to the preschool room, when the teacher returns to the infant room.

Families and teachers should discuss the possibility of the upcoming transition well in advance, so that both parties can begin to think through the implications of such a move. If several children are

At the Janeway Child and Family Centre, when we have a group of infants moving up to the toddler room, we host an orientation meeting. We begin the session with a presentation of what a day might be like in the toddler room. Parents can then see the emphasis we place on a play-based environment both indoors and out and the encouragement we give to a hands-on, sensory approach. We then discuss the similarities and differences between the infant room and the toddler room. We always include information about toddler behaviour—and how we deal with biting, since this is one issue that almost always comes up. We leave lots of time for parents to ask questions. We are also very interested in feedback from parents. It is only through ongoing communication that our program can change to better reflect the needs and interests of the children and their families. We find that having the parents meet together is reassuring for them. We also encourage parents to visit and to feel free to contribute when and where they are able. Theresa, our supervisor, always attends these meetings and is available to answer questions as well.

to be transitioned at the same time, a meeting might be arranged with families to discuss the procedure, to outline the room's approach, to tour the various centres in the room, and to review topics such as developmental norms for this age group and changes in routines. A DVD depicting daily life in the room can be an excellent resource for parents. Along with this meeting, a room handbook prepared by staff and based on the information that is specific for this age group is very reassuring to parents and is a useful tool that they can refer to again and again. A family visit at this time may also support this transition. Above all, teachers should be available to discuss any concerns that family members have.

Exhibit 4.4 demonstrates how the transition to a new playroom can be handled with ease.

EXHIBIT 4.4 Transitioning Children to New Playrooms

Nadia Hall, Margaret McLellan, and Linda Silver developed the following model for transitioning infants to the toddler room.

SUGGESTED STRATEGIES AND IMPLICATIONS

1. PLANNING THE TRANSITION

Understanding the child is the primary goal of this stage. It is vital that both those who are letting go and those who are taking on the care of this child have a sensitive understanding of who the child is and how she behaves. In order for the child to make a secure transition, she must trust that her signals will be read accurately and responded to empathetically. She must feel known, and therefore safe.

When the decision to move the child has been agreed upon by supervisor, staff, and parents, the following procedure can be put into place:

- **Visits to the infant room.** The assigned prospective caregiver visits daily for half an hour with the baby in the infant room. In this way the baby can be observed in her natural context of relating. The infant caregiver in the secure environment can support the infant in this period of acquaintanceship with the new caregiver. This process optimally occurs over a two-week period prior to the transition.
- **Transition conference.** A transition conference brings together a variety of individuals who have or require intimate knowledge of the child—the infant caregiver, toddler caregiver, and parents. Such a meeting offers the opportunity to share information in an organized manner. The meeting occurs after several visits, so that all participants come with some level of understanding of the child. This information will be incorporated into an individualized plan of transition. This also provides a formal opportunity for the infant caregiver to begin to separate from the child and for parents to begin to separate from the infant caregiver.

continued

2. Implementing the Transition

Supporting the child's entry into, and growing comfort level with, the new physical and social environment is the primary goal of this stage. Through a patient and thoughtful process, the child's disruption and sense of loss are minimized. This process ultimately promotes the establishment of new supportive relationships.

- **Two-week adjustment process.** During the minimum two-week transition process, the infant caregiver accompanies the child to the toddler room in order to provide a secure base from which the child can explore and familiarize herself with the physical environment, the people, and the new routines. In week one, time spent in the new room is gradually increased for both the child and caregivers. In week two, the infant caregiver gradually decreases her time in order to allow a relationship to develop between the new caregiver and the child. This should enable the closure of one period and the passage into another. This process must, of course, take into account the child's individual needs and may look different for different children.

- **Transitional objects.** Such objects as blankets, pacifiers, and cuddle toys provide comfort and familiarity, and may be particularly supportive to the child during this period of transition. These objects should be identified during the conference and should be available to the child whenever wanted. Many children have special objects that are important to them and sharing them with their teachers and peers is exciting. It is also an opportunity for everyone to learn about a new object, how to share and take care of them.

- **A transitional book.** This book is a collection of photographs of familiar people and objects (mommy, daddy, room at home, favourite toy, previous caregiver, previous peers, and so on). This book enables the child to refer to familiar and comforting images that reassure and support the child. The book could be kept in the child's own cubby and be available to the child whenever she wants it.

3. Infant Support Worker

Transition times make additional emotional demands both on staff who are losing children with whom they have formed strong bonds and on those who must establish new connections. The realities of group care may not always provide the support required to assist staff and children through this process. To optimize and support all relationships affected by the transition, an infant support worker could facilitate the process. This role is filled, ideally, by someone from the staff (the supervisor, for example) who has an in-depth understanding of attachment, separation, and loss and can therefore support and guide those involved.

In conclusion, this extremely sensitive period in a child's life must be managed with empathetic understanding of the child's experience. Child care can support children and families. Optimally, however, all those involved must work in partnership to bridge and ensure safe passage from infancy to toddlerhood. This careful attention to the child's transition experience builds on the foundation of positive early relationships and can enhance future relationships.

Source: N. Hall, M. McLellan, and L. Silver, "Moving from Infancy to Toddlerhood in Child Care," *Ideas: The Journal of Emotional Well-Being in Child Care* 1, no. 1 (May 1993). Reprinted by permission.

TRANSITIONS FROM CHILD AND FAMILY CENTRES TO SCHOOL ENVIRONMENTS

The Harvard Research Project comments on the transition from child care to school environments:

> Because of the importance of linkages across settings over time, policymakers, practitioners, and researchers recently have begun to focus their attention on the period of transition from preschool to formal schooling. Although research in this area has not focused on which transitions practices relate to specific child outcomes, there is growing consensus that both early childhood settings and elementary schools have a responsibility to support families and help them to sustain their family involvement trajectories. Unfortunately as children transition to public school, teacher and family contact decreases and there is a shift away from parent-initiated communication. Logistical barriers (e.g., no summer salary for teachers, little teacher training in this area, etc.) hinder ideal transition practices. (in Pianta, Taylor, and Cox, 2001: 206)

But when schools openly welcome family engagement, the family's sense of connectedness to the elementary school will ensure a collaborative relationship, and together they can become more focused on providing the best resources to create better child outcomes.

Kreider (2002) states that

> compared to non-preschool parents, parents of children who participated in preschool activities had higher occupational aspirations for their children, more satisfaction with their children's school performance, and greater parent involvement in elementary years at home and in school.

Teachers in early childhood environments can encourage networking among families whose children will be attending the same school, and parents who have already transitioned with an older child may be a valuable resource. The early childhood teacher can also walk the children to the new school as part of a community walk, post pictures of the new school in the playroom, and read children's books that support this transition. We also need to recognize that for many parents this transition may bring some sadness as the child enters a new phase of childhood. One teacher would write a final good-bye letter to the child talking about all of the wonderful things that the child had accomplished in her care. This note was treasured by these families. Teachers will also experience a sense of loss as the child and family move on to a new environment. This is particularly true when several of the children of the same family have been in the centre for a few years and the last child is leaving. Strong bonds and relationships are formed over time and this can be very difficult for everyone involved.

In an ideal situation, early learning environments will be housed in primary school settings so that these relationships will be ongoing. As more provinces move to full-day kindergarten for 4- and 5-year-olds who enter into the school setting, children and families will have an opportunity to spend many years building relationships, thus reducing the anxiety often present when several transitions are necessary.

LATCHKEY KIDS

There are times when school-age children have to leave child care; parents may no longer be able to afford the fees or no programs may be available for the child's age group. While many children successfully make the transition from group care to self-care, others report being bored or lonely, concerned about their personal safety, deprived of opportunities to socialize, or burdened with excessive family responsibilities such as caring for younger siblings. Latchkey children are a growing phenomenon. Jo-Anne Kilpatrick, Executive Director of Sundowners Day Care and Resource Centre in Windsor, Ontario, operates a "Warm Line" designed for children 10 to 12 years of age who are left at home. She reports that children well below the age of 10 are being left at home to care for themselves:

> This little seven-year-old boy … spent all his after school hours alone in his home under his bed, locked in until as late as 6 p.m. each school day evening. The house had to be kept darkened with no light, TV, or radio playing so "people wouldn't know he was home alone." He wasn't allowed to answer the door or use the phone until after his mom got home—well after dark each school winter night. The little guy found out about the Warm Line from a discarded flyer an older child had left on his school playground. Hidden in his lunch bag from his mom, he brought it home and kept our number under his bed. He used it to call when the empty house got too scary or when other older kids from the neighbourhood, knowing he was home alone, taunted him by ringing the doorbell and banging on the door. I'll never forget our last conversation. It was a particularly horrible night for him and he was calling, crying, from the closet of his room. Mom still wasn't home and the "Warm Line" was shutting down for the evening. Out of desperation, I started asking personal questions of him, trying to identify where he lived in case intervention became necessary. This line of questioning is only used when a child is thought to be at risk. In our experience, most children normally have to be discouraged from sharing this type of information to our phone-line staff, because of the inherent trust they have in adults. The child hung up and never called again. I lost him because he had been trained well in how to survive as a latchkey kid … "Don't let anyone know you are alone … keep our family secret and you will be safe." The child's parent, for a lot of good reasons, insulated her son from the dangers of the outside world, but also isolated him from getting help to save himself. I can only guess what scars the chronic isolation, loneliness, and fear have left him with. The lessons we can learn from this one child's nightmare aren't so much about age, as they are about responsibility. We have children who are home alone legally at age 10 who are every bit as isolated and terrified as this young child. The reasons they are home alone, regardless of age, are varied and complex involving societal attitudes, and policies from three levels of government. I know changes are coming in child care … but I also know, at least for one little seven-year-old boy, by the time these changes come to Windsor it is going to be much too late. (in Kilpatrick, 1993: 13)[*]

***

[*]Kilpatrick, J. 1993. "Latchkey Children A National Shame." *Exploring Environment*, p. 13. Reprinted by permission of Lynn Wilson.

In light of this reality, teachers and families can prepare school-age children to take care of themselves by alerting them to potential dangers in their own neighbourhoods and communities. For example, children need to know when play areas are off-limits because of spring run-off. Children should also be provided with a set of house rules relating to cooking and emergency procedures. Teachers can provide emergency training and first-aid courses and teach children how to use the telephone in emergencies.

BOOKS FOR CHILDREN

On My Very First School Day I Met ..., by N. Stiles

I Am Too Absolutely Small for School, by L. Child

First Day Jitters, by J. Danneberg

The Night Before Kindergarten, by N. Wing and J. Durrell

When You Go to Kindergarten, by J. Howe

Welcome to Kindergarten, by A. Rockwell

Do I Have to Go to School?, by P. Thomas and L. Haker

Starting School, by K. Petty, L. Kopper, and J. Pipe

Franklin Goes to School, by P. Bourgeois

Going to School (Usborne First Experiences), by A. Civardi, M. Bates, and S. Cartwright

Starting School, by C. Jenner

My First Day at a New School, by C. Guillain

BOOKS FOR ADULTS

Parent's Survival Guide to Starting School, by K. Beeley

Is Everybody Ready for Kindergarten?: A Tool Kit for Preparing Children and Families, by A. Sancho Passe

Everyday Goodbyes: Starting School and Early Care: A Guide to the Separation Process, by N. Balaban

Children Starting School: A Guide to Successful Transitions and Transfers for Teachers and Assistants, by H. Fabian

Beyond the Bake Sale: The Essential Guide to Family–School Partnerships, by A. Henderson et al.

REFERENCES

Amatea, E. 2009. *Building Culturally Responsive Family–School Relationships*. Merrill.

Barbour, C., N.H. Barbour, and P.A. Scully. 2008. *Families, Schools, and Communities. Building Partnerships for Educating Children*. Pearson Merrill Prentice Hall.

Barker, K. 1993. "Infancy: New Perspective for Caregiving." *Ideas: The Journal of Emotional Well-Being in Child Care* 1 (1). May.

Bell, S.M., and M.D. Ainsworth. 1972. "Infant Crying and Maternal Responsiveness." *Child Development* 43.

Bowlby, J. 1982. *Attachment*. New York: Basic Books.

Brooks, M. 1994. "Family Visits." *Early Childhood Education* 27 (1). Spring–Summer.

Brown, L., and K. Rushowy. 2011. "Teachers See Families' Lives First-Hand." *Toronto Star*. September 3. GT4.

Cullum, A. 1971. *The Geranium on the Window Sill Just Died but Teacher You Went Right On*. Holland: Harlin Quist.

Gestwicki, C. 2004. *Home, School, and Community Relations. A Guide to Working with Families*, 5th ed. New York: Thomson Delmar Learning.

Gorter-Reu, M.S., and J.M. Anderson. 1998. "Home Kits, Family Visits, and More!" *Young Children* 53: 71–74.

Greenman, J. 1988. *Caring Spaces, Learning Places: Children's Environments that Work*. Redmond, WA: Child Care Information Exchange.

Gunnar, M. (n.d.) *The First Years Last Forever: I Am Your Child*. Toronto: Canadian Institute of Child Health.

Haigh, K. 2004. "Creating, Encouraging, and Supporting Relationships at Chicago Commons Child Development Program." In Joanne Hendrick, ed., *Next Steps Toward Teaching the Reggio Way: Accepting the Challenge to Change*. Columbus, OH: Pearson Merrill Prentice Hall.

Hall, N., M. McLellan, and L. Silver. 1993. "Moving from Infancy to Toddlerhood in Child Care." *Ideas: The Journal of Emotional Well-Being in Child Care* 1(1). May.

Hepworth Berger, E. 1991. *Parents as Partners in Education: The School and Home Working Together*, 3rd ed. Toronto: Collier Macmillan Canada.

———. 2008. *Parents as Partners in Education: Families and Schools Working Together*. Columbus, OH: Pearson Merrill Prentice Hall.

Jervis, K., and B.K. Polland. 2007. *Separation*. Washington, DC: National Association for the Education of Young Children.

Kaiser, B., and J.S. Rasminsky. 1994. "Encouraging Parent Participation." *Interaction*. Canadian Child Care Federation. Summer.

Kilpatrick, J. 1993. *Latchkey Children: A National Shame*. Exploring Environment.

Kreider, H. 2002. Getting Parents "Ready" for Kindergarten. The Role of Early Childhood Education. Family Involvement Network of Educators (FINE). Harvard Family Research Project. Retrieved January 28, 2013, from http://www.hfrp.org/publications-resources/browse-our-publications/getting-parents-ready-for-kindergarten-the-role-of-early-childhood-education

Kyle, D., D. McIntyre, K. Miller, and G. Moore. 2002. *Reaching Out: A K-8 Resource for Connecting Families and Schools*. Thousand Oaks, CA: Corwin Press.

Lopez, E.M., H.M. Rosenberg, and H. Westmoreland. 2010. *Parent/Teacher Home Visiting Program, Sacramento, CA: Improving Teacher Effectiveness*. National Family, School, and Community Engagement Working Group. Harvard Family Research Project.

Perlman, M. 2011. "Just Who's Looking After Your Kids?" *Toronto Star*. November 13. A17.

Pianta, D.M., R.C. Taylor, and M.J. Cox. 2001. "Transition Practices: Findings from a National Survey of Kindergarten Teachers." *Early Childhood Education Journal*, 28, 199–206.

Pushor, D. 2007. *Parent Engagement: Creating a Shared World*. Ontario Education Research Symposium. January 18–20.

Rudney, G. 2005. "Every Teacher's Guide to Working with Parents." Corwin Press.

Springate, K.W., and D.A. Stegelin. 1999. *Building School and Community Partnerships through Parent Involvement*. Columbus, OH: Pearson Merrill Prentice Hall.

Weissbourd, B. 1992. "Building Parent Partnerships." *Scholastic Pre-K Today*. August–September.

Created by Ayla

Chapter 5

WAYS TO INVOLVE FAMILIES

Courtesy of Scotia Plaza Child Care Centre

"It's not only children who grow. Parents do too. As much as we watch to see what our children do with their lives, they are watching us to see what we do with ours. I can't tell my children to reach for the sun. All I can do is reach for it, myself."

—*Joyce Maynard*

LEARNING OUTCOMES

After studying this chapter, you will be able to

1. identify and evaluate various strategies for involving families in centre activities

2. review approaches to creating male-friendly environments

3. discuss strategies for developing effective formal and informal family gatherings

4. discuss policies for recruiting, training, and evaluating volunteers

5. review how to plan and evaluate a fundraising project

6. describe strategies for involving families in child-care celebrations

7. describe the roles and responsibilities of family members who serve on the board of directors

8. discuss ways to involve families in the evaluation of the staff and the centre program

STRATEGIES FOR INVOLVING FAMILIES

An alliance with families begins when the family first visits the centre. By the time they actually enrol their child in the centre, family members should be aware of the opportunities for them to become significant partners in the program. Centres should create a welcoming atmosphere by crafting an environment that is aesthetically pleasing and inviting and hiring staff who are genuinely pleased to see the families. Early learning environments should also find innovative ways to maximize the input of busy parents while at the same time setting realistic goals with regard to what can be expected from both teachers and family members. These goals need to be re-evaluated on an ongoing basis to determine their relevance to all parties.

MALE-FRIENDLY ENVIRONMENTS

The role of fathers and significant males in a child's life has changed dramatically within one generation. "The growing interest in the role of men in the family has been triggered by diverse demographic, socio-economic and cultural transformations that have occurred over the past several decades, impacting the formation, stability and overall well-being of families" (United Nations, 2011). As women enter the workforce in increasing numbers, there is an expectation that men will become more actively engaged in family responsibilities. In the past, men have been seen as providers, protectors, and disciplinarians—"Wait until your father gets home" was not an uncommon phrase. For many men, these new responsibilities vary greatly from the roles their own fathers played in their lives; they are in unchartered territory. They have few role models to draw from; their relationships with their fathers were often distant as their fathers were absorbed in work and interests

outside the family or weren't present at all. Unlike mothers who learned from their own mothers, many men are on their own in figuring out the best way to parent and the new ways of parenting! Today men are more likely to be involved in child care, providing emotional support and guidance, and playing a more active role in their community through their children's child-care centres, schools, and extracurricular activities while at the same time assuming more household duties. Men are also becoming more involved in decisions related to family planning and are now more likely to be present at the birth of their child. Despite a worldwide focus and research on the role of men in families, governments have been slow to provide policies that support men's involvement in their families. However, some countries have introduced paternity leave to encourage early attachment and care of their children. As well, there is a need for flexible work arrangements, greater access to joint custody, and education in high school to give young men the skills required to be supportive and nurturing fathers. At the college and university level, child care, social work, and nursing programs should encourage male participation. The media also plays a role in shaping social attitudes and redefining the role of fathers across all cultures. Fathers and other significant males in children's lives—whether grandfathers, uncles, mothers' boyfriends, or stepfathers—need to be included in the family–centre partnership. But these significant males face many stereotypes. Some people see fathers as either invisible or incompetent second-class parents. Many programs for families have traditionally served women and children and have excluded active involvement of men, sometimes because the fathers did not want to participate and at other times because mothers did not want fathers to be involved. Many think that mothers are best suited to be the primary and most influential parent. There is also a communication challenge: while mothers may talk about mothering on a regular basis with each other, fathers are more likely to talk about other topics, and so there is little opportunity for an exchange of information about their fathering role. Special occasions and school events are frequently missed by fathers who are unable to take time off from work, are live-away fathers, are engaged in active military service, or are incarcerated. In early learning environments, we can use technology to support father engagement: video recordings of concerts, band performances, sports events, and just a "day in the life" of their child at the centre can be copied inexpensively to DVDs and given to fathers. Fathers who have only supervised access to their children may also appreciate these types of connections if the court allows.

In a national American survey conducted by *Zero to Three* (2010), it was found that fathers today are not satisfied with work–family balance, they find challenges in a variety of parenting situations, and they need more information regarding social development. The early learning environment must make fathers feel welcome, give them opportunities to interact with their child, and allow them to participate in staff planning and programming. Perhaps if there were more male teachers in early childhood programs, we would see greater father involvement! It is also important that we don't assume that what we know about the differences in male and female experiences are universal; each culture varies in the roles of males and females.

The involvement of fathers or significant males in the raising of our children is an issue that affects all of us. Our own unique personal experiences with our fathers often have a life-long impact. Our society is the mirror of the quality of relationships between parents and their children. It takes a village to raise a child, and it takes a village to support fathers in bringing out the best in their children. Society has a collective responsibility to support and promote positive father involvement. The degree to which we contribute collectively to this goal is a reflection of our commitment to being a truly caring society.

Most early learning environments would likely say that they engage fathers and mothers equally in their interactions. But a director at Pen Green Centre for Children and Their Families in Corby, England, wasn't so sure. She videotaped staff's engagement with mothers and fathers at the beginning and end of the day and, much to their surprise, she found that staff engaged with mothers more frequently verbally and nonverbally, initiated discussions with mothers more frequently, and held longer conversations with them (Levine & Pitt, 1997).

This father and son enjoy time together at the child-care centre.

Men need to feel that they are welcomed and encouraged to actively participate in the centre.

The physical environment of the child and family centre should reflect the fact that fathers are welcome; photographs from magazines or posters that show fathers in nurturing roles will send positive messages. In Fagan and Palm's (2004) research, several fathers suggested that programs would be successful in getting fathers involved if they organized a trip to a sports event. Another father stated, "If it's sports oriented, we'll be there" (2004: 128). He stated this event would give men a chance to network. There are men who are looking to do positive things in the community and bringing fathers together allows the men to talk among themselves and devise some way to contribute more to the early childhood program.

GETTING FATHERS INVOLVED WITH THEIR CHILDREN

With funding from Health Canada, the Canadian Association of Family Resource Programs, the umbrella organization for family resource programs, developed a handbook to assist staff of these programs in helping fathers become more involved in their children's development. Research conducted by McCrae Consulting Associates for the handbook included focus groups across Canada, including fathers and program staff from family resource centres. Some of the findings were as follows:

This father enjoys an early-morning breakfast at the centre.

The Macaulay Child Development Centre and the United Way established *More Than A Haircut* as a one-day pilot project in 2006, in the aftermath of unprecedented youth violence in Toronto and amid growing angst over absentee fathers, particularly in the Caribbean community. Conversations about fathering are being held in local barbershops, a frequent "hangout" for Caribbean men. These conversations, led by African-Canadian men who are fathers themselves, are a chance to find out what others are thinking about being a father, about handling the responsibilities, and about enjoying their children right from the beginning. They talk about how they could better support their wives, girlfriends, fiancées, and former partners in raising their children, and they talk about guns, gangs, and fatherless kids being at higher risk of going astray. They talk about dad's involvement as a crucial ingredient to children's sense of security and self-esteem. As workshop facilitator, Dalton Higgins says, "black-male and black-father bashing seems to be in vogue. In the face of misconceptions and stereotypes, Afro-Canadian fathers need encouragement and camaraderie and a place to address the issues—including poverty, racism, and teen parenthood—that affect them and their children. We're not there to paint a pretty picture. We're there to have frank, blunt discussions." A 30 minute DVD is now available on this project at **http://www.macaulaycentre.org/publications.html**.

Source: Gordon, A. 2008. "They Cut Problems Down To Size," *The Toronto Star*, May 17, L7. Reprinted by permission of Torstar Syndication Services.

- Few supports exist for men.

- Fathers seem to view their role as different from that of their own father.

- Men want to tell their stories.

- An effective way to start supporting fathers is to hold a focus group and ask fathers what they want in the way of support.

- Many program staff said, "We need to be where they [fathers] are, not where we [staff] want them to be."

- Men generally don't seek support unless they are in crisis. Society expects them to be self-reliant and independent.

- Wives, children, and loved ones tend to be the catalyst for men to seek support, so work through them.

- Centres should provide supports without using labels that stigmatize. For example, avoid *anger management* and *deadbeat dad*. *Live-away* or *live-with* language is more appropriate than *noncustodial* parent—custodial language promotes the notion of children as property to be battled over.

The focus on having fathers actively involved in the centre is not meant to minimize the role of mothers or other family members but to develop effective strategies for all those who are actively involved in the child's life.

Child and family centres may also want to consider other male members of the community who may willing to volunteer in the centre or male high school students who need to complete community hours, further educating them about possible career opportunities. Is there a seniors residence near the site? Is there a Big Brothers agency in your community? Some large corporations also allow workers time to provide support to the community.

Courtesy of Richmond Adelaide Child Care Centre

Volunteering can become a very special event for everyone involved!

While I was a bit reluctant to attend my first father–child event at the centre, they have now become something I really look forward to. I'm not always able to be there at drop off and pick up; my wife and I are separated. This was an incredible opportunity for Kennedy and me to spend quality time in a place where she is happy and engaged. The staff at the centre organized a series of events every Saturday morning for two hours over a period of six months—one each month. There were different topics and Kennedy and I enjoyed every one but the best was Cooking Day—we made pasta and sauce from scratch and the staff at the end of the morning had cookbooks written for children available for us to borrow so we could continue our "chefing" at home. This was not just a great time for Kennedy and me, I also got to meet other fathers, and several of us have become quite good friends, and we have the children over for play dates. Most of all, I now feel that I have a closer relationship with the staff. A lot of time and effort went into planning these events, and I know that many of them have families of their own and have given up time with them to be with us.

Obviously, everyone who volunteers in the centre must have appropriate criminal reference checks.

FATHER INVOLVEMENT INITIATIVE

Now called Dad Central Ontario, the Father Involvement Initiative's roots go back to 1997 when Health Canada commissioned a literature review aimed at developing an action plan to promote father involvement in Ontario. It had become clear at that time that fatherlessness presented a challenge in relation to healthy child development and resiliency. With its first report, "Father Involvement: A Supportive Condition to Healthy Child Development," Health Canada developed the process of implementing some of the recommendations that came from the report. From these modest beginnings has evolved a long-term vision and strong commitment that, over time, has led to significant collective achievements and several provincial and national partnerships. The Dad Central website (http://www.cfii.ca/fiion) provides a list of organizations across the country that support fathers in their parenting role and many resources to support educators and families.

Exhibit 5.1 shows how we might measure our effectiveness in our interactions with fathers.

BOOKS FOR CHILDREN

My Dad, by A. Browne

David's Father, by R. Munsch

Dad Goes to School, by M. McNamara and M. Gordon

Just Me and My Dad, by M. Mayer

My Dad Is Awesome, by N. Butterworth

My Daddy and Me, by T. MacNaughton

Daddies Do It Different, by A. Sitomer

BOOKS FOR ADULTS

Father's First Steps: 25 Things Every New Father Should Know, by R. Sears

Handbook of Father Involvement, by N. Cabrera and C. Tamis-Lemonda

Baby Management for Men: A Very Practical Guide, by H. Hanssen

Father for Life: A Journey of Joy, Challenge and Change, by A.A. Brott

The Collected Wisdom of Fathers, by W. Glennon

Fathering Right from the Start: Straight Talk about Pregnancy, Birth and Beyond, by J. Heinowitz and W.F. Horn

Fathering Your Child from the Crib to the Classroom: A Dad's Guide to Years 2–9, by A. Brott

Becoming Dad: Black Men and the Journey to Fatherhood, by L. Pitts Jr.

Crawling: A Father's First Year, by E. Cooper

Engaging Fathers in The Early Years: A Practitioner's Guide, by C. Potter and R. Olley

EXHIBIT 5.1   How Effectively Are Men Involved in Your Program?

The following checklist is intended to include not only fathers but also grandfathers, family friends, and other significant males who may aid teachers in their efforts to provide inclusive male environments. Assign a value of 1, 2, or 3 to each of the statements below, where

1 means we're doing a great job

2 means we're not doing badly

3 means this needs work

1. The philosophy statement of the centre specifically targets the involvement of men in the life of our centre. ____

2. Our philosophy translates into action in our centre. Staff are strongly committed to male involvement and understand its importance. ____

3. Staff have identified who the significant males are in the lives of the children in our centre. ____

4. We evaluate our effectiveness on a regular basis in an effort to improve our connections with fathers. ____

5. Staff understand that bias does exist and are aware of possible barriers to father involvement. ____

6. We understand that differences in male and female experiences are universal, and we make every effort to understand how this will impact on our relationships with the men in our program. ____

7. We make every effort to learn about how the diversity of family forms and culture may influence the fathering role. ____

8. We speak directly to men rather than through their female partners. ____

9. We have male staff members in our centre. ____

10. Staff actively encourage and expect male participation and contact them individually, including live-away fathers. ____

11. We make an effort to include them in the centre, in both indoor and outdoor environments, by inviting them in and letting them know they are welcome. ____

12. We do family visits that are scheduled to include men. ____

13. We know we are responding to male participants' needs and interests because we ask them. We survey men and let them know we value their opinions. ____

14. When fathers are at the centre, we plan activities that are reflective of male socialization, such as physical activities, nature experiences, and other experiences, with input from the fathers themselves. ____

15. Specific activities are carried out that target men. We encourage the formation of groups and help to organize classes on parenting or other issues that are of interest and are relevant to the community. ____

16. We support play-based events, such as Dads and Tots, and opportunities for gatherings at the centre that reflect the interests of fathers and their children at times that are convenient for them. ____

17. When men volunteer, we give them a variety of tasks, not just maintenance and repair. ____

18. Men participate on our board of directors and work on committees. ____

19. Men volunteer in our program, in the playroom, and on field trips, and take us to their place of business. ____

20. Fathers actively seek out staff to discuss issues as they arise and engage in supportive communication. ____

continued

21. When men are in the playroom we use this opportunity to exchange ideas about their child's development. ____

22. With both parents' agreement, we communicate verbally, in a written format and through technology, and encourage fathers to be involved in events at the centre when they are not living with their children. ____

23. We are flexible when we organize family–teacher conferences so that all members of the family can attend. ____

24. Men participating in our centre are encouraged to recruit other men as well as to "mentor" new families. ____

25. We videotape children in our program and include significant males interacting with the children. This DVD is distributed to new families so they know that fathers are welcome. ____

26. We share with a range of local media the initiatives, events, and other centre celebrations highlighting the positive role that men play in our centres. ____

27. Posters, magazine pictures, photos of fathers, and books in our program reflect men from a variety of racial and ethnic backgrounds in nurturing roles, involved in child care, and working in nontraditional jobs. ____

Inside LOOK

There are many helpful resources available for fathers. A few are listed below.

Pamphlet Series

The BC Council for Families, British Columbia's hub for information and resources for and about families, offers the *Fatherhood Pamphlet Series*, with six different titles for fathers.

- *Dads and Babies: Connecting with Your Infant*
- *Dads and Toddlers: Connecting with Your Toddler*
- *Dads and Teens: Connecting with Your Teenager*
- *Dads Away from Home: Keeping the Connection When Work Takes Dad Away*
- *Rookie Moms: Ten Things Every New Dad Should Know*
- *Brochure for Young Fathers: Teen Dads. Your Baby Needs You*

Booklets

Dad Central Ontario: Six 40-page booklets that provide helpful and accessible information on various aspects of fathering:

- *Involved Fathers: A Guide for Today's Dad*
- *Full-time Dad, Part-time Kids: A Guide for Recently Divorced and Separated Fathers*
- *Daddy, Come Play with Me: A Father's Guide to Play with Young Children*
- *Kids We Can Count On: A Father's Guide to Building Character in Children*
- *One Step at a Time: A Guide for Fathers Living in Blended Families*
- *Daddy, I Need You: A Father's Guide to Early Childhood Brain Development.*

Canadian Website for New Fathers

http://newdadmanual.ca

This is a website for new dads that uses car maintenance analogies to offer practical information on topics such as newborn care, new mother care, breastfeeding, and adapting to fatherhood. The website, inspired by the 24-Hour Cribside Assistance Booklet, was developed by the Father Involvement Initiative—Ontario Network.

FAMILY–CENTRE GET-TOGETHERS

Get-togethers can be held for a variety of purposes. Family members may wish to discuss a particular issue as outlined in the bylaws, to share general information, or simply to enjoy one another's company. Families may be surveyed formally and informally to find out what types of gatherings they would like to participate in and what topics are of interest. Families are more likely to attend these events if they are involved from the beginning in their organization.

FAMILY GATHERINGS: FORMAL SESSIONS TO SUPPORT PARENTING SKILLS

FACTORS THAT INFLUENCE PARENTING

Knowledge of child development, personal beliefs and expectations, their own experiences, and the socioeconomic environment are just some factors that influence parenting. The web of family and community is the child's anchor for early development. Families are the first and most powerful influence on children's early learning and development:

> Nurturing, responsive parent–child relationships and parental participation in child-centred activities relate to positive learning outcomes in early childhood. Nurturing relationships provide an emotional refuge for children, fostering the development of a healthy sense of belonging, self-esteem, and well-being. When parents are sensitive and responsive to children's emotions, children are more likely to become socially competent and show better communication skills. (Cornish, 2008: 4)

Parenting is embedded in social and cultural contexts that influence parenting styles. Warm, reciprocal parent–child interactions and fewer life stresses in the home facilitate children's prosocial behaviour. Poverty is related to access to fewer social parenting supports, which in turn is associated with maternal depression and attachment issues. Belsky (2005: i) also states that

> children who were negative, irritable, or aggressive were found to have received less supportive, if not problematic, parenting. Inconsistent, rigid, or irritable explosive discipline, as well as low supervision and involvement, have been closely associated with the development of child conduct problems.

HOW THE CHILD-CARE CENTRE CAN SUPPORT PARENTING

The relationship between an early childhood environment and the families it serves may provide many opportunities for families to connect with one another, share their issues and concerns, and find support and encouragement in their parenting. But those of us who are parents also know that these skills do not come naturally and there are very few of us that don't need help in learning to cope with the parenting role. Very little preparation for parenthood takes place to help families develop their parenting skills but we can all learn. Yet, as Gestwicki (2010: 437) points out,

> knowledge alone is not sufficient to develop parenting competence. So how do we create a continuity of learning between home and the centre? All major efforts at parenting education deal in some way with emotions and attitudes. Feelings about family and parent-child dynamics run deep. Attitudes about power, authority, reciprocity and related issues are often more influential than facts. Parent education must provide a vehicle for dealing with both facts and feelings.[*]

It is also important that families are considered on an equal footing with educators. There is a fine line between providing workshops that may support families in their parenting role and sending the message that parents are deficient and need this remediation. It is also important to acknowledge that many parents will have expertise and, with encouragement, may be willing to share with teachers and other families. A collaborative approach is always more successful than a deficit approach!

It is important that parents have a voice in the types of supports and resources that they need, although

> there are few studies on the topic of what parents want and need in terms of support and resources. When asked about what they would like to see in a parenting support program, many parents indicated that they had clear views about the ways in which support should be offered. Parents often ask for an informal structure where they can feel comfortable to discuss issues with other parents, [with] emphasis on building on existing skills, opportunities for parents themselves to define the agenda, and recognition that each parent has his/her own unique learning style that needs to

---

be nurtured. Parents unanimously rejected the concept of "parenting classes" as they associated them with families where children have been in trouble with either the police, the school or their neighbours. Consequently, the term "group" was preferred since it conveyed a less stigmatizing approach. At a broader level, parents in Johnson's et al's 2005 study indicated the need for universal, nonstigmatized and accessible support and suggested that support would be most appreciated when provided in the familiar setting of the school. (Corter and Arimura, 2006: 22–23)[*]

How do educators start? Walker et al. (2005: 85–104) believe that

effective strategies begin by identifying the early learning and child care needs of families in their communities and then take this information into account when planning the curriculum and pedagogy of the program. Research informs us that when qualified staff deliver family-centred, sustainable support programs that respond to parent needs, parents' confidence and competence is enhanced and the impact on their relationships with their children supports their optimal development. When teachers do connect by reaching out to families, there appears to be a much stronger predictor of family involvement in their children's school progress than family background variables, such as race, ethnicity, social class, marital status or mother's work status.

Although dated, Schorr's research (1997) still rings true today—successful programs share certain attributes; they

- are comprehensive, flexible, responsive, and persevering;
- see children in the context of their families;
- deal with families as parts of neighbourhoods and communities;
- have a long-term preventive orientation, a clear mission, and continue to evolve over time;
- are well managed by competent and committed individuals with clearly identifiable skills;
- operate in settings that encourage practitioners to build strong relationships based on mutual trust and respect; and
- train and support staff to provide high-quality, responsive services. (pp. 17–18)

---

[*] C. Corter and T. Arimura. 2006. *Community Vitality. Literature Review On Parent Support.* Atkinson Centre, Institute of Child Study/Department of Human Development and Applied Psychology, Ontario Institute for Studies in Education/University of Toronto. Prepared For Invest In Kids. June 16. pp. 22–23. Reprinted by permission of the Phoenix Centre for Children and Families.

Sometimes the most effective learning takes place when parents talk to each other about their challenges and strategies for success in smaller gatherings rather than in large groups. It is also an opportunity for families in the same room to network with each other; at times, surprising connections are made. One family was so moved in a meeting by the challenges facing a teen parent in their son's room that they became an important resource and support for that young father.

When we gather with families, we must ensure that

a positive climate is established and risk is eliminated. Different approaches such as role playing, short lectures, open discussion, debates, brainstorming and workshops allow families to learn to use a variety of techniques. Real situations and analogies are used to bring theories to life and positive feedback is used. Problem solving and analysis enable the learner to continue learning beyond the personal contact. (Hepworth Berger and Riojas-Cortez, 2012: 149)

When parents request such support, there are many programs that the centre can make available to assist them in their parenting, and teachers will also benefit. The involvement of teachers as learners is critical to avoid the "teacher as expert" model.

We must also not lose sight of the importance of the community in which our centre or school resides. We must recognize and support the concept that families, early childhood professionals, and healthy communities are key to quality, effective, early childhood programs. Our role is to empower parents, our communities, and ourselves at the same time! Several programs that strive to achieve these goals are discussed below.

THE HANEN LANGUAGE PROGRAM

You Make the Difference in Helping Your Child Learn (Manolson, Ward, and Dodington, 1995), a guidebook and a DVD, is a resource through which parents learn special ways help their child communicate and learn. Language is the single most important predictor of a child's ability to learn. Children learn by engaging in the world around them, and their parents are the most important part of that world. The aims of this resource are to help parents recognize that they have the power and ability to foster their child's communication skills; to give parents specific ways to use everyday activities and play time as opportunities to help their child learn; to help parents become more confident by giving them information and support; and to provide a forum for early identification and referral of children who show signs of language delay. More information about a number of resources for children with and without language delays is available at **http://www.hanen.org/Home.aspx**.

TRIPLE P—POSITIVE PARENTING PROGRAM

Triple P is a world-renowned parenting program that promotes positive, caring relationships between parents and their children and helps parents learn effective management strategies for dealing with a variety of childhood developmental and behavioural issues. Developed by Dr. Matthew Sanders and his colleagues at the University of Queensland, Australia, the program suggests simple routines and small changes that can make a big difference for families. Sanders says,

> it aims to prevent severe behavioural, emotional and developmental problems in children by enhancing the knowledge, skills and confidence of parents. It has five different levels of intervention that operate on a tiered continuum of increasing strength for parents of children from birth to age 16. Delivered by trained practitioners, Triple P aims to build a family friendly environment to support and empower parents. It targets social contexts that influence parents on a day-to-day basis including the mass media, primary health care services, childcare and school systems, work sites, religious organizations and the political system. (in Oates, 2010: 22)[*]

Thirty years of research and evaluation have demonstrated that Triple P is very effective in supporting families. The program has been implemented in a dozen countries around the world and Healthy Child Manitoba is implementing every level of this system province-wide. Find out more at **http://www1.triplep.net**.

CANADIAN PARENTING WORKSHOPS: PREPARING CHILDREN FOR SCHOOL SUCCESS

Developed, field tested, and evaluated by Ryerson University's School of Early Childhood, the Canadian Parenting Workshops are a set of 10 research-based workshops. These workshops have been created specifically for parents with young children. They

include topics of particular interest to parents of preschoolers and elementary aged children, including teaching and learning activities that empower parents; ten workshop modules, fully scripted and ready for use by experienced or novice facilitators; a facilitator's guide; and learning evaluation instruments. (Ryerson University, n.d.)

The workshops have been written by Judith Bernhard, Melinda Freire, and Vickie Mulligan, and published by Chestnut Publishing Group. Further information is available at **http://www.ryerson.ca/ bernhard/research/family-gallery/index.html**.

PATHWAYS TO COMPETENCE FOR YOUNG CHILDREN: A PARENTING PROGRAM

Written by Canadians Sarah Landy and Elizabeth Thompson, *Pathways to Competence for Young Children: A Parenting Program* is designed to help professionals support parents in understanding and managing their child's behaviour while encouraging an active role in guiding social-emotional development. Developed from Sarah Landy's book, *Pathways to Competence*, this manual-and-CD set shows how to set up, lead, and evaluate a parenting program for parents of children from birth to age 7. There are more than 140 parent handouts, instructions on structuring and leading sessions, problem-solving tips, and evaluation guidelines. Field tested for 10 years with hundreds of parents, this program has proved highly successful in improving child behaviour and enhancing parenting skills. Materials can be used for a 10-, 15-, or 20-week parenting group, and professionals can tailor the program to suit the needs of the families. The program is appropriate for a wide range of audiences, including parents with depression, teen mothers, and parents of children with behaviour problems. Visit **http://www2.frp.ca/faireunchoixeclaire/ programdetails_en.asp?pid=113**.

SYSTEMATIC TRAINING FOR EFFECTIVE PARENTING (STEP)

A program developed by Don Dinkmeyer, Gary D. McKay, and Joyce McKay more than 20 years ago, STEP discusses how to improve relationships and establish a democratic atmosphere in the home. The kit contains DVDs, a comprehensive leader's resource guide, and a parent's handbook, which includes material about single parents, stepfamilies, schoolwork, homework, drugs, violence, and

---

[*] Oates, J. 2010. *Supporting Parenting. Early Childhood in Focus 5*. The Open University. Reprinted by permission.

gangs. Kits are available for early childhood and teenaged children. A STEP kit is also available in Spanish. See **http://www.lifematters.com/step.asp**.

PARENT EFFECTIVENESS TRAINING

PET is based on the work of Thomas Gordon, a licensed psychologist who began the program 50 years ago as the first national parent-training system in the United States, and teaches parents how to communicate more effectively with children and offers step-by-step advice for resolving family conflicts so everybody wins. Gordon developed the concept of "I" language and encouraged active listening and win–win problem-solving solutions. His book on this topic is an informative resource. More information can be found at **http://www.gordontraining.com**.

ACTIVE PARENTING NOW

Active Parenting Now, written by Michael H. Popkin, is based on the theories of Alfred Adler and Rudolf Dreikurs. Designed for parents of children ages 5 to 12 years, this program encourages an examination of the goals of misbehaviour, logical consequences, active communication, and family meetings. Parents will acquire skills that help them develop cooperation, responsibility, and self-esteem in their children. They'll also learn positive, nonviolent discipline techniques so they can avoid power struggles. The program kit outlines six sessions and includes a DVD Online parenting class are also available. Visit the Active Parenting Now website at **http://www.activeparenting.com/category/Active_Parenting_Now_in_3**.

BARBARA COLOROSO'S WINNING AT PARENTING

Barbara Coloroso has written extensively on supporting parents with successful and relevant strategies for improving family relationships, and she speaks throughout the world on these important issues. Her cassettes, manuals, and DVDs provide positive strategies for dealing with the challenges of parenting young children. Her work can be explored further in her books: *Winning at Parenting Without Beating Your Kids*; *Kids Are Worth It: Giving Your Child the Gift Of Inner Discipline*; *The Bully, the Bullied and the Bystander: From Pre-School to High School—How Parents and Teachers Help Break the Cycle of Violence*; *Parenting Through Crisis—Helping Kids Through Loss, Grief and Change,* and *Parenting Wit and Wisdom*. Many of these resources are also available on CD or DVD. Coloroso's books are also available in Spanish. Visit **http://www.kidsareworthit.com**.

THE INCREDIBLE YEARS PROGRAM

Developed over 25 years by Carolyn Webster-Stratton, the Incredible Years Program is designed to strengthen young children's social competence and problem-solving abilities while reducing aggression at home and school. It has been positively and rigorously evaluated in community settings in Wales, England, and the United States. The program was developed to promote positive, research-proven parenting and teaching practices that strengthen children's problem-solving abilities and social competency and reduce aggression at home and in the school by using effective nonviolent strategies for managing negative behaviour. The program is presented in four formats: parenting group sessions that focus on basic parenting skills, parental communication, anger management, and promoting children's academic skills; a teacher classroom management series; two-hour weekly small therapy sessions for children; and lesson plans that can be delivered one to three times a week for teachers. More details about the program can be found at **http://www.incredibleyears.com**.

REACHING IN … REACHING OUT (RIRO)

Building on five years of training more than 3500 professionals and paraprofessionals who work with young children, RIRO and its sponsor, the Child and Family Partnership, launched an initiative called *Resilient Parents—Resilient Kids*. The focus is to establish Community Resiliency Hubs in Canadian communities to support families with skills training, information, and resources to help them pass along resilience skills to their children. Resources are available at the website below and include an quarterly e-newsletter. Centres may wish to invite a representative to the centre to discuss this initiative. Visit **http://www.reachinginreachingout.com/resources-parents.htm**.

FILM NIGHT

Many films have been developed for the express purpose of parent education. A film, or two DVDs with opposing viewpoints, might be shown and followed up with a discussion. An excellent DVD that both informs and involves family members is Stanley Greenspan's *Floor Time*.

BOOK NIGHT

With respect to books, family members could be asked to read a relevant book a month in advance. They could then meet to assess the book and discuss controversial issues. An example might be *How to Talk So Kids Will Listen and Listen So Kids Will Talk* by Adele Faber and Elaine Mazlish.

BROWN-BAG LUNCHES

Brown-bag lunch sessions may be most appropriate for family members whose child and family centre is in a workplace environment. One centre held biweekly sessions on issues that parents identified in a survey. Each week either a centre teacher or a parent introduced a different topic about which family members and staff entered into lively discussions. Family members were free to attend all sessions or only those that were of particular interest to them. The lunch provided for the parents encouraged attendance, particularly when the children had a hand in its preparation.

ALUMNI NIGHT

Some families might benefit from advice from "old" parents who have moved on to the school system. They may be able to answer questions about the transition and suggest ways to make the situation less stressful. Alumni can form networks with families to discuss issues relevant to the group. A side benefit may be that alumni are often more than willing to help with fundraising at the centre given the strong connection they may still feel.

FAMILY–TEACHER PANEL DISCUSSIONS

Another way for family members to share their expertise is to hold panel discussions. A topic can be chosen or a series of questions organized and given to the panel in advance. For example, a panel might consist of one teacher and one family member from each of the age groups in the centre.

THE OPEN HOUSE

An open house provides an opportunity for teachers to showcase their playrooms as organized and inviting spaces and to deal with broad programming issues. These events may also be opportunities for families who are transitioning to a new age group in the centre to meet their "new" teachers and discuss the changes that will occur. This is also an opportunity for teachers to share more personal information with the families—why they became teachers and their qualifications. In this way their enthusiasm and dedication to the field will become apparent. Some educators set up interesting activities in each of the learning centres—both indoors and outdoors. Family members can move through the centres, finishing the projects and leaving them behind for their children to see the next day. Other centres asked the children to write down their favourite interest centre and parents were invited to start their visit in that centre. Active involvement in the open house is the best way to engage families rather than sitting listening to the educator explain rules and expectations.

TAKING IT ON THE ROAD

Some educators have taken their meetings to the families. Where many families live in the same apartment building, educators have used party

Each spring we have an open house for family members whose children will be transitioning over the summer months to a new playroom. We have found that families have so many questions about this transition that it is helpful to have everyone together at the same time. We explain to families what they might expect from this age group with respect to their emotional, social, physical, language, and cognitive development. We show a video of the children at "work." Making videos is an integral part of our program and videos are made of special events and of some everyday occurrences. The children are eager to sign them out and take them home, and they allow parents to get to know other families and children in the room. We set up the room so that activities are available at each of the learning centres. We give parents a map with all of the centres located on it and pertinent information recorded. Each centre presents a different challenge. The activities give families a chance to try out the equipment and see firsthand the learning that takes place there. Families receive a handbook that is specific to our room and reviews the material covered during the open house. Finally, we create a bulletin board featuring the work that parents do during the evening. The children are always very excited to see their parents' work the next day!

rooms to hold meetings; even local restaurants close to where the students live have been used. Attendance improved tremendously when meetings were held in such locations and child care was provided (Graham Clay, 2012).

PARTICIPATION DAYS

Whenever family members can participate, the centre should make every effort to accommodate them. To increase family participation in the program, centres may set aside a Saturday for child-care events. Such an arrangement allows for the involvement of families who are unable to take time off work to attend during the week. Since Saturday

may be a religious day for some members of the centre, an evening event might be an alternative.

PREPARING FOR EFFECTIVE MEETINGS

"Why should I worry about asking parents to come to meetings? I've knocked myself out planning and organizing meetings on topics I know parents need to know more about. Most parents don't even bother to show up. Even in the parents who do come, I don't see any changes in their behaviour."

The week before my planned visit to the daycare, my daughter talked of nothing else. She told me how they were decorating the room and how they were preparing a special lunch. When the morning arrived, Tangy was awake long before she needed to be and urged me out of bed so we could have an early start. At the centre the teacher took us through a typical morning and the children led us through a variety of activities. We all sat in the circle and sang songs, did art activities, made towers in the block area, and made a boat in the woodworking centre. I had an opportunity to get to know the children that Tangy talks about at home and to meet some of the other family members. I was a bit uncomfortable in the beginning, but everyone's enthusiasm for the event was overwhelming. Tangy is already planning next year's event.

This comment reflects the "teacher as expert" approach, and it is very unlikely that families in this room would want to come to a meeting where this teacher will tell them what they need to know! The meetings instead should convey the sense that families have a great deal to contribute to the success of the home-to-centre collaboration. Combining meetings for both parties suggests to families that teachers are also interested in life-long learning. If meetings are not properly organized, family members may attend one or two and never return. Their lives are far too busy for them to set aside time for meetings that don't meet their needs. To ensure success, establish an organizing committee of parents and teachers to survey family members to find out what types of meetings they might be interested in attending. In the spirit of "the buck stops here," one person should be designated as the facilitator of the event; depending on the type of meeting, this person could be a family member, a supervisor, or staff person.

FIGURE 5.1   Meeting Topics

Meeting Topics

Sibling rivalry	Gender stereotyping
Superheroes	Infant attachment
Balancing work and family	Computers and education
Sexuality	Community resources for parents
Biting	Childproofing the home
Art experiences in the home	Sleep issues
Divorce/separation	Hospitalization
Effective parenting	Self-esteem
Street proofing	Toilet learning
Physical fitness	Nutrition issues
Challenging behaviour	Fostering a love of books
Child development	Separation issues
Violence and young children	Antibiotics and young children
Media and children	Death
Communication issues	Children's fears
Language development	Stress in children and adults
Curriculum development	Travelling with children
Influence of TV	First aid/CPR
Greening our program	Gardening with children
Preparing a will	Invite a municipal/federal legislator

We asked interested family members to come to the centre to speak to the children about their work experiences or something they wanted to share with the children. We took lots of pictures and the children enjoyed seeing their parents' pictures around the room and recalling the presentations they came to talk to us about. We also made books that told the story of each parent's presentation and the children actively used these in their play. Other children built a relationship with their peers' parents, remembering the wonderful presentations they put on. The children discuss what they learned in the different play areas and what they recalled about certain presentations e.g., "I'm pretending to be a doctor just like Samantha's mom. I'm making latkes like Shahar's mom made for us. I'm wearing the Caribana headdress that Denisha's mom donated to our room."

Source: Reprinted by permission of Mary Bianchi, Esther Exton Child Care Centre, George Brown College.

Although in many cases the early learning environment will serve as an appropriate venue, some meetings may require a larger gathering space. Family members can be good sources of information about locations within the community that can be booked at nominal cost. It may also be possible to find community businesses that might be willing to underwrite the cost of the event or donate materials. In the survey mentioned above, family members should also be asked to state their preferences with respect to meeting times. For example, meetings might be best held at the end of the day with a potluck dinner served. Meetings should also be planned so that family members are able to get their children home in time for their bedtime routines. Conversely, a breakfast meeting may be especially convenient for parents in workplace centres. Families that would struggle to afford a babysitter to attend a meeting may benefit from those held during the day while the children are at

The Regina Early Learning Centre is a child and family development centre that works in partnership with low-income families to provide high-quality early childhood and family support programs. Building respectful relationships with families and creating programming that implements the best in early childhood practice while honouring the values, culture, and goals of parents are hallmarks of the program. The Centre has found providing parent events that combine hands-on experience with guided reflection an effective way of helping parents understand the importance of a play-based, child-centred approach to programming. An example is a parent–teacher supper meeting, which begins with a shared meal with preschool educators and parents. The formal part of the evening begins with parents discussing what they hope their children will learn in preschool. This is followed by parents proceeding to a number of stations where a typical preschool activity is featured. The evening closes with parents reflecting upon what children can learn from the activities they participated in.

Source: Reprinted by permission of Mary Ann McGrath, Executive Director.

the centre. Meetings should always begin promptly at their scheduled time; this will encourage punctuality at future meetings. If guest speakers are to be included, they should come highly recommended and be dynamic and upbeat.

Much thought should go into the preparation of the invitations that are sent home to families; children might assist in the design and, if required, translation should be provided. An invitation from the family members involved in the planning of the meeting may be more effective than one from the centre itself. A variety of media should be used to publicize the upcoming event, and all advertising should be done well in advance. A telephone committee might place calls closer to the event to remind families. A multilingual message might be placed on the centre telephone to encourage participation of all families. A telephone tree or an email list service might also be organized. A personal phone call from an "old" parent to new families with an offer to pick them up may ensure a greater turnout. Having fathers call or email may also encourage other men to attend.

When adults-only events are planned, it is important for the centre to offer child care. Planning special events for the children is one way to encourage families to attend. One centre arranged for the children to be entertained by a magician during a pizza dinner while the parents attended the annual general meeting. Volunteers or students doing their field placements in the centre can be recruited to assist with child care while teachers attend the meeting. Incentives offered for attending, such as a door prize, are often well received. Transportation may be a concern for some families; a car-pool sign-up sheet can assist those parents in need of transportation to or from the meeting. Refreshment breaks also provide an opportunity for social interaction. A meeting's focus is best maintained if refreshments are served at the beginning or end of the meeting. At some events a potluck dinner may be held before the meeting begins. It is always very special for families when their children have taken part in the preparations (by creating table centrepieces, for example, or making punch). Having special displays set up by the children is also a fun incentive to attend. Family members might join teachers in volunteering their services as guest chefs. Letting families know that photos will be taken is another way to encourage participation, as everyone looks forward to seeing the photos after the event.

FIGURE 5.2   Invitation

Join us for a potluck
BREAKFAST
on Tuesday, March 8th
and meet
Sarah Blevens

Sarah is the president of the organization
Parents Against Media Violence.
She will discuss the role families and teachers
can play in advocating for violence-free television.

Tuesday, March 8th
8 a.m.–9 a.m.
Gross Motor Room

The furniture in the meeting room should be comfortable and arranged to facilitate communication among all participants. If visuals are used, care should be taken to ensure that everyone has an unobstructed view.

Copies of the agenda should be circulated before the meeting begins so that families know the expectations; an open invitation to add items is always well received. Additional copies of the agenda should be available at the time of the meeting. Articles or pamphlets relevant to the agenda should be placed in a conspicuous location so families can pick them up as they enter or leave the meeting. These materials can also be provided to parents who were unable to attend the meeting, along with a summary as a valuable postmeeting review for families and teachers. A handwritten note indicating that they were missed is a personal touch many families appreciate.

Inside LOOK

Organizing Effective Meetings: A Checklist

☐ Solicit information from family members on their preferred type of meeting and topic.

☐ Nominate an organizing committee, including teachers and family members, and designate a facilitator.

☐ Coordinate and delegate responsibilities.

☐ Canvass the community for donations to host the event; invite donors.

☐ How much time is needed? Is it a one-time breakfast event or one that is provided over several weeks?

☐ Determine the purpose of the meeting and establish goals.

☐ Invite visitors or guest speakers.

☐ Plan for interpreters, if necessary.

☐ Plan and book an accessible location and an appropriate meeting date and time.

☐ Sign-up for car pooling is posted in advance and parking is available.

☐ Send families a variety of communiqués well in advance.

☐ Set up the family bulletin board to increase interest in the meeting.

☐ Prepare publicity inside and outside the centre.

☐ Arrange for child care.

☐ Order all necessary props and materials.

☐ Prepare a meeting agenda.

☐ Arrange for refreshments that are culturally appropriate (be careful about asking those families who would find it financially difficult to bring in food).

☐ Select, organize, and arrange topic-related displays.

☐ Prepare handouts for families.

☐ View videos ahead of time.

☐ Arrange the furniture to support the format of the meeting.

☐ Secure all necessary equipment (slide projectors, overheads, extension cords, and so forth), test everything before the meeting begins, and ensure the equipment does not block anyone's view.

☐ Adjust the heat or air conditioning.

☐ Remind teachers about personally inviting families to attend.

☐ Telephone or email all families the night before as a final reminder.

☐ Display large signs at entrances and exits on the meeting day.

☐ Have name tags ready.

☐ Make sure the videographer is ready to videotape the event for those who cannot attend.

☐ Assume that everything will go wrong and have back-up plans ready (a flashlight might be useful in an emergency).

HOW TO RUN EFFECTIVE MEETINGS

The facilitator's role is a critical one. Before the meeting begins, the facilitator needs to ensure that the number of attendees is sufficient to reach a quorum, if the meeting is the type that requires one. Unless the bylaws specify a procedure for conducting the meeting, *Robert's Rules of Order* is generally used. The facilitator may wish to begin by taking a few moments to introduce him- or herself or else to be introduced by a member of the organizing committee.

The facilitator should welcome families in a warm and friendly manner. He or she can also use this time to acknowledge guests, to convey the regrets of those unable to attend, to thank those family members and staff who contributed to the organization of the meeting, and to make announcements that are of interest to the group. The location of washrooms and designated smoking areas should be given when the meeting facility is unfamiliar to families. Suggestions for icebreakers are provided below in order to encourage families to socialize with one another.

- *Mixer Bingo for Families of Younger Children:* **In this icebreaker, parents determine which family members fit each of the descriptions shown in Figure 5.3 and write the name of that person on the line provided.**

- *Envelopes:* **As family members arrive, they are given an envelope containing five photocopied pages from an ECE supplier's catalogue, each page depicting a different children's toy. Parents are asked to rank the toys from most expensive to least expensive and share their answers with each other before the facilitator announces the correct responses.**

- *Name Tags:* **Family members are given a tag. They are then asked to decorate the border of the tag (coloured markers are supplied for this purpose). Finished tags are placed in the middle of the floor. Parents are asked to choose a tag for themselves and put their name on it. The person who decorated a particular name tag then identifies himself or herself to the person wearing it.**

- *Photo Name Tags:* **Since most parents are identified as "Renata's mom" or "Connor's dad" by the children and other parents, name tags could be made for each family member that include a wallet-size photo of their child and a space for the parent's name. (When official school photos**

are taken, colour reproductions can be made and stored at the centre for records, individual classroom use, and occasions such as this.)

- *List Making:* **Family members are asked to record on a chart point-form details about their child (for example, favourite child-care lunch, favourite toy or piece of equipment in the playroom, favourite learning centre, favourite outdoor activity).**

- *Sharing Stories:* **Each parent is asked to name one of the most challenging things about raising an infant (or toddler, etc.); a group discussion ensues. Family members in small-group meetings could share one funny (or embarrassing, or touching) story about their child.**

- *Roots:* **Family members write their names on small adhesive notes and, on the world map positioned at the front of the room, place their stickers on their country of origin or the country to which they most closely relate. Discussion can follow on how their roots have influenced their parenting style. Families might also bring in an item that is important to their family and explain its significance.**

- *Treasure Hunt:* **"One of the ways to help parents explore the children's learning environment is to set up a treasure hunt—a search through the classroom looking for designated objects" (Keyser, 2006: 99).***

- *Quilt Making:* **At the beginning of an open house, the kindergarten teachers at one lab school have each family create a square to contribute to a quilt that is made every year and hung in the room.**

- *The Eyes Have It:* **Photos are taken of the children and only their eyes are exposed on the photo. Parents are to find their own child and match the eyes with the child's name.**

- *Scavenger Hunt:* **Families have a tracking sheet and are asked to find things in the centre—their child's name in three different places, the class rabbit (what's his name?), and their child's favourite spot in the outdoor playground. They could also ask their child to show them their favourite book, where Nola the cook works, etc.**

- *Mixer Bingo:* **Create a fill-in-the-blank Bingo game by including comments such as, Can name**

---

* From *Parents to Partners: Building a Family-Centered Early Childhood Program* by Janis Keyser. Copyright © 2006 by Janis Keyser. Reprinted with permission of Redleaf Press, St. Paul, MN; www.redleafpress.org.

two Robert Munsch books; needs a full night's sleep; recently bought a pair of shoes with Velcro; can name a type of cream used for diaper rash etc. and have family members circulate to find someone to sign up beside the comments.

Meetings should be conducted in an atmosphere in which family members feel free to ask questions and discuss issues that are important to them. Some parents may feel vulnerable discussing their parenting role; others may not even attend certain meetings for fear they will be labelled as ineffective parents; still others may feel that some issues are too personal to be discussed in a public forum. As a matter of pure practicality, many English language learners may decline to attend meetings if interpreters are not provided. In fact, if there are a great number of families who are not familiar with English and have a common language, perhaps a better way of reaching these families is to hold the meeting in their home language when there are serious issues to discuss. Therefore, a skillful facilitator will be needed to alleviate any fears or concerns by helping families to understand that they will be safe and their opinions respected.

Another of the facilitator's responsibilities is to find common ground among the diverse participants. Each participant at a meeting brings a different perspective conditioned by age, sex, work experience, cultural background, education, religion, and professional training. In many meetings one or two parents dominate the discussion. The facilitator must be skillful at directing the conversation in such a way that all family members are involved. At the same time, the facilitator must respect the wishes of those parents who would rather listen than actively participate. Timing, pace, and a sense of order are crucial factors in a meeting. The facilitator must be able to read the audience and know when to move on. As a general rule, meetings that involve active participation rather than a lecture format will be more successful. When the group is large, it may be advantageous to break into smaller groups, giving one member the responsibility of being the recorder of the ideas generated then bringing everyone back to the larger group for further discussion. At times when many ideas are formulated, giving people small coloured sticky dots to indicate their most favoured option is a good strategy for organizing divergent ideas. Facilitators should encourage varied opinions and an exchange of ideas. When difficult topics are being discussed, the facilitator must be able to respond to open hostility and be able to ensure that every participant's ideas will be respected and heard. Open debate is a positive strategy for change, but bullying or aggressive tactics must be addressed. Creating a "parking lot" for ideas that are "off topic" is a strategy for acknowledging the speakers ideas with a promise to address the issues later in the meeting or at another time.

The facilitator should use the final minutes of the meeting to summarize what has been discussed and perhaps set a new agenda for tasks that are to be completed or events that are to be planned as a result of the meeting. The end of the meeting might also be a good time to give out special awards or recognize a contribution of a volunteer, a family member, or an educator. The meeting might conclude with a call to parents to bring one other family in the centre to the next meeting.

FOLLOW-UP

Having family members evaluate the meeting can provide teachers and organizers with the information they need to improve future meetings. Families can be asked to complete simple evaluation forms on which the following questions might appear:

1. Was the timing of this meeting convenient for your family?

2. Was enough time allowed for discussion?

3. Did you like the format of this meeting?

4. How well did the speaker cover the topic?

5. What the atmosphere positive and comfortable?

6. What was the most important thing that you learned at the meeting?

7. What information did you wish we had spent more time on?

8. What might we have done differently?

9. What topics would you like to see addressed at future meetings?

Sending a personal note home to families thanking them for attending and participating in the meeting is always a welcome gesture. Any information about upcoming events or future meetings should be included in the note. A record should be kept of those who attended the meetings so that teachers can make a point of encouraging those who did not attend. The meetings might also be videotaped for them and posted on the centre website. Minutes should be taken during the meeting and sent out to families as well as posted in a public place.

FIGURE 5.3 Activities for Informal Gatherings

When attendance at meetings is lower than expected, the organizing committee might reflect on the following questions:

- Did the meeting arise out of interest indicated by a family member survey or was it purely a centre initiative?
- Were families involved in the planning and organizational stages?
- Did the meeting time conflict with family schedules, religious celebrations, or other events in the community?
- Was adequate advance notice given to families?

- Was child care offered so that all families could participate?
- Did teachers in the playrooms actively encourage families to attend and attend themselves?
- Did the organizing committee do a telephone reminder?
- Were signs posted on the day of the event?
- Were interpreters provided, if needed?

Remember that the effectiveness of any parent education program is measured not by how many people come (the "bodies in the building" assessment) but by the effect the program has in changing attitudes and behaviours and increasing parental competence (Gestwicki, 2010: 448).

INFORMAL FAMILY GATHERINGS

Informal gatherings may provide the greatest opportunities for families and teachers to build on their relationships; many families develop friendships that last long past their association with the centre. An informal gathering may consist of small numbers of parents meeting to discuss issues relevant to the specific age group of their children, to share information and expertise, and to socialize. Other opportunities for gatherings may be more playful, for example, a Pet Day on which families bring in their pets. The following overview provides suggestion for such gatherings.

It is important for teachers to encourage newcomer families to participate in informal gatherings. As Murphy Kilbride and Pollard (1990: 36) observe,

> As [immigrant] families learn from each other, they share tips on how to interact with systems and to gain what is needed. This provides a

A camping adventure provides a real opportunity for families and educators to really get to know each other.

very important message to families. As we know, families may represent all levels of adaptation and integration into the new culture. They have each had different experiences and successes (and frustrations) with the system. These [they can share] with each other.

One centre organized a lone-parent informal drop-in group for parents in both the school and the child-care centre. This group meets on a regular basis and discusses a range of topics, including wills, financial planning, children's feelings about separation and divorce, and community resources. Other centres organized fun courses on topics of particular interest to parents (for example, gardening, holiday crafts, sewing). Another centre created a Parent Salon, where the families meet in one another's home on a rotating basis once a month and invite guest speakers to share their expertise. The last half of the meeting is devoted to lively discussion by individual family members about the topic.

As discussed earlier in the chapter, one way for men to explore their feelings, fears, and concerns about parenting is to create men-only discussion groups. These groups provide men with the psychological and physical space they need to talk about their role as fathers. Fathers also indicate that some among them may be intimidated by women because of the widespread assumption that on account of their gender alone women know more about parenting. Common discussion topics may include the changing nature of fatherhood, balancing work and family roles, overcoming stereotypes of fatherhood, shared parenting responsibilities of mothers and fathers, parental burnout and coping mechanisms, and the father's role in influencing child development.

Tobogganing is a great family–centre outing.

Once a year at our centre we rented a Girl Guide campsite for the weekend. All the parents and their children were invited to attend; usually 10 to 15 families participated in this event. The tents were already set up for us, and each family brought its own food. Teachers organized activities during the day, and the families organized the bonfire in the evening. The children absolutely loved being in the woods, participating in scavenger hunts and enjoying simple tasks such as bringing water from the pump. The sense of camaraderie established during this weekend extended well into the year. The children talked about their experience for weeks afterward, and I got to know families in a way that would not have been possible without this event.

The most meaningful meeting I ever attended at the centre was when all the families of toddlers got together to discuss what it was like living with a 2-year-old. I can't tell you how relieved I was to know that other parents were struggling with the same issues that I was, and that I wasn't alone in my feelings. With the support of the teacher, we were able to discuss the issue of biting in the playroom, and I made some new friends in the process. This meeting turned into a monthly event at our centre, and we all looked forward to hearing one another's stories. I think I am a better parent because of this connection.

CHILD AND FAMILY CELEBRATIONS

"When we make choices about what to celebrate, let us be very conscious of who we are doing it for … If we are doing it for the children, let us be conscious of all the subtle messages inherent in what we do and choose things to celebrate that are meaningful, developmentally appropriate, and healthy for them."*

—Neugebauer, 1990: 74

Rituals and celebrations are unique to every family. Even when a celebration is shared by a particular culture, how families celebrate will vary in many different ways. In child and family centres, we have an opportunity to create our own rituals to reflect the many ways in which we celebrate with children and their families. Celebrations for children's birthdays are common in child-care centres. When family members are involved, it becomes a special event. This may mean hosting the event at the end of the day when it is most convenient for the parents but not necessarily the best timing for weary children. The challenge for some families occurs when each birthday party celebration "ups the ante" for the next family—a magician, a juggler, or enormous party loot bags to take home may make it impossible for some families to participate in this way. Therefore many centres have adopted more modest celebrations that focus on the child in a more developmentally appropriate manner.

Celebrations in a child-care centre can be joyous events that promote camaraderie among children, parents, and staff. Encouraging families to share their celebration practices with the centre is critical to the success of the home–centre partnership and so a number of questions must be addressed by families, teachers, and the board of directors when planning celebrations:

- **Will the celebrations reflect the philosophy of the centre?**
- **What role will the families and children play in organizing the celebrations?**

---

* Neugebauer, B. 1990. "Going One Step Further—No Traditional Holidays," *Child Care Information Exchange*, p. 74. Reprinted by permission.

- Will celebrations teach positive values and broaden the children's awareness of others?
- How can the centre ensure that the celebrations are age-appropriate for the children?
- How much time will the centre devote to celebrations?
- How will the centre respond to families who express concerns that holidays are too commercialized?
- If there is little diversity in the centre, should a more comprehensive approach to celebrations be implemented?
- If there is a great deal of diversity in the centre, should every event be celebrated?
- Will everyone feel welcome at the celebrations?
- Is there a procedure in place if a family member objects to a specific celebration—for example, instead of Mother's Day or Father's Day can we have an I Love You Day and invite any person the child is close to?
- How will teachers' time be organized to allow for preparation for these events?
- Can we coordinate celebrations with the school for our school-age children?

Early childhood programs should be involved in celebrations that are meaningful to our children: celebrations that are magical, bigger than life, fantastical, full of hope and power and love, and that make each child feel they belong; festivals that show the brighter side of humanity; music, dance, togetherness, the importance of children, and the power of community to care for children. (Wardle, 1994: 43)[*]

Bonnie Neugebauer (1994:100) suggests the following alternatives to traditional celebrations:

milestones (the first tooth, learning to whistle, printing one's name, moving from one age group to another, tying shoelaces, telling a story, making a friend); points of learning (the number three, worms, the colour red, a favourite story, Thursday); children and families (the birth of a sibling, a grandparent's visit, moving to a new house); a great meal by the cook; a winter picnic; an ice sculpture; inventors; natural and man-made events (a shuttle launch, the first snowflake, puddles, a thunderstorm).[†]

Courtesy of Lynn Wilson

Special events such as this camping adventure are wonderful opportunities for families to share in their children's excitement.

If celebrations are to be meaningful, developmentally appropriate, and healthy, the focus must always be on what is in the best interests of the children. When this focus is absent, the results can be disastrous. Recounts Wardle (1994: 43):

I have experienced early childhood graduations where children cried, staff got mad, and parents literally walked over some children to videotape their own child in cap and gown. The atmosphere was tense; the children were bored. And the entire activity was adult dominated and only for the benefit of adults.[‡]

In some centres, teachers have decided to do away with all celebrations in an effort to not offend anyone, but in doing so they miss wonderful opportunities to celebrate events that are meaningful in the lives of young children and their families. To celebrate our connections with families, don't forget the United Nations International Day of Families in May.

BOOKS FOR CHILDREN

Mama, I'll Give You the World, by R. Schotter and S. Saelig Gallagher

Lighting Our World: A Year of Celebrations, by C. Rondina and J. Oakley

A World of Festivals, by R. Rissman

Holidays Around the World, by C. Otto

---

[*] Wardle, F. 1994. "Beginnings Workshop: Celebrations, Festivals, Holidays: What Should We Be Doing?" *Child Care Information Exchange 100.* November–December, p. 43. Reprinted by permission.

[†] Neugebauer, B. 1994. "Beginnings Workshop: Going One Step Further: No Traditional Holidays." *Child Care Information Exchange.* November–December, p. 100. Reprinted by permission.

[‡] Wardle, F. 1994. "Beginnings Workshop: Celebrations, Festivals, Holidays: What Should We Be Doing?" *Child Care Information Exchange 100.* November–December, p. 43. Reprinted by permission.

One mother has written, "When my son was in junior kindergarten, I suggested to his teacher that she consider [celebrating] festivals reflecting the background of the non-Christian children in the class as well as Easter, Halloween, and Christmas. She showed surprise because the thought had not occurred to her. After some reluctance, she agreed to consider the suggestion if I and other non-Christian parents organized the festivals. This was progress, but she missed the point. For the little children in her class, she was the authority figure, the one with knowledge and power, the one who legitimized learning activities. In terms of legitimacy of what went on in her classroom, they saw the difference between what she planned and initiated and what she allowed to happen.

As a supervisor, I sometimes found it challenging when we had social gatherings with families when all of the children and siblings as well as teachers were all in the centre at the same time. When the children acted out, which was to be expected on these types of special events, no one really knew who should deal with the children when a problem arose. Teachers in the centre were resentful when some adults sat back and chatted to each other while the children engaged in less than desirable interactions, and in other situations the teachers were afraid of embarrassing the parent if they stepped in. From the parent's perspective, I also could tell that they felt as if they were on "our territory" and so seemed reluctant to get engaged with directing their child or others. They worried about creating a situation that would offend us. So in preparation for the event, I explained in the newsletter that we were happy to be hosting the event and this would mean that the teachers would be busy helping to set up and organize so we would appreciate it if the family assumed responsibility for "crowd" control. At the same time, we also wanted families to have time to interact with each other so the teachers organized an activity where the children could be involved, and teachers volunteered to supervise these experiences. This has made a huge difference in our informal gatherings. We could all relax and just have a good time enjoying each other's company!

BOOKS FOR ADULTS

Celebrate! An Anti-Bias Guide to Enjoying Holidays in Early Childhood Programs, by J. Bisson

What If All The Kids Are White? by L.O. Derman Sparks, P.G. Ramsey, and J.O. Edwards

Small World Celebrations! Around the World Holidays to Celebrate with Young Children, by J. Warren, E.S. McKinnon, and M. Hopping Ekberg

Exhibit 5.2 provides a sample of a questionnaire that might be completed by families.

VOLUNTEERS

"Two-thirds of Canadians in 2008 were members of voluntary groups or organizations, an increase in participation since the late 1990s. Four in ten Canadians volunteer with non-profit and charitable organizations, a proportion that fell in the late 1990s, but has been rising since 2000."[*]

—**Canadian Index of Wellbeing (2010: 3)**

[*] Canadian Index of Wellbeing. 2010. Community Vitality, p. 3. Available at http://ciw.ca/reports/en/Domains%20of%20Wellbeing/CommunityVitality/CommunityVitality_ExecutiveSummary.sflb.pdf. Reprinted by permission.

EXHIBIT 5.2 Celebrations: A Questionnaire for Families

1. What special days do you celebrate in your family?
2. How would you like our program to be involved in your celebrations?
3. How do you think we could celebrate everyone's special days in a centre as diverse as ours?
4. What are some of the myths or stereotypes about your culture that you would like us to understand so as not to perpetuate them?
5. How do you feel about celebrations at the centre that are not part of your family's tradition?
6. What can we do to celebrate our centre as an inclusive "human" community?
7. Would you have time to
   - read a favourite story in your first language?
   - share a favourite family recipe?
   - donate articles of clothing that you no longer use for our dress-up corner?

Source: Neugebauer, B. 1994. "Beginnings Workshop: Going One Step Further: No Traditional Holidays," *Child Care Information Exchange*. November–December.

Inside LOOK

One Day at School: *Sae Hae Bok Man Hee Ba Du Se Yo*

My adopted son's preschool class vigorously planned a celebration of the Lunar New Year. No one seemed to know anything about Korean New Year customs. A bit reluctant because of my limited knowledge, I nonetheless took the plunge and volunteered to lead a Korean New Year activity for the class. The one Korean woman with a child in the class shied away from any involvement, so I went ahead on my own. The morning of our special day, we arrived at school with Eric's *han-bok*, which he was refusing to wear at all, 30 purses made from cotton for the children to decorate, and thread with satiny cord, a few pictures, and lots of pennies. I saw my Korean friend there and self-consciously hoped I wouldn't butcher the language I was attempting to teach. To my surprise, when she saw Eric's *han-bok*, she asked if I'd mind if she ran home to get her daughter's. She did, and as a result Eric decided it would be all right to wear his too. What followed was a wonderful morning. The children drew on and threaded their purses. I transported the children via pretend plane to Korea and told them a story about two children anticipating the holiday. Eric and Alice proudly showed off their *han-bok*s to a very admiring audience of their peers. Then I explained the bowing and the words while Myong Ja, Alice's mother, demonstrated and corrected my pronunciation! I was surprised that every child in the class wanted to try bowing. (Of course, the pennies helped.) They loved it; and days later children were still coming up to me and saying, "*Sae Hae Bok Man Hee Ba Du Se Yo*." We repeated our performance for the other class, and the greatest rewards were the pride in Eric's and Alice's faces, the new friendship with a Korean woman, and the delight with which all the children learned about a culture different from their own.

Source: Sheehan, N., and L. Wood. 1993. *Adoption and the Schools Project:* A Guide for Educators, vol. 2. Children's Bureau, Administration for Children, Youth and Families, Office of Human Development Services, U.S. Department of Health and Human Services.

Volunteers are generally motivated by a desire to help others and to feel needed and useful. Most volunteers (93 percent) say they volunteer to assist their community, some to reduce the loneliness and isolation they feel; others in order to enhance their job skills; still others have specific skills they wish to share with others. According to a study by *Volunteer Canada* in conjunction with the

Canadian Centre for Philanthropy, people who give their time to a volunteer activity are happier and healthier in their later years. Much of the benefit comes from being in touch with others and having an impact on their lives.

FAMILY MEMBERS AS VOLUNTEERS

As part of the orientation process, families can be encouraged to volunteer in ways that suit their lifestyles, work commitments, and interests. Based on information gathered in the family visit, the supervisor of the centre should keep a logbook of family members who are willing to serve as volunteers; their areas of expertise and interests could also be recorded. The type of program offered in the centre to some extent determines the kind of volunteers it attracts; in workplace child-care centres, for example, family members may assist during lunch hours or after work whereas in a cooperative early learning environment, family members are expected to volunteer on a regular basis. When asking family members to come and speak of their employment experiences, it is important to include all types of families and their work—doctors as well as those who build homes. When family members come in for the first time to share, to cook, or to help out, when they leave knowing that their support and expertise is much appreciated, it is surprising how much more engaged they feel and more willing to participate more fully. Being appreciated is critical!

When family members volunteer, they send positive messages to their children. Volunteering in meaningful ways gives parents insight into the day-to-day running of the centre and an opportunity to observe firsthand the interactions between the teachers and their child. Family members are more likely to participate when they see that their involvement benefits their child and that their efforts are valued by the centre. Educators benefit by having an extra adult in the room, and they gain an opportunity to more closely observe the parent–child interaction and obtain greater insight into their relationship.

Some fathers want to play an active role in the centre. Once fathers begin to participate, they are often enthusiastic. Some noncustodial fathers may play a more active role than custodial fathers as a way of being part of a child's routine without involving the mother.

Leadership opportunities have been associated with parents' increased sense of efficacy. One effective local program gave parents opportunities to become assistants in a parent–child drop-in readiness centre. These parents recruited other members of their cultural groups; served as translators in the program; and at school-level meetings, took training in running some aspects of the readiness program, such as children's outdoor play time and parent education groups. When parents are given leadership opportunities early, they tend to stay involved over time (Corter and Pelletier, 2005).

Family volunteers should be made aware of the possible reaction of their own child to their presence. The child may resent the time and attention other children receive from his or her parent. The teacher can support this transition by explaining to the children that the volunteer has come to help all of them while at the same time setting aside time for the family member and child to spend with each other.

ELDERS AS VOLUNTEERS

Valuing the attributes and diverse lifestyles of the elderly is a positive experience for children, families, and teachers. As Smith and Newman (1993: 33) observe

> Beyond their benefits to children, older adults make important contributions to the children's families and other program staff. The power of generational roles, for example, can be seen in the way young parents, especially mothers, gravitate to the older adult, the "grandparent," in the classroom.

Courtesy of Lynn Wilson

This father is helping out with T-ball batting practice.

Families have always been an essential part of our program but we decided to take it a step further and start a *Family's in the Classroom Project*. Although you would often find families in our classroom because we have an open-door policy, this was a bit more formal. The idea was to have the children and their families share something that was important to them with their classmates. Families would sign up for a specific day and then we created a calendar for children to refer to as the anticipation for their upcoming day was contagious. It was such a good feeling knowing that this anticipation was also evident with the adults as every child's family signed up and all were very eager! Over the next eight weeks we participated in a variety of experiences; it was powerful that each one was so unique and truly fun!! As a class we did home visits and workplace tours; we hosted extended families, Grandmas who told stories and sang songs, and Nonas who made pasta; and older siblings who conducted soccer clinics, baseball clinics, special bike rides in the community, wacky science experiments and special crafts, camping on the grass; and made special treats. Every family day was documented and the end result was a big thank-you party where each family received a special photo of their experience and a video showcasing each family's contribution. As a facilitator, I found it a moving experience to share in such an incredible project. The willingness of the individual families to share and strengthen our already existing relationship was what made this so successful.

Source: Reprinted by permission of Kelly Antram, RECE, Queen Street Child Care Centre, George Brown College.

COMMUNITY MEMBERS AS VOLUNTEERS

Volunteers may include high school, college, or university students who need fieldwork or community hours; Girl Guides or Boy Scouts; and members of groups and organizations with special interests such as gardening or boating. Busy families will be grateful to centres that

Courtesy of University of Toronto Child Care – Charles Street

This mother volunteers once a week in this early learning environment.

Courtesy of Scotia Plaza Child Care Centre

Elders bring their expertise and knowledge to the child-care centre.

are able to organize out-of-centre events that might not otherwise be available to their children. Centres may want to seek out volunteers who have disabilities or who come from different cultural backgrounds. In centres where staff is predominantly female, male volunteers might be actively recruited; it is important for children to see men in nurturing roles. In centres where the languages spoken by the teachers are not congruent with the families at the centre, contacting community agencies for volunteers who would be willing to provide translation/interpreting skills would be of great benefit. This volunteer might also be willing to hold language classes to help teachers become more proficient in the home language of the families.

In some communities, volunteers can be solicited through a volunteer registry where appropriate criminal reference checks are carried out. Other recruitment methods include posting notices on boards, advertising in local newspapers, or appearing on local cable television or radio shows. With family permission, photographs of the children are a wonderful asset, and it may be possible to set up displays in places such as the local community centre, community colleges, and seniors residences. Staff and families could also speak to friends and acquaintances about doing volunteer work. A formal tour and open house might also generate interest in the community. By establishing

Courtesy of Lynn Wilson

Elders are our greatest connection with the past.

Inside LOOK

The sun drenched common room at the south end of Columbia Garden Village retirement home in Invermere, B.C., is quiet most days. But every Tuesday and Friday, 18 kindergartners from Eileen Madson Primary School arrive in a yellow school bus and take over, turning the home's common room into a classroom, and the home's residents into active participants. The kindergartners go about their lessons, crafts and play time surrounded by the seniors who live there. Some elders watch from the side-lines, others roll up their sleeves and build block towers or indulge in a reading. With fewer children growing up with a grandparent in the home, emerging research suggest they are missing out on rich learning opportunities. The Invermere collaboration is the brainchild of Rocky Mountain School District's superintendent, Paul Carriere and his wife Barbara, a kindergarten teacher. With full co-operation from the administration of the seniors residence and the Ministries of Health and Education the program began. Even on their first day in the home, the children seemed naturally drawn to the elders. As learning partners they're a good match. Reading, for instance, is a skill often preserved long after age has eroded other mental faculties. The students have responded well to the program, referring to the residents as "grandmas and grandpas." One girl even asked her parents if she could have her birthday party at the retirement home. It's taught students about aging, death, and compassion and helped coax others out of their shell. The payoffs can be huge. Barbara Carriere says the seniors make for patient teachers, and the children are at ease around them. "They're just completely accepting of each other," she said. "It makes for a million magic moments."

Source: Hammer, K. 2011. "Kindergarten in a retirement home proves a hit with young and old," *The Globe and Mail*, December 30. © The Globe and Mail. All Rights Reserved.

direct contact with the community via volunteer efforts, teachers are able to disseminate information about the important work being done in child and family centres.

Centres may wish to recruit specific types of resource people. A centre that needs help in the design of its handbook or brochure might contact a local community college and try to enlist the services of students in the graphic arts department. Often community organizations contribute to the child-care centre through fundraising efforts, donating supplies, hosting child-care events, or sharing their expertise. Children can give something back to the community by participating in environmental projects (planting, cleanups); by providing local businesses with original artwork; or by helping seniors with yard work, shopping, and other tasks.

WAYS TO VOLUNTEER

There are many ways in which volunteers can play meaningful roles in the operation of the daycare.

ADMINISTRATIVE DUTIES

* Serving on the board of directors

* Participating on committees organized by the families or board of directors

A wonderful pasta experience is being organized by this community volunteer, who also brings her Garden Club friends to help with the centre's garden.

Courtesy of Lynn Wilson

- Working on hiring committees
- Writing funding proposals
- Typing, filing, and assisting with clerical duties (e.g., photocopying)
- Providing bookkeeping services
- Fundraising
- Helping with public relations activities
- In collaboration with the teachers, finding interesting visitors to the playroom
- Organizing a clothing, boots, shoes, or sports equipment swap
- Organizing a pizza day
- Establishing co-op food purchases for families
- Creating a book exchange: "a parent volunteer might check in the books and issue tickets to be used to 'buy' another one. Children look through the books until they find a book they want and then use the ticket to buy it" (Hepworth Berger and Riojas-Cortez, 2012: 88)*
- Planning for a donation of gently used books and toys that the children no longer need and donating them to a local shelter (this is a great opportunity to help children understand the importance of sharing)

COMMUNICATION TASKS

- Creating a centre website
- Maintaining bulletin boards
- Participating in the production of a regular newsletter
- Preparing media releases
- Creating a telephone tree for distributing centre-wide information
- Being part of a new-family welcoming group
- Organizing translation services for families
- Organizing social events (retirement parties, good-bye events, yearly family reunions, pancake breakfasts, and so on)
- Organizing family discussion groups

*BERGER, EUGENIA HEPWORTH; RIOJAS-CORTEZ, MARI R., PARENTS AS PARTNERS IN EDUCATION: FAMILIES AND SCHOOLS WORKING TOGETHER, 8th Edition, © 2012. Reprinted and Electronically reproduced by permission of Pearson Education, Inc., Upper Saddle River, NJ.

- Serving as a playroom representative
- Establishing a Block Parent group
- Taking photographs during special events and creating a bulletin board
- Creating a history of the child care centre

MAINTENANCE TASKS

- Creating a wish list at the front door to alert everyone to the tasks that need to be completed
- Assisting with centre repairs, painting, cleaning
- Getting garden/greening advice from experts in the community
- Helping children set up a garden in the indoor or outdoor environment and maintaining it
- Creating a butterfly garden
- Building new equipment
- Helping to keep storage areas organized and in good shape both indoors and out
- Assisting with outdoor clean-up
- Tracking dress-up clothes for needed repairs and perhaps sewing new ones

PROGRAM DEVELOPMENT

- Designing project boxes that reflect children's interests
- Designing, organizing, and running a family resource area
- Teaching children the safe use of construction tools while completing woodworking projects
- Serving as the guest "chef" or assisting with cooking projects
- Listening—children have many stories to tell
- Helping over lunch hour or nap time
- Accompanying the children on trips
- Providing one-on-one support for exceptional children
- Videotaping, tape recording, or taking photographs of children during their daily routine or on special occasions
- Sharing expertise with the children (in woodworking, for example, or jewellery-making, pottery skills, or playing musical instruments)

Richmond Adelaide Child Care Centre

Courtesy of Lynn Wilson

Reading, reading, and more reading—an extra lap is always welcome.

Delicious smoothies are in the works with this volunteer!

- Collecting resources and setting up a learning centre

- Helping children learn a new language

- Showing slides or movies about life in other countries or from trips they have taken

- Sharing their expertise about a family celebration

- Sharing information about local history

- Typing children's stories

- Helping children understand computer use and new computer programs

- Playing games with the children both indoors and outdoors

- Coaching in school-age programs (baseball, cricket, basketball, hockey, and so on)

- Creating or collecting dramatic play clothing

- Working with teachers to develop emergent curriculum

How do we connect with newcomers in our communities? An initiative that is possible in many early learning environments is to engage families and extended-family members in creating a community garden. Many newcomer families have difficulty finding foods that were familiar to them in their home country, and the garden is an engaging meeting place for both children and families. Many friendships and relationships are enhanced when planting and harvesting the garden.

TRAINING OF VOLUNTEERS

Clear goals and objectives should be established so that all participants are aware of their roles and responsibilities. Training should involve not only the supervisor but also the teachers who will work with the volunteers. Including pictures or a video of volunteers working with the children is often a positive way to begin and may relieve anxious participants. A video series from the National Association for the Education of Young Children (NAEYC) titled *Caring for Our Children* consists of a set of six 30-minute tapes that show volunteers how to keep young children healthy and safe. In-house videos can also be created to emphasize positive interactions between volunteers and the children.

Volunteers should be provided with a handbook outlining regulations, fire drills, and emergency procedures. The handbook, advises Lowell Krogh (2006), who worked on the NAEYC video series, should

> be clear about what is and isn't permitted on the site: rules for personal use of the telephone, length and flexibility of time for breaks, customs regarding personal use of the refrigerator, and so on. It is embarrassing for people to learn after the fact that they have broken rules they didn't know existed.

The importance of confidentiality must be impressed upon volunteers. Issues that come up in the playroom must not be discussed outside the centre. Volunteers should approach their work in a professional manner and must be reliable and flexible enough to adapt to the busy nature of a childcare centre. The supervisor should monitor the interactions between the teachers and volunteers on an ongoing basis, supporting when necessary and encouraging a positive and nurturing environment.

PREPARING FOR VOLUNTEERS

To prepare children for the arrival of the volunteer, teachers can ask them to think of ways to make the person feel welcome. Children should also be prepared for whatever special circumstances may apply (coping with the presence of a wheelchair, for example, or a cane). It is a good idea to have the volunteer simply observe on the first day. The teacher can make use of "teachable moments" to inform and orient the new volunteer as well as to reinforce the routines and strategies that were learned during training. The teacher should be available to answer the many questions that most volunteers have at this stage. A volunteer who appears difficult or defensive might feel at a loss; however, given a specific task in which they have an interest may make them the teacher's greatest asset. The volunteer should be introduced to the families as well as to the children and made to feel comfortable. A rocking chair on a carpet with lots of big cushions for the children to lie on is a wonderful gathering place.

VOLUNTEER RESPONSIBILITIES: A CHECKLIST

1. Be honest and open with the supervisor and staff, beginning with the interview, regarding intent, goals, needs, and skills so that a good experience is possible for all.

2. Understand the requirements of time and duties of assignments before accepting them, and, once you do accept them, fulfill the commitment to the best of your ability.

3. Work to deserve being treated as a recognized and respected member of the team.

4. Take the commitment seriously enough to participate in planning and evaluating the volunteer program and in whatever training or learning opportunities are available.

5. Share ideas with staff. Volunteers frequently have a fresh perspective that is valuable. However, do not be hurt or resentful if your ideas are not always implemented, for the staff's ideas aren't always carried out either.

6. View staff as allies and mentors, for much can be learned from them.

7. Respect the confidentiality of the centre and its families.

8. Seek and accept honest feedback on performance. Remember, negative feedback is valuable too, when viewed as an opportunity for growth.

9. Serve as goodwill ambassadors and interpreters for the centre and its services in the community at large.

10. Be informed and therefore more effective advocates of change when change is needed.

EVALUATION OF THE VOLUNTEER PROGRAM

Volunteers should regularly receive constructive feedback on their role and interactions in the centre. An evaluation process involving all participants should be in place to identify what has worked well and what areas need improvement. If it is conveyed in a positive manner, most volunteers appreciate the feedback. At the same time, volunteers should also have an opportunity to present their own self-evaluation and feedback on the program and their participation in it. This encourages a stronger sense of belonging and commitment to the centre.

It is important that teachers acknowledge volunteers' contributions (see Figure 5.4 for some ideas) and that they share the administration's enthusiasm for volunteers. Unless teachers are prepared to treat volunteers as coworkers, the chances of successful and meaningful interactions are severely limited. If staff are involved in the initial planning, training, and evaluation process, they are likely to feel a greater commitment to the volunteer program.

When assessing the success of the volunteer program with regard to number of recruits, it is important for teachers to remember that family members may have a good reason for not volunteering: they may lack child care for their own children, they may be ill, or they may already have too many demands on their time. The decision not to volunteer should therefore not be interpreted as lack of enthusiasm for the centre or its teachers. However, families with demanding work schedules can still participate. One busy mother who is a doctor organized an in-depth tour of her workplace for her child's group. Teachers need to understand also that many English language learner family members will not participate unless teachers are particularly encouraging in their recruitment efforts.

FIGURE 5.4 Recognizing Volunteers

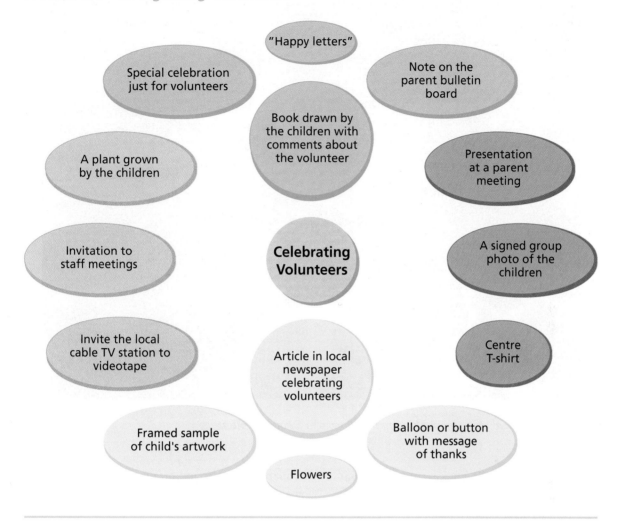

"Happy letters"

Special celebration just for volunteers

Note on the parent bulletin board

Book drawn by the children with comments about the volunteer

A plant grown by the children

Presentation at a parent meeting

Invitation to staff meetings

Celebrating Volunteers

A signed group photo of the children

Invite the local cable TV station to videotape

Article in local newspaper celebrating volunteers

Centre T-shirt

Framed sample of child's artwork

Balloon or button with message of thanks

Flowers

BOOKS FOR ADULTS

Effective Volunteering, by K. Kay and J. Cotton

365 Ideas for Recruiting, Retaining, Motivating, and Rewarding Your Volunteers: A Complete Guide for Non-Profit Organizations, by S. Fader

Connect: How to Double Your Number of Volunteers, by N. Searchy and J. Dykes Henson

FUNDRAISING

It is an unfortunate reality that the economic survival of many programs depends on the fundraising efforts of families and teachers. Fundraising gives those who participate in it an opportunity not only to publicize the centre but also to have fun and build on their relationships with one another. There may also be times when dollars are respectfully diverted into a special fund to help pay for trips or in-centre events that some families may not be able to afford. Before any fundraising begins, the following questions should be asked:

1. Is the activity appropriate for the community?

2. How much money do we have to spend on our fundraising efforts and where will it come from?

3. Will the initial investment in the project be recovered at the end of the event?

4. Will the gains be large enough to warrant undertaking the fundraiser?

5. Who will be responsible for the money and keep appropriate records? Will we need to open a separate bank account?

The children had great fun celebrating the efforts of a favourite volunteer.

6. Do we have the time necessary to carry out the fundraising activity?

7. Will we have enough participation from beginning to end to carry out the project?

8. What materials will we require?

9. How will we handle publicity?

10. Should we hire an outside company to organize the event? Can we afford it? If not, who will coordinate the event?

11. Instead of paying for outside assistance, can we call on families, teachers, and the community whose services we could use?

HOW TO PLAN A SUCCESSFUL FUNDRAISING EVENT

When organizing a fundraising event, it is important to canvass everyone involved—families, teachers, and older children—for their ideas. An organizing committee should be established to oversee the event. It is important at the outset to determine what the community can contribute to the fundraising drive. Are corporate sponsorships available? It is also important to establish a specific goal (to raise $1000 for a new garden, for example) rather than simply to raise money to be allocated at another time.

Whether to hold one large fundraiser each year or several small ones is another decision that has to be made based on the amount of time and number of staff and volunteers available. The date or dates should not conflict with religious celebrations or national or community holidays. Some families prefer not to get involved with fundraising because of their time schedule, and some simply feel too awkward asking friends and neighbours to buy things on a regular basis. Therefore, some families are in a position to make a financial contribution whenever a fundraising event is organized. For other families or those who have more than one child in the centre or school, fundraising can be a financial burden and teachers should be aware of this.

It is important to publicize the event in both the centre and the community. Posters, fliers, newspapers, cable television, Facebook, Twitter, the centre website, and radio are among the vehicles that can be used to publicize the event. A local celebrity may be willing to act as a spokesperson for the centre. Personal invitations to the event can be sent to dignitaries, members of government, and community leaders. Centres may also want to enlist the support of families that have "graduated" from the centre; they may be pleased to come back and see old friends. This is also a good time to have the telephone committee spread the word!

Accurate and up-to-date records of the fundraising event should be kept. Once the event is over, a summary of the efforts should be distributed to families. Records should be kept so that they can be referred to the following year if the event is repeated; this will save a great deal of time.

Unfortunately, not all fundraisers are outright successes. When an event fails to meet expectations, it is important to determine what went wrong and how it can be avoided next time. A survey could be distributed to families to elicit their feelings about the project. Everyone who participated in the event should be thanked through personal letters, bulletin-board displays, acknowledgment in the local newspaper, or on the centre website and in newsletters. As teachers, we must not forget the value of involving parents and older children in projects that contribute to their communities; not all fundraising needs to be self-serving.

FUNDRAISING IDEAS

Many books are available on the subject of fundraising, so the library is a good place to begin your search for ideas. The following list outlines several innovative ways of fundraising, as reported by various centres.

- Sell plants started by the children or sell bulbs in both the spring and the fall; a local garden centre may provide some support.
- Sell calendars decorated with the children's art, or T-shirts or tote bags that school-age children have designed.
- Sell herb vinegars and garlic oils, potpourri, jellies, and jams from produce from the centre garden.
- Take on a newspaper route with proceeds going to supplies for the centre.
- Hold auctions featuring items donated by families and the community; sell raffle tickets (one centre held a monthly raffle with a family member donating a different service each time).

- Create an online auction so that families can participate at their leisure in their own home.
- Hold a fashion show.
- Show a movie, or a series of them, and charge admission.
- Arrange (possibly in collaboration with other centres) a visit by a popular children's singer or theatre group (the performance could take place in a local high school auditorium) or invite a popular guest speaker or storyteller and charge admission.
- Organize bake sales or craft sales (selling parent- and child-made items).
- Buy food or ECE resources in bulk from suppliers and sell to families.
- Organize a bingo or casino night.
- Organize a car wash.
- Produce and sell cookbooks featuring favourite family recipes.
- Hold a wine-tasting event.
- Organize a tour of historical houses.
- Sell fertilizer.
- Organize a community fish fry.
- Hold a walkathon, bikeathon, jumpathon, or readathon.
- Arrange errand services for elderly or bedridden members of the community.
- Sell various services (window washing, lawn mowing, snow shovelling, etc.).
- Hold garage sales.
- Sell magazine subscriptions.
- Have a local pizza shop donate money to the centre on the basis of the number of pizzas sold by families.

BOOKS FOR ADULTS

Effective Fundraising for Non Profits: Real World Strategies That Work, by I.M. Bray

Fundraising for Dummies, by J. Mutz and K. Murray

The Little Book of Gold: Fundraising for Small (and Very Small) Non-Profits, by E. Hanberg

199 Fun and Effective Fundraising Events for Non-Profit Organizations, by R. Helweg and E. Figure Sandlin

Not only do children enjoy face-painting events, but such events can also raise money for their centre.

FAMILIES AS MEMBERS OF A BOARD OF DIRECTORS

This section was contributed by Pat Campbell, faculty, George Brown College.

Many child-care centres, early learning environments and parent co-operatives in this country are run by volunteers who serve on a governing board. This board is responsible for the overall operation of the centre and is elected by the "members" (families) of the centre at an annual general meeting. Some centres have only parents and the supervisors on the board, while others have a few representatives from the larger community. There could be a school principal, a church member, a community centre director, a public health nurse, or others. Most governing boards meet on a monthly basis. The board hires the supervisor and evaluates his or her performance; the supervisor reports to the board on a regular basis. As with any other volunteer organization, there are some years when a strong bond exists and everything seems to work fairly well. In other years, when the board members are new to community work and do not understand what their responsibilities are, more guidance and support are required from an experienced supervisor or outside consultant.

Board training is (strongly) advisable for both experienced and new members. This training serves to clearly refresh and educate all board members about their responsibilities and procedures.

Some child and family centres exist within a larger organization and may serve a function there,

such as a lab school in a community college. These centres often have a parent Advisory Board. This kind of board may invite board members who may meet several times per year to consult with the management of the centres. The members are expected to offer advice and resources and also to raise concerns about current and future issues that affect the quality of care their children are receiving. They have no actual responsibilities to the centre, and their advice and concerns are for consideration only.

The following are specific responsibilities of the most common type. The governing board

- develops all long-range and strategic plans affecting the organization
- ensures that the centre meets the needs of the people it serves through the design, development, and monitoring of appropriate programs
- develops, re-examines, and revises the mission statement, bylaws, and policies that govern the overall operation of the centre
- plans for and carefully monitors the financial solvency of the organization
- ensures that the organization meets all legal standards and government requirements
- maintains complete and accurate records of board meetings and operations
- approves all major contracts involving the organization
- selects the supervisor and delegates to her or him the authority to carry out the policies and deliver the programs
- provides a complete job description for the supervisor and regular performance-based reviews
- ensures that fair hiring and personnel policies are established and maintained
- determines staff responsibilities in job descriptions and sets out working conditions
- negotiates staff salaries and benefits each year
- assists the supervisor to market services, advocate, and fundraise
- works cooperatively at all times with the supervisor and the staff to accomplish objectives
- designs and administers family and staff questionnaires to monitor client satisfaction and program quality
- establishes standing committees that are required to report regularly to the board

- holds annual general meetings as outlined in the bylaws
- ensures regular communication with the general membership
- monitors and responds to government policies
- evaluates their own performance, as a board, in relation to established mission statement and goals
- ensures continuance of the organization through effective board succession

In addition, many provinces and municipalities are now demanding more policies around issues such as working conditions, inclusion, privacy, and financial disclosure. The supervisor will be aware of such changes, and will help craft new policies. The Board must be aware of such changes and ensure that new standards are met. Online resources and training workshops are available in some areas.

In general most supervisors have a close relationship with the governing board of a childcare centre. Many arrange meeting times, meeting places, refreshments, copies of reports and minutes, and even run the meeting itself. Other boards that are more independent will welcome the supervisor, hear his or her report, and carry on board business without help. Staff members may be invited to attend board meetings but do not have a vote. The supervisor's most important role in supporting board governance is to help board members to understand what they can and cannot do. Some inexperienced board members in their enthusiasm will try to intervene in the day-to-day operations of the centre. These responsibilities lie with the supervisor, acting within board policies. The supervisor must also provide board members with as much background information as needed to discuss/decide issues.

Some centres have instituted a system whereby one or two parents in each playroom are designated parent representatives. Their primary role is to keep families abreast of new developments in the centre and to be available to respond to parents' questions and concerns. The names, email addresses and telephone numbers of family representatives may be posted on a centre bulletin board. Some centres invite family representatives to monthly staff meetings. Any family member should be welcome to any board meeting, on the understanding that he or she will not have a vote and will be excluded from discussions of a confidential or financial nature. Confidentiality may become challenging when so many families know each other but personal information about individual families should never be shared with others. Minutes of board meetings, omitting sensitive financial or personnel information, should be posted. This helps families to be informed about, and feel involved in, the centre's operations. A strong board can communicate involvement and enthusiasm. The staff will feel supported and valued, and the families will feel more engaged. This makes it much easier to recruit new board members from among those who already have very full lives.[*]

In addition to the board of directors, committees may be established to encourage family participation. Committees enable families or staff with specialized knowledge to apply their expertise and skills to the centre's advantage. They also provide a means of empowering family members who are unwilling or unable to take on the more demanding task of serving on the board of directors. Small working groups ensure an equitable distribution of responsibilities within the centre. Some examples of committees are finance, fundraising, publicity, social, and newsletter, and committees organized for specific purposes such as redesigning and equipping the outdoor play space, repairing equipment, etc.

Nonprofit organizations are required to hold an annual general meeting to review the previous year's work. Reports are made by the president of the board and an audited financial statement is presented, as well as information from various committees and board members and a report by the supervisor or staff of the centre. This is an opportunity to vote on business items or changes to the bylaws of the organization. Individual family members may bring up situations or events that they have been particularly pleased with. Families also may use the annual general meeting to voice concerns and debate issues relevant to the program and operation of the centre. Additional general meetings can also be called by the board as needed or when a sensitive issue must be voted on. Depending on the centre's bylaws, board members themselves may call full board meetings to discuss an issue, to pass a resolution, or to replace directors. Minutes of board meetings are official records of the centre and should be stored as a historical record and posted for families to see.

---

[*] Reprinted by permission of Patricia Campbell.

THE FAMILY'S ROLE IN EVALUATION

Teachers have a responsibility to continually assess their performance and their interactions with the children, the families, and their colleagues. Evaluations of the teachers by the supervisor and a member of the board of directors should be carried out on a regular basis. Teachers should also provide self-evaluations in which they detail their accomplishments; the areas they would like to target for further improvement;, and their goals, with an action plan for achieving them. It is not enough to evaluate teachers on their ability to provide curriculum for children; it is imperative that they are also evaluated on their family engagement practices.

The supervisor should also be part of a process that requires ongoing evaluation and goal-setting exercises. Educators and families should both be represented in these evaluations of the supervisor, since these parties are affected by the supervisor's ability to provide leadership. Exhibit 5.1 is an example of how we might "measure" our effectiveness in our interactions with fathers.

Teachers and supervisors receive informal feedback from families through their daily exchanges. If families are to be true partners in the operation of the centre, their ideas and criticisms should be of vital importance to the staff and administration. While it may not always be feasible to implement parents' suggestions, families must have their ideas taken seriously and implemented whenever possible. A suggestion box located at the centre allows families to anonymously express their observations, ideas, and comments. The contents of the box must be read and responded to on a regular basis. A centre might acknowledge in its newsletter suggestion-box ideas that have been integrated into the program. Some families may not return surveys because of their busy schedule or because they got lost at the bottom of a knapsack, but they might be more inclined to respond if the survey is posted on the centre website and they can respond electronically.

Another valuable assessment tool is the exit survey. Despite asking for feedback, some families will hold back, afraid that their input may jeopardize their relationships with the teachers and in some instances that their comments if negative would be "taken out" on their child. But exit surveys are perhaps the most honest feedback we will ever receive. Families are leaving the centre and they have nothing to lose in giving us their true opinions.

Other centres distribute parent questionnaires biannually or annually. These assessments can be used to find out

TABLE 5.1   Communication with Families

FAMILIES ARE VIEWED AS THE PRIMARY SOURCE OF LOVE AND CARE	ALWAYS	FREQUENTLY	OCCASIONALLY	SELDOM	NEVER	N/A
A. ECEs recognize differences in family cultures						
• We consult with you about belief systems and preferred practices.						
• Pertinent information is available in different languages.						
• Efforts are made to learn significant words and phrases in families' home language.						
B. Consistent communication is the cornerstone to building confidence and partnership						
• In the orientation process, you received enough information to feel comfortable when your child entered the centre.						
• You receive enough information to feel comfortable when your child moves from room to room.						
• When transitions are to occur, they are gradual and your child's progress is monitored and shared.						
• You receive information via print or electronic material and/or discussions with us.						
• Policies and procedures are outlined in the Family Handbook.						
• There is clear and ongoing communication whenever there is a change in your child's life.						
• The centre supervisor is available for formal or informal discussions.						
• Program plans are posted to keep you informed of day-to-day activities.						
• Menus are posted and you have input into food that is served to the children.						
• The monthly newsletter is informative and gives relevant information about our centre.						
• A resource area (e.g., books, videos, DVDs) is available for your use.						
• Family bulletin boards reflect topics of interest to you.						
C. Families are encouraged to involve themselves in the centre						
• You are welcome in the centre at any time.						
• Meetings are organized with family input and support your parenting role.						
• You are encouraged to participate in events such as field trips, committee work, social gatherings, and volunteering in the playroom or for the advisory board.						
• Your input regarding curriculum is encouraged.						
• You are informed of who the family representatives are.						
• Staff are responsive to your concerns and you are able to influence change in the centre in cooperation with staff.						
• Comments						

Source: Adapted with courtesy of George Brown College.

- the topics families would like to have addressed at meetings and in newsletters
- family ideas about fundraising
- the talents and interests families have that could be shared with the children or be used to improve the centre
- family ideas for field trips
- which committees family members would be willing to serve on
- family ideas about food and ideas for recipes that reflect cultural backgrounds

Family questionnaires should be clear about the purpose of the questionnaire, well designed, and concise (families may not respond to a survey that is

Janeway Child and Family Centre

We hope that the time you have spent with us at Janeway Child and Family Centre has been a positive experience for your child and your family. We would appreciate it if you took a few minutes to give us some feedback about what pleased you and areas in which you feel we could improve our performance. Our focus is always to provide the best possible environment for the children and families in our care, and your comments will give us insight into areas where we could enrich our program.

1. How old was your child when you first enrolled in the centre?

2. As a new parent, how satisfied were you with the orientation you received?

3. Did you find the family visit a helpful part of the orientation process?

4. Have you been satisfied with the care your child has received at the centre as well as our ability to provide a healthy and safe environment:

   - in the infant room ___
   - in the toddler room ___
   - in the preschool room ___
   - in the school-age room ___

5. Did you feel the program met your child's needs emotionally, socially, intellectually, physically, and creatively?

6. Did you feel that staff were friendly, respectful, and professional in their communications with you?

7. Was there a welcoming atmosphere in the centre and did you feel that you and your extended family were able to make spontaneous visits?

8. Did you feel that you were adequately informed about events, meetings, and information related to the centre through newsletters, bulletin boards, telephone calls, electronically, and so on?

9. Did you feel that the supervisor and board of directors were responsive to any concerns or issues that were important to you?

10. Did you feel that you had ample opportunity and encouragement to participate in the centre if you wanted to?

11. Did you feel that the family–teacher conferences were positive opportunities to share information? Was there anything about the conferences that you would like to change?

12. Did you feel the physical environment (indoors and outdoors) was suitable and that adequate toys and materials were available?

13. Would you recommend our centre to another parent?

14. Please feel free to add any other comments.

time consuming). The results of the questionnaires should be communicated to families as soon as possible and acted on when necessary.

INVOLVE FAMILIES IN ADVOCACY

There is no question that families and teachers should be aware of public policy and how it affects families in our country. Municipal, provincial, and federal governments make decisions that affect the quality of life that families can provide for their children. But many teachers and families are hesitant to become involved because they feel powerless and lack the confidence to effect change: they often do not feel they have the time to become involved; they state that they don't know enough about how government legislation affects child care; and, for some families, any involvement with government officials may bring back difficult memories or they may be afraid to get involved. Informed supervisors and teachers can keep families abreast of changes in legislation and impending decisions that will have consequences for their children.

But reporting on research and data is not enough. We need to involve all of the stakeholders and decision makers and engage them in moving from theory to practice. The health and well-being of our children should be of concern to all Canadians—they are our future! With support and encouragement, families can become important allies in this process. Strong bonds are established when staff and families join forces to advocate on behalf of children. Governments at all levels should be pressured to guarantee that early childhood educators are well paid and trained so that they have the ability and time to invite family collaboration and the knowledge to offer parents strategies for developing rich relationships with their children. Many family members who become involved in child-care-related issues are inspired to write to community and city-wide newspapers or government officials, to gather petitions, to appear as interviewees on radio and TV shows, and to attend relevant workshops and conferences. Being involved before elections take place is critical; inviting elected officials to your site to demonstrate the benefits of quality early childhood education can provide useful information for parents. Some parents may be so inspired that they may run for office themselves! It is also important to involve the children in advocacy as well when appropriate and with parental consent. Often parents may accompany their children and staff; many "old graduates" of school-age programs remember their marches on city hall preparing them for a more active civic engagement. Joining professional organizations may also provide guidance and support.

The importance of parents to lobbying efforts on behalf of children is well expressed by Pat Wege, past chairperson of the *Manitoba Child Care Association*:

> It is critical that parents who rely on child care to "keep Canada working" be at the forefront of lobby issues. When our association meets with government, we are often reminded that the majority of parent users are silent on child-care issues. What we say to government is then viewed as self-serving. The future growth and stability of child care in Canada will rest in the hands of parents who must be educated as lobbyists, along with the parents of tomorrow, grandparents, aunts, uncles, employers. Everyone has a stake in child care.[*]

At the 2008 Leighton G. McCarthy Memorial Panel Discussion, Acting On A Vision for Universal Child Care: Integrating Early Childhood Education and Support Services for Families—hosted by the Institute of Child Study in 2008—panel members Professor Carl Corter, Janet Davis, the Honourable Ken Dryden, Paul Tough, Justin Trudeau, and the Honourable Margaret Norrie McCain spoke eloquently about the need for family involvement in advocating for the support systems that they need to raise healthy families. The public needs to be engaged to understand that early experiences get under the skin. We need to help parents understand that they have power and, as advocates for these families, we all need to support their efforts to organize, to speak up on behalf of their families. Every parent should understand how far behind we are; reports from the OECD make it clear that we are lagging behind world efforts for young children and their families in industrialized countries (see Chapter 2). In our own communities, how many people know about the work being done in early childhood? Funding will not come without public engagement.

THE VANIER INSTITUTE OF THE FAMILY

The Vanier Institute of the Family is an organization dedicated to advocating for child care and

---

[*]Reprinted by permission of Pat Wege.

the Canadian family. Its website describes the organization:

> The vision of the Vanier Institute is to make families as important to the life of Canadian society as they are to the lives of individual Canadians.... to create awareness of, and to provide leadership on, the importance and strengths of families in Canada and the challenges they face in their structural, demographic, economic, cultural, and social diversity.

Information from the Institute's research, consultation, and policy development is conveyed through advocacy, education, and communications vehicles to elected officials, policymakers, educators and researchers, the business community, the media, social service professionals, the public, and Canadian families.

The Vanier Institute of the Family, established in 1965 under the patronage of Their Excellencies Governor-General Georges P. Vanier and Madame Pauline Vanier, is a national, charitable organization dedicated to promoting the well-being of Canadian families. It is governed by a volunteer board with regional representation from across Canada. See **http://www.vanierinstitute.ca**.

FAMILY INVOLVEMENT NETWORK OF EDUCATORS

Another important advocacy website is the Family Involvement Network of Educators (FINE)—**http://www.finenetwork.org**—sponsored by the Harvard Family Research Project. It provides an opportunity to exchange ideas, resources, and tools to strengthen the capacity of families, schools, and communities for effective partnership. The site's Publications and Resources section provides a rich and diverse selection of research materials and tools.

CANADIAN CHILD CARE FEDERATION

This section was contributed by Karen Chandler, founding member of the CCCF.

The Canadian Child Care Federation (CCCF) is a national organization that plays a leadership role in research and policy development, providing information services and publications for members and the general public aimed at improving services for young Canadian children and families. CCCF facilitates networks among families, government policymakers, and other relevant organizations. It has numerous projects and services helpful to

practitioners, families, and those working with families, including an award-winning magazine, *Interaction*, which has many articles focused on work with families. One hundred resource sheets are available for families and educators; sample topics include respecting children's rights at home, travelling with infants, and sun safety. This information can be accessed through the Federation's website at **http://www.qualitychildcarecanada.ca**.

CHILD CARE ADVOCACY ASSOCIATION OF CANADA

The Child Care Advocacy Association of Canada (CCAAC) promotes a publicly funded, inclusive, quality, nonprofit child-care system. The nonprofit organization is membership based and regionally representative. It works with provincial and territorial child-care organizations, social justice organizations, and governments to develop policy solutions to child-care issues; presents briefs and submissions to governments; works on initiatives to raise the public profile of child care; and encourages public support for a national child-care system. Visit **http://www.ccaac.ca/home.php**.

CENTRE OF EXCELLENCE FOR EARLY CHILDHOOD DEVELOPMENT

The Centre of Excellence for Early Childhood Development operates under the administrative leadership of the University of Montreal, in partnership with the following organizations:

- **Canadian Childcare Federation, Ottawa, Ontario**
- **Canadian Institute of Child Health, Ottawa, Ontario**
- **IWK Grace Health Centre, Halifax, Nova Scotia**
- **University of British Columbia, Vancouver, British Columbia**
- **Conseil de la Nation Atikamekw, Wemotaci, Quebec**
- **Queen's University, Kingston, Ontario**
- **L'Hopital St-Justine, Montreal, Quebec**
- **Institut de la santé publique du Québec, Quebec City, Quebec**
- **Canadian Paediatric Society, Ottawa, Ontario**
- **Centre de Psycho-Education du Québec, Montreal, Quebec**

These organizations make up the core group that provides direction to the work of the centre, as it supports parents and families to raise children with happy and healthy lifestyles by providing useful, readable information on the early years. Using traditional communication methods such as articles, newsletters, and workshops, as well as multimedia, including videos and CD-ROMs, the centre consolidates expert knowledge on early childhood development and disseminates it to parents and service providers. Visit **http://www.excellence-earlychildhood.ca/home.asp**.

THE CHILDCARE RESOURCE AND RESEARCH UNIT

The Childcare Resource and Research Unit (CRRU) is a valuable Canadian resource. According to its website, it

> focuses on research and policy resources in the context of a high quality system of early childhood education and child care in Canada. The unit was established to provide public education, resources, and consultation on ECEC policy and research; foster and support research in various fields focusing on ECEC; carry out relevant research projects and publish the results. Part of CRRU's mandate is to collect, organize, and synthesize ECEC information resources and to make them widely available. Visit **http://www.childcarecanada.org**, which is updated with new materials weekly basis. A weekly email notification provides links to new resources.

REFERENCES

Belsky, J. 2005. "Social-Contextual Determinants of Parenting." In R.J. Tremblay, R.E. Barr, and R. Peters, eds., *Encyclopedia of Child Development*. Montreal, QC.

Bernhard, J. 2012. "Working with Immigrant Families." The Canadian Parenting Workshop. Retrieved February 15, 2012 from http://www.ryerson.ca/bernhard/research/family-gallery/index.html

Canadian Index of Wellbeing. 2010. Community Vitality. Retrieved January 28, 2013, from http://ciw.ca/reports/en/Domains%20of%20Wellbeing/CommunityVitality/CommunityVitality_ExecutiveSummary.sflb.pdfhttp://ciw.ca/reports/en/Domains%20of%20Wellbeing/CommunityVitality/CommunityVitality_ExecutiveSummary.sflb.pdf

Cornish, M. 2008. *Promising Practices for Partnering with Families in the Early Years*. Information Age Publishing.

Corter, C., and T. Arimura. 2006. "Community Vitality. Literature Review on Parent Support." Atkinson Centre, Institute of Child Study/Department of Human Development and Applied Psychology, Ontario Institute for Studies in Education/University of Toronto. Prepared for *Invest In Kids*. June 16.

Corter, C., and J. Pelletier. 2005. "Parent and Community Involvement in Schools: Policy Panacea or Pandemic?" In N. Bascia, A. Cumming, A. Datnow, K. Leithwood, and D. Livingstone, eds., *International Handbook of Educational Policy* (pp. 295–327). Dordrecht, the Netherlands: Kluwer.

Fagan, J., and G. Palm. 2004. *Fathers and Early Childhood Programs*. New York: Thomson Delmar Learning.

Gestwicki, C. 2010. *Home, School and Community*, 7th ed. Wadsworth Cengage Learning.

Gordon, A. 2008. "They Cut Problems Down to Size." *Toronto Star*. May 17. L7.

Graham Clay, S. 2012. "Communicating with Parents: Strategies for Teachers." Retrieved January 28, 2013, from http://www.adi.org/journal/ss05/Graham-Clay.pdfwww.adi.org/journal/ss05/Graham-Clay.pdf

Hammer, K. 2011. "Kindergarten in a Retirement Home Proves Hit with Young and Old." *The Globe and Mail*. December 31. A6. Retrieved February 20, 2013, from http://www.theglobe andmail.com/news/national/kindergarten-in-a-retirement-home-proves-a-hit-with-young-and-old/article4103165

Hepworth Berger, E., and M. Riojas-Cortez. 2012. *Parents as Partners in Education. Families and Schools Working Together*. Pearson.

Johnson, K., J. Akister, B. McKeigue, and J. Wheater. 2005. "What Does 'Suporting Parents' Mean? Parents' Views." *Practice*, 17(1), 3–14.

Keyser, J. 2006. *From Parents to Partners: Building a Family-Centered Early Childhood Program*. St. Paul, MN: Redleaf Press.

Levine, J., and E.W. Pitt. 1997. "Community Strategies for Responsible Fatherhood: On-Ramps to Connection." *Zero to Three* 18 (1). August–September.

Lightfoot, S. 1978. *Worlds Apart: Relationships Between Families and Schools*. New York: Basic Books.

Lowell Krogh, S. 2006. *Teaching Young Children: Contexts for Learning*. Lawrence Erlbaum Associates.

Manolson, A., B. Ward, and N. Dodington. 1995. *You Make the Difference in Helping Your Child Learn*. The Hanen Centre,

McCormack, L. 2010. "Your Service Is Required." *Zoomer Magazine*.

Murphy Kilbride, K., and J. Pollard. 1990. "Differences in Interactions of Teachers with Visible Minority Children." Retrieved from http://ceris.metropolis.net/Virtual%20Library/education/kilbride1http://ceris.metropolis.net/Virtual%20Library/education/kilbride1

Neugebauer, B. 1990. "Going One Step Further—No Traditional Holidays." *Child Care Information Exchange*.

———. 1994. "Beginnings Workshop: Going One Step Further: No Traditional Holidays." *Child Care Information Exchange*. November–December.

Oates, J. 2010. "Supporting Parenting." *Early Childhood in Focus 5*. The Open University.

Ryerson University. n.d. "Working with Immigrant Families." Retrieved February 23, 2013, from http://www.ryerson.ca/bernhard/research/family-gallery/index.html

Schorr, L. 1997. *Common Purpose: Strengthening Families and Neighborhoods to Rebuild America*. New York: Anchor Books Doubleday.

Sheehan, N., and L. Wood. 1993. *Adoption and the Schools Project: A Guide for Educators*, vol. 2. Children's Bureau, Administration for Children, Youth and Families, Office of Human Development Services, U.S. Department of Health and Human Services.

Smith, T.B., and S. Newman. 1993. "Older Adults in Early Childhood Programs: Why and How." *Young Children*. March.

United Nations. 2011. "Men in Families and Family Policy in a Changing World." Department of Economic and Social Affairs. Retrieved January 28, 2013, from http://www.un.org/esa/socdev/family/docs/men-in-families.pdf

Walker, J.M.T., A.S. Wilkins, J.P. Dallaire, H.M. Sandler, and K.V. Hoover-Dempsey. 2005. "Parental Involvement: Model Revision Through Scale Development." *Elementary School Journal*, 106.

Wardle, F. 1994. "Beginnings Workshop: Celebrations, Festivals, Holidays: What Should We Be Doing?" *Child Care Information Exchange* 100. November–December.

Zero to Three. 2010. *Parenting Infants and Toddlers Today. Research Findings*. Hart Research Association. Retrieved from http://www.zerotothree.org

Created by Siena

Chapter

6

VERBAL COMMUNICATION WITH FAMILIES

Courtesy of University of Toronto Child Care - Charles Street

"Your beliefs become your thoughts. Your thoughts become your words. Your words become your actions. Your actions become your habits. Your habits become your values. Your values become your destiny."

—*Mahatma Gandhi (The Quotations Page, n.d.)*

LEARNING OUTCOMES

After studying this chapter, you will be able to

1. discuss and analyze the strategies for achieving effective communication among family members and educators

2. identify the sources of family–teacher conflict and outline a strategy for conflict resolution

3. summarize the research on day-to-day interactions with families and suggest strategies for making these interactions more meaningful

PRINCIPLES OF EFFECTIVE VERBAL COMMUNICATION

In the field of early childhood education, a teacher's ability to communicate with family members in an effective and responsive manner is the basis on which meaningful relationships are developed. In order to establish a positive climate for communication, educators must acknowledge the critical role that family members should play in the operation and day-to-day functioning of the centre. Teachers' interactions with family members must reflect a belief that the latter are significant members of the child-care team and have a right to be represented when decisions are made that will affect their children. When family members feel valued and believe that their ideas are listened to and acted on, they become more responsive. When this climate of mutual respect is established, the parent, educator, and child all benefit enormously. When educators look for opportunities to support family members, they eliminate the adversarial approach so detrimental to effective and meaningful communication. Since each partnership with each family will be unique, teachers need to be effective and skillful in their interactions.

Powell (1989) identifies three types of parents who use child-care centres. The first type views the centre and the family as *independent* systems; these parents rarely communicate with staff and avoid discussing family matters or child-rearing values. The second type sees themselves as *dependent* on the centre for child-rearing information but communicate little about their families or their expectations for the program. The third type exhibits an *interdependent* pattern of communication; they receive information from the centre and openly share information and family values with the centre. Obviously, the teacher will need to use different interpersonal communication strategies for each of these groups.

There is no question that the building of meaningful relationships between family members and teachers requires a time commitment from all parties, particularly from the teacher. Good educators will embrace this concept and accept that they will not always be financially compensated for the time they commit to establishing a significant alliance with families; nevertheless, the reward for their efforts comes in the form of an effective, meaningful partnership with families and a better working environment.

WHAT MAKES AN EFFECTIVE COMMUNICATOR?

Communication competence is the ability to be both effective and appropriate—that is, to get desired results from others in a manner that maintains the relationship on terms that are acceptable to everyone. According to Adler et al. (2012: 27), "you must have some desire to improve your communication skills with a variety of people. *You need to be open to new ways of thinking and behaviour.* Without an open-minded attitude, a communicator will have trouble interacting competently with people from different backgrounds." Skillful use of a variety of communication styles will help educators adapt to different family approaches.[*]

Despite the fact that competent communication varies from one situation to another, scholars have identified several common denominators that characterize effective communicators in most contexts:

1. *A Large Repertoire of Skills:* **They do not use the same approach in every situation.**

2. *Adaptability:* **They have the ability to choose the right approach for a particular situation.**

3. *Ability to Perform Skillfully:* **Practice is the key to skillful performance.**

4. *Involvement:* **Effective communication takes place when people care about one another and the topic at hand.**

5. *Empathy and Perspective Taking:* **The best chance of developing an effective message occurs when you understand the other person's point of view.**

6. *Cognitive Complexity:* **They have the ability to construct a variety of different frameworks for viewing an issue.**

7. *Self-Monitoring:* **They pay close attention to their own behaviour and use these observations to shape the way they behave** (Adler et al., 2012: 30–33).[†]

The following sections examine various communication strategies that teachers can employ in building this partnership.

***

[*]From Adler, Ronald, et al., *Interplay: The Process of Interpersonal Communication* 3/Ce © Oxford University Press Canada 2012. Reprinted by permission of the publisher.

[†]From Adler, Ronald, et al., *Interplay: The Process of Interpersonal Communication* 3/Ce © Oxford University Press Canada 2012. Reprinted by permission of the publisher.

Many, and sometimes most, of the critical meanings generated in human encounters are elicited by touch, glance, vocal nuance, gestures, or facial expressions with or without the aid of words. From the moment of recognition until the moment of separation, people observe each other with all their senses, hearing pause and intonation, attending to dress and carriage, observing glance and facial tension, as well as noting word choice and syntax. Every harmony or disharmony of signals guides the interpretation of passing mood or enduring attribute. Out of the evaluation of kinetic, vocal and verbal cues, decisions are made to argue or agree, to laugh or blush, to relax or resist, or to continue or cut off conversation.

Source: Brislin in Samovar et al., 2007: 195.

TRUST

In order to establish strong working relationships with families, teachers must be able to establish a basic foundation of trust. This process must begin the first moment families enter the centre. Communicate early and often! Educators who express acceptance, support, and enthusiasm in their initial dealings with families are establishing the groundwork for an effective partnership.

LANGUAGE USE

Initiating, developing, and maintaining positive relationships with families takes considerable skill and effort. Effective verbal communication is critical to the success of the family–teacher relationship. Words can reflect attitudes of respect or disrespect, inclusion or exclusion, judgment or acceptance. The words you choose can facilitate or impede communication. Teachers must be able to

A trusting relationship is the foundation of positive interactions.

Courtesy of Scotia Plaza Child Care Centre

Appropriately used, humour can defuse a difficult situation.

adjust their language interactions based on their understanding of individual family member's styles of communication. They must also avoid the use of accusatory language. "Alex is acting out in the centre. Is something going on at home?" implies that the teacher suspects the problem lies with the parent. The use of more inclusive language to describe the behaviour is more likely to encourage cooperation: "We've noticed that Alex has been very weepy the last few days. Have you noticed this at home?" "Preaching, judging, interrupting, ridiculing, commands, exaggeration, insults, manipulation, control and threats are all communication killers. Avoid them" (Ontario English Catholic Teachers Association, n.d.). When we describe something that we see a family doing well and we acknowledge their efforts in an authentic way, it helps the family to see their strengths.

Additionally, teachers should avoid engaging in ECE shoptalk with family members or peppering their conversations with ECE jargon that will be incomprehensible to many of them. Educators should also avoid using phrases like "Why don't you …?" "If I were you I would …," "I don't think you understand …," "You should …," or any sentence that contains a "but," since it negates everything that comes before it—"That approach is okay, but …"

In order to communicate in a nonjudgmental manner, teachers should make use of "I" language.

Consider this example: Taryn's father is late for the third evening in a row. Rather than saying, "You're late again," adopt a less aggressive approach by using "I" language: "When you're late I feel upset because it means that I will miss my train." A teacher who uses this example of "I" language communicates in a nonaccusatory manner three things: the other person's behaviour, her feelings about it, and the consequences of that behaviour.

Educators should also make an effort to learn key words and phrases in the various languages spoken by the centre's family members, as well as knowing both the names of family members and their correct pronunciation. When communicating with family members whose first language is not English, an interpreter may be required. Dotsch (1999) outlines some ideas for consideration: "Trained professional interpreters are not easy to find. There are many different languages and dialects spoken, interpreters may not be readily available, there may be funding issues, the family may feel embarrassed to ask for an interpreter and finally, some agencies require that families find their own interpreters." She emphasizes the importance of finding professional interpreters who are fluent in the language. They should have a certificate or letter validating their training, and centres should ask for references. It is also helpful if the interpreter has a background in working with families and young children and is familiar with concepts and terminology in early childhood education. It is critical that they be able to interpret information accurately and without distortion. Interpreters should also be cognizant of refugee or immigrant issues and be sensitive to nonverbal responses while displaying equal respect to both parties.

SOME TIPS FOR TEACHERS USING AN INTERPRETER

- Make sure the interpreter is oriented to the purpose of the session, their role, and the process.
- Prepare written information ahead of time for discussion with the family and have it translated if possible.
- Organize the information in a logical sequence.
- Use visuals (props, pictures, animation, gestures).
- Keep content very focused and limited.
- Keep sentences short and simple, and avoid jargon.
- Convey one idea at a time and provide opportunities for questions and discussion.
- Provide summaries instead of detailed information.
- Provide enough pauses for the interpreter to organize the information.
- Verify or clarify the information gathered from the interpreter.
- Be patient enough to let the interpreter communicate uninterrupted.
- Be attentive and maintain interest when the interpreter is speaking to the family.

Check out this website for an interactive evaluation of your communication skills: **http://www.optimalthinking .com/quiz-communication-skills.php.**

VOICE TONE

The tone and delivery of verbal communication carries as much expressive weight as the words spoken. Teachers need to be aware that, however carefully worded, at times, a message expressed in a joking manner may be interpreted as sarcastic and inappropriate by some family members. Teachers also need to monitor the volume of their delivery. Being too soft-spoken can be just as frustrating to the listener as speaking to English language learner parents in a very loud voice under the misguided belief that the greater the volume, the greater the understanding. The speed of delivery also affects the way messages are interpreted. Teachers should observe parents' reactions carefully and,

when in doubt, ask for confirmation that the communication was understood.

NONVERBAL INTERACTION

We cannot not communicate! Our nonverbal interactions with others "speak" for us even if we are not aware of them or did not intend them. "The interconnectedness between the head and nonverbal transmission is evident due the fact that humans are capable of 700,000 different signs it is estimated that humans make over 250,000 facial expressions and 5,000 distinct hand gestures and have over 1,000 catalogue[d] postures" (Phipps, 2008). Most nonverbal messages arrive before the verbal and will influence the interaction; therefore, there are many opportunities for misunderstanding. Most facial expressions last for two or three seconds but micro expressions—which occur when people are concealing how they feel—last for only a fraction of that, just 1/25 of a second. Most of us miss these valuable nonverbal signs but they can provide valuable insight into true feelings. It is not surprising that, at times, we have difficulty interpreting the meaning of our observations.

Our posture or bodily stance also communicates a variety of messages. Some actions serve to block communication—for example, arms folded across the chest, foot tapping, pen flicking, leaning back, staring out a window, or looking at the ceiling. Something as simple as angling your body away from a family member may indicate a lack of interest or concern. Teachers need to be conscious of their nonverbal interactions and aware of the messages they are sending.

Facial expressions that are welcoming—a warm smile upon greeting family members and children, a gentle touch to console a troubled child—contribute to a positive and open climate for communication. But educators who always appear too busy to talk when families arrive convey the message that they are not interested in communicating. Family members who rush into the centre and pick up their child with barely a word to the teachers are also communicating! These are all silent but powerful messages. Teachers need to expand their ability to understand these silent messages. We become more aware of our own patterns of nonverbal communication when we are exposed to those whose patterns are different from ours. As teachers become more familiar with individual families, they will be able to adapt their behaviour accordingly.

Nonverbal communication can send powerful messages.

BOOKS FOR ADULTS

Winning Body Language: Control the Conversation, Command Attention and Convey the Right Message, by M. Bowden

Body Language: Actions Speak Louder Than Words, by P. Surprise

The Silent Language of Leadership: How Body Language Can Help or Hurt How You Lead, by C. Kinsey Goman

The Body Language Handbook: How to Read Everyone's Hidden Thoughts and Intentions, by G. Hartely and M. Karinch

EYE CONTACT

Reactions to various nonverbal behaviours vary significantly from culture to culture and from family member to family member. It is important to know that someone's cultural background doesn't necessarily predict certain behaviours. Few cultural patterns are rigid or apply to all members. For example, not maintaining eye contact may indicate indifference or boredom to one teacher but respect to another. In many Western cultures, a good listener is seen as paying attention if direct eye contact is made with the speaker. Samovar et al. point out in North America, where eye contact is highly valued, eyes serve six communication functions:

- indicate degrees of attentiveness, interest, arousal
- influence attitude change and persuasion
- regulate interaction
- communicate emotions
- define power and status relationships
- assume a centre role in impression management (2007: 210)[*]

However, eye-to-eye contact is not the custom in many Asian or First Nations cultures. In 186 cultures, 67 of them had some belief in the "evil eye" (Samovar et al., 2007: 262). It is a common belief in many cultures that individuals have the power to look at people, animals, or objects and cause them harm. In many cultures talismans are made to ward off the intended curse. Such is the power of the eye!

BOOKS FOR ADULTS

The Power of Eye Contact: Your Secret for Success in Business, Love and Life, by M. Ellsberg

TOUCH

Touch is an important sense and is often used to convey closeness, approval, or support. Handshaking,

[*]SAMOVAR/PORTER/MCDANIEL. *Communication Between Cultures, 6E.* © 2007 Wadsworth, a part of Cengage Learning, Inc. Reproduced by permission. www.cengage.com/permissions

After missing an exam, a Japanese student came to [my] office hours. During the visit, the student continually giggled, averted her eyes, and held her hand over her mouth. From a Western perspective, the student's nonverbal behaviour suggested she was not serious (laughing), deceptive (averting eyes), and very nervous (hand over mouth).... The student offered no reason for missing the exam and did not ask for a retake. She simply apologized for not being there. A third party, however, had already told your author that the student's absence was due to the death of her grandfather. This demonstrates the importance of not assuming that nonverbal feedback in one culture carries the same meaning in another.

Source: SAMOVAR/PORTER/MCDANIEL. *Communication Between Cultures*, 6E. © 2007 Wadsworth, a part of Cengage Learning, Inc. Reproduced by permission. www.cengage.com/permissions

a pat on the back, "high fives," or an arm around a shoulder are just a few of the ways in which we communicate by touch. Touching rules are governed by status, power, and respect. Touch can be perceived as an invasion of personal space in some cultures but a gesture of endearment in others. What may seem to the teacher a simple gesture, for example, touching the top of a child's head, may in fact be interpreted by the parent that the teacher has stolen the child's spirit. Educators need to watch carefully for nonverbal feedback regarding the acceptability of touch.

GESTURES

Gestures are both innate and learned. They are used in all cultures, tend to be tied to speech processes, and usually become automatic. In a large study of 40 cultures, 20 common hand gestures were isolated that had a different meaning in each culture (Morris et al., 1979). Careful use of gestures in intercultural communication is important because gestures that are positive, humorous, or harmless in some cultures can have the opposite meaning in other cultures. Because there are thousands of gestures found in every culture, the teacher will have to do his or her homework!

BOOKS FOR ADULTS

Don't Get Me Wrong! The Global Gestures Guide, by J. Grosse, J. Reker, and F. Bong-Kil

Gestures: The Do's and Taboos of Body Language Around the World, by R.E. Axtell

Field Guide to Gestures: How to Identify and Interpret Virtually Every Gesture Known to Man, by M. Wagner and N. Armstrong

PROXEMICS

Proxemics is the study of how people use the space around them. The amount of distance between you and another person can be interpreted a certain way, and the meaning will change according to the culture. It can mean either an attraction, or can signal intensity. Standing side-to-side can show cooperation, where a face-to-face posture may show competition. Each of us carries around a sort of invisible bubble of personal space wherever we go. Our personal bubbles vary in size according to the culture in which we were raised, the person we're with and the situation. The varying size of our personal space—the distance we put between ourselves and others—gives a non-verbal clue to our feelings. (Sommer in Adler et al., 2012: 199)[*]

Looking at distances that North American communicators use in everyday interaction, Hall (1969) found four, each of which reflects a different way we feel toward others at a given time: intimate distance (out to about 45 centimetres), personal distance (45 centimetres to 1.2 metres), social distance (1.2 metres to 3 metres) and public distance (outward from 3 metres) (Adler, et al., 2012: 200–201).

EFFECTIVE LISTENING

When experts analyze how we communicate, their research tells us that most of us are not good listeners. Although effective listening is critical to relationship building, we listen carefully only a small percentage of the time although "listening is

[*]From Adler, Ronald, et al., *Interplay: The Process of Interpersonal Communication* 3/Ce © Oxford University Press Canada 2012. Reprinted by permission of the publisher.

FIGURE 6.1   Chinese Characters That
Make Up the Verb *to Listen*

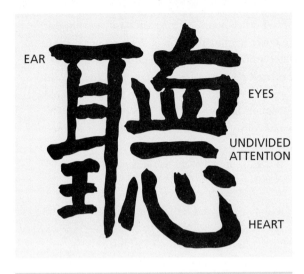

EAR

EYES

UNDIVIDED
ATTENTION

HEART

the heart of effective communication. Listening is more than just hearing sounds. It is the active process of interpreting, understanding, and evaluating the spoken and nonverbal speech as a meaningful message" (Hepworth Berger and Riojas-Cortez, 2012: 124).* Figure 6.1 depicts all of the elements of effective listening.

> We are often overwhelmed by the amount of speech we hear every day; often five or more hours a day. Although we're capable of understanding speech at rates up to 600 words per minute, the average person speaks between 100–140 words per minute. Therefore, we have a lot of "spare time" to spend while someone is talking. The trick is to use this spare time to understand the speaker's ideas better rather than letting our attention wander. (Adler et al., 2012: 219)†

In the playroom, the teacher is bombarded with sounds—music, laughter, blocks crashing—that interfere with the ability to listen carefully. When family members are dropping off their children and relaying messages, it can be very difficult for a teacher to give them the attention they deserve. As family members are speaking, teachers may be listening for signs that the children are restless or need help,

or they may be thinking of what needs to be done in the playroom, or perhaps they are wrapped up in their own personal concerns. In difficult situations, some teachers spend their listening time preparing a rebuttal rather than concentrating on what is being said—a combative approach. Others listen with predetermined attitudes and assumptions about the other person or the matter being discussed. When we listen to only hear what we want to hear, evaluate or judge the speaker, interrupt, or jump to conclusions, we can sabotage our relationships. But *active listening* makes those around us feel appreciated, interesting, and respected. Ordinary conversations emerge on a deeper level, as do our relationships. Listening with intent may in fact reduce misunderstandings and we always learn more when we listen more than we talk.

BOOKS FOR ADULTS

Effective Listening, by M. Green

Are You Really Listening? Keys to Successful Communication, by P.J. Donoghue and M.E. Siegel

ENCOURAGERS

Encouragers are physical and verbal cues that we use to communicate that we are engaged and truly listening to what people are saying and want them to continue. "Examples of encouragers may include nodding your head, saying, 'Yes,' 'Okay,' or 'Mm-hmm.' These encouragers are often used quite readily during casual conversations. Considering your use of encouragers is important, because using them too frequently may cause the person who is talking to feel rushed" (Amatea, 2009: 207).‡

PERCEPTION CHECKING

Misunderstandings frequently arise during communication. Families may misinterpret information that the child brings home, or a child may not understand a teacher's intention. Conversely, a teacher may be unclear about information the child shares about his or her family. Face-to-face interactions may also be misinterpreted. An important strategy teachers can use to verify what family members have

---

*BERGER, EUGENIA HEPWORTH; RIOJAS-CORTEZ, MARI R., PARENTS AS PARTNERS IN EDUCATION: FAMILIES AND SCHOOLS WORKING TOGETHER, 8th Edition, © 2012. Reprinted and Electronically reproduced by permission of Pearson Education, Inc., Upper Saddle River, NJ.

†From Adler, Ronald, et al., *Interplay: The Process of Interpersonal Communication* 3/Ce © Oxford University Press Canada 2012. Reprinted by permission of the publisher.

‡AMATEA, ELLEN S., BUILDING CULTURALLY RESPONSIVE FAMILY-SCHOOL RELATIONSHIPS, 1st Edition, © 2009. Reprinted and Electronically reproduced by permission of Pearson Education, Inc., Upper Saddle River, NJ.

communicated to them is paraphrasing or perception checking. This strategy comprises three steps:

1. a restatement of what the teacher thought the parent meant

2. two or more possible interpretations of the behaviour

3. a request for clarification

The key to perception checking is to restate the other person's comments or nonverbal communication in your own words. Thus, a teacher might say to a parent,

> When you left the centre this morning you seemed upset. I'm not sure if you were worrying about getting to work on time or if there is something about the care we are giving Rashid that you are unhappy with. Is there anything you are feeling uncomfortable about that you would like to share with us?

A perception check can succeed only if the teacher's nonverbal behaviour reflects her words. It is crucial that teachers deal with ambiguous situations as they arise, seeking clarification rather than second-guessing family members or making decisions based on inaccurate information.

SUSPENDING JUDGMENT

Most teachers would agree that it is essential to understand a family member's ideas before forming an opinion, but many of us tend to make snap judgments before hearing them out, especially when a family member's ideas or values conflict with our own. For example, a challenging parent who is critical, complaining, and overprotective may be masking feelings of inadequacy or guilt, or feelings of exclusion.

Our educational, religious, cultural, familial, and socioeconomic backgrounds all influence our perceptions of problems. It is critical that teachers examine their own beliefs for biases that may adversely affect their relationships with family members. Educators may also want to consider their unconscious reactions to family members. For example, teachers who have unresolved hostilities toward their own parents may have difficulty relating to the parents in their centre. "People alienated by unconscious emotional responses," Gestwicki (1992: 126) observes, "will have great difficulty really hearing and speaking to each other clearly."

SELF-MONITORING

Perhaps one of the most effective communication tools teachers can use is monitoring their own behaviour. The ability to be self-reflective, to analyze interactions with family members, and to look for opportunities to improve on skills is the mark of a competent communicator. Adler et al. (2012: 57) believe that

> high self-monitors have the ability to pay attention to their own behaviour and the reactions of others, adjusting their communication to create the desired impression. People who pay attention to themselves are generally able to handle social situations smoothly, often putting others at ease. They are also good "people readers" who can adjust their behaviour to get the desired reaction from others.[*]

GOSSIPING

According to Fox (2003), the subject of gossip is increasingly attracting the attention of researchers across a wide range of disciplines.

---

[*]From Adler, Ronald, et al., *Interplay: The Process of Interpersonal Communication* 3/Ce © Oxford University Press Canada 2012. Reprinted by permission of the publisher.

Inside LOOK

Whenever Samir's parents came to pick him up at the end of the day, he would always be anxious to discuss his artwork or projects with them. It seemed to me that they showed little interest in his work. I used to wish they would be more outwardly expressive and positive about his accomplishments. It wasn't until I was invited to their home and saw Samir's work proudly displayed in a place of honour that I realized they were as pleased with Samir's work as I was. They just celebrated in another way.

VERBAL COMMUNICATION WITH FAMILIES

Teacher: I find it very frustrating dealing with Kelly's mother. She brings Kelly in most mornings after 10:30 a.m. We are often getting ready for our walk, and a few times we have had to wait for her. Not only that, but Kelly misses out on all of the morning activities. I don't think her mother appreciates how inconvenient it is for us. It says in our family manual that the children are all to be in the centre by 9:30 a.m. I have tried to talk to Kelly's mother about this, but she refuses to change her morning routine.

Kelly's mother: I work the night shift and arrive home about the time that Kelly wakes up in the morning. This is the only time during the day that Kelly and I have to ourselves and it is very special to both of us. We have breakfast together, play some of her favourite games, go to the park, and read books. The child-care teachers seem more concerned about their routine. If they were really interested in Kelly and our family, they would see that it is important that we spend this time together. Who are they to suggest that what happens at child care is more important than my relationship with my child? They also seem to forget that I pay for their service.

Yet most of the current research highlights the positive social and psychological functions of gossip: facilitating relationship building, group bonding, clarification of social position and status, reinforcing shared values, conflict resolution and so on. Two-thirds of all human conversation is gossip, because this "vocal grooming" is essential to our social, psychological, and physical well-being.

Many ECE students returning from their field placement experiences relate stories about inappropriate staffroom discussions where teachers gossip about each other and about parents in ways that are hurtful and derogatory.

> I couldn't believe what the teacher was saying about Evan's parents. In front of the whole staff room, students and teachers, she said that if they would just spend more time with Evan, he wouldn't be having these problems at the centre. She went on to describe how Evan's mum dressed for work, that her skirt was too short and she then said that Evan's dad was out of town on business way too often. I didn't know where to look, I was embarrassed and I felt that this teacher had no idea how hurtful her comments were. I wondered if this teacher ever engaged in self-reflection!

Gossiping can undermine relationships between teachers, students, and families. The NAEYC *Code of Ethical Conduct* (2011) states, "We shall maintain confidentiality and shall respect the family's right to privacy, refraining from disclosure of confidential information and intrusion into family life." Leitch

Copeland and Bruno (2001: 23) discuss the necessity of a centre-based policy to

> create a culture of safety, encouragement and respect that is consistent with the Code. The director must assiduously avoid any temptation to listen to the gossip that she abhors. She must articulate the mission, confront gossip and negativity immediately and promote peer responsibility to do the same.… A gossip-free centre culture supports everyone in the centre community and eventually helps them focus on the mission and the work to be done on behalf of children and families.

EMPATHY

According to some researchers, empathy is the most important communication skill. Teachers need to "put themselves in the parent's shoes" and try to identify why family members may be responding this way or why they may be challenging a particular practice in the centre. "One feature that distinguishes effective communication in almost any context is commitment," state Adler and Towne (1993: 34). "In other words, people who seem to care about the relationship communicate better than those who don't." Many family members lead very difficult and tragic lives. Over the course of their careers, teachers may encounter family members who live in abusive relationships, have a spouse in jail, are caring for a dying parent, or have substance-abuse problems. It is the teacher's responsibility to

EXHIBIT 6.1 Nothing Succeeds Like Success: Strategies for Improving Communication

- Get involved. Know the family and children on a personal level. Become familiar with their interests, situations, and values.
- Make a commitment. People who care about a relationship communicate better than those who don't.
- Demonstrate respect for the diversity of families.
- Keep in mind the personal and economic pressures that may be affecting family members.
- The family and the child must be looked at in a cultural context. Learn about cultures and the learning styles predominant in different cultures, but remember that the individual culture of each family may not reflect the traditional cultural ways.
- Learn about the communities in which the families live. What resources are available to support a young and growing family?
- Make sure that family members understand that your role is to function as a team member working *with them* to solve problems.
- Remember the need for privacy. Some conversations that begin on the floor as casual exchanges progress into dialogue that should be private.
- Demonstrate respect for parental concerns and don't respond with "but we've always done things this way here." Be prepared to ask yourself instead "Why not?"
- Ask for more information and listen carefully. Often we don't understand the whole picture.
- Make sure family members have an opportunity to say everything they want to say. Allow enough time for thoughtful discussion.
- Be precise and keep focused on what is best for the child. Remind yourself that the vast majority of parents want the best for their child.
- Consider how vulnerable family members may feel and how they may question their own ability to be effective parents.
- Resist answering a problem with a simple solution and giving advice. There are no quick and simple answers to complex problems.
- Be aware of your feelings and identify them. Use self-monitoring techniques.
- Work on being nondefensive. Remember that hostility inhibits communication.
- Remain calm, take a deep breath, and watch your nonverbal responses.
- Avoid lecturing since this can be interpreted as feeling superior to the families you are working with and will bring forth only defensiveness on their part.
- Never get into a shouting match with a family member. It frightens the children and serves no useful purpose.
- As your confidence grows, defending your expertise will take on less importance.
- Express concerns constructively, in concrete terms, and in a tactful, sensitive manner.
- Ask family members if they have any solutions to their concerns.
- Take action. Respond to requests. What you do is often more important than what you say.
- Check back with family members after a few days to discuss how they are feeling.
- Help family members save face when they know they have acted in an inappropriate fashion. They will thank you for it and may one day return the favour.
- A sincere and well-worded apology should be given to families if you have acted inappropriately.
- Call on more experienced people for help. Use a team approach. Some family issues may be best discussed with the whole staff—but remember that confidentiality is an important consideration.
- Remember that learning is a life-long process. Continue to look for ways (through workshops or courses, for example) in which to improve your communication skills.

Amanda: Being both a teacher and a parent of two young children has given me valuable insight into the struggle many parents experience when trying to work at a full-time job and care for their family at the same time. Last Monday morning, Saorise's mother, Diane, arrived in the infant room. Just by looking at her I could tell that she hadn't had much sleep over the weekend. Saorise is Diane's first baby and she has been colicky and often awake most of the night. As I walked toward Diane to take the baby from her, I asked how the weekend had gone. She looked up at me and burst into tears. I quickly put my arm around her and gave Saorise to another staff. Then I took Diane to the staff room.

Diane: When I walked into the infant room, Amanda asked how our weekend had gone with Saorise. I took one look at her and began to cry. Saorise is 4 months old now and we have had a very difficult time. She cries constantly and no matter what we do we can't get her to calm down. I guess she's not the "perfect" baby we had anticipated. My husband and I take turns getting up with her in the night, but we rarely get more than two or three hours' sleep at a time. Now that I'm back to work, I feel that I just can't cope. I need this job and I'm desperate for this to work out. Amanda and the other staff at the centre have been so helpful. With our parents living in other provinces, the staff at the centre have become our support system. I don't know what I would do without them.

find ways to develop positive relationships with these families, motivated always by what is in the best interest of the child. Few family members in these situations want pity; what many of them will respond to is a genuinely empathetic and caring teacher who is clearly focused on finding ways to involve and support the family with a hopeful approach leading with the family's strengths. This support may also include being part of a team of social workers, probation officers, child protection officers, and so on. Exhibit 6.1 supports the development of strong family/educator relations.

FAMILY–TEACHER CONFLICTS AND STRATEGIES FOR RESOLVING THEM

"If teachers can remember difficult times in their own lives when they relied on a trusted friend, a family member, or perhaps a teacher—people who were patient and understanding—they can draw on this strength to give back to others."

Conflict is inevitable in any meaningful relationship. When conflict occurs, a host of feelings come to the surface: confusion, frustration, anger, disappointment, annoyance. Almost every experienced teacher will tell you that the most difficult interaction they have with families is when they are confronted by an angry parent.

The parent who is bossy, volatile, argumentative can make us question ourselves and our own abilities. New teachers are often taken aback when dealing with this type of conflict for the first time. But if we do not figure out effective and appropriate ways to interact with these parents, we may become apprehensive about communicating with other parents. This may lead to a general discomfort or fear any time we have contact with parents. (Whitaker and Fiore, 2001: ix)

Our role is to act in a sincere, respectful and professional manner no matter how difficult the situation might be. Whether in your personal or professional life, complaints are sources of feedback so let families know you are open to complaints and that you do view them as essential sources of information and an opportunity for improving a relationship or an organization. Welcome complaints!

Some parents will be difficult to deal with; however, without knowing the "back story," we can make assumptions that are misleading and hurtful. Yet there will be times that even the most positive among us will succumb to feelings of extreme

It is the end of the day. Tamara, a preschool teacher, is engaged with two children. A parent enters the playroom and Tamara nods her head in recognition. Tamara leaves the children and begins to busily organize the drying rack on the other side of the room with her back to the parent. The parent picks up her child and leaves the room. Not a word was spoken by either party. Tamara has deliberately chosen not to engage this parent, who she finds distant and difficult to work with. What she doesn't know is that this parent has recently lost her mother whom she had been caring for and whom had been ill for some time. The parent just didn't feel close enough to Tamara to discuss her loss and how it has affected her and her family.

negativity. Unless we take time to understand difficult parents and some of the difficult situations they find themselves in, we will create obstacles to providing the best possible care for this child and this family. Dr. Jenny Jenkins, Atkinson Chair in Early Child Development and Education at OISE/UT at the Summer Institute, 2012, presented *0–3 Years—Research That Informs Policy and Practice*. In her seminar she talked about "getting inside families." We need to break down the barriers and boundaries that prevent us from really getting to know families—by getting inside!

Greenman and Stonehouse (1996: 264) remind us that "if we take any ten or fifteen people, a few will be 'difficult' and one will be 'impossible' and all will be difficult occasionally. It is true of staff and true of parents."

The most difficult parents to form a partnership with are those who are

- critical of the centre and the staff
- irresponsible
- indifferent
- always demanding or uncooperative
- neglectful of their child

However, often, these are the parents who need the most help and support, although they are behaving in ways that are least likely to elicit them. It is the essence of professionalism to serve these parents well.

CAUSES OF CONFLICT

Swick (1992: 129) identifies the two main types of confrontation that occur in early childhood settings:

1. the sudden, unexpected outburst of a parent or teacher
2. the type of emotional discharge that results from a simmering issue that has not been resolved

It is critical for educators to understand that conflict and diverse opinions and approaches are an opportunity for growth and renewal.

BREAKING A RULE

Rules in an early learning environment are important for families and staff:

Rules are sets of standards, laws, or traditions that tell us how to live in relation to each other. Rules may be spoken or unspoken. If we have been informed about a rule, we can discuss, problem solve and make choices. If we are unaware of a rule, we may behave in ways

Scotia Plaza Child Care Centre

Teachers need to maintain a positive approach when interacting with an angry parent.

that are not consistent with that rule. Rules are often embedded in a cultural context; therefore they can contribute to the feeling of cultural discontinuity that some children and families experience at school. When home and school cultures conflict, misunderstanding and even hostility can occur for children, families and teachers. Watch for unspoken rules, especially those related to gender, power, and how we treat each other; discuss them with care. While you may want girls and boys to enjoy cooking experiences, recognize that in some traditional families this may create a conflict. Ask for families' input and assistance when conflict arises over rules. Explain the reasons behind school rules and, equally important, listen to the family. They can share information that may help resolve a problem or address changes that may need to be made in school rules. They may also be willing to modify home rules or talk with their child about the differences between home and school. (Garris Christian, 2006: 5–6)[*]

HIERARCHY

Teachers should make every effort to attempt in their observations of families to understand the importance of hierarchy in the function of the family.

Early childhood professionals may observe family hierarchies based on gender and age and influenced by culture, religion or economic status. At times there may be a clear and strong message but other times it may be difficult to discern. You may observe at the center's family picnic that the males are seated, served and encouraged to eat first. In other families, the elder grandmother may be the decision maker, and everyone may look to her for leadership and guidance. (Garris Christian, 2006: 6)[†]

LACK OF COMMUNICATION

Lack of communication, whether verbal or written, is at the root of most parent–teacher conflicts. Even when the conflict is brought out in the open, it may be perpetuated by the failure of one or both parties to take the other person's position into consideration because of a lack of information.

DIFFERENCES

What makes some people so easy to relate to and others so difficult? Brinkman and Kirschner (2003: 17) believe that

Conflict in a relationship occurs when the emphasis is on the differences, rather than on the similarities. So reducing differences is essential. Success in communication depends on finding common ground, and then trying to redirect the interaction toward a new outcome. Reducing differences can turn conflict into cooperation.

Conflict may arise over issues such as a parent's overprotectiveness, the type of curriculum being delivered, developmental questions (the time at which toilet learning should begin, for example), the setting of limits for children's behaviour, centre menus, the cleanliness of the children at the end

---

[*]Garris, Christian, L. 2006. "Understanding Families. Applying Family Systems Theory To Early Childhood Practice," *Young Children* January: 5-6. © NAEYC. Reprinted with permission.

[†]Garris, Christian, L. 2006. "Understanding Families. Applying Family Systems Theory To Early Childhood Practice," *Young Children* January: 5-6. © NAEYC. Reprinted with permission.

Inside LOOK

Though I teach in the infant room and am a working mother myself, it is sometimes difficult for me to come to terms with my attitudes about working mothers. My parents made great sacrifices so that my mother could stay at home with my sister and me. When a child is brought to the centre ill, or when we enroll infants when they are very young, I can't help thinking that some of these children would be better off at home. I know that I have felt very guilty about going back to work myself, but staying at home wasn't financially viable for me. But I don't know that this is true of some of the parents whose children are at my centre.

of the day, lost clothing, the timely administration of medication, problems in the playroom (for example, one child biting another), families who refuse to have their child tested when the teacher feels this is critical, pushing academic work, and the lack of family involvement to name a few. Differing values may also create conflict as the Inside Look demonstrates.

CENTRE POLICIES

Conflict may also arise over centre policies related to ill children since family members are often overwhelmed when a sick child requires that they stay home from work. For some it may mean the loss of a day's pay, which, in some families, may mean that the rent won't be paid. In some situations, the family may send the child to the centre and thereby create great stress for teachers who are concerned about the well-being of all the children. Even mildly ill children require extra support, and this places even more pressure on teachers, most of whom are already overburdened.

Educators may become resentful of family members who are consistently late when picking up their child. Even if an individual family member is late only occasionally, teachers may, given the total number of families in a centre, find themselves staying behind every night to accommodate tardy families. To deal with this problem, some centres have introduced late fees—a response that only adds to the tension between families and the teachers. What happens when one teacher follows the late fee rules established at the centre and another teacher excuses the lateness?

LACK OF APPRECIATION

Many early childhood educators may be resentful and in conflict with families when they feel that they are not respected and appreciated for the valuable work that they do. This can strain the relationship and be difficult to resolve. Demonstrating a professional approach focused on what is in the best interests of the child is the best option in these circumstances.

HOSTILE TEACHERS

Difficult situations will present themselves; they are inevitable in any early childhood environment. It is how we respond to these situations that is critical. There are times when teachers themselves generate hostile feelings as the following indicates:

My child has just been identified as having Attention Deficit Disorder with Hyperactivity and finally having a diagnosis has helped us to better understand his behaviour. We have shared all of the information from the Child Development Clinic with the teachers and we are more than open to problem-solving strategies that will work at the centre. Yet at the end of the day, one of the teachers seems to delight in recounting all of the negative things that Sam does during the day that had upset her and she most often does this in front of him. I am always so happy to be coming to pick Sam up and this just ruins this end-of-the day connection for me and for him. I feel I have to reprimand him for something that happened at 8:30 in the morning, an event that he has long forgotten. I know if there are serious issues that we need to discuss this, but not in front of Sam and hopefully after we have had time for hugs and positive stories about his day. I have come to dread the pickup time and often hope that teacher will have left, or sometimes I quietly try to go in without her noticing and take Sam home.

WHAT TO SAY: HANDLING DIFFICULT SITUATIONS

Being confronted with an angry family member can feel overwhelming, particularly for an educator in his or her first year of teaching, when getting through the day and dealing with energetic children and balancing family requests seems like a major accomplishment. These teachers especially will need support, reassurance, and encouragement from other team members to know what to say in these situations.

Strong interpersonal communication skills are critical. All early childhood training includes a course on interpersonal communication yet it is one thing to read the theory in the book and another to put it into practice when under pressure. However, there are some practical things that teachers can do when confronted with an angry parent. First, *don't be the first to speak;* many conflicts are escalated when the teacher doesn't hear what the parent has to say. Too often we try to intervene before giving the parent the opportunity to articulate the issues. We are more likely to be successful in problem solving after the parent has spoken and we have provided supportive interactions. The Hostility Curve in Figure 6.2 demonstrates that hostile or angry reactions usually follow a pattern.

Try lowering your voice. When someone is upset, generally speaking, their voice level gets louder.

FIGURE 6.2 Hostility Curve

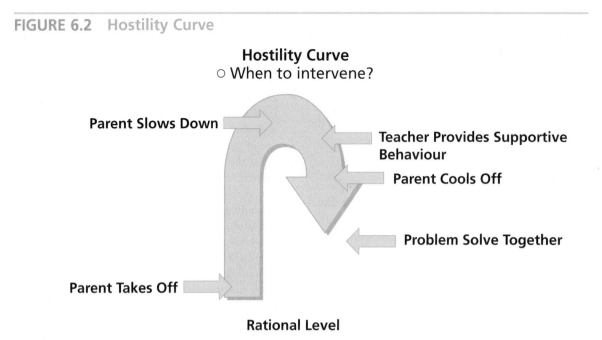

When they hear themselves compared to your calm and quiet voice, they may well lower theirs. Your *voice tone* will send either a positive or a negative message. Even when you are articulate, if your tone is hurried, hostile, or defensive, people may hear something very different from what you intended. In a composed manner, *move closer to the parent*, even though your instincts may tell you to move away. With an open posture, moving closer to may calm the parent. Your body language can send powerful messages. Watch for the parent's reaction to see if this seems appropriate given cultural considerations. Look the parent *directly in the eye* and try not to waiver. It will help you to be seen as more confident and self-assured. There are also times when the parents' concerns are justified and you have perhaps made a mistake. In these situations, always *tell the truth and apologize* when necessary. It is amazing how saying that you are sorry will defuse many difficult encounters. In fact, if you know you have made an error, you are best to call the family before they have a chance to contact you. Again, this will help to defuse the situation. Sometimes angry parents just want someone to *listen with empathy* and concern so they know you really are on their side; this may take time. Make sure you understand both the thoughts and the feelings that go with the concern. Respond to them both! Ask *what he or she would like you to do* about the complaint. Sometimes all a person wants is for someone to hear the complaint and appreciate its legitimacy. The very act of asking proves that you

do welcome concerns and you value the person for bringing it to your attention.

MORE CHALLENGING SITUATIONS

Sometimes situations escalate; these require immediate attention.

- Recognize the person's anger and let them know you understand it. "I can see that you are very upset right now but speaking in an angry voice in front of the children really frightens them. Let's see if the supervisor can come into the room, and let's talk about this privately."

- When tempers flare it may be necessary for the supervisor to step in. "Under no circumstances can you speak to any of the teachers at the centre in an angry way. If you have concerns, we are more than happy to speak to you about these. Please call me and we will make arrangements to meet when you are feeling calmer."

- Keyser (2006: 55–56) suggests empathy and clarification of procedures. For example, if a child was bitten today, start by saying it was very upsetting for everyone:

"We have a lot of experience helping children get through biting. We try to observe when it happens, so we can anticipate it; we give children other things to bite or chew; we let them see that the other person is hurt; and we offer alternative ways for them to express their idea or feeling." It can also be helpful to the parent to know that you have a plan if the behaviour continues. 'Sometimes the biting stops after a few incidents, and other times, it persists for a while. If that happens we will make sure there is a teacher close to Ari most of the time to help keep him and his friends safe.'" (Keyser, 2006: 55–56)*

- "I know that this is very difficult but I cannot allow you to take Muna home. You have been drinking and you should not be driving. I am very happy to call someone in your family or someone on your emergency pick-up list to come to the centre and take both of you home. Who would you like me to call?"

- "I'm so sorry that Cho Hee's mitts have gone missing. I know how annoying this can be. We try very hard to keep everyone's clothing in their cubbies but during the dressing and undressing routine, sometimes things go missing. We will certainly have another look for them. Let me call you at the end of the day when all of the children have been picked up, and I will let you know if I have found them. It would also be really helpful for us if Cho Hee's name was labelled on her clothing."

- "When you are late this often, it is very difficult for the teachers to leave to take care of their own families. It cannot continue to happen. Perhaps we can see if one of the other parents who live near you might be able to pick-up Serge, or perhaps we can help you find another child-care arrangement that works better for you, one that has longer hours to accommodate your work schedule."

THE CONFLICT-RESOLUTION PROCESS

Conflicts between a family member and a teacher should be resolved in such a manner that each party feels it has won. The first step is for the family member and teacher to identify and define the problem in precise terms. The two parties should then discuss the issue, focusing particularly on what needs are not being met and what each party wants. It is important during this phase that both parties make every effort to see the situation from

*From *Parents to Partners: Building a Family-Centered Early Childhood Program* by Janis Keyser. Copyright © 2006 by Janis Keyser. Reprinted with permission of Redleaf Press, St. Paul, MN; www.redleafpress.org.

the other person's point of view. Once the issue is on the table, the next step is to propose and discuss possible solutions. The final step is to implement the agreed-on solution. A further meeting should be scheduled at which the family member and teacher can evaluate the outcome of the conflict resolution and make any necessary adjustments.

Consider the following example of the conflict-resolution process:

Step One: Identify the Issue: Hanesana's mother is concerned that Hanesana is napping at the centre and is not ready for bed at home until late at night.

Step Two: Establish an Appropriate Time for Discussion: Hanesana's mother approaches the teacher with her concern. The teacher and parent agree to meet the next morning, when both parties are available and less likely to be tired at the end of a long day. The supervisor takes over the room so that the teacher can have as much time as is needed to resolve this conflict. They meet in the supervisor's office, where they can have privacy away from the children and they will not be interrupted.

Step Three: Both Parties Outline the Issues: At the meeting, Hanesana's mother explains that it is difficult for her to complete the tasks she needs to do in the evening, as well as study for her exams at school, when Hanesana is unable to settle until late at night. She does not want Hanesana to nap during the day. The teacher explains that it would be difficult to have Hanesana stay up during nap time, since this is the time when staff have their lunches, clean up, and prepare for the afternoon activities. She also explains that Hanesana needs some quiet time, since the child-care day is very busy and tiring.

Step Four: Brainstorm Possible Solutions: Hanesana's mother and the teacher consider each other's points of view with an open mind, and then brainstorm the following ideas:

- Hanesana could visit her younger brother in the infant room and "help out" when her lunch is over.
- Hanesana could take back the kitchen trolley and help the cook with the cleanup routine if the environment is safe.
- Hanesana could assist the teacher when she cleans up in the room and sets up activities for the afternoon.
- Hanesana could have some special materials, available only at nap time, to play with while she rests on her bed until the teacher has

completed her set-up activities. Then she could be encouraged to participate.

- A special quiet space could be organized in the room for Hanesana and other nonsleepers where they are engaged in meaningful activities but respectful of their peers who are sleeping.

- Perhaps when the teachers return from their lunches, the nonsleepers could go outside with one of the teachers. There may be other nonsleepers in other rooms who could be accommodated outside as well.

- A variety of these solutions might be used depending on the ebb and flow of the day.

Step Five: Pick the Best Solution: Hanesana's mother and the teacher agree to this solution: Hanesana will rest on her bed for approximately 20 minutes with special nap-time materials while the teacher tidies the lunch area. The teacher will then set up quiet activities and invite Hanesana to participate. Hanesana's mother also liked the strategy of her daughter being able to visit her brother in the infant room whenever this was feasible.

Step Six: Evaluate: Hanesana's mother and the teacher agree to implement this solution for a week and then meet again to discuss how well it has worked for both parties.

Not all conflicts that arise in a child-care centre are between families and teachers. The conflict resolution strategy outlined above can also be applied to conflicts that arise between teachers or between teachers and administrators. More communication does not necessarily make things better. There are times when it is appropriate to say nothing. If the family member is having a difficult time or if the teacher is upset, it may be best to postpone a discussion until everyone is better able to cope; teachers will need to trust their instincts in this regard.

CULTURES IN CONFLICT
CULTURAL INFLUENCES ON COMMUNICATION

Culture has an enormous impact on our ability to work effectively with families from a culture that may be different from our own:

> Cultural identity is as important in shaping styles of communication as it is in shaping our value system. Every culture is different in the way it defines appropriate listening and speaking behaviours, in its use of body language and eye contact, in its use of silence and the meanings it attaches to silence, in the importance it assigns to taking turns in conversation, in its expectations for formality and informality, and in its understanding of what is appropriate in regard to who addresses whom and under what circumstances, and what is considered polite and impolite. (Chud and Fahlman, 1995: 107)

Exposure to different cultural perspectives provides us with an opportunity to learn more about ourselves and others. Educators must never forget that families will not always see things the way they do and that it is easy to misinterpret a parent's actions.

We need to understand that the way that people communicate during conflicts varies widely from one culture to another. Some cultures encourage

Inside LOOK

A girl named Ana entered kindergarten and proudly wrote her name for the teacher on the first day. The teacher said, "No, that's wrong, Anna has two n's" and the teacher corrected her spelling. Ana went home and told her mother that her name was spelled wrong. Her mother was adamant that the teacher was the one who was wrong. Ana was forced to choose between her mother and her teacher. She chose the teacher. Thirty years later, when Ana told this story, it was with tears running down her cheeks. She said the simple thing that happened in kindergarten affected the way she felt about herself, her family and her culture. At the age of 15, she decided to reclaim her identity, but just talking about it brought more tears. Such a little thing, but such big repercussions!

Source: GONZALEZ-MENA, JANET, 50 STRATEGIES FOR COMMUNICATING AND WORKING WITH DIVERSE FAMILIES, 2nd Edition, © 2010. Reprinted and Electronically reproduced by permission of Pearson Education, Inc., Upper Saddle River, NJ.

a straightforward, self-focused approach; others consider the concerns of the group more important than those of any individual. "These two basic concepts—individualism and collectivism—help make visible how culture influences a person's attitudes, beliefs, values and behaviours. Each orientation is associated with a different set of priorities that often shows up in care and education practices" (Gonzalez-Mena, 2010: 41).*

When teachers and families from two different cultural groups enter into a conflict, neither one may be prepared to understand the conflict from another perspective. Teachers should think twice before they question and challenge family practices that are not harmful to the child and are a reflection of a parent's love and concern. It is also important to remember that not all conflicts are cultural; some may be a family tradition, philosophical ideals, training that has taken place in the past, or an individual family approach that is unique to them.

STRATEGIES FOR RESOLVING CONFLICTS BASED ON CULTURAL DIFFERENCES

We generally find most difficulties arise from the different assumptions concerning the following eight areas, as discussed by Gonzalez-Mena (1993):

1. *Take it slow:* Don't expect to resolve each conflict immediately. Building understandings and relationships takes time. Some conflicts won't be resolved, they'll just be managed. You have to learn to cope with differences when there is no common ground or resolution.

2. *Understand yourself:* Become clear about your own values and goals. Know what you believe in. Have a bottom line, but leave space above it to be flexible.

3. *Become sensitive to your own discomfort:* Tune in on those times when something bothers you instead of just ignoring it and hoping it will go away. Work to identify what specific behaviours of others make you uncomfortable. Try to discover exactly what in yourself creates this discomfort.

4. *Learn about other cultures:* Books, classes, and workshops help, but watch out for stereotypes and biased information. Your best source of information comes from the families in your program. Check out what they believe about their cultures, and see if those beliefs fit with other information you receive. But don't ever make one person a representative of his or her culture. Listen to individuals, take in the information they give you, but don't generalize to whole cultures. Keep your mind open as you learn. Check out your point of view. There's a difference between finding and celebrating diversity and explaining deficiencies.

5. *Find out what the families in your program, individually, want for their children:* What are their goals? What are their caregiving practices? What concerns do they have about their child in your program? Encourage them to talk to you. Encourage them to ask questions. You may find out about cultures this way, or you may find out about individual or familial differences. All are important.

6. *Be a risk taker:* If you are secure enough, you may feel you can afford to make mistakes. Mistakes are a part of cross-cultural communication. It helps to have a good support system behind you when you take risks and make mistakes.

7. *Communicate, dialogue, negotiate:* If you have a chance to build a relationship before getting into negotiations, you're more likely eventually to reach a mutually satisfying point.

8. *Share power:* Empowerment is an important factor in the dialogue–negotiation process. Although some see empowerment (allowing others to experience their own personal power) as threatening, empowerment creates new forms of power. Some teachers and caregivers fear that empowerment means giving away their own power, but this is not true! No one can give personal power, and no one can take it away. We all have our personal power, though we can be discouraged or prevented from recognizing or using it. Sharing power, or empowerment, enhances everyone's power.

Many teachers can easily experience firsthand learning because of the cultural diversity of the parents in their program. To what extent they seize the opportunity depends on their attitudes and openness. I see a progression of attitudes toward differences from awareness, tolerance, and acceptance to respect and appreciation. Beyond that lies celebration, support, and finally using differences as resources to expand and enrich one's own life.

THE CRITICAL CONNECTION: DAY-TO-DAY INTERACTION WITH FAMILIES
HOW MUCH TIME DO WE SPEND IN DISCUSSION?

Daily communication with a meaningful exchange of information between parents and early childhood program staff supports children's development and is a measure of program quality (Zellman and Perlman, 2006). Not surprisingly, most family–staff communication occurs at transition times. Further, family–staff communication occurs two or three times or more a week for most family–staff dyads, with typical conversations lasting less than one minute (Minish, 1986). A study by Endsley and Minish (1991) reveals that approximately two-thirds of these transition-time family–staff communications involve conversations of a median length of *12 seconds* and parent-caregiver communication did not significantly differ in frequency, length, content or usefulness between drop-off and pick-up times.

More recent research by Michal Perlman, OISE/UT (2011), and her colleague Brooke Fletcher studied more than 1087 children being dropped off in the morning in over 100 classrooms in Toronto and Colorado. Ninety-four percent of parents spent an average of *67 seconds* in their child's classroom during morning drop-off, while only 6 percent spent more than 5 minutes in the classroom. In general,

---

EXHIBIT 6.2   Cultures in Conflict

CONTRAST TO NORTH AMERICAN VALUES	NORTH AMERICAN VALUES
1. Individual versus family	
Every individual is perceived in the context of his or her family.	The individual is perceived as a separate entity.
Involvement and dependence on family are encouraged.	Individual responsibility is most important.
Decisions must involve the older respected members of the family.	Decisions must involve the individual as much as possible.
2. Acceptance of others	
Individuals from other cultures react to other people in terms of the whole person, not the role.	North Americans relate to others in terms of their role.
Individuals from contrast cultures tend to accept or reject others completely and have difficulty working with those who are unacceptable.	North Americans don't need to like or agree with someone to avail themselves of his or her services (for example, student and teacher).
3. Social relations	
Differences in status and hierarchical rank are noted and stressed.	Differences in status are minimized to make others feel comfortable.
Communication follows a predictable, formal series of steps that make others feel more comfortable.	A direct, informal style of communicating is also used to achieve the same results.
4. Progress versus fate	
Man is perceived by many cultures in a fatalistic manner, and such things as disease and suffering are accepted more easily.	North Americans believe man is rational and can construct machines and develop techniques to solve problems.
5. Time	
Time is perceived in terms of the right time to do something (supper is when you eat).	Time is perceived in terms of clock time (supper is at 5:30 p.m.).
Time moves slowly; man must integrate himself with the environment, and adapt to it rather than change it.	Time moves quickly, from past to present to future; one must keep up with it, and use it to change and master one's environment.

Source: Miner, M.J., and M.K. Harker. N.d. "Suggested Activities and Material 3, no. 14." *Honouring Diversity*. Ottawa: International Briefing Associates. Reprinted by permission of Michael Miner.

---

communication between parents and staff was limited, with staff providing child-related information to less than 9 percent of parents. Sixty-five percent of parents were greeted by a caregiver either verbally or nonverbally (e.g., smile) upon entering their child's classroom. Of these parents that were greeted, 12 percent were greeted by name. *The remaining 35 percent of parents were never greeted by any of the caregivers present in the classroom while dropping off their children. Twenty-two percent of children were not greeted either verbally or nonverbally by any of the caregivers.* While an improvement from the 1991 study, if adults spent an average of *67 seconds* dropping their children off, it is hard to imagine how authentic, meaningful relationships can develop! How can we get "inside this family" with so little time together? This finding should cause many in the ECE field to re-evaluate their practice and for students to reflect on how this information will impact their performance in their field placement experiences.

WHEN DO THE DISCUSSIONS TAKE PLACE?

While parents seemed to have more time in the afternoon, caregivers were more likely to be free to talk in the morning. Thus it would appear that the ideal communication times for caregivers and parents are at odds. The situation is further complicated by the fact that at the end of the day many parents arrive at the same time to pick up their children. The last half hour that a centre is open is often the busiest, which makes in-depth conversation between families and teachers difficult, if not impossible. Since these transition times are often stressful for families when they have other things on their minds, it is rarely the best time to ask parents to remember details about program policies.

WHAT DO WE DISCUSS?

Family–staff communication can be divided into three areas:

- social exchanges
- sharing of information
- discussion that leads to decision making

Of these, social exchanges are the most frequent. Endsley and Minish (1991) found that greetings, discussion of routine matters, and small talk were followed in frequency by more substantive topics such as the child's behaviour, medical and health

---

EXHIBIT 6.3 Building Meaningful Family–Teacher Interactions

- When possible, schedule staffing so that teachers are available to talk.
- The supervisor should be on the floor during drop-off and pick-up times and alert to show he or she can facilitate this transition.
- Educators should prepare materials and the environment before family members arrive by coming to the centre early.
- Leave tidying up and household tasks at the end of the day until families have left.
- Choose activities at the beginning and end of each day that children can manage on their own, thereby freeing up time for teachers to spend with families.
- Approach family members and children as they arrive and welcome them by name, comment on a new haircut, etc.
- Send positive messages by inviting families into the room and helping them to feel comfortable when they want to play with the children or engage in an activity. Make comfortable adult chairs available.
- Use drop-off and pick-up opportunities to share meaningful observations about the child—something pleasant, a kindness, something touching, or funny, a special art project, etc.
- Schedule private meetings when difficult issues need to be discussed.
- Help families re-engage in a positive manner at the end of the day: "You must ask Charlie how he helped with lunch today!"
- Establish a tracking system to record communications with family members in order to identify those who may require more opportunities to interact with teachers.
- Utilize written communication, telephone calls, centre websites, emails, text messages, etc., in early childhood environments where car pools or busing takes place, or only one parent is involved in drop-off and pick-up, since these factors can significantly reduce face-to-face communication time.

concerns, and the child's day at the centre. Adult-focused and home- or family-focused substantive communication occurred somewhat less frequently, while child-rearing information and cognitive and social-development issues were almost never discussed. Importantly, Endsley and Minish discerned a focus on the adults as people rather than as parents and caregivers. In fact, the adults' health and activities away from the centre were the fifth and sixth most common substantive topics discussed. For some parents, the child-care centre can be a source of adult support and friendship.

WHICH FAMILY MEMBERS DO WE TALK TO THE MOST?

Research suggests that family members of younger children communicate more frequently than family members of older children. Their conversations last longer and are generally more substantive than routine in nature. Parents of infants may wish to spend more time interacting with caregivers because they are a source of information on topics such as feeding and sleeping patterns, and because they generally help to ease the transition from home to child care and vice versa. As the child grows older, families tend to become less dependent on caregivers for practical child-care information. Families of children in after-school care may see staff members at pick-up time but feel less need to spend time conversing, since only a small portion of their child's day is spent in this type of care.

Supervisors have observed that some teachers engage in different behaviours with different parents. For example, a teacher might unconsciously discourage one family member from entering the playroom while inviting another to do so. When considering why they respond more positively to some parents than to others, supervisors need to support teachers in asking themselves several questions:

- Are they gravitating to families whose cultural backgrounds are similar to their own?

- Is race a factor?

- Do they favour families who appear to be more appreciative of their efforts as teachers?

- Do they respond to parents whose interpersonal communication style is similar to theirs?

- Do they assume that parents who are economically disadvantaged are less able parents?

- Are they less tolerant of less-educated parents?

"The truth is that our finest moments are most likely to occur when we are feeling deeply uncomfortable, unhappy or unfulfilled, for it is only in such moments, propelled by our discomfort, that we are likely to step out of our ruts and start searching for different ways or truer answers."

—M. Scott Peck

REFERENCES

Adler, R.B., and N. Towne. 1993. *Looking Out/Looking In*, 7th ed. Fort Worth, TX: Harcourt Brace Jovanovich.

Adler, R.B., L.B. Rosenfeld, R.F. Proctor II, and C. Winder. 2012. *Interplay. The Process of Interpersonal Communication*. Oxford University Press.

Amatea, E. 2009. *Building Culturally Responsive Family-School Relationships*. Pearson.

Brinkman, R., and R. Kirschner. 2003. *Dealing with Difficult People. 24 Lessons for Bringing Out the Best in Everyone*. McGraw-Hill Professional Education.

Brislin, R. 1993. *Understanding Culture's Influence on Behavior*. Fort Worth, TX: Harcourt Brace Jovanovich.

Chud, G., and R. Fahlman. 1995. *Honouring Diversity within Child Care and Early Education*. Ottawa: Ministry of Skills, Training and Labour in conjunction with the Centre for Curriculum and Professional Development.

Code of Ethical Conduct and Statement of Commitment: Guidelines for Responsible Behavior in Early Childhood Education. 2011. Washington, DC: National Association for the Education of Young Children (NAEYC).

Dotsch, J. 1999. *Non-biased Children's Assessments*. Toronto: Bias-Free Early Childhood Services.

Endsley, R.C., and P.A. Minish. 1991. "Parent–Staff Communication in Day Care Centers during Morning and Afternoon Transitions." *Early Childhood Research Quarterly* 6.

Fox, K. 2003. "Evolution, Alienation and Gossip." Social Issues Research Centre. Retrieved February 15, 2013, from http://www.sirc.org/publik/gossip.shtml

Garris Christian, L. 2006. "Understanding Families: Applying Family Systems Theory to Early Childhood Practice." *Young Children*. January.

Gestwicki, C. 1992. *Home, School and Community Relations*, 2nd ed. Albany, NY: Delmar.

Gonzalez-Mena, J. 1993. *Multicultural Issues in Child Care*. Mountain View, CA: Mayfield. 22–23.

———. 2010. *50 Strategies for Communicating and Working with Diverse Families*, 2nd ed. Upper Saddle River, NJ: Pearson.

Greenman, J., and A. Stonehouse. 1996. *Prime Times: A Handbook for Excellence in Infant and Toddler Programs*. St. Paul, MN: Redleaf Press.

Hall, E.T. 1969. *The Hidden Dimension*. New York: Doubleday.

Hepworth Berger, E., and M. Riojas-Cortez. 2012. *Parents as Partners in Education. Families and Schools Working Together*. Upper Saddle River, NJ: Pearson.

Keyser, J. 2006. *From Parents to Partners: Building a Family-Centered Early Childhood Program*. St. Paul, MN: Redleaf Press.

Leitch Copeland, M., and H.E. Bruno. 2001. "Countering Center Gossip." *Child Care Information Exchange* 3.

Miner, M.J., and M.K. Harker. n.d."Suggested Activities and Material 3, no. 14." *Honouring Diversity.* Ottawa: International Briefing Associates.

Minish, P.A. 1986. Creating an Instrument to Assess Parent– Caregiver Communication during Morning Drop-Off and Afternoon Pickup Times in Proprietary Day Care Centers. Unpublished manuscript, University of Georgia, Athens.

Morris, D., P. Collett, P. March, and M. O'Shaughnessy. 1979. *Gestures: Their Origins and Distributions.* New York: Stein and Day.

Ontario English Catholic Teachers Association. n.d. "Positive Professional Parent Teacher Relationships."

Perlman, M. 2011. "Just Who's Looking After Your Kids?" *Toronto Star.* November 13. A17.

Perlman, M., and Fletcher, B.A. 2011. *Examining Informal Parent-Staff Communication.* Ontario Institute for Studies in Education, University of Toronto.

Phipps, R.P. 2008. *Body Language Facts and Statistics.* Retrieved from http://personalpowerinformation.blogspot.com/ 2008/08/body-language-facts-and-statistics.html

Powell, D. R. 1989. Families and Early Childhood Programs. (Research monographs of the National Association for the Education of Young Children No. 3). Washington, DC: National Association for the Education of Young Children.

Quotations Page. n.d. "Mahatma Gandhi." Retrieved January 25, 2013, from http://www.quotationspage.com/ quote/36464.html

Samovar, L.A., R.E. Porter, and R.E. McDaniel. 2007. *Communication between Cultures,* 6th ed. Toronto: Thomson Wadsworth.

Sommer, R. 1969. *Personal Space: The Behavioral Basis Of Design.* Englewood Cliffs, NJ: Prentice Hall.

Swick, K. 1992. *An Early Childhood School—Home Learning Design.* Champaign, IL: Stipes Publishing.

Whitaker, T., and D. Fiore, 2001. "Dealing with Difficult Parents." *Eye on Education.* Retrieved January 29, 2013, from http://www.eyeoneducation.com/bookstore/client/ client_pages/samplechapters/609-8.pdf

Zellman, G., and M. Perlman. 2006. "Parent Involvement in Child Care Settings: Conceptual and Measurement Issues." *Early Child Development and Care.* Preview Article. 1–18.

Created by Hayden

Chapter

7

FAMILY–TEACHER CONFERENCES

mangostock/Shutterstock.com

"Parent-teacher conferences are highly ritualized events, and like most rituals, the form and content can become symbolic or substantive, routine or revelatory, limiting or liberating."

—*Sara Lawrence-Lightfoot (2003)*

LEARNING OUTCOMES

After studying this chapter, you will be able to

1. outline the benefits of conferences for both families and teachers

2. discuss teachers' and families' concerns about conferences

3. heighten awareness of the role of the early childhood educator in supporting families through conferences

4. identify strategies for planning and conducting successful conferences

5. describe strategies for resolving conflicts that may occur during a conference

6. examine follow-up and evaluation procedures

Before beginning this chapter, it is important to note that family–teacher conferences are no more important than any other means of connecting with families. But because of the more formal nature of this type of interaction, conferences sometimes create anxiety for all involved. By being well prepared, however, educators will feel less anxious and will see conferences as opportunities for quality one-on-one time with families. It is a wonderful opportunity to celebrate the lives of the children!

REASONS FOR ORGANIZING CONFERENCES

Conferences allow families and teachers to meet in order to share information that assists both in developing their relationship and in setting appropriate goals for the children. Conferences should be held on a regular basis; some centres schedule them three times a year. Some families, particularly those with infants, may benefit from more frequent meetings. For families that are new to the centre, a family–teacher conference might be arranged after they have been with the centre for a few months. Conferences may be held on fixed dates each year or organized spontaneously to address immediate issues that families and teachers wish to discuss. Either way, these meetings are of particular benefit to families and educators of younger children, who are progressing rapidly through developmental stages.

HOW FAMILIES AND EDUCATORS BENEFIT FROM CONFERENCES

At the conference, families can

- include all family members who are interested in attending

- express their feelings about their child's experience

- discuss their family values

- discuss goals for their child

- ask questions about their child's development

- talk about important family matters such as celebrations, illness, a death in the family

- provide examples of their child's growth and development in the home

- learn more about how they can contribute to their child's development at home

- find out how their child is getting along with other children and adults in the program

- be reassured about the teacher–child relationship when the teacher's insight into their child becomes apparent

- talk over any issues that may be of concern regarding the centre

- ask for clarification about their role in the centre

At the conference, educators can

- encourage family support and involvement in the program

- discuss the centre environment and how it contributes to the development of the child

- explain the developmental milestones that are being reached in the child's life

- gain insight into the family's expectations for both the centre and the child

- find out how the child feels about the centre and about the teacher–child relationship

- be made aware of emerging issues related to the child (for example, developing fears, health concerns, changes in sleep routines)

- learn more about the child's home and community environment

At the conference, both teachers and families can

- strengthen their relationships with each other

- reduce misunderstandings

- raise issues

- identify future goals for the child

- discuss strategies for strengthening the home–centre partnership

CONCERNS ABOUT CONFERENCES
TEACHERS' CONCERNS

1. *No experience with conferences:* I've never done a conference before. I'm not sure what to do or say and I'm not even sure how to start preparing for it. I wish we had some kind of professional development training on how to conduct a conference!

2. *Lack of self-confidence:* I'm a really shy person. I'm fine with the children, but when I have these conferences I feel awkward and uncomfortable. I feel my face turning red, and I stumble over everything I say. I know I have to work on feeling more confident about myself and my skills as a professional. I have the training; I just can't always articulate it the way I should be able to.

3. *Feeling vulnerable:* This is the time when I feel the most vulnerable and defensive. I feel that my abilities and professionalism are challenged by some families. I know there are many emotions at work here, not just mine, and I am sure that parents at times are also feeling vulnerable and defensive.

4. *Personal history:* My parents weren't involved in my school life and I wonder if I react differently to the parents who are very involved in our centre? My mother and my father felt uncomfortable being around my teachers; does my experience growing up impact the relationships I have with the families at our centre?

5. *How do I introduce myself?* I'm not even sure how to greet families at the start of the conference since I know that it is easy to offend someone by doing the wrong thing, so do I shake hands, do I bow? I just feel there is so much for me to learn.

6. *Challenging communication:* I come from a collectivist culture where close intimate contact is accepted behaviour. Hugging, touching, and my style of communication are all part of how I was raised and how I interact with the children. I know that some parents seem put off by my approach and I'm not sure how to effectively deal with them.

7. *Communicating effectively with English language learner families:* My biggest concern is how to have a productive interview with families whose language I don't share. I have several families whose English is limited but whom I can speak to; however, I'm worried that we will not fully understand each other, or I may say something and they may misunderstand my intention and take offence.

8. *Lack of understanding of cultural practices:* With so many diverse families in my program, I am really worried that I just don't have a wide enough worldview to understand the experiences of all of my families. Some parents are very direct and straight to the point, and others are more formal and less direct.

9. *Conflicting attitudes with teachers and families from the same culture:* I know that there are many families in our centre who have a Portuguese background, and so there is an assumption that because I am also Portuguese that we will be on the "same page." But I know that I hold different ideas about child development and schooling that puts me at odds with some of our families.

10. *Being unable to answer parents' questions:* I work hard to prepare for a conference with families because I am terrified that they will ask me a question that I can't answer. I don't want them to think that I'm not knowledgeable. What if I make a mistake?

11. *Not being taken seriously if the teacher has no children of her own:* I sometimes wonder if parents think I don't have a real understanding of what it is like to be a parent because I'm not one myself. I'm still new to the field and several of the parents in the room are the same age as my own parents.

12. *Dealing with an angry parent:* In my personal life I avoid confrontation, because I almost always end up in tears. My greatest fear is that a parent will get angry with me and there will be a confrontation.

13. *Handling issues that are beyond the teacher's control:* The late-fee policy at our centre is a really big issue for one of our parents. I know that he will bring it up at the conference and I'm not sure how I will respond.

14. *Demanding or hard-to-please parents:* I know that I have to work harder at my relationship with Maria's family. They seem so resistant to accepting the limitations of group care, and

their expectations of me seem so high. No matter what I do, I can't seem to please them. I know that when strong feelings arise, it is hard to be objective.

15. *Broaching serious concerns with families:* I'm dreading the interview with Joshua's family. I've been gathering information over the past few months, and have serious concerns about a delay in his development. I know that I have to discuss this with his family, but I'm worried about their reaction and how to best support them.

16. *Not being seen as a professional:* I want to be appreciated by the families. My work with the children is more than a job for me—it is my life's work! Yet some families treat me as though I were nothing more than a babysitter. I don't think these families have an understanding of the time and effort I put into this job. Some parents just don't respect what I do.

17. *Lack of parental interest:* There is not much point in holding conferences at our centre. The families are just not interested in what we have to tell them. They rush in and out, never even asking how things have gone or if there have been any problems.

FAMILY CONCERNS

1. *Being confronted with some wrongdoing on the part of their child:* When I was little, I was the troublemaker in my family. My parents were called into the school several times to talk to the teacher and principal because of something I had done. When we got the letter from the toddler teachers saying they wanted to speak to my wife and me about Jason, all my old fears kicked in.

2. *Being judged by teachers:* I didn't do well at school and always felt intimidated by my teachers. I am very uncomfortable around my son's teachers. I guess I feel that they are making judgments on whether or not I am a good mother. Being a good mother is important to me, and I'm afraid of what they might say.

3. *Having my parenting skills scrutinized:* Amy is my first child, and although I am trying my best I sometimes wish I knew more about how to be a better parent. I'm worried that the teachers are going to quiz me about my parenting techniques, and I won't be able to

provide satisfactory answers. I wish I trusted them enough to just ask for help.

4. *I'm a nuisance:* I never hear from the teachers, I never feel welcome in the centre, and now they want me to come in for a conference. They constantly send the message that they don't want me to be involved and now all of a sudden it is "all hands on deck." Don't they think that there are things that I could contribute to the program? If I call the centre, it's days before anyone even returns my call.

5. *Teachers and their favourites:* The teachers really seem to prefer Sarah and her family. They seem to ignore me when I am in the centre, but they have lots to say to Sarah's parents about how her day went. I'm concerned that the teachers prefer Sarah and her parents over me and my child.

6. *Being informed that my child is not developing "normally":* Our 4-year-old is going through an acting-out phase. What if the teachers tell us he is developing a serious behaviour problem?

7. *Lack of teacher commitment to the well-being of my child:* My biggest concern about the family–teacher conference is not how well Rashid is doing in the program but how much this teacher is really connected to him. Does she really like him? Is she really willing to work with us on his behalf? My son has a unique learning style, and I'm not sure the teacher is willing to accommodate him.

8. *Lack of insight into our family:* We are going through a very difficult time right now; my mother who lives with us has Alzheimer's, and with three children, being a single mother, and working full time, I just don't have time to attend a conference.

9. *Cultural insensitivity on the part of teachers:* Our South Asian heritage is very important to us. We want our child to adjust to his life here in Canada, but we also want to retain the richness of our own culture. Will the centre value our religious and cultural beliefs?

10. *Lack of concern about our dietary practices:* I don't know how to bring this up but the food served at the centre does not reflect the food we eat in our home. I'm worried that the teacher and the cook will think I'm

interfering if I bring this up but Sameer is just not eating the way he should.

11. *Jeopardizing the teacher's relationship with my child:* I have a problem with the nap routine and the length of time Ryan is sleeping. At night he takes hours to settle down because he is not tired but I'm afraid to bring it up because the teachers might get defensive and take it out on Ryan.

12. *Differing school backgrounds:* My schooling was very different from what I see the teachers doing with the children in this centre. We had to be very quiet and respectful of the teachers at all times. We would never have spoken to the teachers in the way the children do at this centre. I think there should be more structure and a greater emphasis on reading and writing. I feel pretty confused about the right way to teach children.

13. *Problems with arrangements for interpreters:* My English-language skills are not good and the teacher has asked me to bring my 12-year-old daughter to interpret for me. But there are things I want to talk about that I do not want my daughter to hear. I know that we should go to the meeting, but we probably won't.

14. *Lack of privacy:* I remember being in a gym full of parents, waiting for an interview with my older daughter's school teachers. Interviews were three minutes long, with one minute allowed for parents to rush to the next teacher. At one point I was so upset with one teacher's comments that I began to cry in front of all those people. I've never attended a conference at a child-care centre before. What if the setup is the same and there is a repeat of my humiliating experience?

It is hardly surprising that all participants in a conference situation may be nervous and unsure of themselves. The information in this chapter should help to alleviate many of these fears and concerns.

STRATEGIES FOR PLANNING THE CONFERENCE
ADVANCE PLANNING

The purpose of family–teacher conferences should be explained in the centre's family handbook and discussed during orientation. In preparing for conferences, a staff meeting is a good place to start so that all staff can problem solve for families who

Documentation is essential to an effective conference.

may have more than one child in the centre, coordinate if an interpreter is needed, and organize where meetings will be held. Most importantly, the centre should take into consideration families' busy schedules. Some families may find early-morning meetings more convenient; others may prefer noon-hour, nap-time, evening, or weekend appointments. Special arrangements might also need to be made for those parents who work shifts or for those who commute great distances. Child care should also be provided for young children so educators and families have this uninterrupted time together. In some cases it may be more feasible to hold the conference at the child's home or at the teacher's home rather than at the centre.

Divorced or separated parents may choose to meet with teachers together or separately. Stepparents, live-in partners, and other family members or individuals who play an important part in the child's life should also be welcome at the conference. Additionally, when necessary, arrangements should be made to include foster families and other support personnel who may be working with their child.

THE CONCEPT OF TIME

Gonzalez-Mena (2008: 47) reminds us that

the concept of time needs to be addressed and what it means to be late. For some people, being early is important and so when the appointed time comes, they are already there and waiting. For others, the goal is to walk in the door one minute before the scheduled time; they don't like to wait. For others, forgivably late means five or so minutes. In some families, clock time has very little meaning and appointments may have even less. In their culture,

Digital Vision/Thinkstock

arriving several hours or even days after the appointed time is within the bounds of courtesy.[*]

In some centres, there is a scheduled 20- to 30-minute time period for each family; other centres are less structured. The length of time available for the meeting should be communicated to families in advance. When necessary, extra time taken for the conference can reduce the follow-up time needed to correct any misunderstanding created by rushing through the conference. Teachers should make sure that the conferences do not conflict with national holidays, religious festivals, or popular events (for example, the last game of the World Cup).

Families should be notified in a variety of ways about the upcoming conference. A letter should be sent home well in advance of the date so that families have an opportunity to organize their schedules. Formal letters on the centre's letterhead may be used but more informal clip-art invitations are also available online to be printed off if more appropriate. English language learner families should receive letters in their own language; if this is not possible, they should be notified in person. Where literacy may be an issue, family members should also be informed verbally. Other communication strategies may include email, fax, text message, a notice in the newsletter with a clip-out portion to be returned to the teacher, or a sign-up poster at the front door. For some families, an online booking that they can make when they have time at home and coordinated by the centre may be the easiest method of ensuring that families attend the conference. This may also be a useful tool when more than one child attends the centre and more than one meeting is to take place. For centres with large numbers, there are a number of commercial booking systems that are available.

*GONZALEZ-MENA, JANET, 50 STRATEGIES FOR COMMUNICATING AND WORKING WITH DIVERSE FAMILIES, 2nd Edition, © 2010. Reprinted and Electronically reproduced by permission of Pearson Education, Inc., Upper Saddle River, NJ.

Janeway Child and Family Centre

NOTIFICATION OF CONFERENCE: SAMPLE LETTER TO FAMILIES

Dear Ms. Khan:

Now that Jamal has been with us for six weeks, we would like to get together with you to discuss his adjustment to our room. We are looking forward to having time to share information about Jamal. During the week of November 3–8 we will be holding our family–teacher conferences. Ms. Ahluwalia will again be available to interpret for you. Child care will also be provided while you are meeting with us. Please sign the list on the parent bulletin board for a time that will be most convenient for you or speak to one of us when you are dropping off Jamal at the centre.

The conference will be an opportunity for you to talk about your feelings about the centre and our program. The following are some of the items that you might like to discuss with us when you come to the conference, but please feel free to add any new ideas or issues:

1. What does Jamal enjoy about being in the centre?
2. What are your feelings about his adjustment to group care?
3. Does he discuss any favourite activities or learning centres in the room?
4. Whom does he like to play with?
5. Does Jamal have any issues that you would like to discuss with us?
6. Do you have any issues that you would like to discuss with us?

Sincerely,
Alexander Dougall, Lindsay Cooper

CONFIRMING THE INTERVIEW

Once all of the times have been coordinated, the teacher should send home a note or an email to officially confirm the date, time, and location of the meeting. To help families prepare for the conference, teachers might invite them to come in beforehand and spend some time observing in the playroom. Teachers may initiate an agenda, but families should also have an opportunity to add their own items as they prepare for the meeting as well.

> Parents and educators need enough information to prepare for the conference no matter who requests it. If parents or teachers are not informed about the nature of the requested meeting, there is the possibility of feeling ambushed by blame fixing and the result is that someone is set in a defensive position. Frustration, anger, fear, discouragement often result and so hope is blanched, the child suffers and the result is far from hopeful for change. The conference should be a celebration of who the child is, what he or she knows and can do, and what the possibilities could be if certain strategies are put in place. The root of evaluation is to "value," [so] the process should be positive. (Cameron, 2012)[*]

---

[*]Cameron, L. 2012. "Ask an expert: Improving parent-teacher interviews." *Canadian Living*. Available at http://www.canadianliving.com/moms/ parenting/ask_an_expert_improving_ parent_teacher _interviews.php. Reprinted by permission of Canadian Living.

TEACHER PREPARATION

Nothing is more frustrating for families than attending a conference in which the teacher speaks in generalities and appears to know little about their child. When preparing for a conference, teachers should consult with other adults who work with the child or who did in the past. As an objective observer of both the child and the teacher, the supervisor is often able to provide valuable insights. It is a good idea to have an experienced teacher or the supervisor take new teachers through the preparation process. It may also be helpful to role-play some of the potential situations during a staff meeting.

Establish the belief that the meeting will be real, meaningful, and relevant for the educator and family members. The meeting must result in productive strategies and hope. It must be honest and fair. Throughout the year, teachers should formally record their observations of the children. Any comments they make at a conference can then be supported by documentation. Record keeping with respect to a child's development can take many forms. One teacher might record milestones and significant events on adhesive notes kept inside her cupboard door until they can be transferred to a binder—indexed for each child—at the end of each week. Another teacher might prepare an index box with file cards organized alphabetically for each child, and then jot down observations

Inside LOOK

Recording Early Learning Observations

The introduction of web-based programs and mobile technologies are new tools that have been added to the ECE's toolbox in order to connect with families. At George Brown College in Ontario, a faculty member became the driving force to develop and create a web-based observation program that is available to not only the child care staff in the centre but also to the families of the children enrolled. This program, known as Recording Early Learning Observations (RELO), allows the child's teachers to record daily observations of individual children, which families can access, with the use of any web-enabled device (smart phone, tablet, computer). Moreover, it also allows families to record their own observations of their child and share that with the teachers in the room. As the recorded observations become the basis of the curriculum, it provides an opportunity for families to make real contributions to the daily curriculum of the program. Creating the occasion to share observations in a meaningful way that is not restricted to drop-off and pick-up times has been an important benefit of the RELO program for families. For ECEs, family access to RELO has given them yet another way in which to connect.

Source: Reprinted by permission of Margaret Isnor, RECE, Faculty, George Brown College.

This teacher is documenting an observation in this RELO program.

throughout the day. Other teachers might record their observations following weekly meetings with other staff. Many new electronic methods for gathering information are also available.

Ongoing record keeping is critical to planning and assessment. According to Martin (2007: 259),

> assessment is a process of gathering information about an individual's behaviour, health indicators, growth, sensory levels, performance in specified tasks, intellectual abilities, social relationships, receptive and expressive language, personality traits, motor skills, spontaneous play activity, potential, or other predetermined criteria. The process may take many forms, including informal observation, standardized tests, teacher appraisal, developmental checklists, parental observations, the individual's own evaluation, medical diagnosis, or any combination of these or other methods.

In many centres, experienced teachers create their own assessment tools using a checklist format. ECE students are not always trained in the use of all assessment tools, but should try to learn from more experienced teachers. Teachers should be mindful of whether the tool is inclusive and reflects the socioeconomic and cultural diversity of the children it assesses. The Nipissing District Developmental Screen (NDDS), which can be accessed at **http:// www.ndds.ca**, is one such inclusive tool.

PORTFOLIOS

Teachers should be in the habit of documenting all interactions and communications with families.

> Documentation in the form of portfolios is a powerful instructional tool because they offer

children, teachers, parents, administrators, and policy makers an opportunity to glimpse the sweep and power of the children's growth and development. When carefully structured, portfolios display the range of a child's work. Above all, they integrate instruction and assessment. (Meisels, 1993: 38)

Portfolios are opportunities for teachers to find creative ways to document learning! Software is also now available so that teachers, children and families can develop electronic portfolios. An example is LifeCubby at **https://www.lifecubby.me**.

A portfolio is a record-keeping system consisting of significant information about a child (health data, work samples, teachers' observations, etc.). The system enables child-care professionals to keep records over time, add items as necessary, evaluate the child's performance, evolve plans to meet the child's needs, and review progress. It enables families to understand their child's progress over time and to become more familiar with what is going on in the playroom.

Martin suggests that a portfolio might contain

- health records;
- family intake forms;
- notes forwarded from previous caregiving agencies;
- observation records;
- developmental checklists;
- parental input in a variety of forms;
- assessment results from standardized tests (attention should be paid to ensure the tests are linguistically and culturally appropriate);
- information from psychologists, social workers, and so forth;
- photographs of special moments in the child's life, things the child has made, and so on;
- special items selected by the child;
- artwork samples;
- samples of the child's writing;
- audiotapes of the child's language, reading, or music;
- videotapes of the child's activities;
- the child's own records-of-achievement journal;
- a learning log of the child's lifetime experiences; and
- questionnaire responses. (2007: 220)

At our centre we are trying a new strategy this year. We have created a checklist that states all the important learning centres in our room as well as important social and emotional areas that we want to highlight. We always have a camera available in the room, and we are using it to take photographs of the children to capture those memorable moments. The checklist with each child's name on it helps us to see what photos we need to collect. We will put the photos into an album for the family and use the album as a tool for discussing their child's development at the family–teacher conference.

When children advance to the next age group in the centre, the portfolio can become a valuable tool for orientating their teachers. When the child leaves the centre to go to another child-care setting or goes into the school system, the portfolio can be an effective and informative way to introduce the child and his family to the new teachers. A communication book that travels with the child through his or her life at the centre may become a treasured family item. It is important to remember that all information gathered about children is confidential and should be stored in a manner that protects their privacy. Portfolios may be used as a marketing and public relations tool—but only after obtaining the families' and child's permission to use the material. In these cases teachers can organize the portfolio materials for families who are considering enrolling their child in the centre.

Educators should review each portfolio to see how well it presents the story of the child's development, then add or subtract pieces as necessary to ensure the story is full and accurate. Portfolios should include less tangible information too: records of the child's enthusiasm, confidence, or kindness, for example. Learning stories can be included that provide real insight into a child's thoughts, feelings, and development. When adding selections of children's work to portfolios, teachers may wish to make a note on why it is significant. School-age children may be interested in contributing their own work and written comments to their portfolios; doing so will provide them with an opportunity to reflect on their own growth and development. The portfolio might also contain notes written by the families, memories, or samples of work completed at home. Educators may also want to consider a travelling portfolio that travels back and forth between home and school with children, families, and teachers adding material.

Gathering information for the portfolio on a regular basis facilitates conference preparation. A table of contents, perhaps organized by areas of development or subject area, with dates of entry should be part of each portfolio. Teachers can use plastic containers, large manila folders, expandable files, binders, or scrapbooks to organize the material. Another possibility is to create an elaborate box, decorating one side as each year passes, to store photographs, records of milestones, videos, artwork, audiotapes, and other relevant items. The centre might also consider hosting a portfolio party where creative portfolios are designed by the children and their families.

This section was contributed by Jane Cawley and Darlene Meecham of Centennial College.

One of the most beneficial aspects of the portfolio process is the rich family involvement. Through observations, work samples, photographs, and audio or video recordings, we are able to share with the family the many "missed and precious" moments on an ongoing and systematic basis. By opening the learning process to the family, we engage them in the life of the centre. This leads to increased trust and respect.

continued

Video portfolios offer families the opportunity to hear language, observe movement, and view the overall development of their own child and of others. They're a great teaching tool! Here are a few examples of how video portfolios touched the lives of our families:

- One of our families moved to Canada from China before their child was born. Many members of their family have never met the child. The father sent the video home, and the entire extended family spent many hours viewing the tape and sharing in her Canadian child-care experience.
- Another parent saved the video of her daughter to view together on Mother's Day. She told us that she cried with joy when she saw her child in action and that it was the best Mother's Day gift she had ever received.
- One mother used the video to help in her child's adjustment after leaving the centre. The child was missing her friends and teachers and they would play the tape every night and laugh as they remembered the happy days at the centre.
- We created a mini-portfolio for one of our new families. The child was experiencing separation anxiety, and the family was experiencing guilt and fear that their child would not adjust to a child-care situation. We put together a small photo album depicting the child's steady progression (from anxiously waiting at the door to onlooker play to parallel play) over a period of several weeks. This effort was greatly appreciated by the families.

Whatever method of portfolio implementation you decide to use, be assured that your parent–teacher relationships will benefit.

Source: Reprinted by permission of Darlene Meecham.

PREPARING THE WAITING AND CONFERENCE AREAS

The location of the meeting should be clearly posted, with multilingual signs provided as necessary. For many families, a conference will be a family affair so be prepared for extra seats to accommodate everyone who arrives. A waiting area should be set up, seating should be comfortable, and articles and handouts should be provided to help families pass the time. This area might include a display of the children's books that are being used in the playroom, a family bulletin board, and photographs of the children. A video of the children during outdoor play could be shown as families wait. Posting a list of appointments and checking names off as each conference is completed gives families a sense of their waiting time. Refreshments (coffee, tea, cookies made by the children) should also be provided.

The conference area itself should be neat and tidy, private, and inviting. Even a simple touch such as fresh flowers will do much to enhance the environment. Paper and writing utensils should be on hand so that families can take notes if they so choose. This may be a helpful strategy if one parent is not able to attend the meeting in order for the attending parent to share more accurately when they get home. To avoid creating a barrier between themselves and the family, teachers should refrain from sitting behind a desk; instead, a round table with adult-size chairs at which both family members and teachers can sit is ideal. Never ask an adult—particularly a very tall father—to sit on a playroom chair! Attention should be given to lighting, ventilation, and the temperature of the room. Of course, cell phones should be turned off during the conference.

SHOULD CHILDREN ATTEND THE CONFERENCE?

As a rule, conferences should not be attended by children who are too young to understand the process. Also, there are times when parents and teachers decide that it is in the best interest of the child not to be present. In some situations the child's presence may inhibit family members from openly discussing family issues. Decisions on children's involvement in conferences should be made on a case-by-case basis.

EARLY LEARNING ENVIRONMENTS AND SCHOOLS WORKING TOGETHER

Teachers in both the school and early learning settings should coordinate and conduct the family conference together when they are housed in the same location. Each teacher sees the child in a different environment, and each has information from his or her own perspective to contribute to the discussion. The child benefits; all the adults working with him or her are apprised of the goals and strategies for achieving them. We need to work toward a united front that blends the skills of the school and the early learning environment. Ongoing communication is critical to providing the best possible experience for the child and his or her family. All children benefit from this approach, but it is especially important for exceptional (special needs and gifted) children when consistency and skill development are critical.

THE ROLE OF THE SUPERVISOR

Though the supervisor may be on hand to greet family members as they arrive, her role in the family–teacher conference is, essentially, an organizational one. Many supervisors meet with staff to review procedures for gathering information on children and presenting it to family members. They also support and problem solve with staff as they prepare for the conference. Supervisors may, however, sit in on some conferences, contributing their expertise and observations. This may be particularly true when a conflict is anticipated.

GETTING STARTED

Consider how to greet the family in a culturally appropriate and welcoming manner. Many families would be pleased to be greeted in their first language: "*Ni Hao*" in Mandarin, "*Dobar Dan*" in Croatian,

or "*Namaste*" in Hindi for example. Some families would expect a very formal greeting, in other families, the father may be seen as the only acceptable individual to engage in a conversation with the teacher. It is up to the teacher to understand which greeting will make the families feel the most welcome.

Family members will bring a variety of attitudes to the conference itself. Some are eager to begin; others appear shy or uncomfortable, and still others will want to socialize first. Some parents may be reluctant to share their concerns because of cultural beliefs related to the authority of the teacher. Many parents would also be surprised to know that the teacher, especially a new teacher, may be as nervous as they are. Therefore, the first few minutes are critical for setting the tone for the conference. It is important for teachers to adjust their conference styles to accommodate individual family members. Parents are not looking for a cold, professional approach. Rather, teachers who develop a "personal touch" in their communication style achieve enhanced school relationships. Similarly, teachers need to convey a value for the "authority and wisdom" of parents (Lawrence-Lightfoot, 2004).

Before beginning, teachers may decide to take families on a tour of the playroom—an especially appropriate gesture for those who are new to the centre or who missed the orientation process. The teacher can explain the child's favourite learning centre and the skills learned there or favourite toys on this tour.

Teachers may want to begin by reviewing the agenda and then giving family members an opportunity to add items they would like to discuss. For some families, a brief explanation of the

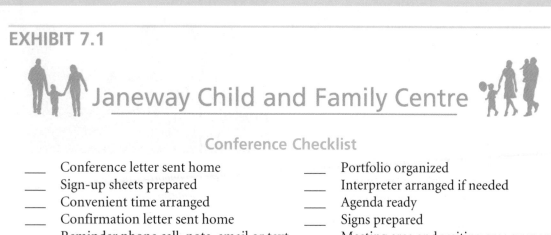

EXHIBIT 7.1

Janeway Child and Family Centre

Conference Checklist

____ Conference letter sent home
____ Sign-up sheets prepared
____ Convenient time arranged
____ Confirmation letter sent home
____ Reminder phone call, note, email or text issued right before the date
____ Child-care services organized, if required

____ Portfolio organized
____ Interpreter arranged if needed
____ Agenda ready
____ Signs prepared
____ Meeting area and waiting area prepared
____ Refreshments organized
____ Support material for families available

purpose and goals of the conference may be helpful. Beginning the conference with some positive comments about the child is a good way to acknowledge the enormous emotional investment that families have in their children.

Some teachers like to get the meeting off to a positive start by commenting on a successful parent–child interaction they have observed: "I've been wanting to tell you that I really admire the way you are so patient with Shanaz at the end of the day. It is such a hectic time and yet you take the time to listen to what he is saying about his day. I can see how proud you are of his accomplishments." Recounting a story that reveals a sensitive or caring moment is another positive way to begin: "Yesterday, one of the children fell on the playground and really hurt herself. Helleca raced over and by the time I got there she had the situation in hand. She was holding the child in her lap and rocking her back and forth. Her empathy and care for others is always evident." A videotape or DVD of the child is also a wonderful way to begin the meeting and can be used as a springboard for discussion. Every parent will be pleased to see their child in action in the playroom or learning in outdoors, especially for those who are not always able to participate or do drop-off and pick-up.

The teacher should stress the importance of families and teachers regularly sharing information. The teacher may then move to a discussion of the child's portfolio. Materials in the portfolio can be used to demonstrate the child's personal development, strengths, and learning goals. Families should be reassured by this demonstration that the teacher has a keen understanding of their child. A well-organized portfolio is a particularly useful tool for inexperienced teachers in that it provides the kind of structure that allows for an effective conference. The teacher should encourage family input into the discussion of the portfolio and it should be clear what goals are being established for the child; strategies for achieving these goals should be reviewed by the teacher and family members.

EFFECTIVE COMMUNICATION

In the busy world of an early childhood environment, it is often challenging to find the time to communicate effectively for many reasons.

> Styles of communication are influenced by individual personality and temperament as well as the rules of talking that people learn in family and culture.... [P]ersonal temperament affects

your communication style. Whether you are an introvert or an extrovert, slow-to-warm or quick-to-warm, flexible or structured will affect your communication strategies and the communication style you develop with different family members in your program. (Keyser, 2006: 35)*

When presenting verbal messages, teachers need to observe the different ways people take in information through sensory modes. A teacher who learns to communicate using words that reflect the way the parent views and interacts with the world should have a better chance of enlisting the parent's cooperation.

As Studer (1993–94: 76) observes, "Teachers need to adjust the conference dynamics to the perceptual modes of their audience. A visual learner wants to see examples, an auditory learner wants to hear examples, and a kinesthetic learner wants to handle materials." Voice tone is a critical element in effective communication. Your tone of voice can convey a wealth of information, ranging from enthusiasm to disinterest to anger. If your tone conveys an undercurrent of anger or frustration, sounds distracted or preoccupied, or is heavy with sarcasm, it will influence how others hear what you are saying and how they interpret your message.

To be effective communicators, teachers must also put their observation skills to work. Family members may be too embarrassed or afraid to say what they are really thinking or feeling. Teachers must look for clues, beyond verbal messages to nonverbal indicators that a parent is becoming upset, restless, or confused, or doesn't understand what has been said. Reflect as well on the impact

Conferences are opportunities to exchange and share important information.

---

* From *Parents to Partners: Building a Family-Centered Early Childhood Program* by Janis Keyser. Copyright © 2006 by Janis Keyser. Reprinted with permission of Redleaf Press, St. Paul, MN; www.redleafpress.org.

Sometimes I have used my own personal experience to help a parent feel more comfortable. I had one parent who broke down in the middle of a conference. As a single mother, she was overwhelmed with the responsibilities of raising her son on her own, and her financial situation was a growing concern. I shared with her my own struggles as a single mother. My ability to reveal my own challenges strengthened our relationship. We had something in common beyond our parent–teacher relationship and I was able to share with her some of the community resources that had helped me.

of culture in interactions between teachers and families; for example, the mother may defer to the father in these discussions.

Effective listening is another critical component of a teacher's communication style. If family members leave feeling that they did not receive an opportunity to discuss their concerns, they may be reluctant to attend another conference. There are times when just being able to talk to a sympathetic teacher who is a good listener helps a family member to resolve his or her problems. Active listening ensures that teachers are connected to both the content and the emotions expressed and demonstrate respect for the family.

As a rule, teachers should be conscious of talking only 50 percent of the time (Hepworth Berger, 2000: 223). They should refrain from changing the topic when family members are speaking, and they should be wary of overwhelming families with too much information. Teachers will have to trust their instincts and be sensitive to families' needs when determining how much information to present at a conference. Teachers should not feel that they need to fill any silences that may occur during the conference. These may in fact be opportunities for a family member to take the lead in the discussion or to reflect on what has been said. There are times when it is important to give up the prepared agenda and just listen to what families are saying. You can demonstrate that you are truly listening by demonstrating attentive behaviours while remaining silent.

QUESTIONING STRATEGIES

The types of questions that teachers ask and how those questions are phrased may either facilitate or undermine communication with family members. Open-ended questions allow families to contribute as much as they feel comfortable doing. The following statements and questions could be used to draw reluctant or hesitant parents into the conversation:

- I've had so much to share with you and now I would really like to get some feedback from you.

- What do you think Sari's feelings are about the preschool room?

- What activities does Sari enjoy at the centre? Are there activities that she doesn't enjoy?

- I've talked about Sari at the centre, but I would like to hear what you hope Sari will enjoy doing here with us.

- What types of responsibilities does Sari have at home?

- How do you feel about your involvement with the centre?

- How can I be more supportive of you and your family?

If a family member makes a statement that indicates concern, the teacher might paraphrase the statement and ask for clarification: "You say that you are having trouble getting Sari to sleep. Could you tell me more about how she reacts when you put her down?" Family members who seem anxious that their parenting skills will be criticized may respond to promptings such as, "Many toddler parents are concerned about behaviour issues, so I wonder how you might be feeling about Sari's interactions at home or at the centre."

SOURCES OF CONFLICT

The Ontario English Catholic Teachers Association's publication *Positive Professional Parent Teacher*

Relationships (n.d.) provides guidelines in six main categories for handling conflict with a parent:

1. *Resources:* Conflicts may occur when resources are limited. A parent of a child with special needs may not understand the lack of resources caused by inadequate government funding. A parent may not understand the teacher's decision over the allocation of scare resources in the classroom. Conflict over the distribution of resources can take many forms—the need for power, the need for recognition, jurisdiction of authority, and assertion of self-esteem.

2. *Psychological Needs:* When psychological factors such as self-esteem, feelings of belonging, or happiness are threatened, people can sometimes become aggressive. A parent who thinks that he or she has been belittled by a teacher or who believes the child has been picked on may lash out.

3. *Values:* People may feel personally attacked if they think their values are threatened. It is not usually the difference in values but the fear that one set of values is dominating. These conflicts can be difficult to resolve.

4. *Divergent Goals:* Conflict may result when a teacher and a parent have completely different goals. A teacher who stresses drama, for example, may come into conflict with a parent who values math and science above all.

5. *Incongruent Role Expectations and Behaviour Norms:* A parent who encourages a child to challenge authority figures may not accept the teacher's discipline of the child for "insubordination."

6. *Incompatible Personalities:* Sometimes conflicts are caused by personality differences.

DEALING WITH DIFFICULT SITUATIONS

No matter how well a person does in his or her job, there are always times when one will have to deal with a difficult situation. Adler et al. (2012: 316) state,

> For many people, the inevitability of conflict is a depressing fact. They think that the existence of ongoing conflict means that there is little chance for happy relationships with others. Effective communicators know differently. They realize that although it's impossible to eliminate conflict, there are ways to manage it effectively. The skilful management of conflict can open the door to healthier, stronger, and more satisfying relationships.*

At times it is our lack of understanding of the cultural context of a situation that may be a cause for concern. Collectivist cultures value cooperation and interdependent relationships and are, at times, in conflict with an individualist culture where independence and competition is valued. For example,

> Andrea and Neil brought their newborn, Alyssa, into their bed at night. They all slept comfortably and Andrea was able to breastfeed easily during the night. Sleeping together even made them feel closer as a family. But their friends, their paediatrician, and their family all warned them to get her into her own bed quickly or she would be spoiled. They were very torn between what felt right and what their culture told them was right. (Wittmer and Peterson, 2006:36)

At the centre, if Alyssa is put to sleep in a sleep room far away from caregivers and other children, she may have a very difficult time during this transition. Andrea and Neil may be shocked to find the babies in a dark room, confined in a crib with no human contact. They may think it unduly harsh to expect preschool children to lie by themselves on a cot a few feet from other children and not be allowed to touch them. Co-sleeping is the norm in many cultures and bedtime and night wakings are not considered a problem.

Meredith Small (1999) writes in *Our Babies, Ourselves* that human contact during sleep assists infants in regulating their body temperature, breathing, and heart rate. Mothers' and infants' sleep cycles are synchronized with each other. SIDS is almost nonexistent in cultures where co-sleeping is commonly practised and breast feeding is certainly more convenient. Children who sleep with someone are less likely to need "transitional items" such as a special blanket or stuffed animal. In families where close contact is more important than early independence, co-sleeping fits. In this situation, to understand cultural differences, teachers and families must communicate with each other. We need to avoid either/or choices and explore how two seemingly opposing views can both be right. "Teachers must be open to diversity and dedicated to respecting all perspectives while

---

*From Adler, Ronald, et al., *Interplay: The Process of Interpersonal Communication* 3/Ce © Oxford University Press Canada 2012. Reprinted by permission of the publisher.

still considering what is in the child's best interests. We need to be creative at finding common ground in order to work in harmony and understanding with all cultures" (Gonzalez-Mena and Bhavnagri, 2001: 91).

THE SANDWICH APPROACH

Many teachers know the value of beginning in a positive manner, celebrating the strengths of the child, dealing with the difficult issue, and then ending again on a positive note—the sandwich approach! When bringing up issues that may be difficult for families to hear, teachers must employ tact and sensitivity. Avoid language that lays blame or judgment or that labels the parent or child. Avoid words such as *behind* or *ahead*, *fast* or *slow*, *normal* or *abnormal*, and words that may trigger feelings of anxiety on the part of parents. Many difficult situations can be handled successfully if the teacher listens and is prepared to help. It is important for the teacher to demonstrate a positive attitude toward accomplishing a goal. Breaking the challenge into manageable parts is often the best strategy for success. Difficult issues should not be sprung unexpectedly on family members or left to the final minutes of the conference. Take care in presenting information so that the message is delivered with tact and sensitivity.

BEHAVIOUR ISSUES

Families are often concerned about behavioural issues. As the following example illustrates, being informed by a teacher that certain behaviours are normal for a particular age group can have a reassuring effect.

Jacob's mother was very worried when she asked the teacher if Jacob was causing trouble at the centre. She was worried about his temper and his inability to listen when spoken to. This active 2-year-old was an engaging child, and after recounting his many positive attributes, the teacher reassured his mother that 2-year-olds often respond this way. At times they are overwhelmed with the many pressure of growing up, are frustrated and haven't the vocabulary to express how they feel. The mother left the conference much relieved and with a growing affection for the teacher.

But no doubt there will be situations that cannot be negotiated between the teacher and the parents, for example, corporal punishment. We need to help parents understand the negative impact of physical coercion and emphasize that it is not allowed under child-care regulations.

BEING PROFESSIONAL UNDER PRESSURE

When families and teachers trust each other, often small annoyances can be overlooked, but we must always remember that very strong emotions will often rise to the surface when families are discussing their children. Professional assertiveness is important when addressing a difficult situation. A parent who becomes angry may be acting out of fear of being misunderstood or not being heard. For some parents, their life situation colours all of their interactions; illness, divorce, change in employment, or financial issues may be causing pressure that makes family life difficult. If the parent is raising honest concerns, it is the teacher's responsibility to address the concern, and it is in the teacher's best interests to respond in a professional, calm manner. Don't try to avoid the problem; if one parent is expressing a concern, the chances are that other parents may also have the same issue. "When confronted by an angry parent, teachers can mask their own nervousness by lowering their voices, moving closer to the parent, and looking the parent straight in the eye" (Whitaker and Fiore, 2001). Gestwicki (2004: 586) advises that "as a conversation proceeds, teachers must be careful that any disagreeing statements concern facts and issues, not personalities. In discussing different viewpoints, participants should use descriptive statements, not evaluative ones. It is easier to deal with descriptions, rather than labels."*

At the same time, teachers should never have to tolerate rudeness, threats, or abuse. Terminate the conference if the parent continues to be intimidating in any way and make an attempt to reschedule the meeting when everyone is calmer. A teacher should never meet on his or her own with a parent who has demonstrated these behaviours in the past; the centre supervisor should attend all future meetings. Teachers should record notes on this interaction in case further follow-up is needed.

At all costs, teachers must avoid discussing other children in the centre. Teachers have a professional responsibility to protect the privacy of the other children and their families. The following is an account of how one teacher handled a parent's attempt to breach that privacy:

---

*From GESTWICKI, *Home, School, and Community Relations*, 7E. © 2010 Cengage Learning. Reproduced by permission. www.cengage.com/permissions.

Katherine's mother was very angry that her daughter had been bitten several times last week in the toddler room. During the conference she insisted that we reveal the name of the child who had bitten her. She planned to have all the other parents sign a petition asking for the removal of the child from the centre and then present the petition to the supervisor. We told her that it was our policy not to reveal the names of children in biting incidents. We then discussed at length the factors that contribute to this behaviour in toddler rooms. Finally, we outlined how we intended to monitor the situation and gave her some articles on biting to take home to read.

An explosive situation can often be defused if the teacher accepts responsibility for an inappropriate action:

As Jane's mother, Sara, arrived at our parent–teacher conference, she noticed that the tips of her daughter's ears were bright pink. I had neglected to put sunscreen on her ears when we went to the park, and her baseball cap had not fully covered her ears. Sara was furious. She approached me in an aggressive manner and shouted at me in front of the children. As I tried to manoeuvre her out of earshot of the children, her eyes filled with tears and she became even more agitated. I waited until she had an opportunity to vent all her feelings and then immediately apologized for my error.

The moment I accepted responsibility for my actions, Sara calmed down. I told her I would place a sign at the exit to remind me to do one final check to make sure that all the children were wearing sunscreen. I was very tempted to tell her that I had many children to care for and that one child had been sick as we were preparing to leave that afternoon, but I made a real effort not to be defensive and to see things from her point of view. It was only after further discussion that I fully understood Sara's concern. Last summer, Jane's older brother had been hospitalized with a serious case of sun poisoning.

When teachers have done something that is inappropriate or a mistake has been made, it is best to contact the parents first. By contacting the parents as soon as possible, much of their anger can be diverted. Apologizing is the single best neutralizer. We will all make mistakes but taking ownership for our errors, apologizing, and having a clear plan of action to prevent a repeat of the error, rather than becoming defensive and denying we did anything wrong, will go a long way to establishing more trusting relationships.

In the following example, the teacher responded to a parent's criticism by being informative rather than defensive:

Manjit's mother was concerned that all we did at the centre was play. She felt that Manjit would not be properly prepared for school. I decided that the best way to explain how play is an integral part of an early childhood education program was to take her on a walking tour of the playroom. I went through each of the learning centres and explained the skills and knowledge that Manjit was acquiring. His mother came away from the conference with a whole new understanding of our program. It is important to help families understand that learning is not a race to reach milestones ahead of everyone else. Children do not benefit from being pushed or overwhelmed by experiences that are not age appropriate. This interaction with this parent made me realize that other parents may have been feeling the same way. I decided that I would create a poster for each of the centres in the room, outlining the skills that the children would be learning through a play-based approach.

One idea to support families' understanding of the many ways in which the environment impacts on children's learning would be to post a list of skills explored in each of the learning centres around the room and in the outdoor environment. See Block Centre poster on the next page for how this might look.

Teaching partners should be careful not to be drawn into a discussion that pits them against one another. It is usually best if the teacher who has the strongest relationship with the family leads the discussion:

When we held our conference with Eugene's mother and father, I was hoping that it would give me an opportunity to strengthen my relationship with them. I felt that Eugene's mother was having a great deal of difficulty accepting me, since I was replacing a teacher in the centre with whom she had been very close. During the conference, I allowed my teaching partner, Patricia, to lead the discussion because the family seemed more comfortable with her. I tried to contribute in a positive manner where appropriate. At the end of the conference, Eugene's mother remarked that Eugene seemed to be adjusting to a new teacher much more easily than she was. I acknowledged her feelings and was pleased that she was able to talk openly about the issue. We are now making real progress in building a more positive relationship.

Criticizing teachers in front of a child who is present during the conference is very confusing for him or her. Even very young children notice negative emotions being expressed. Children often attribute heroic characteristics to their teachers, believing that they actually live at the school! The

Janeway Child and Family Centre

In the Block Centre, I'm learning:

Physical—eye-hand coordination, spatial awareness, gross and fine motor development, visual perception, sensory exploration, hand strength, improved dexterity

Social/Emotional—planning, demonstrating initiative, building on ideas, negotiation, cooperation, sharing, turn taking, respect for others, imagination, confidence, self-esteem

Cognitive—observation, problem solving, experimentation, divergent thinking, logical reasoning, estimating, classification, directionality, order, sequencing, size, shape recognition, patterning, grouping, one-to-one correspondence, matching, sorting, seriation, balance, cause and effect, symmetry, height, weight, gravity, geometry, area, measurement, colours, order, counting, object permanence

Courtesy of Lynn Wilson

Language—labelling, describing and recalling, storytelling, vocabulary development, making signs, recording stories, asking questions, representation, sociodramatic play, reference books

---

child may be confused and uncomfortable about his or her loyalties to both family members and the teacher. Criticizing the teacher in front of the child does not solve the underlying conflict and, in older children, it may result in aggressive and defiant behaviour toward the teacher. As parents discuss issues with their children, they are modelling ways to express problems and frustrations in everyday life. How well are both parties—parents and educators—modelling life skills for the child? A teacher who begins to feel threatened or intimidated during a conference should involve the supervisor or another teacher right away.

A more formal, signed agreement may help parents realize that they also have a parent code of conduct that is expected. Campbell (n.d.) suggests,

> We know how rushed your life is, and how many responsibilities you have. There will be times when you are very frustrated. When you speak to our

staff, remember that other children are present. We cannot allow the children to hear any angry words from parents. This includes the way you speak to your own child in this centre. Children are hurt and frightened by an angry adult. Our responsibility is to protect all the children in our care. We know that you will understand.[*]

Family members may be concerned about administrative or policy matters. On such occasions it is advisable to have the supervisor sit in on the conference:

> Mala's father became visibly upset when he began to talk about the late-fee bill he had just received from the centre. To defuse the situation, I asked our supervisor to join us. She did a great job of outlining the need for the late fee. I honestly believe that he left the conference with a better

---

[*]Reprinted by permission of Patricia Campbell

understanding of the issue. During the conferences it was really reassuring to know that I could call on the supervisor if a situation got out of hand.

There may be times when, despite the efforts of all the participants, it becomes clear that the centre and the family are not a good match. In such situations the centre should do all it can to support the family in exploring alternative care situations.

HELPING PARENTS FIND THEIR STRENGTHS

Some families say that everything at home is "fine." This response can really shut the communication door. It may often be a reflection of a parent's overloaded life, and an acknowledgment of difficulty means one more thing to worry about. A strategy for the teacher may be to mention a few examples that demonstrate situations where the child is having difficulty and then ask, "When this happens at home, what do you do?" Often this lead-in provides an opening for real communication. We need to constantly remember that parents will respond from their heart and are most vulnerable when issues related to their child emerge. Their response may not be what the teacher might expect—they can respond with anger, frustration, withdrawal, and tears. However, the family must know that we have their child's best interests at heart above all and we are anxious to work together to resolve any issue that may arise.

AVOID GIVING ADVICE

It is important that educators be cautious about providing advice, especially unsolicited advice. When parents discuss problems with us, they are not necessarily asking for us to solve their issue:

A teacher is likely not to know the full complexity of the situation and may give inappropriate suggestions. Giving advice tends to distance a teacher from the parent. Parents might quietly listen to this advice while inwardly fuming: "Who does he

think he is? A lot he knows about it anyway—this is my child, not his." Giving advice may usurp the parent's right to decide and may also detract from parents' feelings of competence and self-worth. Giving advice may also be dangerous; when the "expert" suggestions don't work, the expert get the blame and future mistrust. A more effective teacher role may be to help parents move through several steps in problem solving and discovering options that they may follow—"some of the things we've tried in the classroom for that are ...," "let me pass along some ideas that have worked for other parents ...," "do any of these sound like something that could work for you?" (Gestwicki, 2010: 372)[*]

Helping parents lead with their strengths may also be an effective strategy in supporting them when dealing with challenging situations. Ask parents to describe a time when they felt really successful in dealing with their child and help parents look for opportunities to apply it to a different challenge. Our goal is to enable and empower families to make informed decisions themselves.

In other situations, families may find it difficult to express what they are trying to say. If the silence becomes prolonged, teachers can reassure family members by stating that they understand that it is sometimes difficult to put their feelings into words. Simply by acknowledging this, a teacher may help family members feel more comfortable and allow them to proceed.

As the following suggests, openly admitting one's lack of knowledge of a subject is not only honest but also can also bring positive results.

During the conference one of the parents expressed an interest in Kwanza [an African-American cultural festival celebrated annually in late December]. In our most recent newsletter we announced that we would be celebrating Kwanza

*From GESTWICKI, *Home, School, and Community Relations, 7E.* © 2010 Cengage Learning. Reproduced by permission. www.cengage.com/permissions.

Inside LOOK

Grimalda was two days away from going to the hospital to have her tonsils out. During a dramatic-play discussion, she expressed her fears about going in for surgery. She wanted to know whether she could take her teddy bear with her. I shared this with her parents. Soon after, Grimalda was much relieved to know that her favourite stuffed animal would accompany her through the surgery.

in our playroom. This was a new area for me, however, and the parent asked me for more details than I was able to provide. I told her that I was in the midst of my research and would get back to her with the information she had requested. I also invited her to an upcoming circle time at which a family that celebrates Kwanza was going to speak to the children.

There are many topics which arise during a family-teacher conference. The books listed below often reflect these issues:

BOOKS FOR CHILDREN

The Anti-Bullying and Teasing Books for Preschool Classrooms, by B. Sprung, B. Hinitz, and M. Froschl

The Ant Bully, by J. Nickle

The Bully Blockers Club, by T. Bateman

Chester Raccoon and the Big Bad Bully, by A. Penn

Enemy Pie, by D. Munson

Henry and the Bully, by N. Carlson

Andrew's Angry Words, by D. Lachner

Every Time I Blow My Top I Lose My Head, by L. Shapiro and L. Slap-Shelton

Angry Octopus: A Relaxation Story, by L. Lite

Cool Down and Walk Through Anger, by C. Meiners

Hands Are Not For Hitting, by M. Agassi

Hot Stuff to Help Kids Chill Out: The Anger Management Book, by J. Wilde

How to Take the GRRRR Out of Anger, by E. Verdick and M. Lisovskis

I Was So Mad!, by N. Simon

I'm Mad, by E. Crary and J. Whitney

Mad Isn't Bad: A Child's Book about Anger, by M. Mundy

The Penguin Who Lost Her Cool: A Story about Controlling Your Anger, by M. Sobel

The Very Angry Day That Amy Didn't Have, by L. Shapiro

When I Feel Angry, by C. Maude Spelman

When Sophie Gets Angry—Really, Really Angry, by M. Bang

When You're Mad and You Know It, by E. Crary and S. Steelsmith

BOOKS FOR ADULTS

The ABCs of Bullying Prevention: A Comprehensive School-wide Approach, by K. Shore

The Bully, the Bullied, and the Bystander: From Preschool to High School, 2nd ed., by B. Coloroso

Cyberbullying and Cyberthreats: Responding to the Challenge of Online Social Aggression, Threats, and Distress, by N. Willard

Sidestepping the Power Struggle: A Manual for Effective Parenting, by A. Miller and A. Rees

Raise Your Kids without Raising Your Voice: Over 50 Solutions to Everyday Parenting Challenges, by S. Chana

How to Listen So Parents Will Talk and Talk So Parents Will Listen, by J. Sommers-Flanagan and R. Sommers-Flanagan

Time-In Parenting, by O. Weininger

The Incredible Years: A Trouble-Shooting Guide for Parents of Children Aged 3–8, by C. Webster-Stratton

Kids Are Worth It!: Giving Your Child the Gift of Inner Discipline, by B. Coloroso

Pathways to Competence for Young Children: A Parenting Program (Book and CD-ROM), by S. Landy and E. Thompson

The No Cry Discipline Solution: Gentle Ways to Encourage Good Behaviour without Whining, Tantrums and Tears, by E. Pantley

What Am I Feeling?, by J. Gottman and the Talaris Research

Positive Discipline A–Z: 1001 Solutions to Everyday Parenting Problems, by J. Nelsen, L. Lott, and H. Stephen

Positive Discipline: The First Three Years, by J. Nelsen, C. Erwin, and R.A. Duffy

The Everything Parent's Guide to Tantrums, by J. Levine

Please Don't Sit On the Kids: Alternatives to Punitive Discipline, 2nd ed., by C. Cherry

CHILDREN WITH SPECIAL NEEDS

Every teacher is at some point faced with telling a family that she has concerns about their child's development. Early identification of children with special needs is often critical, and educators—as individuals who observe children across time and in a variety of situations—can play an important role in initiating this procedure. "Unfortunately, we sometimes do not refer young children because of the fear of 'labelling' or 'mislabelling' or because we hope the child will 'outgrow' the problem. In too many cases, we do the child and the family no good by not recognizing and acting on a problem" (Abbott and Gold, 1991: 13).

However difficult it may be to break the news to families, teachers have a professional responsibility to share with them the information they will need to be able to support their child. The child's best interest must always be paramount. It is always difficult when telling the truth may cause pain for the family and we must deliver this information with as much sensitivity as we can muster. The information must also be communicated in language that the parents will understand. Assure the parents that if at any time they do not understand, they should not hesitate to ask the teacher to stop so they can ask questions to clarify.

When informing families, teachers need to recognize that during the conference, family members may panic or show signs of anxiety, grief, or depression. These are all common and understandable reactions for parents with children who demonstrate developmental delays. Parents may also respond with anger or denial; they may even blame the teacher or the centre for the child's situation. Abbott and Gold's (1991: 13) advice to the teacher is to "be an active listener and allow them to express their feelings. Be prepared to listen to expressions of anger and sadness. Family members may also blame each other. Try to focus them on the problem." Our role as teachers is to help parents problem solve by sharing our knowledge and experience but we need to have reasonable expectations regarding how and when issues may be resolved. If the relationship between the family and the teacher is strong, the parents may be more willing to accept the information even when the news is difficult.

Inside LOOK

When [Jonah] was four years old, in his second preschool year, other parents started hinting around ... and recommending books and so on. I started getting kind of panicky about what I was doing wrong as a parent, and started to read and find out everything I could about parenting things. Then, out of the blue, one of the preschool teachers said, "I'm giving up on Jonah. I've tried everything I know how to do and nothing works." She had said nothing to me up to that point to indicate she was at her wit's end or needed help with him. So I just burst into tears at this interview. I didn't know how seriously to take what she was saying about Jonah.

On the other hand, I sort of did think [subconsciously] there was something probably wrong with him.... I wish that they [had said] something like "Here's what you can expect of a typical three-year-old or a typical four-year-old. Here are the kinds of behaviours that they all show sometimes, and this is how they should be progressing by the time they've been in preschool for a year or so. Now, there's variation, sure, but that's just a yardstick of normal sorts of behaviour." And I also wish that at parent–teacher conferences or informal chats somebody had said, because obviously they're experienced, "I've been in the business for 15 years. I've seen hundreds of kids come my way and your child is on an extreme end of these sorts of behaviours. I'm not someone who could put a diagnosis on it, but I think this is something that you might want to consider looking at." I felt that there [was] too much of this tiptoeing around, instead of saying what they [saw as] the real difference between my son and other kids.

Source: *SpecialLink*. 1994. 5 (1). October. p. 4. Reprinted by permission of SpecialLink.

I have met parents who have struggled with children who were troubled even as toddlers. After years of hearing about one problem after another, these parents are beaten. They have heard teachers criticize and share their own frustrations with their child. Some teachers may have told them what they should be doing at home to fix the problems. Whether or not they are parents in trouble or the parents of troubled children, these parents need teachers to understand and help. I have watched tension drain from the faces of parents when teachers, instead of showing detachment or criticism, have said, "This must be hard for you. What could be done here at school that would help?" The parents may not know what would help, but they will appreciate a sincere offer. Moreover, there are things that teachers actually can do. They can use the information they have about child and parent development to provide information—when asked. They should be familiar with community resources and know how to access them.

Source: Reprinted with permission of Corwin Press, from G. Rudney, 2005. *Every Teachers Guide To Working With Parents*; permission conveyed through Copyright Clearance Center, Inc.

BOOKS FOR ADULTS

Conducting Effective Conferences with Parents of Children with Disabilities: A Guide for Teachers, by Milton Seligman

WRAPPING UP THE CONFERENCE

Before thanking the family for attending the conference, the teacher can spend a few minutes summarizing the main points to have emerged from the conference; if an action plan is necessary, it should be clear to everyone. Families should also know how and when they can contact the teacher whenever the need arises. Are there specific times when this is more convenient or is communication more open-ended? This is also a good time for the teacher to pass along resources (articles, books, support agency information, and so on) that pertain to issues discussed during the conference and to schedule another conference, if required. Above all, the conference should end on a positive note. This is also a good opportunity to thank families for any contributions they have made to the centre. It is important to personally acknowledge these efforts. Presenting families with a folder of items featuring the child's accomplishments is a wonderful way to conclude the conference. Before the family leaves, the teacher might ask them to leave a note for the child, who will see it the next day.

This teacher is sending home a collection photos of this family's child

Courtesy of Richmond Adelaide Child Care Centre

FOLLOW-UP AND EVALUATION

As soon as the conference is over, the teacher should quickly make notes before the next family arrives. Later, when there is more time to reflect, the teacher can organize this information more formally. It is important that the teacher not take notes during the conference itself, since doing so may be intimidating to some family members. Families might be provided with a written summary of conference highlights; this would be particularly helpful if only one parent was able to attend. A sample format for a conference summary is provided in Exhibit 7.2.

Janeway Child and Family Centre

Family–Teacher Conference Summary

Child's name:_____ Age group: _____

Teacher(s) conducting the conference: _____

Parent's/Parents' name(s): _____

Date of conference: _____

Topics discussed	Action to be taken	Time line

General comments: _____

_____

If the teacher promises during the conference to gather information for families, it is imperative that this be done as soon as possible. When evaluating the conference, teachers should focus particular attention on their own role and how their performance might be improved at future conferences. A sample teacher self-evaluation is provided in Exhibit 7.3. Some families, despite their best efforts, are unable to attend a conference. In these situations when the resources are available, a video conference might be organized using Skype or Google Voice or a home visit scheduled instead.

Sending home a handwritten note after the conference, thanking families for participating, is also not only a nice gesture but also another opportunity to connect with families.

Families should be encouraged to schedule a conference any time that they feel it is necessary. We should welcome an opportunity to provide additional information or allay any concerns as soon as they arise.

Janeway Child and Family Centre

Family–Teacher Conference: Teacher Self-Review

YES	NO	SOMEWHAT	
___	___	___	Did I check to make sure I knew all of the family members' first and last names?
___	___	___	Did I review my files before the interview began?
___	___	___	Did I help the family feel comfortable when they arrived?

___	___	___	Did I greet the family in a culturally appropriate manner?
___	___	___	Was my portfolio complete and reflective of the child?
___	___	___	Did I have the necessary documentation, and was I able to validate my comments with specific examples and materials?
___	___	___	Did I demonstrate that I valued what the family had to offer as the child's first teachers and not consider myself the expert on their child?
___	___	___	Was I able to adapt to the individual family members' level of language use?
___	___	___	Did I demonstrate that I was genuinely interested in what the family had to say by listening attentively and using respectful language?
___	___	___	Was I aware of my own body language throughout the conference as well as that of the family?
___	___	___	Was I mindful in the moment—not fidgeting, not distracted?
___	___	___	Was I open to learning about the child and his or her family?
___	___	___	Did I avoid any judgments in my interactions?
___	___	___	Did I learn anything that will allow me to better support the child?
___	___	___	Was I able to balance my need to have information about the child with respect for the family's privacy?
___	___	___	Did I use open-ended questions that allowed family members to voice their concerns?
___	___	___	Did I give family members an opportunity to talk freely without interruption; was I patient?
___	___	___	Did I listen as much as I talked?
___	___	___	Did I allow the family to express their dissatisfaction with the centre or with my own performance?
___	___	___	Were we able to problem solve together and set positive, measurable goals for the child?
___	___	___	Was a timeline established, if required?
___	___	___	Did I avoid discussing other families or children?
___	___	___	Did I summarize the conference effectively in the last five minutes?
___	___	___	Did I use this conference as an opportunity to explain to the family how they could become more involved in the centre?
___	___	___	Did I acknowledge that not all families may be able to participate in "traditional" ways?
___	___	___	Did I begin and end the conference on positive notes, and was I free with praise?
___	___	___	Was I aware of the timing and pace, and did I begin and end on time?
___	___	___	Did I remember not to use ECE jargon?
___	___	___	Is a partnership developing with this family?
___	___	___	If I promised further feedback or resources, did I follow through in a timely fashion?
___	___	___	Overall, do I think the family felt the conference was productive?
___	___	___	Overall, do I think the meeting was productive?

REFERENCES

Abbott, C.F., and S. Gold. 1991. "Conferring with Parents When You're Concerned That Their Child Needs Special Services." *Young Children*. May.

Adler, R.B., L.B. Rosenfeld, R.F. Proctor II, and C. Winder. 2012. *Interplay: The Process of Interpersonal Communication*, 3rd Canadian ed. New York: Oxford University Press.

Cameron, L. 2012." Ask an Expert: Improving Parent-Teacher Interviews." Retrieved January 31, 2012, from http://www.canadianliving.com/moms/parenting/ask _an_expert_improving_parent_teacher_interviews.php

Campbell, P. n.d. Personal communication.

Gestwicki, C. 2004. *Home, School, and Community Relations*, 5th ed. New York: Thomson Delmar Learning.

———. 2010. *Home, School and Community*, 7th ed. Wadsworth Cengage Learning.

Gonzalez-Mena, J. 2008. *50 Early Childhood Strategies for Working and Communicating with Diverse Families*. Upper Saddle River, NJ: Pearson Prentice Hall.

Gonzalez-Mena, J., and N.P. Bhavnagri. 2001. "Helping ECE Professionals Understand Cultural Differences in Sleeping Practices." *Child Care Information Exchange* 138 (March/April): 91–93.

Hepworth Berger, E. 2000. *Parents as Partners in Education*, 5th ed. Upper Saddle River, NJ: Prentice Hall.

Keyser, J. 2006. *From Parents to Partners: Building a Family-Centered Early Childhood Program*. St. Paul, MN: Redleaf Press.

Lawrence-Lightfoot, S. 2003. *The Essential Conversation: What Parents and Teachers Can Learn from Each Other*. Random House

———. 2004. "Building Bridges from School to Home." *Instructor*, 114(1), 24–28.

Martin, S. 2007. *Take a Look: Observation and Portfolio Assessment in Early Childhood*, 4th ed. Don Mills, ON: Addison-Wesley.

Meisels, S.J. 1993. "Remaking Classroom Assessment with the Work Sampling System." *Young Children*. July.

Ontario English Catholic Teachers Association. n.d. *Positive Professional Parent Teacher Relationships*. Toronto: OECTA.

Rudney, G. 2005. *Every Teacher's Guide to Working with Parents*. Corwin Press.

Small, M. 1999. *Our Babies, Ourselves: How Biology and Culture Shape the Way We Parent*. Anchor.

SpecialLink. 1994. "A Matter of Urgency: Including Children With Special Needs in Child Care in Canada." 5 (1). October.

Studer, J.R. 1993–94. "Listen So That Parents Will Speak." *Childhood Education*. Winter.

Whitaker, T., and D.J. Fiore. 2001. *Dealing with Difficult Parents and with Parents in Difficult Situations*. Larchmont, NY: Eye on Education.

Wittmer, D., and S. Petersen. 2006. *Infant and Toddler Development and Responsive Program Planning: A Relationship-Based Approach*. Upper Saddle River, NJ: Pearson Merrill Prentice Hall.

Created by Ryan

Chapter

8

STAYING CONNECTED

Courtesy of Lynn Wilson

"I never see what has been done; I only see what remains to be done."

—Buddha

LEARNING OUTCOMES

After studying this chapter, you will be able to

1. outline the benefits of effective written communication and its role in developing positive relationships with families

2. describe the kinds of written communication used at the outset of the family–centre partnership

3. discuss the purpose, design, and thematic components of the family handbook

4. discuss the playroom handbook as an extension of the family handbook

5. outline the primary forms of ongoing written communication, from menus to bulletin boards

6. describe how a family resource area might be organized and what items it might contain

7. identify some of the implications of new technologies for the field of early childhood education

THE BENEFITS OF WRITTEN COMMUNICATION

For families who are on tight schedules that don't allow for discussion at either end of the day, or for those who have not as yet built trusting relationships with educators, written material may be an effective way for the centre to communicate. In some two-parent families, only one parent is responsible for pick-up and drop-off duties; it is important to send home information for the rarely seen parent. This also applies when two parents may have joint custody of their child and only one parent visits the centre. In some school-age programs, an older child may pick up the younger family member so parents may rarely visit the centre.

When families first come to the early learning environment, they find out much about the history, organization, and objectives of the program through written materials such as the family handbook and newsletters; written material also is an effective way to continue to keep families informed about the centre, upcoming events, and curriculum issues. It is important to note that this type of communication is a one-way vehicle. More effective is a two-way form of communication that allows families to engage in a written exchange with the educator. This chapter outlines various types of communication, along with strategies for making all forms of communication as effective as possible.

- Create a folder for each child in which all forms of written communication are stored. This might be in the cubby or on a bulletin board, but it should be somewhere families that always know to look for information related to their child and the centre.

- When notes are sent home asking for permission—for example, for a field trip—teachers may want to create a checklist of the children's names, post it in a visible location, and attach it to a file large enough to hold the returning notes. As each family returns their form, the child's name is checked. This way, teachers can keep track at a glance of families who may need a gentle reminder.

- Be careful when a face–to-face meeting would be a more appropriate alternative to a written note. When difficult situations must be addressed, although it may be easier for the teacher to send a note home to avoid conflict, this does little to resolve the issue and, in fact, may make things worse.

It is important for educators to have some sense of how a letter home may be received. For example, a letter asking families to come to a special luncheon may have many different responses. Some parents may quickly take out their iPhones and record the date and time, and put the money requested in an envelope to be returned the next day. In other homes, where English is not the first language there may be difficulty in understanding more than the fact that the teacher wants money and that will mean funds taken out of the food budget for the week. For another family an event during the day means that they would have to take time off work

Inside LOOK

Google Translate is a free app that translates written and spoken words and phrases—65 and 17 languages, respectively—and speaks the translations of 40 languages aloud. It provides phonetic spellings for non-Latin languages.

and will not be paid, a situation they cannot afford. In another home, the timing may mean that they cannot spend time feeding and caring for their aging parent. We need to be "inside families" to understand how our communications will impact each and every family!

INITIAL WRITTEN COMMUNICATION
LETTER OF CONFIRMATION

Any centre that has a reputation for delivering quality care to children will attract the attention of

EXHIBIT 8.1 Guidelines for Written Communication

- Ensure that written communication reflects the needs and interests of the families in the centre.
- Any form of written communication should be considered an "art form." Is the letter visually appealing, eye catching, and engaging?
- Computer programs now enable written communication to be presented in an attractive and accessible format. When appropriate, support the written material with photographs and drawings by children in the centre.
- Use official letterhead of the centre only for formal notifications; some families may be intimidated by this official approach.
- Carefully consider the style of writing to be used; whether informal or formal, it must be appropriate for the intended audience. In some situations, a bulleted format may be the most helpful.
- In some communiqués educators may wish to highlight the most important information at the beginning of the letter in a highlighted box for emphasis.
- Keep in mind the length of the material. Conciseness is generally preferable. If it takes more than five minutes to read, it is too long. Additional material can be made available to families on request.
- Make sure communications go home in plenty of time for parents to respond or to make plans to attend a centre event.
- Consider the tone. Cold, authoritarian, and condescending communications undermine a sense of partnership; for example, use "the children are so excited about our upcoming Pancake Breakfast, and we are all hoping you will be able to attend" rather than "all parents are expected to attend the Pancake Breakfast." Stay positive and respectful since your written communication may have a lasting impact.
- Carefully proofread all written communication prior to distribution. One spelling or grammatical error can alter the families' perception of your work.
- When writing about controversial issues, maintain a positive attitude.
- Remember that a handwritten note is a more personal form of communication and in some situations more appropriate than photocopies of the same note or an email message.
- When photocopying is done, the material should be legible and correctly collated.
- Respect copyright laws.
- Maintain extra copies of the communiqué in case a family's goes missing and make these copies readily available; for example, keep them in a hanging file outside the room.
- Newsletters are often informative and provide real insight into the "workings" of the centre. Copies should be saved to be given to new families during an orientation meeting.
- It is also a good idea for the teacher to keep copies of all written communication in a special file. This may help if a similar note needs to go home with another group of children.
- Communications should be directed to all those who play a significant role in the child's life.
- Remember that any written communication from a centre is a form of publicity. As such, it should reflect a high degree of professionalism.
- Share appropriate communications with the community, it is a form of advocacy.
- Make every effort to have written communications translated into the home languages of all families in the centre. Translated materials should be accompanied with visuals placed in the text where appropriate. Several software translation programs are now available, but they should be used carefully to ensure that the essence of the translated content is captured. The final translated version should be proofread to ensure correctness.

many families in its community. Families who wish to enroll their child in the centre have their names placed on a waiting list. The centre should send families a letter briefly outlining waiting-list procedures.

ORIENTATION FORM

On their first visit to the early learning environment, families may be overwhelmed by the amount of information they are given. A self-contained orientation package with clear instructions on how to complete the required forms can be of great assistance. In some centres, supervisors help families who are not proficient in English complete the forms. Depending on the circumstances, a family member, an interpreter, or another staff member may be called on to assist.

A typical orientation package includes the following:

- an Intake Form
- an Emergency Contact Form
- a Health and Immunization Form
- an Emergency Treatment Release Form
- an Authorization for Pick-up Form
- a Permission-to-Video-and-Photograph Form
- an Excursion Permission Form

INTAKE FORM

Intake forms, such as the one presented here, record background information about the child and the family. Centres may wish to design separate intake forms for different age groups or choose questions from the following form that best suit their needs. It is important to remember that privacy and confidentiality are very important to families, so information gathered on these forms should be treated with respect.

Janeway Child and Family Centre

Dear Mr. Potter and Ms. Chu:

Thank you for your interest in our centre. You have now been officially placed on our waiting list, and we will contact you as soon as a space becomes available. Although spaces are generally allotted on a first-come, first-served basis, priority is given to the siblings of children already enrolled. In addition, since this is a workplace centre, employees working at Janeway Plastics receive priority. The centre's board of directors has the final approval on admissions. Because we have many families on our waiting list at this time, we advise you to contact other centres while you wait to hear from us again. Please find enclosed a checklist that will assist you in choosing a quality child-care setting for you and your family.

Sincerely,

Theresa Sanchez

Theresa Sanchez
Supervisor

Janeway Child and Family Centre

INTAKE FORM FOR INFANTS, TODDLERS, AND JUNIOR PRESCHOOLERS

A. **Personal Information about the Child**

Date enrolled in centre: _____ Health card number: _____

1. Child's name: _____

2. Child's age: _____ Birth date: _____

3. Country of birth: _____ Child's birth weight: _____

4. Was he/she full term? Yes _____ No _____

   If not, how premature? _____

5. Were there any complications or unusual circumstances surrounding the pregnancy and/or delivery?
   Yes _____ No _____

   If yes, please give details: _____

6. Physician's name: _____ Address: _____

   Phone number: _____

7. Has your child had a serious illness or hospitalization? Yes _____ No _____

   If yes, please give details that may affect our care of your child: _____
   _____

8. Does your child receive medication on a daily basis? Yes _____ No _____

   If yes, please give details: _____

9. Does your child have asthma? Yes _____ No _____

   If yes, please describe treatment: _____

10. Does your child have any other allergies or sensitivities? _____
    _____

11. Does your child wear eyeglasses? Yes _____ No _____

12. If your child was adopted and you wish to share this information with us, do you have any specific instructions
    for the centre? _____

13. Does your child have any brothers or sisters? Yes _____ No _____

    If yes, please complete the following:

    Name: _____ Age: _____ Sex: _____

    Name: _____ Age: _____ Sex: _____

    Name: _____ Age: _____ Sex: _____

14. Do these siblings live with you and your child? Yes _____ No _____

15. Are there other family members or friends who also live with the child? Yes _____ No _____

    If yes, please identify: _____

16. Are there any significant adults in your child's life that we should be aware of?
    _____

17. What languages are spoken at home? _____

18. Does your child have any pets? Yes _____ No _____

    If yes, what type of pet and what is its name? _____

B. Information about Household Members

Name: _____

1. Relationship to the child: _____

2. Address: _____

3. Telephone numbers: Residence: _____ Work: _____

4. Cell phone/email address: _____

5. Occupation: _____

6. Place of employment/school: _____

7. Is your place of employment a possible site for a field trip? _____ Yes _____ No

8. Do you have any special interests or hobbies that you would be willing to share with the children? _____
_____

9. Visiting rights of parents, if separated or divorced: _____

10. Is there anyone that needs to receive communications from the centre? _____

Please note: In situations where parents are separated or divorced, the daycare does not have the authority to deny a parent access to his or her children without a court order. If a legal agreement is in place, the centre should have a copy on file.

C. Toileting

1. Has your child learned to use the toilet? Yes _____ No _____

2. Does your child require assistance in the bathroom routine? Yes _____ No _____

3. Does your child signal or use particular words when having a bowel movement or urinating?
Yes _____ No _____ Please describe: _____

4. Does your child have regular bowel movements? Yes _____ No _____
Colour: _____ Consistency: _____

5. If diapers are in use, what type of diaper do you use at home?
Disposable _____ Cloth _____ Combination _____

6. Do you use plastic pants? Yes _____ No _____

7. Is your child prone to diaper rash? Yes _____ No _____
If yes, do you use a special ointment? _____

8. On average, how many times a day would you change your child's diapers? _____

9. Is your child generally dry through the night? Yes _____ No _____

10. Does your child nap with a diaper? Yes _____ No _____

D. Sleeping

1. Does your child experience any sleeping problems? Yes _____ No _____
If yes, please give details: _____

2. How long does your child typically sleep at night? _____

3. What are your child's sleeping patterns for the day? a.m.: _____ p.m.: _____

4. Does your child have a special bedtime routine? Yes _____ No _____
If yes, please describe: _____

5. Does your child sleep with a particular item? Yes _____ No _____
If yes, please identify (toy, pacifier, bottle, special blanket, etc.): _____

6. What kinds of signals does your child give when sleepy? _____

7. How long would your child usually nap during the day? _____

8. If your child has a preferred sleeping position, please describe: _____

9. If you have any special way of helping your child get to sleep, please describe:

   _____

10. Does your child usually sleep in a room by him/herself? Yes _____ No _____

11. Is your child bothered by noise when sleeping? Yes _____ No _____

12. Does your child usually cry when he/she wakes up? Yes _____ No _____

13. Does your child experience nightmares? Yes _____ No _____

    If yes, please give details: _____

14. Does your child have any fears that we should be aware of? Yes _____ No _____

    If yes, please give details: _____

E. Feeding

1. Do you have any concerns about your child's eating habits? Yes _____ No _____

   If yes, please give details: _____

2. Is your child breastfed? Yes _____ No _____

   If yes, is there any way we can support you at the centre so that you can continue to breastfeed?

   _____

3. What type of food does your child eat?

   a. Formula _____ Amount: _____ Frequency: _____

   b. Cereal _____ Amount: _____ Frequency: _____

   c. Strained foods _____ Amount: _____ Frequency: _____

   d. Others: _____

4. Check:

   Your child needs to be fed _____

   Eats slowly _____

   Feeds self with assistance _____

   Eats quickly _____

   Feeds self independently _____

5. If your child drinks from a bottle, please describe his/her preferred drinking position (for example, being held, lying down, sitting up, etc.): _____

6. Check one: Your child drinks from a cup with a lid _____ without a lid _____

7. Are there any food restrictions that we should be aware of? Yes _____ No _____

   If yes, please describe: _____

8. Is your child on a special diet? Yes _____ No _____

   If yes, please give details: _____

9. List your child's favourite foods:

   a. _____ c. _____

   b. _____ d. _____

10. List any foods your child especially dislikes:
   a. _____ c. _____
   b. _____ d. _____

11. What would you consider a normal portion for your child? _____

12. Are there family food preferences that you would like us to honour? _____

F. Other Information

1. What is your child's usual reaction to being bathed or changed by someone other than yourself? _____
_____

2. We would like to know how your child reacts to different situations and people in order to facilitate his/her comfort level:
   a. What does he/she do when you leave him/her alone to go to another room?

   _____

   b. What does he/she do when you leave him/her at home:
      with relatives: _____
      with siblings: _____
      with a babysitter: _____

3. Are there other adults who also take care of your child? Yes _____ No _____

4. Has your child ever been in a group-care setting before? Yes _____ No _____

5. How does your child generally relate to other children? _____

6. How does your child react to situations that make him/her angry or frustrated? _____
_____

7. Describe any strategies for guiding your child's behaviour that you think would be helpful for staff to know:
_____

8. What strategies do you use to comfort your child when he/she is distressed? _____
_____

9. What does your child enjoy doing during the day? What are his/her interests? _____
_____

10. Please describe your child's language skills: _____

11. Please describe any dressing habits that staff should be aware of: _____

12. Please provide any other information about your child that you think the teachers should be aware of:
_____

13. What celebrations are important to your family? _____

14. Please describe any traditions, customs, foods, or symbols associated with this celebration that you would like staff to be aware of: _____

15. Please describe any family values of particular importance to you that you would like the teachers to know about: _____

16. Do you have access to a computer in your home? _____

17. If you have email and would like to receive centre information through this medium, please indicate your email address here: _____

18. Are you available to receive phone calls or text messages during the day? Yes _____ No _____

The completed intake form—plus a family visit—provides teachers with the tools they need to provide a warm, supportive environment that enhances the growth of the whole child—physically, socially, emotionally, cognitively, and creatively.

INCIDENT REPORT/INJURY FORM

In order to keep families informed about serious injuries, centres complete and have families sign an injury report. This form provides families with detailed information about incidents as they occur. A minor fall may result in a bruise that the parent may question a day later; the injury form provides a record of the incident. The centre may give a copy of the report to parents and keep the original in the child's file. The reports also provide centres with information regarding common injuries and opportunities to change practices or the environment. In some provinces, serious occurrence forms are also required to be submitted, for example, to the Ministry.

Janeway Child and Family Centre

HEALTH AND IMMUNIZATION FORM

Each medical officer of health (MOH) in Canada is responsible for the health of children in centres within his or her geographic area. As a requirement for admission to the centre, families need to complete health and immunization forms.

Janeway Child and Family Centre

EMERGENCY CONTACT FORM

Please list below the names of people we should contact, in the event of an emergency, if we are unable to reach you.

Name: _____ Home Phone: _____

Address: _____ Business phone: _____

Relationship to child: _____

Name: _____ Home phone: _____

Address: _____ Business phone: _____

Relationship to child: _____

Janeway Child and Family Centre

EMERGENCY TREATMENT RELEASE FORM

I authorize the Janeway Child and Family Centre to act on my behalf to ensure immediate medical treatment should the staff deem it necessary. I give permission for my child, _____, in the event of an emergency, to receive full medical attention deemed necessary by a physician at the hospital. I understand that my child will be accompanied to the hospital by a child-care staff and that every effort will be made to reach me and/or my emergency contact person. I agree to accept any financial responsibility for any emergency medical care necessary.

Signature of family member: _____

Date: _____ Witness:_____

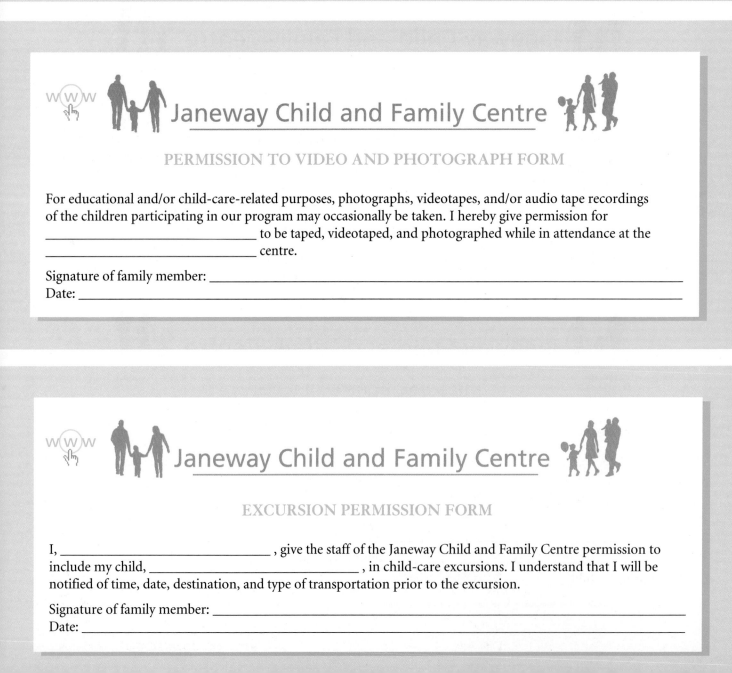

Janeway Child and Family Centre

PERMISSION TO VIDEO AND PHOTOGRAPH FORM

For educational and/or child-care-related purposes, photographs, videotapes, and/or audio tape recordings of the children participating in our program may occasionally be taken. I hereby give permission for _____ to be taped, videotaped, and photographed while in attendance at the _____ centre.

Signature of family member: _____

Date: _____

Janeway Child and Family Centre

EXCURSION PERMISSION FORM

I, _____ , give the staff of the Janeway Child and Family Centre permission to include my child, _____ , in child-care excursions. I understand that I will be notified of time, date, destination, and type of transportation prior to the excursion.

Signature of family member: _____

Date: _____

THE FAMILY HANDBOOK

A well-organized, concise, effectively written, attractively designed family handbook helps families decide if a particular centre meets their needs. The handbook outlines the obligations and responsibilities of the families and staff and provides information on the day-to-day running of the centre. A valuable marketing tool, the handbook can be distributed throughout the community; doctors' offices, local hospitals, community information centres, and schools are all possible distribution points. The diversity and inclusiveness of the centre should be documented in design, photos, and content. If cost is a problem, a smaller brochure outlining the strengths of the program can be distributed instead or the handbook may be made available online on the centre's website. Besides being a useful orientation tool for families who are new to the centre, the handbook serves as a valuable reference for currently enrolled families.

Care should be taken not to include more information than is necessary. Material must be chosen carefully and expressed in a clear and concise fashion. In order to reflect the communities they serve, some centres have their handbook translated into a number of different languages. (One urban centre has translated its handbook into 18 languages.) The handbook should be carefully proofread for grammatical and spelling errors. If possible, a professional copy editor and/or proofreader should be consulted.

Once families have been with the centre for some time, ask them for feedback on the handbook. How effective was it in meeting their needs? They might also be invited to write a testimonial for a revised edition of the handbook:

> I was so excited when we were notified that our baby daughter would have a space at the Janeway Child and Family Centre. It has a wonderful reputation in our community and, after talking to the supervisor of the centre, it seemed like the perfect place for us. I spent a week in the infant room with my daughter and the teachers, helping her make a gradual transition to her new surroundings. Then came the day that I actually had to leave her to return to work! Nothing could have prepared me for the overwhelming sense of loss I felt as I left the centre that first morning. Our daughter giggled and laughed with one of the staff as I waved goodbye (after about five hugs and kisses). I cried all the way to work. For several weeks I got a lump in my throat whenever I left. It is only because of the support and empathy of the staff that I survived those first few weeks.

> They called me at work several hours into the first day to reassure me that things were going well and they greeted me at the end of the day with a photo of our daughter happily playing with a toy. She is now in the senior preschool room and we continue to feel we are a part of a larger family in this centre.

Government officials, doctors, educators, and other community members who have been involved with the centre might also be invited to submit testimonials. These go a long way toward reassuring new families.

DESIGN AND LAYOUT

A handbook's layout and design are critical to its effectiveness, and there are many software programs available to assist in producing a handbook. Photographs and drawings by the children add a personal touch and will encourage families to read the content. A logo for the cover might be designed by staff, parents, children, or a local artist or designer. Some centres differentiate the sections of their handbooks by having them printed on paper of different colours. When choosing coloured paper, check that the text is readable, that the photographs reproduce clearly, and that the colour is not too bold to tire the reader. Other handbooks use tabs to separate sections. Consideration should also be given to factors such as paper quality and binding. Using standard-size paper helps to reduce costs. If the handbook is to retain its professional appearance, it should be reprinted on a regular basis as needed rather than making additions by hand to existing copies.

CONTENTS

The handbook may be divided into the following comprehensive subject areas.

1. WELCOME TO THE CENTRE

The introduction to the handbook should welcome interested families and set the tone for the remainder of the handbook. It should reflect the spirit of the centre and the critical role that families can play. Particularly significant information should be provided here; for example, in a cooperative child-care centre families are required to contribute their time.

2. HISTORY OF THE CENTRE

Many centres have interesting beginnings and parents feel a greater connection to the centre when they understand the often perilous road that centres have travelled. The following excerpt, from the *Campus Community Co-Op Day Care Centre* in downtown Toronto, reflects the tumultuous history of this particular centre:

> About 350 supporters of the Campus Community Co-Op Day Care Centre carried out the first occupation of Simcoe Hall in University of Toronto history today.... Lorenne Smith, assistant philosophy professor and a member of the daycare co-operative, [gave] the crowd a [brief] history of the daycare centre's struggles with the university. "As a woman," Mrs. Smith said, "I find it insulting. It's unthinkable that a woman must give up her career or not be able to work when she needs to support a family because she has children." (*The Varsity,* 1970)

When Lorenne Smith spoke to a crowd of parents and babies at a rally that winter afternoon in 1970, Campus Co-Op had already been in existence for a year, founded by a core of feminists negotiating with university administration to support their Sussex Street daycare centre, staffed entirely by parents and volunteers. Frustrated by the lack of administration interest in supporting mothers who worked for the university—and, by inference, women everywhere—the parents simply took over the Simcoe Hall and began warming bottles and setting up cots.

3. PRACTICAL INFORMATION

This section of the handbook includes the centre's name, mailing address, main telephone number, and information about telephone extensions; an email address or a website address should also be noted. Some centres also provide the telephone numbers of subsidy offices, government ministries related to child care, support groups, and children's help lines. Transportation information might also be included (for example, the nearest subway stop or the number of the connecting bus). If parking is available, outlining the procedures for drop-off and pick-up will be useful. Early learning environments located within a larger complex or a school might provide a map. Finally, this section should include hours of operation, days the centre is closed (statutory holidays, for example), any special days such as religious holidays observed by families in the centre, and information about weather closings. School programs should outline their program for winter, spring, and summer breaks, along with the centre's policy on professional development days.

4. PHILOSOPHY

This section of the handbook helps families decide whether the centre will meet the particular needs of their family. While some centres take a holistic approach to the child, others focus on a particular aspect of child development. Families may, for example, choose a centre that emphasizes creative development in music and the arts. The philosophy statement should reflect not only the centre's beliefs but also the interests and needs of the parents and children in the centre. Some centres use this section to articulate their support for cultural diversity and inclusiveness.

It is not enough for a centre simply to make grand statements about its philosophy. Families must be able to *see* how this philosophy translates into action; this is effectively accomplished by including a list of the centre's goals. These goals summarize the ways in which the families and teachers work together to provide the best possible environment for the children. Each philosophical statement should be accompanied by specific and measurable actions.

5. ADMINISTRATION OF THE CENTRE

The centre can use a simple chart to illustrate its organization by age group. A simplified flowchart gives families an overview of the centre's basic organizational structure. (The cook, the caretaker, and other part-time staff who work at the centre on a regular basis should be included in the chart.)

In the case of kindergarten and school-age programs, the administrative connections between the school setting and the child care should be delineated.

Including photographs in the manual helps to break up the text and, as you can see, a picture is worth a thousand words—a caring teacher and children who are engaged.

6. QUALIFICATIONS OF STAFF

Families should receive relevant information on staff training, education, and work experience. The qualifications of all centre personnel, from cook to bookkeeper to supervisor, should be included here. This section should also include information on specialized training by staff (for example, supporting children with special needs), centre support of staff through ongoing professional development and skills upgrading, and languages spoken by the staff. If ECE students or high school students complete field placements in the centre, this is also relevant information for families.

7. ADMISSION PROCEDURES

Besides clearly explaining admission procedures, this section of the handbook provides information on the admission of children who have received subsidies as well as children with special needs. Health requirements (immunization, doctor's examination, and so on) are clearly outlined. Families who are on a waiting list will want to know the criteria used by the centre in granting spaces.

8. FEE STRUCTURE

One of the most important pieces of information for any new family entering a centre is the cost of the service. Some centres require families to sign a statement that outlines the fee schedule and method of payment; this statement becomes the contract between the centre and the parent.

The fee-structure section should include information on

- registration fees and procedures for payment (cheque or credit card, weekly, biweekly, or monthly payments)

- procedures in the event that families are late with their fees or are unable to pay

- the way sick days and holidays are accounted for in the fee structure

- the administration of income-tax statements

- extra charges above the normal monthly fee for special trips, supplies, breakfast and lunch programs, and so forth

- special arrangements made in the case of parents who are divorced or separated (some centres collect fees only from the custodial parent, because he or she may be the only parent with whom the centre has regular contact)

- special funding or enhancement grants made available to the centre by government or business sources

- withdrawing a child from the centre (financial repercussions should be addressed here)

- review of fees and when families might expect fee increases

- information for families in communities where subsidies may be available

- a contract stating that the family understands the centre's late-fee policy (not all centres with such a policy ask families to sign)

9. PROSOCIAL BEHAVIOUR AND CHILD-ABUSE POLICY

The handbook should clearly outline the centre's strategies for encouraging prosocial behaviour on the part of children. Approaches not condoned or used at the centre might also be mentioned, so that families clearly understand the centre's approach.

Families also need to be aware of the centre's policy on child abuse. For example, staff, family members, and children will not use the following actions in the centre:

- corporal punishment (hitting, shaking, spanking, kicking, pushing, shoving, grabbing, squeezing, pinching)

- deliberate harsh or degrading treatment that would humiliate or undermine a child's self-respect

- abusive or humiliating language, yelling, and screaming

Families should be advised that the staff are required by law to report suspected abuse to local authorities.

The board of directors may, on rare occasions, request that a child be suspended or withdrawn from the centre. It is important for families to understand that while every effort is made to accommodate all children in the centre, there are times when the safety and needs of the group outweigh the needs of one child. In some school-age settings, children under suspension from the school are not allowed in the child-care centre.

Our philosophy at the Janeway Child and Family Centre is that positive reinforcement and encouragement are the most effective means of helping children learn prosocial behaviours. By recognizing personal choice and by allowing the child control over his or her environment, we encourage the child to express feelings and opinions. We provide opportunities for the child to see the validity of different perspectives and to respect the limits created by mutual consent. As teachers, we attempt to model appropriate behaviour by being courteous and by developing warm and trusting relationships with the children.

Source: Reprinted by permission of Lynn Wilson.

10. HEALTH AND EXCLUSION POLICY

The policy regarding exclusion should be very clear to families. For example, Pimento and Kernested (2010: 170) suggest that a child will be excluded if

- the illness prevents the child from participating comfortably in all program activities, including going outside

- the illness results in a greater need for care than the staff can provide without compromising the health, safety, and care of other children

- the illness poses a serious health risk if it spreads to other children or staff, and/or local public health authorities require exclusion

For some families, a child's illness can be a challenge. Many families lack the job flexibility, extended family, or close friends to enable them to care for their ill child. Though it is important to consider the needs of all the children in a group-care situation, supervisors and teachers may occasionally decide that it is in the best interests of the parents and the child to make alternative arrangements. For example, a preschooler with a sprained ankle might easily be accommodated in the toddler room during outdoor time until her injury heals.

This section of the handbook should include the names of agencies that provide emergency care in the community (those agencies that provide translation services should be noted for ESL parents); information about the parents' role with respect to health-related matters; information on the storage and administration of medications at the centre;

information on sunblock and appropriate summer and winter clothing; and dental information. It also explains that the centre is a nonsmoking environment and that toys are disinfected on a regular basis.

11. SAFETY ISSUES

Information on how the centre meets local licensing requirements, which vary from province to province, is imperative. Besides reassuring families that every attempt has been made to ensure that their children are playing in a safe indoor and outdoor environment, this section should provide information on centre procedures for notifying families in the event of a serious injury; information on first-aid training undertaken by staff; and information on fire, theft, and liability insurance. Where applicable, procedures for using security codes or security cards should be given. Families in school-age programs, for example, may need to be aware that certain doors may be locked at certain times and that access is gained only through designated doors. Finally, this section should explain fire-drill and evacuation procedures and name the location of temporary premises in the event of an emergency.

12. FOOD AND NUTRITION POLICY

This section should communicate that good nutrition is an important, intrinsic part of the program. It should discuss how the centre adheres to *Canada's Food Guide* (2011) and information on related issues such as food storage and handling guidelines, the location of menus, and the procedure for notifying families if changes are made to menus. This is an opportunity for the centre to show that the menus reflect the cultural diversity of the children and to invite families to become involved in menu planning.

Procedures for accommodating children with special dietary requirements or restrictions (whether for medical or religious reasons) should be outlined here. Ingredients and methods of preparation are of particular importance to families of children with allergies. For example, some children have such serious nut allergies that centres are responding by turning the centre into peanut-free zones. Menus should emphasize seasonal fruits and vegetables and unprocessed food that is low in sugar and salt content.

Families of babies need to know if the centre provides bottles or solid food. Families of older children need to know the following:

- Does the centre provide a breakfast program?

- Are snacks served?

- How is the lunch program run?

- Are hot lunches or supplements be served?

- Do children bring their own lunch?

- Is junk food (pop, chips, chocolate, and so on) restricted in the children's lunches?

- Can children heat their lunches in a microwave?

- Are garbage-less lunches promoted?

Children should be encouraged to have tasting amounts of all foods offered, with teachers modelling a positive attitude by eating with the children and encouraging a relaxed, comfortable experience.

This section should also explain the centre's policy on celebrations such as birthdays. Does the centre encourage elaborate celebrations involving magicians and loot bags, or are more modest events the norm? A centre generally decides on a policy that reflects the wishes of the majority of families.

13. DROP-OFF AND PICK-UP PROCEDURES

This section outlines procedures for checking in with a staff person in the morning and repeating the procedure in the evening. It should be stressed that drop-offs and pick-ups are easier for everyone involved if a regular routine is followed. If parents know that they will be later than usual, they should notify the centre so that staff can reassure the child. Procedures relating to school-age children must also be explained.

It should be made clear to families that they are responsible for bringing their child to the centre. Some centres will not assume responsibility for a child until he or she is signed in. Other centres will accept older children without a parent being present if a release letter from their parents is on file. Families should be assured in this section that children will be released only to those people they have designated in writing. Parents who are separated or divorced should be advised that the centre does not have the authority to deny a parent access to his or her children without a court order.

14. FIELD TRIPS

This section should reassure families that they will be provided in advance with complete information about any trip that takes the children out of the centre, including the purpose of the event, the itinerary, method of travel, teacher–child ratios, and safety procedures.

15. WHAT TO BRING ON THE FIRST DAY

This section should list the items families are required to bring to the centre on the first day. For the convenience of families, this section could take the form of a checklist, as illustrated in the following box.

The checklist can be adapted to accommodate different age groups. Some centres do not allow

First-Day List

1. Paperwork
   a. Intake Form ___
   b. Health and Immunization Form ___
   c. Permission to Video and Photograph Form ___
   d. Excursion Permission Form ___
   e. Emergency Treatment Release Form ___
   f. Authorization for Pickup Form ___
2. Blanket ___
3. Soft cuddle toy ___
4. Seasonal change of clothing ___
5. Extra socks and underwear ___
6. Diapers if necessary ___
7. Toothbrush and toothpaste ___
8. Bathing suit and towel ___
9. Picture of the family to place in cubby ___

Source: Reprinted by permission of Lynn Wilson

toys, money, or candy to be brought from home; such restrictions should be discussed in advance with families. Families should be advised to label all articles with the child's name.

16. INVOLVING FAMILIES

This section should provide information on the mechanisms for home–centre communication, orientation to the centre, home visits, resources available to families (newsletters, books, videos, family bulletin boards, resource area, and so forth) as well as ways in which families can become actively involved with the centre (for example, by participating in curriculum planning, fundraising events, by volunteering, by sending in "beautiful junk," or by serving on the board of directors).

17. SPECIAL FEATURES

Any special features of the program, such as involvement with an intergenerational program, should be discussed in this section of the family handbook. Sometimes centres that are located close to universities or hospitals are asked to participate in studies or surveys; families should be advised that they may decline if they do not wish their child to participate in special projects. Agencies whose services are available to the centre (developmental assessments and referral services, public health departments, dental and visual screenings, and so on) should be outlined; in the case of school-age programs, information on after-four programs, language classes, and community events could be provided.

THE PLAYROOM HANDBOOK

The playroom handbook provides information about the centre's individual rooms. This benefits both families who are new to the centre and families of children who are moving to new age groups within the early learning environment. Like the Qualifications of Staff section in the family handbook, the playroom handbook might include professional information about the teacher (educational background, length of employment at the centre, and work experience). More personal information (family life, hobbies, etc.) may be included at the teacher's discretion.

The playroom handbook can expand on the centre's philosophical statement by addressing the specific age group. Many parental concerns are alleviated when the ways in which appropriate practice is applied in the playroom are clearly outlined. For example, procedures for dealing with biting in the toddler room might be provided.

The daily schedule should also be discussed, with particular reference to ways in which the philosophy of the centre translates into action in the playroom. The lunch routine, for example, might be described as follows: "In the senior preschool room, the children participate in a family service format. They help themselves and do their own pouring. We feel it is important that the teachers eat with the children, because this offers the children role models for appropriate behaviour and attitudes. The atmosphere is relaxed and social." This statement reinforces the philosophical goal of encouraging self-help skills and a sense of cooperation and sharing. Teachers should point out that the schedule is not "written in stone" but is flexible and changes with the needs and interests of the group.

The playroom handbook should outline the organization of the room and the outdoor environment. Because families may be unfamiliar with the learning centre approach, descriptions of each of the learning centres in the room—from the art centre to the science and exploration centre—might be provided. These descriptions could also be posted in the room near the appropriate learning centres as a source of information for families and visitors to the centre (see Chapter 7). For many families, the outdoor playscape represents a place to burn off energy. It is critical that the handbook outlines the many ways in which learning occurs in the outdoor environment and how critical the connection to nature is to children's development of an environmental ethic.

The handbook should discuss the development of curriculum and provide examples of the way teachers plan and program for the children's individual needs and interests. This section of the handbook will emphasize an emergent curriculum approach. Ongoing activities (swimming lessons, trips to the local library, and so on) and yearly events (such as a pancake breakfast, a summer barbecue, and intergenerational picnics) can be mentioned in this section of the playroom handbook.

DOCUMENTATION AND THE PROJECT APPROACH

Documentation is the process of gathering information about children's ideas, words, and work, as well as documenting the educators' work with the children over time. It is the process of recording and reporting on children's learning through multiple mediums—photographs, written observations and comments, panels, portfolios, booklets, tape recordings, CDs, community displays, etc. Documentation expands the role of the teacher and provides a tool that enables teachers to be more effective in their work with the children. It helps teachers understand children's thinking processes and fosters teachers' facilitation skills. It requires them to become critical thinkers, strong observers of the children, and researchers in the playroom. Teachers must observe, collect data, analyze the information, and then determine the next steps. Documentation is a form of representation that makes children's learning visible.

The type of documentation that teachers do is not so far removed from our own past. Burrington and Sortino (2004) reflect on how our mothers raised us:

> They saved anything—newspaper clippings, school photos, report cards, Sunday school diplomas, obituaries, and even teeth were tucked away. The images and artifacts are by-products of the meaning that we made in our lives. They are like words in the language of our families, fragments of memories. They represent and evoke the time, place, thoughts, and feelings of those particular moments, and we revisit these documents and artifacts of our childhood again and again, with our parents, our siblings, our friends, and our own children.... The documentation on our walls and in our archives is a visual and literary account of events, ideas, projects, learning, people, and community. It represents our history. Our documentation marks the passing of time, honours relationships, celebrates moments, and conveys the inner thoughts and feelings of children and their teachers. We are more present in our daily encounters because we have an identity that is part of something larger. The images of strong, competent, thoughtful children remind us that we have an immense responsibility to the future. (225)

Documentation, in a variety of different forms, has been carried out by educators for many years but as the work at the preschools of Reggio Emilia in northern Italy became more well known, documenting the project approach took on a renewed importance. It informed viewers of the processes children went through in their play and the meaning it had for them. It is a tool that teachers use to record and communicate information to the children themselves, to families, and to colleagues. Like all good stories, the documentation process includes a beginning rooted in observations of the children, a middle, and an end that summarizes what the children have learned over time. This process of documentation involves collaboration with children, colleagues, families, and sometimes community members. Documentation clearly heightens educators' awareness and deepens the insight into the children's journey.

Harris Helm, Beneke, and Steinheimer (1997: 5) state that

> documenting children's learning may be one of the most valuable skills a teacher can learn. Regular and consistent documentation of children's work can benefit teachers in five ways:
>
> 1. Teachers who can document children's learning in a variety of ways are able to respond to demands for accountability.
>
> 2. Teachers who document are more often able to teach children through direct, firsthand, interactive experiences that enhance brain development.
>
> 3. Teachers are more effective when they document.
>
> 4. Teachers who can document children's work are better able to meet special needs.
>
> 5. Children perceive learning to be important and worthwhile when teachers document their learning.[*]

During field placement experiences, ECE students who have an opportunity document the development of a project benefit by

1. Practising and improving observation and recording skills.

2. Increasing their understanding of children's play, thinking, and problem solving.

3. Deepening their understanding of how children make sense of their world and the meaning that they construct.

4. Providing an opportunity for the children to demonstrate the sequence of learning. By telling the story of children's learning, investigations, skill acquisition, and discoveries, students demonstrate their understanding of how learning progresses, and define the beginning, middle,

---

[*]Harris Helm, J., S. Beneke, and K. Steinheimer. 1997. "Documenting Children's Learning," *Childhood Education* 73 (4): 200-205, reprinted by permission of the publisher (Taylor & Francis Ltd, http://www.tandf.co.uk).

Courtesy of Lynn Wilson

Courtesy of Lynn Wilson

The educator and children are documenting their project on oceans.

and end of documentation. When children learn, the content of learning moves from

- concrete to abstract
- simple to complex
- present to future and past
- facts to concepts
- known to unknown

5. Providing a permanent form of communication that can be viewed with children, families, and staff and that allows the student to interact in a meaningful way with families.

6. Providing a permanent record from which further program decisions can be made.

7. Demonstrating respect for the children and their efforts. The children will feel their efforts are valued by the student teacher and other adults in the room.

Documentation panels such as the ones in Figure 8.1 are an opportunity for students to demonstrate their understanding of the learning that is taking place for the children in their care.

Inside LOOK

The Reggio Emilia's Project Approach and the resulting documentation have proved to be an effective means of communicating with families. One parent comments:

I knew that lots of interesting things were happening at the centre as the children and teachers worked on a project about whales. Shakil came home every day with new information and insights to share with us. Since we live near the ocean, whale sightings were not uncommon, but I was struck by the intensity of the learning taking place for these 4- and 5-year-olds. Photos of the children at work, and on their trip to see the whales, and samples of their drawings and stories were placed on bulletin boards at the entrance to the centre for families and children to view. As the work progressed, new documentation was posted on a regular basis, so we were able to monitor the children's headway. One day we were even greeted by whale sounds playing on a tape recorder at the door.

I was impressed by the children's concern for the whales, and through this process they all became media stars. The supervisor contacted a local television station and the children were interviewed and their documentation recorded. What the project documentation demonstrated to me was the children's ability to problem solve and to think in divergent ways well beyond what I thought they were capable of.

Source: Reprinted by permission of Lynn Wilson.

FIGURE 8.1   Student Documentation Panels

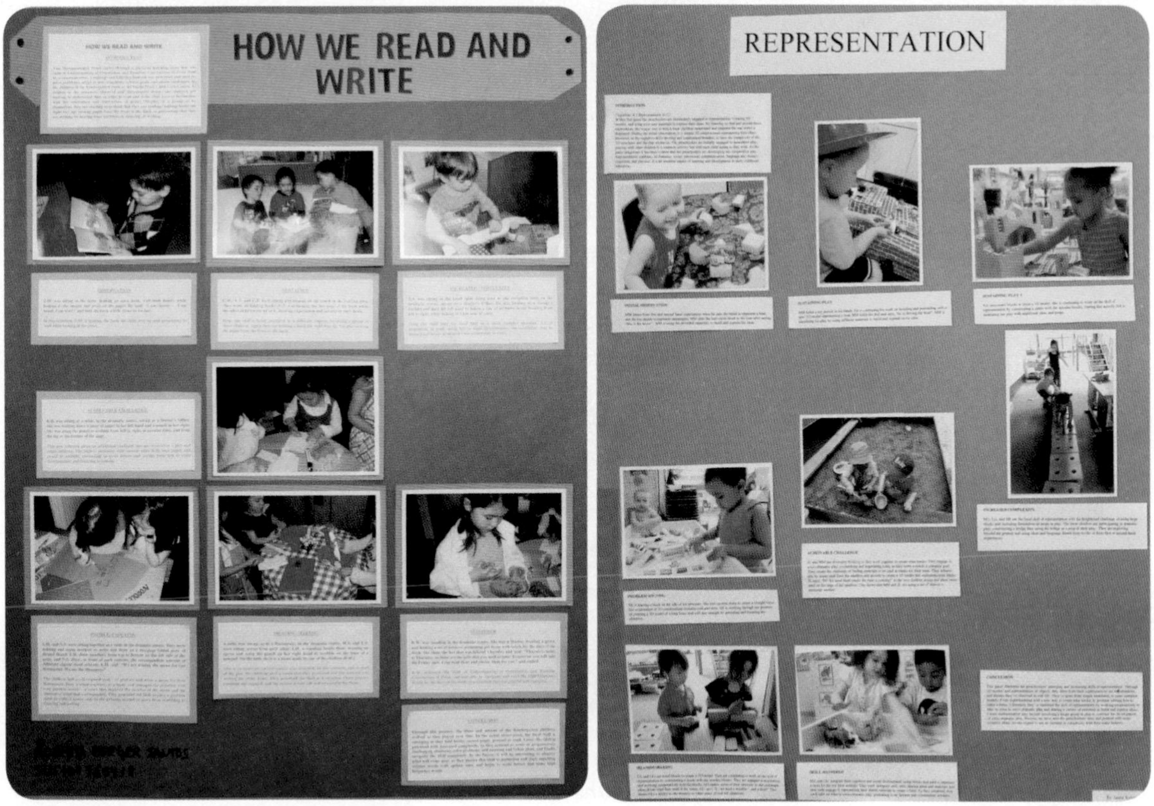

Bertrand (2008: 83) relates how teachers in New Zealand have introduced learning stories (see definition below) to offer snapshots of children's learning and development in action by describing actual, unique experiences:

> Teachers document children's activities and early childhood educators assess what learning and development are taking place and plan for the next steps. The observation, documentation, and analysis of learning stories create a sample of children's learning that is rich in context, articulate, and complete in terms of the situation, the actions and the conclusion. Learning Stories are narrations that document children's engagement in learning experiences, including the analysis or assessment of that learning and the child's emerging developmental skills. The stories and assessments can be presented in the children's portfolios for children, families, and practitioners to read and re-read.*

---

*From BERTRAND. *Understanding, Managing, and Leading, 1E.* © 2008 Nelson Education Ltd. Reproduced by permission. www.cengage.com/permissions.

ONGOING WRITTEN COMMUNICATION

Effective written communication has the potential to help teachers build positive relationships with families. Centres are always looking for effective ways to ensure that families receive written information. Many notices sent with the children never make it home—or they arrive home at the bottom of a knapsack covered in yesterday's lunch. In centres where families pick up information themselves, the information should be placed in an accessible location. A clothesline arranged by the centre entrance, with see-through pockets for each family, provides an efficient pickup system and an easy way for staff to check which families still need to pick up their messages. We must also be aware of the tone of our messages: warnings and messages on the door may well keep parents out. It is also important for families to know that as educators we encourage and welcome their notes when they do not have time to stay for longer periods of time during drop-off and pick-up. This type of communication may be an effective strategy for families with complicated, busy lives.

As each project is completed, a booklet is created to document as a permanent record of the children's work. They are placed in the book centre to which families and children can refer.

This teacher created her own photo book based on her holiday in Peru. The children enjoyed learning about her adventures!

CENTRE MENUS

Menus that are posted in the centre should reflect an understanding of the importance of good nutrition and its positive effects on the health and well-being of the children. Menu selections also should reflect the diversity of the families that the centre serves. Children should have an opportunity to eat food that is familiar to them as well as to try new foods in a positive and encouraging environment. Families should be encouraged to share recipes with the cook at the centre and with other families as well. Some centres produce and sell at fundraisers cookbooks that feature a favourite recipe from each family. If the menus are posted on a bulletin board, nutritional updates, healthy eating information, favourite recipes, etc., can also be highlighted there.

PLANNING FORMS

In order to keep families informed about programming that is happening in the room, a planning form should be posted in an accessible location. The form explains to families what is happening in the centre on a weekly basis. Planning forms provide an opportunity for teachers to share

Menus should be posted in an accessible location.

information about emergent curriculum and appropriate practice both indoors and outdoors. These forms may be continually updated as the children's needs and interests emerge. In many centres, a place is provided to encourage family input into the planned experiences.

DAILY CHARTS

A daily chart is a chart on which both families and staff record information about the child. By providing a way to share pertinent information the daily chart helps to smooth the transition between centre and home. Such charts are particularly useful when they are maintained for infants; knowing when the last feeding has taken place or how well

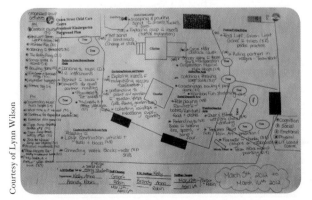

This detailed planning form for outdoor play reassures families that their child's day is well organized and positive learning experiences will take place.

the infant has slept during the night will help a teacher determine how best to support the child. Families can use the chart to record information such as changes to their daily work routine (different phone numbers at which they can be reached, for example). Teachers can use daily charts to record interesting or significant happenings. Ideally, translated versions of charts should be provided to English language learner parents; pictorial charts are another possibility (see Figure 8.2).

At the Esther Exton Child Care Centre, the senior preschoolers contribute to their charts by illustrating some of the highlights of their day. Teachers discuss the chart with the child and record any information the child wishes to add. Rather than use clipboards, some centres use a small binder in which to record daily information about the child. This form of information gathering is often referred to as a communication book. This concept can be expanded to include a booklet that travels between child care and home and in which families and teachers record their observations on a regular basis.

REPORT CARDS

Aronson (1995) says that

report cards are the traditional mode of conveying permanent, written evaluative information regarding student progress and more parents will be receiving these as children enter into full day kindergarten programs. Report cards should be clear and easy for parents to understand. These records

FIGURE 8.2   Infant Chart

INFORMATION CHART–INFANT

Date: _____

Name: _____

Bedtime: _____

Times awake through the night: _____

Wake up time: _____

Early morning feeding: _____

Time of most recent bowel movement: _____

Other comments: _____

_____

_____

_____

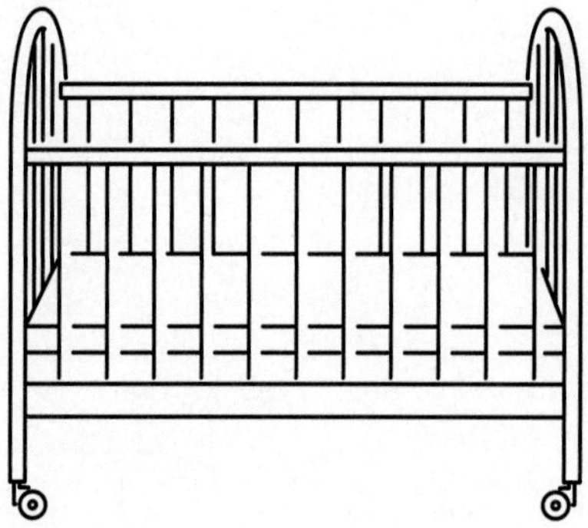

Naptime: _____

_____

_____

Liquids: _____

_____

_____

Diaper change: _____

_____

_____

Activity: _____

_____

_____

Solids: _____

_____

_____

Comments from staff: _____

_____

_____

should provide an analysis of academic development across content areas, information about student strengths and learning style, an assessment of the child's social development, specific goals for the student to work on, and associated suggestions for the parent. (in Graham Clay, n.d.: 119)

Giannetti and Sagarese (1998: 40) point out that

report cards also generally provide an invitation for the parent to respond, usually in written format. Teachers should review parental responses in a timely manner to determine any required follow-up. Carefully prepared report cards, coupled with parent conferences as needed, provide effective communication regarding student learning.

BROCHURES AND FLIERS

It is a good idea for the supervisor to keep a record of where and how families first learned about the centre; with this information, the centre may be better able to market its services to the community. Brochures about the centre can be distributed to local community centres, clinics, health-care professionals, hospitals, and local businesses. The centre can generate further publicity for itself by participating in community events such as fundraising, fairs, parades, and festivals.

In order to emphasize the importance it attaches to family involvement, the centre can design a brochure outlining various strategies for achieving effective communication and summarizing the ways in which families can participate in the day-to-day life of the centre. The brochure is a good place to outline parents' rights and responsibilities and to encourage the active involvement of men in the centre (the brochure could feature photographs of fathers, male teachers, and other men who play a significant role). The early learning environment could also include basic information about community resources and support agencies. Some centre brochures are, in effect, condensed versions of the family handbook. Like family handbooks, brochures can be distributed to appropriate settings throughout the community.

Well-written and informative letters to families about what is happening in the centre are an effective tool for engaging families in the children's experiences. This may encourage them to actively engage the teachers in further discussion and help families feel "in the loop."

Fliers can also serve as an effective information tool. Written material should be concise and translated into languages that reflect the community. Fliers should be colourful, well designed, and attention getting. School-age children might be encouraged to assist with their production.

JOURNALS

In some situations, ongoing journals may be a useful communication tool. Educators use the journal to record their observations of the child during the day and invite families to respond in the evening with written comments or observations of their own; the child may also contribute. This may be a valuable communication tool particularly for children who have specific learning needs. A daily journal may prove to be more than some families can attend to, so a weekly alternative may be more practical. Some educators have the children record their thoughts about centre events or important moments in their child-care life throughout the year. Having the journal bound will make sure important pages don't get lost. When the child leaves the centre, the journal becomes a wonderful memory of the time spent there.

PHOTOS

Some teachers create photo albums to record special events or the day-to-day interactions within the playroom and store them in the book centre. Teachers may encourage photo albums to be signed out and taken home by families. If budgets permit, individual photo albums can also be created. In some centres, finances prohibit printing photos but families could be asked to send in their own photos to create the albums. Other photos could be emailed to families directly. Other centres produce yearbooks featuring photographs of special events and comments from staff, parents, and children. A parent who is adept at photography might volunteer to visually chronicle events at the centre. Photo albums can also be loaned to new families to have a pictorial representation of the types of experiences the children will be engaged in during their time in this room.

Photo albums can also be a wonderful way for ECE students to introduce themselves to a new centre at the beginning of their field placement. One student from Korea created a powerful album of her home in Korea, her parents, siblings, and photos of her as a child the same age as the children in her care. This simple tool allowed her to share her own culture in a meaningful way and paved the way for an impressive beginning.

This journal provides two-way communication between the centre and home and will be a wonderful memory of the child's time in the program.

Inside LOOK

Mary Bianchi, teacher in the Kindergarten program at the Esther Exton Child Care Centres shares an innovative strategy:

In the morning circle, we would often sing "Hello My Friends" in the languages in the room. Children started to talk about the languages they spoke at home, where their family members come from, and other countries they had visited. Children want to learn how to say hello in other languages and learn more about each other. And so, the Family Heritage Book was born! Each child was assigned a page in the book that they took home. Families could add recipes, pictures, photographs—anything that represented their life at home or their heritage. Words were added to the book in different languages, as well as flags, stamps, pictures of cultural festivities, ornaments, or decorations that represent a special holiday. When the book was returned to the centre, the child and sometimes family members shared their page with the rest of the group. The book circulated until everyone had a chance to add something to it. This activity became one of the most popular projects in the room and evolved into other activities. Some expansions included word cards and labels in other languages and simple cooking activities; families brought in figurines and special decorations used during special holidays (dreidels, menorahs, books, ornaments, food boxes, postcards, fabrics, etc.). Families became very involved in this activity.

Source: Reprinted by permission of Mary Bianchi, RECE, Esther Exton Child Care Centre, George Brown College.

This is an example of one of the pages from the Heritage Book.

This clever use of photos helped other families get to know not only this child but his extended family as well.

THE DAILY FLASH

A large dry erasable board, chalkboard, or bulletin board located at the entrance to the playroom provides a space for instant communication to families. The following list suggests some messages that could make up the daily "flash":

- the day's most important events

- the birth of a sibling

- an adoption

- a birthday announcement

- the arrival of a new child to the room

- children who are moving to an older group

- the words to a new song

- quote of the day (a famous quote or a wise or funny comment made by a child)

- menu items that the children particularly enjoyed

- the names of special visitors to the centre

- the name of a new student teacher in the room

- the name of the supply teacher, if a staff member is absent

- a warning about the onset of illness in the room and possible symptoms

- reminders about upcoming events

- items families should bring to the centre the following day

- information about where the children are if they are out of the room ("We are at the park until 4 p.m.")

- digital photos of happenings during the day with a short comment—a great way to highlight milestones or important accomplishments

- a cue for families to start conversations about what took place during the day: "Ask us about what happened with the aquarium today!"

LISTS

Sometimes the simplest gesture can provide the greatest support. Having a list posted on a bulletin board or beside the telephone of all the families who've given permission to provide their address, email address, and telephone number allows families to arrange play dates, create car pools, support each other with babysitting, and stay in touch with each other. With family permission, this could also be sent home in a newsletter.

NEWSLETTERS

The newsletter provides an opportunity for teachers to communicate information about happenings in the centre and within the child-care community. An informative newsletter should reduce the need for individual fliers and reminders to go home to families. A monthly newsletter could be distributed on the same day of each month (the last Friday of the month, for example) so that families come to expect it. If it appears on the same coloured paper or patterned design, and is the same size each time, parents will know what is at the bottom of the knapsack! Every effort should be made to make this communiqué attractive by using different fonts, colour, bullets, boxes, artwork, and photos of the children. There are many templates available for newsletter formats. For example, Microsoft Publisher has many options and Apple users can use iWork. If translations are needed to accommodate English language learner families, financial constraints may require less frequent publication of newsletters; producing fewer newsletters is preferable to excluding English language–learner parents. "Teachers should also consider the length of the newsletter—a rule is 80% of people will spend 30 seconds reading the newsletter, 19% will spend 3 minutes and only 1% will spend 30 minutes reading it" (Recruiting New Teachers, 2001: 33). Centres should draw on the expertise of families when producing the newsletter. The newsletter provides an opportunity for families to contribute and reinforces the need for two-way communication. The newsletter should reflect cultural sensitivity and a high degree of professionalism. The tone of the newsletter and every other form of written communication is critical.

Educators should also be aware of arrangements for joint custody parents and should ensure that all family members receive the newsletter. Back issues of newsletters should be kept on hand to assist with the orientation of families who are new to the centre and also for teachers who may be new to the centre.

Teachers should keep notes on "meaningful moments" in the playroom; these notes can provide the basis of a newsletter anecdote:

> As we were preparing to watch *The Wizard of Oz* with the school-age children, Barrett told his friend Megan that he was worried about watching the video. A staff person reassured Barrett that he could leave the area and play somewhere else if he felt uncomfortable. Megan turned to Barrett, put her arm around his shoulder, and said, "Don't worry, Barrett, I will hug you during the scary parts."

Ideas, photographs, artwork, and other potential newsletter material should be stored in a central file that can be accessed by families or teachers who are working on the newsletter. In school-age programs, children may enjoy producing their own newsletters. Though the content of a newsletter differs from month to month, the inclusion of regular features provides a sense of continuity. Following are suggestions for regular features:

1. *Message from the Supervisor:* In this column the supervisor might deal with centre-specific issues or ECE issues in general. This space could also be used to make announcements about staff and program changes, to acknowledge special contributions by parents or children, to welcome new staff and student teachers, to share special recognition of teachers, or to update families about Health Canada guidelines or warnings, etc.

2. *Teacher of the Month:* Each teacher in the centre could at some point be profiled in the newsletter. Information about teachers' backgrounds, work experiences, philosophies, interests, hobbies, and professional development experiences may be included at their own discretion.

3. *Family of the Month:* Families who have contributed their time and energy should be acknowledged in the newsletter. A positive profile may encourage other families to become active participants in the centre.

4. *Staff News:* Teachers may take turns writing on a specific issue, discussing a professional development workshop they attended, or reviewing a relevant book.

5. *Family to Family:* Families could use this space to address parenting issues by contributing letters or book reviews, asking for suggestions for family trips, etc.

6. *"Families Ask":* Teachers can use this column to respond to questions often asked by families over the years.

7. *News from the Cook:* The centre cook could write about nutrition issues, share favourite recipes with families, recommend

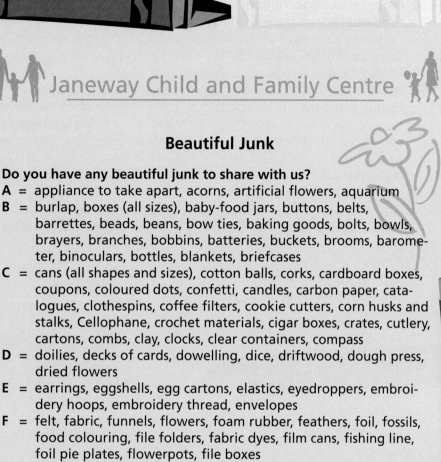

Janeway Child and Family Centre

Beautiful Junk

Do you have any beautiful junk to share with us?

A = appliance to take apart, acorns, artificial flowers, aquarium

B = burlap, boxes (all sizes), baby-food jars, buttons, belts, barrettes, beads, beans, bow ties, baking goods, bolts, bowls, brayers, branches, bobbins, batteries, buckets, brooms, barometer, binoculars, bottles, blankets, briefcases

C = cans (all shapes and sizes), cotton balls, corks, cardboard boxes, coupons, coloured dots, confetti, candles, carbon paper, catalogues, clothespins, coffee filters, cookie cutters, corn husks and stalks, Cellophane, crochet materials, cigar boxes, crates, cutlery, cartons, combs, clay, clocks, clear containers, compass

D = doilies, decks of cards, dowelling, dice, driftwood, dough press, dried flowers

E = earrings, eggshells, egg cartons, elastics, eyedroppers, embroidery hoops, embroidery thread, envelopes

F = felt, fabric, funnels, flowers, foam rubber, feathers, foil, fossils, food colouring, file folders, fabric dyes, film cans, fishing line, foil pie plates, flowerpots, file boxes

G = gloves, garland, greeting cards, gift-wrap, glitter, gems, gourds, grasses, glue, glycerine, garden hose, geoboards, gardening tools

H = hinges, hats, hairpieces, hair accessories, hives, hooks, hammer, hourglass

I = ink pads, ice-cream scoops, ice-cube trays, iron filings

J = jars—all shapes and sizes, juice cans, jewellery, jackets

K = keys, kites, kitchen utensils, knitting materials

L = lids, lace, lunch boxes, leaves, locks

M = milk cartons, meat trays, magazines, magnets, maps, measuring cups and spoons, minerals, moss, moulding, makeup brushes, marbles, metre sticks, magnifying glasses, mirrors

N = newspaper, nuts, neckties, netting, nylons, needles, nails

O = onion skins, onionskin paper

P = paper plates, pie plates, pizza pans, postcards, pine cones, Popsicle sticks, pipe cleaners, paper clips, pails, paint chips, paper bags, place mats, plastic containers, pods, Plexiglas, plastic pipes and tubes, pop carriers, paintbrushes, pinking shears, plumbing parts, paper punch, prisms, pulleys, pans, pitchers, potting soil, Ping-Pong balls, pliers

Q = quilts

continued

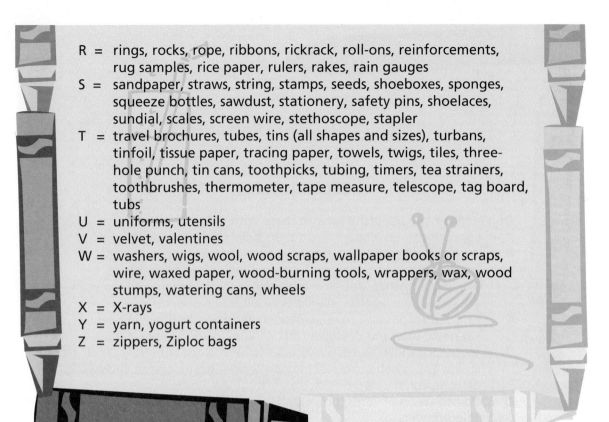

R = rings, rocks, rope, ribbons, rickrack, roll-ons, reinforcements, rug samples, rice paper, rulers, rakes, rain gauges

S = sandpaper, straws, string, stamps, seeds, shoeboxes, sponges, squeeze bottles, sawdust, stationery, safety pins, shoelaces, sundial, scales, screen wire, stethoscope, stapler

T = travel brochures, tubes, tins (all shapes and sizes), turbans, tinfoil, tissue paper, tracing paper, towels, twigs, tiles, three-hole punch, tin cans, toothpicks, tubing, timers, tea strainers, toothbrushes, thermometer, tape measure, telescope, tag board, tubs

U = uniforms, utensils

V = velvet, valentines

W = washers, wigs, wool, wood scraps, wallpaper books or scraps, wire, waxed paper, wood-burning tools, wrappers, wax, wood stumps, watering cans, wheels

X = X-rays

Y = yarn, yogurt containers

Z = zippers, Ziploc bags

good children's cookbooks, and ask families to submit a favourite recipe to share with everyone in the centre. The recipe might also be posted on the bulletin board when the dish is being served, along with a photo of the family.

8. *A Cooking Activity:* Each time the newsletter goes out, it might include a fun cooking experience that children can easily accomplish. Reading, science, and math concepts are all part of cooking!

9. *Feedback to Families:* This section might include a short but powerful message about areas in which families have expressed interest—the importance of play, avoidance of obesity in the early years, early literacy, math activities to do at home, the use of technology in the home, learning outdoors, etc.

10. *Doctor's Report:* A physician affiliated with the centre could use this space to write about child-related health issues and concerns.

11. *Homemade Toy of the Month:* A teacher or a parent could give easy-to-follow instructions

for toy making that both children and parents could participate in.

12. *Activity of the Month:* This column describes the children's favourite activity over the past month.

13. *Book of the Month:* A teacher or parent could review a good children's book or an adult book—for example, Richard Louv's book *Last Child in the Woods, Saving Our Children From Nature Deficit Disorder*!

14. *Committee Reports:* This column gives parent committees an opportunity to update families on their activities.

15. *Report from the Board of Directors:* Here the board of directors can share relevant information.

16. *Resource Area News:* The supervisor could use this space to announce new additions (articles, books, videos, and so on) to the family resource area.

17. *Surveys:* Attaching surveys will most ensure that families will read the newsletter.

18. *Update on the Field:* We want to encourage family members to become advocates for their children and their communities. When something significant occurs, including it in the newsletter helps to keep families informed and involved. For example:

the field of early childhood was deeply saddened by the death of Dr. Fraser Mustard [in 2011] who has been a champion for early childhood. His impassioned campaign calling attention to the crucial first years of life and how brain development during that time sets the stage for health and well-being inspired economists, educators, and politicians around the globe.

Other possible newsletter items include

- information on national and local celebrations (Week of the Child, Children's Book Week, Freedom to Read Week, Family Day, Family Week, International Mud Day!)

- words of popular finger plays and songs

- fun quizzes designed for families

- seasonal suggestions for activities that family members and children can engage in together

- reviews of toys, family television programs, local children's theatre, videos, and parenting magazines

- information on exchanges (babysitting, skates, videos)

- columns on where to get items for children at reasonable prices

- a want ad section where families can network with each other in exchange of goods

- accounts of field trips taken by the children (photos included)

- tips on organizing birthday parties

- highlights of family meetings

- results of family surveys

- a space for community people to share helpful and informative information for families

- announcements of upcoming community workshops, lectures, or seminars on parenting issues, celebrations, etc.

- safety tips (childproofing the home, bicycle safety)

- recipes for modelling clay, silly putty, playdough, etc.

- ideas for keeping children engaged on long car trips

- recipes for tasty and nutritious snacks and ideas for school-age lunch bags

- ideas for healthy and safe outdoor activities

- interviews with children, family members, and teachers

- inspirational poetry

INDIVIDUAL ROOM NEWSLETTERS

In addition to whole-centre newsletters, some centres produce individual room newsletters that reflect the uniqueness of each room and focus on the developmental issues of children in each room's age group. An individual room newsletter might feature upcoming events, developmental milestones, ideas for family participation, issues and concerns (for example, biting in the toddler room, sibling rivalry in the preschool room, street proofing for school-age children), emergent curriculum updates, how families can extend curriculum into the home environment, information about pets in the room, and announcements of the addition of new items (software, toys, books, and so on) to the room. One teacher saw readership of the newsletter increase significantly when she included art contributed by the children and digital photos that showed them at work!

Figure 8.3 is an example how a newsletter can keep families up to date with happenings in the centre.

Newsletters that originate in the room are generally of high interest to families, especially if their children have played a part in producing them. School-agers can play a particularly active role in preparing the newsletter. As families leave a particular room and their child graduates to an older age group, the individual room newsletter provides a perfect forum for acknowledging the contributions these families have made to the centre and to the room.

CALENDARS

Effective communication of daily and upcoming events is critical to the smooth running of the centre. Some centres post a large wipe-off calendar that is clearly visible to families as they arrive. Staff might

FIGURE 8.3   Newsletter

NEWSLETTER

Preschooler Thank-yous

Thanks go out to Christopher's mom, Talin, for her generous gift of watercolours. We are having great fun with such vibrant new colours.

Winter Fun

The preschoolers are all having fun being involved in many different winter activities. Bundled up, we are enjoying all that winter has to offer. Please see the picture of our building projects–winter forts–on the bulletin board outside our room.

Recipes

A few of the preschool parents have expressed an interest in our playdough recipe so here it is:

2 cups flour
1 cup salt
2 tbsp. oil
2 cups water
X amount of food colouring

Cook over medium heat until a solid ball forms.

A New Addition to Our Room

Come and say hello to "Hopper" and "Chomper"! We are learing lots about how to care for our bunnies.

Mr. Abrams, the local veterinarian, has been in to help us set up a happy, safe, and healthy home for our newest furry friends.

Courtesy of Lynn Wilson

Birthdays

Happy 4th birthday to the following preschoolers:

• Emma Bambrick, Jan. 17
• Colombe Nadeau-O'shea, Jan. 31
• Cassidie Baril, Feb. 25

also prepare a calendar of community events that would be of interest to families; this calendar could be posted near the centre entrance or on the family bulletin board. Calendars might be created that suggest different activities that can be carried out at home for each day of the week and for different age groups.

Some rooms have found it helpful to enclose in the newsletter a monthly calendar that outlines upcoming events, fixed experiences such as swimming lessons, library visits, planned field trips, etc. As emergent curriculum unfolds in the room, some planned experiences may be changed to better reflect the children's needs and interests. These changes can be highlighted on the daily flash board.

Many interesting templates are available online. A calendar of events may also appear on the centre's website or individual room websites as well. This is a useful tool to keep families abreast of important happenings.

The older children could make personalized magnets to hold up their own calendar on the fridge. Out-of-date calendars could be placed in a photo album and become a record of the child's time in the room.

HAPPY LETTERS

A happy letter is a communication from a teacher to a family that celebrates something positive about that family's child, whether a memorable moment in his or her life or a kind deed. For families who have been conditioned to believe that any communication from teachers means trouble, the receipt of a happy letter comes as a welcome relief. At the end of a busy day, families appreciate the sight of a happy letter on the child's cubby or locker and what fun for the whole family to open up their mail box and find a letter from the teacher!

When creating a happy letter, teachers are limited only by their imagination. Paper in shapes ranging from animals to birthday cakes can be purchased commercially, but teachers can develop their own letters. One teacher cut out a hand shape, wrote a note in the palm area, and attached it to the child's back for an appropriate "pat on the back." Some teachers buy stickers to create a border around the sheet of paper, and write the message inside. This idea may be replicated with a piece of acetate, so that the children can take off the stickers and reuse them at home. Creative ideas include paper airplanes folded with a special message inside, fancy bags holding a hidden message, bracelets made with bead letters, fortune cookies with messages inside, a message written on a letter cut in the shape of the child's initial, scrolls wrapped in ribbon, and photos of the child completing a special task. Some suggestions for happy letter starters include

Wow! You won't believe what happened today!

____ is a superstar! She …

____ is a hero today! He …

You're terrific because …

HAPPY LETTERS FROM PARENTS

Smiles Made Easy are note cards and envelopes in a tin that start the writer off with a positive thought such as "I love when …" or "I have fun when …" or "I am proud when…." A child or parent can fill out these cards to encourage expressions of gratitude or just an opportunity to share a kind thought. These are fun to include in lunch boxes or under pillows or even mailed home—everyone enjoys receiving a happy letter. This information might be included in a centre newsletter. Smiles Made Easy note cards are available at **http://www.smilesmadeeasy.com**.

HAPPY LETTERS FROM THE CHILD TO THE FAMILY

Some days, children have exciting events that they would like to share with their families. In this situation the teacher can provide fancy paper, interesting blank cards, etc., along with a variety of writing instruments. Sentence starters, such as "Today at the centre I …" can help children get started. The children will look forward to giving these happy letters to their families at the end of the day.

HAPPY LETTERS FROM A PARENT TO A NEW TEACHER

One teacher gives families who are transitioning to her room a blank card to write to her sharing what they want her to know about their child. These letters help the teacher to understand the child on a more intimate basis. Parents often share their hopes and dreams for their family and for their child.

HAPPY LETTERS FROM A FAMILY

For some teachers, their work seems to go unnoticed, and it is only when families take the time to write their own happy letters that teachers can truly feel that their work is valued. The following is an example of a letter written by a family to demonstrate their appreciation and support:

We are happy Queen Street Child Care Centre parents. Our daughter Zoe graduated Kindergarten summer of 2011 and our son Matthew is currently in the Preschool Room. From the very first day at the Centre 5 years ago, we both knew that Queen Street was unlike any other centre we had visited. The staff was, and continues to be kind, energetic, warm, caring and professional. What still strikes us about the staff until this very day, is how happy and positive they are, every single day, to be at work, to look after children. They are a family, and everyone who attends the Centre becomes a part of that family. And at the head of this family is an extraordinary manager and dedicated mentor. She is always available for parents and children, and maintains an open-door policy with her office. Whether it's an issue you need to discuss, a shoulder you need to cry on, or just a chat about life in general, she is always available. Over the years, we have watched our children thrive and flourish during their time at Queen Street. Zoe still pines daily for her Kindergarten

There were times that I thought that my written communication with families went unnoticed. I often sent happy letters through the mail to the children's home, and it was rare that parents would comment. It wasn't until I did a home visit with one of the families that never seemed to provide feedback that I really learned the importance of this simple piece of communication. As I walked into the kitchen, there posted prominently on the refrigerator were all of the happy letters I had sent. Aisha, my kindergartener, took me by the hand and couldn't wait to show me the letters!

years and teachers, while excelling at everything she does at her new school, largely because of her incredible Queen Street experience. Matthew says he never wants to leave the Centre, and we feel the exact same way. It really does take a village to raise great kids, and we are thankful every day for having Queen Street in our village, helping and guiding us, and our children—Patrizia and Chris.*

HAPPY LETTERS TO THE COMMUNITY

Happy letters can also be sent to community members who volunteer or who donate supplies or resources. Children's artwork can be sent along with a thank-you letter. This is also another way of letting people in the community know that exciting things are happening at the centre. In turn, family members will often support businesses in the community that provide resources to the centre.

CARDS AND NOTES

Nothing is quite so special for a child as receiving mail from his or her teacher. A birthday card or get-well card is appreciated by child and parent alike. Children who attend centres or schools that are closed over the summer and re-open in the fall will appreciate a note from the teacher

*Reprinted by permission of Chris Petropoulos.

Jack's eyes shone as he tore open the envelope that had come for him in the mail. As he reached into the letter, he found a small plastic dinosaur that he clutched eagerly, as he handed the letter to his mother to read.

Dear Jack:

Welcome to the Dinosaur Kindergarten Class! We are so excited that you will be coming to our class. We have lots of places ready for you to keep your things and each place will have your name and a special sticker. Your sticker looks like this:

We sent you something special from the Dinosaur teachers. You can bring it to school, too. We will see you at school on Tuesday, August 26!

Your teachers,

Ms. Howell and Ms. Moll

Jack's excitement over receiving mail and the family's satisfaction in this individual welcome to their child created an immediate bond between them and his new teachers. Carrying his dinosaur to school on the first day and knowing that there was a place waiting for him marked with a dinosaur eased Jack's transition into school.

Source: Adapted from Barbour, Barbour, and Scully, 2008: 288.

FIGURE 8.4 Field Trip Letter

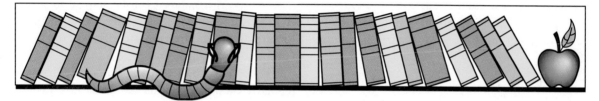

Dear Parents,

On Thursday, February 15, the Kindergarten class will be taking part in a field trip to the Toronto Public Library located at Bloor St. and Spadina Rd. We will be leaving the centre at 12 noon and will return by 2 pm. We will be walking to the library and back to the centre. An early picnic lunch will also be provided. If there are any questions or concerns please feel free to contact Olivia or me. Please sign below before leaving today.

Your cooperation is greatly appreciated.

Thank you.

Renata

Student Teacher

I do/do not (circle one) give my child _____
permission to attend the outing to the Public Library.

I can participate: YES _____

                            NO _____

_____
Signature of Parent

welcoming them back and telling them what they can look forward to when they return. A postcard is a quick and easy method for staying connected to families.

As with all written communication that goes to the home, every effort should be made to create an attractive and eye-catching design (see Figure 8.4). A quick note or Post-it (these come in all kinds of fun shapes and colours) attached to a child's work going home such as "We are so proud of Hyun Ju's effort on her animal drawing. She worked all afternoon on it!" can reinforce the child's efforts and is sure to bring a smile to the parent's face! Varying the format for notes and letters that go home keeps parents interested. For example, when a child needs a new T-shirt for his cubby, the teacher might send the message home on a cut-out form of a T-shirt. Simple but effective!

BULLETIN BOARDS

Bulletin boards do more than communicate information about the teachers and the program. A well-designed, inviting bulletin board can serve as an effective public relations tool for the early learning environment. Besides being visually appealing, bulletin boards should be clearly labelled. The boards should be organized so that the message is clear and located in well-travelled areas. They should also provide a space for families to post messages and respond to teachers or to other families.

Educators should use colour combinations on the board that enhance the overall design of the room. Avoid visual clutter. A *few* complementary colours on all of the boards in the room are preferable to a clash of boards each with its own colour combination. The stronger the colour used, the more attention it will get and we know that colour can affect feelings and behaviour—blue is considered restful and red will stimulate, for example. When designing effective bulletin boards, organization is critical. One strategy is to simply pin everything up on the board with thumbtacks (be careful with them that they don't fall off), then step back and see if it works! Is it visually appealing? Balanced? Too cluttered? All material should stay inside the board and not spill out. Once the visual appearance is deemed satisfactory, the material can be stapled in place. A three-dimensional look is often eye-catching. Pictures of the children are a terrific way to attract families to the board.

The content of bulletin boards should be changed regularly. New information should be added when appropriate. Contributions from families should be especially welcomed. Possible bulletin board items include the following:

- newspaper or magazine articles on subjects of particular interest to families

- general information on the centre (philosophy statement, menus, schedules, licensing documents, and so on)

- photographs of staff accompanied by biographical sketches

- a copy of the most recent newsletter

- a list of people interested in car pools

- movie, video, or book recommendations for specific age groups

- cartoons that express the challenges of parenting

- photo records of field trips or special events in the centre

- congratulations corner to acknowledge new babies, parent donations, special fundraising efforts, and parent volunteers

- a list of volunteers needed, with task descriptions

- a coupon-exchange board or buy-and-sell board

Courtesy of Lynn Wilson

This is an example of what should never happen on a bulletin board!

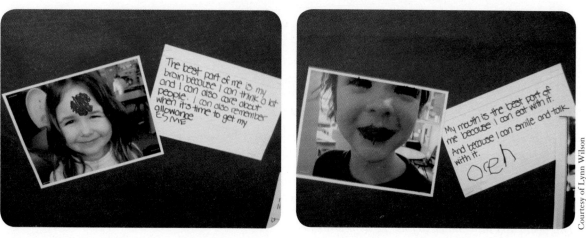

This teacher created a clever board by asking the children to identify the best part of themselves!

- a list of upcoming community events of interest to families

- information on educational opportunities for families

- recipes for playdough, goop, etc.

- guidelines for purchasing appropriate toys and play materials

- postcards from families who are travelling on vacation

- photos of families involved in local community efforts

One centre used Valentine's Day to create a surprise bulletin board for teachers. In the morning (before teachers arrived), the supervisor made heart-shaped pouches and hung them on the bulletin board, one for each teacher. Families, who had been told about the surprise ahead of time, brought in valentines for teachers with messages that expressed appreciation for their work. The surprise bulletin board proved to be an extremely successful morale booster for all concerned.

Another idea is to give families the responsibility for the design and upkeep of one of the bulletin boards in the centre. The board or a family wall may focus on documenting the children and family involvement in the centre. Bulletin boards that are interactive and require family input are an effective way to connect families with one another. A question can be posed at the top of the board such as, "How Are You Supporting Literacy in Your Home?" It may begin with a few parents writing down some suggestions but will often

engage other families to participate: "We read every night before the children go to bed," "We sing all the time," "We have a chalk board on our kitchen wall at Sarah's height and we encourage her to 'write,'" "When we eat breakfast we look for the letters in Kyle's name on the cereal boxes." Other questions might include "What Is Your Favourite Family Meal?" and ask families to write out a recipe for their favourite foods. Photos of each family can be placed beside their recipe. Other questions might include "What Is Your Favourite Place to Take Children in the City?", "Best Tips for Travelling with Children," "Suggestions for Staying Sane over the Holidays," "Words of Wisdom/Proverbs You Grew Up With," "Would Anyone Like to Set Up a Child-Care Exchange One Night a Week?" Other boards might ask for feedback on math or science experiences in the home or learning that takes place in outdoors!

At one centre, the teachers gave each of the families in their room a canvas. Parents were encouraged to design their canvases to reflect their family. As each canvas was returned, it was put up on the bulletin board and proved to be a wonderful opportunity for families to connect with one another.

BULLETIN BOARDS FOR CHILDREN

Bulletin boards for and by children provide opportunities to introduce new concepts and clarify existing ones. They stimulate language development, encourage discussion, provide a record of events that have happened in the centre, and

Courtesy of Lynn Wilson

This board asks the children to find the two classmates who are missing in each class photo.

provide an aesthetic appeal to the environment. The most powerful boards are those that involve the children in manipulating the boards and should be at their eye level. Boards created by and for children provide an opportunity to engage families and visitors to the centre and provide insight into the meaningful interactions that take place between teachers and the children in the centre.

THE FAMILY RESOURCE AREA

While not every centre has space enough to allocate a separate room for a family resource area, it is important that some space, no matter how small, be designated for the purpose of providing materials and resources for families. Regardless of its size or location, the designated family resource area should reflect both the families served and the centre's philosophy. It should also communicate the belief that learning is valued and that sharing resources makes all our lives richer and more meaningful. Teachers can help parents take responsibility for their children's learning outcomes by providing materials and ideas for activities that families can do at home and in the community with their children.

The physical environment should be as inviting as possible—a comfort zone with couches, a coffee table, tables and chairs, carpets, and comfortable chairs. Bookcases, filing cabinets, bulletin boards, and magazine racks help organize the resources available to parents; plants serve to soften the space. Access to a telephone may provide parents with privacy when making important calls. Access to a computer may be the only opportunity some

Courtesy of Lynn Wilson

These examples displayed in the Resource Area may give families ideas of things to do at home.

families have to use technology. If funding allows, a computer lab might be set up for the families to use with an instructor to help those less familiar with technology. Perhaps a local savvy high school student might be willing to lead the class and receive community service hours at the same time! Local service agencies or religious groups, etc., may help with financing this area. There may also be parents who are upgrading their computers who would be willing to donate the older ones to the centre. In some cities, computers and related components that are still in working condition are donated for recycling. Many charities are on these lists; perhaps the centre could also participate in this program.

The space should be adequately lighted. Coffee, tea, fruit juice, and occasional baked goods are always appreciated. A bulletin board can be used to display items parents might like to share with one another; for example, books or articles they have read, items they may want to trade, awards given to family volunteers, children's artwork, lists of food banks, and so forth.

Once the space is established, it must be maintained and organized on a regular basis. A family committee could be created to take over the organization and running of the resource area. Parents will be reluctant to use a space that is cluttered and in disarray. An inventory should be kept of the resource room holdings. A sign-out book should be clearly visible and "how-to" instructions made available to parents in order to keep track of materials.

Centres that have yet to establish a family resource area might begin by surveying parents to find out what resources they would like included. Families may also serve as resources for other parents. They may, for example, be self-employed and offer services that would benefit others. Possible resource items include

- phone and address list of all families (with permission)

- yearly calendar of centre-based events

- photo albums of centre history or events

- books (in the languages spoken in the centre) on child development, parent–child relationships, social issues facing families, behaviour guidance, etc.

- simple phrase books in many languages created by families for other parents and teachers

- ECE journals and parenting or child-development magazines (some family members may be willing to review the material, choosing relevant articles and photocopying them for teachers and families)

- children's health pamphlets and brochures

- articles organized in binders on child-care issues such as safety, nutrition, children's fears, street-proofing, provincial regulations on child care, and so forth

- ECE catalogues that include equipment and play materials

- teacher resource books

- lists of community organizations with accompanying map and phone numbers

- bus schedules, taxi phone numbers

- list of translation services in the community

- copies of old centre newsletters

- posters

- announcements about upcoming community events that might be of interest to families

- trip ideas for families, with vacation tips on, for example, travelling long distances with children

- a list of items for sale or exchange

- brochures designed by the teachers with helpful hints or strategies (tips on reading aloud to children, monitoring television viewing, toileting, and so on)

- videos/DVDs about the centre, on parenting, and for children (parents might want to set up a video exchange)

- community newspapers reflecting the centre's ethnic mix

- CDs and audiotapes

- a recipe book prepared by the cook of the children's favourite recipes, or a recipe exchange board for families

- recycled materials donated by the families for the children's artwork, construction projects, etc.

- parent-initiated babysitting exchange list

- a "borrowing area"—extra umbrellas, hats, mittens, etc.

- clothing-, toy-, or shoe-exchange area

- junk or craft bin, craft bags

- group photos with the names of the children and teachers accompanying

- stationery, calculator, photocopier

- computer and printer to allow parents to research topics on the Internet, create résumés for jobs, complete centre-based projects, etc.

New additions to the family resource area might be noted in the centre newsletter. Families who are leaving the centre might be encouraged to donate items to the resource area. A dedication nameplate representing the family can be included as a way to remember their gift. In one centre each family is invited, on their child's birthday, to add a book to the resource centre in its child's name.

As a way of sharing the responsibilities of the child-care centre, one centre used a large shelving unit in the resource area, on which staff placed a large bin for each teacher, labelled with his or her name. When teachers found themselves out of time but needing work done that was important to the classroom operations, they placed the materials and instructions for completing these tasks inside their bin. Family members who were interested could complete the required task. (Whitaker and Fiore, 2001: 175–176)

This bin approach may also be an opportunity to involve families who cannot spend time at school but want to participate in a meaningful way by taking the bin home and completing the task there.

RESOURCE-AREA EXTRAS
BORROW-A-BOOK PROGRAM

In an effort to encourage an ongoing interest in books, some centres establish borrow-a-book programs. Books can be stored in zip-top bags, which are then punched and hung on hooks on a pegboard. Another strategy is for each child to have his or her own hand-sewn borrow-a-book cloth bag to bring to the resource area. School-age children could sew their own bags and decorate them with fabric paint or embroidery. Under the program, children are invited to choose a book from the collection to take home in their bag. Extra bags should be sewn so that children who leave theirs at home will not be disappointed. Centres that are unable to afford new books for this project may invite parents to donate books as their children outgrow

This is an example of a Borrow-a-Book bag.

them. A booklet may be included for children and their families to write their thoughts about the book, draw a picture, and so on.

STORY BOXES

Story boxes, which can be created by parents or teachers, contain materials and props that are related to a specific story or series of books enjoyed by the children. Each container is identified on the outside to reflect the story inside. Using the *Clifford, the Big Red Dog* series as an example, story box materials might include a Clifford puzzle or CD, a pencil with Clifford designs on it accompanied by red paper, Clifford stickers, story-related finger puppets, photocopies of the pages of the book for the children to put in order along with a clothes line and clothes pins, and so on. An inventory should be included in the story box to ensure that all materials are returned. The story box might also include a response sheet asking parents what their child enjoyed most about the story box and what improvements might be made to it (what new materials might be added, for example). A tip sheet on strategies to support literacy might also be included for families.

VIRTUAL LEARNING

Mass and Cohan (2007) have developed a video program called *Home Connections to Learning*. A video is developed by the children's playroom teachers explaining what new skill is being explored and the families can see the teacher interacting with the children and the hands-on activities that expand or build on their existing math or literacy skills. The take-home video is available to be signed out by parents and is packaged with books, games, and other related activities. Families enjoyed seeing their own children on the video and had a greater understanding of the skills being taught.

SHARE-A-TAPE

Botrie and Wenger (1992: 82) share an interesting classroom strategy that could easily be adapted to school-age programs:

> While studying a unit on our country, we invited parents and/or grandparents, through our newsletters, to share their experiences. Robin's grandparents, both age 78, live in a small town outside of the city and were unable to respond in person. They had both experienced interesting childhoods and were

The Story Box is filled with activities related to the book Bright Eyes, Brown Skin *and was developed by an ECE student during her field placement.*

keen to share their memories with the children in our class. Robin, with tape recorder in hand, visited his grandparents. With their assistance, he formulated a set of ten questions he wanted to pose to these venerable citizens and became an interviewer. Robin, who is a quiet boy in class, blossomed in his role and used strong interviewing skills. His grandparents responded superbly and shared childhood memories that fascinated the students in our class. The program has great potential for strengthening effective language skills.

Families might also enjoy taping their favourite music or singing their favourite songs, nursery rhymes, or lullabies. Teachers may also record the children singing playroom favourites so parents can learn the words and sing along at home.

TRAVELLING SUITCASES

Travelling suitcases are small, inexpensive cases used to store interesting materials that children can take home. In communities where resources for families are limited, items in the suitcases may be kept by the child; for example, a suitcase might contain playdough, a recipe, and a variety of implements. The recipe and playdough would remain at home and only the implements would be returned. Some centres allow the children to choose items in the playroom that they would like to take home in a suitcase overnight or for the weekend. Most children are taught that this is a special privilege and are very responsible about the care and maintenance of the suitcases; however, teachers must expect a certain degree of damage and loss and be prepared to add materials to the suitcases as necessary. Wherever possible, include books related to the contents of the suitcases. Teachers can encourage parents to assist in the development of these travelling kits, which might include the following:

- writing kits (fancy pens, Chinese brushes, notepaper and envelopes, calligraphy pens, erasers, rulers, stamps, and stamp pads)

- games and puzzles

- recipes for favourite centre food

Books can also be stored in clear bags for take-home use as well.

- instructions and materials for simple science experiments family members and children can do together

- projects (friendship bracelets, for example) with instructions and materials

- favourite songbooks and tapes/CDs

- a photo album of all of the children in the group

- instructions and materials for outdoor games (for instance, clue cards for a community treasure hunt)

- musical instruments, CDs, DVDs

- infant activity boards

- sewing cards, needlework, and other craft projects

- dramatic play (jewellery collections, dress-up clothes, puppets, purses)

- manipulatives (such as Lego, Duplo, and Tinkertoys)

- file folder games with a bag of dice or "markers" attached

- art supplies for creative projects such as scissors, smelly markers, oil pastels, glue, fancy paper, and stickers

A special suitcase—prepared by the teachers and children for a sick child—containing get-well notes, a video message, and favourite play room toys might also be kept on hand. If suitcases are in short supply, a backpack is an easy-to-carry substitute.

PORTA PAKS

Developed by Kathy Hartely, a teacher at Orde Street Child Care Centre in Toronto, Porta Paks are simplified versions of travelling suitcases. Consisting of small, unusual play items stored in zip-top bags, they can be taken home by children or used by the centre and taken on bus trips.

Porta Paks for younger children can include such items as sensory "feely bags" and cause-and-effect toys. By using materials that are available in most homes, families can be encouraged to use

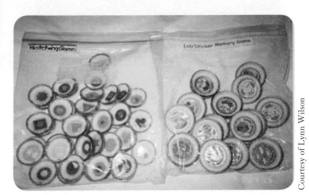

An example of a Porta Pak using baby food jar lids and stickers to create a matching game.

Each of these bags contains instructions and all materials necessary to carry out an activity. The bags can be carried home in travelling suitcases.

the Porta Paks as models for creating their own learning materials. For example, by using juice lids and adding stickers to them, families can make a simple matching game.

TOY LENDING

Toy lending, according to Brock and Dodd (1994: 18),

> affords teachers an opportunity to share quality toys with families and to demonstrate their effectiveness in fostering early literacy development. While parents play with their children, experimenting with different types of toys and modelling ways to use them, they gain a better understanding of the ways children grow and learn. As a result, parents often become more adept at selecting toys to buy their children because they have had access to quality materials.[*]

Families may contribute their own ideas based on the existing resources in the area. In some centres, families encourage other members of the centre to bring in their craft items for sale. In another, one parent created travelling kits. These included tips for travelling with young children as well as a number of travelling games that she invented. The possibilities are endless!

FAMILY INVOLVEMENT STORYBOOK RESOURCES

The Harvard Family Research Project has launched the online Family Involvement Storybook Corner to promote awareness and strategies for assisting families in choosing picture books and other resources through an annotated bibliography for children 4 to 8 years of age. Several resources are downloadable for free along with strategies for effectively engaging teachers and families in children's literacy education. Visit **http://www.hfrp.org/storybook-corner**.

TRAVELLING TEDDY BEAR

> One kindergarten had a traveling teddy bear that was accompanied by a journal intended to record his adventures in the homes he visited. The bear and the journal came in a backpack and went home with a different child each weekend. The idea was for a family member to read parts of the journal to the child and help him or her write additional journal entries, which could be dictated by the child and written by the parent. (Gonzalez-Mena, 2008: 36)[†]

Photos could be taken of the child and the teddy bear and included in a classroom photo album or posted on the centre or playroom website.

EVALUATING THE FAMILY RESOURCE AREA

As adapted from Brock and Dodd (1994: 20), teachers can pose the following questions to family members and children—either verbally or in writing—in order to evaluate the success of the family resource centre.

PARENTS

1. How often do you use the Family Resource Area?
2. Which family member(s) usually shares with your child the books or materials you check out?
3. Tell me about the ways you and your child share books or materials.
4. Have you purchased any of the books or materials that you have checked out from the Family Resource Area? If so, which ones?
5. What new information have you learned about your child as a result of sharing the books or materials from the Family Resource Area?
6. What new information have you learned about parenting as a result of the books or materials you have checked out?[‡]

CHILDREN

1. What are your favourite books to check out?
2. What are your favourite objects, materials, and toys to check out?
3. Tell me how you and your family share the books and materials you check out.

[†]GONZALEZ-MENA, JANET, 50 EARLY CHILDHOOD STRATEGIES FOR WORKING AND COMMUNICATING WITH DIVERSE FAMILIES, 1st Edition, © 2007. Reprinted and Electronically reproduced by permission of Pearson Education, Inc., Upper Saddle River, NJ.

[‡]Brock, D., and Dodd, E. 1994. "A Family Lending Library: Promoting Early Literacy Development," *Young Children* 49 (3): 16–21. © NAEYC. Reprinted with permission.

---

[*]Brock, D., and Dodd, E. 1994. "A Family Lending Library: Promoting Early Literacy Development," *Young Children* 49 (3): 16–21. © NAEYC. Reprinted with permission.

WHERE DO FAMILIES SEEK OUT INFORMATION?

A survey by Best Start Resource Centre (2011) found that

> parents most frequently turned to the Internet, medical professionals, print materials (i.e., books and magazines), and family or friends for information and advice on early child development and parenting, and anticipated they would continue similar information seeking behaviour. Parents indicated that a website is the most useful tool to help them learn about early brain development. They thought they would be most likely to access information about parenting and infant/child development through their health care provider (92%), or parent programs such as Ontario Early Years Centres (74%). The Internet (94%), followed by television (82%) and radio (72%) were the mass media that respondents saw and heard most often.*

TECHNOLOGY AND COMMUNICATION OPPORTUNITIES

> There is no question that the development of new, advanced communication systems over the last twenty years has made our world seem smaller. Communication satellites, sophisticated television transmission equipment, and fibre-optic or wireless connection systems permit people throughout the world to share information and ideas instantaneously. With the simple click of a mouse, you can now "talk" to anyone almost anywhere in the world. (Samovar et al., 2007: 4)†

> Recent immigrants to Canada are more likely to use the Internet (email and text messaging) every day to communicate with relatives and friends. The Internet provides not only increased opportunities for communication locally but also the ability to maintain relationships over long distances. (Adler et al., 2012: 19)‡

Facebook, Twitter, and instant messenger have allowed for a wide range of communication opportunities, and Canada boasts some of the world's highest Internet penetration and social networking usage rates. Yet some families will not have access to technology; even if access is available in local libraries, parents may not have the time or the skills to use them. A computer in the family resource area of the centre may be the only access some families will have to this type of technology. And, for many families, creating opportunities for online communication increases their participation in their children's early learning environment. Communicating online may improve parents' understanding of classroom procedures, philosophies, and policies. Parents may feel more involved in their child's centre and more connected to the educator. This style of communication allows for greater flexibility because families can initiate conversations and express concerns at any time of the day or night. Chatting on online forums can reduce parents' anxiety of meeting face-to-face with educators.

From recipes for playdough, strategies for getting a child to sleep at night, and finding the best price for a new stroller to connecting with other parents with child-rearing challenges, the Internet has dramatically changed how we access and share information. Nevertheless, there are many concerns about the use of technology, such as rising obesity rates, and it may be an useful for families and teachers to come together and discuss the pros and cons of children's use of the Internet, smartphones, amount of TV viewing, etc. As children begin using the Internet at increasingly younger ages, what will ultimately determine the risk level of their online experiences will be the quality of support they receive, not only from their parents, but also from their teachers and from their communities as a whole.

For family-centre partnerships to fully benefit from technology, both parents and teachers must be willing to embrace technology as a communication tool even though a learning curve may result. Some early learning environments are making good use of technology in the classroom and to communicate with parents while others use dated computers with dial-up connections or no Internet access. While computer systems and software have dropped in price over the past few years, for some centres the investment and the monthly costs for Internet access are not financially feasible. Computer programs developed for early learning programs are becoming more sophisticated: in one centre a computer program monitors parent fees; a key pad near the child's cubby allows parents to access the status of their current fees. Some programs alert administrators to upcoming due dates for immunizations for children in the centre and so on.

---

*Adapted/Reprinted with permission by the Best Start Resource Centre.

†SAMOVAR/PORTER/MCDANIEL. *Communication Between Cultures*, 6E. © 2007 Wadsworth, a part of Cengage Learning, Inc. Reproduced by permission. www.cengage.com/permissions

‡From Adler, Ronald, et al., *Interplay: The Process of Interpersonal Communication* 3/Ce © Oxford University Press Canada 2012. Reprinted by permission of the publisher.

SMART BOARDS

In many child-care centres now, computers with educational software are available in the playroom; therefore, monitoring who picks computer time most often and encouraging a balance of active and inactive engagement is critical.

Classrooms are becoming more common with interactive white-boards called SMART Boards transforming learning. Notes on the SMART Board can be filtered by their tags, and moved around the board by educators and children via finger drag. SMART Boards, which were invented by a Calgary-based company, are proliferating; about one-third of classrooms in Canada are now equipped with an interactive whiteboard. In 2008, the province of Alberta announced a three-year, $56 million education initiative that included getting an interactive white-board in every classroom in the province. (Lunau, 2012: 59–61)

How long do you think it will take before white-boards are in programs for children not yet in school settings? As an educator, think of the possibilities!

CENTRE WEBSITES

The centre website can be effective at facilitating family involvement by keeping parents informed by posting information about special events, important dates, photographs, or video segments. It will be important to obtain parental permission to post photos or video clips of the children online and to ensure the security of the site. Permission forms, volunteer opportunities, announcements, fun activities to do at home, links to educational resources, parenting information can all be posted on the website. Parents often find using the school website easier, because it does not require them to know teachers' email addresses. The website should be updated on a regular basis to ensure family interest. Nothing will get parents to the website faster than posting photos of their children that are available 24/7 for sharing with other family members! This is a great way for family members who are not able to get to the site to see their son, daughter, niece, nephew, or grandchild learning and growing! It is also possible to create a response link on the website so that families can comment on centre happenings or share ideas. In centres where some families may not have access to a computer, it may be possible to fundraise or contact an organization that might be willing to donate a computer that can be signed out by families for home use. If this is not possible, informing parents about computer access in the community would be helpful; for example, in local libraries.

It is also important to note that a well-designed website is also a marketing tool that will give prospective parents an insight into the workings of the early childhood environment.

EMAIL

> "Electr[on]ic communication will never be a substitute for the face of someone who with their soul encourages another person to be brave and true."
>
> —adapted from Charles Dickens (Quote Investigator, 2010)

Teachers are using email to communicate with families more frequently because it is a convenient, inexpensive tool to distribute important information about the centre or upcoming events. Notes, messages, newsletters, centre events, and photos of the children can now be sent to many families at once by email. Of course, email should not be used to communicate sensitive information since this information can be saved, printed, or forwarded to others; appropriate discretion should be used. We also need to remember that emails from child-care centres should be professional with an appropriate tone.

BLOGGING AND WEBSITES FOR PARENTS AND TEACHERS

Blogs for parents are gaining popularity. Websites such as **http://www.weewelcome.ca** and **http://www.urbanmoms.ca** are operated for those who want to connect with other mothers. Many controversial topics are raised and there is a forum for women to discuss issues facing mothers. Forums allow women with different viewpoints and parenting styles to exchange information and to learn from a variety of different viewpoints. Online communities are available night and day, and mothers may find that by participating in a forum or by reading a blog they are in contact with mothers outside their own culture or social group and exposed to different ways of doing things, helping them rethink and reframe their own ideas of mothering. More sites for fathers would be a welcome addition to this form of communication.

SKYPE/FACETIME

If families are not able to come to the centre, another option might be to engage in a virtual meeting using Skype or FaceTime but this will depend on the family having access to the Internet and hardware and software that support these programs. For parents who travel, away from home, it is possible to set up web-cams for programs such as Skype or FaceTime to participate in bedtime stories or watch a family event that might have otherwise been missed. When children live far away from a parent or grandparents, this can encourage family connections.

CAMERAS IN THE PLAYROOM

A growing number of centres in Canada and the United States are installing systems that link video cameras in the playroom to websites that families can access from work or home. Most of these systems ensure that security is tight, and encrypted passwords and secure connections make the system hacker-resistant. This system allows parents or relatives to log in at any time during the day to observe the child. Some systems enable photos to be printed out.

At the June Callwood Centre for Young Women, staff at the centre videotape infants once a month. When the family leaves, the DVD is a developmental record of the child as well as his or her interactions with teachers and other children at the centre.

DVDs provide a wonderful opportunity to share the children's day-to-day activities with families who find it hard to spend time on the playroom floor. To facilitate this centre–home communication, educators can record activities that happen outdoors, events in the dramatic play centre, children "reading" to each other, or any of the special events that take place at the centre. This is a simple way for educators to communicate about developmentally appropriate practice. Parents may also get to know the other children in the centre through these images. The DVDs can be signed out by families and, with permission of all families, can be replicated to keep. Siblings, grandparents, aunts, and uncles can share in the DVD at the family's leisure.

THE TELEPHONE AS A COMMUNICATION TOOL

Technology has changed the ways in which telephones are used and will continue to provide alternative ways in which families and teachers can keep in touch. In the past, parents and teachers telephoned each other only when there were problems. Many families will be surprised when the teacher's call is not to raise a concern but to share good news or just catch up.

Contact by telephone or text is immediate and teachers will know that their message has been delivered. Before phoning parents at their workplace, teachers should check that such calls are acceptable to the employer. Teachers might also phone family members at home to ask about a child who has been absent because of illness or another family event; they can also use this time to pass along information that the family might have missed during the child's absence. It is also exciting for the child to speak to the teacher, if he or she is able. If the family uses a speaker phone, the teacher

Janeway Child and Family Centre

SAMPLE TELEPHONE LOG

Date: _____ Time: _____

Child's Name: _____ Parents' Names: _____

Telephone: _____ Teacher: _____

Record of Call:

_____ Busy   _____ Left Message   _____ No Answer   _____ Call-backs

Information Discussed:

Action/Follow up:

_____

_____

may speak to several members of the family at the same time, and when the news is about the child, the child can also hear what is being said. Teachers should consider the timing of a call to the home; no one wants to be disturbed during their dinner hour or during the bedtime routine. There should be an effort to make the conversation short, informative, and to the point. Teaches should stay focused on the reason for the call but be prepared to stay on the phone longer if the parent is inclined to do so. Some teachers make a point of calling each family at home once a month with positive news—"happy calls"—about something the child has accomplished or any good news story! It is an opportunity for families to also share news about their family with the educator—for example, new skating lessons for the child—and, when trust has been established, more difficult and challenging news may be shared. When parents are no longer living together and important news is to be shared, a conference call may also work effectively. When a family member calls the teacher, it is important to return the call as soon as possible. If the topic becomes sensitive, it would be important to arrange for a personal meeting. Some teachers keep track of which family members they have communicated with by phone by creating their own telephone log.

CELL PHONES VERSUS LANDLINES

The availability of cell phones could easily increase parent–teacher communication, yet one reason for the lack of cell phone use in communicating with educators could be the cost involved. Parents may not want to use their cell phone minutes for a parent–teacher phone conference if a landline phone is available. Educators expressed similar concerns regarding the use of their personal cell phone minutes for contacting parents as well as, in some situations, school board policies that prohibit the use of cell phones at school.

> The availability of landline phones may preclude the need for use of cell phones for general communication. Most parents and schools have landline phones and thus the need for cell phone use is limited to situations where there is an immediate need for communication. Cell phones are a technology that although available and convenient, may only be needed for immediate classroom concerns where landline phones are not readily available. (Rogers and Wright, 2012: 48)

THE RIGHT TIME TO CALL THE CENTRE

While telephones in the playrooms allow for a convenient exchange of information, the fact remains that lunch hour, a favourite time for families to call, is often one of the busiest times for staff, as they feed, change, and put the children down for their nap. In school-age lunchrooms there are often large groups of children moving about, involved in getting their lunches microwaved, or heading outdoors, so locating a child may place additional demands on an already busy teacher. A specific time for incoming calls might be arranged so that families and teachers can organize themselves accordingly. At the same time, families should be reassured that all their communications with the centre are welcome.

CALLING TEACHERS AT HOME

Many teachers are happy to give their personal contact information to families in order to support open communication. Some teachers will designate a particular time in the evening when they would be available. This simple gesture sends a powerful message. We know that at times, children go home with imagined slights or misplaced toys and a call to the teacher can alleviate fears or concerns that might have arisen during the day. Parents may also want to connect with a particular teacher whom they may have missed at the end of the day and so a quick phone call can be reassuring. Teachers have found, that almost without exception, parents are respectful of the teacher's "home time" and are grateful for the opportunity to connect.

MASS CALLS

There are times when phone calls to all families are necessary. They are "appropriate for changes in schedule, for example, field trips, reminders about special events and emergencies that affect the whole school—hazardous weather conditions, school closings, etc." (Dyches, Carter and Prater, 2012: 43). Centres might also put in place an information line that enables family members to access a designated extension number for information about their child's playroom. The messages can also be recorded in a variety of languages spoken by the families. Other telephone systems can be established to automatically dial all the numbers designated by the teacher to deliver messages or reminders.

ADVANCE NOTICE

The telephone can also be used to give family members advance warning about any incidents that staff considers serious. For example, if the child has had a fall, a phone call will help parents prepare for a nasty scrape or bump before they arrive. If the teacher involved in a particular incident will be leaving before the family member arrives, it is always a good idea for that teacher to call and explain the situation beforehand rather than have the family member receive the news secondhand from another staff member or, if that is not possible, to call the family at home in the evening. While a positive voice tone may help to deliver your message, the one limitation to phone exchanges is that we cannot see the nonverbal interaction that is taking place. This may place us at a disadvantage particularly when dealing with difficult or challenging issues.

TEXTING

Text messaging is most often used between private mobile phone users, in situations where voice communication is impossible or undesirable, or a quick and easy way to communicate is desired. In many cases, text messaging is less expensive than placing a phone call to another mobile phone. Texting may be more appropriate in reaching family members who may be unable to accept telephone calls; while this is a quick and easy communication format, teachers need to remember to be professional in their communication. Most phones now have a camera that allows for sending photos to families almost instantaneously, an immediate way to capture unexpected moments that can be shared. What a wonderful way to celebrate a child's accomplishment!

THE GOOD THINGS ABOUT TELEVISION

Some parents may be concerned if children are exposed to watching TV in the centre.

> For example, when there is a movie every Friday afternoon, the message educators are sending to parents is that sitting in front of a screen for an extended time must be good practice if the educators highlight it every week in their program. Couple this with the reality that many children, after having sat for an extended period, will then be in a car, bus or stroller for the ride home, followed by more inactivity while the supper is being prepared. Some children even have access to DVD movies on the ride home, as they are now available for use in cars. (Pimento and Kernested, 2010: 340)*

Television is an inescapable part of modern culture and parental concern over how much is too much is a question often asked of educators. We depend on TV for entertainment, news, education, culture, weather, sports, and even music. With the recent explosion in satellite and digital speciality channels, we now have access to an overabundance of both good quality and inappropriate TV content.

*From PIMENTO. *Healthy Foundations in Early Childhood Settings, 4E.* © 2010 Nelson Education Ltd. Reproduced by permission. www.cengage.com/permissions.

Inside LOOK

Sesame Street

Do you remember watching *Sesame Street*? It is the most successful programme in the history of children's television. It has been broadcast to more than 120 million children in 130 nations and is watched by 77 percent of American preschool children. Television producer Joan Ganz Cooney and puppeteer Jim Henson collaborated to form the Children's Television Workshop, and developed the idea of teaching through the perceptual salience of commercial television: quick cuts, animation, and humour with talking puppets and humans posing as narrators. The approach of *Sesame Street* in using direct instruction embedded in an entertaining format that engages children can be found in many early childhood development programs. They are typically organized around specific themes that are relevant to children's daily lives and subject areas such as literacy, math, science, social skills, art and music. Children are encouraged to master specific content such as visual patterns or recognition of colours.

Source: From BERTRAND/GESTWICKI. *Essentials of Early Childhood Education*, 4E. © 2012 Nelson Education Ltd. Reproduced by permission. www.cengage.com/permissions.

In this crowded television environment, the key for parents is to search out high quality TV programs for their children, and whenever possible, enjoy them together as a family. The Media Awareness Network (2012) states the following:

- Because of its ability to create powerful touchstones, TV enables young people to share cultural experiences with others.
- Shared viewing gives family members of all ages an opportunity to spend time together.
- Parents can use TV as a catalyst to get kids reading—following up on TV programs by getting books on the same subjects or reading authors whose work was adapted for the programs.
- Great television can teach kids important values and life lessons.
- TV programs often explore controversial or sensitive issues, which can make it easier for parents and kids to discuss them.
- Educational programming can develop young children's socialization and learning skills.
- News, current events, and historical programming can help make young people more aware of other cultures and people.

Inside LOOK

How to Choose Good TV

The following information may be very helpful to families and their decisions about TV viewing. How can you select viewing that is good for your children? Ask yourself the following questions:

- Does the program actively engage my child, physically or intellectually?
  Television watching doesn't have to be passive. It can prompt questions, kindle curiosity, or teach activities to pursue when the set is off.
- Do I respect this program?
  Parents don't have to like every show their children choose—in fact young people need their own district culture. But parents should trust that a program's creators understand and respect how children grow and learn.

- Does my child see others like himself or herself on television?
  Young children believe that television reflects the real world. To not see people like themselves—in race, ethnicity, or physical ability, for example—may diminish their self-worth. A lack of role models should spark discussion about how TV portrays different types of people.
- How do makers of this program regard my child?
  Some program creators see young people as consumers to be sold to. Others see them as students to be educated, as future citizens to be engaged in the community, or simply as children, whose work is play.

Source: © 2013 MediaSmarts, Ottawa, Canada, The Good Things About Television, http://www.mediasmarts.ca, reproduced with permission.

- Documentaries can help develop critical thinking about society and the world.
- TV can help introduce your family to classic Hollywood films and foreign movies that may not be available in your local video store.
- Cultural programming can open up the world of music and art for young people.*

> "I'm a great believer that any tool that enhances communication has profound effects in terms of how people can learn from each other, and how they can achieve the kind of freedoms that they're interested in."
>
> —*Bill Gates,* Computer World, n.d.

*© 2013 MediaSmarts, Ottawa, Canada, The Good Things About Television, http://www.mediasmarts.ca, reproduced with permission.

REFERENCES

Adler, R.B., L.B. Rosenfeld, R.F. Proctor II, and C. Winder. 2012. *Interplay: The Process of Interpersonal Communication*. 3rd Canadian ed. Toronto: Oxford University Press.

Aronson, M.M. 1995. *Building Communication Partnerships with Parents*. Westminster, CA: Teacher Created Materials.

Barbour, C., N.H. Barbour, and P.A. Scully. 2008. *Families, Schools, and Communities: Building Partnerships for Educating Children*. Columbus, OH: Pearson Merrill Prentice Hall.

Bertrand, J., 2008. *Understanding, Managing, and Leading Early Childhood Programs in Canada*. Toronto: Thomson Nelson.

Bertrand, J., and C. Gestwicki. 2012. *Essentials of Early Childhood Education*. Toronto: Nelson Education.

Best Start Resource Centre. 2011. "Early Brain Development. Parent Knowledge in Ontario, 2011." Retrieved from http://www.beststart.org/resources

Botrie, M., and P. Wenger. 1992. *Teachers and Parents Together*. Markham, ON: Pembroke Publishers.

Brock, D., and E. Dodd. 1994. "A Family Lending Library: Promoting Early Literacy Development." *Young Children* 49 (3): 16–21.

Burrington, B., and S. Sortino. 2004. "In Our Real World: An Anatomy of Documentation." In Joanne Hendrick, ed., *Next Steps toward Teaching the Reggio Way: Accepting the Challenge to Change*. Columbus, OH: Pearson, Merrill Prentice Hall.

Canada's Centre for Digital and Media Literacy. n.d. Retrieved January 28, 2013, from http://www.media-awareness.ca/english/parents/television/good_things_tv.cfm

"Canada's Food Guide." 2011. Retrieved from http://www.hc-sc.gc.ca/fn-an/food-guide-aliment/index-eng.php

Computer World. "The Quotable Bill Gates in His Own Words." Retrieved January 28, 2013, from http://www.computerworld.com/s/article/9101838/The_quotable_Bill_Gates_In_his_own_words

Dyches, T. T., N. Carter, and M.A. Prater. 2012. *A Teacher's Guide to Communicating with Parents: Practical Strategies for Developing Successful Relationships*. Upper Saddle River, NJ: Merrill/Pearson.

Giannetti, C. C., and M.M. Sagarese. 1998. "Turning Parents from Critics into Allies." *Educational Leadership*, 55(8).

Gonzalez-Mena, J. 2008. *50 Early Childhood Strategies for Working and Communicating with Diverse Families*. Columbus, OH: Pearson, Merrill Prentice Hall.

Graham Clay, S. n.d. *Communicating with Parents: Strategies for Teachers*. Retrieved January 31, 2013, from http://www.adi.org/journal/ss05/Graham-Clay.pdf

Harris Helm, J., S. Beneke, and K. Steinheimer. 1997. "Documenting Children's Learning." *Childhood Education*. Summer.

Hewitt, P. 2011. "Autistic Children Use iPad at Toronto School to Reach Out and Communicate." The Canadian Press. May 18.

Holloway, A. 2011. "North America's Techiest Cities." *Connected. Rogers Magazine*. Summer.

Internet World Stats. 2011. "Internet Usage and Population Statistics in North America." Retrieved December 31, 2011, from http://www.internetworldstats.com/stats14.htm.

Lunau, K. 2012. "The Touch-Screen School." *Maclean's*. January 30.

Mass, Y., and K.A. Cohan. 2007. *Home Connection to Learning. Supporting Parents as Teachers*. Washington, DC: NAEYC.

Pimento, B., and D. Kernested. 2010. *Healthy Foundations in Child Care*, 4th ed. Toronto: Nelson Thomson Learning.

Recruiting New Teachers. 2001. *Connect for Success: Building a Teacher, Parent, Teen Alliance. A Toolkit for Middle and High School Teachers*. Belmont, MA: Author.

Rogers, R.H., and V.H. Wright. 2012. "Assessing Technology's Role in Communication between Parents and Middle Schools". *Electronic Journal for the Integration of Technology in Education*, 7: 36–58.

Samovar, L.A., R.E. Porter, and E.R. McDaniel. 2007. *Communication Between Cultures*, 6th ed. Florence, KY: Thomson Wadsworth.

Whitaker, T., and D.J. Fiore. 2001. *Dealing with Difficult Parents*. Larchmont, NY: Eye on Education.

Created by Allison

Chapter

9

FAMILIES WE MAY MEET

"Let us put our heads together and see what life we will make for our children."

—*Sitting Bull, Lakota*

LEARNING OUTCOMES

After studying this chapter, you will be able to

1. identify the diverse families found in Canada today

2. evaluate the role of the educator in supporting families with diverse situations, challenges, strengths, and needs

There is always a danger of organizing information in a way that leads to the assumption that families can be grouped together on the basis of similar characteristics and issues. In fact, nothing could be further from the truth! Regardless of common elements that exist in some families, each is unique. *It is the teacher's responsibility to hear each family's story and to focus on each family's strengths.* To help teachers understand and work with the families they serve and the situations they face, books for both adults and children are useful resources. *Parent Books* offers a comprehensive selection of materials that covers a wide range of issues families and teachers may encounter. Visit **http://www.parentbooks.ca**

ABORIGINAL FAMILIES

"Mary is a teacher in an Aboriginal Head Start program. This is an early intervention program for young Aboriginal children and their families. Mary's sister Sarah teaches in the same program on their reserve. Mary and Sarah have worked with Elders in their communities to design and implement curriculum that includes culture and language, education, health promotion, nutrition, social support programs, and family involvement. Both Mary and Sarah have young daughters who attend this program, and they are pleased that they are all learning Ojibway from an Elder."

According to Statistics Canada, Aboriginal identity refers to those persons who reported identifying with at least one Aboriginal group—North American Indian, Métis, Inuit—and/or those who reported being a Treaty Indian or a Registered Indian as defined by the Indian Act of Canada, and/or those who reported they were members of an Indian band or First Nation.

The terms Indigenous and Aboriginal are used almost synonymously in Canada to refer to the population of peoples who identify themselves as descendents of original habitants.... Some prefer the term Indigenous because it connects to a global advocacy movement of Indigenous peoples who use this term, most notably the Maori in Aotearoa/New Zealand. The term "Aboriginal" was coined in the 1800s by the colonial government in Canada as a catch-all label, and some people refrain from using this term because of its colonial derivation. (Ball et al., 2007)

© Robert Postma/First Light

Native peoples want the right to choose and define the kinds of child-care services that meet their needs.

Others may prefer to be referred to by their nation.

Almost half of the Aboriginal population in Canada are 24 years of age or younger, a higher percentage than that of the same age group in the national population. Most Aboriginals live in the prairies and the territories, but statistics indicate a movement to urban centres with 54 percent of the population living off-reserve. Winnipeg hosts the highest number of Aboriginals in the country with 10 percent of its population claiming Aboriginal roots. Only 0.5 percent of Toronto's and Montreal's populations are Aboriginal. (Norrie McCain, Mustard and McCuaig, 2012: 25).[*]

When discussing Aboriginal families, it is important that we understand the differences among these groups living in Canada. The experiences of an Inuit family living in the Northwest Territories will be vastly different from a Métis family living in Manitoba.

[*] Norrie McCain, M., Mustard, F.J., McCuaig, K. 2012. *Early Years Study 3. Making Decisions Taking Action.* Margaret & Wallace McCain Family Foundation. Reprinted by permission.

The Assembly of First Nations

The Assembly of First Nations (AFN) is the national organization for First Nations (Indian) peoples in Canada. This includes more than 800,000 citizens living in 633 First Nations communities, as well as rural and urban areas. The AFN is an advocacy organization for First Nations and our role is to advance First Nation priorities and objectives as mandated by the Chiefs-in-Assembly. This includes providing an organizing and coordinating role, providing legal and policy analysis, communicating with governments and the general public, facilitating national and regional discussions and facilitating relationship building between the Crown and First Nations.

Source: Submission of the Assembly of First Nations to the United Nations Committee on the Elimination of Racial Discrimination, 2012.

FACTS ABOUT ABORIGINAL FAMILIES AND THEIR CHILDREN

When we examine the lives of Aboriginal children and their families in Canada, we cannot help but be shocked by the following statistics:

- Life expectancy is five to seven times lower than that of other Canadians (Ball, 2008).

- Immunization rates are 20 percent below the general population, leading to high rates of preventable diseases (UNICEF, 2009).

- Aboriginal children are twice as likely to be living with a lone parent or another relative compared to non-Aboriginal children (Statistics Canada, 2011).

- Aboriginal children are more likely to have a teen mother (Statistics Canada, 2011).

- Close to 50 percent of children with chronic conditions on reserve have difficulty accessing health services because of lack of availability of services, facilities, or doctors/nurses within their area (UNICEF, 2009).

- First Nations infant mortality is three to seven times higher the national average and the leading causes of infant death are upper respiratory tract infections and sudden infant death syndrome (SIDS) (UNICEF, 2009).

- Fetal alcohol syndrome disorder (FASD) may affect one in five Inuit and First Nation children.

Lack of access to appropriate resources has made it challenging for First Nations children to have food security. Thus, unbalanced diets and the deterioration of traditional foods have fuelled an obesity epidemic, as 62% of First Nations children living on reserve are either overweight or obese. Unhealthy weight is known to be a precursor for type 2 diabetes among children, and [for] other chronic diseases once they reach adulthood. Another implication of lack of access to a nutritional diet and proper health care services is tooth decay. Ninety-one percent of Aboriginal children are affected by dental decay, with children averaging 7.8 decayed teeth by the age of six.

Source: UNICEF, 2009.

- Tuberculosis (TB) rates in northern Aboriginal communities are four times the national average; the rate of respiratory diseases in Inuit children is the highest in the world.

- Hearing loss and speech and language delays are far greater in Aboriginal communities.

- Sixty-seven percent of Inuit children have some degree of hearing loss, often resulting from chronic ear infections and respiratory infections compounded by an acute shortage of audiologists (MacQueen, 2012).

- There are significant concerns about early school leaving, juvenile detention, incarceration, and juvenile suicide.

- Seventy percent of on-reserve children will never finish high school.

- Only one-quarter of Aboriginal peoples reported that they had enough knowledge of an Aboriginal language to carry on a conversation (Statistics Canada, 2009).

- One hundred and seventeen First Nations communities are under drinking water advisories (UNICEF, 2009).

TABLE 9.1 An Overview

INUIT	MÉTIS	FIRST NATIONS
ABOUT INUIT	**ABOUT THE MÉTIS**	**ABOUT FIRST NATIONS**
For many centuries, outsiders called Inuit "Eskimos," but Inuit prefer the name by which they have always known themselves—Inuit—which means "the people" in their own language, Inuktitut. In 2006, 4 percent of the Aboriginal population identified as Inuit, an 8 percent increase from 2001. About 55,700 Inuit live in 53 communities across the North.	Métis are descendants of marriages of Cree, Ojibway, Saulteaux, and Menominee peoples to French Canadians, Scots, and English. In 2006, an estimated 389,785 people reported as Métis. This population has almost doubled (increasing by 91 percent) since 1996. The Métis represented just 1 percent of the total population of Canada. In 2006, 9 percent of all people in the Northwest Territories reported they were Métis, followed by 6 percent in Manitoba, 5 percent in Saskatchewan, and 3 percent in Alberta and Yukon. Despite their central role in the settlement of Canada, the Métis did not become an officially recognized Aboriginal group until 1982.	First Nations peoples accounted for 60 percent of Aboriginal peoples in 2006. Some 698,025 identified themselves as First Nations. The First Nations population increased 29 percent between 1996 and 2006. There are more than 600 nations across Canada.
WHERE THEY LIVE	**WHERE THEY LIVE**	**WHERE THEY LIVE**
78 percent of the population live in Inuit Nunaat, the Inuktitut expression for "Inuit Homeland" an area of four regions in the Arctic: – 49 percent live in Nunavut. – 19 percent live in Nunavik in northern Quebec. – 6 percent live in the Inuvialuit region of the Northwest Territories. – 4 percent live in Nunatsiavut in northern Labrador.	87 percent of all Métis live in the West and in Ontario in 2006; 7 percent live in Quebec; 5 percent live in Atlantic Canada. The remaining 1 percent live in one of the three territories. 7 out of 10 live in an urban area, and 40,980 Métis live in Winnipeg, the largest Métis population in one location.	40 percent live on-reserve; 60 percent live off-reserve; 75 percent of people living-off reserve live in urban areas. The Prairie provinces are home to young First Nations populations.

INUIT	MÉTIS	FIRST NATIONS
HOUSEHOLDS	**HOUSEHOLDS**	**HOUSEHOLDS**
Eighteen percent of Inuit live in a household that is home to more than one family. Inuit have traditionally lived in family groupings, but the serious shortage of housing in most communities has forced many families to live in cramped conditions.	Overall there has been a decrease in the share of Métis living in crowded homes or in homes needing repairs since 1996. Rural Métis living in rural locations in the Prairie provinces still suffer these conditions.	First Nations people are five times as likely as non-Aboriginal people to live in crowded homes, especially on reserves, with 26 percent living in these conditions, and four times as likely as non-Aboriginals to live in dwellings requiring major repairs.
FAMILY STRUCTURE	**FAMILY STRUCTURE**	**FAMILY STRUCTURE**
In 2006, nearly 70 percent of Inuit children aged 14 and under lived in a family with two parents. Twenty-five percent lived in lone-parent families: about 30 percent lived with a female lone parent and 6 percent with a male lone parent. Four percent lived solely with a grandparent, with no parent or other relatives present.	A total of 54,735 Métis children, or 65 percent of the total, live in a two-parent family, while 27,955 youngsters, or 33 percent, live with a lone parent. The percentage of Métis children living with a lone parent in urban centres is 42 percent, almost double the proportion of 22 percent in rural areas.	Just over one-half (54 percent) of First Nations children live with two parents. Just under one-third (31 percent) of First Nations children aged 14 and under live with a lone mother. Six percent of First Nations children live with a lone father.
LANGUAGE	**LANGUAGE**	**LANGUAGE**
The word *Inuktitut* is routinely used to refer to all Canadian variants of the Inuit traditional language, and it is recognized as one of the official languages of Nunavut and the Northwest Territories. It is spoken in all areas north of the tree line, including parts of the provinces of Newfoundland and Labrador, Quebec, to some extent in northeastern Manitoba, as well as the territories of Nunavut, the Northwest Territories, and traditionally on the Arctic Ocean coast of Yukon. The traditional language is a system of closely interrelated dialects that are not readily comprehensible from one end of the Inuit world to the other.	Michif was a trade language that developed originally in the 1700s between the French/English fur traders and the Cree/Algonkian/ Sioux speakers from Ontario and Manitoba. The most common language is Cree, an Algonquian language. In 2006, 9380 Métis could carry on a conversation in Cree. Older Métis—12 percent of those ages 75 and older—are more likely to speak an Aboriginal language. Less than 3 percent of Métis ages 44 and under speak an Aboriginal language.	Over 60 different languages are spoken by First Nations grouped into distinct language families: Algonquin, Athapascan, Siouan, Salish, Tsimshian, Wakashan, Iroquoian, Haida, Kutenai, and Tlingit. Twenty-nine percent say they can speak well enough to carry on a conversation. The figure is higher for those living on-reserve (51 percent) than off-reserve (12 percent). The language spoken by the largest number of First Nations peoples is Cree, followed by Ojibway.

Source: Statistics Canada 2008. Aboriginal Identity Population by Age Groups, Median Age and Sex, 2006 counts for Canada, Provinces and Territories, Released January 15, 2008; http://www12.statcan.ca/english/census06/data/highlights/aboriginal/pages/Page.cfm?Lang=E&Geo=PR&Code=01&Table=1&Data=Count&Sex=1&Age=1&StartRec=1&Sort=2&Display=Page

HOUSING

The tables above highlight where Inuit, Métis, and First Nations people live, the composition of their households, their family structures, and the languages spoken at home.

CANADA'S AUDITOR GENERAL RAISES CONCERNS

In 2008, in her report on the status of Aboriginals in Canada, Sheila Fraser, Canada's Auditor General stated that while the Indian and Northern Affairs

TABLE 9.2	Where Do Aboriginal People Live?
PROVINCE/TERRITORY	**POPULATION**
Newfoundland and Labrador	23,455
Prince Edward Island	1,730
Nova Scotia	24,175
New Brunswick	17,650
Quebec	108,425
Ontario	242,495
Manitoba	175,395
Saskatchewan	141,890
Alberta	188,365
British Columbia	196,075
Yukon Territory	7,580
Northwest Territories	20,635
Nunavut	24,915

Source: Statistics Canada, 2007. Table 20; http://www12.statcan.ca/english/census06/analysis/aboriginal/tables/table20.htm

Department conducted some studies and began a few new programs, it made little progress on a range of problems cited in 2000, including a large gap in the number of Aboriginal versus non-Aboriginal high school graduates. Ms. Fraser criticized Ottawa for failing Aboriginal children who live on reserves. She pointed out that

> school funding is so inadequate compared to provincial public schools that it will take 28 years for them to catch up to the high school graduation rates of their non-native peers. Most native schools are in communities with fewer than 500 residents, making it difficult to offer a range of services. (Fraser, 2008)

Ontario's former Lieutenant-Governor, James Bartleman, whose mother is Ojibway, was so concerned about the reserves he called "Ontario's Third World" that he sent more than a million books to fill the empty class shelves and began summer literacy camps. He also twinned 100 northern Aboriginal schools with schools in the south, which have pledged to send books.

RESIDENTIAL SCHOOLS

One of the most significant events affecting First Nation communities was the creation of residential schools by the Canadian federal government;

these schools were largely operated by the Anglican, Roman Catholic, Methodist, and Presbyterian churches.

> From the early 1830s to 1996, thousands of First Nation, Inuit, and Métis children were forced to attend residential schools in an attempt to assimilate them into the dominant culture. Over 150,000 children, some as young as four years old, attended the government-funded and church-run residential schools. (Aboriginal Healing Foundation, 2011: 1)

While not all children had negative experiences in these schools, incidents of physical and sexual abuse have been cited by many former students. "Those traumatized by their experiences in the residential school have suffered pervasive loss: loss of identity, loss of family, loss of language, loss of culture" (Aboriginal Healing Foundation, 2011: 3).

Children were placed in the national network of residential schools, which were built far away from reserves so that the children would not attempt to return home and to ensure that the children would be educated in European ways without parental or cultural influences. "The intent of the residential school system was to educate, assimilate, and integrate Aboriginal people into European-Canadian society. In the words of one government official, it was a system designed 'to kill the Indian in the child'" (AFH, 2011: 2).

According to the *Toronto Star* (2007a), a 1996 UN report classed Aboriginal languages in Canada as among the most endangered in the world. Statistics Canada (2007) concluded that only three languages out of 50—Cree, Ojibway, and Inuktitut—had large enough populations to be considered secure from extinction in the long run.

There are estimated to be 80,000 residential school survivors alive today (AFH, 2011: 1), and in 2007, the Government of Canada implemented the Indian Residential School Settlement Agreement. The settlement agreement included Common Experience Payment (CEP) to all surviving former students of federally administered residential schools; the Independent Assessment Process (IAP) to address compensation for physical and sexual abuse; establishment of the Truth and Reconciliation Commission; healing initiatives; and a fund for commemoration projects (AFH, 2011: 5). In 2008, Prime Minister Harper offered a full apology on behalf of Canadians for the Indian

Cree child Thomas Moore, as he appeared in his traditional Cree attire when admitted to the Regina Indian Industrial School.

Residential School System and the impact it had on Aboriginal culture, heritage, and language.

ABORIGINAL FATHERS

This section was contributed by Jessica Ball.

The first study of Aboriginal fathers in Canada was completed by Dr. Jessica Ball at the University of Victoria. She studied a team of Aboriginal fathers from each of five First Nations, as well as some from a number of partnered urban Aboriginal organizations. Questionnaires and interviews were gathered from

73 First Nations and seven Métis fathers who all had at least one child under the age of 5. These Aboriginal fathers emphasized the sociohistorical conditions associated with colonialism that have shaped Indigenous fathers' self-reported challenges in "learning to be a father" and "becoming a man."

Qualitative analyses guided by grounded theory methodology suggested three patterns of response to becoming a father: an avoidance pattern termed "fathers-in-waiting"; learning fathering through play; and stepping up/settling down to fathering responsibilities. Fathers described a gradual

Inside LOOK

As an aboriginal ECE, I think it is important to see positive Aboriginal role models who are proud of who they are. Not stereotypical pictures of an "Indian" dressed up in war tribe gear—feathers and a painted face. We need to see Aboriginals as doctors, police officers, teachers, etc.

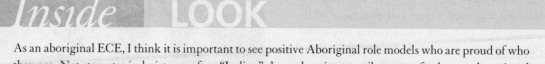

process of accepting and learning fatherhood, often years after the birth of their first child. Widespread shifts in gender roles and constructions of masculinity were identified as reciprocally influential conditions that have enabled some Indigenous men to become more involved in caregiving roles with their children. Fathers pointed to a lack of supports, especially in rural and remote settlements, and especially for men who were raising their children alone. All fathers described incidents where they felt that programs, policies, and society as a whole are biased in favour of mothers (Ball, 2009).

Findings from this study and planned future research will extend community practice beyond a prevailing focus on mothers, and extend fathering theory beyond a prevailing European-heritage perspective. Supporting Indigenous fathers' involvement requires sustained, macro-system, policy-driven efforts to reduce barriers to initiating and sustaining positive engagement with children. Steps include increasing information about declaring paternity on birth records, accessing birth records, and engaging Indigenous fathers with adolescents (e.g., in schools) to promote awareness of how fathers can be important in children's lives (Ball, 2008). ECE practitioners need to acknowledge fathers in children's programs and decision making about children, and work towards implementation of "kith and kin" policies in child protection programs to keep children closer to home (Ball and George, 2006). This project produced a resource kit that includes a documentary DVD that features interviews with First Nations fathers of young children, a booklet for Aboriginal fathers, and a booklet for community-based practitioners. Visit **http://www.ecdip .org/fathers** for more information.

TRADITIONAL EDUCATION

The traditional way of education was by example, experience, and storytelling. The first principle involved was total respect and acceptance of the one to be taught, and that learning was a continuous process from birth to death. It was total continuity without interruption. Its nature was like a fountain that gives many colours and flavours of water and that whoever chose could drink as much or as little as they wanted to whenever they wished. The teaching strictly adhered to the sacredness of life whether of humans, animals or plants.

Source: Art Solomon, Ojibwe Elder, residential school survivor. Visit **http://www.shannonthunder bird.com/residential_schools.htm**.

In traditional Aboriginal approaches to child care, Thomas and Learoyd (1990: i) observe, the child is perceived as a

child of the community. All those people with whom the child comes into regular contact often become part of the "extended family" and as such assume responsibility for the care of the child…. The child in a Native community is raised on values which emphasize autonomy, belonging, mastery and generosity.

Grandparents play a significant role in raising children as they pass on Aboriginal traditions and values.

"Native people firmly believe that children represent the primary means through which a culture can preserve its tradition, heritage, and language. Children are considered the trust of the past and the hope of the future" (Federation of Saskatchewan Indian Nations, 1983). Eva Cardinal, a Cree educator based in Edmonton, states:

Many Aboriginal families want their children to be involved in rituals and ceremonies that recall their traditional past.

My people believe children are a gift from the Creator. Our children are only loaned to us. Children are our future leaders. Children are highly valued. I will not pretend all Native parents act on these beliefs. We have our share of neglect and abuse. But we consider this to be every bit as dysfunctional as the dominant culture does. Our children are precious to us, even when we cannot act on this belief. (1994: 23)[*]

---

[*] Cardinal, E. 1994. "Effective Programming: A Native Perspective." *Early Childhood Education* 27 (1): (Spring– Summer). Reprinted by permission of the Alberta Teachers' Association.

"If it be necessary to punish a child, do it in such a way as to improve his strength or his mind, but lay not your hand upon him for you may damage the possession of your god, his gift to you" (Tribal Laws of the Eastern Algonquin, 2005).

But the challenges of a two-tiered system for health, welfare, and education have created a crisis through inequity on reserves across the country. Schools on reserve come under federal jurisdiction, while children in the provincial/territories receive far greater funding. For example, the school in Attawapiskat First Nation in northern Ontario has

Inside LOOK

Students at Attawapiskat in 2008 had had enough of broken promises and led by 13-year-old student Shannen Koostachin, they travelled to Ottawa to ask for a new school, but then Minister of Indian Affairs Chuck Strahl said it was not possible. There is no timeline in place to provide the community with a new school. Shannen's goal of becoming a lawyer meant she had to leave home to attend high school in a community hundreds of kilometres away. Tragically, while away at school, she died in a car accident. She was 15. Before her death she was nominated for the International Children's Peace Prize. She also spearheaded a campaign that continues to gain momentum and she been re-named "Shannen's Dream" in her honour. Thousands of Indigenous children and youth have rallied behind "Shannen's Dream" which calls for "safe and comfy schools and culturally-based and equitable education" for First Nations students.

Source: First Nations Child and Family Caring Society of Canada, 2012.

http://www.fncaringsociety.ca/shannens-dream

Inside LOOK

In June of 2011, National Inuit Leader Mary Simon, then President of Inuit Tapiriit Kanatami, announced a series of bold new recommendations to empower parents, expand early childhood programs, and gather detailed research data. A total of 10 core investments are set out in *First Canadians, Canadians First: The National Strategy on Inuit Education.* The goal of the Strategy is to graduate more Inuit students and transform early childhood, K-12 and post secondary programs throughout the four Inuit regions of Canada: Nunavut, Nunavik (Northern Quebec), Nunatsiavut (Northern Labrador), and the Inuvialuit Settlement Region of the Northwest Territories. Other recommendations include investing in curriculum development and language resources to create a fully bilingual system based on the Inuit language and one of Canada's two official languages, establishing a standardized writing system so that Inuit across Canada can more easily share teaching materials and published texts, and establishing a university in the Canadian Arctic.

Source: Reprinted by permission of Inuit Tapiriit Kanatami.

been in the news because has been condemned: the land it's built on is contaminated by 50,000 litres of diesel fuel. For the last 10 years, students have used portables that are infested with mice, are freezing in the winter, and are considered serious fire hazards. Unfortunately, Attawapiskat is only one of many schools on reserves in dire need of repair. Another pressing issue is that many reserves do not have high schools, so many Aboriginal students either end their education at Grade Eight or are forced to attend city schools kilometres from their families (Shadow Report, U.N. Committee on the Right of the Child, 2011).

ABORIGINAL FAMILIES IN EARLY LEARNING ENVIRONMENTS

> "Look into the eyes of your child once a moon and see there … the miracle of the Great Spirit."
>
> —**Tribal Laws of the Eastern Algonquin, 2005**

COLLABORATION

In 2005, 160 Aboriginal and non-Aboriginal leaders and 11 national organizations met to discuss opportunities for collaboration in supporting the healthy development of Aboriginal children and youth. Examining the strengths and challenges in the current system, participants engaged in an extensive dialogue to establish core principles for more effective early childhood programs:

- Aboriginal peoples are in the best position to make decisions that affect their children, youth, families, and communities.

- The ability of families to define their own cultural identifies must be respected and not imposed on them by others.

- There is a need to acknowledge discrimination and to articulate the tangible expressions of racism in the system.

- The health and development of Aboriginal children is a balance between the physical, spiritual, emotional, and cognitive sense of self and how these are interrelated with family, community, world and the environment, in the past, present, and future.

- Because culture and language are ways of seeing and understanding the world, the program will be most effective when it can relate to Aboriginal children and their families in that context.

EXHIBIT 9.1   Aboriginal Child-Care Philosophy

Brokenleg and Brendtro (1989) describe four distinct aspects of Aboriginal child-care philosophy:

1. Significance is nurtured in a cultural milieu that celebrates the ethos of belonging. Within Native society, a sense of belonging fashions young people to be more responsive to advice from other clan/band members.… Native youth listen and reflect upon advice given to them by respectful and caring adults. A sense of belonging extends beyond the family, encompassing nature as well.

2. Competency is enhanced by extensive opportunities for mastery. Success and mastery produce social recognition as well as inner satisfaction. Native children are taught to generously acknowledge the achievements of others, but a person who receives honour must always accept this without arrogance. Someone more skilled than oneself is seen as a model, not a competitor.

3. Power is fostered by encouraging the expression of autonomy. As opposed to contemporary white culture's pressure on children to become independent, assertive, and competitive at an early age, the children must first have opportunities to be dependent, learn to respect and value elders, and be taught to obey through explanation for desired behaviour.

4. Virtue is reflected in the preeminent value of generosity. Native children are taught to be generous, unselfish, and to give without expectations. As the Native community is based upon reciprocity, personal wealth and possessions do not elevate one's social status.… Altruism is considered the highest of virtues.

Source: M. Brokenleg and L. Brendtro, "The Circle of Caring: Native American Perspectives on Children and Youth," p. 10. Paper presented to Child Welfare of American International Conference, Washington, DC, 1989. Reprinted by permission of Reclaiming Youth International.

The Aboriginal Children's Survey (ACS) was developed by Statistics Canada and Aboriginal advisors from across the country to assess the early development of Aboriginal children (ages 0 to 5 years) and the social and living conditions in which they are learning and growing. The survey was conducted jointly by Statistics Canada and Human Resources and Social Development Canada (2010). The most common type of child care arrangement for all three groups of Aboriginal children was a daycare centre: 46% of First Nations children living off reserve, 44% of Métis children and 59% of Inuit children in care attended a daycare centre. This was followed by care by a non-relative (18% for First Nations children living off reserve, 22% for Métis, 12% of Inuit children) and care by a relative (17% for all three groups). Seventeen percent of off-reserve First Nations children, 16% of Métis, and 11% of Inuit children were in a nursery school, a preschool, or [an Aboriginal] Head Start program as their main child care arrangement. Many of the child care arrangements for First Nations children living off reserve, Métis children and Inuit children included some Aboriginal cultural content, be that through traditional and cultural values and customs or the use of an Aboriginal language in the child care environment. For example, the majority of Inuit children in care were reported to attend a child care arrangement that promoted traditional Inuit cultural values and customs (67%) and used an Inuit language (66%).

Source: Statistics Canada, 2010.

The program at Misipawistik Cree Nation Head Start Program, in Grand Rapids, Manitoba, is in some respects a typical Head Start Program. However, this program is unique because of its increased collaboration, enhanced training opportunities, child-centred curriculum, and increased opportunities for families and their children to attend a program.

- **Increased collaboration.** The staff works as a collaborative unit. Planning occurs at all levels—coordinator, early childhood educators, cook, and custodian. Additionally, whenever possible all staff, including the cook and the custodian, have the opportunity to attend workshops together. This fosters an enhanced understanding of the child, the family, and the program.
- **Development of training workshops.** The coordinator and staff have developed and continue to develop area workshops to meet the specific training needs of their program and their families. This includes collaboration with other programs within their community. Workshops also include opportunities for families to participate with children in activities designed to enhance family understanding of children's interactions in a practical setting.
- **Child-centred curriculum.** The program embraces a "play-to-learn" philosophy and is continually striving to improve the active play experiences of the children through further education, individual research, and increased resources.
- **Expansion of opportunities.** An additional half-day program is offered for two-year-olds in the community. There is a dual purpose to this activity. First, it provides an opportunity to families who have no access to a program to attend. Second, it provides a bridging to children and families who potentially will participate in the program when the children are three years old.

Source: Reprinted by permission of Dr. Ingrid Crowther, Executive Director, ICC Lifelong Learn Inc.

- Aboriginal children need the best that Aboriginal and non-Aboriginal systems have to offer. For that to happen, the mainstream system needs to make space for Aboriginal concepts.

- Aboriginal people should take the lead role in addressing issues and establishing relationships with non-Aboriginal providers and organizations. These relationships should be characterized by reciprocity, respect, and a balance of power (Bertrand and Gestwicki, 2012: 24).*

THE GENERATIVE CURRICULUM MODEL

This section was contributed by Jessica Ball, coordinator, First Nations Partnership Programs.

Ten partnership programs between the University of Victoria and First Nations communities have explored the value of bringing community Elders and other community resource people alongside mainstream teaching and learning in postsecondary training in order to ensure bicultural, community-relevant, community-involving processes and outcomes. First Nations community partners engage with a curriculum team from the mainstream institution to develop and deliver community-based, culturally sensitive course work leading to a diploma in Child and Youth Care. The program was first offered in 1988 when Saskatchewan's Meadow Lake Tribal Council approached Dr. Alan Pence, a noted early childhood educator, to cooperatively develop a bicultural curriculum that prepared First Nations students to deliver quality child-care programs both on and off the reserve. The partnership resulted in the *Generative Curriculum Model* for creating curriculum, in which cultural knowledge about child development, child-rearing practices, and community life are considered alongside Euro-Western theory, research, and practice. These partnerships have shown the tremendous positive potential of involving the community in every step of program development and delivery, and grounding the development of human service practitioners in intergenerational relationships, community collaboration, and cultural revitalization.†

---

* From BERTRAND/GESTWICKI. *Essentials of Early Childhood Education, 4E.* © 2012 Nelson Education Ltd. Reproduced by permission. www.cengage.com/permissions.

† Reprinted by permission of Jessica Ball.

ABORIGINAL HEAD START (AHS)

Between 1995 and 1998, the Aboriginal Head Start Program in urban and northern communities and on reserves was founded. This program was designed to engage First Nations, Inuit, and Metis children up to 6 years of age to ensure stimulating early learning environments that would nurture the healthy growth and development of Aboriginal children. AHS is locally controlled and designed with early intervention strategies that focus on supporting the physical, developmental, emotional, social, cultural, and spiritual well-being of the children (Norrie McCain, Mustard, and McCuaig, 2012).

Projects typically provide half-day preschool experiences that prepare young Aboriginal children for their school years by meeting their spiritual, emotional, intellectual, and physical needs. All projects provide programming in six core areas:

- *Education and School Readiness:* To foster a desire for life-long learning, focus on early childhood development, and provide children with opportunities to develop school readiness skills.

- *Aboriginal Culture and Language:* To offer an understanding of, respect for, participation in, and responsiveness to the culture and language of children, families, and communities.

- *Parental and Family Involvement:* To acknowledge parents and guardians as the primary teachers and caregivers of the children, ensuring that they play a key role in the planning, development, operation, and evaluation of the program. The Building Strong Spirits program supports extended families in teaching and caring for children, particularly Elders and traditional people.

- *Health Promotion:* To support the family in assuring that the child receives regular preventive health care and professional attention to health problems.

- *Nutrition:* To use a balanced approach to meet children's nutritional needs by using Aboriginal Food Guides comparable to Canada's Food Guide, be respectful of local traditions and customs, and encourage parents' healthy eating habits.

- *Social Support:* To provide opportunities for the child to develop social and emotional skills that are consistent with Aboriginal core values.

Aboriginal Head Start directly involves parents and the community in the management and operation of projects. Parents are supported in their role

I travelled north to Canada's Arctic to work as an instructor in a program called *Educators in Native and Inuit Child Care Services*. I lived in a remote Inuit community in Nunavut (population 750) where traditional knowledge continues to be part of everyday life. I did my best to prepare before I travelled. I read books and talked to people about the language, culture, land, and history but no amount of reading can prepare for your first trip to the arctic. My class consisted of 14 women ranging in age from 18–55 and English was a second language for all of them. The course was competency-based and delivered with an interactive hands-on approach. I modelled all aspects of working in a child-care program (effective interactions with children and adults, guidance strategies, songs, circle time, activities, setting up of learning centres, etc.) for the students in the classroom and then we practised these aspects with the children and families in the child-care centre.

The main goals of the program were for the women to build confidence in their existing skills and to develop new ones, to be introduced to new ideas and tools, and to have opportunities to put it all into practice. Emphasis was always placed on using the Inuktitut language and integrating Inuit culture into program content and values. I recognized that the success of the program and its sustainability rested on my acceptance within the community. I worked to develop partnerships with the Aboriginal Head Start program, the Arctic College Satellite, the local school, and other community organizations, and also to build relationships with Elders. I made every attempt to connect with people by involving myself in community gatherings and demonstrating a genuine interest in the language and culture. I consistently reminded myself that I was a guest and focused on displaying respect and openness to all that was unfamiliar to me. I travelled north to teach Early Childhood Education and returned south with more awareness and knowledge that could be gained only through my experience.

Source: Reprinted by permission of Rachel Brophy, Faculty, George Brown College.

as the child's first and most influential teachers, and the wisdom of Elders is valued. There is no charge to parents for participating in an AHS program.

The Martin Aboriginal Education Initiative (MAEI) celebrates Aboriginal history, culture, and tradition in an effort to raise awareness of Aboriginal issues. Free the Children has joined with MAEI in the We Stand Together Campaign. More information is available at the website: **http://www.maei-ieam.ca/about.html**.

NATIONAL ABORIGINAL DAY

In 1982 the National Indian Brotherhood (now the Assembly of First Nations) launched a national campaign to have June 21 recognized as National Aboriginal Solidarity Day. In cooperation with national Aboriginal organizations, the government of Canada chose June 21 because it is also the summer solstice, the longest day of the year. For generations, many Aboriginal peoples have celebrated their culture and heritage on or near this day. This day is a chance for Canadians to celebrate the rich contributions Aboriginal peoples have made to Canada. Educators should consult the website at the Department of Indian Affairs and Northern Development for more information that they can use to honour this day in the classroom.

An article in the journal *Interaction* (1998) outlines additional strategies for Aboriginal cultural content in early childhood care and education (see Table 9.3).

ROLE OF THE EDUCATOR

- Many teachers in non-Aboriginal child-care centres have little knowledge of values and practices toward children in the Aboriginal community. Child-care staff must ask themselves what stereotypes and assumptions they bring to their teaching of Aboriginal children. Failure to do so can lead to misunderstandings in the playroom.

For example, Aboriginal children who are quiet and shy in a non-Aboriginal child-care setting may be interpreted as being resistant, withdrawn, or noncompliant.

- Teachers should remember that there are many different Aboriginal cultural groups in Canada, and protocols for how to invite and work with Elders and use cultural resources may vary; for example, some songs can be used only by a certain clan or family.

- Aboriginal children's education must ensure two basic principles: (1) family and community involvement and (2) local control and participation in decision making and delivering of curriculum.

- Teachers should recognize that many people may "parent" the child and they should be included in the centre.

- Teachers should understand the cultural differences in behaviour. For example, Aboriginal children are often uncomfortable speaking in front of groups and are more at ease in small-group settings, where they can work in cooperation with others. Also, eye contact is often difficult for them to maintain, since avoiding it is a sign of respect.

- Some children are less verbal and more autonomous at an earlier age. Teachers must recognize that traditional Aboriginal culture places a high value on individual freedom, and Elders give guidance. Strategies best used with young children are modelling, influences from the larger group, and the expectation of positive behaviour.

- Provide parenting information as well as information about workshops and seminars that will help to strengthen parenting skills.

- Teachers should be knowledgeable about health conditions that Aboriginal families may be facing. Given the high incidence of type 2 diabetes in the Aboriginal population, families may be interested in workshops related to preparing nutritious meals based on the Aboriginal Food Guide. It is important to remember that workshops are always more successful and best received when the ideas come from the families themselves.

ROLE OF THE EDUCATOR IN THE ROOM

- The oral language is the Aboriginal way of preserving and understanding culture. Encourage families and Elders to share their oral culture with the children and with the educators in the centre as well. This is a learning opportunity for the whole community.

- Invite an Elder into the centre to explain the cultural relevance of materials that might be placed in the dramatic play centre or others centres both indoors and outdoors so that children learn to treat these resources in a respectful manner.

- When possible, seek out Elders who can spend time in the centre or classroom for extended periods of time.

- Invite families to the centre when they are able to also share their knowledge and expertise—for example, to cook traditional foods, teach language, or demonstrate traditional hunting and fishing methods.

- Materials in the centre should be concrete, real, and relevant to the children and their families, and should reflect an understanding of their history.

- Incorporate Aboriginal stories into story time as well as traditional arts and crafts such as drumming, dancing, throat singing, blanket tossing, string games, or beading (CCCF, 2008).

- Make and serve traditional foods and encourage healthy food choices.

- A diversity of opinion exists on ceremonies such as smudging, naming, and praying; therefore, teachers should consult the families in their program. Traditional opening and closing ceremonies should be observed if relevant to the families in the centre.

- Connect older children to Aboriginal history. Many towns and cities have Aboriginal names with have rich histories that will interest the children. Aboriginal Affairs and Northern Development Canada (2010) explains:

  - **Canada** is from Kanata, meaning "settlement" or "village" in the language of the Huron.

  - **Coquitlam** (British Columbia) is derived from the Salish tribal name Kawayquitlam; this word can be translated as "small red salmon." The name refers to the sockeye salmon common to the area.

  - **Kamloops** (British Columbia) is likely from the Shushwap word kahm-o-loops, which is usually translated as "the meeting of waters." The name refers to the junction of the North and South Thompson rivers at Kamloops.

- **Medicine Hat** (Alberta): is a translation of the Blackfoot word, saamis, meaning "headdress of a medicine man." According to one explanation, the word describes a fight between the Cree and Blackfoot when a Cree medicine man lost his plumed hat in the river.

- **Mississauga** (Ontario): is named after the Mississauga people who live in the area, and describes the mouth of a river. Michi or missi means "many," and saki, "outlet," a river having several outlets.

- **Ottawa** (Ontario): the word comes from the Algonquin term adawe, "to trade." This was the name given to the people who controlled the trade of the river.

- **Gaspé** (Quebec): is a name believed to come from the Mi'kmaq word for "end" or "extremity," referring to the northern limits of their territory.

- **Inuvik** (Northwest Territories): comes from the Inuktitut word meaning "the place of man."*

- Learn words and phrases in the families' language and use them in the playroom and in interactions with families whenever possible.

---

* Aboriginal Affairs and Northern Development Canada. *Aboriginal Place Names. Ottawa:* Aboriginal Affairs and Northern Development Canada, July 2001, http://www.aadnc-aandc.gc.ca/eng/110010001634 6/1100100016350. Reproduced with the permission of the Minister of Public Works and Government Services Canada, 2013.

- Look for CDs with songs in traditional languages and play them both indoors and outdoors.

Head Start programs prepare Aboriginal children for their school years by meeting their spiritual, emotional, intellectual, and physical needs.

TABLE 9.3	How to Include Aboriginal Cultural Content
Do	**Don't**
Do include activities and materials that reflect the specific Aboriginal groups represented in your program, community, and/or geographic region. Whenever possible, involve Aboriginal Elders and families in all aspects of programming. This will help ensure relevance and authenticity for both Aboriginal and non-Aboriginal children.	Don't assume that all Inuit, Métis, Dene, and/or First Nations cultures are alike. While there are many commonalities, there are also major differences between groups and individuals, in terms of history, values, traditions, customs, language, current interests, and concerns. Use materials that accurately reflect both similarities and differences among Aboriginal peoples (e.g., all First Nations people celebrate special events but, depending on their particular band or nation, their celebrations may be quite different).

continued

Do	**Don't**
Do use books, posters, and other resource materials that accurately portray Aboriginal peoples in a wide variety of both traditional and contemporary roles and settings—work, sports, the arts, family activities, and special celebrations. Look for and use books and materials written and illustrated by Aboriginal people.	Don't use stories or pictures that include "I is for Indian" or "E is for Eskimo" as part of the alphabet, or that portray "playing Indian" with feather head-dresses and tomahawks. Such materials stereotype and trivialize Aboriginal people and traditions. Don't make up Aboriginal legends or ceremonies.
Do include Aboriginal traditions, legends, and related materials in a meaningful context and in age-appropriate ways. When focusing on the past, do so for both Aboriginal and other cultures, in order to avoid stereotyping or romanticizing the "olden days" only for Aboriginal peoples (e.g., "I wonder what each of our grandmothers wore [ate, played with, etc.] when they were little girls").	Don't use materials that show Aboriginal people in a stereotypical or exclusively historical context—wearing buckskins, living in igloos or teepees, or living off the land with bows and arrows.
Do include lots of opportunities for outdoor play and contact with plants and animals, as part of strengthening children's appreciation of the natural world.	Don't assume that all Aboriginal children, especially those living in urban areas, are "connected to the land" and familiar with their traditional, land-based heritage.
Do represent Aboriginal families as living in both urban and rural environments and as having a range of perspectives and views on ecological issues.	Don't represent Aboriginal peoples as living only in the wilderness, on reserves, or in small communities. Don't portray them as the "first ecologists."
Do acknowledge and accommodate different learning styles, experiences, and goals. Examples of some Aboriginal children's preferred learning styles include more learning through watching and imitating, self-directed experiences and trial-and-error, rather than through following verbal instructions; more emphasis on cooperation and group learning activities, rather than on competition or individual performance and achievement; more focus on a holistic or global approach to learning, rather than emphasis on learning about an abstract subject (e.g., numbers and letters) out of context from daily living.	Don't assume that all children learn the same way or that one child-care program fits all when dealing with children and families from Aboriginal and/or minority culture backgrounds. A child- and family-centred approach means introducing new learning opportunities while also reflecting and reinforcing for children what's familiar and comfortable from home.

Source: CCCF, 1998. "Aboriginal Cultural Content in Early Childhood Care and Education," *Interaction* 12, (2). Reprinted by permission.

- Use written language to label items around the room in the first language of the children in the centre.
- Provide books and magazines written and illustrated by Aboriginal people.
- Encourage the children to write their names in their traditional language.
- Give examples of Aboriginal heroes and present them as role models for children.

- Avoid segregating children by placing them into cultural groups when doing activities in the room.
- Participate with the families in the centre in community celebrations, ceremonies, and gatherings.
- Teachers should spend time creating a positive learning environment outdoors because a fundamental Aboriginal principle is living in harmony with nature. Richardson (1994) believes that

schools for Native children should be designed with large, open spaces. They should take into account aspects of the medicine wheel and spirituality; be alive with plants, water, and animals; and encourage the Native spirit by including skylights and bare ground where sweat lodge ceremonies can be performed. Once schools show that being Native is an act of being, Native children feel good about themselves and the school they attend. (27)

BOOKS FOR ADULTS

Supporting Indigenous Children's Development, by J. Ball and A. Pence

Developing Culturally Focused Aboriginal Early Childhood Education Programs: A Handbook, BC Aboriginal Child Care Society (**http://www.acc-society.bc.ca**)

THE VISITING SCHOOLS PROGRAM

This program is a partnership between the Native Canadian Centre of Toronto and Indian and Northern Affairs Canada. It is an interactive project to help promote and foster a greater understanding of Aboriginal peoples in Canada and their distinct culture. Children are exposed to the teachings and traditions of First Nations, Inuit, and Métis people. A standard presentation revolves around the pow-wow format, which includes the drum and various styles of dancing. Some of the topics covered are the contributions of Aboriginal people throughout history, traditional stories and oral teachings, the six styles of dancing, the significance of the drum, and the different nations of people within the Native community. Also offered are specialized workshops such as traditional bread making and lessons in dream catcher assembly.

BOOKS FOR CHILDREN

Shannen and the Dream for a School, by J. Wilson

The Salmon Twins, by C. Simpson

Sky Sisters, by J. Bourdeau Waboose and B. Deines

The Polar Bear Son: An Inuit Tale, by L. Dabcovich

Solomon's Tree, by A. Spalding and J. Wilson

Secret of the Dance, by A. Spalding and D. Gait

The Elders Are Watching, by R. Henry Vickers

BOOKS FOR ADULTS

Rethinking Columbus: The Next 500 Years, by B. Bigelow and B. Peterson

Aboriginal Languages and Education: The Canadian Experience, by S. Morris

Broken Circle: The Dark Legacy of Indian Residential Schools, by T. Fontaine

Iroquois: The Six Nations Confederacy, by J. Duden

Canada's First Nations: A History of the Founding Peoples from Earliest Times, by O. Dickason

A Concise History of Canada's First Nations, by O. Dickason

A People's Dream: Aboriginal Self-Government in Canada, by D. Russell

MULTIRACIAL FAMILIES

"Since my son started daycare, I've heard a lot of comments about how beautiful or exotic biracial children look, and a lot of discussion about how to deal with the hair—that's a hot topic. As my child gets older, though, I expect the issues will get tougher. Which group will he identify more with? Will he have to choose? Which group will he hang out with in school? Will there be a mixed group? Somehow I doubt it, but if there is, will they be cool or uncool? Then I ask myself how I can best prepare my son for this uncharted course he must take. And of course the answer is he must have a strong sense of self.

He must be confident in his knowledge of who he is when people ask him to declare 'what' he is—black or white. So what can his daycare teachers do now for my son? They can make sure there are biracial families and children in the books he reads and the pictures he sees. They can make sure he feels he belongs, that his family is accepted, and they can support his developing personality to build all the self-esteem he's going to need to be confident in whatever group he finds himself."

—Lucy Patterson

Mixed race or multiracial people are those whose ancestors come from multiple races.

> Mixed-race people have a long history in North America, starting with the Métis, unions between French traders and native women in the 1700s. Mixed-race families have several variations: marriage and common-law unions between visible and non-visible minority individuals; children born to such parents, both within and outside of marriage; and children adopted internationally or transracially within Canada. (Ward and Belanger, 2011: 43)[*]

There were 289,420 mixed-race couples, married and common-law, in 2006—one third more than recorded in the 2001 census. In terms of generational status, the proportion of mixed unions rises with the length of time spent in Canada. Among *first-generation* visible minority Canadians (those born outside Canada), 12 percent were in mixed-union couples. For *second-generation* Canadians who were members of a visible minority group, the proportion in a mixed union was 51 percent. It reached 69 percent for *third-generation* visible minority Canadians. Mixed unions are an urban phenomenon: In 2006, 5.1 percent of all couples who lived in a census metropolitan area were in mixed unions, compared with 1.4 percent of couples who lived outside these areas. In Vancouver, 8.5 percent of couples were in mixed unions, the highest proportion among metropolitan areas (Statistics Canada, 2006c).

According to Hune-Brown (2013), "as a group, mixed-race couples were young and urban and tended to be more highly educated: one in three people in mixed-race relationships had a university degree, versus just one in five people in non-mixed unions."

As the population grows, more and more mixed-race people appear in the media. Golfer Tiger Woods is a perfect example as he identifies his mixed race heritage as Cablinasian—Caucasian, Black, American Indian, and Asian. Actress Jennifer Beals has an Irish mother and African American father; supermodel Naomi Campbell is of Jamaican and Chinese descent. All have appeared on "most beautiful people" lists. Johnny Depp claims Irish, German, and Cherokee ancestry; Angelina Jolie's parents were French Canadian and Iroquois (mother) and Czechoslovakian (father); and Keanu Reeves' parents were English (mother) and Hawaiian Chinese (father). Canada's former governor general Michaëlle Jean and her husband, Jean-Daniel Lafond, are a prominent interracial couple.

Wendy Roth, a sociologist at the University of British Columbia, reasons that intermarriage and mixed unions prove so interesting because they serve as a litmus test of social relations between different groups. Mixed unions have experienced a steady, though not huge, increase; the fact that it continues to be steady in different censuses suggests that barriers between cultural groups are diminishing. The vast majority of interracial couples in the last census (85 percent) involve a white person and a visible minority, and 15 percent are marriages among couples from two different visible minority groups. (La Rose, 2008)[†]

Multiracial people are helping us rethink what it means to be Canadian because, in addition to exploring their own identities, mixed-race people are challenging our notions of race, ethnicity, and national identity. This has implications for public policy and for society as a whole. Murphy Kilbride et al. (1998: 20–21) state,

> Children with multiple ethnoracial origins (for example, white European and black Caribbean, Asian and African, South Asian and Latin American) have reported in recent Canadian research that their experience of racial exclusion by other groups of children is minimal in early childhood, but increases as other children become aware of racial differences in new and hostile ways. Biracial children, for example, can find themselves rejected by others who come from both parents' racial groups: white peers may shun them as black, for instance, and black peers may have doubts about their "blackness" and presume that their experiences are so different that a biracial individual cannot understand a black individual's situation.... Biracial and multiracial children can assist educators in developing new sensitivities, as we move

Mixed-race people are challenging our notions of race, ethnicity, and national identity.

---

[*] From WARD. *The Family Dynamic, 5E.* © 2011 Nelson Education Ltd. Reproduced by permission. www.cengage.com/permissions.

[†] Lauren La Rose / The Canadian Press

from a presumption that all children in a group we consider to be visible minorities have similar challenges in our society to the more careful distinction among the actual experiences that children have.*

For some mixed-race people, the priority is to move beyond race completely, or to refuse to be defined by classic notions of race. Some say that

---

* Murphy Kilbride, K., J. Pollard, M. Friendly, and J. Dotsch. 1998. *Early Differences Experienced by Visible Minority Children*. Metropolis–Toronto Centre of Excellence. Research and Policy. Reprinted by permission of Kenise Kilbride.

gender, class, religion, language, location, occupation, age are all more important than race (Khoo, 2007).

Today, as reported by La Rose (2008), the groups least likely to marry another religion, according to a 2006 Statistics Canada study, are Sikhs, Muslims, and Hindus. For many parents, religious differences are the hardest to overcome. "Japanese immigrants are the most likely minority group to enter into a mixed union (74.7 percent), with Latin Americans (47 percent) and Blacks (40.6 percent) following. In contrast, Chinese and

Inside LOOK

I have a multiracial family. Our heritage is Irish, Jamaican, Chinese, and West Indian. My two boys are dark skinned with beautiful brown eyes, and my daughter has flaming red hair and blue eyes! I am often asked if my red-haired child is adopted; despite the fact that we are open in our discussions of our cultural heritage, I wonder what the impact of questions such as these will have on her long term?

EXHIBIT 9.2   A Model for Biracial Identity Development

W.S. Carlos Poston (1990) has conducted research on American biracial children that has looked at two main issues for them: their personal identity, including their self-esteem, self-worth, and interpersonal competence; and the reference group orientation, including racial identity, racial esteem, and racial ideology. Poston then developed a model for biracial identity development that includes five stages individuals may pass through toward a healthy biracial identity:

1. **Personal identity.** Very young children are not always aware of membership in a particular ethnic or racial group; identity is primarily based on personal factors developed within the family context.

2. **Choice of group categorization.** This can be a time of crisis and alienation, as children feel pushed to choose a racial identity in order to belong to peer, family, or social groups. Hall (as cited by Poston, 1990) identified several key factors influencing this choice: status of the groups at issue, social support from parents and other family members, and personal factors like language, appearance, age, political involvement, cultural knowledge, and so on.

3. **Enmeshment and denial.** Choosing, as a result of external pressures, one identity that isn't fully expressive of one's family background can produce confusion, guilt, and a sense of disloyalty to the parent whose background is omitted in a monoracial identity.

4. **Appreciation.** At this stage, individuals begin to appreciate their various sources of identity and broaden their reference group orientation and may begin to learn about their heritages, but still tend to identify with one group, influenced by factors prevalent in their choice phase.

5. **Integration.** Individuals now recognize and value all their sources of identity and develop a secure, integrated identity.

Source: W.S. Carlos Poston, 1990. "The Biracial Identity Development Model: A Needed Addition," *Journal of Counselling and Development* 69 (2): 152–55. Reprinted by permission.

South Asians are among the least likely to form a union outside their group" (La Rose, 2008). One hypothesis, put forth by Siad, Kassam, and Bhattacharya (2007) for this breakdown of likelihoods is that the Japanese have been in Canada longer and the idea of intermarriage does not seem strange to the third generation (La Rose, 2008).*

ROLE OF THE EDUCATOR

- Teachers need to examine their own feelings about interracial marriage or preconceived ideas about biracial people and ask whether a bias may interfere with their ability to support these families.

- Be sensitive to every family. Each family is unique and should be treated as such; no one should be stereotyped.

- Find out what terminology parents are using and use this to support their choice.

- When families share their ethnoracial heritage, teachers should ask how families would like to see it celebrated in the early learning environment. What will be important issues for them? Would they be willing to share with the children?

- Consider engaging in a program such as Seeds of Empathy (Chapter 2) with an infant from a multiracial family.

- Attend cultural celebrations in the community with the children to encourage greater interest and understanding of the complexities and diversity of all peoples.

- Celebrate people in the both the local and larger community who are multiracial.

ROLE OF THE EDUCATOR IN THE ROOM

- Teachers should provide experiences and opportunities that allow for the child's positive identification of both parents and their cultures.

- Show multiracial families as only one of many types of families in discussions and family-related activities.

- Encourage children's natural curiosity to talk and ask questions about similarities and differences in physical appearance.

- Provide a safe place for children to discuss racial issues, feelings, and reactions to unkind comments.

- If necessary, respond quickly and clearly, stating that any type of teasing or name calling will not be tolerated. Clearly this applies to all situations including any of the children in the group.

- Help older children by role-playing how they might handle bullying.

- Many multiracial children do not see themselves represented in learning materials. Be vigilant in looking for resources, dolls, books, photos, posters, puzzles, videos, etc., that support positive images of multiracial families.

- When celebrating special religious or cultural events, assure children that no one cultural experience is greater or more important than another.

- Incorporate a wide range of food from all cultures.

- Music and dance are powerful connections to cultures. Celebrate!

BOOKS FOR CHILDREN

A Touch of the Zebras, by I. Sadu
Hot, Sour, Salty, Sweet, by S. Smith
Black Is Brown Is Tan, by E. Arnold McCully
Black, White, Just Right, by I. Trivas
The Colour of Us, by K. Katz
All the Colours of the Race, by A. Adoff

BOOKS FOR ADULTS

Does Anyone Else Look Like Me? A Parent's Guide to Raising Multiracial Children, by D. Jackson Nakazawa
Of Many Colours: Portraits of Multiracial Families, by G. Kaeser, P. Gillespie, and G. Valentine
Tomorrow's Children: Meeting the Needs of Multiracial and Multiethnic Children at Home, in Early Childhood Programs, and at School, by F. Wardle
White Chocolate, by E. Atkins Bowman
Everyday Acts Against Racism: Raising Children in a Multiracial World, by M. Reddy

---

* Lauren La Rose / The Canadian Press

OLDER FAMILIES

> "Sylvie, 36, and Carlos, 42, have lived together for 12 years. Sylvie is an editor at a large publishing firm, and Carlos is a successful lawyer. The couple lives in a condominium in downtown Vancouver. Sylvie is three months pregnant. Both she and Carlos are looking forward to being parents. They made the decision to have this child after much discussion about how their lifestyle and relationship would be affected. Sylvie hopes that she will be able to work from home for the first few years of the baby's life."

Women in Canada in their 40s who have preschool children are still in the minority, but the phenomenon is not as uncommon as it was 25 years ago. In 2006, nearly 1 out of 10 women ages 40 to 44 had a preschool child, more than double the proportion observed in 1986 (8.9 percent versus 4.3 percent). According to studies by demographers and sociologists, the increase in the proportion of older mothers with young children is primarily due to higher educational attainment among women and greater labour market participation by women. University graduates complete their studies later, are more likely to participate in the labour market, and have different expectations regarding their family roles and life in general. As Lochhead (2000) found, for many young men and women, there are powerful and economic incentives to delay childbirth:

> Marrying and having children later allows young people opportunity to pursue post-secondary education, and additional time to gain employment experience and security in a highly competitive labour market. In addition, many women are able to pursue the goal of financial independence through education and employment prior to marriage and family. Today's first time mothers and fathers are not only older, but on average, have more formal education, are more likely to be part of a dual earner family, and as a result, have considerably higher family incomes.

Despite the importance of education, the impact of other factors and the considerable changes in values, particularly regarding women's role in society and the labour market, should not be underestimated. The fact that young people's transitions to adulthood are occurring later and in a less linear manner than in the past has also affected the timing of the first birth for many women. Leaving the parental home, landing a full-time job, forming a stable union, and buying a home are all taking place, on average, at a more advanced age. Of course, the later young adults make these transitions, the greater the likelihood that there will be a delay in having children.

Research suggests that women who have children after age 35 have more financial resources and more life experience, and are more satisfied with their career and marital situation than women who become mothers earlier. In general, women who delayed childbearing were in a better socioeconomic situation when their first child was born. In particular, they were better educated, more likely to live in a family whose income was in excess of $50,000, more likely to have a university degree, and more likely to own their home. They were also much more likely to have a management position in their workplace (Gregory, 2007).

How does a later pregnancy impact a mother's health? Vezina and Turcotte (2009) found that

> later pregnancy is associated with certain risks, such as greater prevalence of low birth weight and premature delivery (or false labour), and higher incidence of gestational hypertension and pregnancy diabetes. Although medical advances have substantially improved the survival rates of premature babies, researchers have shown that prematurity could saddle both families and society with financial costs and a significant burden in terms of the additional care required. Moreover, children born to older women (especially women aged 45 or older) are more likely to have chromosomal abnormalities. Aside from the health effects, the fact that women are older when they give birth for the first time may have an impact on

Balancing a career and a young family can be a challenge.

population renewal through births. The chances of getting pregnant and giving birth decline as women age: 91% of women succeed in getting pregnant at age 30, compared with 77% at age 35 and 53% at age 40. The older a woman is at first birth, the fewer children she is likely to have.

As women age and become less fertile, they may turn to reproductive technologies, which for some result in multiple births. Some older women may have another child when they enter into a second marriage.

Maurin (2007: 161) reports on research at McGill University's Reproductive Centre where young women freeze their eggs for future use, believing that "It's the age of the eggs, not the age of the woman, that makes all the difference." There is no question that this technology, though still new, has the potential to allow women the choice to have children on their own schedule.

Children of older parents experience both benefits and challenges;

> Children who are born to older parents usually benefit from the financial and emotional stability that their parents have developed over the years, as well as the attention given by parents who have waited a long time to have children. But children of older parents also face specific challenges as parents often become frail when their children are still young. Older parents need to plan for the guardianship of their children, and children can become burdened with the anxiety about their parents' health and mortality. Children with older parents may have to care for their parents before their own adult lives are established. (Riedman, Lamanna, and Nelson, 2003: 334–45)*

Because their family may no longer live in the same vicinity, many new older parents look to books, magazines, and the Internet for advice. Arnup (2003) asks,

> So what is the situation now that parenting books and magazines have become a multimillion dollar industry? Things are probably even more confusing. There are so many experts dispensing advice using many different methods and approaches. It can be overwhelming for new mothers, especially at a time when they may be vulnerable.

Arnup points out that today's older parents are used to being competent and successful at what

they do. Being new parents, "while wonderful and thrilling, can make them feel nervous, inexperienced, and terrified of making mistakes."

New and inexperienced teachers may encounter parents who are the same age as their own parents, possibly creating a sense of unease. A form of accommodation will need to be established between the two parties—one that takes into account the age difference while allowing the teacher to feel confident about her skills and training. Like all parents, older parents who see the teacher celebrating the accomplishments of their child will also see the benefits of the family–teacher partnership.

ROLE OF THE EDUCATOR

- When dealing with older families, the recent graduate must remember that she brings with her specific expertise that allows her to be a meaningful partner in contributing to every child's total well-being.

- Adopting a professional approach, exhibiting a strong understanding of child development, and expressing genuine interest in the children are some of the ways in which inexperienced teachers can begin to build significant relationships with older parents.

- Older parents may have well-established careers in areas that may be complementary to the business of running the child-care centre. Teachers can encourage them to become more involved in the centre.

- Linking older parents with other parents in a similar situation at the centre may develop into a support network.

ROLE OF THE EDUCATOR IN THE ROOM

- As they learn more about the life cycle, some school-age children may be fearful that their parents will die. Teachers can reassure children by helping them focus on the present.

- Some children may find it difficult, particularly if they are the youngest in a larger family, being "parented" by older siblings as well as their parents. Stories about younger children as "heroes," managing independently, may be helpful.

- Books, posters, and photographs in the centre should reflect parents of all ages.

* From LAMANNA/RIEDMAN/NELSON. *Marriages and Families, 1E*. © 2003 Nelson Education Ltd. Reproduced by permission. www.cengage.com/permissions

GRANDPARENTS RAISING THEIR GRANDCHILDREN: SKIP-GENERATION FAMILIES

> "When Grandmothers speak, the earth will be healed."
>
> —Hopi Prophecy
> (The Whirling Rainbow, n.d.)

"Ed and Kerri are in their late 50s. Their 18-year-old daughter, Leslee, is the mother of a two-and-a-half-year-old, Erin. Leslee lives on social assistance in a small basement apartment. She continues to go to school, and it is there that Erin attends a daycare centre recently built for teen parents. Leslee is trying to complete her high school education, but her attendance is erratic and her grades are falling. Although she curtailed her drug use while she was pregnant with Erin, she is using drugs again. Ed and Kerri are very concerned about the well-being of both Leslee and Erin. Several months ago they found Leslee unconscious from a drug overdose in her apartment and Erin crying hysterically. Since then, Erin has been living with Ed and Kerri. A reluctant Leslee has entered a drug-rehabilitation program in a nearby city. Erin is still attending the daycare at Leslee's school."

Skip-generation families are a growing phenomenon that crosses all ethnic groups in urban and rural communities across the country and all socioeconomic groups; it includes grandparents in their 40s as well as those in their 70s. A skip-generation family is one in which a child lives with one or both grandparents without the presence of a parent or middle generation. In 2011, 30,005 children ages 14 and under, or 0.5 percent of all children in this age group, lived in skip-generation families. This proportion is relatively unchanged since 2001. About 57.8 percent of grandchildren in skip-generation families lived with a grandparent couple, while the remaining 42.2 percent lived with only one grandparent. Across Canada, the highest numbers of skip-generation families in 2011 were found in Nunavut (2.2 percent), the Northwest Territories (1.8 percent), and Saskatchewan (1.4 percent).

Two racial groups are substantially overrepresented among Canadian grandparent caregivers: black Canadians and First Nation Canadians. Many Caribbean Canadian grandparents cited economic necessity and high levels of migration from the Islands as reasons promoting such patterns of shared caregiving. The willingness of First Nation grandparents to provide care may be influenced by traditional involvement of extended kin in child care in Aboriginal communities (Fuller-Thomson, 2005).

Grandchildren move into this situation either through a legal process or a family agreement. There are various reasons for this situation, including

- a parent's drug or alcohol abuse may result in a court-ordered removal of the child or children
- a parent dies
- child abuse and neglect are present
- a parent has a serious or terminal illness
- a parent has been incarcerated
- a parent is experiencing mental illness
- parental unemployment
- divorce or desertion has changed the family

While many grandparents may willingly take on this responsibility, the financial and psychological demands may exceed their existing resources. According to Amatea (2009: 119),

> researchers have reported that children in the care of grandparents are often exceptionally needy, due to a combination of congenital and environmental factors. Many grandparented children have experienced abuse and neglect as a result of living with a drug-involved or otherwise poorly functioning parent. As a result, grandparented children deal with many troubling emotions such as grief and loss, guilt, fear, embarrassment and anger.[*]

KINSHIP CARE

The Child Welfare League of America (2005) defines kinship care as the "full time nurturing and protection of children who must be separated from their parents by relatives, members of their tribe or clans, godparents, stepparents or other adults who have a kinship bond with a child." The group Grand Parenting Again Canada, which strives to provide support and information for skip-generation families, believes that the involvement of kin as alternative caregivers could prevent the

[*] AMATEA, ELLEN S., BUILDING CULTURALLY RESPONSIVE FAMILY-SCHOOL RELATIONSHIPS, 1st Edition, © 2009. Reprinted and Electronically reproduced by permission of Pearson Education, Inc., Upper Saddle River, NJ.

Courtesy of Lynn Wilson

Many grandparents are raising their grandchildren.

need for children to go into foster care. Preliminary research outcomes indicate that kinship care homes reduce the number of moves experienced by children, are less traumatic, and permit continuity of care within or close to the family.

Throughout Canada there are a number of kinship care programs run through Children's Aid Society (CAS) organizations. One such program is the Calgary Rock View Program in Alberta, which seeks kin rights from the moment of the child's intake. In the programs,

> families receive a per diem and social work support similar to foster families. Alberta reports that the cost of children in kinship care is not lowered, but outcomes for children are improved and foster care resources are less strained. Rocky View has moved at least 60 children from foster care into kinship care since 1998. (Grand Parenting Again Canada, n.d.)

Unfortunately, the traditional concept of the nuclear family affects government policies and professional practices; as a result, they often do not reflect the growing diversity in family structures, and many make it difficult for grandparents to access adequate support for their family. For example, if grandparents decide to become foster parents in order to access funding, they give up their rights to decisions affecting the child. When undertaking research on grandmothers raising their grandchildren, Callahan, Brown, McKenzie, and Whittington (in press) gained insight into why grandmothers took on the care of their grandchildren.

> Some feared that if they did not, the government safety net, child welfare, would take [the grandchildren] into foster care. They considered this a far worse option than providing that care themselves. Some were worried that if government got involved in the situation, then they may

lose custody of their grandchildren because social workers would think that they were too old to be parents again or that they had done a bad job with their own children and thus should not be parents again.

Fuller-Thomson (2005) found that "Grandmother caregivers were poorer, less likely to be married, more likely to be out of the labour force and more than twice as likely to provide 60 or more hours per week of unpaid child care than were grandfathers." For some retired grandparents, financial necessity may mean that they will have to re-enter the workforce as they struggle to meet the needs of their "new" family. For others their finances may be further strained as they attempt to gain legal custody of their grandchildren. Some may lose their life savings and even their homes in these legal battles. The cost of placing the children in child care may be prohibitive, especially for those living on a small pension, but would provide the much needed support system from which many grandparents would benefit.

There are many emotional issues for both grandparents and their grandchildren. Miles (n.d.: 1) states,

> Many grandparents who are parenting their grandchildren are deprived of a positive relationship with their own child. In fact, many start their role grieving an actual or emotional death of their child. 'That's not my daughter," one woman said. "Drugs have taken over. That's not the girl I raised, love, and nurtured." Thus, grandparents are often dealing with feelings of failure, guilt and embarrassment.

Grandparents may also be faced with a situation in which they have physical custody of the child but not legal custody. Gaining legal custody or guardianship can be a costly process and at the same time requires the termination of the rights of the child's parent. If the grandparent hopes that his or her own child may at one point be ready to assume their parental role again, they may be unwilling to proceed with legal guardianship.

Of course, the children are affected too. According to CANGRANDS, a Canadian grandparents' advocacy and support organization,

> many of the grandchildren in these families are angry with their parents, confused by their absence, and divided in their loyalties. They may be afraid of showing affection to their grandparents in front of their parents or vice versa. Because children who have been separated from their parents have already experi-

enced much emotional turmoil, grandparents are often confused about what parenting approach to take. Some grandparents decide that discipline will only make a child feel lonelier and more punished, so they become very permissive; these grandparents may become overprotective of their grandchildren. On the other hand, some grandparents worry that their grandchildren will repeat the virulent behaviour of their parents, and so decide to impose rigid rules and penalties. (CANGRANDS, 2003: 1)

The lives of grandparents change dramatically when young children come to live with them. In a study by Jendrek Platt (1993: 620), "almost half of all custodial grandparents reported problems with family and friends, the first line of defence for most people in times of stress." However, this same study also found that "almost two-thirds of the custodial grandparents reported having more of a purpose for living because of providing care to their grandchild; the grandchild keeps them young, active, and 'in shape.'" According to Miles (n.d.: 1), "In the best of circumstances, the renewal can be both biological and emotional, adding new social networks and experiencing emotional self-fulfilment in being able to support the positive development of a generation that carries a family forward." Many grandmothers may find themselves in a familiar role but for some grandfathers, who spent very little time with their own children, it may be a more difficult adjustment:

> Grandparents may not necessarily be retired or in compromised health. Grandparents themselves may be single, working full time or still have younger children of their own in the house. They may believe that this will be a temporary arrangement and that the birth parents will assume responsibility as soon as they are able. In actuality, the dependent relationship may last years, and the extended family may make a permanent commitment to the children. (Rockwell, Andre, and Hawley, 2010: 68–69)

Many grandparents report that their grown grandchildren are incredibly supportive and continue to be actively involved in their lives. However, as the grandparents age, they worry about who will care for the children if one or both of the grandparent dies.

If financial impediments to grandparents were removed, many children who are currently in foster care could be returned to their extended family members. The continued lack of government initiatives to provide adequate financial resources to those grandparents who need it is a challenge for all concerned.

Inside LOOK

Jan is a 29-year-old college student and the mother of a two-year-old daughter. She comes from St. Lucia, which she left at the age of eight. Jan's mother moved from St. Lucia to Toronto in 1968 with the hope of getting settled in Canada and then sending for her two daughters so they could have a better life and education in their new home. From the age of seven until the age of eight, Jan lived with her grandmother and sister in St. Lucia. "My grandmother was very strict. We were brought up with the expectation of proper behaviour at all times, and especially that we would show respect to our elders. Because my sister was four years older than me, I was expected to respect her as well and do what she said. Gramma was from the old school, a devout Catholic, who stressed the importance of self-discipline and study. I don't remember my grandmother expressing affection readily. When I was eight, we moved to Canada to join my mother. The pattern of interaction between me and my sister stayed the same throughout my childhood. My mother was a single working mother who relied on my sister's help in raising me and maintaining the household. Even today, all these years later, when I talk about my parents I really am referring to my sister and my mother."

Source: From Shimoni and Baxter, *Working with Families* 4/e © Pearson Canada 2008. Reprinted by permission of the publisher.

NONCUSTODIAL GRANDPARENTS AS PART OF THE EXTENDED FAMILY

The impact of grandparent involvement varies significantly between families. Age of grandparents, age of grandchildren, geographical differences, and relationships of grandparents with the family will all be a factor.

> Studies indicate four different categories of grandparenthood: the custodial grandparent, the nearby grandparent, the distant grandparent, and the emotionally remote grandparent. Directly or indirectly, grandparents express to their grandchildren a value system and philosophy of how children are to be instructed, whether morally, religiously, culturally or intellectually. Caring and supporting grandparents, living nearby or in a distant area, who keep close contact with their families, will have considerable influence. (Barbour, Barbour, and Scully, 2008: 220–222)

A child's bond with his or her grandparents can be enormously strong. Grandparents often offer a safe and nurturing environment where their grandchildren are loved unconditionally. Many grandparents express the joy of loving and caring for their grandchildren without the worries and concerns that plagued them as parents!

Many grandparents look back on their own role as a parent, and realize they have learned a

Grandparents can provide enormous support to a young and growing family.

great deal that benefits their interactions with their grandchildren.

To understand multigenerational families, it is important for educators to gain insight into the roles that many individuals may play in the family unit.

> Multigenerational families, in which parents, grandparents, other relatives and even friends live together is growing more and more common Nonrelated adults of the same culture and community are often invited to join families and to share child care responsibilities. Although these close friends may have no formal kinship ties, they may be expected to participate in a form of co-parenting. In times of economic hardship, informal adoptions may occur in which friends assume roles identical to those of birth parents. Because so many children live in extended families, professionals who care for young children must consider the influence of many different family and non-family adults in children's lives.[†] (Trawick-Smith, 2010: 464–472)

- Many grandparents will not have had experience in child-care settings and teachers will need to spend time with them to explain the program, policies, procedures, etc.

If I Had My Child To Raise Over Again*
by Diana Loomans

If I had my child to raise over again,

I'd finger paint more, and point the finger less.
I'd do less correcting and more connecting.

I'd take my eyes off my watch and watch with my eyes.
I would care to know less and know to care more.

I'd take more hikes and fly more kites.
I'd stop playing serious and seriously play.

I'd run through more fields and gaze at more stars.
I'd do more hugging and less tugging.

I would be firm less often and affirm much more.
I'd build self-esteem first, and the house later.

I'd teach less about the love of power,
and more about the power of love.

It matters not whether my child is big or small;
From this day forth, I'll cherish it all.

www.dianaloomans.com

---

* Diana Loomans, If I Had My Child to Raise Over Again. www.dianaloomans.com. Reprinted by permission.

[†] TRAWICK-SMITH, JEFFREY, EARLY CHILDHOOD DEVELOPMENT: A MULTICULTURAL PERSPECTIVE, 5th Edition, © 2010. Reprinted and Electronically reproduced by permission of Pearson Education, Inc., Upper Saddle River, NJ.

- Grandparents may need up-to-date information about child development and parenting strategies, and teachers should be prepared to supply information or resources whenever possible.
- Linking grandparents with relevant community resources or support agencies is another service teachers can provide. For example, Robyn's Nest, at http://**www.robynsnest.com**, is a comprehensive interactive community website for parents, grandparents, teachers, and families, featuring expert parenting advice, a chat room, and bulletin boards.

ROLE OF THE EDUCATOR

- Accessing other programs in the community may give grandparents some respite time. Some grandparents may not even be aware that these resources exist in their community or think that only parents are eligible for this type of support.
- For those raising children with special needs, children who have been victimized, or children who have suffered neglect in their previous environment, accurate information can help grandparents better understand their grandchild's particular needs and how they can best support them.
- In situations where the mother or father plays a continuing role, the ground rules for communication among all the parties need to be clearly established. Legal restrictions may impose barriers for access to information so teachers need to be informed.
- Children may feel a sense of abandonment even if they are happy living with their grandparents. The teacher's close link with the family is critical in supporting both the child and the grandparents.
- Teachers can put grandparents in touch with other families or teachers who might be able to help them with the drop-off, pick-up, or other reciprocal arrangements.
- It is important for teachers to realize and be understanding of the fact that even those grandparents who enjoy raising their grandchildren may at times feel angry and resentful and concerned about their financial situation and dramatic change in lifestyle.

ROLE OF THE EDUCATOR IN THE ROOM

- A family in which a child lives with his or her grandparents is just another type of family that is respected in the playroom. A growing collection of children's books that feature seniors as main characters and specific books about grandparents raising their grandchildren can be used in the playroom. Selecting a variety of books that present diversity in behaviours, appearance, and roles helps to raise awareness and sensitivity on the part of all the children. Posters, photographs, and other visual materials posted in the room should also reflect this family type.
- Having the child keep a journal where appropriate and creating a comprehensive portfolio of the child's accomplishments may be an important reminder of the time spent in the centre and may become an important communication tool if the child is reunited with his or her biological parents.
- Active grandparents can dispel many myths about physical, intellectual, and emotional loss with aging and, if possible, should be invited into the playroom to share their expertise, skills, etc. Grandparent involvement in the centre is something teachers and grandparents need to determine on a case-by-case basis.
- In 1994, the Canadian Parliament set aside a special day—the second Sunday in September—for grandparents. Teachers can celebrate this important date with the children and their families.
- Though many grandparents will be able to keep up with their energetic grandchildren, others may struggle with failing health. Teachers can support these grandparents by helping their grandchildren with boots and snow pants and other potentially difficult tasks.
- Others may be unable to attend school events or visit the child's classroom. Alternative forms of communication must then be considered, remembering that some grandparents may not have access to a computer. Transportation may also be an issue, and perhaps a staff or another family may be able to assist.

AN INNOVATIVE PROGRAM— GRANDFAMILIES HOUSE

GrandFamilies House has 26 units and was developed in an abandoned nursing home. It has a playground, daycare centre, and enrichment program for all ages. Located in Boston, it meets the special needs of the burgeoning population of grandparents raising grandchildren (Mehren, 1999).

BOOKS FOR CHILDREN

Chelsea's Tree, by M. McCarn

Robert Lives with His Grandparents, by M. Whitmore Hickman

Sometimes It's Grandmas and Grampas Not Mommies and Daddies, by G. Byrne

My Two Grannies, by F. Benjamin

BOOKS FOR ADULTS

Living with Your Grandchildren: A Guide for Grandparents, by J. Lee and L. Cowan

Grandparents as Parents: A Survival Guide for Raising a Second Family, by S. deToledo and D. Edler Brown

The Sacred Work of Grandparents Raising Grandchildren, by E.K. Williams

Successfully Raising Grandchildren, by K.D. Barnes Sr. and B. Barnes

Born Into Love: The Unconditional Love of Grandparents Raising Their Grandchildren, by P. O'Connor

Raising Our Children's Children, by D. Doucette-Dudman

Ticklebelly Hill: Grandparents Raising Grandchildren, by H. Osborne

At Grandma's House We … Stay, S. Houtman

Second Time Around: Help for Grandparents Who Raise Their Children's Kids, by J. Callander

FOSTER FAMILIES

"Binh and Lee have been foster parents for more than 20 children in the past 16 years. They have cared for newborn infants, young children, and teenagers. They have two biological children, ages 12 and 10. While some of their foster children stay for only two or three weeks, others have been with them for many years. Recently, they adopted 8-year-old Riley, who has lived with them for six years."

Foster care is a temporary arrangement, usually made between a family in distress and a child-welfare agency, whereby a child is placed in the care of a foster family until he or she can be returned to the family of origin or placed for adoption.

The 2011 census counted foster children for the first time. Foster children ages 14 and under accounted for 0.5 percent of children in Canada. Among foster children ages 14 and under, 29.0 percent were ages 0 to 4, 29.9 percent were ages 5 to 9, and 41.1 percent were ages 10 to 14. A total of 17,410 households were home to at least one foster child ages 14 and under. Of these households, 45.1 percent included one foster child, 28.8 percent included two foster children, and 26.2 percent included three or more foster children (Durnford, 2012).

Sheila Durnford, president of the Canadian Foster Family Association (2012), believes that foster parents play a vital role in enabling children and youth placed in their care to become mature, responsible productive adults. They open their hearts and homes to children and youth in need of a safe, nurturing, loving home. They may be experienced parents, young couples who are raising their own children, or single people. Foster parents are commonly mature, flexible, child-focused, patient, and understanding. They enjoy family life, can cope with stress, respect and accept other cultures, are financially stable, and are willing to learn. Foster parents work as part of the professional team toward the goal of family reunification. CFFA works in collaboration with the provincial and territorial foster family associations and other national organizations involved with children and youth in care to enhance foster care across Canada.

http://www.canadianfosterfamilyassociation.ca

Guidelines published by the Canadian Foster Family Association are intended to ensure that all children in Canada receive good care while living in foster families. But one of the challenges facing the nation is the acute shortage of foster families. For example, according to the Canadian Press (2012) in Saskatchewan, an estimated 500 of children in care were in overcrowded foster homes at the end of 2010. Perhaps now that census data is available, provinces that fund foster care will share best practices to enhance the lives of those children in foster situations.

Prior to the granting of foster parent status, a social worker usually does a home visit in order to assess the family's suitability. Other requirements include a police check and a medical examination. This procedure varies from province to province, but the intent in every jurisdiction is to ensure

Aboriginal children are three times as likely to be in foster care as non-Aboriginal children, according to the Assembly of First Nations. Many are taken from their communities and put into non-Aboriginal homes. Children often come into the care of child and family services not for abuse but rather because their families are unable to provide the necessities of life. On March 5, 2007, the Assembly of First Nations launched a human rights complaint against the government for failing to stop the increase of Aboriginal children in care. The Assembly argues that there are too many Aboriginal children in foster care—up to 27,000 as of 2010—and the First Nations need more money to deal with the situation. The number of kids in apprehension has increased by 65 percent, a statistic that reflects the circumstances in communities, but that also includes children suffering from difficulties such as fetal alcohol syndrome, and suffering from poverty (Ferris-Manning and Zandstra, 2003). The Commission assessed the complaint and in September 2008 referred it to a separate organization called the Canadian Human Rights Tribunal for a full hearing. The Auditor General of Canada in her 2011 report notes that although the federal government has made some efforts to fix the program by making the enhanced funding arrangement available in more areas of the country, progress overall has been unsatisfactory.

Source: Nation Talk, n.d.

stable environments for foster children. Foster parents need detailed information about what life was like for the foster child before coming into their home and how the child's history might affect his or her behaviour and development. Foster care rates range from $25 to $30 a day and vary from province to province but it is clear that this is not adequate. Because of the lack of resources and the large number of foster children, it is impossible to scrutinize every home on a regular basis. As such, foster children are more vulnerable to neglect and even abuse (Montgomery, 2008).

In a random sample of five Ontario Children's Aid Societies, Philp (2007) found that psychotropic drugs are being prescribed to almost half— 47 percent—of the Crown wards (children in permanent CAS care). The prescriptions were to treat depression, ADD, anxiety, and other mental health problems. With histories of abuse, neglect, and loss, children in foster care often bear psychological scars unknown to most of their peers. The high percentage of prescriptions, however, kindles fears that the agencies are overusing medication with the province's most vulnerable children.

Many children entering foster care tend to be older and to have more emotional and physical challenges; many have been victims of abuse and neglect. The long-term consequences may be the main reason that they have so many difficulties[*] (Trawick-Smith, 2010: 468). By the time they arrive at a child-care centre, older foster children may have lived with several foster families, each with its own set of expectations and standards. Some children are moved from home to home, as foster families are unable to deal with their behaviour. Entering a new environment can be an anxious experience for foster children, many of whom have spent their lives in a state of uncertainty. Given the problems foster children can bring into the family, and given that mothers are increasingly likely to be employed outside the home, foster families are in short supply. Foster children often experience an average of seven foster home placements over the course of their childhood (Bokma, 2008).

Since foster care is seen as a temporary phase for the child, contact between the child and his or her birth parents is encouraged so that the move home will be smoother. Some children who are placed in foster homes develop well, particularly if they remain in the same home for the duration of their time away from their birth parents (Barber and Delfabbro, 2006). Certainly, foster care can be

[*] TRAWICK-SMITH, JEFFREY, EARLY CHILDHOOD DEVELOPMENT: A MULTICULTURAL PERSPECTIVE, 5th Edition, © 2010. Reprinted and Electronically reproduced by permission of Pearson Education, Inc., Upper Saddle River, NJ.

preferable to continued exposure to the psychological or physical dangers of an abusive family. However, many children respond poorly to foster care. They have frequent conflicts with foster family members and are more likely to exhibit behaviour problems in school (Dance, Rushton, and Quinton, 2002). They tend to lag behind their nonfoster care peers academically (Finkelstein, Wamsley, and Miranda, 2002).

An attempt is also made to keep siblings together when planning foster care arrangements because children who are able to remain with their siblings show more positive emotional development than those who are separated (Hegar, 2005; Leathers, 2005). However, sibling separation is very common, because of the reluctance of foster parents to take more than one child. "Separated siblings report a greater sense of loss and feelings of not belonging within their new foster family. They are more likely to be disruptive, more likely to be transferred from one foster home to another, and less likely to be permanently adopted"* (Trawick-Smith, 2010: 468).

Further complicating the lives of foster children is that many foster children "age" out of the system at 18. In some jurisdictions, this has been extended to 21 but many wish that this could be further extended to age 25, when most would be finished postsecondary education (Ontario Association of Children's Aid Societies, n.d.). Many foster children are compelled to leave the only stable environment they may have known. And where will they go?

> While counselling and financial support of about $1,000 per month is available through the Extended Care Maintenance program until the child turns 21, Canadian and international research shows that between 40 percent and 60 percent of these youth end up homeless. The combination of homelessness and lack of education means the vast majority of them have trouble finding work and rely heavily on welfare. They are more likely to become involved in the criminal justice system to become parents too early, and to suffer from mental health and substance abuse problems.† (Monsebraaten, 2011)

---

* TRAWICK-SMITH, JEFFREY, EARLY CHILDHOOD DEVELOPMENT: A MULTICULTURAL PERSPECTIVE, 5th Edition, © 2010. Reprinted and Electronically reproduced by permission of Pearson Education, Inc., Upper Saddle River, NJ.

† Monsebraaten, L. 2011. "Foster Kids Struggle To Make It As Adults," *The Toronto Star*, June 12, A1. Reprinted by permission of Torstar Syndication Services.

Foster families need to be sensitive to the needs of their own children as well. These children have to share their parents and adjust their position within the family (for example, the status of each child may change when a foster child arrives). At times the rules may be different for the foster child, depending on his or her needs. The other children in the family may resent this and will need extra support.

ROLE OF THE EDUCATOR

- Gather appropriate background information. For example, will the child be with the centre on a temporary or long-term basis?

- Teachers need to display sensitivity when gathering information and respect confidentiality.

- Know the court arrangements. Is the biological parent permitted to visit the child at the program or pick up the child? If so, under what circumstances?

- It is crucial that all parties—social workers, foster families, teachers, and other significant adults—meet and plan ways to create a warm and nurturing environment for the child.

- It is important to support the foster family. Share information on the child's strengths, strategies that work successfully, and activities the child enjoys.

- If the child is to be moved to a new foster home, teachers may offer to meet with the new family to discuss the child, sharing their expertise and knowledge. This may be reassuring to the child.

ROLE OF THE EDUCATOR IN THE ROOM

- Discuss foster families as just one of many types of families to be respected in the playroom.

- Be mindful of other children and their response to the foster child. Foster children are often vulnerable to teasing or bullying.

- Foster children can become over-stimulated or distracted by noisy, busy environments or clutter. Try as much as possible to create an environment that is quiet, consistent, and highly predictable. Try to anticipate "meltdowns" and intervene before problems escalate using a kind and gentle voice, empathetic statements and gentle touch (Wotherspoon and Petrowski, 2008: 19).

When Amy, age seven, goes to sleep at night, she doesn't dream about games and parties, or even about monsters. She dreams of social workers and wakes up screaming. In her nightmares social workers snatch her from home. In real life, Amy, a ward of the foster care system, lived with six families before she was six, shuttled back and forth between foster homes and the home of her mother, who was unable to care for the girl's sickle cell anemia.

Source: Azar, 1999.

- Be respectful of the child's personal boundaries when trying to engage him or her in activities. This also applies to situations where the teacher may attempt to provide warmth and affection.

- Foster children may test the limits in a new centre by challenging teachers to "give up on them." Catch the child doing things right and celebrate accomplishments. Consistency and perseverance are key, and realistic expectations are important.

- Empower children to make their own decisions and choices and accept responsibility for their outcomes.

- Encourage foster families to participate in the centre as you would any new family.

- When older foster children leave the centre to move in with an adoptive family, it's a time for celebration, but teachers should listen to and acknowledge any fears or concerns.

- A child's move to a new foster family presents its own problems. Teachers can express their connection to the child and let him or her know that they will miss the child. Teachers and children can continue to correspond.

- Photographs, special projects, and artwork can be important keepsakes for departing foster children. Teachers may consider having the children create a special booklet in which each child records a special event or meaningful moment shared with the foster child. This is important, because children often are moved to new locations and leave behind treasured possessions.

BOOKS FOR CHILDREN

Maybe Days: A Book for Children in Foster Care, J. Wilgocki

Finding the Right Spot: When Kids Can't Live with Their Parents, by J. Levy

Kids Are Important: A Book for Young Children in Foster Care, by J. Nelson

Families Change: A Book for Children Experiencing Termination of Parental Rights, by J. Nelson and M. Gallagher

Zachary's New Home: A Story for Foster and Adopted Children, by G. Blomquist, B. Blomquist, and M. Lemieux

The Star: A Story to Help Young Children Understand Foster Care, by C. Miller Lovell

BOOKS FOR ADULTS

Another Place at the Table, by K. Harrison

The Supportive Foster Parent: "Be There for Me," by K. Gopal

On Their Own: What Happens to Kids When They Age Out of the Foster Care System, by M. Shirk and G. Strangler

Building a Home Within: Meeting the Emotional Needs of Children and Youth in Foster Care, by T. Heineman

A Guidebook for Raising Foster Children, by S. McNair Blatt

ADOPTIVE FAMILIES

"Ever since she was a young girl, Elaine knew that she wanted to adopt a child. Her best friend was adopted and she felt that adoption would be a wonderful way to have a family. Elaine and her husband, Linton, started the process through their local Children's Aid Society. They attended parent training seminars, met with parent support groups, and met with a social worker who would complete their home study. On October 8, 2008, Elaine and Linton met with their children for the first time: Tara (age 5) and her brother Mark (age 7). Like any transition, the placement was not without its obstacles; however, Tara, Mark, Elaine, and Linton are all doing very well in a home filled with love and support."

Adopting a child can be an exciting and anxious time for a family.

Adoption is the legal transfer of parental rights and obligations from birth parents to adoptive parents: the adoptive parents become the legal parents of the child or teenager. Adoption is a permanent, legally binding arrangement. It is estimated that one in five persons will be touched by adoption in his or her lifetime. We do not have information about stepchild adoption in Canada.

In Canada, adoption is a provincially mandated issue and each province and territory has its own rules and regulations on all aspects of adoption. As such, the prospective adoption process must comply with the policies and procedures that exist in the family's province or territory of residence.

DOMESTIC ADOPTION (ADOPTIONS WITHIN CANADA)

In Canada, there are two types of domestic adoption: public adoption and private adoption.

PUBLIC ADOPTION

Public adoption is an adoption arranged through a provincial ministry or an agency funded by government. Since public agencies are government funded, they provide services at no cost. An example of a public agency is a Children's Aid Society.

Given the different provincial mandates surrounding adoption in Canada, reliable and up-to-date national numbers on adoption, foster children, and children in care are difficult to gather. The most reliable information from Adoption Council of Canada is that there are more than 80,000 children in the care of child welfare organizations across Canada. More than 30,000 of these children have parents whose parental rights have been terminated by the courts and are permanent wards of governments—meaning the courts have ruled they probably won't be returned to their birth families (Adoption Council of Canada, n.d.).

One of the biggest myths about adoption in Canada is that there are no Canadian children available for adoption. Fortunately, the Adoption Council of Canada educates Canadians about children available for adoption across the country, particularly through its program Canada's Waiting Children. Its website, **http://www.canadaswaitingkids.ca**, contains photos and background information about children who are currently in the care of provincial, territorial, and First Nations agencies.

PRIVATE ADOPTION

In Canada, private adoption is an adoption arranged by a privately funded, licensed adoption agency. Private agencies are nongovernment bodies licensed by the province in which the agency operates. Private agencies charge fees for their services and usually involve the adoption of infants. Some children in blended families are adopted by their stepparent.

OPENNESS IN ADOPTION

Birth parents and adoptive parents often agree to have an open adoption, with ongoing contact between their families. Their open adoption agreement may be verbal or written, but it is not legally binding. The agreement spells out how much contact will exist, and it might specify the frequency and manner of contact between adoptive and birth families or between siblings placed separately. The families might exchange

When Michael was four, he asked, "Mommy, was I the most beautiful of all my brothers?" Confused, his mother asked him to explain. "Did you and Daddy pick me because I was the most beautiful of all my brothers at the hospital?" Finally, his mother understood. Michael seemed to have the notion that his adoptive parents came to the hospital and chose him from his "brothers." His mother reassured him that even though he was quite beautiful, he had no brothers remaining at the hospital from whom he was chosen. Michael's question is one indication that, even as young as four-years-old, he had begun the complicated psychological search for self.

Source: SPRINGATE, KAY WRIGHT; STEGELIN, DOLORES A., BUILDING SCHOOL AND COMMUNITY PARTNERSHIPS THROUGH PARENT INVOLVEMENT, 1st Edition, © 1999. Reprinted and Electronically reproduced by permission of Pearson Education, Inc., Upper Saddle River, NJ.

letters and photos, either directly or through an agency, or schedule phone calls and visits.

According to the Adoption Council of Canada's website at **http://www.adoption.ca**, there are two types of open adoptions: open and semi-open. In an open adoption, the families exchange names and addresses, and have a full and ongoing relationship. In a semi-open adoption, the families exchange nonidentifying information, such as messages and photos, through an intermediary. They do not, however, know each other's last names or addresses. These are, clearly, very different from a closed adoption, in which confidentiality is the rule. The families do not share identifying information and have no contact (Adoption Council of Canada, 2008).

INTER-COUNTRY ADOPTION

Many families look outside the country to adopt a child.

Inter-country adoption is an adoption of a child living in a different country from the adoptive parent(s). Canada has recently seen a decline in inter-country adoptions, partially because adoption agencies are facing many challenges such as greater paper work, tougher international regulations, higher fees for adoption, longer waiting times and fewer young children available.

On average, it now takes $35,000 to $45,000 to complete an adoption:

- $15,000—flights, hotel stay

- $15,000—fees paid to adoption country including court costs, fees paid to the child's orphanage after a match is made

- $15,000—fees paid in Canada, social worker to do a home study, adoption training[*] (Pearce, 2012)

Although many families have adopted from China, numbers have plummeted since 2006; "the more stringent regulations put in place by the Chinese government have resulted in far longer wait times, [and] they no longer allow adoptions by single moms, same-sex couples, obese parents or those with alcoholic parents or cancer in the family"[†] (Pearce, 2012). Therefore, some families are now choosing to adopt from other countries. Ethiopia is also making it harder to adopt because of its own domestic policies. Most provinces have suspended Haitian adoptions because of irregularities after the 2010 earthquake, such as adoptions being arranged without a proper search for birth parents. Also on the no-adoption list are Guatemala, Cambodia, and Nepal, for allegations of unethical or illegal practices including payments being made to birth mothers for giving up their babies.

THE HAGUE CONVENTION ON INTER-COUNTRY ADOPTION

Historically, a lack of regulation and the potential for financial gain contributed to the development of services in which profit took priority over the best interests of children. Resulting abuses include

[*] Pearce, T. 2012. "The painful new realities of international adoption," *The Globe and Mail*, February 17. © The Globe and Mail Inc. All Rights Reserved.

[†] Pearce, T. 2012. "The painful new realities of international adoption," *The Globe and Mail*, February 17. © The Globe and Mail Inc. All Rights Reserved.

TABLE 9.4	International Adoptions to Canada, Top 10 Source Countries, 2008–2010		
	2008	*2009*	*2010*
China	431	451	472
Haiti	147	141	172
U.S.	182	253	148
Vietnam	111	159	139
Ethiopia	187	170	112
Russia	91	121	102
South Korea	98	93	98
Philippines	118	86	88
Colombia	53	41	62
India	54	59	55
All countries	**1915**	**2122**	**1946**

Source: Reprinted by permission of Robin Hilborn.

the sale and abduction of children, the coercion of parents, bribery, and trafficking. Many countries around the world, including Canada, have recognized these risks and ratified the *Hague Convention on Inter-Country Adoption*, which is designed to put into action the principles of the UN Convention on the Rights of the Child. These rights include ensuring that adoption is authorized only by competent authorities, that inter-country adoption enjoys the same safeguards and standards that apply in national adoptions, that inter-country adoption does not result in improper financial gain, and that efforts have been made to find the child a permanent home in his or her country of origin. Canada ratified the agreement in 1996.

Children who are adopted out of the country face unique challenges. Not only have these children lost their homeland but also many will never be able to connect with family members and friends. It may be difficult for these children to develop a sense of identity in the absence of others from their culture. As a racially diverse family, it must be recognized that although race may not be an issue within the parent's home, it remains a societal issue.

Children may also come to Canada with health problems that may be unknown to the new parents. It is critical that these children receive testing that reflects the potential health issues from their country.

Information sharing varies: some families may have only limited information about the birth mother and father; others have photographs, medical records, and even letters or videos from the birth parents; still others may have face-to-face contact. A range of openness exists in adoption and the child's best interests are always kept at the forefront.

TRANSRACIAL ADOPTION

Transracial adoptions may occur within Canada, as families may adopt a child that is of a different race

Inside LOOK

When our son turned 2 years old, I made a book for him about his arrival (at 3 and a half months) and about our family. He is now almost 3 and has asked to hear *Eric's Story* many times. Once he told a friend, "I'm 'dopted—it's in my book." A few days ago we were reading the book again, and he had a reaction that touched me deeply. When we turned to the page with his foster mother's picture and read, "The nice lady loved him and was sad to see him go, but she knew that he was his mommy and daddy's special baby … She was happy he would be with them," Eric's eyes filled with tears. He seemed to be experiencing such a deep emotion that I felt he needed to just sit for a moment. These tears seemed to come from the depth of his soul. I asked why he was so sad. He only said, "Sad … sad," and pointed to the picture. We simply sat together for a while, then we talked about it a little. For about an hour he continued to be subdued and inward. Although I cannot know the meaning of this for Eric, I felt I had received a gift in seeing briefly into the depth of my child's being. It brought to mind how sad leaving and loss really is and how valuable a shared moment of deep feeling can be.

Source: Bonnie Malouf, quoted in N. Sheehan and L. Wood, *Adoption and the Schools Project: A Guide for Educators* (Washington, DC: Department of Health and Human Services, 1993)

or ethnicity from their own. Many people are under the impression that race "doesn't matter," but they soon come to find that it is one of the most challenging and complicated issues faced in transracial adoption. When preparing a child for intrusive questions or difficult situations, it is important to discuss race and racism with the child, and to establish a trusting atmosphere for open communication. Teachers should be empathetic and acknowledge the importance of this issue to the child, making the child privy to their understanding; in this way, the child's trust will be strengthened. By talking about racism, discrimination, and prejudice, teachers help the child—and all children in their care—understand the issues of equality for all.

FAMILY ADJUSTMENT

All members of the family undergo a major transition and adjustment period when a new child enters their care. In some situations, the news of the adoption comes quickly, giving family members little time to prepare for their new role. It is important for teachers to also focus on the siblings of the newly adopted child. If other children are being negatively affected by the new family member, parents may feel guilty and responsible for destroying the equilibrium of the family they once knew. Parents may even resent the new child for causing distress in the other children. New children may struggle with understanding the new family rules and expectations; they may want to fit it and yet don't know how. Teachers can play a supportive role in these situations by understanding that other children in the family will need extra support (Wheeler, 2004).

As children reach school age, they begin to comprehend that they were born to another family and

> may begin to grieve the loss of their biological family. The grief reactions can be overt or hidden. They may stop asking questions or go silent on the topic. They also realize that not everyone else is adopted and they wonder "Why didn't they keep me? Where is my birth mum, is she sad because she lost me, do I have birth brothers and sisters, are they looking for me, what if they find me, does my birth mum want me back, does she think about me?" Furthermore, a child who remembers abuse may be fearful that the abuser will find him.* (Sheehan and Wood, 1993: 38–39)

---

* Sheehan, N., and L. Wood. 1993. *Adoption and the Schools Project: A Guide for Educators*. Washington, DC: Department of Health and Human Services.

When little information is available about the birth parents, children may create their own fantasy. Older children generally have a more difficult time adjusting to adoption because many have well-developed defence mechanisms that enabled them to survive the hard times of their lives. They are not likely to drop these defences and become open, loving, and grateful children quickly (Wheeler, 2004).

Children who are adopted may carry with them an emotional connection to their biological family even though they are no longer living with them. They will have unanswered questions about their background and about why they were put up for adoption. Some children may feel that they were adopted because they were unworthy of their biological families. "Even worse," Edwards and Sodhi (1992: 6) observe, "[children] are often expected to feel grateful for being adopted. Expecting gratitude denies the fact that adoption means a child's life was marked by loss."

It is not uncommon for families formed by adoption to require support. Birth parents, adoptive

Rob Marmion/Shutterstock.com

Siblings of a newly adopted child will also have a period of adjustment as a new member is added to the family.

EXHIBIT 9.3 Talking with Your Child about Adoption: Guidelines for Adoptive Parents

1. **Start Early:** Even though your child may not understand, it's practice for you. Your child, even as an infant or toddler, gets to hear the word "adopted" in a positive context.

2. **Be Honest:** If you don't know the answer, say so. Show that you share your child's curiosity and that you would like to know too.

3. **Use Positive Adoption Language:** Use positive language, for example, "biological parent" as opposed to "real parent."

4. **Answer the Questions Your Child Asks:** *If* you are not sure what the question really is, ask your child what they mean.

5. **Include Information About Your Child's Actual Birth If You Have This:** Many adoptees report that they have grown up thinking that they weren't born like other people are because nobody talks about their birth.

6. **Don't Wait for Your Child to Raise the Subject:** Keep the communication lines open. Raise the subject every once in a while by saying for example, "I was remembering when we adopted you and we made the trip to …" or "I was just thinking of your birth mother and wondering if you ever think about her …"

7. **Once Is Not Enough:** Your child's understanding is developing and growing all the time. Don't assume that your child got all the details that you told them the last time.

8. **Paint a Positive Picture of the Birth Parents:** Refer to them by name if known. Your positive attitude is very important to building your child's self-esteem.

9. **Acknowledge and Accept Your Child's Feelings:** Listen for the feelings behind your child's comments and questions. Curiosity and sadness are natural responses to being adopted. Don't take your child's expressions about wanting to see their birth family as a reflection on you or your parenting. We don't like to see our children experiencing sadness or pain, but adoption is a mixture of joy and pain, loss and gain for all of us. Acknowledge this and help to make your child feel comfortable about talking about it.

10. **Prepare a Lifebook of Photos and the Adoption Story:** Be sure to include birth family information, foster family, orphanage, etc., as applicable. Include photos of birth family if available.

11. **Check Out Your Child's Understanding from Time to Time:** Tell her "Mary was asking about … [something to do with adoption]." What would you say to her?" Read about child development and children's understanding of adoption.

12. **Reach Out to Others:** Join a support group. Talk to other adoptive parents, share and learn from them. Consult an adoption professional, if you feel the need. If you are troubled by some of the issues you face as an adoptive parent, reach out. Others can help you work through these issues so that you can be comfortable in talking with your child about adoption. Make sure your child gets to know other adopted children.

Source: Fenton, P. 2004, "Talking With Your Child About Adoption – Guidelines For Adoptive Parents," *Adoption Roundup: Journal of the Adoption Council of Ontario*, Winter. Reprinted by permission of the Adoption Council of Ontario.

parents, and adopted children may benefit from support services. Informal supports are available through adoption groups; through special events, seminars, and workshops; and through the Internet. More formal services are available through experienced adoption professionals.

ROLE OF THE EDUCATOR

Pat Fenton, former executive director of the Adoption Council of Ontario shares her insights with teachers:

Like all families, adoptive families are unique, and each adoption story is in turn unique. Rather than a one-time legal event, adoption is now understood as an on-going developmental process that is a blend of joy and pain, loss and gain. Some adoptive families have concerns that professionals don't really understand adoption and its dynamics, and consequently they are reluctant to share adoption information. [The parents] would like to have confidence that their child's teacher can be an ally and play a supportive role in promoting understanding of adoption as a fully accepted means of family formation.*

- Teachers need to respect families' wishes as to how much information is to be shared with the children and other staff members. Teachers should never share the information they do have about an adoptive situation without obtaining the approval of the family and/or the child. Some families may choose not to disclose the adoption (even on the intake form), and teachers may never know the details of the child's situation.

- Teachers should emphasize the "belongingness" definition of a family, rather than the circumstances surrounding a child's birth (Stroud, Stroud, and Staley, 1999).

- A single parent adopting a child may need a strong support network.

- Adoptive parents are faced with a whole new set of challenges, particularly if the child has special needs. We know that early intervention in these situations is critical.

- Adoptive families often don't seek help early enough. Educators could help parents by finding out what support services are available in their community and referring families to adoption support groups or play groups for adoptive families (an easy way to meet others and make lifelong friends) and to websites where many people go for support.

- Check with local adoptive parent groups—they welcome the opportunity to offer resources, workshops, book suggestions, and speakers.

- Teachers should be willing to meet with social workers or foster families if the adoptive parents feel an exchange of information would be helpful in the support of the child.

- Each November, the North American Council on Adoptable Children and the Adoption Council of Canada sponsors National Adoption Awareness Month. This may be a good time

---

* Reprinted by permission of Patricia Fenton.

to display books on adoption (both children's and adult) and to ask parents who have been adopted to share their stories with the children.

- Many adoptive families celebrate the anniversary of their child's adoption. Teachers can discuss with families whether they would like this day to be celebrated in the centre as well.

ROLE OF THE EDUCATOR IN THE ROOM

- Including adoptive families as examples in discussions of kinds of families can help to normalize the adoption experience.

- If a child has a baby born into his family, mention that some children join their family by adoption.

- Whether adopted children are in the group or not, teachers should bring adoptive families into playroom discussions.

- Teachers need to be aware of the reaction of siblings who may also be in the centre. A number of children's books view the adoption process from the point of view of the child already in the family.

- Teacher observations of the child in his or her day-to-day interaction with adults and children are especially important to the families, who are bound to have concerns about the development of the child, particularly if little background information is available.

- Teachers may want to include in their program information about a child's country if he or she has been adopted from overseas; many families welcome the opportunity for children to share in their dual heritage.

- Older adopted children who have had a difficult and perhaps traumatic beginning need to be linked with teachers who are warm and nurturing and able to clearly articulate realistic expectations and limits.

- Some children may act in a way that appears to the teacher to have no bearing on the particular event or moment. The behaviour may be the result of something that triggers an unpleasant memory, an act of abuse, or other traumatic situation for the child. Families may be able to help teachers identify some of the stressful situations that trigger these unpleasant memories.

- Consistent routines and procedures provide the child with a sense of stability. Teachers should be aware that some children find changes in staff—or abrupt departures from the normal routine—highly unsettling. Others have difficulty building relationships with adults. Teachers will need to be patient.

- Teachers who themselves come from adopted families may choose to share the positive experiences that they have had.

- Be sensitive to the challenges an adopted child may face when asked to do assignments or class activities such as bringing in baby photos or doing a family tree.

- Teachers should be sensitive about asking for such materials as baby photos, since these may not be available to the adopted child. However, creating family booklets with photos of their present-day lives is a great way to share the diversity that exists in families.

- When assigning family-related projects to older children, teachers should give adopted children wide latitude in deciding what to share. When describing the project to the children, the teacher may use an adopted family as an example.

- Use books or tell stories that include adoptive families and adopted children. Today there are many children's books available, but these do not reflect all the ways in which children are adopted; therefore, they should be chosen with care. Families may have already created their own more personalized family books and might be willing to share these with the children.

- Teachers should avoid showing movies or videos that depict adopted children as "out of control" or "bad."

- Teachers should guard against the negative impact of adopt-a-theme programs. As Johnston (1993: 119) points out, these programs range from the adopt-an-animal program of zoos across the country, to silly not-for-profit fundraising ideas, such as adopt-a-rubber-duck river races, sponsored by a local radio station to benefit a food bank, city adopt-a-park and adopt-a-pothole programs, commercial adopt-a-product promotions, to Humane Society animal placement programs. Those of us who are parents by adoption and adoption activists, however, believe that such programs trivialize a very serious topic and that they further myths and misconceptions about this family planning method to yet another generation of children. Unfortunately, they turn upon a kind of "save the rejects" image that may seem cute and harmless to grownups but which confuses concrete-thinking children—be they adopted or not.*

- Teachers need to be consistent in their use of positive adoption language. As Edwards and Sodhi (1992: 21) observe,

Positive adoption language can stop the spread of misconceptions such as these. By using positive

---

* Johnston, P. 1993. *Adoption and the Schools Project: A Guide for Educators*. Washington, DC: Department of Health and Human Services.

Inside LOOK

I usually "forget" that I didn't birth Tanya until I am "reminded" by strangers or new acquaintances whose curiosity results in unintentional insensitivity. "Is Tanya your grandchild?" or "Who is Tanya's mother?" are common questions when it is obvious that Tanya is biracial and I am not. I guess it's human nature to try and connect the dots. However, I wish the person would think first about how my child will feel about the question. We have two daughters, one by birth and one by adoption. There is never any question that we are "real" parents to both of them. But we are aware that we can't know what Tanya's experience of being biracial is like, and we respond to her need to be connected to her racial and ethnocultural backgrounds. This enriches our lives as we benefit from involvement in Afro-Caribbean culture. Like all parents, we hope that both our children won't have too many closed doors through their childhood and adolescence, but we also know that challenging life experiences build strength of character. Supportive teachers along the way for Tanya continue to validate her as an individual whose blueprint includes her racial background and adopted family, realities that contribute to who she is.

adoption language, we educate others about adoption. We choose emotionally "correct" words over emotionally laden words. We speak and write in positive adoption language with the hope of impacting others so that this language will someday become the norm.

Using the term *birth parent* rather than *real parent*, or *biological parent* rather than *natural parent* are examples of positive versus negative language.

BOOKS FOR CHILDREN

What Is Adoption?, by S. Stergianis.

Adoptive Families Are Families for Keeps: Activity Book, by L. Cowan

Bringing Asha Home, by U. Krishnaswami

Finding Joy, by M. Coste

Journey Home, by L. McKay, Jr.

My Family Is Forever, by N. Carlson

My Mei Mei, by E. Young

A Sister for Matthew, by P. Kennedy

The Starlight Baby, by G. Shields

We Are Adopted, by J. Moore Mallinos

I Love You Like Crazy Cakes, by R. Lewis and J. Dyer

Over The Moon: An Adoption Tale, by K. Katz

I Don't Have Your Eyes, by C.A. Kitze

Did My First Mother Love Me? A Story For An Adopted Child, by K. Miller

BOOKS FOR ADULTS

What Is Adoption? Helping Non-Adopted Children Understand Adoption, by S. Stergianis and R. McDowall

Born In Our Hearts: Stories of Adoption, by F. Casey and M.C. Casey

The Post Adoption Blues: Overcoming the Unforeseen Challenges of Adoption, by K. Foli and J. Thompson

Becoming a Family: Promoting Healthy Attachments with Your Adopted Child, by L. Eshleman

From China with Love: A Long Road to Motherhood, by E. Buchanan

LESBIAN, GAY, BISEXUAL, TRANSSEXUAL, TRANSGENDERED, AND QUEER FAMILIES (LGBTQ)

"Sarah and Monique have been living together for five years. Sarah is a teacher and Monique owns her own catering business. They live in a small house with Sarah's 7-year-old daughter, Megan, from her first marriage. Monique is six months pregnant with a baby conceived through insemination. Sarah, Monique, and Megan are all looking forward to the birth of this child."

Individuals and parents who identify as lesbian, gay, bisexual, transsexual (people who want their bodies to match the gender they feel they truly are), transgendered (anyone whose gender identity falls outside the stereotypical expected behaviours of men and women), and queer (historically a derogatory term that has been reclaimed, with a movement underway to use it in a positive way) may also include individuals who are questioning (a person who is questioning his or her sexual orientation or gender identity), intersex (a person who may be born with external female genitalia but internal male reproductive anatomy) and two-spirited (First Nations people who believe in the existence of three genders: male, female, and male-female).

FACTS ABOUT LGBTQ

The 2011 census counted 64,575 same-sex couples, with 32.5 percent married, nearly double the 2006 share. The 2006 to 2011 period marks the first five-year period during which same-sex couples could legally marry.

The Toronto District School Board (2011) points out important dates for LGBTQ:

- Prime Minister Pierre Trudeau's amendments pass into the Criminal Code, decriminalizing homosexuality in Canada in 1969.[*]

- In May 1995, Ontario becomes the first province to legalize adoption by same-sex couples. British Columbia, Alberta, and Nova Scotia followed suit.

---

[*] Toronto District School Board. 2011. *Equitable And Inclusive Schools. Challenging Homophobia and Heterosexism. A K-12 Curriculum. Resource Guide.* www.tdsb.on.ca. Reprinted by permission.

- The federal government passed Bill C-33, which adds "sexual orientation" to the Canadian Human Rights Act in 1996.

- In May 1999, Canada's Supreme Court ruled same-sex couples should have the same benefits and obligations as opposite-sex common-law couples, and equal access to benefits from social programs to which they contribute

- In 1999, Alberta courts first agreed to let same-sex partners adopt each other's biological children, but those in New Brunswick had to wait until 2004 to do so.

- July 19, 2005, Bill C-38 was passed by the Senate, officially legalizing same-sex marriage in all of Canada. Canada became the fourth country in the world to legalize same-sex marriage, after the Netherlands, Belgium, and Spain.

Corbett (1993: 31) asks how many early childhood teachers have considered "that in our care are children who will grow up to be lesbian and gay adults and that while a handful may show early indications of seeming 'different' in some way, the vast majority will offer no clue to even the most observant eye."*

Teachers must challenge the issues of heterosexism, that is, the belief that all people are or should be heterosexual and that heterosexuality is inherently superior to and preferable to homosexuality or bisexuality. In a society that tells gays and lesbians constantly through our laws, our acted-out prejudices, and our ignorant and uncaring behaviour that they are unacceptable human beings, how do we attempt to rear a generation that accepts homosexuality as a

---

* Corbett, S. 1993. "A Complicated Bias," *Young Children*, March: 31. © NAEYC. Reprinted with permission.

Inside LOOK

In March 2009, Egale Canada partnered with the University of Winnipeg and undertook a study to identify the forms and extent of the experiences of homophobic incidents at schools in Canada and measures being taken by schools to combat this common form of bullying. Some of the key findings included:

- LGBTQ students were more likely than non-LGBTQ individuals to report that staff never intervened when homophobic comments were made.
- Nine out of ten transgender students, six out of ten LGB students, and three out of ten straight students were verbally harassed because of their expression of gender.
- Three-quarters of LGBTQ students and 95 percent of transgender students felt unsafe at school, compared to one-fifth of straight students.
- Over half of LGBTQ students did not feel accepted at school, and almost half felt they could not be themselves, compared to one-fifth of straight students.
- Three-quarters of LGBTQ students feel unsafe in at least one place at school, such as change rooms, washrooms, and hallways.
- Half of straight students agree that at least one part of their school is unsafe for LGBTQ students.
- Three-quarters of all participating students reported hearing expressions such as "that's so gay" every day in school.

Source: Reprinted by permission of EGALE Canada.

According to the Canadian Centre for Justice Statistics report *Hate Crime in Canada* (2006) and the 2007 Toronto Police Service *Annual Hate/Bias Crime Statistical Report*:

- Sexual orientation was one of the top three motivations for hate crimes.
- 56.3 percent of all hate crimes motivated by sexual orientation were violent.
- The second most likely place for hate crimes to be committed was in educational facilities.
- Hate crimes predominantly affected youth: approximately one-half of all victims and three-quarters of those accused were between the ages of twelve and twenty-four.

Source: Safe Schools Action Team. 2008.

fact of life? Greenspoon (1998: 18) states that "there is a perception that issues related to people's sexual orientation is a moral question, often with religious prohibitions, rather than a question of diversity and equal rights." Gonzalez-Mena (2007: 119) argues that we must unlearn biases around sexual orientation and gender identity:*

> Oppression is oppression and you don't want to have any part of it—either supporting oppressive systems, practicing discrimination yourself or harboring internal oppression. Recognize that taking on challenges make you stronger. Struggling with your own religious beliefs and honouring all families at the same time may seem overwhelming. If the struggle isn't within you, you may find it among colleagues, or among families themselves. It may be hard to facilitate relationships with these struggles going on, but you have to do your best.

Janmohamed (2006) points out that "although LGBTQ parents have fought hard to win the right to be recognized as parents legally through the birth and adoption process, LGBTQ families continue to face isolation and homophobia in their day-to-day experiences or parenting and social interaction."†

Courtesy of Lynn Wilson

Kim, Julie, and Charley celebrating at their wedding.

* GONZALEZ-MENA, JANET, 50 EARLY CHILDHOOD STRATEGIES FOR WORKING AND COMMUNICATING WITH DIVERSE FAMILIES, 1st Edition, © 2007. Reprinted and Electronically reproduced by permission of Pearson Education, Inc., Upper Saddle River, NJ.

† Janmohamed, Z. 2006. *Building Bridges: Lesbian, Gay, Bisexual, Transgender, Transsexual and Queer Families in Early Childhood Education*. Toronto: Ontario Coalition for Better Child Care. Reprinted by permission of the publisher.

Inside LOOK

In the context of the early childhood professional preparation program, the pedagogical approach to understand diversity and difference is often laid out in environmental scans that enable one lecture to focus on immigrants and refugees, and the next on children being raised by grandparents and the next on the needs of English language learners. Although the provincial program standards sets expectations that early childhood educators will graduate with knowledge about diversity and equity, the approach in early childhood training is focused more on how to enable families with diverse backgrounds with transitions into early childhood programs rather than dwelling more deeply into the social and pedagogical differences of the individual family construct. This approach assumes commonality in the traditional conceptual framework of family and is in fact extended to "same-sex" families. If that same-sex coupling is married, it is given more legitimacy—somehow, the symbolic nature of marriage and its heteronormative promise, softens the image that queers don't just have sex all the time. They also raise children, spend time at the grocery store, negotiate drop-offs and pick-ups and generally operate in the heteronormative framework of a nuclear family unit. This construct also perpetuates a newly created normative framework of lesbian or gay parents without recognizing the growing population of trans people having children in seemingly heterosexual relationships that go far beyond the commonly understood family construct. Ideas about how families operate are infused throughout early childhood teacher training programs and as a result, educational institutions can implicitly and explicitly foster foundational knowledge that promotes a hegemonic or dominant perspective.

Source: Reprinted by permission of Zeenat Janmohamed, Atkinson Centre, OISE/UT.

Julie and I have been together for the last five years. We are both police officers and met on this job. We found that we share much in common, including wanting to start a family together. Julie is our daughter's biological mother. I am much older than Julie (we are actually 16 years apart in age, but it doesn't feel that way…). We had Charley back in June of 2010 and she is a joy for us both. We are now talking about having a second child and hope to start the process soon. If we are lucky we will have a second sweet child and our lives will be fulfilled in the way that we always hoped. I can honestly say that our police family has been extremely supportive in every respect. Charley's godparents are both police officers as well and we have had nothing but positive energy from both our work environments. I can say, being a police officer for just over 25 years now, that the membership has come a long way in terms of acceptance of the gay population and family diversity. This is a step in the right direction.

Source: Reprinted by permission of Kimberly Gross.

Kate and Amy have been partners for 10 years and in 2009 they were married in front of a large group of friends and family. The majority of their friends are straight couples living parallel lives to Kate and Amy. However their friend's lives continued to develop into families while they struggled to build a family of their own. Shortly after their wedding, Kate and Amy began the process of having their first child through donor insemination. Looking back, they had no idea it would be three years later and they would still be trying. The process has been a trying and difficult time for both of them. Months of getting excited about the potential and possibility of pregnancy only to be repeatedly disappointed has taken its toll. Thankfully, the process has not been without its positive aspects. The fertility clinic where Kate and Amy have been having their insemination has treated them as any other couple struggling through issues of infertility. Staff have been considerate and caring as well as aware of their individual needs and concerns. This has meant the world to Kate and Amy as it allows them to feel like there is one less thing for them to be disappointed about in a process that has been full of letdowns. It has also made Kate and Amy hopeful about the future, knowing that perhaps society has progressed to an extent where their sexual orientation will not be an issue that their child will have to face.

Update: Kate and Amy are now proud parents of twins—Hanlan and Edgar—born September 30, 2012!

Source: Reprinted by permission of Amy Davey.

Since the mid-1980s, when so many lesbians began pursuing motherhood that it was labelled the Lavender Baby Boom, support for LGBTQ parents has become easier to find. Toronto has the LGBTQ Parenting Network, Montreal has the LGBT Family Coalition, and Vancouver has Queer Families. There are even summer camps such as Camp Ten Oaks in Quebec's Gatineau Hills, founded in 2004 by a lesbian couple who felt their children could use a space to canoe, hike, and camp without awkward scrutiny. As members grew older, staff created Project Acorn, a leadership program for GLBT teens and kids of same-sex couples. (Balkissoon, 2011).

GAY MALE TEACHERS

Janmohamed (2006) quotes Campbell and Forrester who discuss the problems facing a gay male teachers:

> I am painfully aware of the assumptions that are often made about a male who demonstrates an interest in working with young children. Those who hold such stereotypes to be true may ultimately dismiss this passion as dangerously pathological. This fear may be further compounded by the fact that gay men, in particular, are falsely regarded by some to be frequent abusers of young children. Although these sweeping generalizations remain unsubstantiated by reputable research they continue to pervade mainstream public consciousness and serve as a potential barrier to my relationships with parents in particular. As a gay teacher, I have made a concerted effort to include homosexuality as an integral component to anti-bias education within the classroom … it is important for children to learn and know about the many differences in their world. The fact that someone may have two moms or two dads, or that their friend's parent might not have always been a woman or man, is fact, not fiction. In fact, early childhood educators need to be aware that the children may also be experiencing gender identity issues and need to be cared for in an environment that is accepting of all people. Early Childhood Educators have the responsibility to create environments that are safe for all children and families.[*]

GAY FATHERS

A summary of research into factors relating to parenting by nonheterosexual fathers was conducted by Rachel Epstein and Scott Duggan (2006) and provides us with insight into the challenges faced by those who are fathers in a heterosexual relationship, fathers in the context of gay identity, and those who are not yet fathers.

- The extreme invisibility of gay fathers is connected to a lack of programs and services supporting them.

- Many gay fathers give up the desire to parent when they come out because they are affected by negative stereotypes about gay men and parenting.

- Many formerly straight fathers believe that they will not be able to gain access to their children through the court system. Research is required to determine how gay fathers fare in Canadian courts, and whether these men's fears are based on legal realities, and/or perceived homophobia and heterosexism in the court system—particularly stereotypes about gay men as pedophiles and resulting fears about gay men being near young children.

- Participants identified many issues related to coming out to children and spouses, including fear of the children's and spouse's homophobia and the consequences of this homophobia on access to children.

- Gay men who have children after coming out, face other challenging issues. Most significant are the complexities involved in adoption, surrogacy, or co-parenting arrangements. Participants describe the time, energy, and financial resources required, and the emotional toll of the process (Father Involvement Research Alliance, n.d.).

http://www.fira.ca/

LGBTQ FAMILIES AND THEIR CHILDREN

Many same-sex parents feel that there is a need for them to constantly defend their family structure while constantly being compared to heterosexual family models:

> Lesbian parents talk about feeling that they are being viewed through a lens that foregrounds their lesbianism, and that attributes any problems their children experience at school, or any nonconforming behaviours on the part of their children, as stemming from the sexual orientation of the parents. Some, conscious of the tendency for their behaviour to be viewed as "lesbian behaviour," are reluctant to make waves, fearing that it will have negative repercussions for their children. While many have had positive experiences with individual teachers, they also describe their parenting status as being tolerated but not acknowledged in the classroom. (Epstein, 2003: 91–92)[†]

HOW ARE THE CHILDREN DOING?

What can we learn about gender roles and assignments of tasks and household responsibilities that may differ from heterosexual family structures? Epstein (2003: 175) reports Stacey and Biblarz's meta-analysis of 21 studies of the children of

---

[*] Janmohamed, Z. 2006. *Building Bridges: Lesbian, Gay, Bisexual, Transgender, Transsexual and Queer Families in Early Childhood Education*. Toronto: Ontario Coalition for Better Child Care. Reprinted by permission of the publisher.

[†] Reprinted by permission of Rachel Epstein.

Stephen and I publicly adopted our first child, a 9-month-old boy, in 1998. While both Stephen and I were fully included in the adoption process, I was the only one who could legally be Ronan's adoptive parent. Ronan was subsequently adopted by Stephen in a separate court application the following year, thereby giving both of us equal and legal guardianship of our son. Conversely, in 2002, when Stephen and I adopted our second boy, Josh, who was 1 year old at the time, we were able to adopt together in one application to the courts. Within three short years, the Canadian laws went from not recognizing Stephen and me as common-law, to including same sex common-law in the government's definition of a family. Not only are we accepted as a family in the eyes of the government but also our friends, family, and the children's educators have opened their arms and minds to our lifestyle. We are so thankful to have had an opportunity to be involved with two different daycare centres where staff have not only accepted us, but also asked all the right questions to make us and our children feel welcomed, loved, and important. When special days roll around such as Mother's Day or Father's Day, the kids are welcomed to make cards and gifts for their dad and papa, and the daycare staff are consistently aware and supportive of our family differences.

Source: Reprinted by permission of Byron Silver, Family Service Toronto.

Several years ago, when my daughter was about 3, her daycare teacher approached me at the end of the day. The preschool room was doing a family unit, and the teacher had asked each child to say something about their mother and father. "Jesse got really angry," the teacher told me, "and insisted that she didn't have a father. I told her that every child has a father somewhere. Then she got really mad, and started yelling, 'I don't have a father.'" The teacher looked at me, waiting for my sympathetic response to her story. Instead, I responded in shock and outrage. "She was right," I said. "She doesn't have a father." When she looked puzzled, I continued: "Obviously every child has a biological father somewhere, but Jesse does not have a social father. So from her point of view, she was right. I hope you never contradict her explanation of her family again."

Ten years later I still feel upset when I think of that incident. If I had one message to convey to teachers it would be this: "Listen to the children. They will tell you what you need to know." Lesbian and gay families have many ways of defining themselves. Some families may have two mothers. Others may refer to themselves as Mommy and Bonnie or Suey or Mary. In some cases where the original lesbian parents have split up, there may be even more than two mothers. Children born into a heterosexual marriage may have a father; children whose conception is the result of alternative insemination generally do not have a father. Attempting to define what a lesbian or gay family looks like, and trying to impose that definition on children, will do far more harm than good. Teachers must also realize that some lesbian and gay families may choose not to disclose their sexual orientation, because of employment or family concerns. In such cases, pushing children to provide details of their family life may put considerable stress on both the child and the family.

Source: Reprinted by permission of Katherine Arnup, Associate Professor, Canadian Studies, Carleton University.

lesbians conducted between 1981 and 1998. From this research they concluded that

the children of lesbians differ in "modest but interesting ways" from children with straight parents. They attribute some of these differences to the ways that gender and sexual orientation interact to create new kinds of family structures and processes. Some differences they highlight are discussed below:

- Children with lesbian moms exhibit an increased awareness and empathy toward social difference and tend to describe themselves in ways that indicate higher self-esteem and better mental health than do the children of other moms.

- Children of lesbians appear less traditionally gender-typed. For example, lesbians' daughters may be more than twice as likely to aspire to non-traditional jobs, and lesbians' sons are less aggressive than those raised by heterosexual mothers.

- Two women co-parenting may create a synergistic energy pattern that brings more egalitarian, compatible, shared parenting and time spent with children, greater understanding of children, and closeness and communication between parents and children.

Balkissoon (2011) agrees:

A series of studies in Canada and elsewhere over the past decade has found that the children of lesbians aren't just well-adjusted—they excel. On average, kids with two moms seem to be more confident and less aggressive than those raised by a mom and a dad. They are open-minded, affectionate and less susceptible to anxiety and depression.

Teachers and administrators often lack knowledge of the resources to support them in addressing gay and lesbian issues, but more and more helpful material has become available. One resource that can be invaluable is a document from the Toronto District School Board, published in 2011. *Challenging Homophobia and Heterosexim: A K-12 Curriculum Resource Guide* is filled with practical teaching ideas and many community resources.

ROLE OF THE EDUCATOR

As teachers we need to be aware of rigid models of gender behaviour and how that influences homophobia, bullying, and discrimination—and gender-based violence. Antihomophobia education is about respect of difference and recognition of the human rights guaranteed by the *Canadian Charter of Rights and Freedoms*. LGBTQ families engage in their lifestyles at great personal risk and cost. Their commitment to parenting demands our respect. Gay and lesbian families are obviously concerned about protecting their children from homophobia. Older children, in particular, may be reluctant to disclose their family situation to teachers and other children for fear of inviting a negative reaction. While some gay and lesbian parents feel comfortable discussing their family situation with supervisors and teachers, others fear that disclosure will stigmatize their child and invite censure or criticism. Wickens (1993) relates the comments of two fathers who did not disclose their family situation until the last few months of their child's time in preschool but who offered full disclosure when the child entered public school.

Inside LOOK

Audre Lorde writes about what it means to be the child of a lesbian of colour:

There are certain basic requirements of any child—food, clothing, shelter, love. So what makes our children different: We do. Gays and Lesbians of Color are different because we are embattled by reason of our sexuality and our Color, and if there is any lesson we must teach our children, it is that difference is a creative force for change, that survival and struggle for the future is not a theoretical issue. It is the very texture of our lives.

Source: Lorde, in Pollack and Vaughn 1987: 313.

It was a learning thing. The learning was that there is no choice but to bring it up. There's no way to hide it. Not that we were doing it so much on the conscious level. But it's much more wise to be open about it because you don't have a choice anyway. The child is going to tell everyone. Then it's much harder to explain it all after the fact. It's much easier to be out right at the start. It's also giving a very negative message that what you're doing is wrong. So how can a child have a clear, positive concept and understanding about what this relationship is about if someone's telling him not to tell anybody?* (Wickens, 1993: 26–27)

Educators can play a significant role in supporting same-sex families as they enter early learning environments. Trawick-Smith (2010: 467) states that

one factor that differentiated the proud same sex families from the anxious ones was the level of support provided by schools and teachers. The better adjusted parents and children reported having teachers who were open, relaxed, and accepting of gay and lesbian families. These teachers took steps to include discussions of all different kinds of families in their curriculum.†

---

* Wickens, E. 1993. "I Will Have a Child in My Class with Two Moms," *Young Children*, March: 26-27. © NAEYC. Reprinted with permission.

† TRAWICK-SMITH, JEFFREY, EARLY CHILDHOOD DEVELOPMENT: A MULTICULTURAL PERSPECTIVE, 5th Edition, © 2010. Reprinted and Electronically reproduced by permission of Pearson Education, Inc., Upper Saddle River, NJ.

One supervisor points out that

on my door is a pink triangle, once a designation of a homosexual person during the Nazi regime, that meant persecution, arrest and for far too many, extermination in a concentration camp. Today it is a symbol of gay pride and liberation. The triangle is a reminder of the suffering and persecution of those that came before us. The triangle is my effort to let parents, staff and anyone who enters our building know that gay families and gay staff are in a safe and welcoming place.

- When dealing with gay and lesbian families, it is critical that teachers examine their own values and attitudes for possible biases. Children are very astute and pick up on a teacher's confirming or disconfirming attitude.

- "Compassion, sensitivity and accurate information are resources needed by all professionals supporting and serving the homosexual family" (Hildebrand et al., 2008: 349).

- The supervisor of the centre must lead the way in creating centre safety for staff and for families and ensure that anti-oppression policies are in place. The centre's written philosophy and practice should reflect the Human Rights Code Section 4, which "provides that every person has a right to freedom from discrimination …"

Inside LOOK

Silence

Silence has a powerful voice, especially when it excludes the people most important to children, the people who keep them safe, and tuck them into bed at night and feed them and love them—their family. Even when it is not the intention of an educator to create harm, it may in fact be the result. Here is an example: A lesbian mother overheard her second grade daughter, Jenny, and her best friend, Rita, having a conversation in the other room:

    Jenny: "I hate having two moms!"

    Rita: "Why?"

    Jenny: "I hate it when the teacher says 'Take this home to your mom or dad.'"

    The educator involved probably had no idea that her words would impact Jenny this way. Through our everyday actions and language in the classroom, we convey messages of acceptance or rejection, of "normalcy" or strangeness that teach a child whether or not they are welcomed, valued, and included in this world. Jenny was given the message that she and her family didn't belong.

Source: Burt, T. and Klinger Lesser, L. 2008. "Lesbian, Gay, Bisexual and Transgendered (LGBT) Families," *Exchange*, September/October, p. 1. Reprinted by permission.

- Supervisors may need to provide in-service training where teachers have an opportunity to talk with gay and lesbian members of their community and ask honest and frank questions that will help them in working with both children and parents. Supervisors can also plan online sessions with staff to explore the many Internet sources of information and support to same-sex families.

- Be proactive. Advertise that your program is LGBTQ friendly to attract both staff and families.

- Create a positive atmosphere by learning the differences between tolerance, acceptance, celebration, and advocacy for same-sex families.

- Teachers should view a parent as a child's mother or father, not as the child's gay father or lesbian mother. Parents should be made to feel welcome and included right from the beginning of their association with the centre.

- Ask families how they would like to be referred to since some labels or terminology may be offensive to some. Options include *same-sex family* or *gay or lesbian family*. Always use the same language used by the parents and their children.

- Teachers need to use appropriate non-discriminatory language. Avoid the use of common offensive phrases that denigrate same-sex individuals—for example, referring to strange or unusual objects or occurrences as "gay." Encourage inclusive language with older children to avoid the assumption that everyone is heterosexual. Use terms such as *partner* or *significant other* in place of *boyfriend*, *girlfriend*, *husband*, or *wife*.

- Don't assume that all LGBTQ families will have the same needs or the same lifestyle. Each family must be celebrated for its uniqueness. LGBTQ families cross all socioeconomic, racial, and cultural backgrounds and may be at various stages of being "out."

- Protecting confidentiality is an important teacher responsibility. Do not disclose or "out" an individual. Teachers need to respect and honour the rights of parents to maintain silence about their homosexuality.

- Registration forms and all centre-generated written communication should include "parent and/or co-parent," replacing the traditional "mother and father."

- Family visits may be particularly important for some LGBTQ families so privacy can be ensured and a fuller discussion can take place.

- Gay and lesbian parents may feel constant pressure to exceed societal expectations of parenting—to prove that the benefits of raising children in a gay or lesbian family parallel those offered by their heterosexual counterparts. Teachers should be sensitive to these issues for all families.

- Teachers need to be prepared to challenge insensitive jokes or antigay or lesbian comments by adults in the centre in the same way that they would challenge any racist slur. Don't be a silent witness to hate speech. The centre needs to reflect this fundamental principle in the working environment and in all its interactions. Teachers must take personal responsibility and be prepared to intervene when necessary.

- If teachers are uncomfortable with the way in which their colleagues are handling same-sex families in their centre, professional development workshops would be a positive strategy for challenging negative attitudes. Resource people are available in the community to carry out these workshops in a positive and sensitive manner.

- Teachers should consider that a colleague may be gay or lesbian and afraid to disclose his or her orientation for fear of harassment and discrimination. How can you contribute to a safe and inclusive work environment?

- Teachers should also be mindful that members of the LGBTQ community have suffered death, and grieving continues to play a role in many of their lives. Compassion and empathy is the role of the educator.

ROLE OF THE EDUCATOR IN THE ROOM

- When gay and lesbian families visit the centre, they should see representations of themselves. "How must the scores of children living with gay parents feel," Corbett asks, "never to see any representation of their lives in any book, any song, or any television program?"* (1993: 31). Books, photos of families in the room, posters, and artwork should reflect all families.

---

* Corbett, S. 1993. "A Complicated Bias," *Young Children*, March: 31. © NAEYC. Reprinted with permission.

The first Rainbow Flag was designed in 1978 by Gilbert Baker, a San Francisco artist, who created the flag in response to a local activist's call for a community symbol. (This was before the pink triangle was popularly used as a symbol of pride.) Using the five-striped "Flag of the Race" as his inspiration, Baker designed a flag with eight stripes: pink, red, orange, yellow, green, blue, indigo, and violet. According to Baker, those colours represented, respectively: sexuality, life, healing, sun, nature, art, harmony, and spirit. In the true spirit of Betsy Ross, Baker dyed and sewed the material for the first flag himself. (Ast, 2011: 14)

nito/Shutterstock.com

- Recognizable symbols in the classroom such as rainbow flags, safety zone stickers, or LGBT (lesbian, gay, bisexual, and transgender) posters raise awareness.

- Children will ask many questions such as, "Is homosexuality against religion?" "What if you find out you're gay and your religion thinks it's wrong?" Teachers may respond with something like the following: "Sometimes even within the same religion people disagree. Some consider homosexuality a sin, others consider it a personal choice, while others consider it a gift from God. There are gays, lesbians, and bisexuals in every religious group around the globe" (Changes in Me, 2011).

- If children use names such as "fag," "dyke," etc., teach the children what the words mean and how they are hurtful and let them know that this language will not be tolerated.

- With older children, hold open discussions about discrimination and its consequences. Guests from the community might be invited to share appropriate information with the children.

- When teachers are unsure of how to handle a situation that might arise, they are encouraged to discuss strategies with the gay or lesbian family. The family is the best resource and may have many helpful suggestions.

- When dealing with younger children, it is sufficient for teachers to explore the concept that all families are different and that each is acceptable. For school-age children, a more detailed explanation may be in order. It may be helpful to discuss with older children the many talented politicians, writers, athletes, actors, and musicians who are gay or lesbian: Giorgio Armani, Anderson Cooper, Ellen Degeneres, Melissa Etheridge, Rick Mercer, Elton John, k.d. lang, Alexander McQueen, Harvey Milk, Rosie O'Donnell, Brian Orser, Mark Tewksbury, Andy Warhol.

- Hoy Crawford (1996:7) says,

There is general societal homophobia which results in parents' and teachers' concern about children's play where they are acting out non-stereotypical gender roles. "Tomboy" or "sissy" play looks like stereotypical "gay behaviour," and any child who exhibits this behaviour may be shamed and marginalized. All children suffer because of these narrow limits of what is deemed to be acceptable.... Gender and racial stereotypes hamper the growth of individuals by limiting their expectations for themselves.

Teachers need to support all types of play for boys and girls in the program and actively engage the children in challenging stereotypical approaches to games, toys, and activities. Discuss with the children why stereotyping based on gender is wrong.

- Take the children to a large department toy store, or examine advertising flyers and examine how the toys are arranged and the target audience. Do they see a stereotypical display?
- Display posters for community activities, resources, agencies, etc., for all families in the child-care centre. Learn about what is available in the community for LGBT families.
- Activities need to be inclusive—for example, create two Mother's or Father's Day cards (or call it Family Day to include all family structures).
- In child care we celebrate everything in order to include everyone! Celebrate Pride Day!

PRIDE LIBRARY

The Pride Library is a project of the University of Western Ontario Research Facility for Gay and Lesbian Studies, the first of its kind in Canada. Its focus is to provide Canadians with reliable information on LGBT family issues in a variety of scholarly and popular forms—academic books, specialist periodicals, magazine articles, documentary videos, parenting manuals, and children's books. The website is **http://www.uwo.ca/pridelib**.

PFLAG

In 1972, Morton Manford was physically attacked at a gay rights demonstration in New York. Morty's parents, Jeanne and Jules Manford, saw the attack in a local newscast and witnessed the failure of the police to intervene. Their outrage turned them into activists. "In 1972, Jeanne Manford marched beside her gay son in a New York City Gay Pride parade. Overwhelmed by the positive reactions from participants and observers, she and her husband went on to launch Parents, Families and Friends of Lesbians and Gays (PFLAG) (Hildebrand et al, 2008: 335).

Today, PFLAG Canada is the only national grassroots organization that deals with sexual orientation and gender identity issues from a family perspective, providing support, education and resources to families, friends and colleagues with questions or concerns, 24 hours a day, 7 days a week. As of 2012, PFLAG Canada has more than 70 chapters and contacts across Canada, with representation in nine Canadian provinces. One family comments

We are very proud of our gay son, our first born. He did not choose to be gay any more than we chose to be straight. He lives his life with courage, dignity, and good humour, in a positive relationship.... He is loved and respected by his four younger siblings and a large extended family. If you met him you would say, "What a fine young man." And you would be right. We wouldn't have had the courage to have chosen to parent a gay person, but we have come to feel that it is a privilege.* (PFLAG, n.d.)

More information about the group can be found on its website at **http://www.pflag.ca**.

QUEER PARENTING PROGRAMS
THE 519 CHURCH STREET COMMUNITY CENTRE, TORONTO, ONTARIO

The 519 Church Street Community Centre is an exemplary program for LGBTTQ families. Visit the website at **http://www.the519.org**.

BOOKS FOR CHILDREN

123: A Family Counting Book, by B. Combs
ABC: A Family Alphabet Book, by B. Combs
Best Best Colors/Los Mejores Colores, by E. Hoffman
Felicia's Favourite Story, by L. Newman
Saturday Is Pattyday, by L. Newman
Asha's Mums, by R. Elwin and M. Paulse
Daddy's Roommate, by M. Willhoite
The Family Book, by T. Parr
Heather Has Two Mommies, by L. Newman
Molly's Family, by N. Garden
Mom and Mum Are Getting Married, by K. Selterington
William's Doll, by C. Zolotow
Are You a Boy or a Girl?, by J. Karleen Pendleton
My Two Uncles, by J. Vigna
Gloria Goes to Gay Pride, by L. Newman
How My Family Came to Be: Daddy, Papa and Me, by A.R. Alrich and M. Motz

---

* Reprinted by permission of PFLAG Canada.

Who's in a Family?, by R. Skutch

Bedtime for Baby Teddy, by T. Arc-Dekker

BOOKS FOR ADULTS

LGBT-Parent Families: Innovation in Research and Implications for Practice, by A.E. Goldberg and K.R. Allen

For Lesbian Parents: Your Guide to Helping Your Family Grow Up Happy, Healthy and Proud, by S. Johnson and E. O'Connor

Gay Dads: Transitions to Adoptive Fatherhood, by A. Goldberg

Who's Your Daddy, a collection of essays edited by R. Epstein

The Ultimate Guide to Pregnancy for Lesbians: How to Stay Sane and Care for Yourself from Preconception through Birth, by R. Pepper

Families of Value: Personal Profiles of Pioneering Lesbian and Gay Parents, by R. Bernstein

A Gay Couple's Journey through Surrogacy: Intended Fathers, by M. Menichiello

The Lesbian Parenting Book: A Guide to Creating Families and Raising Children, 2nd ed., by D.M. Clunis and G.D. Green

Home Fronts, by J. Wells

TEEN FAMILIES

"Kristy, 18, lives with her mother, a younger brother and sister, and her stepfather. Kristy's mother has just given birth to Dana, her first child with Kristy's stepfather. Kristy is two months pregnant. She is in her last year of high school and has been involved with her boyfriend, Emilio, for two years. Kristy and Emilio have decided that they want to parent the baby. Because they both want to finish high school, they will continue to live with their families once the baby is born. Kristy is aware that having two infants in the house will be a challenge, but her parents have been very supportive. Kristy and Emilio plan to move in together once they graduate."

Over the last two decades, teen pregnancy in Canada has continued to drop, indicating that young women are doing a good job of controlling and protecting their reproductive health. But there are variations across the country as Figure 9.1 illustrates.

It is important to remember that the statistics in Figure 9.1 reflect teen births, which is not the same thing as teen pregnancies, which include births, abortions, and miscarriages, and is a truer picture of teens dealing with pregnancy.

FIGURE 9.1   Teen Pregnancy

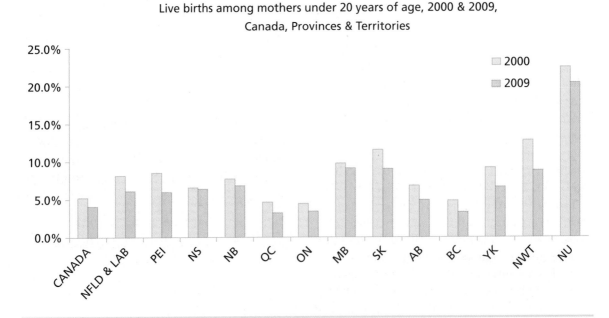

Live births among mothers under 20 years of age, 2000 & 2009, Canada, Provinces & Territories

Source: Statistics Canada. Table 102-4503—Live births, by age of mother, Canada, provinces and territories, annual, CANSIM (database).

Quebec, British Columbia and Ontario have particularly low teen birth rates, in part because of urbanization and the availability of abortion. For Canada as a whole, nearly half of pregnant adolescents give birth because they, their parents, or their boyfriends prefer to have a baby or object to abortion on moral grounds.* (Ambert, 2012: 225)

Only 17.8 percent of all general hospitals in Canada perform abortions, with some jurisdictions, such as Prince Edward Island and Nunavut, offering no hospital abortion services at all (Arthur, 2012).

According to Rotermann (2005), the average age of first sexual experience for both male and females is 16.5 years in Canada, and approximately two thirds of Canadians have their first sexual experience in their teenage years.

A study that interviewed pregnant or parenting adolescents found other factors which predict risky sexual behaviour that could lead to teenage pregnancy: presence of a family member with a drinking problem, physical assault by a family member, early age of first drunkenness, excessive sexualisation of the mass media combined with a relative absence of sexual education in the schools and limited access to contraception in the community. (McDaniel and Tepperman, 2011: 163)

While the federal government has put guidelines in place for sex education, programs differ by school board, school, and classroom. The programs are not uniform enough across the country to make a consistent contribution to the health of Canadian youth.

DEMANDS OF PARENTHOOD

When we consider adolescent development, we know that teens are developing their self-identity, are seeking peer acceptance, may have concerns about their body image, and are striving for independence. They are experiencing mood changes and experimenting with adult behaviours and formulating their sex roles. How will these developmental tasks impact on a teenager who finds out that she is pregnant or that he will be a father?

Ambert (2006) gathers research that points out that for some young women, having a baby may be a form of social status: the young woman has someone to love, gets a lot of attention from her family, and, for a period of time, receives a great deal of peer interest.

Ambert (2006) also provides evidence that the rates of teen pregnancy increase in families where there are sexually active siblings. In families where the mothers are openly sexually active with a variety of men and where there is little parental supervision, the incidence is also likely to increase. A smaller but significant number of teenagers become pregnant through coerced sex: at least 20 percent of teen mothers have experienced involuntary intercourse.† (Shimoni and Baxter, 2008: 120)

The McCreary Centre Society (2008) indicates, though, that soon changes:

Regardless of age, most new parents discover that the care demands of a newborn require changes in lifestyle, perspectives, expectations and aspirations. For teens, balancing parenthood and school as well as work can be challenging, particularly where the resources and supports for young moms are insufficient (BC Council for Families, 2009). To be effective as parents and to reach their full potential, teen parents need access to health care and social and economic supports (prenatal counselling, childcare subsidies, affordable housing, etc....), and to personal, parenting and career mentoring, coaching, and guidance. These supports help them build confidence and acquire skills and knowledge regarding child development and parenting so they and their children can thrive.‡ (in Vanier Institute of the Family, 2012a)

The days of shame and stigmatization have lessened in some cultures and although it may be now more socially acceptable to have a child out of wedlock, there are still serious health risks for the babies of teen mothers, including low birth weights and associated health problems. Dryburgh (2003: 1) points out that the mothers themselves are at risk of various health problems, including "anemia, hypertension, renal disease, eclampsia and depressive disorders. As well, teenagers who engage in unprotected sex are putting their own health at risk of sexually transmitted infections." Shimoni and Baxter (2008: 41) concur: "Children of teen mothers are more likely to suffer from health risks associated with low birth weight and/or prematurity, mainly due to the high rate of cigarette smoking among teenage mothers: over 45 percent of teenage mothers smoke."§ An individual marrying for the first time in his or her teens faces a risk of a marital breakdown that is almost two times higher than that of a person who married between the ages of 25 and 29 (Statistics Canada, 2006b).

---

* From Ambert, *Changing Families: Relationships in Context* 2/e © Pearson Canada 2010. Reprinted by permission of the publisher.

† From Shimoni and Baxter, *Working with Families* 4/e © Pearson Canada 2008. Reprinted by permission of the publisher.

‡ Vanier Institute of the Family. 2012. "Fascinating Families," *Teen Pregnancy: Supporting Young Parents*, (May 23) Issue 46. Reprinted by permission of The Vanier Institute of the Family.

§ From Shimoni and Baxter, *Working with Families* 4/e © Pearson Canada 2008. Reprinted by permission of the publisher.

Compared to their childless peers, teen mothers face a greater chance of living in poverty with low career and educational prospects. This is even more likely if they have more than one child (Zabin et al., 1992; Nock, 1998; Solomon and Liefeld, 1998). Teen mothers are also more likely to marry early and have a higher rate of divorce (Manning, 1993). This situation tends to be repeated in children of teen parents, who are more likely to have lower academic achievements and early, unmarried pregnancies (Hayes, 1987; Alexander and Guyer, 1993). Geronimus (1991) is careful to point out that it is not certain how much of this results from other background characteristics (such as living in poverty), rather than specifically from teen pregnancy. Teens also run the risk of violence, which is more likely to start during pregnancy. Unfortunately, teen parents often become stereotyped as "losers," though this negative societal image overlooks their diversity, experiences, and educational and career aspirations (Camarena et al., 1998).

> According to one analysis of national data, teen parents are more responsible than other teenagers. Furthermore, teen mothers are less likely than their childless female peers to drink alcohol or socialize with friends who do; teen fathers who acknowledge their child tend to be employed or engage in other "socially productive work," such as volunteering, more than their male peers. (Riedman, Lamanna, and Nelson, 2003: 342)

> Balancing motherhood with selfhood, particularly adolescent selfhood, calls for maturity, psychological strength, and a full complement of family and external supports. To be a student (and often a worker), a daughter, a friend, a girlfriend, and a mother is demanding for anyone. To assume these roles at 16, within a milieu in which there is virtually no margin for error, requires extraordinary talent and fortitude. (Musick, 1990: 24)

We must celebrate that many teen parents do manage with great courage and sacrifice to love and care for their child. With support from the community, much can be accomplished.

Many compelling issues and concerns face teen families. Will they receive adequate prenatal and postnatal medical and nutritional care for themselves and their child? How will they support themselves and their child? What impact will the child have on their education? Are they prepared for the realities of parenthood? What kind of input can they expect from their own families? Will they be able to handle the expenses associated with raising a child (babysitters, transportation, child-care services, dentists, and so on)? Have they come to terms with the new restrictions on their independence and their consequences (for example, diminished social life)? Where will they live?

For teen families, this will be a time of redefining themselves and discovering how the child affects their personal as well as professional lives. Some young parents feel resentful at times and trapped in their new lifestyle. Some receive a great deal of support from their extended families; 60 percent of Canadians 20 to 24 years of age still live with their parents, and pregnant teens may feel they will have more support in raising their child if they stay at home. In fact, 30 to 50 percent of teen mothers continue to reside in their family of origin up to two years postpartum (Ambert, 2006).

> Others teens must cope with their new circumstances entirely on their own. One trend observed by Pauline Paterson, director of the YWCA's girls and family programs, is a phenomenon called "multi-daddying." Teen moms are having more than one baby with various fathers as a way of forming bonds with new men in their lives, another way that adolescents are putting their stamp on parenthood and establishing new family models. (Gulli, 2008)

YOUNG FATHERS

Babies' fathers often have a background similar to that of the young mothers. According to Moffitt et al. (2002),

> young men who are highly antisocial produce nearly three times the percentage of babies than do more prosocial young men by the time they reach the age of 26. Fathers with a history of incarceration are more than twice as likely to have had children by two or more partners.[*] (in Ambert, 2012: 227)

Becoming a young father is life changing. Some men will take on these new responsibilities in a way that reflects their care and concern for the mother and child, leaving school to find a job to support their new family and changing social patterns. Others will initially be involved but later, as expectations and commitment increase, they may spend less and less time with the family. Others will never make a commitment to their family and will abdicate all responsibilities. It is clear that young fathers need more coordinated support. Some of this may come from grandparents and friends of the family but more structured and supportive community agencies need to develop programs to support young fathers in their new role. Clearly more research is also needed in this area.

In June, Lindsay Kretschmer, 25, will graduate from Centennial College's three-year creative advertising program. In the audience will be her seven-year-old daughter Emilee. Getting by with two part-time jobs and student loans, Kretschmer has won awards and accolades for her volunteerism and leadership, including being honoured as a YWCA Young Woman of Distinction in 2002. She left home at 13, bunking first with friends and then living on her own, and she found out at 17 that she was pregnant. For some young women, becoming a mother is a turning point in their lives, giving them direction and purpose. They draw on inner strength and community resources to cope with the challenges of teen parenting. Clearly this was the case for Lindsay. She was inspired by the many people who helped her dream big and not to "limit yourself," including the unique Literature For Life Program which brings group discussions on books to young mothers. She not only attended the program when she was a new mother but has also worked for it in a variety of positions including group leader. A success story!

Source: Crawford, T. 2008. "Teen Moms Beat Odds To Succeed," *The Toronto Star*, March 11. Reprinted by permission of Torstar Syndication Services.

ROLE OF THE EDUCATOR

- It is important to remember that adolescent parents will vary greatly and many are competent parents. Teachers who come in contact with teen families must be available to provide support with a focus on the best interests of the child.

- When working with teen families, teachers need to establish an atmosphere of trust and respect. Teen families are more open about their experiences and problems if they feel that the teacher is willing to listen in a nonjudgmental manner.

- Maintaining confidentiality is critical.

- Like all parents, teen parents should be consulted and encouraged to contribute to the program as they are able.

- In a quality early learning environment, teen families receive practical advice on matters such as housing, financial options, and family planning.

- As a source of additional support, teens should be encouraged to build relationships with other teen families or other families in the centre.

- Teachers need to remember that young fathers need support and encouragement; they are struggling with role expectations that they may not be able to live up to and societal attitudes that are often hostile and rejecting.

- Make families aware of the Kids Help Phone 1-800-668-6868 and that telephone help lines are available for parents in many provinces.

- Teachers should be alert to times when parents could use respite care and help to connect them to appropriate community resources.

- The evidence is very clear in regards to education: a teen parent who completes his or her education has a better chance of economic stability and a personal sense of achievement. Teachers can provide information about full-time and part-time programs at local high schools, alternative schools, colleges, or universities.

ROLE OF THE EDUCATOR IN THE ROOM

- Teens should see strategies for dealing with infants modelled by the staff.

- Be involved, celebrate, and praise teen parents' efforts with their child.

- Family visits may be a valuable opportunity to support teen parents.

- The early learning environments could offer programs that focus on strengthening parenting skills, father's groups, cooking programs that help parents prepare inexpensive yet nutritionally sound meals, first aid courses, etc.

- Programs should be flexible enough to support teen parents who are trying to balance school and their personal life.

- Teachers can encourage the supportive partnerships that often develop between families in the centre.

Community Support: Jessie's Centre (The June Callwood Centre for Young Women)

This section was contributed by Maritza Sanchez, executive director.

Jessie's Centre is a nonprofit, charitable organization funded by the Ministry of Children and Youth Services, the City of Toronto, Public Health Canada, the United Way, corporations, foundations, and private donors; it provides comprehensive programs in collaboration with the Toronto Board of Education and Public Health. It was established in 1982 in recognition of the large number of teenage parents who were struggling to raise their children, sometimes without adequate financial resources, family support, affordable housing, child-care facilities, and access to parenting information and health services. Each year, Jessie's Centre

This teen mother decided to raise her child without the support of the father.

serves about 500 young families. Programs include pregnancy counselling, individual support and counselling, health services, nursery drop-in and parent relief, housing assistance, 24-hour respite care, prenatal and parenting groups, high school credit courses, and a variety of discussion and support groups.

Jessie's Centre has many regular volunteers who work in child-care, tutoring, labour support, and administration as well as a 15-member board of directors from a broad spectrum of backgrounds that includes graduates of the agency. In 1998, Jessie's was chosen by United Way to receive Success By 6 funding. This grant has allowed Jessie's to expand many of its parenting services and create the Community Education Project, through which the staff and parents act as educators and ambassadors to schools and organizations throughout Toronto. In 2002, Jessie's initiated the Intensive Parenting program. Jessie's Centre mission is supported by a feminist, anti-oppression framework. The agency attempts to empower young families through both the direct services available at the agency and individual and systemic advocacy to assist their access to community support and entitlements.

Source: Reprinted by permission of Maritza Sanchez.

SEPARATED, DIVORCED, JOINT-CUSTODY, AND LONE-PARENT FAMILIES

"Monique, 25, has been living alone with her two children, ages 2 and 4, since her husband left her when she became pregnant with her youngest. Monique has divorced her husband, who has since disappeared from their lives. In defiance of a court order, he has not paid any child support in two years. Monique lives on welfare in an inner-city

housing project in Halifax. She is about to enter a government-sponsored training project that allows her to go back to school while her children attend a local child-care centre. Monique put aside her ambition to become an occupational therapist when she became pregnant with her first child. Now she is excited at the prospect of a new, independent life for herself and her children.

Junlin and her former partner, John, have two children ages 6 and 8 years. The court has awarded joint custody to both parents. Financially able to do so, they have purchased two semi-detached homes that are side by side. They have a formalized routine, with each parent having the children live with him or her one week at a time but the children move freely back and forth. Junlin and John both feel that this arrangement is in the best interests of all concerned.

Tani is a 37-year-old financially independent teacher. For some time she has been thinking about having a child. Tani is not in a serious relationship, but she realizes that her biological clock is ticking and she is considering asking a man she has been intimate with in the past to be the biological father of her child. However, she wants to raise her child without the help or involvement of this man. She has a strong support network of family and friends."

ATTITUDES TO MARRIAGE

Overall, fewer couples are getting married, but among highly educated people, a more traditional idea of marriage seems to be taking hold. In a widely cited 2010 report from the *National Marriage Project* (2010) at the University of Virginia, college and university graduates reported the highest levels of marital happiness … We're waiting longer to get married, picking our partners more carefully and are sometimes more willing to work on a marriage. Countless Gen X and Yers lived through their parents' divorces, and seem anxious about not repeating their mistakes. In Canada, the typical age of first marriage was 31 for men and 29 for women in 2008. This partly helps to explains the shrinking divorce rate; getting married before 25 is a risk factor for splitting up. About 70 percent of couples have now lived together before they tie the knot. A person's age, religion, education level, income and family background all have major implications for how long a marriage lasts.[*] (Lunau, 2011:53)

How do children of divorced parents view marriage?

The Vanier Institute reports that 86 percent of high school students surveyed, including 78 percent of the teens whose own parents had not stayed together, expect a lifelong marriage. From magazine advertisements to children's books, and even more pervasively from television shows, the attractive vision of husband, wife and children beams at us. What has been called the "Leave It To Beaver Syndrome" has given several viewing generations, including those who are now our leaders and legislators, a clear yardstick against which to measure desirable family characteristics and measure guilt and negative feelings when reality does not match the ideal.[†] (Gestwicki, 2010: 25)

A clear majority of Canadians of all ages, fully 80 percent, report that they intend on getting married at some point. No less than 90 percent of teens ages 15 to 19 years state that they expect to get married, and 88 percent say that they expect to stay with the same partner for life (Bilby, 2009).

---

[*] Lunau, K. 2001. "Young, divorced and stigmatized," *Maclean's*, November 28, Vol. 124, no. 46, pp. 53-55. Reprinted by permission.

[†] From GESTWICKI, *Home, School, and Community Relations, 7E.* © 2010 Cengage Learning. Reproduced by permission. www.cengage.com/permissions.

Inside LOOK

The Top Ten Characteristics That People Want in a Partner

1. Honesty
2. Kindness
3. Respect
4. Compatibility
5. Humour
6. Dependability
7. Love
8. Values
9. Religious Commonality
10. Communication

continued

DIVORCE

Four in 10 of the Canadian couples who married in 2008 will be divorced by 2035, according to a report from the Vanier Institute of the Family (2011) and the rate has been relatively stable for more than a decade. Divorce is a process that involves loss, grief, anger, endings, and new patterns and rituals. Divorce may be the best option for some families and the relief it brings may be in the best interests of all concerned. With the passing of the *Divorce Act* in 1968, grounds for divorce were extended to include "no-fault" divorce based on separation for at least three years; the separation period was revised to one year in 1986. The easing of Canada's divorce laws, combined with other social changes, marked a significant shift in the way Canadians perceived marriage and divorce. According to the *Toronto Star* (2007b), Canadian common-law relationships last, on average, 4.3 years whereas the average length of a Canadian marriage is 14.3 years.

Despite the divorce rate's dramatic increase over the past 30 years, Canadians' marital stability measures well internationally. The Canadian divorce rate is lower than that of most industrialized nations; the American rate is almost double. Gary Direnfield discusses the state of Canadian divorces on his website **http://www.yoursocialworker.com**.

He estimates that 80 percent of divorces are low conflict (the parents able to manage between themselves, cooperate, and inform the daycare of their situation to support the child). In the other 20 percent of divorces, 5 to 10 percent can be classified as medium conflict (the parents require outside resources and operate separately from the daycare) and 5 to 10 percent are high conflict (the parents involve the court system in the divorce and may draw the daycare into conflict as a source of data to support their position or to restrict access to information and/or the child). Only 2 to 3 percent of divorces will go to trial (Direnfeld, n.d.).

Second marriages are more likely than first marriages to end in divorce; the divorce rate for second marriages is about 10 percent higher than in first marriages. More research is needed in this area.

IMPACT ON CHILDREN AND PARENTS

In their 25-year study on divorce, Wallerstein, Lewis, and Blakeslee state that

children who grow up in post divorce families experience not only one loss, that of the intact family, but a series of losses as people come and go. Divorce is a life-transforming experience. They claim that divorce is almost always more devastating for children than for their

The Supporting Families Experiencing Separation and Divorce Initiative (SFI) is a new, five-year family law strategy that began on April 1, 2009. The Government of Canada has funded the SFI to help reduce the stress on families when parents separate or divorce. Parents in these circumstances often carry a heavy burden of negative emotion and financial worry. All too often, these emotions interfere with their ability to make good decisions on behalf of their children. The "best interests of the child"—the core principle used to determine parenting arrangements in Canada—can be obscured or even lost when conflict between parents leads them into destructive battles about child support, parenting arrangements, residential arrangements and sometimes spousal support.

Through the Supporting Families Fund, the Government of Canada will devote $122 million between 2009 and 2014 to funding family justice services run by provinces and territories. Services like mediation, parent information sessions and support recalculation services (available in some provinces) will all help parents come to lasting but flexible agreements that are in the best interests of their children—all without going to court. The Government will also continue to provide funding for provincial and territorial efforts to enforce family orders and agreements.

Source: The Supporting Families Experiencing Separation and Divorce Initiative, http://www.justice.gc.ca/eng/pi/fcy-fea/abo-apr/index.html, Department of Justice Canada, 2009. Reproduced with the permission of the Minister of Public Works and Government Services Canada, 2013.

parents, and that the effects of divorce are often long-lasting. Longitudinal studies indicate that children's fundamental attitudes about society and about themselves can be forever changed by divorce and by related events experienced in the years afterward. They state that we have not fully appreciated how divorce continues to shape the lives of young people after they reach full adulthood. (Wallerstein, Lewis, and Blakeslee, 2000, in Gestwicki, 2010: 548)

Furstenberg and Cherlin (2001: 493) quote psychologists Chase-Lansdale and Hetherington, who labelled

the first two years following a separation as a "crisis period" for adults and children. The crisis begins for children with shock, anxiety, and anger upon learning of the breakup (the harmful effects on children of marital conflict may begin well before the breakup). For children, divorce strikes at the very core of their world, but we need to be cautious about the conclusions we reach about the socioemotional consequences of divorce for children and their parents. For adults the immediate aftermath is a dismaying and difficult time. It is especially trying for mothers who retain custody of the children. During the crisis period, it is important to address the following two needs of children: "additional emotional support as they

struggle to adapt to the breakup; and the structure provided by a reasonably predictable daily routine. (Furstenberg and Cherlin, 2001: 493)

We know very little about the impact of divorce on very young children but preschoolers may demonstrate fearful, anxious, or aggressive behaviour or want the comfort of security objects that they had put aside. Some children may withdraw and toileting issues may arise. Older children have a better understanding of the impact of divorce but, like younger children, may demonstrate great sadness at their loss, and this is especially true if the absent parent is rarely present. These children may feel a divided loyalty and often may feel caught in the middle if the separation is acrimonious. However, it is difficult for many single parents to constantly and consistently meet these needs. Single parents, depressed and worried themselves, are often unable to comfort their children and, as a result, their children lose some of the support they need. Many single parents feel anxious and overburdened and let daily schedules slip. There is also evidence, from a number of psychological studies, to suggest that the fallout of the crisis period is worse for boys than for girls, though boys and girls react to stress differently and this may be a factor.

Most parents and their children recover from the trauma of the separation "crisis period" within two or three years. In some situations, the child may be separated from his or her biological parent as well as siblings and have less contact with aunts, uncles, and grandparents, compounding the stress of the separation. Eventually, though, wounds from the breakup heal and both parents and children are able to stabilize their lives. Furstenberg and Cherlin (2001: 493) note, "With the exception of some difficulties between single mothers and their sons, parent–child relationships generally improve. And the majority of children, it seems, return to normal development with time." Many people enter into another relationship at some point in their lives and this bring with it new joys and challenges.

When mothers are given custody of their children, fathers often struggle in their new role. Often their visits are playtimes with very little guidance offered to the children. More often than not, if grandparents are located nearby, the father will take the children to their home where he can receive the support of his extended family.

JOINT CUSTODY

Both the *Children's Law Reform Act* and the *Divorce Act* enable a Canadian court to award custody to both parents. Joint custody, which includes several options, is an agreement in which legal and physical custody of the children is shared between the two parents. In one option, the parents together make all decisions regarding the children and the children live part-time with each parent; in another form of joint custody, there is joint legal custody but the children physically reside with one parent.

Parents often try to create living arrangements that support the children. In some situations the parents try to locate close to each other; in others the children stay in the home and the parents come and go, creating a greater sense of continuity. These arrangements may be more challenging when an infant is involved, especially is the mother is breast-feeding.

An interesting shift in how divorced parents care for their children is highlighted in *Reconcilable Differences* by Cate Cochran. Many parents, though

FIGURE 9.2 The Divorce Onion

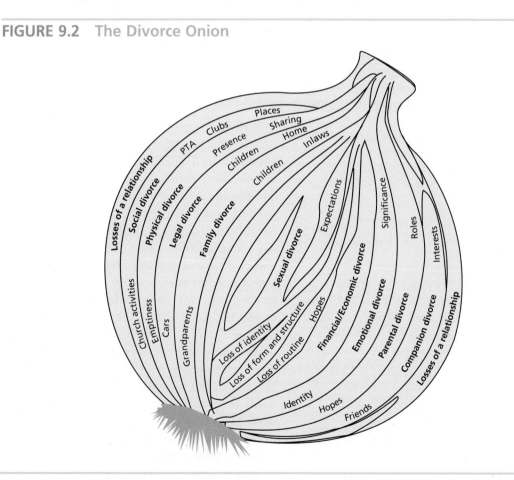

Source: From GESTWICKI, *Home, School, & Community Relations, 5E.* © 2004 Cengage Learning. Reproduced by permission. www.cengage.com/permissions

For Pat Hinds the hardest thing about separating from her husband seven years ago was abandoning the family home and moving her three children to the only place she could afford: a rundown, low-income housing complex in northwest Calgary. Garbage was strewn everywhere, the fences and playground equipment were crumbling, and the grass was long and untended because none of the tenants owned a lawn mower. "The first thing I did was sit down and cry," recalls Hinds. "Then I thought, I can crawl in a hole and die—or I can change it." Hinds chose the latter. In addition to working full-time and raising her kids, she spearheaded a major cleanup campaign. Hinds and her neighbours held bottle drives and sold old toys to raise enough money to buy two lawn mowers. They successfully lobbied the city and their landlords to replace the playground gear and fences. They even convinced Calgary retailers to donate flowers they could plant. Last week, in recognition of her community service, Hinds became one of 46,000 Canadians to receive a commemorative medal marking Queen Elizabeth's golden jubilee.

Source: Wickens, B. 2002. "How we live," *Maclean's*, November 2, Vol. 115, no. 44, pp. 46. Reprinted by permission.

not able to continue in a marital relationship, are looking for innovative living arrangements that allow their children close proximity to both parents and with create interruption to their routine. In some cases, parents live on different floors of the same house, live side-by-side, or live in close proximity to each other.

CUSTODIAL AND NONCUSTODIAL PARENTS

The moving back and forth between custodial and noncustodial parent and possible custodial disagreements can at times result in difficult situations at the centre. A photograph of the noncustodial parent should always be on file.

All educators must be apprised of these custody agreements to ensure that a child is not released to a noncustodial parent without authorization. Educators should be cautious if the noncustodial parent arrives on a day other than the one that had been agreed on. Staff can't assume that releasing the child is acceptable to the other parent simply because it's a different day. Parents, not strangers, are responsible for most child abductions. What do staff do when an unauthorized noncustodial parent insists that the program release the child to him or her? Educators may face a verbal or physical confrontation with this parent. In this situation, staff need to:

- Calmly ask the parent to move to an area with more privacy (more than one educator

should be with the parent) or at least have staff move all children away or outside.

- Have someone call the custodial parent so he or she knows what is happening. Depending on their rapport, the custodial parent may be able to talk to the other parent or quickly come to the program.

- Call the police if the parent loses control or tries to leave with the child.[*] (Pimento and Kernested, 2010: 435)

SEPARATED AND LONE PARENTS

The term *single parent* or *lone parent* may be misleading.

Although a mother or father may not live with the child, other nonparent adults may. These individuals, grandparents, other relatives, older siblings or friends perform significant family roles, including child caregiving. Furthermore an absent parent may still remain active in a child's life and provide child rearing and financial support. For this and many other reasons, we should not assume that single parenting has a negative effect on children.[†] (Trawick-Smith, 2010: 466)

[*] From PIMENTO. *Healthy Foundations in Early Childhood Settings,* 4E. © 2010 Nelson Education Ltd. Reproduced by permission. www.cengage.com/permissions

[†] TRAWICK-SMITH, JEFFREY, EARLY CHILDHOOD DEVELOPMENT: A MULTICULTURAL PERSPECTIVE, 5th Edition, © 2010. Reprinted and Electronically reproduced by permission of Pearson Education, Inc., Upper Saddle River, NJ.

Close to one in five (19.3 percent) children ages 14 and under lived with lone parents in 2011, up slightly from 18.0 percent in 2001. Of these 1,078,575 children, 82.3 percent lived with female lone parents. "Since the 1980's, non-resident fathers have gained more legal rights to make decisions about their children's welfare and more divorced fathers now maintain contact with their children. However, about a third of non-resident fathers lose contact"* (Baker, 2010: 167). When fathers have been involved in parenting before the separation they are more likely to continue their involvement with their children even when they have a new partner or another child. But if the mother remarries, this is not always the case. "Cooperative parenting results in more frequent father-child contact, a better relationship, and more responsive fathering"[†] (Ward and Belanger, 2011: 253).

When are men more likely to be single parents? "Men tend to become single parents in the middle and late years of the life cycle—few are lone parents in their teens or 20s. Men are lone parents for shorter periods than women too, because they are more likely to marry or cohabit than mothers"[‡] (Ward and Belanger, 2011: 236). The after-tax income of female lone-parent families in Canada was $37,400 in 2009 while the income for two-parent families was $75,600 (Statistics Canada, 2013. There are many reasons why women suffer economically when separating.

> On average, women earn less than men. In addition, lone fathers tend to be older and better educated, have more labour force experience, and have older children. For many, their careers are established before they become lone parents and their children are already school-aged. The low levels of child support awarded by the courts and the high number of men who do not comply with the court orders are significant causes of the financial hardship experienced by many lone mothers and their children.[§] (Vanier Institute, 1994: 83–84)

---

* From Baker, Maureen, *Choices and Constraints in Family Life* 2/e © Oxford University Press Canada 2010. Reprinted by permission of the publisher.

[†] From WARD. *The Family Dynamic*, 5E. © 2011 Nelson Education Ltd. Reproduced by permission. www.cengage.com/permissions.

[‡] From WARD. *The Family Dynamic*, 5E. © 2011 Nelson Education Ltd. Reproduced by permission. www.cengage.com/permissions.

[§] Vanier Institute of the Family. 1994. "Profiling Canada's Families." Ottawa: Vanier Institute of the Family. Reprinted by permission of The Vanier Institute of the Family.

ONE-CHILD FAMILIES

Families choosing to have one child are no longer unusual; and there is a worldwide trend in this direction. For many families, the decision is a monetary one. For others, nature will make the decision. Investment in fertility treatments is costly and emotionally very difficult. "At a time when both parents work and the cost of housing, food and post-secondary education is skyrocketing, onlies more often get the benefit of their parents' undivided attention and luxuries that kids from large families rarely get" (Kopun, 2011).

ATTACHED BUT APART
TRANSNATIONAL FAMILIES

Some families are transnational—they live in different countries but consider themselves a family. They may be forced to live across national boundaries for personal, economic, or political reasons. This may be the case for many immigrant and refugee families who come to Canada in order to find work so that they might bring their children here for a better life. This family undergoes many stressors and the distance may keep them apart for many years. They face unique parenting challenges before and after the parents reunite. Often those in Canada send remittances to their home country where these funds may be used to support multiple family members; in other situations, Canadian families depend on support from abroad. For these families, kinship is perceived as a cornerstone value and providing for them is part of their obligation. Reuniting can bring both joy and challenges.

> When they are reunited, especially after unexpectedly long separations, some parents and children have drifted apart. Some children become resentful for having been left behind, some rebel against the heightened levels of discipline and control parents/mothers try to re-establish and still others struggle to fit in once they are in Canada. It is important for educators to be attuned to these families. Berhard et al. (2006) found that service providers were usually not aware of the range of problems experienced by some of these families, especially the mothers. The shame and stigma some felt after leaving children behind often caused them to keep to themselves and stay "off the radar" of social services. (in Albanese, 2009: 150)

In other situations, one of the parents may work far from home and return only when his or her job allows. Another emerging family profile comprises

Fasih, who trained as a gynecologist in her native India, lives in Mississauga with her two teenage children while her husband, Syed, works in Jeddah, Saudi Arabia. They have been apart for more than two years, communicating mainly by phone and reuniting just twice a year. She is one of hundreds of South Asian women, many of Pakistani origin, who live with their kids while their husbands work in the Middle East. Many immigrate to Canada as families, but the men, unable to find work in their professions, eventually move to the Middle East. They all struggle with the challenges of loneliness, single parenting, long-distance marriage and the fear of spousal infidelity, a foreign bureaucracy, and a new culture. The stress of being on their own takes its toll both mentally and physically for both husbands and wives, but many women also find a new person in themselves, a new-found independence, the one positive offshoot of living without their husbands (Aulakh, 2011: A8–9).

family members who decide that they will be happiest as a family when the adults live in two separate locations but consider themselves a family.

INCARCERATED PARENT

In some situations a mother or father may be a lone parent not by choice but because their spouse or partner has been incarcerated (see Chapter 10 for more information on this family type).

MILITARY FAMILIES

There are 57,352 military families in the Canadian Forces (Vanier Institute of the Family, 2012b). (A military family refers to a member of the Canadian Forces [Army, Navy, and Air Force], either Regular Force or Reserve Force, and his or her spouse/partner with or without children). Seventy-five percent of military couples have children and there are 64,262 children under the age of 18 with a parent in the military (Department of National Defence, 2012, cited in Vanier Institute of the Family, 2012b).

Members of military families may spend a great deal of time apart. Canadian troops actively participated in combat duty in Afghanistan from 2002 until 2011, and approximately 950 military personnel remain in Afghanistan as part of NATO's International Security Assistance Force. During the nine years of combat, 158 Canadian soldiers were killed and the Department of National Defence reports that 1,859 military personnel were injured or wounded. In his report to Parliament as a member of the Standing Committee on National Defence, Casson (2007: 2) states,

when Canadian Forces personnel deploy away from home, whether on a ship patrolling the Arabian Sea, or in surveillance aircraft patrolling Afghanistan airspace, or in a dusty pair of boots patrolling the villages of Zhari district, their military families continue to serve at home. Wives and husbands carry the burden of managing family life while their spouse completes a tour of duty in or near Afghanistan. Sons and daughters worry about Mom or Dad. Mothers and fathers worry about the circumstances of a serving son or daughter. Other close loved ones share the stress and concern.… Their role in keeping the home front happy and stable is of prime operational importance because it allows our fighting men and women to concentrate on their mission.[*]

It is important for educators who work with military families to understand the many stressors that may affect children and their parents. In addition to financial concerns, three unique stressor events for military families have been documented: mandated relocations, separation from family members, and reuniting with family members. The frequent and mandated moves required of military families also demand a great deal of adjustment and adaptation from them. Not only must the household reorganize for a new living space, but the relocation is likely to involve major geographic distance, sometimes internationally. New climates and cultural change also provide challenges for families. Both positive and negative effects have been documented for children in such relocations. The loss of social networks—family,

[*] Casson, R. 2007. *Canadian Forces In Afghanistan. Report of the Standing Committee on National Defence.* 39th Parliament, 1st Session. Reprinted by permission of the House of Commons.

friends, coworkers, and community—as well as concern about finding new social networks in the next community is a source of stress for adults as well as children. Caring for children when a family member has been deployed is always challenging. However, this challenge might be exacerbated when the military family member is a single parent or when both parents are deployed to active duty. Very little research has been done to examine children's fears and concerns when a parent is serving in a war zone[*] (Couchenour and Chrisman, 2011: 158–159).

Zero to Three: The Duty to Care training series helps professionals understand ways to support young children when family members are deployed as well as when they are reunited. This is a comprehensive resource and can be found at **http://www.zerotothree.org/about-us/funded-projects/military-families**.

BOOKS FOR CHILDREN

Lily Hates Goodbyes, by N. Stoltenberg
Dear Baby I'm Watching Over You, by M. Braught
Love Lizzie: Letters to a Military Mom, by L. Tucker McElroy and D. Paterson

BOOKS FOR ADULTS

Parent's Guide to the Military Child During Deployment and Reunion, by The National Child Traumatic Stress Network

---

* From COUCHENOUR/CHRISMAN. *Families, Schools and Communities*, 4E. © 2011 Wadsworth, a part of Cengage Learning, Inc. Reproduced by permission. www.cengage.com/permissions.

Deployment: Strategies for Working with Kids in Military Families, by K. Petty

LONE-PARENT FAMILIES BY CHOICE

It is becoming increasingly acceptable for single people to adopt children. As well, some women have a child through artificial insemination, by a surrogate mother, or with a consenting partner who will have little or no role in the child's life. When a single mother has a good income, her child's development is similar to that of a comparable married mother's child. The good news is that according to the National Longitudinal Survey of Child and Youth (NLSCY, 2007), most single parents are doing a good job of raising their children, and most children of lone-parent families show no problems; despite the emotional, social, and financial pressures involved when one adult is responsible for all child-rearing and household duties, the outcomes for most children are no different from those for children in two-parent households. Despite the growing number of people raising children on their own, there may still be societal bias against those who are single or never having been married.

Children of single parents by choice are at an advantage over those who fell into single parenting. Since their parents go into parenthood with their eyes wide open, they are well prepared financially and emotionally for the challenges of single parenthood. Children of single parents by choice haven't seen divorce and fighting as other children of single parents have. (Ambert, in O'Connell, 2007)

Inside LOOK

Choosing to have a child by myself was not an easy decision to make. Being a mother was something I knew I wanted, but finding the elusive "Mr. Right" was proving to be a harder task than I'd imagined. I knew I didn't want to risk waking up one day and have it be too late for me to have a child. So, after much debate, I chose to forge ahead with what has been the best decision I have ever made. Being a mother, single or not, is no easy task. It takes a lot of work, and I can't imagine doing it without the support of my family, especially my mother. At the end of every day I have the privilege of tucking this sweet boy in bed and knowing that life couldn't be more perfect. I am his world and I hope that I can provide him with everything he deserves and give him back everything he has given me.

Many single parents successfully raise happy well-adjusted children.

Inside LOOK

I met Stephanie and her daughter, Madison, when my preschooler and I joined the centre. The staff introduced us to each other, and it wasn't long before we realized that, as single mothers by choice, we were struggling with many of the same issues. Both of us were renting small but expensive apartments. We served on a newsletter committee at the centre and became very good friends over the next six months. When Stephanie's lease was coming up for renewal, she started to look for a bigger and less expensive residence. One morning she showed me a newspaper listing for a wonderful house with a garden in the back yard. If we combined our two incomes, we quickly calculated, we could afford to rent this house. Three years later, we continue to share the house with our two children. What started out as a financial decision turned into one of the major supports in my life! We are a family—not in the traditional sense but certainly in terms of the emotional support we give each other.

WIDOWED PARENTS

Some parents found themselves to be lone parents through illness or death. Single parents who have been widowed deal not only with the same issues as divorced or separated parents but also with the grief associated with losing their life partner. Death often strikes suddenly, leaving the widowed person unprepared to cope with single parenting. There are very few supports for young widows or widowers raising children on their own and, for most, it means redefining their life. A widow described her life as

walking on ice. You can walk along just like everyone else, but there are those days where you step on a crack and you don't know it until the cold slushy water washes over your head. Then you struggle out and keep walking. With time, the cracks may be spaced out a little further from each other, but they are always there.

MacLean (2003: L9) states, "The thing about being a widow is being alone, being the only one responsible for everything and needing to ask for help in a way you never had to before." Teachers can be a lifeline in situations like these.

ROLE OF THE EDUCATOR

- Teachers may first need to examine their own feelings and emotional reactions about divorce, separation, and single parenting. We bring our own histories to our teaching practice. Divorce or separation may trigger intense feelings and teachers need to make every effort to contain these to provide the best possible support to the families and their children.

- If teachers are not in touch with their own feelings, they may react very emotionally themselves. Researchers cite situations in which teachers actually cried, took the side of one or the other parent, gave the parents personal advice, scolded parents and encouraged them not to divorce, or referred parents inappropriately (Wright, Stegelin, and Hartle, 2007: 193–194).

- Separating or divorcing parents require non-judgmental support from teachers, who should refrain from taking sides and instead maintain a neutral position. Avoid being drawn into taking sides or placing blame. Avoid reporting on the "other" parent. Parents need to respect our boundaries.

  A neutral, positive and hopeful approach will always be best. Look for ways to see the strengths in families!

- Teachers may be the first people outside the family to become aware of a family's changing needs. They can help by referring families to support services such as social workers or counsellors (Rockwell, Andre, and Hawley, 2010: 57).

- It is also important for teachers to remember that parents may find themselves overwhelmed by the issues they are facing in the separation or divorce and may not be as emotionally or physically available to their children as they might be when they have had more time to work through their situation. Providing stability in the time the child is with the teacher may the greatest benefit that the teacher can provide.

- People going through a divorce tell their divorce stories frequently. However, when meeting with parents, teachers should keep the focus on the child's development, safety, and stability (Hildebrand et al., 2008: 267).

- Although the details of a separation or divorce agreement may seem personal and private, some details should be shared with the centre. Teachers and supervisors need to know, for example, whether both parents have the right to make inquiries and be given information about the child, new contact information for the parent who may no longer be living in the home, whether both parents want to be informed of school events, who should be contacted during emergencies, etc.

- Unless the court orders otherwise, a spouse who is granted access to a child of the marriage has the right to make inquiries and to be given information.

- Teachers should work to create a climate of trust so that parents feel comfortable about approaching them when issues arise.

- The child-care centre must be seen as a secure and stable place for the child and all family members. For children whose parents are in conflict, the child-care centre may be a respite from the conflict.

- Teachers should know the names of all significant members of the child's family since the surnames names may not be the same.

- Parents may be too caught up in their own grief and anger to fully appreciate their child's needs. This does not mean that they are uncaring or unconcerned, only that their circumstances have left them feeling paralyzed and depressed.

- Ongoing communication between families and teachers is important. During this difficult time, teachers can advise parents of support groups or agencies that may be of assistance. Teachers must remember the limitations of their training and redirect family members to community counselling.

- Teachers can provide print resources about divorce and children's books to help them explain divorce in a developmentally appropriate manner; these should be accessible in the Family Resource Area.

- If parents are interested in common issues, such a budgeting or preparing a will, because of their changed circumstances, the centre could facilitate such workshops at the families' request or link families to community resources.

- In some situations, and with permission of the parents, teachers may offer to share their insights about the child with social workers or psychologists who are working with him or her or attend counselling sessions with a child who may have lost a parent through divorce or death.

- One of the greatest challenges facing some newly separated or newly divorced parents is living on a reduced income. Some parents benefit from an extended fee-payment schedule. It is also important to recognize that some lone parents are not in any financial difficulty. Never make assumptions. If a parent is struggling financially, be cautious about asking for extra money for field trips or special lessons offered in the centre.

- Depending on the circumstances, teachers may decide not to ask parents to contribute time and effort to centre activities. Additional responsibility or pressure may be the last thing these parents need. For others, involvement in the centre is a welcome relief from their day-to-day life.

- Parents who enter into joint-custody family living are generally anxious for the process to succeed, and clearly both parties are focused on providing a stable situation for their child. It takes a great deal of cooperation and coordination in order to experience success, and teachers should look for opportunities to support all parties.

- Workshops may be provided to help families, especially blended families, to create new family traditions. Having family members share their most significant traditions will be a memorable opportunity for sharing.

- Some lone parents may be lonely. They find themselves gradually excluded from contact with couples and at a loss to know how to handle holidays without a spouse. Notices about community activities such as meetings of Parents Without Partners (see below) or We Care (for those whose spouse has died) should be routinely posted. Organizations such as Big Brothers and Big Sisters may also provide much needed support to children, who may also be lonely.

ROLE OF THE EDUCATOR IN THE ROOM

- Teachers can assist children by providing a stable environment and predictable routines.

- Teachers need to guard against feeling so sorry for the child that they become less insistent in maintaining expectations for routines and behaviour. Predictability and the security that can be found in routines is critical for the child.

- Teachers should be prepared for uncharacteristic or regressive behaviours on the part of the child (sucking thumb, wetting pants, and so on) and help families understand that these changes are not uncommon when children are dealing with stress.

- "Children who are quiet, helpful and positive during the divorce process can be feeling just as stressed and grief-stricken as those who are acting out and confronting authority" (Hildebrand et al., 2008: 267).

- The book centre should have reading material for children that reflects all families, including books about children living in one-parent, divorced, separated, or joint-custody families. Many resources in this area are now available.

- Though many children welcome an opportunity to discuss what is happening in their family, others are reluctant and withdraw. Teachers should take their cue from the child. Newman (1993: 121) advises teachers to "help the child to understand that anger is part of the process of grieving, a necessary part. Help them to separate their anger at the behaviour of a parent from the love they have for the person."

- Providing a "soft" space in the room where the child can go in order to self-regulate will be beneficial. The teacher may want to stay with the child and use this one-on-one time to talk, read, or just engage the child in conversations that have nothing to do with their situation. It is an opportunity to reinforce that the child is valued and cared for.

- Though it is important to keep the child busy and engaged, reasonable limits should be maintained. Teachers may wish to consider holding off on events that may further confuse or worry the child (for example, moving the child to another age group).

- When children ask questions about separation and divorce, teachers should provide age-appropriate information that is respectful of the parents' wishes and in the best interests of the child. Children need to understand why the divorce happened and to hear the explanation in age-appropriate language.

- Older children may benefit from talking to other children who have experienced divorce and may seek these children out. When possible, these discussions are best monitored when possible by a trusted teacher.

- Teachers should reassure children that they are not to blame for the separation or divorce. Besides looking for opportunities to engage in one-on-one interaction with the child, teachers should plan activities (dramatic play, creative movement, music, water play, woodworking, art, puppetry, felt board stories, journal writing and so on) that allow for and encourage the expression of feelings.

- Some children will respond by drawing, writing, or acting out their feelings in the dramatic play centre. Children should be encouraged to do so.

- Having a bulletin board with photographs of all the families at the centre will help children see that their family is similar to others and may provide some comfort to them.

- Most children want to know what changes will take place in their lives. If the teacher is unsure of how to respond, she may relay the child's concerns to the parent (or parents). Additionally, many children fear that they will not see the parent who leaves. Teachers can share this concern with the family if the child expresses it.

- In a joint-custody situation, effective communication is especially important. As children move back and forth between parental residences, it is easy to see how communication may break down. Creating a journal that stays in the child's cubby with important information may facilitate drop-off and pick-up when both parents are involved and on different schedules.

- Teachers should be prepared for an adjustment period as the child moves between two homes and two different sets of expectations and parenting styles. Monday morning and Fridays may be times when the child needs extra support and reminders of what is to take place.

- It may be helpful for parents with joint custody to have a complete set of clothing, special toys, extras the child would want, etc., stored at the centre in case something is forgotten during a transition.

Children's artwork may often reflect strong feelings.

Paul Volker created an inventive communication tool (http://www.ourfamilywizard.com) to eliminate conflict among divorced or separated family members trying to coordinate their schedules. This online calendar and message board allows parents to record information about their timetables, track parenting time, record their expenses, and create a visitation schedule for their child without personal contact. Grandparents and other important people in the child's life may also be granted access to the site. Children may also have limited access to this tool so that they too are able to participate in the process. This inventive use to technology is a fee-based service that can also be accessed through mobile phones.

- Having school supplies handy may support a school-age child in transition; knowing the supplies are available at the centre can reduce the child's anxiety about not being prepared for school.

A teacher can guide children to work through feelings by encouraging discussion and understanding and accepting a child's reactions:

"It can be pretty scary not to have both your daddy and your mommy living in your house together anymore." "Sometimes children get pretty mad at their mommy and daddy when they change a lot of things in their family." "You're going to your Dad's for Thanksgiving? Sometimes it is hard to do new things, but I'll bet you'll have fun."* (Gestwicki, 2004: 427)

PARENTS WITHOUT PARTNERS

Parents Without Partners is an important social networking organization that supports single parents and their children. With many chapters throughout Canada, this nonprofit organization provides friendship and guidance for those experiencing the challenges of single parenting. More information is available at http://www.parentswithoutpartners.org.

BLENDED FAMILIES

"Julie and George have recently married. Both have been married before. Julie has two children, ages 3 and 5, and George has a son, Brent, age 9. Brent lives with his mother but visits George and Julie every other weekend,

one night every week, and for longer periods of time during the summer. Julie and George are considering having a child together."

Census data tell us that 557,950 children ages 14 and under lived in stepfamilies in 2011, or 10.0 percent of children in private households. Among these children, most were stepchildren themselves (63.1 percent). The remainder were children of both parents in a couple but also lived with stepsiblings. One of the biggest challenges facing blended families is reconciling and harmonizing long-entrenched attitudes, values, and routines that may be at considerable variance. The new-found need to share power and decision making can place further strain on relationships. Parents in blended situations may fantasize that everyone will be accepting and life will be harmonious—a fantasy in direct competition with that of their children who fantasize that their biological parents will get back together again. Shifting roles among blended family members can be a source of apprehension and confusion. Children may compete with children of the stepparent over the sharing of space, toys, and, most importantly, their biological parent. "Children in blended families experience higher levels of parental conflict than do other children." (Couchenour and Chrisman, 2000: 97). Children in remarriage, whether they are stepchildren or a new child born to the remarriage with stepchildren, have on average less positive outcomes than children whose parents have never divorced. These results are fairly consistent throughout the Western world. At this point, no solid explanation exists because this research is very new (Marks, 2006, in Ambert, 2012: 374).

---

* From GESTWICKI, *Home, School, and Community Relations,* 7E. © 2010 Cengage Learning. Reproduced by permission. www.cengage.com/permissions.

Stepfamilies often experience financial problems, especially when fathers are supporting children in more than one household. These financial difficulties may lead to more general disputes about the fair allocation of resources, time, and attention. Research also notes that young children fare better than older children in stepfamilies because adaptation is easier at an earlier age before allegiances are developed to the absent parent. Research on stepfamilies reports that the role of stepmother is more ambiguous and stressful than the role of stepfather, and find that mothers are described as being more negative towards step-parenting than are fathers.[*] (Baker, 2010: 165)

Riedman, Lamanna, and Nelson (2003: 512) show how the lack of a "cultural script" may play into this: "Relationships in immediate remarried families and with kin are often complex, yet there are virtually no social prescriptions and few consistent legal rules to clarify roles and relationships. The lack of cultural guidelines is clearest in the stepparent role."[†]

There is no question that many families struggle in their attempts to figure out the best and most advantageous roles for all of the players. Ward and Belanger (2011: 266) state,

One of the main difficulties in remarriage families is that there are too many candidates for the available roles. This fact affects the stepparent in particular. The children already have two biological parents and are not usually interested in replacing them. If the new spouse tries to take over the role of the parent of the same sex, he or she will meet resistance and resentment from the children. North American culture has no terms to identify these new relationships other than adding "step" before mother, brother, and so on.

Wright, Stegelin, and Hartle (2007: 198) agree that even in the most well-adjusted blended families, both boys and girls report feelings of loss for their original family and its unique characteristics. Emotional responses to remarriage depend significantly on how the new relationship has been explained and integrated into the child's living situation. Most stepchildren report feelings of anger, hostility, denial, loss, anxiety, fear, excitement, curiosity, hesitancy, happiness, jealousy, and unrealistic expectations. Because the child has already experienced one major loss (one parent from the original family), she or he may fear future abandonment by the remaining primary parent, the new stepparent or both. Adjustment to the new reconstituted family take years.

Conflict can break out over many issues, from meals that are too different from what the children are used to eating to behaviour guidance. A key time for discomfort is any special event involving the child. Guilt frequently plays a role in blended relationships. A divorced father who lives with his new wife's children and sees his biological children only intermittently may be especially prone to feelings of guilt.

Jennifer Jenkins, a professor of human development and applied psychology at the University of Toronto, collaborated with researchers in Rochester and Britain to study 296 children from 127 families in England. Studying the families over a period of time allowed researchers to see the extent to which children and adult partners influence each other. Children who saw their parents arguing about them showed increasing behaviour problems at school including defiance, impulsiveness, shouting, and aggression. In turn, those problems led to more marital conflict at home. The results were even more pronounced in families with stepchildren. What's new about this research is the finding that it is a two-way street, with challenging children often provoking arguments between their parents. She states, "kids who are a bit more difficult create more stresses in a family and more stresses in a family contribute to kids being more difficult. It's absolutely not about blame or people feeling responsible. It's about complicated interactions" (Gordon, 2005: D5).

ROLE OF THE EDUCATOR

- Keep the lines of communication open with all of the members of this extended family.

- Always check the surnames of the children and the parents, because they may not be the same.

- Depending on the conditions of custody, biological parents should not be excluded. Teachers may communicate with biological parents by phone, by letter, or by inviting them to visit the child at the centre. Some blended families may want to come to the centre together. Teachers will know that maintaining a healthy relationship with the ex-spouse will help to make the transition as smooth as possible for everyone involved.

---

[*] From Baker, *Maureen, Choices and Constraints in Family Life 2/e* © Oxford University Press Canada 2010. Reprinted by permission of the publisher.

[†] From LAMANNA/RIEDMAN/NELSON. *Marriages and Families, 1E.* © 2003 Nelson Education Ltd. Reproduced by permission. www.cengage.com/permissions

Bibby (2005) reported that

respondents who had entered a new marital relationship that involved step-parenting reported very positively on their experience. About 80 percent characterized their new relationships as being much happier than their earlier ones. About the same proportion said that they had adjusted very or fairly well to their new partner's children and that the children had adjusted well to them. Men were slightly more positive than women, and those who had been previously married were more positive than those who had never previously married before entering a new combined family with a previously attached spouse and children. However, only about 56 percent of step-children, when asked to look back on their childhoods, reported they got on well with step-parents while 65 percent reported similarly about relations with stepsibling. Significant numbers of grown stepchildren are thus indicating strain in the combined family, though it is not clear that this strain is inherently worse than in intact families (Cheal, 2010: 77).

Blended families become even more complex if this happens more than once. For the mature children of some families this ultimately adds extensive obligations to a multiplicity of aging parents along with their other responsibilities as adults. Children of combined families may well find themselves in late middle age with four or more parents to assist in their declining years, parents who may have experienced financial reversals in their lives due to family dissolution and who may have remained the poorer for it (McKie in Cheal, 2010: 78).

- Recognize cultural and ethnic differences among blended families.
- Link families with others in the same situation, if appropriate and desired.
- Make sure that notices about relevant local agencies or resources are posted for families to see.
- Help parents find time for themselves. One centre has a date night where the children sleep over at the centre and the parents have time for themselves.

ROLE OF THE EDUCATOR IN THE ROOM

- Teachers shouldn't automatically expect problems from a blended-family; many children make a successful transition. A child with involved parents and stepparents is twice blessed!
- Help the children set realistic expectations about stepfamily life.
- Teachers should observe children closely and be active listeners, helping them to articulate their feelings. Help children understand that it takes time for a new blended family to get to

know one another. A common issue for children is the embarrassment over the divorce and remarriage. It is important to acknowledge the child's feelings.

- Do not use terms such as *broken home*. Ask parents whether they prefer *reconstituted, step,* or *blended*. Children can devalue themselves if they hear terms that appear to be derogatory. Other children might conclude that some students are different and inferior (Hepworth Berger, 2004: 118).
- Confusion is the order of the day for some children who have to learn to become members of two households. Transitions to one of these homes at the end of the week often happen in child-care centres. Teachers can help the child to organize and prepare for this adjustment.
- Teachers should be sensitive to the fact that the child's order in the family has likely changed. It's a big transition to go from being the "baby" of the family to being a middle child, or to go from having only sisters to having a brother as well. These adjustments to new siblings often are brought on abruptly in contrast to the gradual adjustment of a newborn sibling.

- In the playroom, teachers should encourage discussion and provide books, tapes, and other materials that send positive messages about blended families. Teachers should avoid material that depicts stepparents in a negative way, such as fairy tales.

- Provide opportunities through sensory experiences, art, drama, etc., for children to express their emotions.

- Teachers should identify positive personality traits of the new parent and how mutual interests may benefit the child.

- The stepmother or stepfather might be invited to the playroom to share a talent or an interest, or just to visit. Let the child be the tour guide.

- Be aware of when transitions are taking place in the child's life (visitation, changes in their schedule) and be sensitive to their needs.

BOOKS FOR CHILDREN

Two Homes, by C. Masurel

When My Parents Forgot How to Be Friends, by J. Moore-Mallinos

The Not So Wicked Stepmother, by L. Boyd

Amber Waiting, by N. Gregory

A Day with Dad, by B. Homberg

Do I Have a Daddy? A Story about a Single Parent Child, by J. Warren Lindsay

Daddy's Getting Married, by J. Moore-Mallinos

BOOKS FOR ADULTS

Creative Interventions for Children of Divorce, by L. Lowensiten

The Practical Guide to Weekend Parenting, by D. Hewitt

Remarried with Children: 10 Secrets for Successfully Blending and Extending Your Family, by B. LeBey

Single Parenting That Works: 6 Keys to Raising Happy Healthy Children in a Single Parent Home, by K. Leman

Single by Chance, Mothers by Choice, by R. Hertz

Stay Close: 40 Clever Ways to Connect with Kids When You're Apart, by T. Gemelke

My Father Married Your Mother: Writers Talk About Stepparents, Stepchildren, and Everyone in Between, by A. Burt

NEWCOMER FAMILIES
IMMIGRANT FAMILIES

"Miguel came to Canada from Portugal. He was sponsored by his brother, who had come several years earlier, and Miguel left behind his wife and three children. More than two years passed before Miguel was able to afford to bring his family to Canada and to complete all the government requirements. The separation was difficult for the entire family. Adjusting to a new environment has been particularly challenging for his wife, Maria. Though there is a large Portuguese community where they live, she misses her parents and siblings and a different way of life."

"Why do people move? What makes them uproot and leave everything they've known for a great unknown beyond the horizon? Why enter a jungle of foreignness when everything is new, strange, and difficult? The answer is the same the world over: people move in the hope of a better life."

—**Yann Martel, author of *Life of Pi***

There is no question that immigration is at an all-time high not just in Canada but around the world because of factors such as war, famine, or poverty.

Each year, about 2.3 percent of the world's population, or 146 million people move from one country to another. The major migration streams flow into North America, the oil-rich areas of the Middle East, and the industrial economics of western Europe and Asia. Currently, seven of the world's wealthiest nations (including Canada, Germany, France, the United Kingdom, and the United States) shelter about one-third of the world's migrant population but less than one-fifth of the world's total populations. (Witt and Hermiston, 2010: 303)

MULTICULTURALISM IN CANADA

In 1967, Canada's immigration policy was changed so that preferential entry based on the place of origin replaced the points system. In 1971, Canada was the first country to adopt multiculturalism as an official policy. All Canadians are guaranteed equality before the law and equality of opportunity regardless of their place of origin. Canada affirmed the value and dignity of all citizens regardless of their racial or ethnic origins, their language, or their religious affiliation. In 1977, Parliament passed the *Canadian Human Rights Act*, barring discrimination on the basis of race, sex, age, national or ethnic origin, colour, and religion. In 1982, the *Charter of Rights and Freedoms* was adopted and, in 1985, the *Multicultural Act* was passed. It recognized the existence of diverse communities and the use of languages other than English and French; it also acknowledged the freedom of those who want to preserve and enhance their cultural heritage.

As Canadians we should be proud of our multicultural heritage. Adams (2007a) believes that

> the Canadian concept of multiculturalism, where people value, celebrate and preserve their cultural heritage rather than becoming assimilated into the dominant culture, helps to create this microcosm of global diversity.* (in Adler et al., 2012: 21)

Moving to a new country is never easy. Differences between customs from the "old" country and life in Canada may be a source of conflict in immigrant families. Many families find Canadian ways different from the traditional life that they have left behind. Leaving behind family members is particularly difficult for women, some of whom may leave their children in the care of others while they come to Canada as domestic workers. Language may also be a concern if they do not speak English or French and many immigrants believe that Canada will be the answer to their prayers. However, they may face economic hardship here: credentials or experience may not be recognized in Canada and immigrants without much education often face poverty.

It is also important to note that when we talk about problems being associated with a new language, we are talking about two ideas: language acquisition and the ways of speaking unique to the new culture. Both of these can delay the adaptation process. Harper (in Samovar, Porter, and McDaniel, 2007: 352) summarizes this view when she notes, "lack of language skills is a strong barrier to effective cultural adjustment and communication whereas lack of knowledge concerning the ways of speaking of a particular group will reduce the level of understanding that we can achieve with our counterparts."†

New immigrants also feel intimidated in situations where their lack of English makes it difficult to communicate, such as in an emergency room of a hospital when interpreters may not be available and staff do not understand their cultural practices.

Recent immigrants are more likely to live in three-generation households than people born in Canada. Such households are most common in British Columbia and Ontario where there are areas with high concentrations of newcomers. Those coming from developing regions, especially South

---

* From Adler, Ronald, et al., *Interplay: The Process of Interpersonal Communication* 3/Ce © Oxford University Press Canada 2012. Reprinted by permission of the publisher.

† SAMOVAR/PORTER/MCDANIEL. *Communication Between Cultures, 6E.* © 2007 Wadsworth, a part of Cengage Learning, Inc. Reproduced by permission. www.cengage.com/permissions

Inside LOOK

Hiteshini Jugessur is a Community Outreach Worker at the South Asian Women's Community Centre in Montreal, Quebec. The organization was first started in July 1981 by a group of nine women from Indian and Pakistan. These women recognized that immigrant women from visible and ethnic minorities experienced great handicaps in integrating into the Canadian way of life. In addition, the socio-cultural background of South Asian women was a contributing factor in the difficulties they faced. In some respects these problems were unique to South Asian women because their cultural traditions kept them more isolated than many other immigrant groups. The core objective of the organization is to help South Asian women develop their potential to the fullest, to raise their social and community awareness, and to facilitate their access to mainstream life in this country (Mawani, 2004: 15).

Asia, prefer to live with relatives, even in crowded quarters, than to live with nonrelatives. Often, older individuals have come to join their younger relatives; the older relatives are not eligible for welfare or government pensions for a considerable length of time after arrival and rely on the financial resources of younger relatives. There is also a growing concern about the access to services for new Canadians.

Paul Anisef and Kenise Murphy Kilbride of the Joint Centre of Excellence for Research on Immigration and Settlement and Joanna Ochocka and Rich Janzen of the Centre for Research and Education in Human Services completed *Parenting Issues of Newcomer Families in Ontario* (2001), a study that explored the issues faced by immigrant parents within diverse ethnic backgrounds in Toronto, Ottawa, and Waterloo. The study focused on families in 12 language groups who had arrived in the past three years. Their findings showed that most participants were optimistic of their children's future in Canada. Participants often said that they were hoping their children would have a better life than they themselves had. These high expectations were held despite the fact that many parents were struggling to provide for their families here in Canada. Study participants put major emphasis on education and school. They often found a second job or borrowed money to help children concentrate on education. A significant number of parents, however, also expressed fear of their sons' involvement in drugs and violence and their daughters' in premarital sexual relationships.

Recommendations emerged in 11 areas where families felt the need for additional support to enhance fulfilling their responsibilities as parents: education, language support (English learning and translation), culture, first language and religion, extracurricular activities for children, family housing, employment-related supports, specific parenting support, holistic family support, mental health, collaboration among service providers and funders, and further research and information. Some recommendations are in areas where most parents articulate the need for assistance, such as finding child care and housing that is both good and affordable or successfully guiding teenagers. (Anisef et. al., Executive Summary, 2001: 4–5)

While children may acclimatize quickly in their new environment, parents are often slower to do so. This presents a challenge in that roles may be reversed. Children may need to translate for their parents if English or French is not well established and they may be embarrassed as their parents hold on to "the old ways." Conversely, parents worry that their children are less respectful and that they will lose their connection to their home country.

The financial status of new immigrants is often a concern. "Immigrants who have been in Canada fewer than 10 years have a greater risk of poverty especially in large cities. Rates were highest among those who had been in Canada for one to two years"* (Ward and Belanger, 2011: 354).

Newcomer parents, especially fathers, believed their job-related difficulties since their arrival had negatively influenced their roles as parents. Their decreased job-related status and financial constraints had decreased their self-confidence and lowered their esteem as parents. On the other hand, a large number of fathers also indicated that their families had become closer and benefited because they were at home more (if unemployed) or that their diminished capacity to earn money had led to more mutual support within the family. (Anisef et. al, 2001: 4)

MIGRANT FAMILIES

Educators may work with children whose parents are migrant workers. Many of these parents work long hours in difficult circumstances to provide for their families. Poor health in both migrant workers and their children is a concern. These families may relocate on a regular basis, preventing them from accessing consistent medical care. Wages are often

---

* From WARD. *The Family Dynamic*, 5E. © 2011 Nelson Education Ltd. Reproduced by permission. www.cengage.com/permissions.

Inside LOOK

Sagher Chatta's children are just preschoolers, but the Pakistani immigrant is bracing himself for "big time" culture clash down the road. Once his daughter, 4, and son, 18 months are in full time school, they may balk at speaking Urdu at home. They may pull away from some of the Muslim traditions they are being raised with. In a decade, they'll be forging their own identities, merging their Pakistani roots with Canadian teen culture. He's prepared to negotiate and give the kids freedom to make their own choices. But he realizes it might not be easy. That's one reason that about 40 other men have assembled at the Ahmadiyya Muslim Community Canada Mosque in Maple, Ontario. Inside, fathers, grandfathers, and young men hoping one day to become dads gather in the men's prayer hall to participate in a six week program on fatherhood run by dads and for men only. During the 90 minute evening sessions, the men discuss such topics as reading and playing with young children, discipline without physical force, postpartum depression, and the cultural and spiritual aspects of child rearing. Five of the six sessions are in Urdu and the accompanying workbook *What a Difference a Dad Makes* is also in Urdu. It is also available in nine other languages. For the first time the program is being delivered in a place of worship, in hopes of reaching more dads who need support. It will soon be launched in a synagogue and in Sikh and Hindu temples.

Source: Gordon, A. 2008. "Immigrant Men Learn How to Broaden Paternal Role," *The Toronto Star*, May 17, L1. Reprinted by permission of Torstar Syndication Services.

Inspired Immigrants!

Olivia Chow, a Hong Kong–born immigrant, is one of the most credible and well-respected politicians of our times. Her political involvement started when Vietnamese Boat People began to arrive in Canada. She also supported people of her ethnic community and the fact that she spoke both English and Cantonese allowed her a unique perspective and an understanding of both cultures. Chow joined the New Democratic Party and became one of the first elected Asian woman school board trustees in 1985 and the first Asian woman councillor in Metro Toronto six years later. She joined husband Jack Layton in Ottawa, by representing her riding of Trinity-Spadina. She continues to work diligently for the rights of all Canadians.

Keinan "K'naan" Abdi Warsame

Keinan was fortunate to leave his native Somalia with his mother and two siblings on the last commercial flight that left the country before civil war broke out. He came to Toronto's Rexdale neighbourhood and, despite the fact that he could not speak English, taught himself hip-hop and rap diction, copying the lyrics and style phonetically. After becoming known for poetry, he was invited to the 50th anniversary of the United Nations Commission for Refugees where he received a standing ovation for his spoken-word poetry. K'naan has scaled most of Canada's music industry's heights, receiving a Juno Award for his song "Wavin' Flag," which was selected as the official anthem of the 2010 FIFA World Cup in South Africa. Music is his passion and part of his family's story: his aunt Magool was a well-known singer in Somalia and he's the grandson of famed Somali poet Haji Mohamed. The 34-year-old father of two creates a mix of rap, hip-hop, spoken word and rock that transcends the world music category.

Source: Suhasini, G., and Jetelina, M. 2012. "The Top 25," *Canadian Immigrant* (Ontario Edition), June. Reprinted by permission of Margaret Jetelina, Editor, Canadian Immigrant, www.canadianimmigrant.ca.

---

very low, the work is physically hard and often dangerous.

Many immigrants are suspicious, rightly or wrongly, that involvement with schools will bring official scrutiny about their legal status. Some migrant parents come from cultures that tend to leave school activities and contact to the professionals. Often migrant parents are not educated or comfortable in a school setting. And still more do not have the language ability to communicate comfortably with teachers and others in education programs.[*] (Gestwicki, 2010: 448)

REFUGEE FAMILIES

"Zara, her husband, and their two sons fled Syria when she found out that her husband, who had participated in mass protests in

[*] From GESTWICKI, *Home, School, and Community Relations, 7E.*
© 2010 Cengage Learning. Reproduced by permission.
www.cengage.com/permissions.

Damascus, was about to be apprehended by the local militia. There were also rumours that Zara was on a "pick-up" list after she was seen delivering anti-government flyers. Although they had no relatives in Canada, the family came to Toronto and found housing. Zara's husband had trouble adjusting to a new society. Unable to find work, he went to work in Egypt, leaving Zara with the two boys. Zara knows that she will never be able to go back to her country to see her family and her children will never know their grandparents, uncles, aunts, or cousins."

The 1951 Refugee Convention establishing United Nations High Commission for Refugees (UNHCR) spells out that a refugee is someone who

owing to a well-founded fear of being persecuted for reasons of race, religion, nationality, membership of a particular social group or political opinion, is outside the country of his nationality, and is unable to, or owing to such fear, is unwilling to avail himself of the protection of that country. (UNHCR, 2013)

In 2012, UNHCR stated that 33,924,475 refugees have been identified but the true estimate is believed to be closer to 43.7 million. Eighty percent of the world's refugees are women and children, many of whom have been displaced by armed conflicts (Evans, 2012).

The process of flight for many refugees is usually frightening, dangerous, and extremely stressful

Inside LOOK

In my first placement, we had a new child come into the kindergarten room at the same time that I arrived. He was new to Canada and new to child-care centres. He had some problems with language, not necessarily understanding but more so expressing himself in positive ways. I took it upon myself to help Daniel adjust. I had cut and laminated different emotion cards (a picture and a written word) and action cards so that at any point of the day, he could point to the card that best represented what he was feeling. By the end of my seven-week placement, he had improved so much! Instead of lashing out and throwing toys, he started to tell me his feelings instead. It was a great feeling of accomplishment for me but Daniel benefited most. He was able to integrate more successfully into the room and with his peers.

Source: Reprinted by permission of Anik van Draanen, RECE.

Courtesy of Lynn Wilson

These cards provide a visual cue for children who are English learners. These cards are also used with children with other special needs such as those with autism.

and there is no guarantee that refugees will find a safe haven. Some refugees may sneak through the countryside, often at night, while attempting to avoid discovery by the police or military, and live in constant fear with little or inappropriate food, clothing, or shelter. Others may live in refugee camps in their efforts to find safety. For refugees who have survived torture, the disruption of life and patterns of normalcy can last for years, prolonging stress (Berdichevsky, n.d.).

VICTIMS OF TORTURE

The Canadian Centre for Victims of Torture aids survivors of torture. Although it is shocking to associate children with torture, it is a reality that children suffer from oppression, war, and torture directly or indirectly. In the 20th century, children have increasingly become the target of oppressive regimes. Organized violence can affect children in numerous ways. Direct forms of torture used on adults have also been carried out on children. They include kidnapping; rape; forced labour and executions; and witnessing scenes of extreme violence such as murder, rape, beatings, or torture of others, including one's parents. Living in a war zone, which is often the case for refugees, has a disorganizing and traumatizing effect on the entire family. Trauma of this sort, occurring before or after a child's birth, can limit or damage the parenting skills of the parents. As a result, they may be preoccupied, depressed, anxious, in mourning, or otherwise incapable of properly caring for their child or children.

Few early childhood educators are prepared for the impact of dealing with families who have been confined to camps, separated from their loved ones, or subjected to the threat of military or civilian violence. "It is estimated that 50 percent of the people living in refugee camps are children, many of whom have spent their entire lives there" (Fantino, 1993: 2). Children and youths who have lived through a war may exhibit a wide range of symptoms. This variation of symptoms depends on the nature of the trauma, the child's developmental stage, the child's gender, the dynamics of the child's family and available supports, and the child's personality. These children may have recurring nightmares and have trouble distinguishing between reality and fantasy, as well as anxieties and insecurities that cause them to perceive every aspect of the world as being unsafe and frightening. It is important for healing to take place in a supportive environment such as within the realm of the family. Healing is dependent on the family's remaining structure, its protective and nurturing qualities, the degree to which the family adapts to the new culture, and the degree to which the child adjusts to a new life—at school, with peers, and with a new culture and language.

Inside LOOK

In the multicultural city of Toronto, many children come from different cultural and ethnic backgrounds. Because of the different perspectives regarding respect for teachers in class and the concept of teachers' authority, Chinese children are usually very quiet. They may listen to teachers without actively responding to the teacher's questions. I found that both in my college classrooms and in early childhood environments, this was very noticeable. In an interactive teaching environment like here in Canada, passive students may result in teachers who don't know this cultural difference feeling disrespected or even frustrated. They may label these children or students as unresponsive, shy, quiet, or unable to talk. I grew up with the belief "Modesty helps one to go forward, whereas conceit makes one lag behind." Like many others, my parents and teachers reminded me not to be proud of myself, that there was always someone better than me. Because of this influence, I grew up into a person without high self-esteem like many other Chinese children. So, teachers, please balance the power you have over children according to their cultural differences and their parents' expectations.

FIGURE 9.3 Refugee Child's Drawing

The Canadian Immigrant Integration Program (CIIP) was created by the Association of Canadian Community Colleges (ACCC) in 2007 with the Canadian government's support to better prepare newcomers for economic integration, while still in their country of origin. Over the years, too many immigrants have landed in Canada with false impressions of how easy it will be to get a job that meets their qualifications, particularly in licensed fields, and this program aims to prevent that misinformation. This free voluntary program operates through regional offices around the world and about 14,000 people have graduated. The program provides an overview of the job market, resume skills and referrals in Canada as well as providing relevant websites concerning licensing, credential assessment, language assessment etc. Top questions range from labour market information, schooling, childcare and the weather! According to the participants surveyed, almost all (96 percent) said they were going to take further action to prepare themselves before leaving for Canada.

Source: Suhasini, G., and Jetelina, M. 2012. "The Top 25," *Canadian Immigrant* (Ontario Edition), June. Reprinted by permission of Margaret Jetelina, Editor, Canadian Immigrant, www.canadianimmigrant.ca.

The Vancouver Association for Survivors of Torture says,

> Talking about these traumatic experiences is not a threat to their psychological well-being, nor a challenge to their ability to "grow out" of those experiences. On the contrary, children may need validation of those experiences, support and help to learn how to cope with the memories of traumatic experiences. (in DeAndrade, 1992: 10)

Despite their often high educational qualifications, many immigrant parents are able to find employment only in the low-paying service sector. This has an enormous impact on the family unit. The lack of affordable quality child care is another issue for these families who may have limited incomes.

The NLSCY shows that immigrant children have fewer emotional and behavioural problems than children born in Canada—despite the fact that almost 30 percent of immigrant children live in poverty, an environment that is often associated with poor mental health. Furthermore, immigrant children come from families that are less dysfunctional and whose parents are in better mental health (National Research Conference, 1998: 103).

ROLE OF THE EDUCATOR

- It is critical that educators become knowledgeable about world issues where persecution, religious persecution, and racial discrimination occur. A greater understanding of where families have come from will lay the foundation for a stronger relationship.

- Teachers need to be familiar with the symptoms of culture shock and watch for them. Teachers should also be aware of their own reactions to each family's story, particularly those who have come from war-torn countries. Teachers may well be overwhelmed by the trauma the family has suffered and may need to seek support themselves.

- It is hard to be alone in a new country and it is important for teachers to be alert to parents who may be experiencing depression or prolonged sadness:

> At first I did not know what was happening to me. I cried all day. I could not sleep. Nothing was going right. I was lucky, a woman at my mosque noticed that I was unhappy and she kept talking and talking to me. It was because of her that I

went to see a social worker. The next time it happened, I knew what to do. I called a psychologist right away. Depression is very, very bad. (Farida from Syria in CAMH, 2001: 35)

- Some families may want to maintain traditional ways while others may want their children to quickly assimilate into the dominant culture; it is important for the teacher to understand how she can best support each of these families.

- Be sensitive to the fact that many family members may have held important occupations in their homeland and may be embarrassed by the menial jobs they have had to take in order to survive in Canada.

- Whenever possible, consider a family visit. Seeing families in their home environment where they are confident, using their home language, and engaging all family members is often in contrast to the hesitant parent who may be trying to communicate in an unfamiliar language in a child-care setting.

- Some immigrant and refugee families will face prejudice and preconceived ideas about who they are; it is important to support the family in as many ways possible as they face these issues.

- Discrimination may come from Canadians who have been here for a long time or from other newcomers. It can be based on race, ethnic group, or religion. Teachers should be aware of historical events that may contribute to some families struggling with each other, even within the same ethnic community.

- Teachers should listen to what the families have to say about their dreams for themselves and their children. This insight will provide opportunities to provide meaningful support.

- A family who lived in a rural community may be dealing with the additional stresses and confusion of adjusting to urban life for the first time.

- Find out which families and children have never experienced a cold climate and help prepare them for winter by setting up a winter clothing exchange program.

- It is important to link families with agencies in the community that may be specifically helpful to the individual needs of these families: English or French language classes; churches, mosques, temples, and other religious or spiritual places; volunteer organizations; sports clubs; fitness classes at the local community centre; the local library; immigrant settlement agency; self-help groups; Kids Help Line; Telehealth lines; clinics, etc.

- Infant Mental Health Promotion Project (IMP), Department of Psychiatry, the Hospital for Sick Children, Toronto: The IMP project designs and runs innovative training programs for service providers from different disciplines; develops teaching materials and information on infant development and parent-child relationships; offers information and support to service providers; and develops models and training for community workers in the use of innovative, practical interventions for infants and their families. This project work may be particularly relevant for those working with newcomer families (**http://www.sickkids.on.ca/imp**).

- If meaningful resources for immigrant and refugee families are not present in a community, teachers can collaborate with families to make them happen.

- Ethnic associations may contribute flyers and notices in the students' home languages regarding city agencies, food banks, employment centres, and adult English classes. These should be displayed prominently for all families. Teachers can create a "What's in Our Community" booklet for families new to the centre to help them access the resources they need, translating it if possible.

- Where English is not a family's first language, they may prefer written communication instead so they can review it at their leisure.

- Important notices should be translated into the languages of the families in the centre and posted where they can be seen and used to inform.

- Do not use student interpreters if there is access to staff interpreters or ethnic agencies. Parents may not want to share information with a student or a child who has greater English fluency.

EXHIBIT 9.4   Supporting Immigrant or Refugee Families: An Information Checklist

Meyers (2007) provides a checklist of questions for teachers who are working with young immigrant or refugee children.

- **Are the parents alive and are they together with the children?** I have had students from Hong Kong with an absent parent, as well as children from war-torn countries, whose parents have been killed, imprisoned, or are missing.
- **Have the siblings been separated? How long and where?** Often, one child is given over to a trusted relative who is ready to immigrate. In other cases, an older sibling has come ahead and paved the way for the rest of the family. Sometimes, it takes years before the whole family can be reunited.
- **Have all the siblings had schooling? In which languages?** Many older students have had some training in English in their homeland but usually the lessons were grammar-based. Students may read and write basic English but they do not understand the rapid pace of our speech and they lack experience speaking in English. Younger siblings may not even know our alphabet system. Moreover, students who have resided in several countries often have learned to read and write in a language that is different from the language(s) spoken in their homes.
- **Has the family joined friends or relatives in the new country?** A family is fortunate if they have relatives or associates who can assist with translations and explain our customs. Such assistance helps to reduce the initial impact of culture shock that all immigrants experience. (Many of us have heard the story about the Vietnamese family who had just got settled in their new home only to be terrorized on their first night by masked hooligans who kept up a steady barrage of screaming and knocking on the door. It was Halloween.)
- **What is the family's immigration status?** A refugee is initially not allowed to work in this country and that may give you some indication of the family's financial status. It is especially important to know this information if there are several children within that family who may be asked for trip monies.

continued

- **Is there someone in the home who can speak any English?** If a student is highly motivated and if there is someone in the home who can assist with homework, then language acquisition can be speeded up. It is also important to know if school notices will be understood in the home.

- **Is anyone in the household employed?** The D. family from Egypt had seven children. The older two went to work to support their mum and siblings. They spoke little English and did not get a chance to learn English on the job. The younger children, however, acquired English rapidly and became the family translators. During the first winter the children did not have appropriate clothes so the teacher introduced the family to the local Red Cross.

- **Does the family have knowledge of its ethnic associations in our city?** Knowing where to turn for assistance and advice is essential for all of us, and is even more so for a new immigrant family with few cultural connections to this new country.

- **Has the child witnessed or been the victim of any trauma before or during the move to our country?** Information from parents can indicate if a student(s) has either witnessed or been a victim of trauma. It is better to ascertain such information and be forewarned, than to observe signs of post trauma stress syndrome (PTSS) in a child during class. Symptoms may include a lack of affect, extreme behaviors (passivity or aggression), incontinence, or poor social skills.

- **Is the family here for business, for example, a three-year term?** The motivation to learn to communicate in a new language may not be as great if children think they will be "going home" soon.

- **Does a family member have previous experience with North American culture and/or education?** A family member with knowledge of North American norms will be a great asset to his/her family in every way.

Source: From MEYERS M. *Teaching to Diversity, 4E.* © 1993 Nelson Education Ltd. Reproduced by permission. www.cengage.com/permissions.

- Consider how families will celebrate holidays. It is very lonely to spend these special times alone. Teachers might consider inviting the family to their own homes to include them in the celebration.

The process of acculturation becomes a life-long challenge for every member of a family that migrates to this country. Parents struggle to keep what is really valued to them and to their cultural community, while at the same time trying to facilitate their children's integration into Canadian society. The struggle to find a balance goes well beyond the initial years of resettlement and adaptation to their new environment; it arises over and over throughout the different life stages families face. It ultimately redefines and permeates almost every aspect of their lives and every decision they make in building a future in Canada. (Mawani, 2004: 22)

Blackburn (1999) states, "Even in the midst of war and poverty, traditional cultural rituals, celebrations, and gatherings can be adjusted to the conditions to enable individuals and families to either maintain or reestablish a sense of community and a sense of self." Community events can be an important opportunity to gather with others in familiar rituals and customs and be a catalyst for hope and healing.

ROLE OF THE EDUCATOR IN THE ROOM

- Some children will benefit from an extended orientation to the program, with a family member staying with them for a longer period of time. Each child will respond differently to the new setting.

- Be prepared for dissonance caused by the difference in expectations for children in their homes and in the early learning environment. Talk to families to learn more about their expectations.

- Parents and children might be unfamiliar with the English language. Teachers can reassure a

Courtesy of Lynn Wilson

Newcomer families should be encouraged to participate in the early learning environment in ways that support their transition to a new cultural experience.

child and at the same time demonstrate respect for his or her identity by learning a few key words in the child's first language, or by using student translators informally for minor things: to reassure, give directions, or state procedures.

- Foster an atmosphere of acceptance in class, in which children feel comfortable expressing themselves in their home languages. Teachers should also provide books and materials that reflect students' heritages. Children benefit enormously when they are invited to participate in an enviornment of respect and friendliness.

- Roma Chumak-Horbatsch, Ryerson University's School of Early Childhood Education faculty, encourages teachers to "support families who want their children to be bilingual to read regularly, write letters to relatives in their home country, sing songs and play in their home language, buy colourful sticky notes and write the names of objects in the home language and stick the notes on the objects" (Calabresi, 2011: 40).

- Be aware of the kinds of activities and assignments that relate to the child's family or the family's history,which may be painful, unavailable, or unkown. Asking abut the origin of a child's name or for baby pictures can be a problem for children who were adopted past infancy. Asking a family to share artefacts can be painful if they fled from their homeland with only the clothes on their backs* (Gonzalez-Mena, 2010: 2).

- Teachers can help the children find ways to contribute to the program in significant and meaningful ways and focus on the child's strengths.

- Naptime may frighten children, and teachers should be prepared for this. Don't belittle children's behaviours; listen patiently to what the children say (or ask parents) and take the fears seriously.

- Teachers can learn breathing and relaxation techniques. Yoga for children before naptime would be a great opportunity for children to collect themselves. Some parents may also benefit from participating in these relaxation experiences.

- Teachers should be prepared to adapt to family expectations for toileting (for example, washing rather than wiping, using only one hand) and feeding routines and dietary requirements.

- Ample time should be provided in the dramatic play centre. By observing carefully, teachers may gain insight into the challenges the child might be facing since many act out their feelings during their play situations. Teachers can use the observed behaviours to deal with issues at a more appropriate time.

- The dramatic play area should reflect the many ways in which food is prepared.

- The outdoor space should provide children with ample opportunities to run, draw, read, and play games that are familiar to them.

- Many families may have remedies for illnesses with which teachers may not be familiar. This is a great opportunity to learn more about health practices in other cultures.

  Dotsch (1994: 25–26) suggests a number of strategies that teachers can adopt during this difficult time.

* GONZALEZ-MENA, JANET, 50 STRATEGIES FOR COMMUNICATING AND WORKING WITH DIVERSE FAMILIES, 2nd Edition, © 2010. Reprinted and Electronically reproduced by permission of Pearson Education, Inc., Upper Saddle River, NJ.

With the first separation from the parent, symptoms of extreme anxiety may occur, such as screaming, vomiting, and shaking. In some cases it may be necessary to recall the parent. Anger, too, may be displayed, as well as crying, or great despondency. When a child exhibits this behaviour, the teacher must approach the child slowly and gradually, offering gestures of comfort only when the child is ready to allow them. Sometimes it may be another child who will fulfil this role; but if effective strategies are implemented, as confidence comes, the child will begin to play with toys, allow a teacher to help, and accept food.[*]

- The following recommendations, made by Bernhard and Freire (1994), will give teachers a better understanding of how to facilitate the adjustment and recovery process of refugee families. Educators need professional development time to upgrade their education and better equip themselves to respond to the needs of the refugee population.

- ECE outcomes and competencies should stress preparation to enable caregivers to work with populations of different ethnolinguistic backgrounds. In the case of the refugee population, training and education should also address posttraumatic stress disorder[†] and other challenges associated with the refugee experience.

- In their practicum, students should have appropriate supervision while working with children of refugees. Caregivers need to be made aware of the particular needs of refugee families and children. They need to be aware, too, of their own important position as potential family stabilizers.

ECE programs should include education on cross-cultural and bilingual child-rearing practices; on the value of first-language maintenance and second-language learning.

Nirdosh (1998: 5) summarizes the situation succinctly:

> It is critical that we interact with refugee children and their families in ways that do not revictimize them. We need to learn how to support these families by seeking out community resources and further developing our understanding through professional development of the stressful and often life-threatening experiences suffered by these families. This may be the greatest challenge a teacher may face—but we can make a difference!

---

[*] Dotsch, J. 1994. "Supporting the New Immigrant/Refugee Family in Child Care." *Interaction* 8 (2). Summer. Reprinted by permission.

[†] Bernhard, J., and M. Freire. 1994. "Latino Refugee Children: Families of War and Persecution in the ECE System." *Interaction* 8 (2). Summer. Reprinted by permission.

Inside LOOK

Three-year-old Ly Ly can hear the noise as she nears the room. She doesn't know what to expect, but her mother has told her that she is now old enough to go to "school." A strange-looking woman has come close to her and is saying something she doesn't understand. She hides her head in her mother's skirt because the noise and confusion are overwhelming. Some bigger boys race by and she begins to cry. Her mother looks very uncomfortable and embarrassed. The teacher has told her that it will be easier for Ly Ly if she leaves quickly. The mother hesitates because she has never left her daughter before. She departs with tears in her eyes as Ly Ly screams, cries, and kicks the door. When the mother tries to go back, she is told through a crack in the door that she really should leave because she is making her daughter more upset. Ly Ly can see and hear her mother through the crack in the door. Maybe her mother will never come back and she will be trapped with these strange people forever. Suddenly, another adult pulls her away from the door. Ly Ly frantically tries to escape but is no match for the much stronger teacher.

So many things have changed in Ly Ly's life—her home, her toys, the place where she sleeps, even the people with whom she lives. If only the parent had been encouraged to stay; if only one of the teachers had been able to speak some Vietnamese so that Ly Ly could feel more secure; if only the teacher had had some training in the experience of separation and how the trauma of immigration affects children.

Source: Dotsch, J. 1994. "Supporting the New Immigrant/Refugee Family in Child Care," *Interaction* 8, no. 2, Summer. Reprinted by permission.

THE MOSAIC FAMILY RESOURCE CENTRE, CALGARY, AB

The Mosaic Centre is a family resource centre, hosted by the Calgary Immigrant Aid Society (CIAS), for immigrant and refugee families with children ages 6 and under. Developed with input from community agencies, community members, staff, and consultants, the centre provides multi-tiered preventive and intervention services. The partners in this project share the belief that the health and well-being of young children need to be addressed within the framework of the family and the community. The Mosaic Centre is designed to ensure easy access to direct services that are culturally sensitive and adapted to specific needs of the population. A wide range of programs is provided to support the family as a unit as well as the individual health, educational, and psychosocial needs of parents and children. The use of first language is extensive in all program aspects. There is a well-equipped multi-age playroom, as well as an open space for large motor activities, comfortable spaces for adults to sit and talk, and a kitchen for preparation of snacks. The Saturday Morning Playgroup has worked well in attracting immigrant fathers and their children. Fathers have appreciated the choice and the range of activities, and the opportunity to socialize with other fathers.

BOOKS FOR CHILDREN

Our New Home: Immigrant Children Speak, by E. Hearn and M. Milne

Being Muslim: A Groundwood Guide, by H. Siddiqui

The Best Eid Ever, by A. Mobin-Uddin

In the Small, Small Night, by J. Kurtz

Our Global Community Series, by L. Easterling

Our New Home: Immigrant Children Speak, by E. Hearn and M. Milne

Making It Home: Real Life Stories from Children Forced to Flee, by B. Naidoo

From Far Away, by Robert Munsch

Hannah Is My Name: A Young Immigrant Story, by B. Yang

BOOKS FOR ADULTS

Women and Wars, by C. Cohn

Exceptional People: How Migration Shaped Our World and Will Define Our Future, by G. Cameron and M. Balarajan

Refugees Worldwide, by R. Munson, D. Elliott, and U.A. Segal

English Language Learners: The Essential Guide, by D. Freeman and Y. Freeman

Empowering Children through Art and Expression, by B. St. Thomas and P. Johnson

Let's Celebrate Canada's Special Days, by C. Parry

Refugees in a Global Era, by P. Marflett

REFERENCES

Aboriginal Affairs and Northern Development Canada. 2010. "Aboriginal Place Names." Retrieved January 29, 2013, from http://www.aadnc-aandc.gc.ca/eng/1100100016346

Aboriginal Healing Foundation (AHF) and Legacy of Hope Foundation. 2011. Retrieved February 4, 2013, from http://www.legacyofhope.ca/downloads/hope-and-healing-en.pdf

Adams, M. 2007. "Surprise, Canadian Pluralism Is Working." *Environics Research Group News.* 20 November.

Adler, R.B., L.B. Rosenfeld, R.R. Proctor II, and C. Winder. 2012. *Interplay. The Process of Interpersonal Communication.* New York: Oxford University Press.

Adoption Council of Canada. n.d. Retrieved February 4, 2013, from http://www.adoption.ca/myths-and-realities

Albanese, P. 2009. *Children in Canada Today.* Toronto: Oxford University Press.

Alexander, C.S., and B. Guyer. 1993. "Adolescent Pregnancy: Occurrence and Consequences." *Pediatric Annals* 22: 85–88.

Amatea, E. 2009. *Building Culturally Responsive Family-School Relationships.* Upper Saddle River, NJ: Pearson.

Ambert, A. 2006. *One-Parent Families: Characteristics, Causes, Consequences, and Issues.* Ottawa: The Vanier Institute of the Family.

———. 2012. *Changing Families. Relationships in Context*, 2nd ed. Toronto: Pearson.

Anisef, P., K. Murphy Kilbride, J. Ochocka, and R. Janzen. 2001. *Study on Parenting Issues of Newcomer Families in Ontario.* Kitchener, ON: Centre for Research and Education in Human Services (CREHS). Joint Centre of Excellence for Research on Immigration and Settlement (CERIS).

Arnup, K. 2003. "Parenting in the 21st Century." Retrieved from http://www.carleton.ca/cu/research/spring2001/article4.html

Arthur, J. 2012. *Liberal MP Paul Steckle Introduces Bill to Ban Abortions After 20 Weeks.* Abortion Rights Coalition of Canada. Retrieved February 4, 2013, from http://www.arcc-cdac.ca/action/bill_c338.html

Ast, D. 2011. "Challenging Homophobia and Heterosexism: A K-12 Curriculum Resource Guide." Toronto District School Board.

Aulakh, R. 2011. "Colony of Wives Thrive." *Toronto Star*. May 29.

Azar, B. 1999. "Foster Children Get a Taste of Stability. "American Psychological Association. Retrieved from http://www.apa.org/monitor/nov95/orphana.html

Baker, M. 2010. *Choices and Constraints in Family Life*. Toronto: Oxford University Press.

Balkissoon, D. 2011. "The Seven Habits of Highly Effective Lesbian Families." *The Globe and Mail*. November 5. Section F.

Ball, J. 2008. "Policies and Practice Reforms to Promote Positive Transitions to Fatherhood among Aboriginal Young Men. "*Horizons: Government of Canada Policy Research Initiative* 10 (1): 52–59.

———. 2009. "Indigenous Fathers' Involvement in Reconstituting 'Circles of Care'" *American Journal of Community Psychology*.

Ball, J., and R.T. George. 2006. "Policies and Practices Affecting Aboriginal Fathers' Involvement with their Children." In J.P. White, S.K. Wingert, P. Maxim, and D. Beavon, eds., *Aboriginal Policy Research: Moving Forward, Making a Difference*. Toronto: Thompson Educational Press.

Ball, J., C. Roberge, L. Joe, and R. George. 2007. "Fatherhood: Indigenous Men's Journeys." Retrieved February 4, 2013, from http://ecdip.org/docs/pdf/IF%204%20pg%20summary.pdf

Barbour, C., N.H. Barbour, and P.A. Scully 2008. *Families, Schools, and Communities. Building Partnerships for Educating Children*. Pearson Merrill Prentice Hall.

Barbour, J., and P. Delfabbro. 2006. "Children's Adjustment to Long-Term Foster Care." *Children and Youth Services Review*, 27. 329–340.

Becker, G. 1991. *A Treatise on the Family*. Cambridge, MA: Harvard University Press.

Berdichevsky, R. n.d. *The Continuing Ordeal: Long Term Needs of Survivors of Torture*. Centre for Victims of Torture. Retrieved February 4, 2013, from http://ccvt.org/publications/online-publications/the-continuing-ordeallong-term-needs-of-survivors-of-torture

Bernhard, J., and M. Freire. 1994. "Latino Refugee Children: Families of War and Persecution in the ECE System." *Interaction* 8 (2). Summer.

Bernhard, J., P. Landolt, and L. Goldring, 2006. "Transnational, Multi-local Motherhood: Experiences of Separation and Reunification Among Latin American Families in Canada." *Policy Matters* 24.1-6.

Bertrand, J., and C. Geswicki. 2012. *Essentials of Early Childhood Education*. Nelson Education.

Bibby, R. 2004. "The Future Families Project: A Survey of Canadian Hopes and Dreams." Retrieved from http://www.vifamily.ca

———. 2005. *Future Families Project: A Survey of Canadian Hopes and Dreams*. Ottawa: Vanier Institute of the Family.

Bilby, R. 2009. *The Emerging Millennials: How Canada's Newest Generation Is Responding to Change and Choice*. Lethbridge: Project Canada Books.

Blackburn, C.A. 1999. "Resilient Children and Families." Retrieved from http://www.ecdgroup.com/cn/claudia.html

Bokma, A. 2008. "Being a Foster Care Family." *Canadian Living*. Retrieved February 4, 2013, from http://www.canadianliving.com/relationships/friends_and_family/being_a_foster_care_family.php

British Columbia Council for Families. 2012. "Family Roles and Responsibilities." *Vanier Institute of the Family*. Vol. 42. No. 2.

Brokenleg, M., and L. Brendtro. 1989. The Circle of Caring: Native American Perspectives on Children and Youth. Paper presented to Child Welfare of American International Conference, Washington, DC. 10.

Burt, T., and L. Klinger Lesser. 2008. "Lesbian, Gay, Bisexual and Transgendered (LGBT) Families." *Exchange*. September/October.

Calabresi, A.P. 2011. "Language Power." *Canadian Immigrant*. 8(9).

Callahan, M., L. Brown, P. McKenzie, and B. Whittington. In press. *Knitting Up the Raveled Sleeve of Care: Grandmothers Making Families with Their Grandchildren*.

Camarena, P.M., K. Minor, T. Melmer, and C. Ferrie. 1998. "The Nature and Support of Adolescent Mothers' Life Aspirations." *Family Relations* 47 (2). 129–37.

CAMH Centre for Addiction and Mental Health. Citizenship and Immigration Canada. 2001. *Alone in Canada: 21 Ways to Make It Better. A Self-Help Guide for Single Newcomers*.

Canadian Centre for Justice Statistics. 2006. *Hate Crime in Canada*. Profile Series. Retrieved from www.statcan.gc.ca/pub/85f0033m/85f0033m2008017-eng.pdf

Canadian Child Care Federation. 2008. "Encouraging Aboriginal Cultural Identity at Home and in Child Care." Retrieved February 22, 2013, from http://www.cccf-fcsge.ca/wp-content/uploads/RS_92-e.pdf

Canadian Press. 2012. "Canadian Foster Care in Crisis Experts Say." February 19. Retrieved February 4, 2013, from http://www.cbc.ca/news/canada/story/2012/02/19/foster-care-cp.html

CANGRANDS. 2003. "Tips for Grandparents Raising Grandchildren and Other Family Members." Retrieved February 4, 2013, from http://www.cangrands.com/grgtips.htm

Cardinal, E. 1994. "Effective Programming: A Native Perspective." *Early Childhood Education* 27 (1). Spring–Summer.

Carlson, M.J., and F.F. Furstenberg, Jr. 2006. "The Prevalence and Correlates of Multipartnered Fertility Among U.S. Parents." *Journal of Marriage and Family*, 68. 718–732.

Casson, R. 2007. *Canadian Forces in Afghanistan. Report of the Standing Committee on National Defence*. 39th Parliament, 1st Session.

Changes in Me: A Resource for Educators On Puberty And Adolescent Development. 2011. Healthy Sexuality Program, Peel Public Health.

Cheal, D. 2010. *Canadian Families Today. New Perspectives*. Oxford University Press.

Child Welfare League of America. 2005. Kinship Care: Fact Sheet. Retrieved February 4, 2013, from http://www.cwla.org/programs/kinship/factsheet.htm

Citizenship and Immigration Canada. 2010. "Welcome to Canada: What You Should Know." July 21. Retrieved February 22, 2013, from http://www.cic.gc.ca/english/resources/publications/welcome/wel-03e.asp

————. 2011. RDM at March 2011, and GCMS on May 31, 2011. Transmitted Oct. 26, 2011. Summations by Robin Hilborn, Family Helper, www.familyhelper.net. Retrieved February 20, 2013, from http://www.familyhelper.net/news/111027stats.html

Corbett, S. 1993. "A Complicated Bias." *Young Children.* March.

Couchenour, D., and K. Chrisman. 2000. *Families, Schools and Communities: Together for Young Children.* New York: Delmar Thomson Learning.

————. 2011. *Families, Schools and Communities. Together for Young Children.* 4th ed. Belmont, CA: Wadsworth, Cengage Learning.

Crawford, T. 2008. "Teen Moms Beat Odds to Succeed." *Toronto Star.* March 11. Section L.

Dance, C., A. Rushton, and D. Quinton. 2002. "Emotional Abuse in Early Childhood: Relationships with Progress in Subsequent Family Placement." *Journal of Child Psychology and Psychiatry*, 43. 395–407.

DeAndrade, Y. 1992. *VAST Project: Children and PTSD.* Vancouver: Vancouver Association for Survivors of Torture.

Department of Justice, 2012. "The Supporting Families Experiencing Separation and Divorce Initiative." August 28. Retrieved February 2, 2013, from http://www.justice.gc.ca/eng/pi/fcy-fea/abo-apr/index.html

Direnfeld, Gary. n.d. Workshop material. Retrieved from http://www.yoursocialworker.com

Dotsch, J. 1994. "Supporting the New Immigrant/Refugee Family in Child Care." *Interaction* 8 (2). Summer.

Dryburgh, H. 2003. *Teenage Pregnancy* 12 (1). Catalogue 82-003. Ottawa: Statistics Canada.

Durnford, S. 2012. Canadian Foster Family Association. Retrieved from http://www.canadianfosterfamily association.ca

Edwards, L., and S. Sodhi. 1992. *Me and My Families: A Handbook on Adoption and Foster Care for School Professionals.* Washington, DC: Department of Health and Human Services.

Epstein, R. 2003. "Lesbian Families." In M. Lynn, ed., *Voices: Essays on Canadian Families.* Toronto: Nelson Thomson Learning.

Epstein, R., and S. Duggan. 2006. *Father Involvement Community Research Forum* Spring. Father Involvement Research Alliance. Retrieved from www.fira.ca/cms/documents/44/Gay_Fathers.pdf

Evans, M. 2012. "World Refugee Day—20th June 2012." *Earth Times.* Retrieved February 4, 2013, from http://www.earthtimes.org/politics/world-refugee-day-2012/2046

Fantino, A. 1993. "Refugee Children in Canada: Reshaping Identity." Speech given to the Canadian Council for Refugees, Calgary. November 11–13.

Father Involvement Research Alliance, n.d. "Gay Fathers Cluster." Retrieved February 1, 2013, from http://www.fira.ca/cms/documents/44/Gay_Fathers.pdf

Federation of Saskatchewan Indian Nations. 1993. Retrieved from http://www.FSIN.com

Fenton, P. 2004. "Talking with Your Child about Adoption: Guidelines for Adoptive Parents." *Adoption Roundup: Journal of the Adoption Council of Ontario.* Winter.

Ferris-Manning, and C., Zandstra, M. 2003. *Children in Care in Canada. A Summary of Current Issues and Trends with Recommendations for Future Research.* Toronto: Centre of Excellence for Child Welfare.

Finkelstein, M., M. Wamsley, and D. Miranda. 2002. *What Keeps Children in Foster Care from Succeeding in School?* New York: Vera Institute of Justice.

First Nations Child and Family Caring Society of Canada. 2012. "Shannen's Dream." Retrieved from http://www.fncaringsociety.ca/shannens-dream

Fontaine, P. 2007. "Improving Quality of Life for First Nations People." *Toronto Star.* February 5. A15.

Fraser, S. 2008. Chapter 4—First Nations Child and Family Services Program—Indian and Northern Affairs Canada. Retrieved from http://www.oag-bvg.gc.ca/internet/English/parl_oag_200805_04_e_30700.html#hd3d

Freeman, R. 1994. "Outcomes of Divorce for Children. *"Profiling Canada's Families.* Ottawa: Vanier Institute of the Family.

Fuller-Thomson, E. 2005. "A Profile of Skipped Generations families." McMaster University, Social and Economic Dimensions of an Aging Population (SEDAP) Research Paper No. 132; Furstenberg, F., and A.J. Cherlin. 2001. "Children's Adjustment to Divorce." In B. Fox, ed., *Family Patterns Gender Relations*, 2nd ed. New York: Oxford University Press.

Geronimus, A.T. 1991. "Teenage Childbearing and Social and Reproductive Disadvantage: The Evolution of Complex Questions and the Demise of Simple Answers." *Family Relations* 40 (4) (October). 463–471.

Gestwicki, C. 2004. *Home School and Community Relations*, 5th ed. New York: Thomson Delmar Learning.

————. 2010. *Home School and Community Relations*, 7th ed. New York: Thomson Delmar Learning.

Gonzalez-Mena, J. 2010. *50 Early Childhood Strategies for Working and Communicating with Diverse Families.* Columbus, OH: Pearson/Merrill Prentice Hall.

————. 2007. *50 Early Childhood Strategies for Working and Communicating with Diverse Families.* Columbus, OH: Pearson/Merrill Prentice Hall.

Gordon, A. 2005. "Family Feuding a Two-Way Street." *Toronto Star.* February 11. D5.

————. 2008. "Immigrant Men Learn How to Broaden Paternal Role." *Toronto Star.* May 17. L1.

Gower, R. 2005. "Opening Doors to Understanding and Acceptance." In Z. Janmohamed, ed., *Building Bridges, Lesbian, Gay, Bisexual, Transsexual, Transgender and Queer Families in Early Childhood Education.* Toronto: Ontario Coalition for Better Child Care.

Grand Parenting Again Canada. n.d. "Kinship Care." Retrieved from http://www.grandparentingagain.ca/?page_id=31

Greenspoon, B. 1998. "Addressing Gay and Lesbian Issues." *Interaction* 12 (2).

Gregory, E. 2007. *Ready: Why Women Are Embracing the New Later Motherhood.* Philadelphia, PA: Basic Books.

Gulli, C. 2008. "Suddenly Teen Pregnancy Is Cool?" *Maclean's.* January 28.

Hall, C.C.I. 1980. The Ethnic Identity of Racially Mixed People: A Study of Black- Japanese. Unpublished doctoral dissertation, University of California, Los Angeles.

Harper, A.M. 1997. Cultural Adaptation and Intercultural Communication: Some Barriers and Bridges. Paper presented at the Annual Convention of the Western Speech Communication Association. Monterey, California. February 13.

Hayes, C.D. 1987. *Risking the Future: Adolescent Sexuality, Pregnancy and Childbearing*. Vol. 1. Washington, DC: National Academy Press.

Health Canada. n.d. "Aboriginal Head Start." Retrieved February 22, 2013, from http://www.hc-sc.gc.ca/fniah -spnia/famil/develop/ahsor-papa_intro-eng.php

Hegar, R. L. 2005. "Sibling Placement in Foster Care and Adoption: An Overview of International Research." *Children and Youth Services Review*, 27, pp. 717–739.

Hepworth Berger, E. 2004. *Parents as Partners in Education: Families and Schools Working Together*, 6th ed. Toronto: Prentice Hall.

Hildebrand, V., L. Aotaki Phenice, M. McPhail Gray, and R. Pena Hines. 2008. *Knowing and Serving Diverse Families*. 3rd ed. Pearson Merrill Prentice Hall.

Hoy Crawford, S. 1996. *Beyond Dolls and Guns: 101 Ways to Help Children Avoid Gender Bias*. Portsmouth, NH: Heinemann.

Hune-Brown, N. 2013. "Mixie Me." *Toronto Life*. March. 40

International Research." *Children and Youth Services Review*, 27. 717–739.

Inuit Tapiriit Kanatami, 2011. "Report Sets Out First-Ever National Goals for Inuit Education." Media Release. June 16. Retrieved January 29, 2013, from https://www.itk.ca/ media/media-release/visionary-report-sets-out-first-ever -national-goals-inuit-education

Janmohamed, Z. 2006. *Building Bridges: Lesbian, Gay, Bisexual, Transgender, Transsexual and Queer Families in Early Childhood Education*. Toronto: Ontario Coalition for Better Child Care.

Jendrek Platt, J. 1993. "Grandparents Who Parent Their Grandchildren: Effects on Lifestyle." *Journal of Marriage and the Family* 55 (August).

Johnston, P. 1993. *Adoption and the Schools Project: A Guide for Educators*. Washington, DC: Department of Health and Human Services.

Khoo, L. 2007. "Mixed Blessings. Mixed-Race Identity." *CBC Radio's The Current*. September 7.

Kopun, F. 2011. "Families with One Child Are Growing in Number Around the World." *Toronto Star*. August 25. Retrieved February 4, 2013, from http://www.thestar .com/parentcentral/news%20&%20features/specials%20 and%20features/article/1044380--families-with-one -child-are-growing-in-number-around-the-world

Kowaleski-Jones, L., and F.L. Mott. 1998. "Sex, Contraception and Childbearing among High-Risk Youth: Do Different Factors Influence Males and Females?" *Family Planning Perspective*s 30 (4). 163–169.

La Rose, L. 2008. "Mixed Race Marriages on the Rise." *Toronto Star*. April 2.

Leathers, S. J. 2005. "Separation from Siblings: Associations with Placement Adaption and Outcomes Among Adolescents in Long-Term Foster Care." *Children and Youth Services Review*, 27. 793–819.

Lochhead, C. 2000." The Trend toward Delayed First Childbirth: Health and Social Implications." *A Profile of Mothers and Fathers in Canada: 1971–1996*. Ottawa, ON: Policy Division of Health Canada.

Lorde, A. 1987. "Turning the Beat Around: Lesbian Parenting 1986." In S. Pollack and J. Vaughn, eds., *Politics of the Heart*. New York: Firebrand.

Lunau, K. 2011. "Young, Divorced and Stigmatized." *Maclean's*. November 28.

MacLean, J. 2003. No How-to Guide for Catastrophe. Widowhood Not Meant for the Young. *Toronto Star*. 6 September. L9.

MacQueen, K. 2012. "Hard of Hearing." *Maclean's*. March 28.

Manning, W.D. 1993." Marriage and Cohabitation Following Premarital Conception." *Journal of Marriage and the Family* 55 (3). 839–850.

Marks, G.N. 2006. "Family Size, Family Type and Student Achievement: Cross-National Differences and the Role of Socioeconomic and School Factors." *Journal of Comparative Family Studies*, 37. 18–24.

Maurin, R. 2007. "Special Delivery." *Fashion*. November.

Mawani, F.N. 2004. *Attachment Across Cultures*. National Advisory Panel.

McCreary Centre Society. 2008. "A Picture of Health. British Columbia Adolescent Health Survey. " Retrieved from http://www.mcs.bc.ca/pdf/AHS%20IV%20March%20 30%20Final.pdf

McDaniel, S.A., and L. Tepperman. 2011. *Close Relations. An Introduction to the Sociology of Families*. Toronto: Pearson Canada.

Mehren, E. 1999. "Grandparents Raising Their Children's Children." *Toronto Star*. January 30. L9.

Meyers, M. 1993. *Teaching to Diversity: Teaching and Learning in the Multi-Ethnic Classroom*. Toronto: Irwin.

Miles, S.C. n.d. "Grandparents Raising Grandchildren." Retrieved February 4, 2013, from http://www.wvu.edu/ ~exten/inforest/pubs/fypubs/240.wl.pdf

Moffitt, T.E., A. Caspi, H. Harrington, and B. Milne. 2002. "Males on the Life-Course—Persistent and Adolescence-Limited Antisocial Pathways: Follow-up at Age 26." *Development and Psychopathology*, 14. 179–206.

Monsebraaten, L. 2011. "Foster Kids Struggle to Make It as Adults." *Toronto Star*. June 12. A1.

Montegomery, S. 2008. "Foster Parents Charged: Accused of Sexually Abusing Children." *The Montreal Gazette*. April 15.

Murphy Kilbride, K., J. Pollard, M. Friendly, and J. Dotsch. 1998. *Early Differences Experienced by Visible Minority Children*. Toronto: Metropolis–Toronto Centre of Excellence. Research and Policy.

Musick, J.S. 1990. "Adolescents as Mothers: The Being and the Doing." *Zero to Three*. December.

Nation Talk, n.d. Retrieved February 1, 2013, from http://www .nationtalk.ca/modules/news/article.php?storyid=50487

National Longitudinal Survey of Child and Youth. 2007. "Detailed Information for 2006–2007 (Cycle 7)." Retrieved from http://www23.statcan.gc.ca/imdb/p2SV.pl?Function =getSurvey&SurvId=4450&SurvVer=1&InstaId=16044& InstaVer=7&SDDS=4450&lang=en&db=imdb&adm=8 &dis=2

National Marriage Project. 2010. "The State of Our Union—Marriage in America." University of Virginia. Retrieved from http://www.dss.virginia.gov/files/about/sfi/intro

National Research Conference. 1998. *Linking Research to Policy*. Banff, AB: National Research Conference.

Need Great Info, 2012. Retrieved February 1, 2013, from http://www.needgreatinfo.com/parenting.html

Newman, F. 1993. *Children in Crisis: Support for Teachers and Parents*. Toronto: Scholastic Canada.

Nirdosh, S. 1998. "Refugee Families: Reactions to Stress and Trauma." *Early Childhood Diversity Network Canada Newsletter*. Fall.

Nock, S.L. 1998. "A Comparison of Marriages and Cohabiting Relationships." *Journal of Family Issues* 16 (1). 53–76.

Norrie McCain, M., F.J. Mustard, and K. McCuaig. 2012. *Early Years Study 3—Making Decisions, Taking Action*. May. Toronto: Margaret & Wallace McCain Family Foundation.

O'Connell, D. 2007. *Single Parenting by Choice*. Parents Canada. Retrieved February 4, 2013, from http://www.parents canada.com/family-life/single-parenting-by-choice

Ontario Association of Children's Aid Societies. n.d. "Why Build Bridges to Belonging." Retrieved February 4, 2013, from http://www2.oacas.org/pubs/building_bridges/en/31.html

Parents without Partners. n.d. "Mission Statement." Retrieved from http://www.parentswithoutpartners.org/about.htm

Pearce, T. 2012. "The Painful New Realities of International Adoption." *The Globe and Mail*. February 18. A8. Retrieved February 20, 2013, from http://www.theglobe andmail.com/life/parenting/the-painful-new-realities-of -international-adoption/article547159

PFLAG. n.d. "Stories." Retrieved from http://www.pflag.ca

Philp, M. 2007. "Nearly Half of Children in Crown Care Are Medicated." *The Globe and Mail*. June 9. A1.

Pimento, B., and D. Kernested. 2010. *Healthy Foundations in Child Care*, 4th ed. Toronto: Nelson Thomson Learning.

Pitt, S. 2004. "Kinda Brown." *Tree House Canadian Family*. March. 28.

Pollack, S., and J. Vaughn. 1987. *Politics of the Heart: A Lesbian Parenting Anthology*. Ithaca, NY: Firebrand Books.

Poston, Carlos W.S. 1990. "The Biracial Identity Development Model: A Needed Edition." *Journal of Counselling and Development* 69. 152–55.

Richardson, B. 1994. "Improving Native Education." *Early Childhood Education* 27 (1). Spring–Summer.

Riedman, A., M.A. Lamanna, and A. Nelson. 2003. *Marriages and Families*. Toronto: Thomson Nelson.

Rockwell, R.E., L.C. Andre, and M.K. Hawley. 2010. *Families and Educators as Partners*. Wadsworth Cengage Learning.

Rotermann. M. 2005. "Sex, condoms and STDs among young people." *Health Reports* 16(3), 39–45. Retrieved November 15, 2012, from http://www.sexualityandu.ca/resource -library/statistics/age-at-first-intercourse1

Safe Schools Action Team. 2008. *Shaping a Culture of Respect in Our Schools: Promoting Safe and Healthy Relationships*, Ontario Ministry of Education, Toronto: Queen's Printer for Ontario, 2008. Retrieved February 1, 2013, from http://www.edu.gov.on.ca/eng/teachers/RespectCulture.pdf

Samovar, L.A., R.E. Porter, and R.E. McDaniel. 2007. *Communication between Cultures*, 6th ed. Toronto: Thomson Wadsworth.

Shadow Report. 2011. *Honouring the Children*. The United Nations Committee on the Rights of the Child, First Nations Child and Family Caring Society of Canada, and KAIROS: Canadian Ecumenical Justice Initiatives. October 24.

Sheehan, N., and L. Wood. 1993. *Adoption and the Schools Project: A Guide for Educators*. Washington, DC: Department of Health and Human Services.

Shimoni, R., and J. Baxter. 2008. *Working with Families*, 4th ed. Toronto: Pearson Addison Wesley.

Siad, S., A. Kassam, and S. Bhattacharya. 2007. "Mixing and Matching, to Mom's Chagrin." *Toronto Star*. July 1. A1.

Soloman, R., and C.P. Liefeld. 1998. "Effectiveness of a Family Support Center Approach to Adolescent Mothers: Repeat Pregnancy and School Drop-Out Rates." *Family Relations* 47 (2). 139–144.

Springate, K.W., and D.A. Stegelin. 1999. *Building School and Community Partnerships through Parent Involvement*. Columbus, OH: Merrill Prentice Hall.

Stacey, J., and Biblarz, T. 2001. "(How) Does the Sexual Orientation of Parents Matter?" *American Sociological Review*, 66. 159–183.

Statistics Canada. 2006a. "Aboriginal Peoples in Canada in 2006: Inuit, Métis and First Nations, 2006 Census. Table 20." Retrieved from http://www.12.statcan.ca/english/census06/analysis/aboriginal/children.cfm

———. 2006b. "The Risk of First and Second Marriage Dissolution." *The Daily*. June 28. Retrieved from http://www.statcan.ca/Daily/English/060628/d060628b.htm

———. 2006c. "Study: A Portrait of Mixed Ethnocultural Couples." Retrieved February 4, 2013, from http://www.statcan.gc.ca/daily-quotidien/100420/dq100420b-eng.htm

———. 2007. *Census 2006 Analysis Series*. Retrieved from http://www.12.statcan.ca/english/census06/analysis/index.cfm

———. 2009. "Aboriginal Languages in Canada. Emerging Trends and Perspectives on Second Language Acquisition." Mary Jane Norris. Retrieved February 22, 2013, from http://www.statcan.gc.ca/pub/11-008-x/2007001/9628-eng .htm

———. 2010. "Child Care for First Nations Children Living Off Reserve, Métis Children, and Inuit Children." Leanne C. Findlay and Dafna E. Kohen, October 19. Retrieved February 2, 2013, from http://www.statcan.gc.ca/pub/11 -008-x/2010002/article/11344-eng.htm

———. 2011. "2006 Census: Aboriginal Peoples in Canada in 2006. Inuit, Metis and First Nations 2006 Census." Retrieved February 22, 2013, from http://www12.statcan .ca/census-recensement/2006/as-sa/97-558/p4-eng.cfm

———. 2013. "Selected Income Concepts by Main Family Type." *The Daily*. Retrieved February 22, 2013, from http://www.statcan.gc.ca/daily-quotidien/110615/t110615b1-eng.htm

Stroud, J.E., J.C. Stroud, and L.M. Staley. 1999. "Adopted Children in the Early Childhood Classroom." *Early Childhood Education Journal*, 24(4). 229-234

Submission of the Assembly of First Nations to the United Nations. Committee on the Elimination of Racial Discrimination, 80th Session, February 13–March 9, 2012, United Nations, Geneva, Response to Canada's 19th and 20th Periodic Reports. Retrieved February 20, 2013, from http://www.afn.ca/index.php/en/news-media/latest-news/assembly-of-first-nations-calls-for-stable -and-equitable-funding-for-f

Suhasini, G., and M. Jetelina. 2012. "The Top 25." *Canadian Immigrant. Ontario Edition*. June.

The 519. 2013. *Queer and Trans Family Programs. Overview and Schedule: 2013*. Retrieved from http://www.the519 .org/programsservices/familyandchildren/familyplanning andpre-natalcourses

Thomas, L., and S. Learoyd. 1990. "Native Child Care: In the Spirit of Caring. Speech delivered to the Native Council of Canada, Ottawa." January.

Toronto District School Board. 2011. "Equitable and Inclusive Schools. Challenging Homophobia and Heterosexism. A K-12 Curriculum." Resource Guide. Retrieved from http://www.tdsb.on.ca

Toronto Star. 2007a. "Aboriginal Languages." *Toronto Star*. February 18. 1A.

———. 2007b. "Divorce Canadian Style." *Toronto Star*. June 23. L12.

———. 2007c. "Parents of Multiracial Children, Grownups Say the Darnedest Things." *Toronto Star*. April 7. L5.

Trawick-Smith, J. 2010. *Early Childhood Development. A Multicultural Perspective*. Merrill.

Tribal Laws of the Eastern Algonquin. 2005. "Temagami Native Web." Retrieved February 4, 2013, from http://temagami.nativeweb.org/tribal-laws.html

UNICEF. 2009. "Canadian Supplement to the State of the World's Children." Aboriginal Children's Health: Leaving No Child Behind. Retrieved February 4, 2013, from http://www.unicef.ca/sites/default/files/imce_uploads/DISCOVER/OUR%20WORK/ADVOCACY/DOMESTIC/POLICY%20ADVOCACY/DOCS/Leaving%20no%20child%20behind%2009.pdf

Vanier Institute of the Family. 1994. "Profiling Canada's Families." Pamphlet. Ottawa: Vanier Institute of the Family.

———. 2011. "4 in 10 Marriages End in Divorce." *Fascinating Families* 26(41). Retrieved February 22, 2013, from http://www.vanierinstitute.ca/modules/news/newsitem.php?ItemId=74

———. 2012a. "Teen Pregnancy: Supporting Young Parents." *Fascinating Families* (23) 46.

———. 2012b. "Military Families—By the Numbers." Retrieved February 4, 2013, from http://www.vanierinstitute.ca/modules/news/newsitem.php?ItemId=472

Vezina, M., and M. Turcotte. 2009. "Forty-year-old Mothers of Pre-school Children: A Profile." Statistics Canada. Retrieved February 4, 2013, from http://www.statcan.gc.ca/pub/11-008-x/2009002/article/10918-eng.htm

Wallerstein, J., J. Lewis, and S. Blakeslee. 2000. *The Unexpected Legacy of Divorce: A Twenty-five Year Landmark Study*. New York: Hyperion Press.

Ward, M., and M. Belanger. 2011. *The Family Dynamic: A Canadian Perspective*, 5th ed. Toronto: Nelson.

Wheeler, L. 2004. "Adopting an Older Child: How to Help Yourself and Your Child." *Adoption Roundup: Journal of the Adoption Council of Ontario*. April.

Whirling Rainbow. n.d. Retrieved January 29, 2013, from http://whirlingrainbow.com/online%20heartofone.htm

Wickens, E. 1993. "I Will Have a Child in My Class with Two Moms." *Young Children*. March.

———. 2002."How We Live. *Maclean's*. November 4.

Wigod, R. 2000. "Conference Celebrates Unique Education: There Are Hundreds of Innovative College Programs That Often Go Unnoticed by Many Who Benefit. "*Vancouver Sun*. May 1.

Witt, J., and A. Hermiston. 2010. *SOC: A Matter of Perspective*. Whitby, ON: McGraw Hill.

Wotherspoon, E., and N. Petrowski. 2008. "Supporting the Social-Emotional Development of Infants and Toddlers in Foster Care." *IMP: The Newsletter of Infant Mental Health Promotion*. Volume 52. Winter.

Wright, K., D.A. Stegelin, and L. Hartle. 2007. *Building Family, School, and Community Partnerships*, 3rd ed. Upper Saddle River, NJ: Pearson/Merrill Prentice Hall.

Zabin, L.S., R. Wong, R.M. Weinick, and M.R. Emerson. 1992. "Dependency in Urban Black Families Following the Birth of an Adolescent's Child." *Journal of Marriage and the Family* 54 (3). August. 496–507.

Created by Julian

Chapter 10

FAMILIES IN TRANSITION: ISSUES FACING MANY FAMILIES

Monkey Business Images/Shutterstock

"While all children are born equal, they don't all have the same opportunities to flourish … nothing in today's society is more disgraceful than the marginalization of some young people who are driven to isolation and despair. We must not tolerate such disparities."

—Michaëlle Jean, Former Governor General of Canada, September 27, 2005
(in World Vision Canadian Programs, 2005–2010)

LEARNING OUTCOMES

After studying this chapter, you will be able to

1. analyze the impact of becoming a parent, the stages of parenthood, and the ways parenting styles influence children

2. discuss the impact of siblings on the family unit

3. assess the needs of families with children with special needs and develop strategies for supporting them

4. discuss the impact on families when an adult member has a chronic illness or disability, or when a death occurs

5. identify issues for families when a natural disaster occurs

6. explore the issues of substance abuse and its impact on families

7. identify the challenges facing families living with violence

8. examine the needs of families when one member is incarcerated

In this chapter we will explore the role of parenting and issues that may affect any of the families that you have been reading about in this text or may meet in your early learning environment. In Canada today, many families are struggling in their role as parents:

> Chemical dependency, economic concerns, marital discord, illness of parents and family members, homelessness, limited human resources and a variety of other issues may play roles in the scarcity of emotional and physical parenting. Yes, this does happen with far greater frequency than children deserve. However, with support, many parents do overcome such issues to return to parenting and to become better parents. Our goal is to nurture the growth and development of children. This is our common ground. (Wright, Streglin, and Hartle, 2007: 274)

PARENTAL EXPECTATIONS

From the outset, despite our preconceived notions about children and childhood, infants force parents to rethink who they are and how they do things. Ambert (1997) notes that

> despite what parents expected their infants to be like, each baby requires different types of care that shape parents' perceptions of and experiences surrounding the "easiness" of their baby. "Easy" babies make parents feel adequate, happy, rewarded, and successful as parents, while more "challenging"' demanding, or less healthy babies often make them feel inadequate, stressed, and ineffective (Albanese, 2009: 59).

RESEARCH ON PARENTING

The report *Vital Communities, Vital Support* takes an in-depth look at parents' parenting behaviour, their knowledge about how children grow and develop, their confidence in parenting, and how each of these elements are related. According to research,

- *there is not enough positive parenting and too much negative parenting by Canadian parents.* Fathers in particular are struggling. Fifteen percent of mothers and nearly 30 percent of fathers have insufficient levels of positive parenting, and 25 percent of mothers and 30 percent of fathers have excessive levels of negative parenting. And this happens across all socio-demographic groups—it is not confined to parents with low income and education.

- *Parents' knowledge about child development is substantially lacking.* Only half of mothers and one third of fathers demonstrate high knowledge about how children grow and develop. There is significant room for improvement in parents' knowledge of child development.

- *Parents' lack of confidence in their parenting is even greater than their lack of knowledge about child development.* Only one third of mothers and one quarter of fathers have high confidence in their parenting. Why does this matter? Because both high knowledge about child development and high confidence in parenting are associated with high quality parenting behaviours for both mothers and fathers.

- *Too many parents feel left to handle new parenthood on their own.* Only about half of parents felt they received enough emotional and practical support when they first became parents. It is not only at the time they become parents that today's parents of young children do not feel supported in their role as parents. No more than half of the parents surveyed feel they receive strong support for their parenting role from any of their close relationships—their spouse/partners, their own parents or from their extended family and friends, and only about one quarter of parents reported strong support from their neighbourhood community. (Crill Russell et al., n.d.; emphasis added)*

---

* C. Crill Russell, et al. *Vital Communities, Vital Support. How Well Do Canada's Communities Support Parents Of Young Children? Phase 2 Report. What Parents Tell Us.* (Pembroke, Phoenix Centre). Reprinted by permission of the Phoenix Centre for Children and Families.

This survey, as well as Invest in Kids' earlier research, tells us Canadian parents are committed to their role. They understand that being a parent is the most important thing that they will do, but they feel unsupported and vulnerable. Many do not truly understand how children grow and develop and what their role is as a parent in maximizing this development. As a society, we need to provide the necessary supports for parents to develop the skills they need and the confidence to carry them out.

STAGES AND STYLES OF PARENTING

Despite the many pressures on modern-day families and the shifting roles of men and women, the birth of a child remains perhaps the most joyous event a family can experience. With the arrival of a baby, parents embark on an exciting journey that will last for the rest of their lives.

STAGES OF PARENTING

Children change everything! Few parents are prepared for the amazing and challenging role they now will play. Galinsky (1987: 86) summarizes her views on how parenthood changes adults:

> Taking care of a small, dependent, growing person is transforming, because it brings us in touch with our baser side, it exposes our vulnerabilities as well as our nobility. We lose our sense of self, only to find it and have it change again and again. We learn to nurture and care. Often our fantasies are laid bare, our dreams are in a constant tug of war with realities. And perhaps we grow. In the end, we have learned more about ourselves, about the cycles of life, and humanity itself. Most parents describe themselves as more responsible, more accepting, more generous than before they had children.

Galinsky (1987) also outlines the six stages of parenthood:

- *Image-making:* Parents prepare for pregnancy and for changes in themselves and in their relationships with others.

- *Nurturing:* From the birth until the child is 18 to 24 months, parents balance their own needs with the child's and set priorities.

- *Authority:* From the child's second birthday and lasting two to three years, parents become rule givers and enforcers as they attempt to set structure and order in place.

- *Interpretive:* From the child's preschool period and extending to adolescence, parents interpret the world for their children, teaching morals and values.

- *Interdependent:* Parents share their power with the children.

- *Departure:* Parents evaluate themselves as the children prepare to leave home.

PARENTING STYLES

A parenting style is a general approach to socializing children that includes the amount of warmth, communication, and control parents provide, along with their expectations for children's mature behaviour. Diana Baumrind (1967) devised a system for categorizing parenting styles—Authoritative, Authoritarian, Permissive-Indulgent and Permissive-Neglectful (see Table 10.1).

A survey of 23,000 children and their parents asked 23 questions about their parenting styles in 1994 and 1996 and found that one third of parents are what American psychologist Barbara Coloroso terms "backbones"—the most positive parents who provide a

Inside LOOK

A Canadian study of close to 3,000 children (ages 2–11) from 96 different Canadian neighbourhoods found that children had high levels of physical aggression and lower pro-social behaviour in families where more punitive parenting (highly disciplinary) was used (Romano et al., 2005 in Albanese, 2009: 73).

TABLE 10.1	Diana Baumrind's Classification of Parenting Styles	
PARENTING STYLE	DESCRIPTION	EXPECTED CHILD OUTCOMES
Authoritative	Parent is democratic, warm, and encourages communication when problems arise. Makes final, firm decisions about punishments or rules. Expects a moderate level of maturity in children.	Many children of authoritative parents become highly competent, socially, emotionally, and intellectually. They are more cooperative with teachers and peers and are more independent.
Authoritarian	Parent is very controlling and allows no discussion when making demands. Provides less warmth in interactions.	Many children of authoritarian parents are less independent, have poor relationships with peers, and can be either submissive or aggressive. They tend to be more distrustful of others.
Permissive-Indulgent	Parent provides much warmth and encourages children to "speak their minds." Does not set rules for children and strives to create an environment of complete freedom. Social responsibility and maturity are not emphasized.	Many children of permissive-indulgent are less competent socially and intellectually. They are less independent and socially responsible. They have difficulty with self-control and learning rules and routines in school.
Permissive-Neglectful	Parent is generally detached and less warm. Is less responsive to the child's needs or bids for attention. No effort is made to guide or control behaviour.	Many children with permissive-neglectful parents are less competent, intellectually and socially. They have difficulty with self-control and exhibit conduct problems in school.

Source: Trawick-Smith, J. 2009. *Early Childhood Development: A Multicultural Perspective.* 5th ed. Prentice Hall. 478.

loving, caring environment; encourage independence; are consistent; and provide one-on-one interaction. One quarter are "brick walls"—inflexible, authoritarian, and demanding—and another one-quarter are considered "jellyfish"—irresponsible parents.

Parents display a variety of parenting styles, some of which may be very different from those by which they themselves were raised. They bring their own history and social skills to the process of parenting.

Other factors that affect parenting include

- the shift in parental roles and responsibilities, which has created new stressors as families attempt to find balance in their new lifestyle

- the age of parents

- the gender of the children (boys may be raised differently from girls, in accordance with cultural and social ideas about gender roles)

- parents in the same family having different styles of parenting

Parenting style has a bigger impact on children's behaviour than any other influence, including poverty or being raised by a single parent.

Being a parent is a multifaceted and challenging opportunity to support and contribute to the growth and development of a child. Parental

Parenting style has a bigger impact on a child's behaviour than any other factor.

competence involves behavioural, affective, and cognitive components; parental self-efficacy is an important competency component. For example, the following findings have been reported about parents with high self-efficacy:

- They believe that they have the ability to effectively and positively influence the development and behaviour of their children and engage in positive parenting behaviours (Coleman and Karraker, 1998).

- They are more responsive to the needs of their children and they engage in direct interactions with their children (Mash and Johnston, 1983).

- They exhibit active coping strategies (Wells-Parker, Miller, and Topping, 1990).

- They perceive fewer behavioural problems in their children (Johnston and Mash, 1989).

The opposite is true for parents with low self-efficacy:

- They have higher rates of depression (Teti and Gelfand, 1991).

- They demonstrate greater defensive and controlling behaviour (Donovan, Leavitt, and Walsh, 1990).

- They have greater perceptions of child difficulties (Halpern, Anders, Garcia Coll, and Hua, 1994).

- They report higher stress levels (Wells-Parker, Miller, and Topping, 1990).

- They have a passive parental coping style, focus more on problems in relationships, demonstrate

more negative affect, experience elevated autonomic arousal, feel helpless in the role of parent, and use punitive disciplinary strategies (Bugental and Cortez, 1988; Bugental and Shennum, 1984, in Pelletier and Brent, 2002: 4–5).

Parents who are considered "successful" value children's learning and play an active role in their child's early learning environments and beyond. They encourage peer-to-peer relationships and are involved with their children in activities and experiences in their community. These social networks bind the community together and parents often advocate at the local, provincial, and federal level on behalf of families in their community.

Invest in Kids worked on four critical fronts to provide all of us with the skills we needed to make a difference in the lives of young families:

1. *Supporting discovery:* Identify what works by searching out and supporting best practices and model approaches; identify what's important by pinpointing gaps between knowledge and practice; work to develop a better understanding of the attitudes, behaviours, and needs of Canadians when it comes to caring for our youngest children.

2. *Changing the climate:* Work to create a social environment that enhances understanding of the critical importance of our children's earliest years and the crucial role that all of us play in determining a child's future.

3. *Providing the tools:* Develop educational resources such as videos, booklets, magazine supplements, and posters that equip parents,

Ninety-two percent of parents believe that parenting is the most important thing they will ever do.

caregivers, and other Canadians with the knowledge and skills they need to nurture children best.

4. *Turning theory into practice:* Support training through workshops, conferences, and curricula to help professionals develop more proactive and effective healthy-child development practices.

BEST START RESOURCE CENTRE, 2011

The Best Start Resource Centre 2011 Ontario survey of parental knowledge about early brain development examined the attitudes and knowledge of parents of children aged 0–6 years. Despite their understanding of child development, some parents felt that responding to infant cues might spoil them: 12% of parents felt that for infants and babies up to one year of age, their cries and signals did not indicate a genuine need for parental attention. 31% of respondents believed that picking up an infant every time s/he cries will spoil them.

Results of this survey clearly showed that parents want simple, practical, research-based information (i.e. tips, activities, approaches, do's and don'ts), to help guide them to doing what's best for their baby or child, and their developing brain, at each stage of development. Specific areas parents were interested in include, but were not limited to: Recommendations for nurturing developing brains with healthy nutrition (including breastfeeding); suggestions for stimulating the five senses through daily experiences; characteristics of safe, engaging environments for babies and young children; ways to strengthen the infant-parent or primary caregiver relationship (i.e. infant attachment) and to promote its importance for healthy (brain) development. (Source: Best Start Resource Centre, 2011)[*]

SIBLINGS

Recent research suggests that sibling relationships may have as much, or more, influence on the development of children than the parent–child relationship (Tucker and Updegraff, 2009; Kluger, 2006). "Almost 80 percent of Canadians have at least one sibling. It is an important type of family relationship and one that outlasts the parent–child relationship" (Ambert, 2006). As children grow, in many households, siblings will spend more time together than they will with their parents or their peers. Older siblings may well provide cultural socialization and are often required to spend time caring for younger brothers and sisters. "Sometimes they play a direct role in promoting learning. It is not uncommon for an older sister or brother to give the names of objects, provide toys, and stimulate cognitive development. This teaching role becomes even more pronounced as children get older" (Trawick-Smith, 2009: 471)[†]. Conflicts are an inevitable part of family life but when siblings do not get along with each other, this can have a huge impact on the family dynamic. This is particularly true when this involves bullying, physical interactions, and hurtful comments.

Younger siblings that have aggressive older siblings are at risk for problems with conduct, academics and peers yet older siblings can serve as a buffer for younger siblings in times of family upheaval. Older children who have difficult temperaments

---

[*]Adapted/Reprinted with permission by the Best Start Resource Centre.

[†] TRAWICK-SMITH, JEFFREY, EARLY CHILDHOOD DEVELOPMENT: A MULTICULTURAL PERSPECTIVE, 5th Edition, © 2010. Reprinted and Electronically reproduced by permission of Pearson Education, Inc., Upper Saddle River, NJ.

or special needs may influence parental ability to provide appropriate nurturance to younger siblings. When differential treatment is seen as unfair by siblings, issues may arise. Poor emotional and behavioural functioning may occur when children perceive that siblings receive more warmth from parents than they do. (Couchenour and Chrisman, 2011: 67–68)[*]

As families grow, the news of an approaching child will have an impact on all members of the family. It can be exciting and unsettling at the same time for a young child. Changes in the child's routine should not coincide, if possible, with the arrival of the new baby. Some hospitals run sibling workshops in which the upcoming event is explained in age-appropriate terms. The infant room staff might invite the child to practise helping out with the babies. The child-care centre might also support the child by setting up the dramatic play centre as a nursery with a variety of dolls and materials borrowed from the infant room. The family could also be invited to the centre, with their preschooler(s) taking the lead to introduce the baby to his or her friends.

Sibling rivalry is inescapable in most families. Some children initially make a wonderful connection with the new baby, only to have issues of territory or jealousy surface later in the baby's life as he or she becomes more mobile. Anderson and Rice (1992) found that "girls demonstrated more positive behaviours, such as empathy and support, toward brothers and sisters than did boys, but they showed equal amounts of aggression and hostility as boys." In some stepfamilies and divorced families we see more negative sibling relationships due to the complexity of the relationships but for many children, the positive outweighs the negatives.

---

[*] From COUCHENOUR/CHRISMAN. *Families, Schools and Communities, 4E.* © 2011 Wadsworth, a part of Cengage Learning, Inc. Reproduced by permission. www.cengage.com/permissions.

Courtesy of Lynn Wilson

Off to a great start with this new sister!

BOOKS FOR CHILDREN

Waiting for the Sun, by A. Lohans

Welcome Precious, by N. Grimes

Waiting for Baby, by R. Fuller

Hello Baby, by L. Rockwell

The New Baby, by M. Mayer

When the New Baby Comes, I'm Moving Out, by M. Alexander

Baby on the Way and What Baby Needs, by W. Sears, M. Sears, C. Watts Kelly, and R. Andriani

How to Drive Your Sister Crazy, by D. Shore and L. Rankin

Babies Can't Eat Kimchee!, by N. Pats

Baby Baby, Blah Blah Blah, by J. Shipton

Babies Don't Eat Pizza: A Big Kid's Book About Baby Brothers and Baby Sisters, by D. Danzig

Brothers: Best Friends Growing Up, by S. Ramrattan Smith and B. Smith

Bratty Brothers and Selfish Sisters: All About Sibling Rivalry, by R.W. Alley

Oh, Brother … Oh, Sister. A Sister's Guide to Getting Along, by B. Whitney and L. Cornell

BOOKS FOR ADULTS

Siblings Without Rivalry: How to Help Your Children Live Together So You Can Live Too, by A. Faber and E. Mazlish

Understanding Sibling Rivalry—The Brazelton Way, by T. Brazelton and J. Sparrow

Beyond Sibling Rivalry: How to Help Your Children Become Co-operative, Caring and Compassionate, by P. Goldenthal

101 Activities for Siblings Who Squabble, by L. Aber

The Everything Parent's Guide to Raising Siblings: Tips to Eliminate Rivalry, Avoid Favouritism and Keep the Peace, by L. Sorina

Making Brothers and Sisters Best Friends: How to Fight the Good Fight at Home, by S. Mally, S. Mally, and G. Mally

Loving Each One Best: A Caring and Practical Approach to Raising Siblings, by N. Samalin and C. Whitney

The Sibling Effect: What the Bonds Among Brothers and Sisters Reveal About Us, by J. Kluger

FAMILIES WITH CHILDREN WHO HAVE SPECIAL NEEDS

The past few decades have brought enormous changes to the ways in which families, teachers, and governments define the place of children with special needs in early learning environments. Medical advances have made it possible for children with serious medical issues to survive and, as a result, we are seeing more and more of these children in early learning environments. "Five large Canadian studies have reported that 25–30 percent of five-year olds in the general population are developmentally delayed at school entry in one or more of crucial school-readiness skills" (Doherty, 2008: 30).

Although the concept of inclusiveness has become increasingly entrenched in ECE practice and philosophy, barriers to the successful integration of children with special needs in traditional settings persist. The presence of a child with special needs can place enormous demands on a family, and we must be committed to providing comprehensive, coordinated, and family-focused services that will provide the support that this family will need.

The response of parents to their child's disability and the feelings associated with it can significantly affect the parent–teacher partnership. All members of the family are affected when a child has special needs. Within the family itself, there are increased pressures that may exacerbate existing issues, and divorce rates are higher in this family type. Siblings will also feel the pressure as parents attempt to provide the best possible care for their child with special needs. Parental involvement is critical but as observed by Krajicek and Moore (1993: 13),

Teachers may need support from families to learn how to use specialized equipment.

it does not occur until parents have adapted to the children's disabilities. Not all parents adjust. Those who do become committed to all facets of the care of their infants and toddlers with special needs. These parents realize the benefits that they and their children alike derive from quality child care.

Not surprisingly, the more severe the child's disability, the greater the impact on the family situation. Some families may benefit from counselling that will help the family face continuing periods of grief and assistance in handling the special problems and environmental adjustments that having a child with a disability entails. Counselling may help parents understand the diagnosis, educational planning, and future prognosis. Sessions also provide a forum in which parents can openly express and work through any feelings of anger, fear, and anxiety, as well as teach self-help skills, group relaxation, self-praise, and self-instruction. As siblings are an important aspect of family-centred practice, in many cases the counselling sessions will actively involve them (Winzer, 2008). Many families may also want to form groups of parents who have children with similar disabilities. McMaster University researchers conducted a study of nine parent-run support groups in Ontario to explore the groups' perceived effect in providing parents with support, reducing stress, and improving parents' ability to deal with disability issues. Results indicated substantial benefits for those belonging to the groups. Parents were seen to gain increased skills, a greater sense of power, and a sense of belonging. Participants were able to connect with each other and provide support and skills to deal with the day-to-day issues of raising a child with special needs (Winzer, 2008).

The financial pressures and the lack of child care and support from their employers places many families at even greater risk A two-year study, commissioned by the Canadian Union of Postal Workers and co-authored by Sharon Hope Irwin and University of Guelph family studies professor Donna Lero, was the first Canadian research on the employment barriers that parents of children with special needs experience. According to parent respondents,

- 39 percent worked reduced hours
- 26 percent changed jobs
- 46 percent altered their work schedule
- 68 percent turned down overtime
- 27 percent passed up a promotion

Inside LOOK

We have been through sleepless nights, toilet training, temper tantrums, food allergies, first day of school, discipline, behaviour challenges, medications, tube feeding, specialized equipment needs, government programs, graduation, planning for the future—these are some of the challenges parents face when raising children with special needs. Most parents look to others for guidance, advice, and comfort and found it in other parents. When our children have disabilities, we especially need one another. We want to talk to another parent who has "been there." When parents are raising children with disabilities, they are usually in uncharted territory, even the people who are closest to us—our families and friends—may have difficulty knowing how to support us best and may distance themselves. This can leave families isolated and on their own.

The Hamilton Family Network brings families together by connecting parents to one another for information and emotional support. Resource Parents are trained and experienced so they can offer support to other parents. Families are carefully matched based on disability and/or a specific challenge that arises from the child's disability. The support Resource Parents offer to other parents is the foundation upon which rests all the other work of the Network. Visit **http://www.hfnet.ca/**.

Source: Family Alliance Ontario. 2007. "Is Your World Touched by Disability? So Is Ours!" *The Compass*, Vol. 12, No. 1: 4. Reprinted by permission of Family Alliance Ontario.

Inside LOOK

Children's Futures Start with Birth

What might have been considered alternative therapies at one time have now become mainstream strategies for supporting children and their families. One such example is chiropractic services. Deirdre Edwards, a health lecturer and clinician with 40 years of healthcare experience, continues private chiropractic practice in England. She states that "children need adequate rest and sleep to assimilate, regenerate and restore cell growth and health enabling them to be receptive for learning". Unlike adults who portray symptoms of lethargy, slowness & delayed response rate when suffering sleep loss; children have a heightened activity rate, an inability to concentrate and portray out of character behavioural swings. Deirdre advocates a healthy nervous system with optimum neural interplay from the brain and spinal cord throughout the body, pervading neurons to all parts of the body efficiently without interruption. Interruption can cause discomfort and pain affecting sleep, which in turn impacts health and learning. The research indicates successful outcomes through cranial or skeletal checks and gentle treatment by a skilled paediatric chiropractor can ensure the integrity of the nervous system.

A five year study in a private clinic in England revealed children can present with behavioural and developmental problems related to their birth. The clinical studies revealed many did not sleep as much as they should for their age and developmental requirements. The study of 145 record cards revealed many of these children suffered some form of trauma at birth, and had been unsettled, unpredictable, cried inconsolably, with sleep problems since and were often described as "naughty children" seeking labels for this behaviour (attention deficit, attention deficit hyperactivity, autism, sensory cognitive dysfunction, clumsy). From the records it was found that all children in the study presented with one or more areas of neurological dysfunction—all with delay in some area of development, some marginally

continued

delayed, some with more severe social, language and motor delay. Chiropractic treatment helped these children. The results endorsed the suitability and benefit of certain types of chiropractic and advocates wider recognition, accessibility and use. The published article requested heightened awareness by midwives, health workers, educationalists to intervene earlier and refer to qualified Paediatric Chiropractors. Gentle Chiropractic intervention would be a simple low cost application and solution to the spiralling costs of treating, teaching and assisting children with developmental delays later in life.

Source: Reprinted by permission of Deirdre Edwards.

- 64 percent of two-parent families with one parent unemployed reported their child's special needs as the major factor in losing their job

- 88 percent said they felt tired and overloaded

- 90 percent said they were stressed as they tried to balance work and family obligations (Monsebraaten, 1998)

Parents may also face isolation, particularly if the child has a disability that draws attention in

Inside LOOK

Innovative Program at Canada Post

In 1996, a special-needs pilot project became one of 12 programs funded by the CUPW Child Care Fund. As stipulated in the most recent union contract, Canada Post puts $250,000 into the Child Care Fund every three months. Bankrolled by the corporation and developed and coordinated by the Canadian Union of Postal Workers, the special needs project helps parents pay for extra costs related to children's disabilities. It also offers families support and advice by phone, points them in the direction of community resources, improves their advocacy skills, and keeps them in touch with each other through a regular newsletter. Today,

- 93 percent of parents say it has reduced over-all family stress levels

- 99 percent say it has reduced financial stress

- 81 percent feel it has improved their morale and effectiveness at work

Child care coordinator Jamie Kass and board member of the Child Care Human Resources Sector Council states that among participants, 80 percent say the additional support they've been able to afford has helped their child's language, academic, and recreational skills. Ninety percent say their child is happier and has more self-esteem.

A book the union has published on the project, *Moving Mountains: Work, Family and Children with Special Needs*, is available through its website: **http://www.cupw.ca/index.cfm/ci_id/4911/la_id/1.htm.**

Source: Henderson, H. 2003. "Centennial Infant and Child Centre: Project Invests in Workers and Kids With Special Needs," *The Toronto Star*, 25 January, K11. Reprinted by permission of Torstar Syndication Services.

public. Family members may prefer to remain within the safety of their own home. Consideration must also be given to different cultural responses to disability. Some cultures view disability as fate and as something that must be endured. Other cultures see disability as the result of something the mother did wrong in pregnancy or as punishment for a sin, thus the family's fault and the family's responsibility. Such families find it difficult to accept, let alone seek, assistance from nonfamily members (Doherty-Derkowski, 1994). In working with families from a variety of cultural backgrounds, teachers must consider that families' language differences may be one major barrier to participation or engaging support for their family. Teachers need to be aware of religious beliefs and family traditions that might impact on the family dynamic.

FIGURE 10.1   Parental Reactions to Their Child's Disability

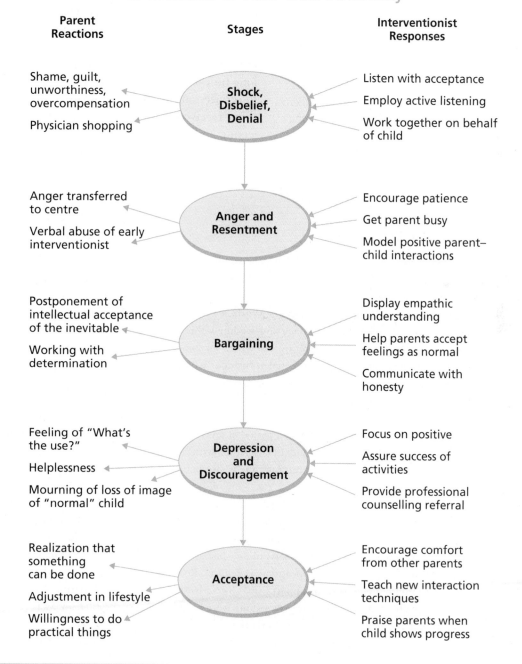

Source: COOK, RUTH E.; TESSIER, ANNETTE; KLEIN, M. DIANE, ADAPTING EARLY CHILDHOOD CURRICULA FOR CHILDREN IN INCLUSIVE SETTINGS, 5th Edition, © 2000. Reprinted and Electronically reproduced by permission of Pearson Education, Inc., Upper Saddle River, NJ.

According to Greey (1995: 19–20), many cultures intertwine health beliefs and attitudes towards disability with Christian, Muslim, Jewish, Hindu, or Buddhist religious or spiritual beliefs. Consequently, if a family believes that ghosts, demons, or evil spirits inhabit the body of a child with special needs, rituals of expiation will be much more highly valued than the support services of an infant development worker.

Cultural beliefs may have a significant impact on parents' expectations about their child's behaviour and ability:

> Families are sometimes fatalistic in their outlook regarding the potential their child might have and are reluctant to accept support. A family's attitude may be "well, this is the way he was born and we just have to live with it." On the other hand, parents who have a child with challenging behaviour or a disability may have to deal with isolation, blame, shame or other forms of stigma in the community. It is essential that staff take the time to understand how family members make sense of their child's experience and behaviours. Parents can benefit from the support of other families with similar experiences who share culturally appropriate information about strategies they have found useful. (Bradley and Kibera, 2007: 41)

HOW PARENTS CAN SUPPORT TEACHERS

It is vital for parents of children with special needs to have a sense of control over what happens with their children. When other people make important decisions about a child without the parent's input, the parent feels powerless and dependent. It takes a long time to gain a balance between feeling entitled to services and feeling humbly grateful for everything received. Families can help teachers by collecting and submitting medical records, providing background information for staff on the child's

Inside LOOK

It was difficult for us to accept the fact that Matthew wasn't just a high-energy child who needed teachers who would be accepting of his needs and just plain liked being with him. We felt he needed someone who could see that he was bright and had many strengths. We spent a lot of time blaming the teachers in the program for being too harsh and for having Matthew sit on a time-out chair many times during the day. We were worried about his self-image and we knew this behaviour strategy was wrong! He was quickly becoming the "bad kid" in the room, and whenever something went wrong he was assumed responsible. Virtually every night we were greeted at the door with another list of inappropriate things Matthew had done. Finally we met with the supervisor to discuss our concerns.

She said the teachers in the room were at a loss as to what to do with Matthew. None of the strategies they had tried seemed to work. She suggested that we have Matthew undergo an assessment at our local children's hospital. We reluctantly agreed. Over a period of several months Matthew was given a battery of tests. They revealed that he had attention deficit disorder with hyperactivity. He is now on medication and is calmer, happier, and able to concentrate. He is also building positive relationships with the children and teachers.

In retrospect I realize that we didn't want to believe there was something different about Matthew. It was easier to blame the teachers than to accept the truth. The teachers have since shared with us that although they had known something was not quite right with Matthew, they had not the expertise to identify a child with attention deficit disorder. Instead they had attributed much of what was happening with Matthew to what they saw as our inappropriate parenting. Recently, the teachers met with us and Matthew's doctor to find out how best to support him. Once adversaries, we are now partners. It's too bad that so much valuable time was lost while we adults were busy blaming each other for Matthew's behaviour—because in the end it was Matthew who suffered.

condition, monitoring and assisting in individualizing the training so that procedures are geared specifically to the child, keeping staff up to date on developments, health issues, etc., and assisting staff in advocating for necessary supports.

Research confirms that inclusion quality does not happen by itself. Practices including adjustments and modifications to the physical environment, equipment and materials, director's attitude and involvement, staff support, staff training, therapies, individual program plans, parents, involvement of typical children, boards or similar units, and preparing for transition to school are all critical to inclusion quality. Confidence, competence and commitment grow as staff work with a variety of children with special needs and benefit from supports that facilitate their success. (CCCF, 2009)*

ROLE OF THE TEACHER

- Teachers need to help families see that the disability or the label is just one small piece of who the child is. We need to stress that these are ordinary children with somewhat extraordinary needs for support. Not surprisingly, it is often the family that teaches this to the teacher.

- Teachers need to know that the stages parents with a child with a disability will go through are not necessarily linear. Each family is unique; some will cope effectively and others may struggle, feeling helpless and lost. A wise teacher will know the difference and adjust and accommodate to the best of his or her ability.

- Teachers need to appreciate that every member of the family will be impacted by a child with special needs.

- Teachers must understand that parents need to have hope; lack of hope paralyzes families.

- Strong communication skills—verbal and written—and an appreciation of cultural responses to children with special needs are important.

- Teachers need to have a strong child development background, and the ability to seek answers and to use resources to learn how best to support families.

- Teachers should share teaching strategies and new research information with the family on a regular basis through informal meetings and written and electronic communication.

- When exceptional children join the centre, it may be the first opportunity parents have had to see their child in a setting with children his or her own age. Teachers should encourage parents to look for ways in which the children are similar rather than different.

- As exceptional children grow older, the gap between them and the other children may become more apparent. Teachers need to continue to stress the gains children make.

- Parents—some of whom are coping without the assistance of family and friends—require teachers' support. English language learner families in particular may have trouble communicating with doctors and other medical professionals. Teachers can help by assisting parents with medical terminology, liaising, and so on.

- Teachers should be prepared to work with other professionals in the support of families.

- Like all families, parents of children with special needs are looking for teachers who will accept their children and not resent the extra time and effort they might require.

- Teachers must be flexible enough to adapt activities, the environment, and out-of-centre experiences so all children can participate. In the case of wheelchairs, teachers need to check the accessibility of outside locations when arranging field trips or outings for the children.

- Teachers who work with exceptional children need to be sensitive to the financial, medical, and emotional challenges parents may be facing.

- Other family members and children (if age appropriate) in the centre should be given a simple, matter-of-fact explanation of the child's disability. The parents of the child could be part of this discussion, providing information about medication, special equipment, toileting procedures, and so forth. It is important that everyone who works with the child has an understanding of how special equipment works.

- In cases where the exceptional child has siblings who are also enrolled in the centre, teachers

* Canadian Child Care Federation (CCCF). 2009. Resource Sheet #97. How Do You Know That You Are Moving Toward Inclusion? http://www.cccf-fcsge.ca/publications/resourcesheets_en.html. Reprinted by permission.

should do everything they can to support these children, who may resent the fact that their brother or sister receives more attention than they do, who may have to deal with negative reactions to the disability from their peers, and who may be pressured by their parents to excel in order to "make up" for the child with special needs. They may also be given additional household responsibilities as well as being involved in caring for their sibling.

- Above all, teachers should demonstrate respect, concern, empathy, and a sincere desire to work cooperatively with families.

SPECIALINK

SpeciaLink's goal is to expand the quality and quantity of opportunities for inclusion in child care, recreation, education, and other community settings, to young children with special needs and their families. SpeciaLink is a helpline, clearinghouse, and virtual resource and research centre, and provides personalized responses to specific questions, as well as referrals and links to other organizations and sources of help, information, and technical assistance including curriculum development and program evaluation. SpeciaLink provides fact sheets, books and videos, as well as

Inside LOOK

Our son, Jeffrey, has spina bifida. As I think back over the teachers he has had, one in particular always comes to mind. He was constantly asking me how he could support Jeffrey, and the effort he put into trying to put those ideas into place made him different from any other teacher that we had encountered. Nothing was impossible in this school-age program. The teacher would research and visit trip sites in advance to find the best possible routes for Jeffrey. There was never any question that Jeffrey wouldn't be included in any outing. This teacher was constantly focusing on Jeffrey's self-esteem.

One of his most successful ideas came when he located a wheelchair and held wheelchair races in the hallways. Jeffrey raced the teachers and the other children—and he always won! We have encountered many wonderful teachers, but what made this one different was that he saw Jeffrey as a whole person. He also recognized that we were the experts on Jeffrey's condition, and he worked with us to provide the best possible environment for him. He will never really know how much we appreciated his total acceptance of Jeffrey and the energy and enthusiasm he demonstrated!

Source: Reprinted by permission of Julie Cowie.

Inside LOOK

A friend asked me today if I had a dream for my special needs son Alexander. When I thought about this, I always thought that Alexander and my daughter would have their own dreams and as their mother I would do everything I could to make their dreams come true. But upon more reflection, I realized that I do have a dream for Alex. I want him to know that he is loved not only by those of us in his family but also by his friends. I hope that they will invite him to their parties, that they will want to sit beside him in circle, and that they will hold his hand when he struggles up the stairs. Along the way I can only hope that he is surrounded by peers who want to be with Alexander because he is their friend.

training in partnership with community organizations. SpeciaLink is committed to research that is informed and shaped by practice, and builds from the experiences of real-world child care with its limitations and its strengths. It connects researchers and policymakers with inclusive practices on the frontline. By identifying innovative practices, testing them, and presenting them to the wider field and to policymakers, SpeciaLink helps improve practice and inform policy. The SpeciaLink Early Childhood Inclusion Quality Scale, used by trained early childhood professionals, can be an effective, reliable tool to determine the quality of inclusion in child-care programs and the capacities of programs to improve inclusion quality. More information about SpeciaLink and the Quality Scale is available online at **http://www.specialinkcanada.org**.

BOOKS FOR CHILDREN

Oliver Onion: The Onion Who Learns to Accept and Be Himself, by D. Murrell (Autism)

The Sibling Slam Book: What It's Really Like to Have a Brother or Sister with Special Needs, by D. Meyer

What to Do When Your Brain Gets Stuck: A Kid's Guide to Overcoming OCD, by D. Huebner

Don't Call Me Special, by P. Thomas and L. Harker

We Can Do It!, by L. Dwight

What's Wrong with Timmy?, by M. Shriver and S. Speidel

Someone Just Like You, by T. Brown

Since We Are Friends: An Autism Picture Book, by C. Shally and D. Harrington

BOOKS FOR ADULTS

Cup of Comfort for Parents of Children with Autism: Stories of Hope and Everyday Success, by D. Flutie, L. Flutie, and C. Sell

More Than a Mom: Living a Full and Balanced Life When Your Child Has Special Needs, by H. Fawcett and A. Baskin

Driven to Distraction: Recognizing and Coping with Attention Deficit Disorder from Childhood through Adulthood, by E. Hallowell and J. Ratey

Breakthrough: Parenting for Children with Special Needs, by J. Winter

Parenting a Child with Sensory Processing Disorder: A Family Guide to Understanding and Supporting Your Sensory Sensitive Child, by C. Auer and S.L. Blumberg

Parenting Your Complex Child: Become a Powerful Advocate for the Autistic, Down Syndrome, PDD, Bipolar or Other Special Needs Child, by P.L. Morgan

Reflections from a Different Journey: What Adults with Disabilities Want All Parents to Know, by S. Klein and J. Kemp

The Secret Life of the Dyslexic Child, by R. Frank and K. Livingston

Autism Heroes: Portraits of Families Meeting the Challenge, by B. Firestone

Kids in the Syndrome Mix of ADHD, LD, Asperger's, Tourette's, Bipolar and More!, by M. Kutscher

Living with FASD: A Guide for Parents, by S. Graefe

Living with Prenatal Drug Exposure: A Guide for Parents, by L. Cowan and J. Lee

Hothouse Kids: The Dilemma of the Gifted Child, by A. Quart

Teaching by Design: Using Your Computer to Create Materials for Students with Learning Disabilities, by K. Voss

MENTAL HEALTH, CHRONIC ILLNESS, OR DISABILITY IN FAMILIES

For every parent who feels successful in his or her role, there are parents who are addicted, dysfunctional, or suffering from a mental illness, or who have limited skills or resources for support in the parental role. A child may have difficulty coming to terms with or understanding a parent's mental illness.

Research shows a significant connection between family dysfunction and mental health problems among children. The *National Longitudinal Survey of Children and Youth* (NLSCY) measures family functioning by looking at how well a family works together. It found that

Most children of people with psychiatric disorders find that mental illness in a parent is a tragic event that uproots their entire life. Strange, unpredictable behaviours in a loved one can be devastating, and a child's anxiety can be high as they struggle with each episode of illness. When Trudi Ford's husband was hospitalized with bi-polar disorder, Ford, who works with the United Way, turned to co-workers for help. She found the Family Association for Mental Health Everywhere (FAME), a group that offers support services for families affected by mental illness. "I found FAME and personally got support through their group sessions, but I was very interested in the fameKIDS program." FameKIDS helps children between the ages of 6 and 12 understand a family member's mental illness at an age-appropriate level in a safe, blame-free environment. Ford's daughter has been involved for a year now and the change has been substantial. "She's totally blossomed. My daughter really loves going to the sessions with the counsellors and finds it awesome to be with other kids whose family members have mental illnesses. Just being able to talk about mental illness and knowing she wasn't going to hurt our feelings, that she could ask whatever she wanted and no one would judge her was fantastic. It's a big, safe space for her." Hailey now better understands her father's mental illness and she has also developed a healthy scientific curiosity in neurology and how the brain works.

Source: Reprinted by permission of Trudi Ford, United Way Peel Region.

"Dysfunctional" families experience a great deal of stress in their daily lives. They often live in poverty and have few social supports. The challenge for many families is finding appropriate care for their child.

A growing concern also exists for children suffering from mental illnesses, that is, children who are depressed, or who have anxiety, schizophrenia, or bipolar or conduct disorders; roughly one in five Canadian children suffer from these illnesses and a lack of services and funds is a huge crisis. With an average of only 10 child psychiatrists graduating each year, and with cuts to education and social service funding, there are fewer social workers and psychologists available in schools and in communities to intervene early and refer children at risk for help (Gordon, 2005: D5).[*]

Teachers may also encounter families where a parent has a mental health issue, chronic illness, or disability that may affect his or her parenting and ability to provide for the family.

From an article published in *Child and Adolescent Psychiatry and Mental Health* in 2009, a group of Ontario based researchers used data from the Canadian Community Health Survey to estimate that there were 570,000 children under the age of 12—about 12.1%—who lived with parents who had mood, anxiety or substance abuse disorders in the year leading up to the survey. The study authors believe the real number was higher. (Smith, 2012)

The majority of children live with parents who report that they are in very good or excellent health. But that rate has been declining. One in three individuals will experience a mental health problem at some point in their lives. In Canada, that translates into more than 10 million people. It's been estimated that mental illness costs the Canadian economy $33 billion each year in disability and lost productivity. Another $6 billion to $8 billion is spent annually to treat mental disorders. More hospital days are consumed by people with a mental illness than by those with cancer and heart disease combined. At the same time, research shows that two-thirds of adults who experience mental illness never seek help; for adolescents, the figure is 75 percent (Andrews, 2008).[†]

In a speech at the Empire Club of Canada, the Honourable Michael Kirby, Chair of the Mental

---

[*]Gordon, A. 2005. "Crisis in Children's Mental Health," *The Toronto Star*, February 11, D5. Reprinted by permission of Torstar Syndication Services.

[†]Andrews, G. 2008. "Primed To Heal: Delivering Effective Mental Health Care," *Maclean's*, March 17. Reprinted by permission of Gavin Andrews.

Health Commission of Canada, stated that children's mental health issues in this country are reaching crisis proportions. Early diagnosis is critical but the lack of doctors trained in diagnosing and in treating mental health issues exacerbates the problem. In a recent survey, 38 percent of parents are embarrassed to say that their child has a mental health issue. This reinforces the notion that the stigma attached to a mental health issues continues to plague effective treatment. We must help bring these issues out of the shadows.

FACTS ABOUT DEPRESSION AND ANXIETY

Depression and anxiety disorders are the fastest rising health issues in Canada today and impact relationships, work, and family life. While only a small minority of children live with depressed parents, the impact on the child's well-being can be significant. Parents who are depressed are often withdrawn, tired, and despondent about the future, which creates a very stressful family environment.

Unfortunately, children in low-income families are more likely to live with a parent who is depressed.

> In 2000, 20 percent of children in low-income families (under $30,000 per year) had a parent who was depressed, compared to 6 percent of children in families with incomes over $60,000. (Canadian Council on Social Development, 2006: 14)

When teachers are working with parents whom they believe may be depressed, they should look for indicators; mothers

> look at their infants less often, touch them less often, have fewer positive facial expressions, and vocalize with infants less often than do non-depressed mothers ... babies of depressed mothers are fussier, more irritable, and less active than are babies of non-depressed mothers. Depression in babies is observed at birth. They have higher sensory thresholds and therefore need more stimulation to respond. They already show flat affect and low activity levels. Babies of mothers who are successfully treated for depression show no long-term adverse effects of their infant experience. Because the effects of mothers' depression on infants' behaviour are reversible, interventions to help depressed mothers and their infants are essential. (Brooks, 2006: 268)

SERIOUS ILLNESS

Families in which a serious illness is diagnosed will need time to adjust and adapt to the situation. Initially most of the attention is focused on the person who is ill and the needs of others in the family are often ignored. Household chores, meals, and supervision of the children may go by the wayside. Over time this may result in a crisis situation as the carer's ability to meet all of the needs of the family go unanswered. He or she may in fact become ill while attempting to cope with all of the demands placed on him or her.

Helping children understand the severity of the situation requires a great deal of tact and sensitivity. Hamilton (2003: 8) provides some strategies for helping parents explain serious illness to children:

- Tell your children what is happening as soon as possible. They will sense that something is wrong. It is far better for them to hear it from you than find out another way.

- Tell all your children at the same time, even if there is an age gap. The younger ones may not understand at the level of the older ones, but they will feel included. When the children know there are no secrets, they will be better able to support each other.

- Be open and honest. Children need your trust more than ever right now. Don't risk losing it.

- Children tend to cope best when they are well informed and there are no surprises about what is happening. Keep children up to date.

- Let other people caring for the children know how you have explained things and give them some direction on how to respond to children's questions, fears, and behaviours. Some parents write down explanations or answers to questions so that others will know how to respond to the children.

- Sometimes, different generations have different ideas of how or when to include children when something like this happens. Some believe you shouldn't tell or involve children because you don't want to upset them. Some believe children should be protected from the pain. Experts now believe we should not protect children from what is happening in their own family and that children will have a smoother adjustment to change if they feel included and if they know, to their level of understanding, what is going on. Children then have the opportunity to work at, and to work through their feelings at the same time as everyone else. A check to gauge that you are open and honest with children is if you can talk freely with other adults on the phone or face to face, and not have to be too careful about what you are saying because the kids are around. For example, use the word *cancer*. Let them hear it first from you.

- Explain the treatments planned for the near future or as much as you know. Will the parent be in hospital or at home? Will his or her appearance change? What will be the likely side effects of the disease or treatment?

- Explain how things will change for the children, and who will be looking after them. Will they be staying in their own home? Will they still be going to their usual activities? If plans are still uncertain/unknown, tell them you will let them know as soon as you know. Try to give your children even a rough idea of the length of time the treatment and recovery may take: months; by the season ("maybe after the end of the summer"); by a certain holiday or celebration; or "We just don't know how long Mommy is going to be sick," "I am going to be sick for a long time before I can get better."

- It is amazing what children can hear in the neighbourhood, at school, or at a friend's house. Explain how information can get mixed up and what they should do if they hear something that conflicts with what you've told them.

- For many parents, the hardest thing about explaining serious illness to their children is talking about the dying issue. As uncomfortable as it may be, this issue needs to be addressed in one of your early conversations. If you don't address it, children will think it is off limits to discuss and it becomes a barrier to completely open communication. "Right now the doctors feel I am going to do fine and that I will get better, but if anything changes I will let you know."

WHEN A CHILD IS HOSPITALIZED

Children may be taken to hospitals for routine procedures, for an illness that may mean a longer stay, and to emergency wards because of injuries.

At some point in their career, teachers may also be faced with a child who is chronically or terminally ill. Children are highly compassionate and ask many questions about children with skin rashes, hair loss (caused by chemotherapy), and so on. Staff should use this opportunity to teach the children about the illness and to encourage their sense of concern and caring. One teacher recounts his story:

> In our 10-plus school-age program we were all devastated when we learned that Jason had a brain tumour that would require surgery and chemotherapy. We waited anxiously for several months for the results of the tests. Fortunately the prognosis was positive. While we awaited Jason's return to our group, the children knew that he had lost most of his hair, since many of us had visited him during his recovery at the hospital and at home. A group of the boys approached me about shaving their heads, so that when Jason came back he wouldn't feel so awkward. I was moved by their compassion for Jason and their ability to look for a way to make his return a happy one. With their parents' permission we all visited the local barber, and the next morning when Jason arrived with his family, he was greeted by a roomful of bald heads including mine!

Hospital-based programs have been shown to be effective in reducing the anxieties of children who are facing a period of hospitalization. Teachers can invite people involved in these programs to visit the playroom for a demonstration and discussion of the hospital stay. Children can touch and play with the medical equipment they will see on the day of their procedure. They will also be given age-appropriate information about how the equipment is used.

Teachers can encourage children to act out their concerns by setting up the dramatic play centre to reflect a hospital theme. Drawing and other art activities also allow for meaningful self-expression. The following information can be gathered so that the child can be prepared and reassured:

- How long will the child be hospitalized?

- Will there be other children in the room?

- Will there be X-rays, anesthetic, blood tests, urine tests, etc.?

- Can the child bring a comfort toy into the operating room?

- Will it be acceptable to bring other familiar objects—toys, books, clothes—from home?

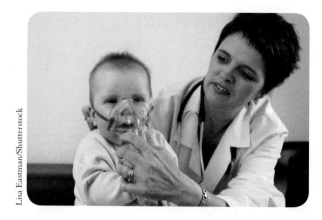

A hospital stay can be a difficult and challenging time for children and their families.

- How will the child feel after the surgery or treatment?

- What are the rules about visiting, parental involvement, sleeping over, etc.?

- What will the meals be like?

- Will television be available?

- What play facilities are available in the hospital?

Children are most concerned about interacting with new people and whether they will be in pain.

One of the hardest things for children to understand is that something that hurts or feels strange is actually helping them; however, anticipation and not knowing can make it worse. Family members should encourage their child to express their feelings and listen carefully for the questions the child might ask and the ones he or she doesn't ask. For parents, a loss of control and a sense of helplessness create only more anxiety and fear. Hospitalization will affect the whole family so it is important that accurate and age-appropriate information is also given to siblings.

DISABILITY AND SUCCESSFUL PARENTING

Society frequently views parents with disabilities, especially mothers, as totally dependent individuals who have somehow committed an immoral act by becoming parents (Fine and Asch, 1988; Finger, 1991). Mothers with disabilities, in particular, "shoulder the burden of society's perception of them as incompetents who have irresponsibly become mothers who will, along with their offspring, unquestionably become a burden on society" (Baskin and Riggs, 1988: 240). Nothing could be further from the truth.

Inside LOOK

When Yun's parents informed us that she was taken to the hospital, it was a difficult time for all of us at the centre and particularly for her kindergarten friends. Initially we did not know what the diagnosis was, but when we learned that she had childhood leukemia, we understood why she had appeared so tired and short of breath, and had frequent nose bleeds. We were encouraged when her parents shared that 90 percent of this type of leukemia goes into remission, but we knew that Yun and her family had difficult days ahead. She responded to the chemotherapy but was nauseated and losing her hair. As a group we decided that we must do what we could to support this family. Teachers in the kindergarten took turns visiting Yun at the hospital, bringing letters and drawings from her peers that she happily posted in her room. The supervisor brought some interesting puzzles and books on Yun's favourite topic—dinosaurs! On another visit we took a video that we had made with all of the children singing get-well songs. We played the video in the hospital playroom, and this drew a great crowd. Other teachers took food to the home and since the parents were spending so much time at the hospital, they appreciated a home-cooked meal. We are happy to say that Yun is now back in the centre with us in full remission!

FAMILIES IN TRANSITION: ISSUES FACING MANY FAMILIES

Blackford and Israelite (2003: 135) believe that the disability of a parent must be understood not merely as a problem for the family that must be "fixed" through a medicalized therapeutic approach. Instead, it is important to acknowledge problems that rest outside the individual and to question the extent to which barriers to successful parenting are societally imposed.... A narrow view of families with a parent with a disability that focuses only on what happens inside the family fails to sufficiently take into account stigma and ableism in the larger society. Such a view results in what has been called "blaming the victim."

Dr. Blackford's 1990 findings in a study conducted with Persons United for Self Help in northeastern Ontario show children and their parents with various disabilities creating flexible family systems that are not always bound by traditional expectations of the division of labour with regard to age, gender, and physical condition. Many family members were more accepting of difference in their relationships outside the family. Children and parents lived in and for the moment, rather than constantly anticipating the future. These results suggest that consideration of families with parents with disabilities can enlarge our view of what family life could or should be (reported in Blackford and Israelite, 2003).

BOOKS FOR CHILDREN

Wishing Wellness: A Workbook for Children of Parents with Mental Illness, by L.A. Clarke

Living Well with Serious Illness, by M.E. Heegaard

Mom and the Polka Dot Boo Boo: A Gentle Story Explaining Breast Cancer to a Young Child, by E. Sutherland

Hair for Mama, by K. Tinkham

Imagine a Rainbow: A Child's Guide for Soothing Pain, by B.S. Miles

Sammy's Mommy Has Cancer, by S. Kohlenberg

Can I Catch It Like a Cold? A Story to Help Children Understand a Parent's Depression, by the Centre for Addiction and Mental Health

Is a Worry Worrying You?, by F. Wolff and H.M. Savitz

BOOKS FOR ADULTS

The Ghost in the House: Real Mothers Talk about Maternal Depression, Raising Children and How They Cope, by T. Thompson

The Mother-to-Mother Postpartum Depression Book: Real Stories from Women Who Lived Through It and Recovered, by S. Poulin

We Carry Each Other: Getting through Life's Toughest Times, by E. Langshur and S. Langshur

Every Day Counts: Lessons in Love, Faith and Resilience from Children Facing Illness, by M. Sirois

Helping Your Child Cope with Your Cancer: A Guide for Parents and Family, by P. Van Drenoot

Can I Still Kiss You? Answering Your Child's Questions about Cancer, by N. Russell

How to Help Children through a Parent's Serious Illness: Supportive, Practical Advice from a Leading Child Life Specialist, by K. McCue

Preparing the Children: Information and Ideas for Families Facing Terminal Illness and Death, by K. Nussbaum

DEATH IN THE FAMILY

In 2003 in Canada, 3,561 children under the age of 19 years died, many of them after long terminal illnesses. In the same year, 16,053 adults between the ages of 20 and 49 years died. It is likely that many of these adults were parents, leaving children under the age of 21. These numbers mean that a very large number of children are affected by death and dying every year in Canada (Statistics Canada, 2006a). How close the child was to the person who died, how the death occurred (after a long illness or a sudden or violent death), and whether the child saw the person after death may all be factors in how the child will manage during this difficult time. There is no question that a death in the family alters the family makeup and often creates new roles for family members.

Much of our understanding about death and dying has been influenced by Elisabeth Kubler-Ross (1974). She identifies the process of grieving as moving through five stages: shock and denial; anger and protest; bargaining; depression and despair; and, finally, adjustment and acceptance. Recently these stages have been challenged by others who believe that each individual's reaction to death is different, and some may never go through all of the stages listed above. Hadad (2008) suggests that children's attitudes toward death are very much coloured by whether their parents have discussed death with them, how their parents handle death within the family, and whether the end of life has remained a hidden subject. If the child witnesses a grieving parent behaving stoically and showing little emotion when a loved one dies, the message communicated is that emotions should not be displayed, no matter what pain is felt. The child may then retain into adulthood the idea that public displays of grief are not acceptable and that the difficulty a grieving person may have in dealing with daily life is a sign of weakness or psychological disorder. However, if the child sees family members showing their grief, the message received is that grief is acceptable and expected. If a child has been inculcated into a religious belief, it plays a large part in determining attitudes toward death. Depending on the beliefs, children may form an attitude of calm acceptance of death or a fear of final judgment. Cultural background also influences a family's attitudes and its practices. Children may also feel they have caused the death and are responsible.

For instance, five-year-old Sam screamed at his older brother, "I hate you, and I wish you were dead!" He was haunted with the idea that his words created his brother's murder the following day. Due to Sam's age-appropriate egocentrism and magical perception, he saw himself as the centre of the universe, capable of creating and destroying at will the world around him. Reversibility also characterizes children's grieving. For example, Jack, a five-year-old first-grader was very sad after his dad died in a plane crash. Age-appropriately, he perceived death as reversible and told his friends and family that his dad was coming back. Jack even wrote his dad a letter and waited and waited for the mailman to bring back a response. (Goldman, 2004: 168)[*]

The media will also colour a child's interpretation of death. Estimates vary but some suggest that by the time children graduate from elementary school, they will have witnessed at least 8,000 murders on television alone. This clearly may distort their true understanding of death and its permanence. When death occurs, it is important to ask children what they want to know and then work toward finding the answers.

When a child, a sibling, a parent, or an extended family member dies, or when a death occurs through miscarriage or stillbirth, it is a difficult time for everyone involved. It is important for the teacher to know the cultural and religious practices of the family. In some instances, teachers may be active participants in the grieving process (e.g., attending the funeral) and in other situations, the family will prefer a more private arrangement. Sending food to the home or doing drop-off and pick-up if the child is attending the centre may be another way of supporting the family. Teachers should find out how mourning is conducted in cultures that may be different from their own.

---

[*] Goldman, L. 2004. "Counseling with children in contemporary society," *Journal of Mental Health Counseling* 26 (2, April): 168. Reprinted by permission of the American Mental Health Counselors Association.

Inside LOOK

When I was three, my father passed away, leaving my mother to raise my sister, who was 6 at the time, and me. What I remember as most painful was doing crafts for Father's Day. All of the teachers knew that I didn't have a father, but they still had the whole class do the craft. I write this because I want us as ECEs to know that even young children may have to face losing a parent, and teachers should know about the history of the families in the centre and be sensitive to this issue. Years later this memory still stays with me.

Source: Reprinted by permission of Justina Dorrington.

TABLE 10.2	Overview of Children's Understanding of and Reactions to Death	
AGE	**CONCEPTS**	**NORMAL BEHAVIOUR**
Less than 3 years	Little understanding of death Sense of separation or abandonment	Increased crying Fussiness Clinginess Regression in sleep, eating and elimination behaviours Resistance to change
3–6 years	Death is seen as temporary or reversible Magical thinking	Sadness Aggression Magical thinking Regression Nightmares Bladder/bowel problems Noncompliance
6–9 years	Gradual comprehension that death is final Some magical thinking Personification of death	Guilt Compulsive caregiving Phobias Possessiveness Aggression Regression Difficulty expressing grief Difficulty concentrating Psychosomatic symptoms
9–12 years	Cognitive awareness of death and its finality Difficulty conceiving of his or her own death or that of a loved one Concrete reasoning about how and why death occurs	Defiance Phobias Possessiveness Aggression Psychosomatic symptoms
12+ years	Death is irreversible, universal, and inevitable Abstract and philosophical reasoning Understand all people and self must die, but believe death is in the distant future	Anger Defiance Risk taking Increased sexual activity Substance abuse Aggression Possessiveness Psychosomatic symptoms Suicidal ideation

Goldman, L. 2004. "Counseling with children in contemporary society," *Journal of Mental Health Counseling* 26 (2, April): 168. Reprinted by permission of the American Mental Health Counselors Association.

Parents may also ask if the teacher thinks the child should attend the funeral and how to support the child during this difficult process. The answers will depend on the age of the child, religious teachings, and cultural influences. For some children, attending the funeral may be a way of bringing closure to a difficult family time; for others, it may create more anxiety. Each child's reaction will be unique and so there is no right or wrong answer. In some situations, finding a way to honour the person who has passed—for example, by creating a photo album, finding a special picture of the loved one to put into a frame, drawing and framing pictures of happy times together—may help the child deal with the loss. Planting a tree or building a special garden may also honour the memory. Many of these strategies will also be important if a child has died at the centre; classmates will need support and an opportunity to celebrate the life of their friend. There are many wonderful books that have been written to explain death (see the list at the end of this section).

ROLE OF THE TEACHER

The symptoms of grief are wide and varied. The Dougy Center for Grieving Children in Portland, Oregon, has worked with thousands of grieving children and teens since 1982. Their advice to teachers? When in doubt, ask a child what helps and the child will tell you. It is also important that teachers be alert to behaviours that may require interventions by mental health counsellors.

The centre has created a booklet, *35 Ways to Help a Grieving Child*. The suggestions included in the pamphlet are invaluable and all teachers are encouraged to explore this publication and to visit **http://www.dougy.org** to discover additional resources. The following 15 suggestions are particularly relevant in a child-care centre:

1. Listen.
2. Be honest. Never lie to a child.
3. Don't force kids to talk but answer the questions they ask—even the hard ones.
4. Talk about and remember the person who died.
5. Expect and allow all kinds of emotions.
6. Encourage consistency and routines. Set limits and rules and enforce them.
7. Understand that grief looks different at different ages and respect differences in grieving styles.
8. Get out the crayons, pens, pencils, paint, and chalk.
9. Run! Jump! Play! (Or find other ways to release energy and emotions.)
10. Help the child at naptimes. Sleep may come hard for grieving children.
11. Resist being overprotective.
12. Remember: "Playing" is "grieving."
13. Remember special days that impact the child.

Inside LOOK

Rainbows: Guiding Kids Through Life's Storms

Rainbows is an international not-for-profit organization that fosters emotional healing among children grieving a loss from a life-altering crisis. These losses, among others, include separation, divorce, death, incarceration, and foster care. Often youth are expected to accept the changes in their family or sort out their feelings alone. They can become "silent mourners," and, often confused and angry, they reveal their pain by acting out with negative behaviour and withdrawing in unhealthy ways. Rainbows provides a safe and supportive environment for participants to process their feelings, build self esteem, and learn positive coping tools to last a lifetime—because "it doesn't need to hurt forever." This is accomplished through our unique 12-week peer support programs available from preschool through to adult. Rainbows partners with the community to make the program available free of charge to children and youth in 1,620 trained sites located in more than 496 Canadian communities. These sites include schools, social service organizations, community centres, and places of worship. The National Office of Rainbows Canada is located in Barrie, Ontario. Rainbows Canada is a National Chapter of Rainbows International. For more information on this program, visit **http://www.rainbows.ca**. The international organization is at **http://www.rainbows.org**.

Source: Rainbows Canada. n.d.

14. Be available for children when they need you and hug with permission.

15. Take care of yourself and do your own grieving and ask for help if you need it. (Dougy Centre, 2012)*

Other strategies may include making a photo collage of the person who has died; in the process of collecting the photos, many stories may arise that help to create important memories. Families may hold a special activity on the anniversary of the person's death, birthday, holidays, etc., to commemorate the person who has passed.

BOOKS FOR CHILDREN

Lifetimes, by B. Mellonie

I'll Always Love You, by H. Wilhelm

When Dinosaurs Die: A Guide to Understanding Death, by L. Krasny Brown and M. Brown

I Miss You! A First Look at Death, by P. Thomas and L. Harker

When Your Grandparent Dies: A Child's Guide to Good Grief, by V. Ryan and R.W. Alley

The Tenth Good Thing About Barney, by J. Viorst

BOOKS FOR ADULTS

Why Did You Die? Activities to Help Children Cope With Grief and Loss, by E. Leeuwenburgh and E. Goldring

Creative Interventions for Bereaved Children, by L. Lowensiten

Kids Grieve Too! A Handbook for Parents, by T. Easthope

When Children Grieve: For Adults to Help Children Deal with Death, Divorce, Pet Loss, Moving and Other Losses, by J.W. James, R. Friedman, and L. Matthews

Help Me Say Goodbye: Activities for Helping Kids Cope When a Special Person Dies, by J. Silverman

When Someone Dies: An Accessible Guide to Bereavement for People with Learning Disabilities, by M. Mansfield

FAMILIES COPING WITH A NATURAL DISASTER

Fire, hurricanes, tornadoes, flooding, earthquakes, and other natural disasters have always been part of our existence; however, very little research exists that examines their impact on young children. We have all seen the devastation of the tsunami in Southeast Asia in 2005; the earthquakes in China and Haiti; and, closer to home, the Slave Lake wildfire; the flooding of the Red, Assiniboine, and Souris Rivers; the 2011 North American blizzard; and the devastation caused by Hurricanes Igor and Juan.

Many factors contribute to how well children and their families recover from such disasters. According to the National Association of School Psychologists (NASP, Brock et al., 2005), common symptoms exhibited by children following a natural disaster include the following:

• **Preschoolers:** thumb sucking, bedwetting, clinging to parents, sleep disturbances, loss of

---

* Reprinted by permission of The Dougy Center.

appetite, fear of the dark, regression in behaviour, and withdrawal from friends and routines

- Elementary school children: irritability, aggressiveness, clinginess, nightmares, school avoidance, poor concentration, and withdrawal from activities and friends

However, children who exhibit symptoms usually improve in two weeks to a month (Amatea, 2009: 351).[*]

ROLE OF THE TEACHER

It is important to remember that many families and children may be affected in unique ways and that it is important for the teacher to understand the implications of these experiences, to the best of his or her abilities. For example, one family's home might be destroyed in a wildfire while their neighbour's home was spared. This invokes all kinds of feelings on the part of both families, including survivor guilt and complete helplessness.

In some settings a trauma response team may be available to provide expertise and support. These professionals are trained to deal with difficult issues and will be an important support to families and to teachers. The stability of the centre will be critical in the time right after the disaster, and a calm and reassuring approach by teachers is critical. Keeping to schedules as much as possible will give the children the security of a normal routine. Allowing the children to talk about their experiences, and to express them through art, dramatic play, and/or written work will be important.

BOOKS FOR CHILDREN

Eyewitness Books: Natural Disasters, by C. Watts and T. Day

Surviving Hurricanes, by E. Raum

I Know What to Do: A Kid's Guide to Natural Disasters, by B. Mark, A. Layton, and M. Chesworth

BOOKS FOR ADULTS

Children and Natural Disasters, by K. Anderberg

Child Survivors of Natural Disasters: From Hurricanes to Tornados, by A. Hitt and Z. Hitt

FAMILIES IN WHICH THERE IS SUBSTANCE ABUSE

Alcoholism is a disease with physical, psychological, and social repercussions. Although there is no conclusive evidence of a genetic predisposition to the

---

[*] AMATEA, ELLEN S., BUILDING CULTURALLY RESPONSIVE FAMILY-SCHOOL RELATIONSHIPS, 1st Edition, © 2009. Reprinted and Electronically reproduced by permission of Pearson Education, Inc., Upper Saddle River, NJ.

Inside LOOK

Major findings from the Canadian Alcohol and Drug Use Monitoring Survey (Health Canada, 2010) are based on telephone interviews with 13,615 respondents, across all 10 provinces, which represent 25,957,435 Canadian residents, ages 15 years and older.

- Among Canadians 15 years and older, the prevalence of past-year cannabis use decreased from 14.1 percent in 2004 to 10.7 percent in 2010.
- Among Canadians 15 years and older, the prevalence of past-year use of cocaine or crack decreased from 1.9 percent in 2004 to 1.2 percent in 2010, while past-year use of hallucinogens (0.9 percent), ecstasy (0.7 percent), and speed (0.5 percent) is comparable to the rates of use reported in 2004.
- The rates of psychoactive pharmaceutical use and abuse remain comparable to the rates reported in 2009: 26.0 percent of respondents ages 15 years and older indicated that they had used an opioid pain reliever, a stimulant, or a sedative or tranquilizer in the past year, while 0.3 percent reported that they had used any of these drugs to get high in the past year.
- The prevalence of heavy frequent drinking among youth 15 to 24 years of age was approximately three times as high as the rate for adults 25 years and older (9.4 percent versus 3.3 percent).

Source: Health Canada, 2010.

disease, studies show that 50 to 80 percent of alcoholics have a close alcoholic relative. Ward (2002: 291) refers to an "alcoholic family system" rather than to "a family with an alcoholic member" because so much of family life focuses on the alcohol abuse that it becomes the main organizer; that is, the entire family system is involved with alcoholism.

According to Boyd-Webb (2003), some common stressors for children living in substance-abusing families are

- living in dangerous neighbourhoods, often with unstable housing arrangements and frequent moves
- financial strain and often homelessness
- lack of family or other social support system
- parents with poor coping and management skills
- addicted parents are sometimes so consumed with the need to obtain and use drugs that children may be neglected, abandoned or abused
- parents who have active drug use problems may be arrested and jailed often, leaving children as wards of the state if no relatives can care for them
- family life is often chaotic, leaving children anxious and unsettled (in amatea, 2009: 350)*

Robinson (1990: 69) observes that children of alcoholics

* AMATEA, ELLEN S., BUILDING CULTURALLY RESPONSIVE FAMILY-SCHOOL RELATIONSHIPS, 1st Edition, © 2009. Reprinted and Electronically reproduced by permission of Pearson Education, Inc., Upper Saddle River, NJ.

are at higher than average risk of becoming alcoholics, workaholics, compulsive gamblers, compulsive spenders, or sex and drug addicts. Eating disorders are also common. The bedrock of these problems is laid in the preschool years. Early identification can lead to primary intervention that can interrupt the disease cycle before it is implanted and before it takes its toll on the child physically, cognitively, emotionally, and socially.[†]

Robinson (1990: 71) goes on to explain that children of alcoholics, are "children of fear: They are afraid of what is happening at home and terrified that something awful is going to happen to them. Many of them cope by building walls around themselves."[‡] Stark (1987: 59), agrees that fear is a major factor in the lives of children of alcoholics. As parents argue and the tension escalates, children fear that someone will be hurt; they fear not only for themselves but also for their parent. Children worry about accidents—a fall, a fire—or that the parent may die. Although young children should be building relationships with other children, many avoid contact and live in isolation out of embarrassment and fear of reprisals from their peers.

Children may also withhold information about their alcoholic parent from not only their peers but also other adult family members and teachers.

† Robinson, B.E. 1990. "The Teacher's Role in Working with Children of Alcoholic Parents," *Young Children*. May: 69–72. © NAEYC. Reprinted with permission.

‡ 1990. "The Teacher's Role in Working with Children of Alcoholic Parents," *Young Children*. May: 69–72. © NAEYC. Reprinted with permission.

Inside LOOK

Steve, age 35, has been an alcoholic for 20 years. He has three young daughters. Until a year ago, his children and wife had existed only in the peripheral haze beyond his bottle. "I wanted to do what I wanted to do. I drank whatever money there was. I stayed out for days and nights. When I was home, I beat my children. I wasn't able to function." After attending a fathers' support group, Steve has not had a drink for a year. He continues to have marital strife but the fathers' support group helped him cope with these problems separately, and to pursue a relationship with his children he has never had. "What I learned the most is a personal identity as a father. I've learned to look at my children as individuals, and to spend time with them. I'm dealing with the stress and I take time for myself. I have a little more patience and a little more tolerance. I don't let the kids get control of me. I know my limitations."

Source: De La Barrera, J., and Masterson, D. 1988. "Support Group Helps Troubled Fathers Learn Parenting Skills," *Children Today*, March-April, pp. 10–13.

Depression may also be a factor for these children. In some situations, children may take on the parenting role in the family, caring for younger siblings and for the parent.

Newborns born to addicted women can have life-long problems. Weston et al. (1989: 3) state that "child-care providers may have drug-exposed infants who are irritable and hypersensitive to external stimulation; exhibit feeding and sleeping problems; have tone, reflex and movement abnormalities; and produce decreased vocalizations." Many parents who are addicted are not able to provide the nurturing that children need, and the economic well-being of the family may well be jeopardized when adults lose jobs because of addiction. All substances alter, in varying degrees, an individual's state of consciousness, memory, affect regulation, and impulse control.

A growing number of Canadian babies are being born with neonatal abstinence syndrome (NAS), an addiction to prescription opioids, the painkillers fuelling Canada's fastest-growing addiction—and the methadone used to treat it. In 2011,

> at least 1,057 babies were born in Canada with NAS, an 18 per cent increase over the year before, according to the Canadian Institute for Health Information. In Ontario, that number increased by a third in a year; in Manitoba, it more than doubled. (Mehler Paperny, 2012)[*]

Canadians pop more prescription opioids than almost any country in the world, behind the United States and Belgium.

> Last fall [2011] Ontario became one of the first jurisdictions in North America to design modernized guidelines setting out a standard of care for NAS. The recommendations include testing women of childbearing age for substance use and diagnosing babies with neonatal abstinence using the same updated scoring system. Diagnosed, the condition is treatable. Babies are swaddled and given tiny doses of morphine to ease their withdrawal and monitored for weeks or months in a bassinet in a neo-natal ICU before they're slowly weaned off. But that diagnosis depends on a woman telling her obstetrician she's an addict or a doctor recognizing symptoms once the baby is born. If NAS goes undiagnosed, it can prove serious or fatal.... Some of these babies need to stay in hospital up to 40 or 50 days for $1,000 per day in hospital care clearly adding huge costs to the country's already overextended health-care budgets. (Mehler Paperny, 2012)[†]

ROLE OF THE TEACHER

Robinson (1990: 70–71) suggests ways teachers can help:

- Play therapy—the use of creative materials such as clay, water, sand, and paint—may help the children express their feelings and provide soothing, calming experiences. Teachers need to help children recognize and label their emotions.

- Many homes are in a constant state of upheaval. A sense of order and consistency in the daily routines in the child-care centre is critical.

- Teachers need to educate themselves about the adverse consequences for children who live with an alcoholic or a drug-addicted parent. Insecurity and loss of control are two of the psychological consequences.

---

[*] Paperny, A.M., 2012. "Treating the tiny victims of Canada's fastest-growing addiction," *The Globe and Mail*, January 6. © The Globe and Mail. All Rights Reserved.

[†] Paperny, A.M., 2012. "Treating the tiny victims of Canada's fastest-growing addiction," *The Globe and Mail*, January 6. © The Globe and Mail. All Rights Reserved.

- Teachers can help children by giving them appropriate choices and challenges to allow them to manage and control their lives. Empowering children through decision making in the classroom will help battle children's fear and dependency.*

- Teachers can further restore children's sense of security by establishing positive, loving relationships with them and by setting clear and consistent limits. Some children will test the limits since they are used to making decisions for themselves without adult supervision or intervention.

- Finding one-on-one time for these children is crucial.

- Some children believe that the substance abuse is somehow their fault; teachers need to reassure them that this is an adult problem.

- Teachers must follow through on promises made to the children.

- Many of these children become adept at hiding their feelings. Observe them carefully and look for opportunities to build bridges.

- Older children may be provided with information on alcoholism; a number of children's books are available to assist teachers in this endeavour.

- While teachers must make every effort to support children of alcoholics, they also need to understand that they "cannot replace the alcoholic parent and should not try to do so. Allowing the child to become too dependent on you would be a disservice, because this child must continue to deal with the alcoholism long after leaving your classroom" (70).†

Pimento and Kernested (2010: 436) offer the following:

A teacher who feels that a parent is under the influence of alcohol or drugs and in no condition to pick up his or her child after school (especially in a car) might suggest that the parent take a cab home or even offer to drive the family herself. There may also be a family friend who might be willing to assist in this situation. It is no easy thing to challenge parents who may respond angrily to what they perceive as interference. Under such circumstances, however, the child's well-being is the most important consideration and from both an ethical and legal perspective, educators cannot release a child to someone who could cause the child harm.

If the parent is belligerent or confrontational, or wants to or has already taken the child from the program and is driving away, call the police and tell them that a drunk driver is leaving the program with a child. If possible, provide the police with the make, model and colour of the car as well as the licence plate number.

Diane Buhler, executive director of the organization Parents Against Drugs, has this advice for teachers:

The most typical concern of child-care centres in the area of substance abuse is primary prevention. For young children, this means discussing situations involving those drugs—medicine, caffeine, and tobacco—that are part of daily living. For example, when daycare providers dispense medication, they can communicate respect for the powerful effects of the drug. Possible messages include:

- Even a little too much medicine can hurt you.

- Some medicines look like candy and that is why medicine must be kept in a safe place.

- We use medicine only if we really need it.

- Only trusted adults can give you medicine.

Other thoughts to consider:

- Other teachable opportunities are present in the daycare schedule; for example, when kindergarten children are accompanied to their school program, they often encounter teenagers who are smoking. A daycare worker could discuss the addictive nature of tobacco with the children and assure them that the best choice is not to start smoking in the first place.

- Other issues regarding substance abuse that may arise concern the well-being of a child if the daycare has reason to believe that the primary caregivers are abusing alcohol or other drugs. Children in these circumstances have the potential of suffering neglect or even abuse—the usual reporting procedures need to be followed.

- Children who grow up in families where an immediate family member or frequent visitor abuses alcohol or other drugs can begin to develop anxieties and other behaviour patterns that are characteristic of children of alcoholics. These characteristics can range from being overly responsible or "parentified" to being overly suspicious and withdrawn. A daycare provider cannot necessarily ascertain that familial substance abuse is the cause of these behaviours but should be aware that the possibility exists.

* Robinson, B.E. 1990. "The Teacher's Role in Working with Children of Alcoholic Parents," *Young Children*. May: 69-72. © NAEYC. Reprinted with permission.

† Robinson, B.E. 1990. "The Teacher's Role in Working with Children of Alcoholic Parents," *Young Children*. May: 69-72. © NAEYC. Reprinted with permission.

BREAKING THE CYCLE: A SUCCESS STORY

Breaking the Cycle (BTC) is an early identification and prevention program designed to reduce risk and to enhance the development for substance-exposed children (prenatal to 6 years) by providing services that address maternal addiction problems and the mother–child relationship through a community-based cross-systemic model.

Families receive integrated addictions counselling, health/medical services, parenting support, development screening and assessment, early childhood interventions, child care, access to an FASD Diagnostic Clinic, and basic needs support in a single access setting in downtown Toronto, with home visitation and street outreach components. (Mothercraft, 2012)[*]

One mother, Venus Carter, provides insight into the challenges she faced:

I was worried about the baby and how I could stop using [the drug] and stay clean when all I had known for years was how to survive on the street. I really wanted Jamai but I was terrified he'd be taken from me. You want this baby but you want this drug, too. If you're an addict, it's a tough choice.[†]

Venus says her baby son Jamai is alive and well today only because of her own willpower, bolstered by Breaking the Cycle (Dineen, 1995: B3).

BOOKS FOR CHILDREN

Wishes and Worries: A Story to Help Children Understand a Parent Who Drinks Too Much, by the Centre for Addiction and Mental Health

Moon Pie, by S. Mason

I Wish My Daddy Didn't Drink So Much, by J. Vigna

BOOKS FOR ADULTS

In the Realm of Hungry Ghosts: Close Encounters with Addiction, by G. Mate

Addiction Proof Your Child: A Realistic Approach to Preventing Drug, Alcohol and Other Dependencies, by S. Peele

Trouble Don't Last Always: When a Child Becomes a 4-Year-Old Parent, by S. Lenard Rico Salter

Working with Children and Families Affected by Substance Abuse: A Guide for Early Childhood Education and Human Service Staff, by K. Pullan Watkins and L. Durant

Addiction: Why They Just Can't Stop, by R. Books

HOMELESSNESS AND SHELTER LIFE

We often have a stereotypical idea of who a street person might be—an adult male suffering from mental illness or addictions; however, the truth is that homeless families with children are everywhere (Gonzalez-Mena: 2010). Homelessness is a reality for many families in communities large and small, urban or rural, following welfare cuts, increased rents, and lack of employment. The very nature of homeless families makes counting them nearly impossible. Regardless of how a homeless family is defined, no current, accurate, or comprehensive statistics are available regarding the number of such families in Canada. The situation is further complicated by the fact that Canada is one of the few countries without a national housing policy. The federal government downloaded housing costs and responsibilities to the provinces in the early 1990s. Families who have always been self-sufficient and suddenly find themselves without employment face tremendous psychological adjustments as well as the obvious difficulty of providing shelter and food. Families struggling with low-income issues for the first time may be embarrassed about their situation and not sure of where to turn in their own community.

In 2006 and 2007, Canada West Foundation researchers studied street-level social problems in Western cities. Serious concerns were identified in Vancouver, Calgary, and Edmonton where people living on the street in shelters were on the increase (Ward and Belanger, 2011). "Currently, in Toronto, each night, over 5,000 persons are homeless: about 90 percent sleep in 64 shelters" (Chiu et al., 2009). Of increasing concern is the fact that "over 300 children are born to homeless women each year" (Ogilvie, 2010 in Ambert, 2012: 133).

SHELTER LIFE

Life as a homeless woman or child can mean life on the streets, life in substandard housing, life in a

---

[*] From Mothercraft, 2012. "Breaking the cycle," http://www.mothercraft .ca/index.pho?g=early-interverntion-programs. Reprinted with permission.

[†] Dineen, J.M. 1995. "For Jamai's Sake," *The Toronto Star*, 22 September: B3. Reprinted by permission of Torstar Syndication Services.

series of motel rooms, or a life of enforced dependency on the welfare system. In Canada, "about 30 percent of the homeless are women. They are usually less noticeable than men partly because they fear child protection services will take their children" (Ward and Belanger, 2011: 357). Despite this, many homeless women with children have no other option but to seek out a shelter.

> While shelters provide a welcome relief from the street, families who use them often live in very cramped conditions and members are sometimes separated. Once in shelters, mothers encounter many difficulties in fulfilling their parental role. For instance, they no longer have control over the daily routine of their family life, whether it is bedtime or other rituals. (Ambert, 2012: 135)

For homeless children there is a loss of much of what they have known. They may no longer go to their child-care centre or school and may be placed in a new school that for older children creates the anxiety of trying to fit in. They may be ashamed of their circumstances and worry that their peers will find out they are homeless. Anger, aggressive behaviour, and resentment may surface as children struggle to understand their situation. They may also be estranged from their grandparents and other family members, meaning the loss of another support system. Many of these children display anxiety and insecurities, and they may experience sleep issues or revert to stages of development that previously had been well established.

Ward (1998: 363) points out the negative effects of shelter life:

> Like other poor children, those living in shelters suffer in both their health and education, but the effects are more extreme. Usually by the time families reach shelters, they have already moved several times, staying with friends and relatives, perhaps even sleeping in a car. As a result, children often have a high number of respiratory infections and other illnesses. They also suffer psychologically. Two-thirds of homeless parents report an increase in their children's acting-out behaviour.

ROLE OF THE TEACHER

- **The child-care centre or school may be the only stable environment for the family during its period of homelessness. Given these circumstances, the teacher plays a vital role in supporting parents and children who are living in shelters.**

- **Families may need assistance in settling into their new environment. Children may require individualized attention and extra reassurance, not only when they are in a shelter but also during their reintegration into the community.**

Inside LOOK

The following excerpt from the *Toronto Star* offers illuminating details about life in a homeless shelter:

> Every year about 3,000 school children in Toronto live in homeless shelters. Yet despite this long-standing problem—the number of affected children has remained steady for the last five years—there are no government or school board policies to ensure the educational and emotional needs of these vulnerable children are being met, says *Lost in the Shuffle*, the first Canadian study on the issue. "As long as governments allow family homelessness to continue, it is necessary to understand the educational experiences of homeless children and to put in place the supports they need for educational success," says the report by Toronto's Community Social Planning Council and Aisling Discoveries Child and Family Centre. Even though school enrolment from a shelter happened within a day or two, educational assessments and enrolment in special needs programs were "subject to delays and a serious impediment to education," the study says. A majority of these children have experienced or witnessed violence that can cause behaviour that interferes with learning, the study found, and yet access to support and training for teachers is uneven. Parents reported difficulty finding a quiet space in shelters for their children to do homework and said a lack of access to computers was a problem for kids in higher grades.

Source: Monsebraaten, L. 2007. "Homeless Kids Neglected. Report Says Education, Emotional Support Lacking For Students Living In Shelters," *The Toronto Star*, October 1. Reprinted by permission of Torstar Syndication Services.

- The loss of a home robs a child of the familiarity and sense of place most of us take for granted.

- Many of these children live in crisis much of the time, and the child-care setting should be a low-key, caring environment.

- Teachers need to be vigilant in their efforts to protect these children from ridicule or censure from their peers.

- The child may appreciate a space to call his or her own, where he or she can keep personal things.

- Having extra clothing on hand, particularly in the cold weather, may also be helpful.

- Giving the child breakfast upon arriving at the centre, lunch, and a hearty snack at the end of the day will ensure adequate nutritional needs are met.

- Taking and giving photos of the children to the families may be such a small but important memento as some families may not have the resources to take photos on their own.

- Creating books or journals with photos when possible will also be an important reminder of happy times at the centre.

- Around holidays, teachers should help the family to provide positive memories for their child. These can include making small gifts and participating in events with other families, such as "fun day" programs, class picnics, sports days, etc. (Rockwell, Andre, and Hawley, 2010: 62).

- Educators should be aware when planning activities that these families will not have the financial resources to participate in experiences that require funds. Perhaps teachers could engage in a fundraising event to provide financial support for out-of-centre experiences for all the children in the centre.

- Teachers must also prepare for the fact that they may have these families for only a short stay at the centre; many shelters have time limits and families are forced to move on.

- Whenever possible, communicating with the shelter staff with the family's permission may open up opportunities for further support. The extra effort on the part of teachers can make a great difference in building positive and healthy relationships between staff and these families.

BOOKS FOR CHILDREN

Fly Away Home, by E. Bunting and R. Himler

The Lady Who Lived in a Car, by S. Hubbard

A Shelter in Our Car, by M. Gunning and E. Pedlar

The Cardboard Shack Beneath the Bridge, by T. Huff

The Teddy Bear, by D. McPhail

December, by E. Bunting

Lily and the Paper Man, by R. Upjohn

The Family Under the Bridge, by N. Savage Carlson

The Lady in the Box, by A. McGovern

Inside LOOK

Trish Horrigan, a child advocate with a family residence program, provides the following glimpse into the lives of homeless families. She suggests ways in which teachers can support these families:

A number of Canadian families have no place to call home. These are the men, women, and children who find themselves seeking refuge in shelters and hostels. Some have been evicted, forced to leave unsafe living conditions; some are fleeing domestic violence; others are new immigrants to Canada. No matter the circumstances, all of these families are facing crisis. They have left behind their homes, friends, and belongings. This is a stressful time for parents and their children. The relations between families and other members of the community are strongly affected by this stress, including relations between parent and teacher. Factors that might affect parent–teacher interaction include the following:

- Living in a shelter environment that is crowded, unstable, and without privacy leads to high levels of stress.

continued

- A transient lifestyle may prevent parents from developing an affiliation with a particular child-care centre or school. Members of the family may see themselves as temporary members of the community and therefore make no effort to forge a lasting relationship.
- Newly arrived immigrant families may have limited or no English skills. Also, the cultural background of the family will often dictate the level of interaction with teachers and caregivers. For example, parents from some countries may view teachers as authority figures and feel it inappropriate to question them.
- Mothers fleeing an abusive relationship may be hesitant to enroll their children in a school or child-care setting because of concerns for their physical or emotional safety. Trust is a critical issue for these families.

Source: Reprinted by permission of Trish Horrigan, Review Officer, Toronto Hostel Services.

BOOKS FOR ADULTS

Homelessness: Making and Unmaking a Crisis, by J. Layton

Homelessness, Housing and Mental Health, by C. Forchuk, R. Csiernik, and E. Jensen

Homelessness, by A. Gillard

Homelessness, Poverty and Unemployment, by S.J. Thompson

Dying for a Home, by C. Crowe

Street Stories: 100 Years of Homelessness in Vancouver, by M. Barnholden and N. Newman

Can't Get There from Here, by T. Strasser

FAMILIES LIVING WITH ABUSE AND VIOLENCE

FAMILY VIOLENCE

This information in this section is based on excerpts from two publications developed by Boost Child Abuse Prevention and Intervention: Making a Difference: The Community Responds to Child Abuse, *6th edition, by Pearl Rimer (2009);* and Looking for Angelina: A Learning Guide on Family Violence, *by Giselle Rishchynski, Pearl Rimer, and Jonah Rimer (2009). We gratefully acknowledge Pearl Rimer's contribution and participation.*

Home is supposed to be the safest place of all. However, family violence remains a pervasive and persistent issue in Canada and around the world. At least one in three women globally has been beaten, coerced into sex, or abused in some other way, most often by someone she knows, including her husband or another male family member (UNICEF, 2006). Family violence can be found across all ethnic, cultural, racial, and class backgrounds (Menjivar and Salcido, 2002) and "violence and abuse toward an intimate partner is arguably the most common form of violence in society" (Wolfe and Feiring, 2000: 360).

The reality of family violence in Canada is staggering. Research reveals that 29 percent of women in Canada are affected by men's violence (UNFPA, 2000) and

between 70–85 percent of women who are sexually assaulted are assaulted by men they know. As outlined by Johnson (1996: 127), of all incidents of sexual assault, 24 percent took place in the victim's home, 20 percent in the perpetrator's home, 10 percent in someone else's home, 25 percent in a car, and 21 percent in a public place.

In 2004 and 2009, Statistics Canada reported that spousal violence against Aboriginal women is three times higher than for non-Aboriginal women. Aboriginal woman were also significantly more likely than non-Aboriginal women to report the most severe and life-threatening forms of violence, including being beaten or choked, having had a gun or knife used against them, or being sexually assaulted. (in Perreault, 2011)

Amnesty International (2004) reports that "Aboriginal women aged 25–44 are five times more

---

* Reprinted by permission of Pearl Rimer.

likely than other Canadian women of the same age to die of violence" (14). Annually, between 1991 and 2010, "45–87 women were murdered by their spouse and dating violence claimed the lives of 10–32 females" (Sinha et al., 2010: 50–51).

This is only part of the picture. Statistics Canada does not include boyfriend/girlfriend or extra-marital relationships in its intimate partner assault or homicide total, and until 2010, did not include dating violence within a definition of family violence. In addition, as with most illegal and hidden behaviours, the prevalence of family violence is unknown. Underreporting occurs for many reasons, including victims who do not recognize that the behaviour is abusive and illegal, shame, self-blame, fear of retaliation by the offender, loss of financial security, uncertainty if immigration status will be affected, fear that the children will be

FIGURE 10.2 "I Hide in the Closet"

I hide in the closet when my dad hits my mom.

Reprinted by permission of Pearl Rimer.

taken away, and hope that the violence will stop. Underreporting is also the result of family, friends, and neighbours who feel that what goes on in other people's homes is a private matter.

Family violence has psychological, physical, social, and economic impacts for victims, families, and society. The federal government estimates that the annual direct medical costs related to violence against women is $1.1 billion (World Health Organization, 2004), a figure that rises to $4 billion a year when social services, lost productivity, lost earnings, and police, courts, and prison costs are taken into account (Greaves, Hankivsky, and Kingston-Riechers, 1995; Ontario Women's Directorate, 1997). The University of British Columbia conducted the first Canadian study to comprehensively identify the range of economic costs for services used by women who leave a violent partner. According to the study, the cost to Canadians of this type of violence is an estimated $6.9 billion a year, which represents expenditures related to health, legal and social services (e.g., medical visits, counselling, legal aid, child protection, unemployment insurance, social assistance, food banks) (UBC, 2011).

Family violence is based on an imbalance of power. The aim of family violence is to frighten, intimidate, and control. Family violence is defined as "the systemic use of tactics to establish and maintain power and control over the thoughts, feelings and conduct of an intimate partner" (Duffy and Momirov, 1997: 137). Klein (2005) further explains

> Domestic violence is not about relationships, good or bad … It is about abusers and their use of violence. Domestic violence is … not accidental violence … Abusers do not strike their partners because they are out of control. They strike their partners to maintain control over them, humiliate and debase them, isolate them, or punish them for asserting their independence.

Family violence is also referred to as woman abuse, intimate partner violence, domestic violence, spousal violence, spousal assault, and violence against women. The use of the term *family violence* throughout this section does not indicate gender neutrality, but rather is an attempt to convey that the intimate partner, along with the children and youth exposed to the violence, are impacted by violence in the home.

Family violence erupts in many families, and does not exist solely in male–female relationships.

Family violence is also found in same-sex relationships and in homes where extended families live together. In heterosexual relationships, men are not the only perpetrators of family violence. However, statistically, women are most likely to be victimized by family violence and the perpetrator is likely to be her male partner. Therefore, in this section the partner being abused is referred to using feminine terms and the abuser using masculine terms.

Overall, the violence experienced by women tends to be more severe and more often repeated than the violence directed at men. Women are more likely than men to be the victims of family violence such as physical assault, sexual assault, criminal harassment/stalking, and homicide. Female victims of family violence are more likely than males to report being injured, require medical attention, experience multiple assaults, and fear for their lives and the lives of their children. About 60 percent of female homicides in Canada are committed by current partners or estranged partners with a history of family violence (Statistics Canada, 2006b). Women are also more likely to be killed because of their partner's jealousy.

"The 2010 report of *Family Violence in Canada: A Statistical Profile* states that in the previous decade, jealousy was a factor in the homicide of a spouse or dating partner, accounting for 24% of cases" (Sinha, 2012: 39).

FORMS OF FAMILY VIOLENCE

Family violence can take the form of physical, sexual, emotional, spiritual, or financial harm. While these categories are helpful in understanding family violence, it is important to realize that many individuals experience more than one form of violence.

- *Physical abuse* includes all acts that result in physical harm, as well as threats to harm the partner and/or children. Examples of physical abuse include pushing, kicking, slapping, choking, restraining, and using a weapon/ object. Physical intimidation (e.g., eye contact, destroying property) and threats of violence (e.g., "you know what's coming next," the making of a fist, the displaying of a weapon) are psychological elements of physical abuse.

- *Psychological/emotional abuse* tactics are often effectively used to control and intimidate partners, particularly by isolating the victim (especially if there are disability, economic dependence, and language barriers).

- *Sexual abuse* includes, but is not limited to, forced sexual acts, sexual accusations, use of sexually degrading language, and sexual assault accompanied by threats of or actual violence.

- *Emotional abuse* is the most common type of abusive behaviour and also the most varied and complex. The three most common forms of emotional abuse are name calling or put-downs; jealousy and not wanting the victim to talk to other people; and demanding to know who she is with and where she is at all times (General Social Survey, 2004). Emotional/psychological abuse also includes blaming the victim for the abusive behaviour; harassment (e.g., stalking); controlling and/or monitoring friendships and the use of the car and telephone; spiritual abuse (e.g., interfering with her ability to practise her chosen religion); and keeping the victim in a state of fear. The presence of emotional abuse is the largest risk factor and greatest predictor of physical violence (Johnson, 1996) and sexual violence (Statistics Canada, 2006b).

- *Financial/economic abuse* includes, but is not limited to, the abuser controlling all of the financial matters and decisions; keeping the victim from obtaining employment, or taking away her paycheques, making the victim dependent on him for money; enforcing a strict allowance that does not allow the victim to pay for basic necessities; and making her account for every penny.

RISK OF FAMILY VIOLENCE

Young women between the ages of 15–24 are most at risk for interpersonal violence. Experiencing violence as a child is a risk factor for being a victim or perpetrator of intimate partner violence. The 2009 General Social Survey (GSS) found that spousal victims of physical and sexual assault were more likely than other victims of violent crime to have been victimized as a child. (Sinha, 2012: 33)

Other individuals at high risk for family violence are women who have just separated from a partner or are deciding to separate; pregnant women (40 percent of woman abuse incidents begin during pregnancy (Noel and Yam, 1992; Rodgers, 1994); Aboriginal women; women in common-law relationships; and women with disabilities. For some women and their children it may be safer to stay in the relationship than leave; violence often escalates when abusers sense that their victims are trying to leave or are using outside intervention. In 79 percent of the domestic homicide cases in Ontario (from 2002 to 2005), women were murdered during a pending or actual separation (DVDRC, 2005). The risk of homicide is higher in the first two months after separation (Daly and Wilson, 1993). In his book entitled *The War on Women*, Vallée (2007) addresses the question of "Why does she stay?" It comes down to fear: "Unless you have personally experienced that fear, it can be almost impossible to comprehend. But anyone who does understand it would never proclaim, "I don't know why she stayed. I wouldn't put up with it for a minute" (36).

CHILD ABUSE

David Finkelhor (a world-renowned expert on child abuse) bluntly states, "Children are most arguably the most criminally victimized people in society" (2008: 3). Finkelhor goes on to say, "In reality, most studies now confirm that children face frequencies of assaultive violence far above the levels that most adults encounter, although this really is not widely recognized" (2008: 100). Statistics Canada has stated that children and youth under 18 years of age are more at risk of physical and sexual abuse than adults, confirming Finkelhor's comments (Ogrodnik, 2010; Sinha, 2012).

Generally, child abuse is categorized into four major conditions: neglect, physical abuse, sexual abuse, and emotional abuse. Although these divisions may be useful in principle, it is common for a child to suffer more than one form of abuse. For example, children who have been physically abused may also have been told that they are bad or stupid and that they deserve what they are getting, resulting in emotional consequences to the children. The description of child abuse under each section below does *not* necessarily reflect the legal definition of child abuse.

- *Neglect* occurs when a parent or caregiver does not provide for the basic emotional and physical needs of the child on an ongoing basis. Neglect includes not providing the proper food, clothing, housing, supervision, safe surroundings, personal health care, medical and emotional care, and education. Children who are neglected physically and emotionally may not develop normally. The consequences of neglect can be very serious, particularly for young children, with some children suffering permanent harm.

- *Physical abuse* includes all acts by a caregiver that result in physical harm to a child. Physical abuse may happen if a child is punished harshly, even though the parent or caregiver may not have meant to hurt the child. Examples of physical abuse include bruises; marks in the shape of objects or handprints; shaking; burns; human bite marks; fractures of the skull, arms, legs, or ribs; and female genital mutilation. Physical abuse may result in a minor injury (such as a bruise) or a more serious injury that could cause lasting damage or death (for example, from shaking a child). Inappropriate punishment includes, but is not limited to, anything that leaves a mark on the child or the use of an object to strike a child. Although cultural factors play a role in caring for and/or disciplining children, injuring a child is unacceptable.

- *Sexual abuse* occurs when a person uses power over a child to involve the child in any sexual act. The power of the abuser can lie in his or her age, intellectual or physical development, relationship of authority over the child, and/or the child's degree of dependency. The sexual act is intended to gratify the needs of the abuser. "Touching" is not the only criteria in defining sexual abuse. It includes acts such as fondling; genital stimulation; oral sex; inserting fingers, a penis, or objects in the vagina or anus; exposing oneself; sexual exploitation over the Internet; as well as exposing a child to, or involving a child in, pornography or prostitution. The offender may engage the child in the sexual activity through threats, bribes, force, lies, or by taking advantage of the child's trust. Most of the time, the offender is someone known to the child and trusted by the child or family.

- *Emotional abuse* is the continual use of any of the following by a parent or caregiver when interacting or disciplining a child: rejecting (e.g., "I wish you were never born"); criticizing (e.g., "Why can't you do anything right?"); insulting (e.g., "I can't believe you would be so stupid"); humiliating (e.g., embarrassing a child in front of other people); isolating (e.g., not allowing a child to play with friends; terrorizing (e.g., "The police will come and take you away"); corrupting (e.g., frequently swearing in front of the child or getting the child to participate in things against the law); not responding to a child's emotional needs; or punishing a child for exploring the environment. Children who are exposed to violence in their homes may suffer emotional harm.

The four types of child abuse can occur at the hands of individual caregivers or on a larger scale. Abusive and damaging acts can occur in institutional settings with responsibility for children if caregivers do not supervise children adequately; use harmful methods of controlling children; use drugs inappropriately to manage children's behaviour; use harsh disciplinary measures such as corporal punishment, isolation, or withholding food; use excessive force when trying to deal with a child who is "out of control"; or do not report the knowledge of any abusive behaviour toward children in the setting. Societal abuse refers to acts of commission or omission on the part of society as a whole that result in children suffering; for example, society's knowledge and acceptance of children living in poverty.

PREVALENCE OF CHILD ABUSE

The following statistics are the findings of the *Canadian Incidence Study of Reported Child Abuse and Neglect—2008*, the third nationwide study to examine the incidence of reported child abuse in Canada (Trocmé et al., 2001):

- In 2008, there were an estimated 39.16 investigations of child abuse per 1,000 children in Canada.

- The two most frequently substantiated forms of maltreatment were exposure to intimate partner violence (34 percent) and neglect (34 percent), in total accounting for 68 percent of child maltreatment investigations.

- Physical abuse[1] comprised 20 percent of substantiated cases, followed by emotional maltreatment (9 percent), and sexual abuse (3 percent).

INTERNET SEXUAL EXPLOITATION

Sexual exploitation of children on the Internet encompasses three major forms of maltreatment against children:

- child pornography (more appropriately termed "child sexual abuse images")

- child luring/unwanted sexual solicitation

- child prostitution/child sex tourism

Canadian police estimate that there are more than 100,000 websites that contain thousands of child abuse images (Alcoba, 2008).

> In 2007, it was estimated that there were 500,000 individuals actively involved in the trafficking of child sexual abuse images (i.e., child pornography) on the Internet, and over 5 million unique child sexual abuse images on the Internet. There are over 750,000 pedophiles online at any given time. (Office of the Federal Ombudsman for Victims of Crime, 2007: 5)

A large percentage of child pornography is produced in Western nations (Canada, United States, and the United Kingdom): "North America is one of the top producers of child abusive images" (CTV Newsnet, 2009). According to Cooper (2006), 50 percent of collected images between 2000 and 2001 were of children ages 5 or younger. The majority of offenders who produce child abuse media are known to their victims. Fifty percent of all child sexual abuse images are made by family members (Cooper, 2007). "In child pornography cases where the child was identified, 35% of the abusers were related to the child (26% of whom were a parent). In 78% of cases, the abuser was known to the child (e.g., a family friend, neighbour, coach) and had legitimate and prolonged access to the child" (Canadian Centre for Child Protection, 2009: 18).

> Child victims are increasingly younger and the images are more violent in response to a growing appetite for live streaming of child sexual abuse on the Internet. Often mistaken as victimless or merely image-based offences, most child pornography/luring offences in Ontario involve the actual sexual exploitation, rape and sexual torture of children, including infants, on camera. (Ontario Provincial Police, 2009)

Internet use knows no borders, and identifying and rescuing children is very difficult and time consuming. "There are more than five million children worldwide drawn into child prostitution and child sex tourism, including more than 200,000 in Canada" (Flowers, 2001: 149–150).

CHILD HOMICIDES

According to Statistics Canada (2001), about 100 child homicides, on average, are documented by the police every year across Canada. Data consistently has shown that the majority of family-related homicides against children and youth are committed by parents. According to Statistics Canada (2011; Sinha, 2012), between 2000 and 2010

- 84 percent of victims under the age of 18 were killed by a parent

- infants less than 1 year experienced higher rates of family-related homicide compared to older children

- the rate of family-related homicide against infants was nearly triple the rate of 1- to 3-year-olds, the next highest age group

- parents were accused in family-related homicides against infants under age 1 in approximately 98 percent of cases, and in 90 percent of family homicides of children 1 to 3 years old.

> As with family violence, it is difficult to determine the extent of child abuse, since so many cases go unreported, and infant homicides may be underreported since some cases of accidental deaths (e.g., falls) could actually be due to child abuse. Homicides of children and youth may also be underreported since some deaths caused by intentional injury may be misclassified as resulting from natural or undetermined causes. (Ogrodnik, 2010: 16)

THE OVERLAP BETWEEN FAMILY VIOLENCE AND CHILD ABUSE

Exposure to family violence goes beyond actually witnessing (i.e., seeing) violent episodes. It refers to the multiple ways in which children are exposed to family violence:

- directly seeing and/or hearing the violence (e.g., the children are hiding under the covers, but can hear what is going on)

- being used as a pawn by the perpetrator (e.g., the perpetrator threatens to hurt the children if their mother does not cooperate; the perpetrator uses the children as "spies" and interrogates them about their mother's activities)

- sustaining injury during the violence (e.g., a child is injured while trying to protect another family member)

- experiencing the physical, emotional, and psychological repercussions of violence (e.g., a family member is physically injured; living in a tense environment dominated by fear; child protection and/or police intervention).

As expressed by Newton (2001),

Domestic violence can severely impair a parent's ability to nurture the development of their children. Mothers who are abused may be depressed or preoccupied with the violence. They may be emotionally withdrawn or numb, irritable or have feelings of hopelessness. The result can be a parent who is less emotionally available to their children or unable to care for their children's basic needs. Battering fathers are less affectionate, less available, and less rational in dealing with their children.

It is impossible to accurately determine how many children are exposed to abuse and violence in their own families, but the statistics below clearly indicate that it is a pervasive and troubling problem:

- Eleven to 23 percent of all Canadian children witness some violence against their mother in the home. It is estimated that two to six children in each classroom have witnessed some form of woman abuse in the home over the past year (Sudermann and Jaffe, 1999).

- Studies estimate that 60 to 80 percent of children in families where woman abuse occurs either see or overhear it (Jaffe, Wolfe, and Wilson, 1990).

- In 2009 in Canada, 52 percent of spousal victims with children reported that their children heard or saw assaults on them in the previous five years. This was an increase from 43 percent in 2004 (Sinha, 2012: 6).[2] The form and consequences of spousal assaults witnessed by children tended to be more severe, compared with violence where children were not present (e.g., threats/assaults with a gun or knife, physical injuries). Spousal victims with children present were also three times more likely than others to fear for their lives (32 percent versus 7 percent) and to take time

off from their daily activities (31 percent versus 9 percent) (Ibid: 70).

- Studies that have explored the prevalence of child abuse in homes where domestic violence occurs indicate that in 26 to 78 percent of cases, the children are also being abused (Bowen, 2000; Bowker, Arbitell, and McFerron, 1988; Edleson, 1999; Straus and Gelles, 1990; Suh and Abel, 1990).

- In studies of child abuse, about 50 percent of the cases also involve the abuse of the child's mother (Sudermann and Jaffe, 1999).

The *Canadian Maternity Experiences Survey* estimated that 6% of mothers 15 years of age and older who had recently given birth experienced abuse or violence at the hand of a spouse, partner or boyfriend within the previous 2 years. This represents approximately 4,300 mothers that were either physically or sexually victimized by their partner. Almost 3/4 (74%) of these mothers indicated the violence started before they were pregnant, and almost 1/3 (32%) said they were abused during the pregnancy (29% said that their partner knew that they were pregnant when the abuse occurred). Another 27% reported that the violence occurred after the birth of their child. (Public Health Agency of Canada, 2009: 96)

- In Canada, between April 1, 2009, and March 31, 2010, there were over 64,500 admissions of women to shelters across Canada (452 admissions per 100,000 women). The following statistics are the findings of the "snapshot date" of April 15, 2010 (i.e., information collected on women being served in shelters on a specific date) from the report *Shelters for Abused Women in Canada, 2010* (Burczycka and Cotter, 2011):

  - Abuse was the reason 71 percent of women sought refuge.

  - 74 percent of women with parental responsibilities brought their children into the shelter with them (on average, these women were admitted with two children).

  - The desire to protect their children from suffering or witnessing abuse was a significant motivating factor for women to seek shelter.

- Between 1995 and 2004, in 4.4 percent of the spousal homicides in Canada, children of the perpetrators were also killed (Statistics Canada, 2006a).

"If domestic violence calls are dangerous, emotionally charged, and volatile for police officers, the accused and the victim, they are equally as distressing and frightening—if not more so—for children at the scene" (Benoit and Gibson, 2006: 7).

THE POSSIBLE IMPACT OF ABUSE ON CHILDREN

Where there is family violence, the home environment in which these children live is often described as "toxic"; in many cases, the children's well-being and development are severely compromised. There is often an atmosphere of fear, anxiety, anger, and tension that permeates the home, even when incidents of physical abuse are not happening (Sudermann and Jaffe, 1999).

Children who have witnessed the abuse of their mothers often experience the same types of emotional and behavioural problems experienced by children who have been abused themselves (Sudermann and Jaffe, 1999). These may include symptoms of posttraumatic stress disorder, lower self-esteem and social competence, aggressive behaviour, conduct problems, anxiety, and depression (The Future of Children, 1999: 2).

Like all other forms of abuse against children, the extent of sexual exploitation of children over the Internet is unknown, and the effects of Internet sexual exploitation are not fully understood (Rimer, 2007). Generally, the trauma suffered by victims of child pornography is longer lasting and harder to alleviate (Palmer, 2004). There is also the added dimension that there is a permanent record of the abuse that will be on the Internet forever, out of the victim's control (Palmer, 2005; Cooper, 2006).

The section below explains how the impact of child abuse, violence, and exploitation may manifest in children.

SELF-BLAME

- Some children feel they are responsible for what happens to them and around them. When they are abused, they often blame themselves. They may think they deserved the physical abuse because they were bad, or the sexual abuse because they wanted love or accepted presents from the offender. Many children feel responsible for their mother's suffering and their father's anger.

- Some children feel guilty because they did not try to stop the abuser, especially if a family member was hurt. Many children tried to protect themselves, but failed. As a result, they do not try anymore. This is a type of learned helplessness.

- Children may experience a deep sense of shame, or feel different, damaged, and alone. The sense of shame and secrecy can affect their ability to express feelings openly (Jaffe, Wolfe, and Wilson, 1990).

FEAR

- Children who have been abused or have been exposed to family violence are often left in fear of those they know and trust—the world is no longer a safe place.

- Children may be afraid of rejection, upset, or other negative reactions, either from family, from friends, or, in some cases, by the offender. This may be emphasized if there are specific cultural taboos or expectations around disclosing matters relating to abuse.

- Children may also be afraid that the threats the abuser has used will come true (e.g., the disclosure will result in the breakup of the family); that they themselves or someone they love will be hurt or killed; and that they will be abandoned if someone finds out about the abuse.

POWERLESS AND VULNERABLE

- Children feel powerless to protect themselves: nothing they did stopped the abuse of themselves or others, or they had no way to stop it.

- Some children are isolated, with no one to help or support them; some children may think that no one has the ability to stop the abuser.

- Children may lose faith in themselves, others, and their future. Having experienced the world as unsafe and unloving, they fall into despair and give up hope that their needs will be met.

- Exposure to family violence teaches children that being male equals being powerful and abusive, and being female equals being punished and victimized. They learn that power and violence are ways to deal with decision making, conflict resolution, and stress release. Boys, particularly, may be aggressive in their relationships with their mothers, girlfriends, or partners, while girls are more likely to be victims of domestic and sexual violence (Moore et al., 1990; Hagemann-White, 2006). It has also been suggested that "because of their own familiarity with violence and abuse during their earlier development, some vulnerable youth may have particular difficulty recognizing their own abusive behavior in romantic relationships or their options to terminate an abusive romantic relationship" (Wolfe and Feiring, 2000: 362).

BETRAYAL

- Children learn that a trusted person has hurt them or someone they care about, causing them to feel angry, betrayed, confused, and depressed.

- Children often feel confused because they love the abuser. Should they be loyal to the abuser or tell what happened?

- Children who have been betrayed often have trouble trusting others and forming healthy relationships.

DESTRUCTIVENESS

- Children who grow up in violent environments may engage in self-destructive behaviour, including self-mutilation, frightening displays of rage, eating disorders, substance abuse, prostitution, suicidal or homicidal tendencies, and involvement in criminal activity.

- A study by Jaffe, Wolfe, and Wilson (1990) reported that 70 percent of young offenders charged with crimes against people have witnessed violence in their families. Longitudinal studies on delinquency have shown that children who develop a "deviant career" are more likely to have parents who are abusive toward their partners, compared to those not exposed to interparental violence (Steinberg, 2000).

LOSS

Children who have been abused may suffer many losses:

- They lose the innocence and trust of childhood.

- Gone is a sense of control over their environments.

- Normal patterns of growth and development, including problems with eating, sleeping, developing healthy relationships, normal sexuality, and school are affected.

- Normal emotional attachments to primary caregivers erode: the most important protective factor for children exposed to violence is a secure relationship with an adult, most often a parent. Research by Zeanah et al. (1999) revealed that mothers who experienced more serious partner violence were more likely to have infants with disorganized attachments to their mothers. Problems with bonding and attachment to the primary caregiver can lead to a fragile foundation that is associated with a myriad of adverse effects in intellectual, emotional, social and behavioural functioning, including delayed development in motor, language, cognitive, and learning skills; difficulty expressing and regulating emotions; aggression; mental health problems; dysfunctional relationships; substance addiction; and delinquency and criminal activity (Benoit, 2005; Benoit and Gibson, 2006; Cohen, Cole, and Szrom, 2011: 4; Cuthbert, Rayns, and Stanley, 2011: 22; Perry, 2002: 95).

- The prevalent belief that young children, particularly infants, are not impacted by stress or traumatized in the way that teenagers and adults are is simply untrue. Neurological and psychological research has revealed that brain development is negatively affected when children, including very young children, are exposed to substantial stresses and trauma, such as child abuse and exposure to family violence. This has implications for how an individual responds biologically, physically, cognitively, and emotionally to stressful situations; a range of mental health problems (e.g., depression and anxiety); emotional regulation, impulsivity, and aggression; cognitive and social processing; and physical stress-related problems (Benoit, 2005; Benoit and Gibson, 2006 Cohen, Cole, and Szrom, 2011: 3; Healy, 2004; McCrory, McCrory, De Brito, and Viding, 2011; Mohr and Fantuzzo, 2000; National Scientific Council on the Developing Child, 2005, 2010; Perry, 1995, 2004; Rossman and Ho, 2000).

- In some cases, the abuser isolates the children or the children choose not to bring friends home for fear that the violence may be uncovered. As a result, these children may not develop positive peer relationships or learn important social skills. Peer friendships are also negatively affected for those children who respond to family violence with withdrawn or aggressive behaviour. Bullying and victimization in school are associated with exposure to interparental violence (Baldry, 2003).

- On disclosure, there may be removal from homes and families, the community, and other caregivers; children may worry about who will take care of them.

Effects of exposure to abuse and violence in childhood may persist into adulthood and last a lifetime. They include difficulty establishing and maintaining relationships; misuse of power and control; substance abuse; self-destructive behaviour (e.g., suicidal tendencies, eating disorders); posttraumatic stress disorder; anxiety; depression; poor self-esteem; and health problems (e.g., heart disease, hypertension, stroke, diabetes) (Felitti, et al., 1998; The National Children's Advocacy Center, 2011).

ROLE OF THE TEACHER
REPORTING SUSPICIONS OF CHILD ABUSE AND FAMILY VIOLENCE

Each province and territory in Canada has its own legislation with respect to child abuse and "a child in need of protection" or "child whose security or development is in danger," although they all address neglect, physical, sexual, and emotional abuse, and the death of a parent. Each province and territory addresses the age of a child who is entitled to protection under the law, the duty to report, confidentiality, and failure to report. It is imperative that all individuals who provide services to children and families be familiar with their current provincial/territorial legislation with respect to the children's protection; this means keeping up-to-date on any relevant legislative changes.

When one form of abuse is suspected or identified, it is important to be tuned into the possible indicators of other types of abuse occurring within the same family. In situations where there are concerns or doubts as to whether or not the indicators support suspicions of child abuse or family violence

and reporting requirements, it is best *not* to ask anyone else to help you decide if the call should be made; instead, consult with a worker from the local child protection agency. It is also advisable to consult with a child protection worker before informing a parent/caregiver that you are consulting/reporting to a child protection agency, or that you have already done so. To do so could jeopardize the child and/or the investigation and court proceedings. If you acquire additional information or new suspicions arise, call the child protection agency again—do not take for granted that a child protection agency knows about the present situation or issues, even if the child protection agency is or has been involved with the family.

The *Criminal Code of Canada* sets out offences relating to neglect and physical abuse of children (e.g., abandonment, assault), sexual abuse (e.g., invitation to sexual touching, sexual exploitation), and the age of consent regarding sexual acts. The *Criminal Code* does *not* include a specific charge for "woman abuse" or "partner abuse"; however, an alleged abuser may be charged with any number of relevant criminal offences (e.g., forcible confinement, criminal harassment, attempted murder).

HELPING PARENTS WHEN THEIR CHILD HAS BEEN ABUSED

Coping with the crisis of a child's abuse and disclosure can be distressing and exhausting for parents/caregivers. It is the parent's response to the child's disclosure that is so important to the child's recovery. Parents need help staying calm for their children and providing stability and reassurance while everyone is coping with what happens after suspicions of child abuse are disclosed. Parents may ask staff/caregivers for information and advice. The following information will assist in helping those who are in need of support.

- A child's experience of abuse may cause tremendous stress and disruption in the family. A difficult period for children and families is to be expected. Try to maintain consistent routines and limits, avoiding other new or challenging experiences and unnecessary separations from primary caregivers.

- The child's siblings may be afraid of what will happen or feel guilty for not protecting the child. It is also possible that other children in the family may have been abused.

- Children communicate in their own way. Encourage children to talk by being a good listener and trying to stay calm, no matter what the child says. Let the child talk about what happened using his or her own words, without adding words or asking leading questions, which may confuse the child and affect an investigation.

- Accept any temporary regression in the child's behaviour (e.g., bed-wetting). It may be advisable for parents/caregivers to supervise the child more closely, setting clear limits on aggressive and hurtful behaviours. Children need to be reassured that their feelings, fears, and behaviours that seem babyish or out of control are normal after this type of experience. With time they will feel more like themselves.

- Some children may need night-time comforts and strategies to cope with bedtime fears. If asked, a child may be able to tell parents what she or he needs (e.g., a night light, leaving the bedroom door open at night). It is helpful to try to protect children from re-exposure to frightening situations and reminders of the abuse.

- This is a time when parents may question their beliefs about themselves as parents and protectors, their ability to judge people, feelings about the world as a safe place, and justice. Their own memories of abuse may also be triggered. It is important to get help or advice, not only for their children but also for themselves. Direct parents to the appropriate community resources to help with emotional, economic, legal, and/or safety issues.

- Encourage parents to talk about their own feelings with someone they trust. It is normal for parents to feel helpless and guilty especially if they feel that they did not protect their child. Many parents think about things over and over, trying to understand what has happened, being fearful that the abuse will happen again.

- Although parents' feelings need to be acknowledged, remind them that expressing intense feelings to the child and minimizing or exaggerating the child's trauma may overwhelm and frighten a child. Children should not have to worry about whether or not their parents are coping; it is the job of grown-ups to look after the children.

- Encourage parents to role model healthy communication and interactions, solutions for conflicts, positive discipline, and positive strategies for coping.

- Recommend to parents that they should tell the child's doctor about the allegation of abuse. Parents may want the doctor to check the child for health reasons and/or to discuss getting help. The child may also need reassurance if he or she is worried about anything.

- Advise parents to contact a child protection agency with their suspicions, concerns, or questions. Parents can help the investigation by cooperating.

- Suggest to parents that they keep notes on further developments or disclosures and their observations of their child's behaviour. This information may be helpful to the investigation and to the support people working with the child and the family.

- Reinforce to parents that even if legal proceedings do not result in charges or a conviction, the child is to be believed and commended for his or her efforts. The child should never be blamed for whatever happens.

- Parents must decide whether or not, and when, to tell others about the abuse. Suggest to parents that they listen to the child's feelings as to who should be told. Ask them to respect the child's rights to privacy and confidentiality.

- Suggesting family outings and fun activities will help to reduce the stress for everyone.

- It can be reassuring to remind everyone that the passage of time will help reduce stress and anxiety.

HELPING CHILDREN WHO HAVE EXPERIENCED ABUSE

Staff plan and implement many of the strategies below for *all* children enrolled in a program. However, the goals and strategies are especially critical for children who have been victims of abuse and/or family violence. Remember that many children express their pain, fear, anger, despair, and other feelings through play and "misbehaviour." Seek the advice of appropriate professionals if needed; knowledge of atypical development and therapies is a specialized area. Children are resilient, and with supports for themselves and their families, they can heal and thrive (adapted from Rimer and Prager, 1998).

Children in a state of fear retrieve information from the world differently than children who feel calm. In a state of calm, we use the higher, more complex parts of our brain to process and act on information. In a state of fear, we use the lower, more primitive parts of our brain. As the perceived threat level goes up, the less thoughtful and the more reactive our responses become. Actions in this state may be governed by emotional and reactive styles.... The traumatized child lives in an aroused state, ill-prepared to learn from social, emotional, and other life experiences. She is living in the minute and may not fully appreciate the consequences of her actions. (Perry, 2004)

- Help children to develop positive self-esteem.

  - Plan activities where success is built in, based on the children's age, development, and realistic expectations.

  - Give positive reinforcement for accomplishments and desired behaviour.

  - Display the children's accomplishments.

  - Reinforce through discussion and activities that women and men are both valued and respected, and should never be controlled through violence.

- Help children to trust.

  - Establish limits and routines and be consistent.

  - Be loving and affectionate, and respect children who may need more time before feeling comfortable with being touched.

  - Allow children to safely express anger without the fear of punishment.

  - Spend one-on-one time so children feel cared for and listened to.

- Help children to gain control over their environment, since many children who have experienced abuse and family violence had little or no control in their environment.

- Help children to identify and express emotions.

  - Name emotions.

  - Plan sensory and dramatic play activities.

- Provide books and other materials that help children learn about feelings.

- Show children healthy ways to express anger and solve problems without hurting themselves or others.

- Accept children's need to talk about fears, sadness, and losses experienced because of abuse.

- Help children to learn to communicate.

  - Speak to children calmly.

  - Use a firm but kind tone when asking children to do things or when expressing disapproval.

  - Give children the message that it is okay to ask questions and say how they feel.

  - Spend time talking and listening.

  - Plan activities that encourage language and listening skills.

- Help children to identify and solve problem situations.

  - Teach children that they have choices and how to make the best choice.

  - Use positive methods to guide children's behaviour.

  - Plan activities that require problem solving.

  - Solve any conflicts that happen with nonviolent methods, and role-model calm, nonaggressive ways of dealing with anger.

- Help children to resume developmental progress.

  - Plan activities that help practise motor and language skills.

  - Support positive relationships with friends.

  - Help children with schoolwork.

- Help children to develop a safety plan.

  - Teach children how to dial 911 (i.e., practise memorizing the phone number; teach them to leave the phone off the hook until police arrive).

  - Help children to choose a neighbour they can go to for help.

  - Plan how to keep safe during a violent scene (e.g., identify a safe spot to hide; do not try to stop the fight).

VIOLENCE PREVENTION

Early childhood educators have an important role to play in preventing child abuse and family violence by maintaining an environment for children and families that is physically and psychologically safe; modelling healthy relationships; developing policies and practices to prevent abuse and violence; identifying and responding effectively to children believed to be at risk; participating in advocacy; and being responsive to the needs of their communities.

Prevention materials have changed considerably in the past decade, so be sure that you are using materials that are up-to-date and developmentally appropriate. For example, the reality is that most children are harmed by someone they know and trust (Fallon et al., 2005; Statistics Canada, 2011; Sinha, 2012), so the focus should *not* be on "stranger danger."

Although there has been considerable progress in Canada in the understanding and response to child abuse and family violence, the prevalence of violence, the extension of victimization into the virtual world, and lack of universal services and supports mean that we must continue to address these issues. Participation in preventing abuse and violence in Canadian homes and communities can be accomplished on individual, collective, and societal levels.

- Examine and challenge personal values and relationships with family members, children, colleagues, and others.

- Participate in personal and professional development to update knowledge and skills, keeping current with relevant legislation and research. Subscribe to related journals, mailing lists, and websites.

- Learn about the dynamics of abuse and violence, indicators, how to respond to disclosure, and reporting responsibilities. Follow through on your legal and moral responsibility to report.

- Develop a philosophy, goals, and programs for children's learning about relationships and sexuality that build self-esteem and potential, regardless of gender and ability, and teach peaceful problem solving and conflict resolution; making good choices; respect; understanding of individual rights and responsibilities; and how and where to get help. All of these help to lessen children's vulnerability to abuse and promote healthy relationships.

- Model equality in relationships and the positive use of power.

- Choose language carefully, refraining from racist and sexist words and derogatory labels, and challenge sexist jokes and discriminatory practices.

- Be open to discussion with parents about parenting, discipline, early intervention, and other related topics, and provide opportunities for parents to meet together. Help parents and caregivers to understand how to meet the physical and emotional needs of children. Examine barriers that might prevent working with parents as partners.

- Maintain an up-to-date list of community resources and agencies. Include resources specific to the cultural and language mix represented in the agency.

Inside LOOK

To reduce fever, fatigue, headaches, asthma, muscle/tendon injuries, digestive disorders, urinary tract infections, and coughs, many cultures have a variety of treatments that may be interpreted by the uneducated as some as a form of abuse. These treatments may include cupping, in which a heated glass is placed upside down on the chest or back, and it is taken off when it has cooled; this creates a vacuum that results in red, ring-shaped marks. Spooning involves rubbing a spoon vigorously back and forth across the person's body, often on the back or neck. A similar treatment—coining—uses a coin to rub the back, neck, stomach, chest, upper arms, forehead, and temples after applying oil along the acupuncture meridians. For many, these treatments "rub out" evil winds or spirits and restore good health.

http://www.neighboursfriendsandfamilies.ca

This valuable and resourceful website—*Neighbours, Friends and Families*—supports a public education campaign to raise awareness of the signs of woman abuse so that those close to an at-risk woman or an abusive man can help. Dr. Peter Jaffe, academic director, Centre for Education and Research on Violence Against Women and Children, states on the website,

> In the majority of cases there were several risk factors that family, friends or co-workers could have identified. Had they understood the significance of what they were seeing, they might have been able to inform the person who became the victim of the risk or they may have been able to intervene with the abusive man. We want to change public attitudes so that everybody, whether a friend, neighbour or a family doctor, will look at this issue differently and respond.

> The organization provides brochures such as "How You Can Identify and Help Women at Risk of Abuse," "How to Talk to Men Who Are Abusive," and "Safety Planning for Women Who Are Abused"; a Community Action Kit to organize in your community; and a video.

- Advocate on behalf of children and families, encouraging those in positions of responsibility to recognize the issues surrounding child abuse and family violence.

- Become an active member of organizations that battle the acceptance of violence in our society, including child pornography, children/youth in the sex trade, and the negative influence of the media.

- Be an active participant in building bridges with other services and resources in the community, including child protection and police services.

Children should *never* be given the message that they are responsible for protecting themselves, nor should staff and parents expect a child to protect him- or herself. This is the responsibility of those who care for children and the community at large.

Osofsky summarizes that "protecting children and facilitating their development is a family's most basic function" (2003: 162).

A Very Touching Book, by J. Hindman

Today I Feel Silly and Other Moods That Make My Day, by J.L. Curtis

The Cloud, by H. Cumming

The Way I Feel, by J. Cain

I'm Gonna Like Me: Letting Off a Little Self-Esteem, by J.L. Curtis and L. Cornell

I Like Myself, by K. Beaumont

The Hurt, by T. Doleski

A Boy and a Bear: The Children's Relaxation Book, by L. Lite

Stress Relief for Kids: Taming Your Dragons (Creative Relaxation Activities for Home and School), by M. Belknap

A Terrible Thing Happened: A Story for Children Who Have Witnessed Violence or Trauma, by M. Holmes

BOOKS FOR CHILDREN

I'm a Great Little Kid Series, by L. Grossman (*Now I See How Great I Can Be; Respect Is Correct; It's No Joke, My Telephone Broke; Sam Speaks Out; Charlene's Choice; A Tale Worth Telling*)

BOOKS FOR ADULTS

Cruel But Not Unusual: Violence in Canadian Families, by R. Alaggia and C. Vine

Safe Kids, Safe Families, by S. Wilson

Protecting the Gift: Keeping Children and Teenagers Safe (and Parents Sane), by G. De Becker

Childhood Victimization: Violence, Crime, and Abuse in the Lives of Young People, by D. Finkelhor

The War on Women, by E. Armour and J. Hurshman

Criminal Domestic Violence in Canadian Homes, by B. Vallée

KIDS HAVE STRESS TOO

In his book *The Hurried Child,* David Elkind (1981) suggests that stress is the wear and tear on our bodies that is produced by the very process of living. One of the greatest contributors to stress in children's lives is hurry—to get ready, to go from one place to another, to do well, and to grow up. Family upheavals from death or divorce, family health problems, tension, and quarrelling in the home lead to children's fear, anxiety, and emotional overload, and contribute to chronic stress. Signs and signals that indicate a child might be experiencing undue stress include

- recurring headaches, tummy aches, or neck pain

- increased irritability, sadness, panic, anger

- being more quiet than usual

- trouble relaxing or sleeping

- lethargy, daydreaming, withdrawal from activities

- excessive energy or restlessness

- reverting to less mature behaviours

- nervous habits such as nail biting, hair twisting, thumb sucking, or sighing deeply

- subtle reactions, a strained look, frowning

- trouble getting along with friends (CCCF, 2001:19)[*]

Kids Have Stress Too, an education program for preschoolers to children aged 9 years, may help educators and families find effective ways to provide support. Claire McDerment, co-chair of Kids Have Stress Too (**http://www.ecdss.ca**) states that stress can affect children's physical, emotional, social, and intellectual well-being. Extreme stress can have a negative effect on brain development in very young children; they have a weakened immune system and are three times as likely to

[*] Canadian Child Care Federation (CCCF). 2001. *Resource Sheet #19. Stress In Children.* http://www.bcfcca.ca/pdfs/participant_resources_3/Stress%20in%20Children.pdf. Reprinted by permission.

Inside LOOK

My Toes Feel Like Spaghetti: An Exploration of Relaxation Strategies for Preschool Children

A Yukon-based project which teaches relaxation procedures such as breathing, progressive muscle relaxation and yoga to three- to five-year-old children was designed to encourage effective coping strategies. Providing young children with skills and strategies to cope enhances their abilities to respond and adapt effectively to a variety of situations. The early intervention workers observed the children to be calmer after engaging in these experiences. Parents also talked about the transfer of skills at home. The workers also reported that incorporating relaxation activities into the routine appeared to increase the children's abilities to focus and attend to activities promoting self-control, cooperativeness and positive interactions. The workers also described similar benefits for themselves; feeling calmer after they gained the skill and confidence level to lead the activities and engage the children. One worker noted, "My voice level has gone down, it is not so high pitched and I am aware of my tone." Providing children with skills and competencies to enhance their coping abilities at a young age promotes life-long practices of independence, wellness and self-care. The children's eagerness to participate in and then adopt the relaxation procedures (to tense their toes like popsicle sticks and then relax them like spaghetti) provides a foundation for pre-schoolers to acquire relaxation strategies that will allow them to respond to future stressful experiences in an effective, healthy manner.

Source: L. Corniere and S. Armstrong, 2008-2009. "My Toes Feel Like Spaghetti: An Exploration of Relaxation Strategies for Preschool Children," *IMPRINT: The Newsletter of Infant Mental Health Promotion* Vol. 52, Winter, pages 9–11, The Hospital for Sick Children, Infant Mental Health Promotion, Toronto. Reprinted by permission.

Yoga 4 Kids

Under the leadership of Director Sherry LeBlanc, this program is based upon the yoga practices of Kundalini Yoga and Integral Hatha Yoga (**http://www.yoga4kids.org**). It is specifically developed to suit the needs and abilities of children. The program combines dynamic movements, postures, and simple breath and mantra meditations with game playing, singing, storytelling, and deep relaxation into an integrated and holistic program of physical fitness, education, and social and self awareness. Family yoga is also an option that strengthens the bond between parent and child. Yoga therapy is also available for children with special needs. These programs help children be calm, inwardly focused, and to value silence and stillness among others.

catch respiratory infections. Children report that their stress comes from many different factors:

- moving to a new home or school or starting school for the first time

- having too much to do; kids need some quiet time

- feeling different from other kids, or being teased or bullied

- fighting or arguing among family members, or not getting along well with brothers or sisters

- having trouble with schoolwork

- being yelled at by family, friends, or teachers

- having a family break up

- feeling lonely and unloved

The program was developed by the Psychology Foundation of Canada, Toronto Public Health, and the Toronto District School Board Stress Management Committee. It includes a facilitator resource guide and provides training for those who wish to become facilitators. The Preschool Program is designed for teachers of young children and provides strategies for creating a caring environment where adults model a peaceful and relaxed program. The Preschool Program also supports teachers in helping children identify the symptoms of stress, the physical and emotional changes that take place, and strategies for reducing stress.

Information is available from the Psychology Foundation of Canada (**http://www.psychology foundation.org**).

BOOKS FOR CHILDREN

My Daddy Is a Pretzel: Yoga for Parents and Children, by B. Baptiste

The Yoga Adventure for Children: Playing, Dancing, Moving, Breathing, Relaxing, by H. Purperhart

A Boy and a Bear: The Children's Relaxation Book, by L. Lite

Cool Cats, Calm Kids: Relaxation and Stress Management for Young People, by M. Williams

Don't Pop Your Cork on Mondays! The Children's Anti-Stress Book, by A. Moser and D. Pilkey

Stress Relief for Kids: Taming Your Dragons, by M. Belknap

When My Worries Get Too Big: A Relaxation Books for Children Who Live with Anxiety, by K. Dunn Buron

Be the Boss of Your Body: Kit with Stress Book and Self Care for Kids, by T. Culbert and R. Kajander

Stress Can Really Get on Your Nerves, by T. Romain and E. Verdick

BOOKS FOR ADULTS

The Hurried Child: Growing Up Too Fast and Too Soon, by D. Elkind

10 Mindful Minutes: Giving Our Children and Ourselves the Social and Emotional Skills to Reduce Stress and Anxiety for Healthier, Happy Lives, by G. Hawn, W. Holden, and D.J. Siegel

Growing Up Brave: Expert Strategies for Helping Your Child Overcome Fear, Stress and Anxiety, by D.B. Pincus

The Highly Sensitive Child, by E. Aron

Ties That Stress: The New Family Imbalance, by D. Elkind

The Worried Child, by P. Foxman

RESILIENT CHILDREN

What helps children overcome difficult life experiences? What makes for resilient children, those who are able to demonstrate positive outcomes even when in high-risk situations? One important element is the child's temperament. Resilient children are easy children: active, affectionate, and good natured. These children seem to bring forth positive responses in the adults who care for them, and they learn early to cope through both self-sufficiency and asking for help when they need it (Werner, 1995).

Children can become more resilient even in families where there is a great deal of turmoil when they are supported by "at least one family member who is emotionally competent, stable, and willing to nurture that child. Further, community members, especially teachers, are often seen as a source of support when at-risk children are facing crises. Characteristics of these teachers are that they listened to the children, challenged them, and rooted for them" (Werner, 1995: 83, in Couchenour and Chrisman 2000: 78).

A child's temperament influences parental interactions.

Courtesy of Scotia Plaza Child Care Centre

FAMILIES FROM WHICH A PARENT IS INCARCERATED

Families from which a parent is incarcerated require skillful interactions on the part of the teacher. Understanding more about the profile of both female and male offenders in the country is perhaps the best place to start.

FEMALE OFFENDERS

- According to Thompson (2011), more than half of female inmates in Canadian federal facilities are ages 20 to 34, and 85 percent of incarcerated women are mothers.

- More than one third (37 percent) of women sentenced to a prison term are Aboriginal, an alarming number in a country where less than 3 percent of the population is First Nations, Métis, or Inuit.

- Drug offenders comprise more than one quarter of all female federal inmates in Canada.

- Women convicted of various property offences make up the majority of female inmates in provincial and territorial prisons.

Crimes by women are usually driven by survival, exploitation by others, escape from abusive families or relationships, or the search for love, acceptance and belonging. The sample of women surveyed matched the expected profile: young mothers of young children, high levels of unemployment and early school leaving, low levels of father involvement with the children and an over-representation of Aboriginal and visible minority women. Theirs are oftentimes fragile family units, living in unsafe neighbourhoods, poor, socially marginalized, isolated from good family support. A stay in custody, even a brief one, is more likely to compromise their success in life than assist it. (Cunningham and Baker, 2011)*

MALE OFFENDERS

- In Canada, nearly half of all male prisoners in federal prisons are between the ages of 25 and 34.

- Younger men make up a higher proportion of the provincial and territorial prison population—about one quarter of male inmates in such facilities are between the ages of 20 and 24.

* Cunningham, A., and Baker, L. 2011. "Waiting For Mommy: Children of Incarcerated Women," *Transition*, Vol. 42 (Summer), No 2. Reprinted by permission of The Vanier Institute of the Family.

Stress Test for Children

STRESS	POINTS	CHILD'S SCORE
Parent Dies	100	
Parents Divorce	73	
Parent Separate	65	
Separation from Parent (foster placement, termination of parental rights)	65	
Parent Travels as Part of Job	63	
Close Family Member Dies	63	
Personal Illness or Injury	53	
Parent Remarries	50	
Parent Loses Job	47	
Parents Reconcile After Separation	45	
Mother Goes to Work	45	
Change In Health of a Family Member	44	
Mother Becomes Pregnant	40	
School Difficulties	39	
Birth of a Sibling	39	
School Readjustment (new teacher)	39	
Change in Family's Financial Condition	38	
Injury or Illness of a Close Friend	37	
Starts New (or changes) Extracurricular Activity (music, Brownies, etc.)	36	
Change in Number of Fights with Siblings	35	
Exposed to Violence at School	31	
Theft of Personal Possessions	30	
Changes Responsibilities at Home	29	
Older Brother or Sister Leaves Home	29	
Trouble with Grandparents	29	
Outstanding Personal Achievement	28	
Move to Another City	26	
Move to Another Part of Town	26	
Receives or Loses a Pet	25	
Changes in Personal Habits	24	
Trouble with a Teacher	24	
Changes in Hours with Baby Sitter or Day Care Centre	20	
Move to a New House in Same School District	20	
Changes to a New School	20	
Changes in Play Habits	19	
Vacations with Family	19	
Change in Friends	18	
Attends Summer Camp	17	
Changes Sleeping Habits	16	
Change in Number of Family Get-Togethers	15	
Changes Eating Habits	15	
Changes Amount of TV Viewing	13	
Birthday Party	12	
Punished for Not "Telling The Truth"	11	
Child's Total Score		

Add child's total score: score below 150 = average stress load, score between 150–300 = higher than average chance of stress symptoms, score above 300 = high likelihood of serious change in health and/or behaviour.

Source: From *The Worried Child: Recognizing Anxiety in Children and Helping Them Heal*. Excerpted with permission from Hunter House Inc., Publishers. © 2004 by Paul Foxman, PhD. To order call (800) 266-5592, fax (510) 865-4295, or visit www.hunterhouse.com. To order on Amazon, go to http://amzn.com/0897934202.

- Nearly three quarters of male federal inmates are Caucasian, while the government classifies one-sixth as Aboriginal.

- The majority of all male inmates are single.

- Roughly half of all male inmates in Canada are imprisoned for violent crimes, such as homicide, assault, and robbery.

- Approximately one quarter of all male federal inmates are imprisoned for homicide, while less than one tenth are incarcerated for drug offences.

Many fathers who are incarcerated experience a great sense of guilt and loss about the disruptions and challenges they have caused for their children and family.

For many children, parental incarceration often creates additional challenges, such as financial instability and material hardship, instability in family relationships and structure, residential mobility, school behaviour and performance problems, shame and social and/or institutional stigma. Having a parent in jail can have rippling effects on children's home life, school performance and mental well-being. Though many reports claim that maternal incarceration is more destabilizing for children, the reality is, whether it is Mom or Dad, or both, many children in Canada are affected by a parent behind bars. (MacNaull, 2011)

CHILDREN OF OFFENDERS

About 20,000 Canadian children experience a separation from an incarcerated parent each year (Cunningham and Baker, 2011). This separation can be especially difficult for children. However, family visits are possible. Anyone sentenced to more than two years in prison can be granted private family visits, which can include spouses, children, common-law partners, siblings, grandparents, friends, etc.,

for up to 72 hours; these visits may occur every two months. Some prisoners are barred from the program either because there is a risk of family or conjugal violence or because they have access to other programs for maintaining family ties, particularly unsupervised leaves (Vacheret, 2007).

Cunningham and Baker (2011) stated,

one-third of women worried that their children's current placement might not be safe, possibly because 85% had no time to make child-care arrangements prior to admission, typically because of an unexpected arrest. What may result is reliance on convenient but inappropriate caregivers, including when teenagers are left to care for younger siblings. Almost half of the children (43%) had to leave their homes, to move in with relatives or, for one-fifth, into foster care. For half of the children with siblings, this meant a separation from brothers and sisters. These disruptions occur at a time when stability and predictability are needed most by these vulnerable youngsters. Unlike separations for other reasons, such as military service or hospitalizations, children quickly realize that the situation is something to be embarrassed about, something to keep hidden from others such as teachers. This isolates them from sources of potential support.[*]

Many studies document a statistical association between parental incarceration and an elevated likelihood of later incarceration among their children. For example, Cunningham and Baker (2011: 2) found that

40% of the provincially sentenced women surveyed in their study had themselves been separated from a parent by incarceration during childhood. Among the mothers of teenaged children, about

---

[*] Cunningham, A., and Baker, L. 2011. "Waiting For Mommy: Children of Incarcerated Women," *Transition*, Vol. 42 (Summer), No 2. Reprinted by permission of The Vanier Institute of the Family.

Inside LOOK

It is difficult, if not impossible, to ensure equality before the law for Native people in our criminal courts when so many Native people do not understand the nature of the charges against them, the implications of a plea, the basic court procedures and legal terminology, or their right to speak on their own behalf or to request legal counsel.

Source: Department of Justice Canada, Aboriginal Courtwork Program, n.d.

From Imprisonment to Integration

First developed in 1998, *Stride* is an innovative program of Community Justice Initiatives (CJI)—a non-profit organization ... located in Kitchener that facilitates community-based solutions to conflict and crime through a central philosophy of restorative justice. Restorative justice is a way of approaching conflict and crime by addressing the needs of the victim, holding the offender accountable and including the broader community in the process. CJI and its programs have been recognized and emulated worldwide. Simply put, *Stride* expands the options available to women and their children, facilitating meaningful changes in their lives and supporting the development of positive coping strategies and constructive participation in society. In all its many facets, the program challenges and inspires the community to get involved, to be a part of the solution. A just community works toward addressing the root causes of crime and conflict and takes every opportunity to support the healing of all parties involved in an effort to see that it is never repeated. *Stride* strives for that which is restorative, not only for fractured people, families and relationships, but for communities at large.

Source: Thompson, J. 2011. "Striding Toward A Just Community," *Transition: Families and Incarceration*, Vol. 42 (Summer) No. 2. Reprinted by permission of The Vanier Institute of the Family.

half of those youngsters had already served a period of time in youth custody. Even without this research, we know enough to suggest that prison sentences and remand of women rarely make the public safer, often break down fragile family units, and impair a woman's ability to support herself and retain custody of her children. Prison is often the default option in the absence of more effective—and less costly—services such as addictions treatment, shelter, or hospitalization.[*]

There is no question that the overrepresentation of Aboriginals in the criminal justice system is an ongoing concern. The Aboriginal Justice Strategy (AJS) comprises community-based justice programs cost-shared with provincial and territorial governments, as well as capacity-building activities to support Aboriginal communities' involvement in the local administration of justice. These activities include diversion or alternative measures; community sentencing circles and peacemaking; mediation and arbitration in family and civil cases; and court/community justice programs. AJS programs supported to date have been managed by First Nations and tribal councils, community groups, urban Aboriginal coalitions, Inuit hamlets, Métis organizations, and other nonprofit organizations.

The Canadian Families and Corrections Network (CFCN) is a voluntary-sector agency whose mandate is "building stronger and safer communities by assisting families affected by criminal behaviour, incarceration and community reintegration." With over 20 years in business, CFCN understands that families are the ones who deal with the financial harm, geographical separation, stigma, emotional harm, ostracism from the community, lack of knowledge, and emotional cycle of incarceration. CFCN focuses on the needs of families across Canada as victims of the results both of criminal behaviour and of having a family member incarcerated. The organization offers services, programs, and assistance to help reduce the consequences of incarceration on the family. In 2011, the United Nations recognized CFCN's work, mainly *Jeffrey Goes to Jail* (a resource storybook for families with children), on the Day of the Child in Geneva, Switzerland.

- **Children Visiting Prisons in Kingston, Ontario,** runs a variety of programs and supports for families. These include a children's activity area normalizing the visiting experience for children without normalizing crime, prison, or incarceration, as well as parenting workshops strengthening the parent–child bond.

- **The House of Hope in Ottawa** offers family support services, such as support groups for women with a partner in prison, for children,

[*] Cunningham, A., and Baker, L. 2011. "Waiting For Mommy: Children of Incarcerated Women," *Transition*, Vol. 42 (Summer), No 2. Reprinted by permission of The Vanier Institute of the Family.

and for youths; a drop-in centre; short-term counselling; and information and referrals. Contact them at http://www.ohhaonline.ca/house_of_hope.htm.

ROLE OF THE TEACHER

Families and Corrections Network (FCN), an American organization for and about families of prisoners, is an outstanding resource for students and teachers. One important resource for fathers is the Children of Prisoners Library. This is a special collection of pamphlets and readings for incarcerated fathers, their families, their children, and those who work with their children. The library is open around the clock to millions of computer users via the Internet at **http://www.fcnetwork.org/cpl/cplindex.html**.

The organization has found that children ask or want to ask their incarcerated parents four main questions:

- Where are you?
- Why are you there?
- When are you coming home?
- Are you okay?

There are also two questions in the hearts and minds of prisoners' children that they rarely ask:

- Do you blame me?
- Do you love me?

These questions can come in many forms. Some children ask them directly; others beat around the bush. Some act out their questions by getting into trouble or confronting adults with challenging or aggressive behaviours.

Some parents find discussing this information very painful. They avoid telling the child or make up stories about the absent parent being in the hospital, in the military, away at school, working in another province, etc. Although lying to the children is intended to minimize feelings of shame and stigma, in fact it may increase these feelings by creating a family secret. Parents need to weigh three choices: tell the truth and let it be out in the open, tell the truth and ask the children to keep it quiet, or make up a story. Parents, and teachers if they are included, then have to judge the dangers of each option to the child's emotional health.

- Be a consistent, caring teacher who understands that children love their parents even when they have committed a crime.

- Do not speak negatively about the incarcerated parent.

- Be sensitive and responsive to the needs of the child who may feel angry, sad, confused, and worried. Provide ample opportunities for children to express their feelings in all forms—dramatic play, art, written work, etc.

- Research books on this topic to help children understand the prison system.

- Provide consistent, predictable routines in the centre with reasonable boundaries.

- Answer the children's questions. Teachers should do this only after discussions with the family.

- Tell children the truth, which is often easier to accept than what they might imagine. Children understand the idea of being punished for breaking the rules but they need simple descriptions of the offence—"Dad hurt someone," "Mom stole something." Older children will have more questions and may need more detail.

- Reassure the child. Often when one parent is incarcerated, the child can become very attached and worried that the remaining parent will be taken away.

- With family approval, collect examples of the child's work or photos of the child in the playroom for him or her to share with the parent by mail. Children might begin a picture or a story that the parent adds to and mail it back and forth.

- Give the child concrete examples of how long the parent will be away. The concept of time is difficult for a young child to understand so they will need specifics—three summers, four birthdays, etc.

- The stigma of incarceration is challenging for some children but the level of difficulty experienced may reflect the family's view of incarceration. If the family feels that the incarceration is more the result of social prejudice and less about the individual, children in these families may feel less stigma.

- Reassure older children that the incarcerated parent is safe, secure, and able to manage. Describing what the parent has access to is sometimes helpful—"Your mother has a bed and books to read," for example.

- Reassure children that they are not to blame for their parent's mistakes.

- Support and encourage the remaining parent. Help by finding agencies or organizations that will support families in their situation; other parents may need practical community support on issues such as budgeting and legal concerns.

BOOKS FOR CHILDREN

Visiting Day, by J. Woodson

Amber Was Brave, Essie Was Smart, by V. Williams

Jakeman, by D. Ellis

What Will Happen to Me?, by H. Zehr and L. Stutsman Amstutz

BOOKS FOR ADULTS

All Alone in the World: Children of the Incarcerated, by N. Bernstein

Imprisoned Fathers and Their Children, by G. Boswell

My Daddy Is in Jail: Story, Discussion Guide and Small Group Activities for Grades K to 5, by J. Bender

Loving Through Bars: Children with Parents in Prison, by C. Martone

War on the Family: Mothers in Prison and Families They Leave Behind, by R. Golden

ENDNOTES

1. The *Canadian Incidence Study of Reported Child Abuse and Neglect—2003* found that inappropriate punishment was a factor in 75 percent of substantiated cases of physical abuse; contrary to the common belief that child abuse in the result of pathological behaviour, this statistic indicates that most physical abuse is the result of punishment (Durrant and Ensom, 2006: 2), although the caregiver may not have intended to harm the child.

2. This is an underestimation since respondents were asked only about their children seeing or hearing physical or sexual assaults, and were not asked about children's exposure to emotional or verbal spousal violence or indirect exposure to violence. In addition, underestimation may occur if parents are unaware of their children's exposure to the violence, or if parents do not disclose their children's involvement for fear of repercussions or feelings of shame (Sinha, 2012: 68).

REFERENCES

Albanese, P. 2009. *Children in Canada Today*. Toronto: Oxford University Press.

Alcoba, N. 2008. "Child-Porn Fighter to Head Cybercrime Research Centre." *National Post*. March 21

Amatea, E. 2009. *Building Culturally Responsive Family-School Relationship*. Upper Saddle River, NJ: Merrill.

Ambert, A. 1997. *Parents, Children and Adolescents: Interactive Relationships and Development in Context*. New York: The Haworth Press.

————. 2006. *Changing Families: Relationships in Context.* Toronto: Pearson Education Canada.

————. 2012. *Changing Families: Relationships in Context,* 2nd ed. Toronto: Pearson Education Canada.

Amnesty International. 2004. *Stolen Sisters: A Human Rights Response to Discrimination and Violence Against Indigenous Women in Canada.* October. Retrieved from http://www.amnesty.org/en/library/info/AMR20/003/2004

Anderson, E.R., and A.M. Rice. 1992. "Sibling Relationships During Remarriage." *Monographs of the Society for Research in Child Development,* 57 (2–3), Serial No. 227. 149–177.

Andrews, G. 2008. "Primed to Heal: Delivering Effective Mental Health Care." *Maclean's.* March 17.

Baldry, A.C. 2003. "Bullying in Schools and Exposure to Domestic Violence." *Child Abuse and Neglect* 27. 713–732.

Baskin, B.H., and E.P. Riggs. 1988. "Mothers Who Are Disabled." In B. Birns and D.F. Day, eds., *Different Faces of Motherhood.* New York: Plenum Press.

Baumrind, D. 1967. "Child Care Practices Anteceding Three Patterns of Preschool Patterns." *Genetic Psychology Monographs,* 75. 43–88.

Beating and Child Abuse." In K. Yilo and M. Borad, eds. *Perspectives on Wife Abuse.* Newbury, CA: Sage Publications.

Benoit, D. 2005. "Efficacy of Attachment-based Interventions." University of Toronto and the Hospital for Sick Children. April. *Encyclopedia of Early Childhood Development.* Retrieved from http://www.child-encyclopedia.com

Benoit, D., and A. Gibson. 2006. "Impact of Violence on Children." *IMPrint: The Newsletter of Infant Mental Health Promotion* (IMP) 46. 6–10.

Best Start Resource Centre. 2011. "Early Brain Development: Parent Knowledge in Ontario, 2011." Retrieved from http://www.beststart.org/resources/hlthy_chld_dev

Blackford, K.A., and N.K. Israelite. 2003. "Families and Parents with Disabilities." In Marion Lynn, ed., *Voices: Essays on Canadian Families,* 2nd ed. Toronto: Nelson Thomson Learning.

Bowen, K. 2000. "Child Abuse and Domestic Violence in Families of Children Seen for Suspected Child Abuse." *Clinical Pediatrics* 39(1). 33–40.

Bowker, L.G., M. Arbitell, and J.R. McFerron. 1988. "On the Relationship Between Wife Beating and Child Abuse." In K. Yllo and M. Bograd, eds. *Perspectives on Wife Abuse.* Newsberry Park, CA: Sage.

Bradley, J. and P. Kibera. 2007. *Closing the Gap! Culture and the Promotion of Inclusion in Child Care. Spotlight on Young Children and Families.* Washington, D.C. NAEYC.

Brock, S.E., S.R. Jimerson, and K. Cowan. National Association of School Psychologists. 2005. "Responding to Hurricane Katrina. Understanding Responses of Children and Youth." Retrieved February 17, 2013, from http://www.teachersandfamilies.com/open/parent/katrina-cope.cfm

Brooks, J. 1997. *Parenting,* 2nd ed. Mountainview, CA: Mayfield Publishing Company.

————. 2006. *The Process of Parenting.* New York: McGraw Hill.

Bugental, D.B., and V.L. Cortez. 1988. "Physiological Reactivity to Responsive and Unresponsive Children as Moderated by Perceived Control." *Child Development* 59. 686–693.

Bugental, D.B., and W.A. Shennum. 1984. "'Difficult' Children as Elicitors and Targets of Adult Communication Patterns: An Attributional-Behavioral Transactional Analysis." *Monographs of the Society for Research in Child Development,* 49 (Serial No. 205).

Burczycka, M. and A. Cotter. 2011. "Shelters for Abused Women in Canada. 2010." Stats Canada. June 27. Retrieved February 11, 2013, from http://www.statcan.gc.ca/pub/85-002-x/85-002-x2011001-eng.htm

Canadian Alcohol and Drug Use Monitoring Survey. 2010. Retrieved February 11, 2013, from http://www.hc-sc.gc.ca/hc-ps/drugs-drogues/stat/_2010/summary-sommaire-eng.php

Canadian Centre for Child Protection. 2009. "A Child Sexual Prevention Kit." Parent Guide. Retrieved February 11, 2013, from http://www.teatreetells.ca/pdfs/parentguide_lowres.pdf

Canadian Child Care Federation (CCCF). 2001. "Resource Sheet 19. Stress in Children." Retrieved February 11, 2013, from http://www.bcfcca.ca/pdfs/participant_resources_3/Stress%20in%20Children.pdf

————. 2009. "Resource Sheet 97. How Do You Know That You Are Moving Toward Inclusion?" Retrieved from http://www.cccf-fcsge.ca/publications/resourcesheets_en.html

Canadian Council on Social Development. 2006. "The Progress of Canada's Children and Youth." *Family Life.* Ottawa: Health Canada.

Carson, L. 1987. *Integration Means All Our Children Belong.* Fredericton: Department of Education, Student Services Branch.

Chiu, S., D.A. Redelmeier, G. Tolomiczendo, A. Kiss, and S.W. Hwang. 2009. "The Health of Homeless Immigrants." National Institute of Health. Retrieved February 17, 2013, from http://www.ncbi.nlm.nih.gov/pmc/articles/PMC2773541/

Coleman, P.K. and K.H. Karraker. 1998. "Self-efficacy and Parenting Quality: Findings and Future Applications." *Developmental Review,* 18. 30–46.

Cooper, S.W. 2006. *Congressional Opening Statement of Sharon W. Copper, MD.* Retrieved from http://energy commerce.house.gov/reparchives/108/Hearings/04042006hearing1820/Cooper.pdf

————. 2007. Age Determination. Presentation at the Provincial Strategy to Protect Children from Sexual Abuse and Exploitation on the Internet, Multidisciplinary Training Conference. Gravenhurst, Ontario, March 5–7.

Corniere, L. and S. Armstrong. 2008–2009. "My Toes Feel Like Spaghetti: An Exploration of Relaxation Strategies for Preschool Children." *Infant Mental Health Promotion* (IMP). Vol. 52. Winter.

Couchenour, D. and Chrisman, K. 2000. *Families, Schools and Communities. Together for Young Children.* Delmar Learning.

————. 2011. *Families, School, and Communities: Together for Young Children,* 4th ed. Wadsworth Cengage Learning.

Crawford, T. 2007. "Jailed But Not Yet Found Guilty" *Toronto Star.* August 11. L12.

Crill Russell, C., W. Birnbaum, W.R. Avison, and P. Ioannone. n.d. "Vital Communities, Vital Support. How Well Do Canada's Communities Support Parents of Young Children? Phase 2 Report." *What Parents Tell Us. Invest In Kids.*

CTV Newsnet. 2009. "31 Charged After Ontario's Largest Ever Child Porn Sting." Retrieved February 11, 2013, from http://toronto.ctvnews.ca/31-charged-after-ont-s-largest-ever-child-porn-sting-1.367547

Cunningham, A., and L. Baker. 2011. "Waiting for Mommy: Children of Incarcerated Women." *Transition*. Summer, 42(2).

Cuthbert, C., G. Rayns, and K. Stanley. 2011 *All Babies Count*. London, UK: NSPCC.

Daly, M., and M. Wilson. 1993. "Spousal Homicide Risk and Estrangement." *Violence and Victims*, 8(11). 3–16.

De La Barrera, J., and D. Masterson. 1988. "Support Group Helps Troubled Fathers Learn Parenting Skills." *Children Today*. March–April.

Dineen, J.M. 1995. "For Jamai's Sake. "*Toronto Star,* September 22. B3.

Doherty, G. 2008. *Ensuring the Best Start in Life*. Institute for Research on Public Policy. 30.

Doherty-Derkowski, G. 1994. *Quality Matters: Excellence in Early Childhood Programs*. Don Mills, ON: Addison-Wesley.

Donovan, W.L., L.A. Leavitt, and R.Q. Walsh. 1990. "Maternal Self-efficacy: Illusory Control and Its Effect on Susceptibility to Learned Helplessness." *Child Development*, 61. 1638–1647.

Dougy Center. 2012. The National Centre for Grieving Children and Their Families. *35 Ways to Help a Grieving Child*. Retrieved February 17, 2013, from http://www.dougy.org/books-dvds/books

Duffy, A., and J. Momirov. 1997. *Family Violence: A Canadian Introduction*. Toronto: James Lorimer and Company.

Durrant, J., and R. Ensom. 2006. "Physical Punishment of Children. Lessons from 20 Years of Research." *CMAJ*. Retrieved from www.nospank.net/durrant&ensom.pdf

Edleson, J.L. 1999. "The Overlap between Child Maltreatment and Woman Battery." *Violence Against Women* 5(2). 134–154.

Elkind, D. 1981. *The Hurried Child: Growing Up Too Fast and Too Soon*. Da Capo Press.

Fallon, B., N. Trocmé, J. Fluke, B. MacLaurin, L. Tonmyr, and Y. Yuan. In press. "Methodological Challenges in Measuring Child Maltreatment." *Child Abuse and Neglect*.

Family Alliance Ontario. 2007. "Is Your World Touched by Disability? So Is Ours!" *The Compass*. Spring 12(1). 4.

Federal Ombudsman for Victims of Crime Recommends Changes to Address Internet-Facilitated Child Sexual Abuse. 2009. Ottawa. June 2. Retrieved February 17, 2013, from http://www.victimsfirst.gc.ca/media/news-nouv/nr-cp/2009/20090602.html

Felitti V.J., R. Anda, D. Nordenberg, et al. 1998. "The Relationship of Childhood Abuse and Household Dysfunction to Many of the Leading Causes of Death in Adults: The Adverse Childhood Experiences (ACE) Study." *American Journal of Preventive Medicine*. May 14(4). 245–258.

Finger, A. 1991. *Past Due: A Story of Disability, Pregnancy and Birth*. London: The Woman's Press.

Finkelhor, D. 2008. *Victimization Violence, Crime and Abuse in The Loves Of Young People*. New York: Oxford Press.

Flowers, R.B. 2001. The Sex Trade Industry's Worldwide Exploitation of Children [Electronic version]. *Annals of the American Academy of Political and Social Science*, 575. 147–157. Retrieved from http://www.du.edu/korbel/hrhw/.../trafficking/Globalization.pdf

Foxman, F. 2003. *The Worried Child*. Alameda, CA: Hunter House.

Future of Children. 1999. *Domestic Violence and Children* 9(3). Winter.

Galinsky, E. 1987. *The Six Stages of Parenthood*. Addison Wesley Publishing.

General Social Survey (GSS) on Victimization. 2004. Catalogue no. 85-565-XIE, Cycle 18. Ottawa: Statistics Canada.

General Social Survey (GSS), An Overview. 2009. Online Catalogue no. 89F0115X. Statistics Canada: Minister of Industry. Retrieved February 17, 2013, from http://www.statcan.gc.ca/pub/89f0115x/89f0115x2009001-eng.htm

Goldman, L. 2004. "Counseling with Children in Contemporary Society." *Journal of Mental Health Counseling*. April, 26(2).

Gonzalez-Mena, J. 2010. *50 Strategies for Communicating and Working with Diverse Families*, 2nd ed. Upper Saddle River, NJ: Pearson.

Gordon, A. 2005. "Crisis in Children's Mental Health." *Toronto Star*. February 11. D5.

Greaves, L., O. Hankivsky, and J. Kingston-Riechers. 1995. *Selected Estimates of the Costs of Violence Against Women*. London, ON: Centre for Research on Violence Against Women and Children.

Greey, M. 1995. *Honouring Diversity: A Cross-Cultural Approach to Infant Development for Babies with Special Needs*. Toronto: Centennial Infant and Child Centre.

Haas, G.A. 2008. *The Impact of Intimate Partner Violence on the Children*. Presentation for ACT Against Violence Leadership Seminar, Washington, DC. March 27.

Hadad, M. 2008. *The Ultimate Challenge: Coping with Death, Dying and Bereavement*. Toronto: Thomson Nelson.

Hagemann-White, C. 2006. *Combating Violence Against Women, Stocktaking Study on the Measures and Actions Taken in Council of Europe Member States*. Directorate Strasbourg, France: General of Human Rights, Council of Europe.

Halpern L.F., T.F. Anders, C. Garcia-Coll, and J. Hua. 1994. "Infant Temperament: Is There a Relation Between Sleep-Wake States and Maternal Nighttime Behavior?" *Infant Behavior and Development* 17. 255–263.

Hamilton, J. 2003. *When a Parent Is Sick. Helping Parents Explain Serious Illness to Children*. Lawrencetown Beach, NS: Pottersfield Press.

Health Canada. 2010. "Canadian Alcohol and Drug Use Monitoring Survey." Retrieved February 17, 2013, from http://www.hc-sc.gc.ca/hc-ps/drugs-drogues/stat/_2010/summary-sommaire-eng.php

Healy, Margaret. 2004. "Child Pornography: An International Perspective." August 2. Retrieved February 11, 2013, from http://www.crime-research.org/articles/536/

Henderson, H. 2003. "Centennial Infant and Child Centre. Project Invests in Workers and Kids with Special Needs." *Toronto Star*. January 25.

Howland Thompson, S. 1998. "Working with Children of Substance-Abusing Parents." *Young Children*. January.

Irwin, S. 1993. "SpeciaLink: The Road to Mainstream Child Care." *Focus*. October.

Jaffe, P.G., D. Wolfe, and S. Wilson. 1990. *Children of Battered Women: Issues in Child Development and Intervention Planning*. Newbury Park, CA: Sage Publications. January.

Johnson, H. 1996. *Dangerous Domains: Violence Against Women in Canada*. Toronto: Nelson Canada.

Johnston, C., and E.J. Mash. 1989. "A Measure of Parenting Satisfaction and Efficacy." *Journal of Clinical Child Psychology* 18(2).167–175.

Klein, Andrew. 2005. *A Report to the U.S. House of Representatives House Ways and Means Committee*, February 10. Retrieved from http://waysandmeans.house .gov/hearings.asp?formmode=view&id=2960

Kluger, J. 2006. "The New Science of Siblings." *Time Magazine*. July 10.

Krajicek, M.J., and C.A. Moore. 1993. "Child Care for Infants and Toddlers with Disabilities and Chronic Illness." *Focus on Exceptional Children* 25(8).

Kubler Ross, E. 1974. *On Death and Dying*. New York: Simon and Schuster.

MacNaull, S. 2011. "What About Dad?", *Transition* VI. Retrieved February 11, 2013, from http://www.vanier institute.ca/include/get.php?nodeid=1636

Mash, E. J., and C. Johnston. 1983. "Parental Perceptions of Child Behavior Problems, Parenting Self-Esteem, and Mothers' Reported Stress in Younger and Older Hyperactive and Normal Children." *Journal of Consulting and Clinical Psychology*, 51. 86–99.

McCrory, E.J.P., S. De Brito, and E. Viding. 2011. "The Neuroscience and Genetics of Childhood Maltreatment." In D. Skuse, H. Bruce, L. Dowdney, and D. Mrazek, eds. *Child Psychology and Psychiatry,* 1st ed. London, UK: Wiley. 121–127.

Mehler Paperny, A. 2012. "Treating the Tiny Victims of Canada's Fastest Growing Addiction." January 6. *The Globe and Mail*. Retrieved February 11, 2013, from http://www.theglobeandmail.com/life/health-and-fitness/ health/conditions/treating-the-tiny-victims-of-canadas -fastest-growing-addiction/article547509

Menjivar, C., and O. Salcido. 2002. "Immigrant Women and Domestic Violence: Common Experiences in Different Countries." *Gender and Society,* 16(6). 898–920.

Mohr, W.K., and J.W. Fantuzzo. 2000. "The Neglected Variable of Physiology in Domestic Violence." In R. Geffner, P. Jaffe, and M. Sudermann, eds., *Children Exposed to Domestic Violence: Current Issues in Research, Intervention, Prevention, and Policy Development*. New York: The Haworth Maltreatment and Trauma Press.

Monsebraaten, L. 1998. "Working Parents of Disabled Severely Stressed, Report Says." *Toronto Star*. November 2. A3.

———. 2007. "Homeless Kids Neglected." *Toronto Star*. October 1. Retrieved February 11, 2013, from http:// www.thestar.com/GTA/Education/article/262153

Moore, T., D. Peplar, B. Weisberg, L. Hammond, J. Waddell., and L. Weiser. 1990. "Research on Children from Violent Families." *Canada's Mental Health*, Vol. 38, June/September.

Mothercraft. 2012. "Breaking the Cycle." Retrieved February 11, 2013, from http://www.mothercraft.ca/index .php?q=early-intervention-programs

National Children's Advocacy Center. 2011. Retrieved February 11, 2013, from http://www.nationalcac.org

National Scientific Council on the Developing Child. 2005. "Excessive Stress Alters the Architecture of the Brain." Retrieved February 24, 2013, from http://www.developing child.harvard.edu

———. 2010. "Persistent Fear and Anxiety Can Affect Young Children's Learning and Development." Working Paper

9. Retrieved from http://www.developingchild.harvard .edu/activities/council

Newton, C.J. 2001. "Domestic Violence: An Overview." *Mental Health Journal*. February. Retrieved February 11, 2013, from http://www.aaets.org/article145.htm

Noel, N., and M. Yam. 1992. "Domestic Violence: The Pregnant Battered Woman." *Women's Health,* 27(4).

OACAS of Canada. 2009–2010. "The Voice of Child Welfare in Ontario." Annual Report. Retrieved February 11, 2013, from www.oacas.org/pubs/oacas/annual/10annual _web.pdf

Office of the Federation Ombudsman for Victims of Crime. 2007. "Shifting the Conversation. Special Report." Government of Canada. Retrieved from http:// www.victimsfirst.gc.ca/pdf/ShiftingConversation.pdf

Ogilvie, M. 2010. "Pregnant, Homeless and Invisible in Toronto." March 13. Retrieved February 11, 2013, from http://www.thestar.com/news/gta/article/779450

Ogrodnik, L. 2010. "Child and Youth Victims of Police- reported Violent Crime, 2008." Canadian Centre for Justice Statistics Profile Series. Catalogue no. 85F0033X. No. 23. Ottawa: Statistics Canada.

Ontario Provincial Police. 2009. Press Release. "Child Pornography and Child Sexual Abuse and Exploitation on the Internet." Retrieved February 17, 2013, from http://www.opp.ca/ecms/index.php?id=489

Ontario Women's Directorate. 1997. *Prevention of Violence Against Women: It's Everyone's Responsibility*.

Osofsky, J. 2003. *Children, Youth and Violence: Searching for Solutions*. New York: The Guilford Press

Palmer, T. 2005. "Behind the Screen—Children who are the Subjects of Abusive Images." In E. Quayle and M. Taylor, eds., *Viewing Child Pornography on the Internet: Understanding the Offence, Managing the Offender, Helping the Victims* (ch. 5). Dorset, UK: Russell House Publishing.

Pelletier, J., and J. M. Brent. 2002. "Parent Participation in Childrens' School Readiness: The Effects of Parental Self-Efficacy, Cultural Diversity and Teacher Strategies." *International Journal of Early Childhood* 34(1).

Perreault, Samuel. 2011. *Self-reported Internet victimization in Canada, 2009*. Juristat. Ottawa: Statistics Canada. Catalogue No. 85-002-X. Retrieved February 11, 2013, from http://www.statcan.gc.ca/pub/85-002-x/2011001/ article/11530-eng.pdf

Perry, B.D. 1995. "Incubated in Terror: Neurodevelopmental Factors in the Cycle of Violence." In J. Osofsky, ed. *Children, Youth and Violence: Searching for Solutions*. New York: The Guilford Press.

———. 2002. "Childhood Experience and the Expression of Genetic Potential: What Childhood Neglect Tells Us About Nature and Nurture." Retrieved February 11, 2013, from http://www.childtrauma.org/images/stories/ Articles/mindbrain.pdf

———. 2004. *Maltreatment and the Developing Child: How Early Childhood Experience Shapes Child and Culture*. Inaugural Lecture, The Margaret McCain Lecture Series, Centre for Children and Families in the Justice System, London, Ontario. September 23. Retrieved February 11, 2013, from http://www.lfcc.on.ca/mccain/ perry1.html

Pimento, B., and D. Kernested. 2000. *Healthy Foundations in Child Care*. Toronto: Nelson Thomson Learning.

Public Health Agency of Canada. 2009. "What Mothers Say: The Canadian Maternity Experiences Survey." Retrieved February 11, 2013, from http://www.phac-aspc.gc.ca/rhs-ssg/pdf/survey-eng.pdf

Rainbows: Guiding Children Through Life's Storms. 2013. "History of Rainbows." Retrieved February 24, 2013, from http://www.rainbows.ca/History-Of-Rainbows.htm

Rimer, P. 2007. *Making a Difference: The Community Responds to Child Abuse,* 5th ed. Toronto: Boost Child Abuse Prevention and Intervention.

Rimer, P., and B. Prager. 1998. *Reaching Out: Working Together to Identify and Respond to Child Victims of Abuse*. Toronto: ITP Nelson.

Rishchynski, G., P. Rimer, and J. Rimer. 2009. *Looking for Angelina: A Learning Guide on Family Violence*. Toronto: Second Story Press.

Robinson, B.E. 1990. "The Teacher's Role in Working with Children of Alcoholic Parents." *Young Children*. May.

Rockwell, R.E., L.C. Andre, and M.K. Hawley. 2010. *Families and Educators as Partners*. Belmont, CA: Cengage Learning.

Rodgers, K. 1994. "Wife Assault: The Findings of a National Survey." *Juristat* 14(9), Catalogue no. 85-002-XPE. Ottawa: Statistics Canada.

Romano, E., R.E. Tremblay, B. Boulerice, and R. Swisher. 2005. "Multilevel Correlates of Childhood Physical Aggression and Prosocial Behavior." *Journal of Abnormal Child Psychology*, 33(5). 565–578.

Rossman, B., and J. Ho. 2000. "Posttraumatic Response and Children Exposed to Parental Violence." In R. Geffner, P. Jaffe, and M. Sudermann, eds. *Children Exposed to Domestic Violence: Current Issues in Research, Intervention, Prevention, and Policy Development*. New York: The Haworth Maltreatment and Trauma Press.

San Franscisco Children of Incarcerated Parents Partnerships. 2005. Retrieved February 17, 2013, from http://www.sfcipp.org/images/brochure.pdf

Sinha et al. 2010. "Family Violence in Canada. A Statistical Profile." May 22. Juristat 85-002-X. Retrieved February 11, 2013, from http://www.statcan.gc.ca/pub/85-002-x/2012001/article/11643-eng.pdf

Sinha, M. 2012. "Section 2. Violence Against Intimate Partners." Statistics Canada. Retrieved February 11, 2013, from http://www.statcan.gc.ca/pub/85-002-x/2012001/article/11643/11643-2-eng.htm

Smith, J. 2012. "Daddy's Having a Bad Day Today." *The Toronto Star*. 1.

Stark, E. 1987. "Forgotten Victims: Children of Alcoholics." *Psychology Today*.

Statistics Canada. 2001. *Family Violence in Canada: A Statistical Profile 2001*. Catalogue no. 85-224-XIE. Ottawa: Statistics Canada.

———. 2006a. *Family Violence in Canada: A Statistical Profile 2006*. Catalogue no. 85-224-XIE. Canadian Centre for Justice Statistics. Ottawa: Statistics Canada.

———. 2006b. *Measuring Violence Against Women: Statistical Trends* 2006. Catalogue no. 85-570-XWE. Ottawa: Statistics Canada.

Steinberg, L. 2000. Youth Violence: "Do Parents and Families Make a Difference?" *National Institute of Justice Journal* 2, 30–38.

Straus, M.A., and R.J. Gelles. 1990. "Societal Change and Change in Family Violence from 1975 to 1985 as Revealed by Two National Surveys." In M.A. Strauss and R.J. Gelles, eds. *Physical Violence in American Families: Risk Factors and Adaptations to Violence in 8,145 families.* New Brunswick: Transaction Publishers.

Sudermann, M., and P. Jaffe. 1999. *A Handbook for Health and Social Service Providers and Educators on Children Exposed to Woman Abuse/Family Violence.* The Family Violence Prevention Unit, Health Canada. Ottawa: Minister of Public Works and Government Services Canada.

Suh, E., and E.M. Abel. 1990. "The Impact of Spousal Violence on the Children of the Abused." *Journal of Independent Social Work* 4(4), 27–34.

Teti, D.M., and D.M. Gelfand. 1991. "Behavioral Competence among Mothers of Infants in the First Year: The Mediational Role of Maternal Self-Efficacy." *Child Development*, 62. 918–929.

Thompson, J. 2011. "Striding Toward a Just Community." *Transition: Families and Incarceration* 42(2).

Trawick-Smith, J. 2009. *Early Childhood Development: A Multicultural Perspective*, 5th ed. Upper Saddle River, NJ: Prentice Hall.

Trocmé, N., et al. 2001. *Canadian Incidence Study of Reported Child Abuse and Neglect: Final Report*. Ottawa: Minister of Public Works and Government Services Canada.

Tucker, C.J., and K. Updegraff 2009. "The Relative Contributions of Parents and Siblings to Child and Adolescent Development." In L. Kramer and K.J. Conger, eds. *Sibling as Agents of Socialization: New Directions for Child and Adolescent Development*. 126. 13–28.

UBC. 2011. "Annual Cost of Violence Pegged At $6.9 Billion After Women Leave Abusive Partners." October 11. Retrieved February 11, 2013, from http://www.publicaffairs.ubc.ca/2011/10/11/annual-cost-of-violence-pegged-at-6-9b-after-women-leave-abusive-partners-ubc-research

UNFPA. 2000. Annual Report. Retrieved February 11, 2013, from www.unfpa.org/public/publications/pid/2580

UNICEF. 2006. "Some of the Biggest Victims of Domestic Violence Are the Smallest." Retrieved February 11, 2013, from http://www.unicef.org/evaldatabase/index_35151.html

Vacheret, M. 2007. "Private Family Visits in Canada, Between Rehabilitation and Stricter Control: Portrait of a System." Retrieved February 11, 2013, from http://champpenal.revues.org/document2322.html

Vallée, B. 2007. *The War on Women: Elly Armour, Jane Hurshman, and Criminal Domestic Violence in Canadian Homes*. Toronto: Key Porter Books.

Ward, M. 2002. *The Family Dynamic: A Canadian Perspective*. Toronto: Nelson Canada.

Ward, M., and M. Belanger. 2011. *The Family Dynamic: A Canadian Perspective,* 5th edition. Toronto: Nelson Canada.

Wax, I.F. 1996. "Don't Give Up the Dream." *Learning Disabilities Association of Toronto* 1(4). May–June.

Wells-Parker, E., D.I. Miller, and J.S. Topping. 1990. "Development of Control-of-outcome Scales and

Self-efficacy Scales for Women in Four Life Roles." *Journal of Personality Assessment*, 54(3/4). 564–575.

Werner, E.E. 1995. "Resilience in Development." *Current Directions in Psychological Science*. June. 81–85.

Weston, D.R., B. Ivins, B. Zuckerman, C. Jones, and R. Lopez. 1989. "Drug-Exposed Babies." *Research and Clinical Issues, Zero to Three* 9, no. 5.

Wilson, M., and M. Daly. 1992. "Who Kills Whom in Spouse Killings? On the Exceptional Sex Ratio of Spousal Homicides in the United States." *Criminology*, 30. 189–215.

Winzer, M. 2008. *Children with Exceptionalities in Canadian Classrooms*, 8th ed. Upper Saddle River, NJ: Pearson Publishing.

Wolfe, D., and C. Feiring. 2000. "Dating Violence Through the Lens of Adolescent Romantic Relationships." *Child Maltreatment* 5(4). 360–363.

World Health Organization. 2004. *The Economic Dimensions of Interpersonal Violence*. Geneva, Switzerland: Department of Injuries and Violence Prevention, World Health Organization. Retrieved February 11, 2013, from http://whqlibdoc.who.int/publications/2004/9241591609.pdf

World Vision Canadian Programs. "Partnering for Peace and Well-Being in the Lives of Canadian Children. 2005–2010." Retrieved February 11, 2013, from http://www.worldvision.ca/Programs

Wright, K., D.A. Stegelin, and L. Hartle. 2007. *Building Family, School, and Community Partnerships*. 3rd ed. Upper Saddle River, NJ: Pearson.

Zeanah, C.H., B. Danis, L. Hirshberg, D. Benoit, D. Miller, and S.S. Heller. 1999. "Disorganized Attachment Associated with Partner Violence: A Research Note." *Infant Mental Health Journal* 20. 77–86.

Created by Boden

Chapter 11

WORKING WITH FAMILIES: AN INTERNATIONAL PERSPECTIVE

Sarah Nicholl/Shutterstock

"You must be the change you most wish to see in the world."

Gandhi (The Quotations Page, n.d.)

LEARNING OUTCOMES

After studying this chapter, you will be able to

1. evaluate the implications of the UN Convention on the Rights of the Child and the Convention on the Elimination of All Forms of Discrimination to determine how they influence the development of early childhood services at home and abroad

2. consider the impact of the Millennium Development Goals and their implication for the health and well-being of children and mothers

3. discuss the implications of war and conflict on families

4. consider the impact of early childhood education worldwide

5. evaluate organizations and early childhood graduates in their role of supporting families in the global community

In this chapter we move beyond our Canadian borders and take a more global look at children and their families and the conditions that influence their well-being.

THE CONVENTION ON THE RIGHTS OF THE CHILD

In celebration of the 20-year anniversary of the adoption of the Declaration of the Rights of the Child, the United Nations declared 1979 to be the International Year of the Child. Its goal was to focus attention on children living in poorer nations, many of whom were undernourished and receiving inadequate health care and educational services. The original 1959 declaration challenged countries and governments across the world to review the status of children and to focus attention on improving the quality of life for children everywhere. In 1989—on the 30th anniversary—the United Nations Convention on the Rights of the Child (CRC) was adopted. The UN Convention differed from the declaration in that it was a comprehensive, binding treaty consisting of 54 articles, 44 of which established that children should be treated as individuals with their own rights, and 10 that required states to put mechanisms in place to facilitate these changes. The convention has been ratified by 193 national states and is the most widely supported international human rights instrument in the world. As of 2012, only two nation states—Somalia and the United States— had not yet ratified the convention!

As we review the intent of the UN Convention on the Rights of the Child and its impact on Canadian children, it is clear that there is much work to be done. The fundamental ideology expressed in the convention must serve as the basis for Canadians' work with children and families. Many policies offered in Europe are more extensive and generous: although there are important differences across France, Germany, Finland, and Sweden, family policies in each of these countries reflect a tradition of acknowledging social responsibility for children. Canadian policies, like those in the United States,

The world focuses on improving the quality of life for all children through the United Nations Convention on the Rights of the Child.

often reflect the attitude that children are the private responsibility of their parents. As a result, the outcomes for European families look much better than outcomes in Canada.

In 1994, Richard Reid, director with the United Nations International Children's Fund (UNICEF), noted in his keynote address at the International Conference on Children's Rights:

It has been four years since the world's countries adopted, unanimously, the Convention on the Rights of the Child at the General Assembly of the United Nations. Looking back across the world over those few years—at the avalanche of stepped-up violence against children, at the burned-out villages of the scores of savage new ethnic wars, at the streets of the big cities, and at dysfunctional homes—all of this mayhem played out, somehow, side by side with wonderfully steady gains in child health and solid advances in basic education. Can anyone ... tell where the hands of the world's crisis

There is still much to be done to improve the quality of life for so many children.

clock for children stand at this moment? Does the clock say dawn, with daylight ahead of us, or are we approaching midnight? In all this uncertain mix of hope and bleakness, there is one thing we can be sure of. And that is that the Convention on the Rights of the Child is here to stay, each day more steadily afoot in the world. While other national treaties languish, the Children's Convention has swept the world in four years; more countries have bound themselves to it than any other global humanitarian treaty in history. It is a rising tide that soon enough will begin to lift all boats. All of us who work for children need to capitalize on this gathering force. (Reid, 1994)

Unfortunately today, almost 20 years later, his words ring true, we still struggle for a world in which children can live healthy, safe, and peaceful lives.

MONITORING CHILD RIGHTS

The UN Committee on the Rights of the Child (UNCRC) is the body of independent experts that monitors the implementation of the Convention on the Rights of the Child by state parties. The UNCRC meets in Geneva, normally holding three sessions per year. Canada, like all countries, is required to submit regular reports to the UNCRC on the implementation of child rights in their countries. It also monitors implementation of two optional protocols to the convention, on the involvement of children in armed conflict and on the sale of children, child prostitution, and child pornography. A third protocol was approved by the UN General Assembly in 2011 that will allow individual children to submit complaints with respect to their rights under the convention. Ratification is expected in 2012 (Office of the United Nations High Commissioner for Human Rights, 2012).

Goals of the organization:

1. To strengthen understanding of the human rights of all young children and to draw States parties' attention to their obligations towards young children.

2. To comment on the specific features of early childhood that impact on the realization of rights.

3. To encourage recognition of young children as social actors from the beginning of life, with particular interests, capacities and vulnerabilities, and of requirements for protection, guidance and support in the exercise of their rights.

4. To draw attention to diversities within early childhood that need to be taken into account when implementing the Convention, including diversities in young children's circumstances, in the quality of their experiences and in the influences shaping their development.

5. To point to variations in cultural expectations and treatment of children, including local customs and practices that should be respected, except where they contravene the rights of the child.

6. To emphasize the vulnerability of young children to poverty, discrimination, family breakdown and multiple other adversities that violate their rights and undermine their well-being.

7. To contribute to the realization of rights for all young children through formulation and promotion of comprehensive policies, laws, programmes, practices, professional training and research focused on rights in early childhood. (UNESCO, n.d.)

AMNESTY INTERNATIONAL

"Being unwanted, unloved, uncared for, forgotten by everybody, I think that is a much greater hunger, a much greater poverty than the person who has nothing to eat."

—**Mother Teresa (Welcome to the Fast Family, n.d.)**

There are many organizations that work to end human rights abuses but perhaps the most well known and most effective is Amnesty International. This worldwide organization has activists in more than 150 countries and more than 3 million supporters.

The United Nations Universal Declaration of Human Rights is the foundation of Amnesty International's work. Its focus is ensuring that everyone in the human family, both male and female enjoys freedom of speech and belief and freedom from fear and want. These human rights should be protected by the rule of law. Amnesty International is independent of any government, political leanings, economic interests, or religion. It is funded largely by members and by public donations. Amnesty International is particularly focused on ensuring that children's human rights are protected. Because of their vulnerability and dependency on adults, many children are in situations where they are not seen as individuals with their own rights.

> Children are tortured and ill-treated by state officials, detained in appalling conditions, and sentenced to death. Countless thousands are killed and maimed in armed conflicts. Millions are forced by poverty or abuse to live on the streets where they are vulnerable to abuse. Millions more work at exploitative or hazardous jobs or are victims of child trafficking and forced prostitution. Discriminatory attitudes and practices mean girl children suffer gender-specific abuses, such as female genital mutilation, and are particularly vulnerable to other forms of abuse, including rape. (Amnesty International, 2006)

www **http://www.amnesty.ca**

ELIMINATION OF ALL FORMS OF DISCRIMINATION AGAINST WOMEN

In 1980, Canada signed the Convention on the Elimination of All Forms of Discrimination against Women (CEDAW). This treaty has been ratified worldwide by all but six countries—the United States, Iran, Sudan, Somalia, Palau, and Tonga. Every year, representatives of Member States gather at UN Headquarters in New York to evaluate progress on gender equality, identify challenges, set global standards, and formulate concrete policies to promote gender equality and women's empowerment worldwide. In 2012, the commission adopted six resolutions:

1. Ending female genital mutilation

2. Situation of and assistance to Palestinian women

3. Release of women and children taken hostage, including those subsequently imprisoned, in armed conflicts

4. Gender equality and the empowerment of women in natural disasters

5. Eliminating maternal mortality and morbidity through the empowerment of women

6. Indigenous women: key actors in poverty and hunger eradication* (United Nations Women, 2012)

UNITED NATIONS MILLENNIUM DEVELOPMENT GOALS

World leaders came together in New York on September 25, 2008, to renew commitments to achieving the Millennium Development Goals and to set out concrete plans and practical steps for action. All 189 United Nations member states have pledged to do the following by 2015:

1. Eradicate extreme poverty and hunger:

   • Reduce by half the proportion of people living on less than a dollar a day and the proportion of people suffering from hunger.

2. Achieve universal primary education:

   • Ensure that all boys and girls complete primary education.

3. Promote gender equality and empower women:

   • Eliminate gender disparity in primary and secondary education at all levels by 2015.

4. Reduce child mortality:

   • Reduce by two-thirds the mortality rate among children under five.

5. Improve maternal health:

   • Reduce by three-quarters the maternal mortality ratio.

6. Combat HIV/AIDS, malaria and other diseases:

   • Halt and reverse the spread of HIV/AIDS, malaria and other major diseases.

7. Ensure environmental sustainability:

   • Integrate the principles of sustainable development into country policies and programs; reverse loss of environmental resources.

   • Reduce by half the proportion of people without sustainable access to safe drinking water.

---

*United Nations Women. 2012. Convention On The Elimination Of All Forms Of Discrimination Against Women (CEDAW). Available at http://www.un.org/womenwatch/daw/csw/56sess.htm#resolutions. Reprinted by permission of the United Nations.

- Achieve significant improvement in lives of at least 100 million slum dwellers, by 2020.

8. Develop a global partnership for development:

- Develop further an open trading and financial system that is rule-based, predictable and non-discriminatory including a commitment to good governance, development and poverty reduction.

- Address the least developed countries' special needs including tariff- and quota-free access for their exports; enhanced debt relief; cancellation of official bilateral debt; and more development assistance for countries committed to poverty reduction.

- Address the needs of landlocked and small island developing states.

Birute Vijeikiene/Shutterstock

The Millennium Development Goals form a blueprint for a global partnership to provide primary education for all children.

Inside LOOK

- 783 million people in the world do not have access to safe water. This is roughly one in ten of the world's population (WHO/UNICEF Joint Monitoring Programme (JMP) Report 2012 update).
- Around 700,000 children die every year from diarrhoea caused by unsafe water and poor sanitation; that's almost 2,000 children a day (WaterAid 2012/WHO 2008/The Lancet 2012).
- 2.5 billion people in the world do not have access to adequate sanitation, almost two fifths of the world's population (WHO/UNICEF Joint Monitoring Programme (JMP) Report 2012 update).

Source: Water Aid International, n.d. Retrieved February 12, 2013, from http://www.wateraid.org/international/what_we_do/statistics/default.asp

The international community must recognize the need to finance and organize the effective distribution of a broad spectrum of medical aid to the world's neediest.

- With pharmaceutical companies provide access to affordable essential drugs in developing countries.

- With the private sector, make available new technologies.* (United Nations, 2008)

EARLY CHILDHOOD DEVELOPMENT

Around the world, many governments are not in a position to meet the Millennium Development Goal that ensures universal primary education. The worsening global markets further threaten governments' commitment to education for children under 5. The Organisation for Economic Co-operation and Development (OECD) suggests that at least 1 percent of GDP needs to be spend on early childhood education to ensure that children are receiving quality services. "Some central and eastern European and South American countries budget 0.4% for pre-school education, while the figure is as low as 0.1% in Kenya, Nepal and Tajikistan. Nicaragua and Senegal spend less than 0.02%" (Alexander, 2011). Although UNICEF, Save the Children, the Aga Khan Foundation, Step by Step, and the World Bank continue to support early childhood initiatives, unless a substantial increase is seen in government allocations, the poorest segments of the world's population will continue to endure inequities, and the children who are most likely to benefit from early childhood development program will continue to be the least likely to have access to them (Alexander, 2011: 2).

WORLD FOOD PRICES SOAR

One of the challenges of the recession has been volatility and increasing food prices, and their effect on global hunger. The UN Food and Agricultural Organization (FAO) reports that 925 million people are identified as living in hunger. In developing countries the poorest people are the hardest hit, spending more than 60 to 80 percent of their family income on food.

In this turbulent scenario it is those who are least able to cope who will bear the brunt of the impact. Food aid and other measures to reduce the increasing burden on the poorest are made more difficult by the global economic crisis, which has left even wealthier countries deep in debt.[†] (Arnold, 2011: A4)

CHILD SURVIVAL: A GLOBAL PERSPECTIVE

Although child mortality rates have dropped over the past 20 years, too many children still die from diseases that are treatable and preventable. Nearly all of these children live in 60 developing countries. UNICEF (2012) states that 7.6 million children died before the age of 5 in 2010.

More than one-third of these children die during the first month of life, usually at home and without access to essential health services and basic commodities that might save their lives. Some children succumb to respiratory or diarrhoeal infections that are no longer threats in industrialized countries, malaria, AIDS or they are victims of early childhood diseases, such as

Increases in global food prices threaten food security and the well-being of millions of people.

---

*United Nations. 2008. *End Poverty 2015: Millennium Goals.* Available at http://www.un.org/millenniumgoals. Reprinted by permission of the United Nations.

†Ward, O. 2011. "Food Price Rise Takes Huge Toll On World's Poor," *The Toronto Star*, April 18, A4. Reprinted by permission of Torstar Syndication Services.

measles, that are easily prevented through vaccines. An underlying cause in up to half of the under-five deaths is under-nutrition, a condition which deprives a young child's body and mind of the nutrients needed for growth and development. Unsafe water, poor sanitation, and inadequate hygiene also contribute to child mortality and morbidity. Poverty is at the root of the problem. (State of the World's Children, 2008)[*]

*UNICEF. 2007. The State of the World's Children, 2008: Child Survival. New York: United Nations. Available at http://www.unicef.org/sowc08/report/report.php. Reprinted by permission of UNICEF.

Further complicating the issues are female illiteracy, early pregnancy, and geographic isolation and political marginalization.

When comparing 200 countries and the number of deaths of infants under 1 year per 1,000 births, the following countries had the most and least deaths, respectively:

MOST DEATHS:

1.	Angola	175.9
2.	Afghanistan	149.2
3.	Niger	112.22

4.	Mali	111.35
5.	Somalia	105.56

LEAST DEATHS:

1.	Monaco	1.79
2.	Singapore	2.32
3.	Bermuda	2.47
4.	Sweden	2.74
5.	Japan	2.78

Shockingly, Canada ranks 182th of the 221 countries at 4.85. (Index Mundi, n.d.). As we near the 2015 deadline for the Millennium Development Goals (MDG) we know that much more must be done to reduce child mortality.

FEMALE FETICIDE

In an editorial in the *Canadian Medical Association Journal*, editor Rajendra Kale argues that doctors should withhold the sex of a fetus from parents until 30 weeks into a pregnancy to prevent the possibility of female feticide—the termination of a pregnancy because of a preference for sons over daughters. The practice, which reportedly occurs in the millions in place such as India and China, is not common in Canada or condoned in any way by the Asian community. But there is evidence it happens here, says Kale. Withholding the sex of the fetus is a simple fix to what he rightly describes as "discrimination against women in its most extreme form." (*Maclean's*, 2012). In India, gender detection has been illegal since 1994 yet female fetuses continue to be terminated. Indian parents provide fewer resources to female children, including food and health care; therefore, it is not surprising that more girls die in their first years than do boys.

The Indian central government and many state administrations have used a variety of policy instruments in recent years to try to erode the prejudice against girl children. These include providing payments to parents at the birth of a girl, providing girls with bicycles and grants for secondary education, and making regular payments intended to provide a girl with dowry at the age of 18. This latter initiative recognizes the fact that while the practice of dowry is also illegal, it is still widely practised, and that the need to provide dowry and thus "give away" many family assets is a major reason why families do not want girls.* (Nolen, 2011: A23)

UNDERLYING AND STRUCTURAL CAUSES OF MATERNAL AND CHILD MORTALITY

Save the Children's *State of the World's Mothers* 2011 report ranks 164 countries on women's access to health care, education, and opportunities for a better life.

Every minute, at least one woman dies from complications related to pregnancy or childbirth—that

---

*Nolen, S. 2011. "Rate of aborted female fetuses increases in India," *The Globe and Mail*, April 1. © The Globe and Mail. All Rights Reserved.

TABLE 11.1   2011 Mother's Index Rankings

TOP 10 BEST PLACES TO BE A MOTHER		BOTTOM 10 WORST PLACES TO BE A MOTHER	
RANK	COUNTRY	RANK	COUNTRY
1	Norway	155	Central African Republic
2	Australia	156	Sudan
3	Iceland	157	Mali
4	Sweden	158	Eritrea
5	Denmark	159	DR Congo
6	New Zealand	160	Chad
7	Finland	161	Yemen
8	Belgium	162	Guinea-Bissau
9	Netherlands	163	Niger
10	France	164	Afghanistan

Canada ranks 20th on this scale.
Source: Reprinted by permission of Save the Children.

means 529,000 women a year. In addition, for every woman who dies in childbirth, around 20 more suffer injury, infection or disease—approximately 10 million women each year. Five direct complications account for more than 70% of maternal deaths:

- haemorrhage (25%),
- infection (15%),
- unsafe abortion (13%),
- eclampsia (very high blood pressure leading to seizures—12%), and
- obstructed labour (8%).

These women are dying in staggering numbers because they did not have access to safe high quality health care or they could not afford it. These deaths leave approximately one million children motherless every year. We also know that these children are 10 times more likely to die within two years of their mother's death.[*] (WHO, 2012b)

EMPOWERING WOMEN TO ADVANCE MATERNAL, NEWBORN, AND CHILD HEALTH

Despite the importance of maternal health, one in four pregnant women receives no antenatal care and more than 40 percent give birth without the assistance of a skilled attendant. Empowering women, especially at the community level, is essential. The lack of status for many women in their families and communities is a contributing factor to their lack of influence in health-related decisions. This is particularly true for women in South Asia and sub-Saharan Africa:

In Burkina Faso, Mali, and Nigeria, almost 75 percent of women respondents reported that husbands alone make decisions about women's health care. In South Asia, Bangladesh, and Nepal, this ratio was around 50 percent. The situation is often most severe in rural areas or in urban slums, where women are largely illiterate and suffer from socio-cultural barriers to accessing health services, such as restrictions on leaving their homes or on interacting with strangers, and frequently do not have access to a health centre or a health clinic.

A number of community health worker programs that train primarily women have successfully circumvented gender-based barriers to utilization of health services. In Bangladesh, the community health

workers who have been trained are married, middle-aged women, and their "doorstep" health services allow women to circumvent purdah restrictions that prevent them from leaving their homes to access health facilities on their own[†] (UNICEF, 2007: 20).

HIV AND AIDS

HIV/AIDS is a disease of the immune system caused by the human immunodeficiency virus. It is transmitted largely through unprotected sexual intercourse; contaminated blood transfusions and needles; and mother-to-child transmission during pregnancy, delivery, or breastfeeding. Young women are particularly vulnerable to contacting HIV/AIDS because of their physiology and because of the power imbalances in their relationships with men. Researchers are working worldwide to develop a cure or vaccine to combat this disease. Currently, only antiretroviral treatments have been

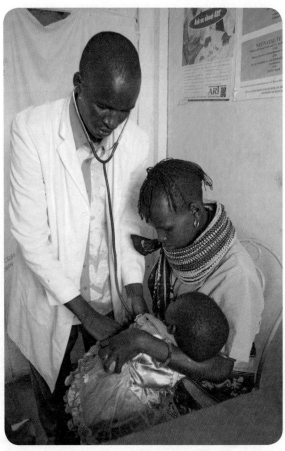

spirit of america/Shutterstock.com

Ninety percent of mother-to-child transmissions of HIV occur in Africa.

---

[*]World Health Organization. 2013. "Why do so many women still die in pregnancy or child birth, 2012." http://www.who.int/features/qa/12/en/. Reprinted by permission.

[†]UNICEF. 2007. The State of the World's Children, 2008: Child Survival. New York: United Nations. P. 20 Available at http:// www.unicef.org/sowc08/report/report.php. Reprinted by permission of UNICEF.

shown to slow the spread of the disease. These medications are very expensive, meaning they are unavailable to many victims in developing countries. There are still many misconceptions about HIV/AIDS and discrimination is of great concern. The numbers of those infected are staggering.

> An estimated 34 million people were living with HIV as of 2010; 3.4 million of them were children under 15 years, and about 16.8 million were women. Every day, over 7,000 persons became infected with HIV and about 5,000 persons died from AIDS, mostly because of inadequate access to HIV prevention care and treatment services. Roughly 17.1 million children under the age of 18 have lost one or both parents to AIDS, and millions more have been affected, with a vastly increased risk of poverty, homelessness, school dropout, discrimination and loss of life opportunities. (UNICEF, 2011)

Preventing new infections is the first line of defence against AIDS. It is also the best way to protect the next generation. Once a pregnant woman is infected with HIV, there is a 35 percent chance that without intervention she will pass the virus on to her newborn during pregnancy, birth, or breastfeeding. Antiretroviral drug therapy can greatly reduce the chances that transmission will occur and is essential to stemming the rise in child mortality rates in countries where AIDS has reached epidemic levels. With appropriate drugs and proper care, infants who are HIV-positive can remain healthy indefinitely (UNICEF, 2007: 42).

MALARIA

Despite the fact that interventions such as insecticide-treated nets and spraying of homes have increased, malaria continues to be a risk for about half of the world's population. In 2010, an estimated 216 million cases resulted in approximately 655,000 deaths, 86 percent of which occurred in children under the age of 5 (WHO, 2012).

URBAN AND RURAL ISSUES

UNICEF's report, *The State of the World's Children 2012*, outlines the risks for the hundreds of millions of children who live in urban slums without any access to even the most basic of services, at risk from violence and exploitation as well as the dangers associated with living near railroad tracks, busy streets, or garbage dumps. Children living in slums are also the least likely to attend school. The report states that by 2050, 70 percent of all people will live in urban areas—already 30 percent live in slum conditions. In Africa, the statistics are even more startling where rate is 60 percent.

Jean Marc Giboux/Getty Images

The UN's Health Agency reports that a shortage of 4.3 million doctors, nurses, and other health workers is hampering the fight against AIDS and other fatal diseases.

Every disadvantaged child bears witness to a moral offense: the failure to secure her or his rights to survive, thrive and participate in society. And every excluded child represents a missed opportunity—because when society fails to extend to urban children the services and protection that would enable them to develop as productive and creative individuals, it loses the social, cultural and economic contributions they could have made. (Lake, 2012)

WAR AND TERRORISM

> "It'll be a great day when education gets all the money it wants and the Air Force has to hold a bake sale to buy bombers."
>
> **—Anonymous**

War and terrorism has an enormous impact on the lives of civilians caught up in conflict.

War Child (**http://www.warchild.ca**) reports that

> 60 million people have been killed in wars during the 20th century and today more than 30 wars and conflicts rage around the world. Over 80 percent of war casualties are civilians, mainly women and children. Children are among the first casualties of any armed conflict, always the most vulnerable and innocent of victims. In the last decade alone 1.5 million children have died in wars, 4 million have been disabled, and a further 10 million traumatized. (War Child, n.d.)

Of the 11 countries in which 20 percent or more of children die before age 5—Afghanistan, Angola, Burkina Faso, Chad, the Democratic Republic of the Congo, Equatorial Guinea, Guinea-Bissau, Liberia, Mali, Niger, and Sierra Leone—more than half have suffered a major armed conflict since 1989 (UNICEF, 2007). The severe psychological wounds that war inflicts on children can scar them for life, crippling the very generations that must one day rebuild their devastated countries. Young girls and women pay a terrible price when sexualized violence is used as a tool in genocide and conflict zones around the world.

CHILD SOLDIERS

Child Soldiers International considers the term *child soldier* to be equivalent to the following description of children associated with armed forces or groups:

> … any person below 18 years of age who is, or who has been, recruited or used by an armed force or armed group in any capacity, including but not limited to children, boys and girls, used as fighters, cooks, porters, spies or for sexual purposes. It does not only refer to a child who is taking, or has taken, a direct part in hostilities. (UNICEF, 2007)

Child Soldiers International concur with the UNICEF report:

> Child soldiers perform a range of tasks including participation in combat, laying mines and explosives; scouting, spying, acting as decoys, couriers or guards; training, drill or other preparations; logistics and support functions, portering, cooking and domestic labour; and sexual slavery or other recruitment for sexual purposes. (Child Soldiers International, 2012)

It is impossible to accurately report on the number of child soldiers but they exist all over the world in many conflict zones.

KAREL PRINSLOO/ASSOCIATED PRESS

Many children under the age of 18 serve in government forces or armed rebel groups.

Feminist and activist Gloria Steinem is coordinating a website called *Women Under Seige*.

The website, part journalistic part advocacy, details horrific stories of rape and sexual violence in places like the Democratic Republic of the Congo, Rwanda, Libya, and Bosnia as well as long-unspoken cases from the Holocaust. Steinem knew there were lessons to be learned from those experiences and the stories of women in conflict zones. Women Under Siege is an offshoot of the *Women's Media Centre*—a non-profit media advocacy group which Steinem began in 2005 along with actress Jane Fonda and writer Robin Morgan. 'There are many heroic organizations working against women's violence," Steinem said. "What we hope to contribute is connections among and between these outbreaks of violence. The hope is that the world will see the connections and do something." The website features a blog of guest essays and first-person accounts of sexualized violence, including an essay by CBS reporter Lara Logan, who was sexually assaulted while covering protests in Cairo's Tahrir Square in 2011. (Black, 2012)

http://action.womensmediacenter.com/sites/siege/index.php/

Source: Black, D. 2012. "Steinem Website Fights Rape In War Zones," *The Toronto Star*, February 11, A27. Reprinted by permission of Torstar Syndication Services.

In Canada, young people between 12 and 18 years can enroll in sea, army, or air cadets. This program is funded through Canada's National Defence Department. According to Albanese (2009), some would consider this recruitment or training of child soldiers.

CHILDREN AND DISABILITY

Children are extremely vulnerable to disability. One of the significant contributors to child death and disability in former war zones is the explosive remnants of war. According to UNICEF (2006), explosive remnants of war, including land mines and unexploded ordnance (grenades and cluster bombs), pose a huge threat to children and their families in more than 80 countries, most of which are no longer engaged in war.

Of the 15,000 or 20,000 people who are killed or disabled each year by these deadly weapons of war, at least 20 percent are children. An estimated 85 percent of child victims die before they can get medical attention. Of those who live, most of their families cannot afford life-saving or reconstructive surgery or rehabilitative care for their disabilities. Many of the problems facing mine-injured children and their families are similar to those facing all disabled children, particularly those in countries where health services are damaged, inadequate, and/or underfunded. (Schwartz and Scott, 2010: 434)

For more information on Canada's role in eradicating land mines, visit Mines Action Canada at **http://www.minesactioncanada.org/about**.

SUPPORTING CHILDREN IN POSTEMERGENCY SITUATIONS

In *Early Childhood Matters* (2005), Save the Children outlines seven critical types of protection that children require in disaster areas and war zones:

1. Protection from physical harm
2. Protection from exploitation and gender-based violence
3. Protection from gender-based psychosocial distress

As Canadians we should be proud of the work being done by Michaëlle Jean, former Governor General of Canada.

The Canadian Press/Paul Chiasson

Syria, 2012

The following are quotes by the children of Syria:

Bilal, 13—The army came to our village … and they were shouting, "We are not going to kill you; we are here to protect you." They were lying. They killed so many people.

Hamza, 10—I told my father that I wanted to stay here and if I die here I die as a martyr for the sake of my country.

Jameel, 13—On a cousin who died during escape: I just cannot explain to you. It feels like your heart has been torn away. He was dying in front of me and I could not save him.

Radwan, 12—On escaping, hiding in the back seat of a car: I am asking myself why I did not take a good look at it [his house]. (Shephard, 2012)

Source: Shephard, M. 2012. "Children of the revolution," *The Toronto Star*, February 4, WD4-5. Reprinted by permission of Torstar Syndication Services

4. Protection from gender-based recruitment into armed groups

5. Protection from family separation

6. Protection from abuses related to forced displacement

7. Protection from denial of children's access to quality education.*

COGNITIVE POTENTIAL

Grantham-McGregor et. al (2007) outline the conservative estimate that more than 200 million children

*Reprinted by permission of Save the Children.

under 5 years of age fail to reach their potential in cognitive development because of poverty, poor health and nutrition, and deficient care. Sub-Saharan African countries have the highest percentage of disadvantaged children but the largest number live in South Asia. The children will subsequently do poorly in school and are likely to transfer poverty to the next generation. Grantham-McGregor et al. estimate that this loss of human potential is associated with a more than 20 percent deficit in adult income and will have implications for national development: "The problem of poor child development will remain unless a substantial effort is made to mount

The children of the world had a voice at the UN Special Session on Children in 2002.

STEPHEN CHERNIN/ASSOCIATED PRESS

EXHIBIT 11.1   UN Special Session on Children

A WORLD FIT FOR US

We are the world's children.

We are the victims of exploitation and abuse.

We are street children.

We are the children of war.

We are the victims and orphans of HIV/AIDS.

We are denied good-quality education and health care.

We are victims of political, economic, cultural, religious, and environmental discrimination.

We are children whose voices are not being heard: it is time we are taken into account.

We want a world fit for children, because a world fit for us is a world fit for everyone.

Children made history on May 8, 2002, when two child delegates from the Children's Forum addressed the opening session of the United Nations General Assembly Special Session on Children in New York. It was the first time ever that children formally addressed the General Assembly on behalf of children. The Special Session, which continued through May 10, was itself a landmark, the first such session devoted exclusively to children and the first to include them as official delegates. Four priority themes of the outcome document were these:

- Promoting Healthy Lives
- Providing Quality Education for All
- Protecting Children Against Abuse, Exploitation, and Violence
- Combatting HIV/AIDS

Source: UN Special Session on Children United Nations. 2002. "A World Fit For Us." United Nations: Special Session on Children. Available at http://www.unicef.org/specialsession/documentation/childrens-statement.htm. Reprinted by permission of UNICEF.

appropriate integrated programs. There is increasing evidence that early interventions can help prevent the loss of potential in affected children and improvements can happen rapidly" (Grantham-McGregor et al., 2007: 67). Engle et al. (2007: 239) agree: "Providing services directly to children and including an active parenting and skill-building component is a more effective strategy than providing information alone."

HOW TECHNOLOGY IS CHANGING THE WORLD

Mobile devices outnumbered humans in 2012 according to network firm Cisco's latest analysis of global mobile data traffic. By 2016, it predicts that there will be 10 billion mobile connected devices around the world (BBC, 2012). Unfortunately, a digital divide persists, and not everyone—especially not the less affluent—can access the Internet. In Africa, for example, only 3.6 percent of the population has access to the Internet (This Day Live, 2012). One way to address this divide is to provide computing technology to those people who do not have it. The One Laptop per Child (OLPC) campaign seeks to do just that (**http://laptop.org**). In 2005, Nicholas Negroponte

of the Massachusetts Institute of Technology (MIT) announced his successful development of a low-cost computer called the XO. His goal was to ensure that the 1.2 billion children in the developing world would have one of his computers. His goal was to sell the laptop for $100 with its wireless hook-up and a battery that would last five years. His hope was that foundations and governments of developed countries would fund the distribution of the computers so that children would receive them free (Witt and Hermiston, 2010).

Today, roughly 2 million children and teachers in Latin America are currently part of an OLPC project, with another 500,000 in Africa and the rest of the world. Their largest national partners include **Uruguay** (the first major country in the world to provide every elementary school child with a laptop), **Peru** (their largest deployment, involving over 8,300 schools), Argentina, Mexico, and Rwanda. Other significant projects have been started in Gaza, Afghanistan, Haiti, Ethiopia, and Mongolia. Every school represents a learning hub, a node in a globally shared resource for learning.[*] (One Laptop per Child, n.d.)

*Reprinted by permission of One Laptop Per Child

INNOVATIVE PROGRAMS

This section was contributed by Moira Luccock, Operational Director Children's Services, 2012.

SURE START, ENGLAND

Sure Start was launched in 1998 with the aim of improving the well-being and health of young children and their parents through centres providing universal integrated services. In 2003 the Government announced its intention to set up a Sure Start Children's Centre in each of [the] 20 most deprived wards in England. In 2012 there were more than 3,600 Centres, each providing the following core services:

- Child and family health services, ranging from health visitors to breastfeeding support
- High-quality child-care and early learning options
- Advice on parenting, access to specialist services such as speech therapy, healthy eating, and help managing money
- Services of a dentist or dietician
- Stop-smoking clinic
- Parenting classes
- Assistance in improving English if not first language.
- Support to find work or training opportunities; links to local Jobcenter Plus

Children's Centres are open to all children and parents in that catchment area. Services are available from pregnancy until the child enters reception class at primary school. Many of the services are free; for example, access to midwives and health visitors. Payment is required for child-care services but there is support through free early learning for 3- and 4-year-olds and tax credits for those eligible for help.

The Government directly funded Sure Start until 2006; then local authorities were given funding to set up centres to meet local needs. While multiagency integrated services continue to be required to deliver the core services, Local Authorities have discretion about how and who will manage the Children's Centres and how commissioning arrangements work. Local authorities must ensure that all children's centres within their remit set up an advisory board to drive quality and improvement of services. Children's Centres are subject to regulation now and are inspected against key indicators on a regular basis. Many Sure Start Children's Centres continue to be managed by Children's charities such

as Action for Children, which has continued to be a leader in ensuring parents and carers have a key partnership role in service design and delivery and are active participants on advisory boards.

In March 2008 the latest evaluation report on 3-year-olds and their families showed positive outcomes such as children displaying more independence and positive behaviour and parents offering a better home learning environment. A strong indicator of successful Sure Start Children's Centres is leadership. A National Programme of Integrated Children's Leadership (NPQIL) was introduced by the Government and is now the standard qualification required for working in a Sure Start Centre.

There is consensus across all political parties that early intervention in the early years of a child's life is critical to a child's reaching his or her potential to become an active, fulfilled citizen contributing to the economic and social well-being of the community. Children's Centres are a key social support mechanism that is a core part of our investment in the future of our children in the UK.[*]

NATIONAL MATERNAL-CHILD PROGRAM, EDUCA A TU HIJO PROGRAM, CUBA

This section was contributed by Maxine Brown, ECE faculty.

In the early years, Cuban children and families are supported by an interprofessional team of health care professionals, ECEs, and primary teachers in their local communities. Comprehensive health and educational programs are provided from the point of conception through the primary school years. Health care professionals provide prenatal/antenatal care and immunization through the National Maternal–Child Program. Families receive an average of 12 prenatal home visits. Preschool programs for working parents are provided through the national Infantile Circulos Program (Infant Circles) for 2- to 5-year-olds. Teachers conduct home visits and developmental assessments prior to the child's enrolment in the program.

The Educa a Tu Hijo Program (Growing up with Your Child) for newborns to 6-year-olds is a community-based, family-centred early childhood development service provided to families within their local community. The primary schools also provide many services to the whole family such as

---

[*]Reprinted by permission of Moira Luccock, former Operational Director Children's Services.

School-age children in Havana, Cuba.

recreation, art, literacy, library, and computer programs that run after school and on weekends. Some schools offer Grandparent Programs, which are run by local grandparents. These life skills programs offer training in skills such as weaving, sewing, etc. In addition, primary schools offer the OPJM Program (Organization of Pioneers of Jose Marti), is a cultural program that promotes understanding of the natural environment and Cuban culture through field trips to the countryside. The benefits of these programs are clearly evident given that Cuba has the highest literacy rates in the Caribbean.*

CANADIANS MAKING A DIFFERENCE ON THE WORLD FRONT

"If you don't like the way the world is, you change it. You have an obligation to change it. You just do it one step at a time."

—Marion Wright Edelman
(Thinkexist.com. n.d.)

*Reprinted by permission of Maxine Brown.

It is an impossible task within one textbook to list all of the incredible organizations and individuals in Canada that are making a difference. However, some examples are highlighted below.

STEPHEN LEWIS FOUNDATION

"The Foundation will never cease its work at the grassroots in Africa until the AIDS pandemic is defeated."

—Stephen Lewis

Stephen Lewis is a Canadian politician, broadcaster, and diplomat. He was the Special Envoy for HIV/AIDS in Africa to United Nations Secretary-General Kofi Annan and is chair of the Stephen Lewis Foundation. He is a distinguished visiting professor at Ryerson University and codirector of AIDS-Free World, an international AIDS advocacy organization in the United States. He was awarded the Order of Canada in 2003. His book *Race Against Time* (Anansi Press) should be required reading for all students, no matter what their discipline.

His work in Africa has had a profound impact, and the Stephen Lewis Foundation, established in 2003, is one of the outcomes. Visit **http://www .stephenlewisfoundation.org**.

As outlined on the foundation's website,

HIV and AIDS have had an especially devastating effect on children across Africa. Tens of millions have been orphaned—including 14.8 million children under the age of 18—and still countless others are being left vulnerable as a direct result of the devastation wreaked on families and communities. Young women—often the first to be pulled out of school to help care for dying mothers and raise families of orphaned siblings—are particularly vulnerable, increasing their chances of contracting HIV.* (Stephen Lewis Foundation, n.d., "What We Do")

Older children are often caring for their younger siblings.

Since 2003, the foundation has funded over 700 initiatives, partnering with 300 community-based organizations in the 15 African countries hardest hit by the pandemic. Funds are provided to care for women who are ill and struggling to survive; to support orphans and other children affected by AIDS by providing food and school fees; and to assist the efforts of people living with HIV/AIDS who have openly declared their status.

African grandmothers are central to the life of their communities. With almost no support, they have stepped forward to care for millions of children orphaned by AIDS, sometimes as many as ten to fifteen in one household. They display astonishing reserves of love, courage and emotional resilience, even while grieving the loss of their own adult children. Canadians have raised an astonishing $16.5 million for African grandmothers through the Grandmothers to Grandmothers Campaign.† (Stephen Lewis Foundation, n.d., "Get Involved")

Africa has become a continent of orphans— nearly 15 million children have been orphaned by AIDS. Grandmothers bury their own adult children and step into the breach, caring for the

*Reprinted by permission of the Stephen Lewis Foundation.

†Reprinted by permission of the Stephen Lewis Foundation.

Inside LOOK

Sam Terry doesn't want to be known as "that fundraiser girl." But when you are a month shy of your 15th birthday and have built one school in Nepal and are outfitting another, that horse has definitely left the barn. The teen from Barnwell, Alberta, a small ranching community outside of Taber, juggles basketball, the honour roll, and rodeo competitions with public speaking. It's how she raised her first $32,000 before she'd even graduated from elementary school. Sam's message is straightforward: "My theory is that life is like a lottery and we got the winning ticket, but you could share your prize with everyone." Young Canadians form a "powerhouse of giving," according to a 2008 survey commissioned by Mackenzie Investments, which sponsors a yearly contest to highlight Canada's top teen philanthropists. [Teens are] donating time—100 million hours a year—and money, with approximately three million Canadians between 13 and 19 giving an average of $293 a year, while engaging in fundraising activities that contribute an additional $516. They're driven by the fact that they truly believe they can make a difference. Sam has a similar take. "Adults think with their heads; kids think with their hearts. Whenever I'm telling my story to kids, it's not 'What's my financial obligation?' It's just, 'What can I do now?'" Looking to tap into this action-based altruism is a wide range of organizations, from churches and service clubs to youth-driven global initiatives such as Free The Children.

Source: Youngblut, S. 2011. "Teen who built a school in Nepal is more than just 'that fundraiser girl'," *The Globe and Mail*, November 4. © The Globe and Mail. All Rights Reserved.

orphaned children left behind. They have no time to grieve their losses, little to no financial resources, deteriorating health, and limited support to bridge the generation gap and help their grandchildren work through the trauma of losing their parents. Despite these hardships, these courageous women have become the heart of the response to AIDS in Africa.[*] (Stephen Lewis Foundation, 2011)

FREE THE CHILDREN

Craig Kielburger is a household name in Canada. At the age of 12 he began his fight against child labour. With his brother Marc, he created Free the Children, a network of children helping children through education. Winner of the World's Children's Prize for the Rights of the Child (also known as the Children's Nobel Prize) and many other awards of note, Craig's work continues to grow in numbers and in substance.

According to the Free the Children website (http://www.freethechildren.com),

> the primary goals of the organization are to free children from poverty and exploitation and free young people from the notion that they are powerless to affect positive change in the world. Through domestic empowerment programs and leadership training, Free the Children inspires young people to develop as socially conscious global citizens and become agents of change for their peers around the world. Free the Children has built more than 650 schools around the world which now teach over 55,000 children every day. One million people have been provided access to clean drinking water, health care and improved sanitation facilities and thirty thousand women have been equipped to become economically self-sufficient.[†] (Free the Children, 2012)

We Day, which began in 2007 with 7,000 young people attending, is now an annual event in eight cities across the country with more than 100,000 people participating and being inspired to become active global citizens. We Day's 3.3 million Facebook "likes" makes it the largest social media cause in Canada and one of the largest in the world.

WAR CHILD

War and terrorism has an enormous impact on the lives of civilians caught up in conflict. Responding to the needs of children surrounded by violent conflict, Dr. Samantha Nutt created War Child (http://www.warchild.ca), an organization that has "grown from one volunteer with a cell phone" to "an award-winning non-profit with a dedicated staff of over 200." War Child reaches out to the children affected by war and provides access to education and justice. One of the organization's main goals is to raise awareness of the impact of war on communities; for example:

- More than 2 million children have died as a direct result of armed conflict over the last decade.

- Newborns in developing countries are 8 times as likely to die in childhood as those in industrialized countries.

- Over the last decade, 20 million children have been forced to flee their homes because of conflict and human rights violations.

War Child's vision is "a world where no child knows war." Visit http://www.warchild.ca.

SLEEPING CHILDREN AROUND THE WORLD (SCAW)

Murray Dryden (father of NHL star Ken Dryden) was on a trip to India when, coming home in the evening from a meeting, he tripped over children sleeping in the street. Believing that every child has the right to a place to sleep, in 1970 Murray and Margaret Dryden established Sleeping Children Around the World. Since that day, SCAW has raised over $23 million to provide bedkits for children in 33 countries. What is unique about this organization is that 100 percent of all donations is spent on the bedkits. All volunteers contribute their own time and travel at their own expense to ensure these bedkits get to the children. For $35.00 each kit will contain a mat or mattress, pillow, sheet, blanket, mosquito net (longer lasting insecticide nets in malaria hotspots), clothes, and school supplies. The kits are prepared with the support of local organizations in each country. Every child is photographed with their bedkit showing the donor's name and country and this photo is mailed back to the original donor. In 2009, SCAW reached their millionth child! (Sleeping Children Around the World, n.d.).

Visit http://www.scaw.org/about/index.html.

---

[*]Reprinted by permission of The Stephen Lewis Foundation.

[†]Reprinted by permission of Free the Children.

Sleeping Children Around the World is successful because of its grass-roots approach.

Courtesy of Sleeping Children Around the World

SAVE THE CHILDREN CANADA

Save the Children Canada has worked tirelessly for the last 91 years in Canada and overseas in support of children's human rights.

> Save the Children is the world's leading independent organization for children, delivering programs and improving children's lives in 120 countries worldwide. Working toward a world in which every child attains the right to survival, protection, development and participation, Save the Children's mission is to inspire breakthroughs in the way the world treats children and to achieve immediate and lasting change in their lives. Save the Children is committed to long-term development at the grassroots level through partnerships with local communities, government bodies and international organizations. (Save the Children Canada, n.d.)

Visit **http://www.savethechildren.ca**.

PACE CANADA: PROJECT FOR ADVANCEMENT OF CHILDHOOD EDUCATION

PACE Canada was founded in 1987 by Dr. Mavis Burke. With many awards to her name she was bestowed with the Order of Ontario in 1999 in recognition of her many contributions. PACE promotes early childhood education at home and in Jamaica with a special focus on children of preschool age in situations of racial, cultural, or economic disadvantage. The Adopt-a-School program provides assistance to Jamaican Basic Schools (ages 3 to 5) in areas of need identified by local community committees. For $1 a day, sponsors can adopt a school by selecting the parish or location of their choice. The David Appelt Bursary, awarded by PACE, is available to a second-year ECE student studying at a Canadian college and a similar PACE scholarship is available for a Jamaican ECE student. One of PACE's exciting initiatives is the Mobile Computer Buses—*Tech de Bus*, and *Tech de Bus2*. The buses go from school to school to teach 4- to 6-year-olds computer skills (Pace Canada, n.d.).

Visit **http://www.pacecanada.org**.

EDUCATION BEYOND BORDERS

Education Beyond Borders is an international nonprofit, nondenominational non-governmental organization focused on providing education in developing countries. Its mandate is to provide professional development for teachers and to support community education. Inspired by UNESCO's directive, it focuses on building "self-reliance, health,

Strong relationships are built between ECE students and the children with whom they are working in Jamaica!

EXHIBIT 11.2   Students Speak!

Russell Everett and Erin Corcoran are two of over 200 students from the School of Early Childhood at George Brown College who have completed a field placement in Jamaica over the past 10 years as part of the college's focus on international opportunities for students. Their comments demonstrate the tremendous impact an international field experience can have on an ECE student.

RUSSELL EVERETT

The most inspiring thing about our learning experience in Jamaica was that I realized there are people all over the world striving to better the lives of children because it brings them an ultimate sense of joy knowing they've changed the world just by bettering the life of one child.

Source: Reprinted by permission of Russell Everett.

ERIN CORCORAN

Being in Jamaica has made me realize that one of the best ways to learn and understand yourself better is by being open to learning and understanding others. There really has been an exchange of cultural "gold" that has enriched my life.

Source: Reprinted by permission of Erin Corcoran.

---

and capacity of education. The organization is made up of teachers and volunteers supported by those who believe in education as a passport to an optimistic future" (Education Beyond Borders, n.d.).

Visit **http://www.educationbeyondborders.org**.

THE CONSULTATIVE GROUP ON EARLY CHILDHOOD CARE AND DEVELOPMENT

This section was contributed by Louise Zimanyi, Director of The Consultative Group on Early Childhood

Care and Development, Ryerson Polytechnic University, School of Early Childhood Education

The Consultative Group on Early Childhood Care and Development (CG) is a global alliance for ECCD with strong links to regional networks and platforms including development agencies, civil society organizations, and professionals with expertise and experience in the ECCD field around the world. The CG works to facilitate a broad-based understanding of the importance of ECCD for social development and poverty reduction and to improve investments, policies, and actions that support the holistic development of young children (prenatal to 8 years).*

Led by a Secretariat and governed by an elected Executive Board, the CG actively identifies gaps, critical issues and emerging areas of needs and demands related to ECCD and to initiate and collaborate on innovative communication efforts to effect change at different levels. Through strong collaboration with and technical support to active and emerging ECCD regional networks, the CG works to facilitate South-South knowledge sharing and ensures that national and regional perspectives inform global advocacy and communication strategies and vice versa.

The CG's global work aims to support key ECCD stakeholders and others engaged in the design, implementation, and evaluation of ECCD programs in low- and middle-income countries. Specifically, the CG works to

- Expand, synthesize, and communicate key findings in research and major publications on ECCD as the volume of evidence as well as interest increases. The CG works to identify emerging issues, through consultation with its partners and others, and to respond through communication materials and advocacy.

- Extend and develop links to programmatic areas that are important for ECCD, such as disabilities, social protection, media and information technology, child protection, sustainable development and climate change, humanitarian assistance, and linguistic/cultural preservation/ reinforcement.

- Provide a global perspective on key ECCD issues—participation of networks from the major regions of the world gives the CG access

to information that individual agencies are not always able to source on their own in a timely manner. This global reach enables it to develop a comprehensive perspective on issues and provide guidance on ECCD that is not available through any other entity.

- Increase its capacity to convene major international agencies, NGOs, academic institutions, specialists, and regional networks to effect global policy change for young children.

For more information, visit **http://www .ecdgroup.com.**

HELPING CHILDREN COPE

For those educators working with older school-age children, active involvement in peace and aid organizations may help these children feel positive about their contributions to others while sensitizing them to the broader worldview. Many global issues are unsettling and may create real concerns on the part of the children. The National Association of School Psychologists (NASP) also has an informative website—Helping Children Cope in Unsettling Times: Tips for Parents and Teachers—at **http://www.nasponline.org.**

EARLY CHILDHOOD GRADUATES: WAYS THAT YOU CAN MAKE A DIFFERENCE
TEACHER SHORTAGE

The United Nations estimates that 8 million extra teachers will be needed worldwide by 2015 (Provost, 2011).

A teacher shortage on this scale could not only become the most serious challenge our profession has ever faced, it could also pose a serious threat to the survival of our public school systems worldwide. There is widespread concern about teacher quality, as well as pay and working conditions for education workers. (Van Leeuwen, 2007)

ARE YOU A GOOD CANDIDATE FOR WORKING ABROAD?

The world needs early childhood educators but would you be a good candidate for work in the international community? Kealy et al. (2001) researched the

---

*Reprinted by permission of Louise Zimanyi, Director of The Consultative Group on Early Childhood Care and Development, Ryerson Polytechnic University, School of Early Childhood Education.

International Competencies

	1	2	3	4	5
GETTING AROUND SKILLS					
• Ability to use unfamiliar transportation and communications systems					
• Awareness of travel documents required, local policies and laws					
• Awareness of security issues and potential strategies to travel safely					
KNOWING WHERE COUNTRIES FIT					
• Knowledge of your own background: country (countries) history, politics and culture(s)					
• Awareness of the impact of events, culture, politics and geography upon history					
• Awareness of global issues and current events					
• Awareness of how events and cultures in one country impact on other countries					
• Knowledge of the socio-economic, political and cultural aspects of specific countries					
COMMUNICATION SKILLS					
• Ability to develop relationships with people from backgrounds different than your own by respectfully and actively clarifying that your own behaviour is congruent with the norm of cultures other than your own					
• Ability to actively and respectfully listen (e.g. suspend own assumptions)					
• Ability to use body language that is understood by people from backgrounds other than your own (e.g. attentive to verbal and non verbal cues)					
• Ability to use the appropriate level of formality in situations different than ones your are used to					
• Ability to demonstrate culturally appropriate caring and relationship-building behaviour					
INTERCULTURAL SKILLS					
• Curiosity about differences in people and between people					
• Ability to identify the differences in people versus cultural differences					
• Ability to identify similarities and differences within and between world cultures					
• Ability to establish a rapport matched to styles of a context different than your own					
• Ability to identify and understand religious issues and how they impact social, cultural and political realities					
• Ability to maintain personal autonomy while showing respect for others					
• Ability to suspend personal assumptions and understand the assumptions under which other people operate					
PROBLEM SOLVING/DECISION MAKING SKILLS					
• Ability to obtain information about another culture/country/environment through the use of various mediums including the internet etc.					
• Positive attitude toward learning new things, toward change					
• Ability to suspend personal assumptions (tolerate ambiguity) and assess information about environments other than your own					

	1	2	3	4	5
• Understanding of the assumptions under which other people operate					
• Exercising of good judgment related to the most appropriate course of action that balances your values with values different than your own					
• Personal strategy for understanding of and participation in local, national and international issues					
• Ability to negotiate agreement with in a win-win way especially with people from backgrounds different than your own					
• Acquisition of new ways to solve problems as a result of learning about other cultures					
PROFESSIONAL COMPETENCE					
• Subject area of knowledge, skills and background is demonstrated with skill					
• Ability to work in teams especially with people from cultures other than your own					
• Ability to plan strategically, especially in situations different that your own					
• Changes in the way you practice your profession as a result of learning about it's practice in socio-economic, political and cultural settings different than your own					

Inside LOOK

Canadians Studying Abroad

When 25 university presidents converged in Ottawa (February 2012), several of them cautioned that more home-grown students need to study outside their own backyard to develop strong worldwide connections and an instinct to innovate. "Canadian students are not big travellers in comparison to, say, Americans or New Zealanders or Australians, and they don't even travel that much from province to province," says Queen's University president Daniel Woolf. About 9 in 10 Canadian students go to university in their home province, and evidence suggests a large proportion choose a school within 20 kilometres of home. Only 12 per cent of undergraduates have an international placement or exchange experience, according to a 2009 survey—reason to fear the experience of many students is too parochial given high demand for the ability to work and think globally. Most universities have dozens, even hundreds of partnerships with schools abroad, but only a fraction of students take advantage of them, especially early in their studies, said Dalhousie University president Tom Traves. "It exposes you, it transforms you, changes you as a person—you never see the world in the same way again," he said. Dr. Traves worries the public still sees study abroad as frivolous, making student travel a tough political sell. Most trips are funded out of strained university budgets, through in-house fundraising or out of students' pockets. By contrast, the Brazilian government recently promised to spend $2 billion sending 75,000 more of its students abroad. "If you put in place a broad national strategy along these lines, I don't think it would cost big money in the context of the total budget of the federal government—we're talking tens of millions of dollars, not hundreds. That would be astonishing and have a huge impact." (Bradshaw, 2012)

Unfortunately, statistics on college students were not available at publication.

Source: Bradshaw, J. 2012. "University leaders want more Canadians to study abroad," *The Globe and Mail*, February 2. © The Globe and Mail. All Rights Reserved.

I never anticipated how much teaching and living abroad would enrich my life, both professionally and personally. Imagine culture, language, tradition, travel, and education all in one! Mexico has given me just that, not to mention three years of irreplaceable teaching experience. My preschoolers teach me something new about their beautiful country every day, and they have inspired me to continue with this work throughout my life. Ordinary people accomplish the extraordinary every day—from three-year-olds learning in an English Immersion environment to the teachers who lead them. There are children in every corner of this planet who need people to care for, teach, and cherish them. You can never imagine how much working abroad gives back to you. Get out there. Live. Laugh. Love. Learn.

Source: Reprinted by permission of Marcia Kuehnen.

personal characteristics shared by those most effective in the transfer of skills in an international setting in their book *A Profile of the Interculturally Effective Person*. The International Competencies rating scale presented is an adaptation of a questionnaire used for George Brown College ECE students travelling abroad. Which competencies do you think you exhibit and which ones require more work?

ORGANIZATIONS FOR VOLUNTEERING

> *"**Never doubt** that a small group of committed people can change the world. Indeed, it is the only thing that ever has."*
>
> —**Margaret Mead (Book Browse. n.d.)**

There are many organizations that provide positive international experiences for ECE graduates working with children; a few are listed below.

CANADIAN INTERNATIONAL DEVELOPMENT AGENCY INTERNATIONAL YOUTH INTERNSHIP PROGRAM

As outlined on the Canadian International Development Agency (CIDA) website at **http://www.acdi-cida.gc.ca/internships**.

The International Youth Internship Program (IYIP) is focused on Canadians between 19–30 years of age with a post-secondary diploma. Through this organization, young people would have an opportunity to work in a developing country developing their personal and professional growth while supporting Canada's international development goals. (CIDA, 2012)

CANADA WORLD YOUTH

http://cwy-jcm.com

Founded in 1971 by senator Jacques Hebert, Canada World Youth (CWY) is a world leader in developing international educational programs for young people aged 15 to 35. A non-profit organisation, CWY is dedicated to enriching the lives of young people that have a desire to become informed and active global citizens. CWY programs are designed to help youth experience the world for themselves, learn about other cultures and diverse Canadian communities while developing leadership and communication skills. In 2011–12, 1,103 young volunteers took part in Canada World Youth's programs, 794 were Canadians and 309 were from our partner countries. 26.6% of the Canadian volunteers were Aboriginal youth and 14.4% represented a visible minority group.

Working in partnership with local organizations, the majority of Canada World Youth programs have a phase in Canada and a phase in one of the partner countries which include Indonesia, Vietnam, Mali, Ghana, Benin, South Africa, Kenya, Tanzania, Mozambique, Ukraine, Bolivia, Honduras, Nicaragua and Peru.* (Canada World Youth, 2012)

*Reprinted by permission of Canada World Youth.

INTERNATIONAL ECE STUDENTS

Many students, particularly those in urban centres, have come to Canada to study Early Childhood Education. Studying abroad can be a challenging time. The Canadian Bureau for International Education (CBIE) found in its 2009 survey on international student satisfaction that students in Canada struggle most with

> finding accommodations, cultural and racial sensitivities, immigration and institutional presence outside Canada, and integrating with their Canadian peers. Although it is solely a student's responsibility to maintain his or her immigration status and obey immigration regulations while in Canada, colleges and universities understand the stressful nature of immigration and do their best to help students through the red tape. When asked whether they have experienced any form of racism or discrimination as an international student in Canada, the CBIE's survey found that about six in 10 indicated they have not. Still, many international students do grapple with cultural and racial sensitivities, and having to cope alone with these cultural stresses can exacerbate the situation, lead to isolation, and ultimately create an unpleasant experience during a time that should be of fulfilment and growth. Many students comment that the biggest obstacle has been the winter![*] (Hansen, 2011)

The cost of tuition is a challenge for many students whose families face enormous financial burdens to send their children abroad. Canadian tuitions for most arts and science programs are heavily subsidized by the government. A Canadian student would pay $6,100, while an international student will pay full cost for their education at $17,200—a staggering difference! "It comes as little surprise then that many Canadian schools eagerly welcome international students, who brought $6.5 billion to the Canadian economy in 2008 alone" (Hansen, 2011: 22–24).

INTERNATIONAL INSTITUTE FOR PEACE THROUGH TOURISM

Since its founding in 1986, IIPT has been committed to making travel and tourism the world's first "global peace industry" and the belief that every traveler is potentially an "Ambassador for Peace." IIPT's first Global Conference: Tourism—A Vital Force for Peace (Vancouver 1988) introduced a "Higher Purpose of Tourism" that includes the key role of travel and tourism in:

- Promoting international understanding among peoples
- Collaboration among Nations
- Protecting the environment and preserving biodiversity
- Enhancing cultures and valuing heritage
- Sustainable development
- Poverty reduction and
- Healing wounds of conflict and reconciliation through tourism, culture, and sports.

Visit **http://www.ipt.org**.

IIPT CREDO OF THE PEACEFUL TRAVELER©

Grateful for the opportunity to travel and to experience the world and because peace begins with the individual, I affirm my personal responsibility and commitment to:

- journey with an open mind and gentle heart;
- accept with grace and gratitude the diversity I encounter;
- revere and protect the natural environment which sustains all life;
- appreciate all cultures I discover;
- respect and thank my hosts for their welcome;
- offer my hand in friendship to everyone I meet;
- support travel services that share these views and act upon them; and
- by my spirit, words, and actions encourage others to travel the world in peace.[†]

> "There are no boundaries in the real Planet Earth. No United States, no Soviet Union, no China, no Taiwan, East Germany or West. Rivers flow unimpeded across the swaths of continents. The persistent tides—the pulse of the sea—do not discriminate, they push against all the varied shores on Earth."
>
> —**Jacques-Yves Cousteau, Oceanographer and Explorer (Not Crazy, n.d.)**

---

[*]Hansen, D. 2011. "The Student Experience," *Canadian Immigrant*, 8 (9). Reprinted by permission of Denise Hansen.

[†]IIPT Credo of the Peaceful Traveler © International Institute for Peace through Tourism. www.iipt.org. Reprinted by permission.

THE FINAL WORD

"One Day …
Youngsters will learn words they will not understand.
Children from India will ask:
What is hunger?
Children from Alabama will ask:
What is racial segregation?
Children from Hiroshima will ask:
What is an atomic bomb?
Children at school will ask:
What is war?
You will answer them.
You will tell them.
Those words are not used any more,
Like stagecoaches, galleys or slavery—
Words no longer meaningful.
That is why they have been removed from dictionaries."

—Martin Luther King Jr. (Shoah, n.d.)

REFERENCES

Albanese, P. 2009. *Children in Canada Today*. New York: Oxford University Press.

Alexander, G. 2011. "Should New Research on under 5's Reshape Our Approach to Development. " UNICEF's Innocenti Research Centre. Retrieved February 22, 2013, from http://www.guardian.co.uk/global-development/poverty-matters/2011/sep/23/early-child-development-mdgs

Amnesty International. 2006. "The Human Rights of Children: Overview." Retrieved from http://www.amnesty.ca

Arnold, T. 2011. "Food Price Rise Takes Huge Toll on World's Poor." *Toronto Star*. April 18.

BBC. 2012. "More Mobiles than Humans in 2012, Says Cisco." February 15. Retrieved February 22, 2013, from http://www.bbc.co.uk/news/technology-17047406

Black, D. 2012. "Steinem Website Fights Rape in War Zones." *Toronto Star*. February 11. A27.

Book Browse. n.d. Retrieved February 13, 2013, from http://www.bookbrowse.com/quotes/detail/index.cfm?quote_number=88

Bradshaw, J. 2012. "University Leaders Want More Canadians to Study Abroad." *The Globe and Mail*. February 3. A4. Retrieved February 20, 2013, from http://www.theglobeandmail.com/news/national/university-leaders-want-more-canadians-to-study-abroad/article543333

Canada World Youth. n.d. "About Us." Retrieved from http://www.cwy-jcm.org/en/aboutus

Canadian Bureau for International Education (CBIE). 2009. Retrieved from http://www.cbie-bcei.ca

Cannon, M. 2010. "Canadians in Haiti." *Zoomer Magazine*.

Child Soldiers International. 2012. Retrieved February 13, 2013, from http://www.child-soldiers.org/home

Convention on the Elimination of All Forms of Discrimination Against Women. Office of the United Nations High Commission for Human Rights. Retrieved February 22, 2013, from http://www.un.org/womenwatch/daw/cedaw

Education Beyond Borders. n.d. Retrieved February 13, 2013, from http://www.educationbeyondborders.org

Engle, P.L., M. Black, J.R. Behrman, M. Cabral de Mello, P.J. Gertler, L. Kapiriri, R. Martorell, and M. Eming Young. 2007. "Strategies to Avoid the Loss of Developmental Potential in More Than 200 Million Children in the Developing World." *The Lancet* 369 (January 6). 239.

Food and Agricultural Organization of the United Nations (FAO). 2012. "Initiative on Soaring Food Prices." Retrieved February 22, 2013, from http://www.fao.org/isfp/about/en

Gates, M. 2007. "The Other Side of the Mat: Uniting for Maternal, Newborn and Child Survival and Health." *The State of the World's Children, 2008: Child Survival*. New York: UNICEF, 2007. Retrieved from http://www.unicef.org/sowc08/docs/sowc08.pdf

Grantham-McGregor, S., Y. Bun Cheung, S. Cueto, P. Glewwe, L. Richter, and B. Strupp. 2007. "Developmental Potential in the First Five Years for Children in Developing Countries." *The Lancet* 369 (January 6). 67.

Gustafsson, L.H. 1986. *Children in Emergencies. Action for Children: Unfinished Business*. Report of the NGO Forum organized by UNICEF New York: Radda Barnen International.

Hansen, D. 2011. "The Student Experience." *Canadian Immigrant*, 8(9).

Index Mundi. n.d. Retrieved February 13, 2013, from http://www.indexmundi.com/g/r.aspx?v=29

International Institute for Peace Through Tourism. 2003. "Credo of the Peaceful Traveler." Retrieved February 13, 2013, from http://www.iipt.org/credo.html

Kealy, D., T. Vulpe, D. Protheroe, and D. MacDonald. 2001. *A Profile of the Interculturally Effective Person*. Ottawa: Centre for Intercultural Learning, Canadian Foreign Service Institute/Department of Foreign Affairs and International Trade.

Lake, A. 2012. *The State of the World's Children*, Foreword. Retrieved February 12, 2013, http://www.unicef.org

Macleans. 2012. "Bad News: An Abhorrent Practice." January 30. 8.

Nolen, S. 2011. "Rate of Aborted Female Fetuses Increases in India." *The Globe and Mail*. April 2. Retrieved February 20, 2013, from http://www.theglobeandmail.com/news/world/rate-of-aborted-female-fetuses-increases-in-india/article580726

Not Crazy. n.d. Retrieved February 13, 2013, from http://forum.notcrazy.net/index.php?topic=6965.0

Office of the United Nations High Commissioner for Human Rights. 2012. Retrieved February 13, 2013, from http://www2.ohchr.org/english/bodies/crc

One Laptop per Child. n.d. Retrieved February 13, 2013, from http://laptop.org

Pace Canada. Retrieved February 13, 2013, from http://www.pacecanada.org

Provost, C. 2011. "Global Teacher Shortage Threatens Progress on Education." *The Guardian, U.K.* October 7. Retrieved February 13, 2013, from http://www.guardian.co.uk/education/teacher-shortages

Quotations Page. n.d. "Gandhi." Retrieved February 11, 2013, from http://www.quotationspage.com/quote/27184.html

Rabson, M. 2012. "Canada's Food Policies Hurt Poor: UN Envoy." Republished from the Winnipeg Free Press print edition May 17, A6. Retrieved February 22, 2013, from http://www.winnipegfreepress.com/local/canadas-food-policies-hurt-poor-un-envoy-151840815.html

Reid, R. 1994. Keynote Address for the World Conference on Human Rights, 1994, Vienna, Austria.

Save the Children. 2005. "Responses to Young Children in Post-Emergency Situations." In *Early Childhood Matters #104*. Bernard Van Leer Foundation.

———. 2011. "2011 Mother's Index Rankings." Retrieved from http://www.savethechildren.org

———. n.d. "What We Do." Retrieved February 13, 2013, from http://www.savethechildren.ca

Schwartz, M., and B.M. Scott. 2010. *Marriages and Families,* 6th ed. Upper Saddle River, NJ: Prentice Hall.

Shephard, M. 2012. "Children of the Revolution." *Toronto Star.* February 4. WD4–5.

Shoah. n.d. Retrieved February 13, 2013, from http://www.shoah.org.uk/2012/01/01/happy-new-year-one-day-children-will-ask-what-is-war

Sleeping Children Around The World. n.d. Retrieved February 13, 2013, from http://www.scaw.org/about/index.html

Stephen Lewis Foundation. n.d. Retrieved February 13, 2013, from http://www.stephenlewisfoundation.org/assets/files/Materials%20-%20General/SLF%20G2G%20Flyer%20ENG%20March%202011.pdf

———. n.d. Retrieved February 13, 2013, from http://www.stephenlewisfoundation.org/what-we-do/areas-of-work/children-affected-by-aids

———. 2011. "Turning the Tide of AIDS in Africa," from http://www.stephenlewisfoundation.org/assets/files/Materials%20-%20General/SLF%20G2G%20Flyer%20ENG%20March%202011.pdf.

Thinkexist.com. n.d. "Marian Wright Edelman." Retrieved February 13, 2013, from http://thinkexist.com/quotation/if_you_don_t_like_the_way_the_world_is-you_change/215839.html

This Day Live. 2012. "WAFICT: Bridging Digital Divide through Broadband." Retrieved February 22, 2013, from http://www.thisdaylive.com/articles/wafict-bridging-digital-divide-through-broadband/116019

UNESCO. n.d. Retrieved from http://www.unesco.org/new/en/unesco

UNICEF. 2006. "Saving Children from the Tragedy of Landmines." April 4. Retrieved February 13, 2013, from http://www.unicef.org/media/media_32034.html

———. 2007. "Paris Principles and Guidelines on Children Associated with Armed Forces or Armed Groups." February. Retrieved February 22, 2013, from http://www.unicef.org/emerg/files/ParisPrinciples310107English.pdf

———. 2007. *The State of the World's Children, 2008: Child Survival.* New York: United Nations. Retrieved February 13, 2013, from http://www.unicef.org/sowc08/report/report.php

———. 2011. "Child Info." http://www.childinfo.org/hiv_aids.html

———. 2012. "Young Child Survival and Development." Retrieved February 13, 2013, from http://www.unicef.org/childsurvival/index.html

United Nations. 2002. "A World Fit for Us." *United Nations: Special Session on Children.* Retrieved February 13, 2013, from http://www.unicef.org/specialsession/documentation/childrens-statement.htm.

———. 2008. "End Poverty 2015: Millennium Goals." Retrieved February 13, 2013, from http://www.un.org/millenniumgoals

United Nations Regional Information Centre for Western Europe. 2012. "One Third of All Food Wasted!" Retrieved March 29, 2013, from http://www.unric.org/en/food-waste/27133-one-third-of-all-food-wasted

United Nations Women. 2012. Convention on the Elimination of All Forms of Discrimination Against Women (CEDAW). Retrieved February 13, 2013, from http://www.un.org/womenwatch/daw/csw/56sess.htm#resolutions

Van Leeuwen, F. 2007. Keynote Address for the Education International 5th World Congress, Berlin, Germany. Retrieved from http://www.ei-ie.org/worldcongress2007/ei-ie/index5e0c.html?Id=191&SkipRec=2

Volunteer Canada. n.d. Retrieved from http://volunteer.ca

War Child. n.d. Retrieved February 13, 2013, from http://www.warchild.ca.

Water Aid International. n.d. Retrieved February 12, 2013, from http://www.wateraid.org/international/what_we_do/statistics/default.asp

Welcome to the Fast Family. n.d. Retrieved February 12, 2013, from http://www.thefastfamily.org/motherteresaquotes.html

Witt, J., and A. Hermiston, 2010. *SOC: A Matter of Perspective.* Whitby, ON: McGraw Hill Ryerson.

World Health Organization. 2012a. "World Health Statistics." Retrieved February 13, 2013, from http://www.who.int/gho/publications/world_health_statistics/2012/en

———. 2012b. "Why Do So Many Women Still Die In Pregnancy or Childbirth?" Retrieved February 13, 2013, from http://www.who.int/features/qa/12/en/index.html

World Vision. 2007. *Child View: The Magazine for Child Sponsors.* Fall: 5.

Youngblut, S. 2011. "Teen who built a school in Nepal is more than just 'that fundraiser girl.'" *The Globe and Mail.* November 5. A4.

Created by Iris

INDEX